The Dog Lover's Companion to the Pacific Northwest

2ND EDITION

Val Mallinson

AVALON
TRAVEL

THE DOG LOVER'S COMPANION TO THE PACIFIC NORTHWEST
THE INSIDE SCOOP ON WHERE TO TAKE YOUR DOG

Published by
Avalon Travel
a member of the Perseus Books Group
1700 Fourth Street
Berkeley, CA 94710, USA

Printing History
1st edition—May 2005
2nd edition—May 2009
5 4 3 2 1

ISBN-10: 1-59880-032-9
ISBN-13: 978-1-59880-032-6
ISSN: 1553-135X

Editor and Series Manager: Shaharazade Husain
Copy Editor: Kay Elliott
Designer: Jacob Goolkasian
Graphics Coordinator: Elizabeth Jang
Production Coordinator: Elizabeth Jang
Map Editor: Brice Ticen
Cartographers: Kat Bennett, Brice Ticen

Cover and Interior Illustrations by Phil Frank

Printed in the United States of America by R.R. Donnelley

ABOUT THE AUTHOR

This is the story of how a washed-up copy-writer, a puppy-mill puppy with a broken back, and a dog who lived in a cage in a barn overcame all obstacles to bring more joy to people and their pets.

© J.Nichole Smith / www.dane-dane.com

Val Mallinson believes that beauty and hilarity are everywhere you look. Bitten by the travel bug early, she has explored all 50 states, a dozen European countries, Mexico, and the Caribbean. Val's love of dogs began even earlier, thanks to her childhood companion Keegan, who waited, nose pressed to the window, for her to come home from kindergarten. Her favorite bedtime story was *The Pokey Little Puppy,* which also forecast a love of dessert. After being seduced by her mother's adopted dog Thumper, Val adopted two miniature dachshunds, Cooper and Isis, from purebred rescue.

Cooper spent the first year of his life locked in a cage in a barn. When he broke free, he vowed from that day forward to chase as many squirrels through the world's forests as the length of his extendable leash would allow. Isis spent her working years as a dog-bed demo model and nanny to eight fussy Italian greyhound show dogs. It was back-breaking work, literally. Post surgery for spinal cord injuries, she chose to retire to a life of leisure in the back seat of Val's Prius.

Before devoting herself to the position of chauffeur and stenographer for the Wonder Wieners, Val survived a decade in the fast-paced and glamorous world of advertising and marketing copywriting. She penned snappy copy for extinct dot-coms, as well as for a large software company in Redmond, Washington. She helped author the stylish travel guide *Moon Metro Seattle,* and her writing and photography appear in *Bark, Seattle Metropolitan, Northwest Travel, Northwest Palate,* and *CityDog* magazines. With her husband, Steve, she has lived in Seattle for fifteen years.

In the course of writing *The Dog Lover's Companion to the Pacific Northwest,* and *The Dog Lover's Companion to Seattle,* the Dachsie Twins have slept in the car in a downpour and eaten kibble off the cold, hard ground. They've learned how to navigate using the (bleep)-ing GPS, endured the admiration of excitable toddlers, and scratched at rashes caused by field grass allergies. It's been worth every moment.

For those who rescue dogs and other innocents

CONTENTS

Puget Sound Islands 111

Everett and Vicinity 135

North Seattle 165

Central Seattle 185

The Eastside 225

South Seattle 251

Tacoma and Olympia 275

Southwest Washington. 299

North Cascades 327

Central Washington 361

OREGON 391

North Coast 393

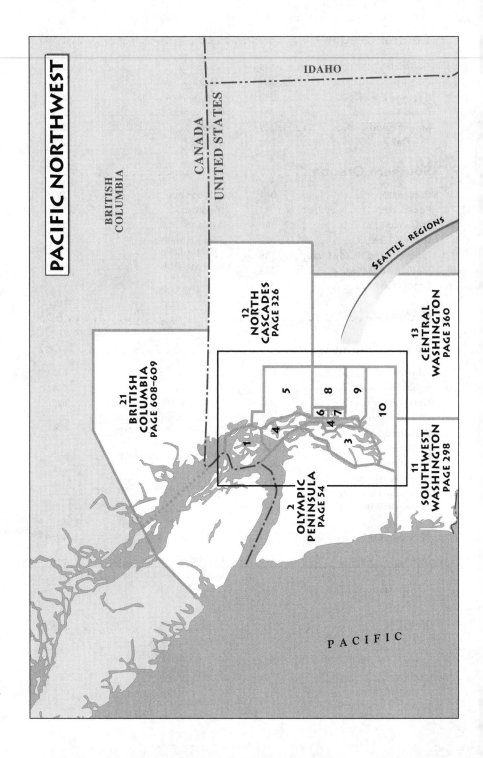

PACIFIC NORTHWEST

IDAHO

CANADA
UNITED STATES

BRITISH
COLUMBIA

SEATTLE REGIONS

12
NORTH
CASCADES
PAGE 326

21
BRITISH
COLUMBIA
PAGE 608–609

13
CENTRAL
WASHINGTON
PAGE 360

5
4
6
8
7
4
9
10
1
3

2
OLYMPIC
PENINSULA
PAGE 54

11
SOUTHWEST
WASHINGTON
PAGE 298

PACIFIC

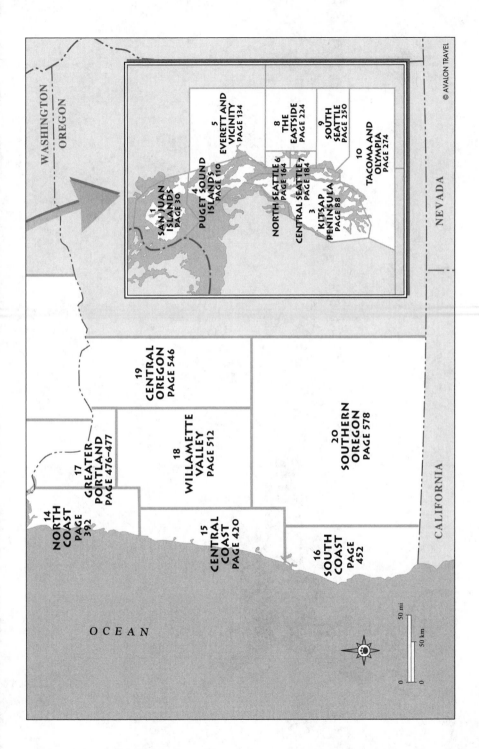

Introduction

In our demand-filled lives, the faithful creatures who sit at our feet expect so little of us. In exchange for lifelong devotion, all they ask is to be fed and to have someplace warm and dry to sleep. For bringing joy and laughter into our lives, all they hope for in return is an occasional tummy rub and some play-time. For unconditional love, they demand only to remain glued to our sides, always, always, always allowed to go wherever we are going. That is, unless we are going to the v-e-t.

At our house, going on a trip without the dogs is rarely an option. We can't handle the guilt. Copernicus Maximus the Red, a.k.a. Cooper, or Coop for short, mourns our departure from his perch at the picture window, his devastation clearly visible in his hangdog posture. The Goddess Isis is much more direct in expressing her displeasure. At the first key jangle, she runs to the door to the garage. As the door closes behind us without her, she protests, using a high-pitched, staccato bark reserved for these occasions. I-can't-be-lieve-you-are-leav-ing-with-out-ME!

Why shouldn't they protest? They know the big wide world out there holds more wonders than they can possibly fit into their short dog lifetimes. For the Dachsie Twins, even a trip to the dry cleaners is full of new sensory pleasures.

Truth be told, we don't want to go anywhere without the kids, for the dogs are our children, hairy, four-legged, and speech-challenged though they may be. Seeing the Pacific Northwest through the eyes of the Wonder Wieners makes the region's natural beauty and endless recreation opportunities seem even more wondrous. Every city looks prettier from the perspective of its parks. They are right, there are marvels out here.

Native Americans treasured the secrets of the Pacific Northwest for thousands of years. Their oral legends and petroglyphs tell of its abundance. Of giant forests sheltering elk and wildlife to hunt, hillsides thick with brambles yielding sweet blackberries, and oceans and rivers teeming with steelhead and the sacred salmon. The Lewis and Clark Expedition of 1805–1806 brought the mysteries of what was called the Oregon Territory to the attention of European settlers back east. Meriwether Lewis explored Washington and Oregon with his faithful Newfoundland named Seaman at his side, and his journals are bursting with drawings and details of native flora, fauna, and natural phenomenon the likes of which the Corps of Discovery had never seen. From 1843 to 1869, hundreds of thousands of pioneers endured dangerous journeys and immense hardships to reach this promised land at the end of the Oregon Trail.

Thanks in part to this book, our hope is that you don't have to suffer any hardships traveling the Pacific Northwest with your pets. Coop 'n' Isis worked their weenie hindquarters off for you, to sniff out romps with the highest fun factor, the choicest eats where dogs are allowed, and the nicest digs for slumber parties. They discovered, more often than not, that dogs are a natural fit into the relaxed, casual, outdoor lifestyle of the region. On their journey, the Dachshund Duo met dogs who hike, bike, kayak, fish, and ride river rafts and motorcycles with their humans. International outdoor outfitters are headquartered here, such as Eddie Bauer, REI, Nike, and RuffWear.

What will you find on your travels in the Pacific Northwest? Steve, dad of Cooper and Isis, declares his love for the region because it has big water *and* big mountains. The marine heritage of the Northwest Coast is everywhere: ferries, lighthouses, beaches, islands, inland waterways, bridges, marine parks, and people who live on houseboats. No matter how many times you see it, the power of the Pacific Ocean never diminishes. As for the mountains, despite 150 years of logging, there are deep forests and wilderness areas with towering conifers that will astound you. This combination of surf and turf yields the highest concentration of parks, beaches, and recreation opportunities we think you'll find anywhere.

Let's face it, our pets are natural fitness coaches, preferring their calorie-burning activities to take place in the great outdoors. People are demanding more quality time with their pets, and are working together to make it happen. Since the first edition of the book, you'll discover dozens of new off-leash areas, and many more are in the works. The dog park trend is spreading to smaller cities and outlying areas.

For at least half of the year, you'll also find mud. It is said that the Eskimo peoples of the world have a hundred names for different qualities of snow. So, too, do residents of the Pacific Northwest have many ways to describe rain, from mist and drizzle on through to showers with sun breaks and raining cats and dogs. This precipitation nourishes the greenery and flowers that give the region its nicknames: Evergreen State for Washington, Emerald City for Seattle, and City of Roses for Portland. Embrace mud, jump in mud puddles, take a therapeutic mud bath, and make mud pies. Enjoy it without judgment, as your dog does, or like you did when you were a kid. Bring raincoats and towels for everybody, and cover your car seats.

If you simply can not stand the wet dog smell a minute longer, don't despair—simply head east. Starting at the eastern slope of the Cascade Mountains, it is typically warm and dry. In this book, you can count on the locations in the Central Washington and Central Oregon chapters to have an average of 300 sunny days a year. Some even say Pacific Northwesterners exaggerate reports of rainfall to prevent more people from moving here, thus keeping all of the region's desirable qualities to themselves. Honestly, the sun starts peeking through in April, and it can be dry and temperate through Indian summer in September.

While rumors of rain may be exaggerated, everything you've ever heard about the regional obsession with coffee is true. No matter how backwoods or one-horse a town, there will be an espresso shack, even if it doubles as the post office and gas station. It is not just a beverage, it is a way of life.

Which brings us back to the reason we are here. Cooper and Isis hope that this guide will help make traveling with your dogs a way of life. Every park, place to eat, and place to stay has passed the inspection of these hounds' fine-tuned senses. Coop 'n' Isis dug up dog events, unearthed the fanciest pet boutiques, and scratched under the surface of dog day care centers to include a few they deemed most worthy. Each pupportunity has been carefully rated and described to make your travels easier. You can fit your dog into your favorite outdoor passion, whether it's hitting every farmers market and roadside fruit and vegetable stand in sight, climbing every mountain, or fording every stream. As we researched this book, we fell in love with the region's beauty over and over again, from the mountains to the prairies to the oceans white with foam. The Wonder Wieners hope your discoveries in the Pacific Northwest will be no less wonderful.

The Paws Scale

At some point, we've got to face the facts: Humans and dogs have different tastes. We like eating chocolate and smelling lavender and covering our bodies with soft clothes. They like eating roadkill and smelling each other's unmentionables and covering their bodies with slug slime.

The parks, beaches, and recreation areas in this book are rated with a dog in mind. Maybe your favorite park has lush gardens, a duck pond, a few acres of perfectly manicured lawns, and sweeping views of a nearby skyline. But unless your dog can run leash-free, swim in the pond, and roll in the grass, that park may not deserve a very high rating from your pet's perspective.

The lowest rating you'll come across in this book is the fire hydrant 🐾. When you see this symbol, it means the park is merely worth a squat. Visit one of these parks only if your dog can't hold it any longer. These pit stops have virtually no other redeeming qualities for canines.

Beyond that, the paws scale starts at one paw 🐾 and goes up to four paws 🐾🐾🐾🐾. A one-paw park isn't a dog's idea of a great time. Maybe it's a tiny park with only a few trees and too many kids running around. Or perhaps it's a magnificent national park that bans dogs from every inch of land except paved roads and a few campsites. Four-paw parks, on the other hand, are places your dog will drag you to visit. Some of these areas come as close to dog heaven as you can imagine. Many have lakes for swimming or hundreds of acres for hiking. Some are small, fenced-in areas where leash-free dogs can tear around without danger of running into the road. Many four-paw parks give you the option of letting your dog off-leash (although most have restrictions, which are detailed in the park description).

In addition to finding paws and hydrants, you'll also notice an occasional foot symbol 👣 in this book. The foot means the park offers something special for humans. After all, you deserve a reward for being such a good chauffeur.

This book is not meant to be a comprehensive guide to all of the parks in the Pacific Northwest. This region suffers from a happy problem of excessive recreational opportunities. We struggled not to become overwhelmed or jaded as we selected the best, largest, most convenient, and dog-friendliest parks to include in the guide. Most areas have so many wonderful parks that we had to make tough choices about which to include and which to leave out. A few places have such a limited supply of parks that, for the sake of dogs living and visiting there, we listed parks that wouldn't otherwise be worth mentioning.

Since signposts are spotty and street names are notoriously confusing, we've given detailed directions to all the parks from the nearest major roadway or city center. Pacific Northwesterners have a reputation for being as helpful as they are adventurous, all too glad to give you directions that will get you hopelessly lost on their favorite backdoor route to somewhere obscure. It certainly can't hurt to pick up a detailed street map before you and your dog set out on your travels.

He, She, It

In this book, whether neutered, spayed, or au naturel, dogs are never referred to as *it.* They are either *he* or *she.* Cooper and Isis insisted we alternate pronouns so no dog reading this book will feel left out.

To Leash or Not to Leash...

This is not a question that plagues dogs' minds. Ask just about any normal, red-blooded American dog if she'd prefer to play off-leash, and she'll say, "Arf!" (Translation: "That's a rhetorical question, right?") No question about it, most dogs would give their canine teeth to frolic about without that cumbersome leash.

Whenever you see the running dog 🐕 in this book, you'll know that under certain circumstances, your dog can run around in leash-free bliss. Some parks have off-leash hours, marked by the time 🐕 symbol. Fortunately, the Pacific Northwest is home to dozens of such parks, and the trend is growing. The rest of the parks require leashes. We wish we could write about the parks where dogs get away with being scofflaws. Unfortunately, those would be the first ones animal control patrols would hit. We can't advocate breaking the law, but if you're tempted, please follow your conscience and use common sense.

Also, just because dogs are permitted off-leash in certain areas doesn't

necessarily mean you should let your dog run free. Unless you're sure your dog will come back when you call or will never stray more than a few yards from your side, you should probably keep her leashed. An otherwise docile homebody can turn into a savage hunter if the right prey is near. A curious wet-nose could perturb the rattlesnakes that are common in high desert areas or run into a bear or cougar in the woods. In pursuit of a strange scent, your dog could easily get lost in an unfamiliar area.

Crowded or popular areas, especially beaches, can be full of unpredictable children and other dogs who may not be as well behaved as yours. It's a tug of war out there. People who've had bad experiences with dogs are demanding stricter leash laws everywhere or the banning of "those mongrels" altogether from public places. When faced with increasing limits, dog lovers want more designated places where their pets can play without fear of negative consequences. The rope is stretched thin and tensions are tight.

In short, be careful out there. If your dog needs leash-free exercise but you don't have her under complete voice control, she'll be happy to know that several beaches permit well-behaved, leashless pooches, as do a growing number of beautiful, fenced-in dog exercise areas.

As for general leash restrictions, Washington State Parks require dogs to be on an eight-foot or shorter leash. Oregon State Parks limit it to a six-foot or shorter lead, and this is the standard that is rapidly being adopted throughout the region.

There's No Business Like Dog Business

There's nothing appealing about bending down with a plastic bag or a piece of newspaper on a chilly morning and grabbing the steaming remnants of what your dog ate for dinner the night before. Worse yet, you have to hang onto it until you can find a trash can. Blech! It's enough to make you wish you could train your pooch to sit on the potty. But as gross as it can be to scoop the poop, it's worse to step in it. It's really bad if a child falls in it, or—gag!—starts eating it. The funniest name for poop we heard on our travels was WMDs—Wanton Mongrel Defecations—but there's nothing funny about a poop-filled park. Have you ever walked into a park where few people clean up after their dogs? You don't want to be there any more than anyone else does.

Unscooped poop is one of a dog's worst enemies. Public policies banning dogs from parks are enacted because of it. Good Pacific Northwest parks and beaches that permit dogs are in danger of closing their gates to all canines because of the negligent behavior of a few owners. A worst-case scenario is already in place in several communities—dogs are banned from all parks. Their only exercise is a leashed sidewalk stroll. That's no way to live.

Be responsible and clean up after your dog everywhere you go. Stuff plastic bags in your jacket, purse, car, pants pockets—anywhere you might be able to pull one out when needed. Don't count on the parks to provide them. Even when we found places with bag dispensers, they were more often empty than not. If you're squeamish about the squishy sensation, try one of those cardboard or plastic bag pooper-scoopers sold at pet stores. If you don't like bending down, buy a long-handled scoop. You get the point—there's a pooper-scooper for every preference.

And here's one for you: If your dog does his business in the woods, and nobody is there to see it, do you still have to pick up? Yes! Pack out what you pack in, and that includes the poop. As forest lands get ever increasing usage, the only way to keep them pristine is to do your part. Here's another radical thought: Pick up extra while you're out and about—garbage, dog droppings, whatever. It's convenient that Cooper and Isis have very petite poop, so there's usually room left over in the bag. If enough people do it, we might just be able to guilt everyone into picking up after themselves and their pets.

Etiquette Rex:
The Well-Mannered Mutt

While cleaning up after your dog is your responsibility, a dog in a public place has his own responsibilities. Of course, it really boils down to your responsibility again, but the burden of action is on your dog. Etiquette for restaurants and hotels is covered in other sections of this chapter. What follows are some fundamental rules of dog etiquette. We'll go through it quickly, but if your dog's a slow reader, he can read it again: no vicious dogs; no jumping on people; no incessant barking; no leg lifts on kayaks, backpacks, human legs, or any other personal objects; dogs should come when they're called; and they should stay on command.

Nobody's perfect, but do your best to remedy any problems. It takes patience and consistency. For example, Isis considers it her personal duty to vocally defend the car from passersby. So, we keep a squirt bottle on hand to quench her tendency to bark. In Cooper's mind, he's obeying the "Come!" command as long as he's vaguely and eventually headed in the right direction, and you can forget about it altogether if there are squirrels in the general vicinity, which means he's on leash more often than not. Every time there's a problem between someone's dog and someone else, we all stand to lose more of our hard-earned privileges to enjoy parks with our pets. Know your dog's limits or leash him. If you must, avoid situations that bring out the worst in your best friend.

The basic rules for dog parks are fairly consistent as well, and we've compiled a master list from our experience: no puppies under four months or females in heat; keep dogs from fighting and biting; leash your pets on entry and exit and in parking lots; be aware and keep your dog under voice control; ensure that your dog is properly vaccinated and licensed; and, you guessed it, pick up poop.

Safety First

A few essentials will keep your traveling dog happy and healthy.

Beat the Heat: If you must leave your dog alone in the car for a few minutes, do so only if it's cool out and you can park in the shade. Never, ever, ever leave a dog in a car with the windows rolled up all the way. Even if it seems cool, the sun's heat passing through the window can kill a dog in a matter of minutes. Roll down the window enough so your dog gets air, but not so much that there's danger of your dog getting out or someone breaking in. Make sure your dog has plenty of water.

You also have to watch out for heat exposure when your car is in motion. Certain cars, particularly hatchbacks, can make a dog in the backseat extra hot, even while you feel okay in the driver's seat.

Try to time your vacation so you don't visit a place when it's extremely warm. Dogs and heat don't get along, especially if your dog is a true Pacific Northwesterner who thinks anything over 80 degrees is blistering. The opposite is also true. If your dog lives in a hot climate and you take him to a cold and rainy place, it may not be a healthy shift. Check with your vet if you have any doubts. Spring and fall are the best times to travel, when parks are less crowded anyway.

Water: Water your dog frequently. Dogs on the road may drink even more than they do at home. Take regular water breaks, or bring a bowl and set it on the floor so your dog always has access to water. We use a thick clay bowl on a rubber car mat, which comes in really handy on Oregon's curvy roads. When hiking, be sure to carry enough for you and a thirsty dog. Those folding cloth bowls you can find at outdoor stores are worth their weightlessness in gold.

Rest Stops: Stop and unwater your dog. There's nothing more miserable than being stuck in a car when you can't find a rest stop. No matter how tightly you cross your legs and try to think of the desert, you're certain you'll burst within the next minute… so imagine how a dog feels when the urge strikes, and he can't tell you the problem. There are plenty of rest stops along the major freeways. We've also included many parks close to freeways for dogs who need a good stretch with their bathroom break.

How frequently you stop depends on your dog's bladder. Cooper can hold it all day, whereas Isis is whining for a potty stop at every park. If your dog is constantly running out the doggy door at home to relieve himself, you may want to stop every hour. Others can go significantly longer without being uncomfortable. Our vet says to stop every two hours as a matter of course. Watch for any signs of restlessness and gauge it for yourself.

Car Safety: Even the experts differ on how a dog should travel in a car. Some suggest dog safety belts, available at pet-supply stores. Others firmly believe in keeping a dog kenneled. They say it's safer for the dog if there's an accident, and it's safer for the driver because there's no dog underfoot.

Because of their diminutive stature, Isis and Cooper have a car seat in the back that lifts them to the level of the car window and secures their harnesses to the seat belt. That way, they can stick their snouts out of the windows to smell to world go by with some level of security. There's still the danger that a tire could kick up a pebble or a bee could buzz by, so we open the car window just enough to stick out a little snout.

Planes: Air travel is even more controversial. We're fortunate that our tiny bundles of joy can fly with us in the passenger cabin, but it still costs at least $75 a head each way. We'd rather find a way to drive the distance or leave them back at home with a friend or at the pampered pets inn. Val lost a childhood dog due to a heat-induced stroke from being left on the tarmac too long in his crate. There are other dangers, such as runway delays, when the cargo section is not pressurized on the ground, or the risk of connecting flights when a dog ends up in Auckland, New Zealand, while his people go to Oakland. Change can be stressful enough on a pet without being separated from his loved ones and thrown in the cargo hold like a piece of luggage.

If you need to transport your dog by plane, it is critical to fly nonstop, and make sure you schedule takeoff and arrival times when the temperature is below 80°F and above 35°F. All airlines require fees, and most will ask for a health certificate and proof of rabies vaccination.

The question of tranquilizing a dog for a plane journey causes the most contention. Some vets think it's insane to give a dog a sedative before flying. They say a dog will be calmer and less fearful without a disorienting drug. Others think it's crazy not to afford your dog the little relaxation she might not otherwise get without a tranquilizer. Discuss the issue with your vet, who will take into account the trip length and your dog's personality. Cooper prefers the mild sedative effect of a children's antihistamine.

The Ultimate Doggy Bag

Your dog can't pack her own bags, and even if she could, she'd fill them with dog biscuits and squeaky toys. It's important to stash some of those in your dog's vacation kit, but other handy items to bring along are bowls, bedding, a brush, towels (for those inevitable muddy days), a first-aid kit, pooper-scoopers, water, food, prescription drugs, a lint roller, and, of course, this book.

Make sure your dog is wearing her license, identification tag, and rabies tag. We advocate a microchip for your dog in addition to the ever-present collar. On a long trip, you may want to bring along your dog's rabies certificate. We pray it'll never happen, but it's a good idea to bring a couple of photos of your dog to show around, should you ever get separated.

You can snap a disposable ID on your dog's collar, too, showing a cell phone number and the name, address, and phone number of where you'll be staying, or of a friend who'll be home to field calls. That way, if your dog should get lost, at least the finder won't be calling your empty house.

Some people think dogs should drink only water brought from home, so their bodies don't have to get used to too many new things at once. Although Cooper and Isis turn up their noses at water from anywhere other than a bottle poured in their bowl, we've never heard of anyone having a problem giving their dogs tap water from any parts of the Pacific Northwest. Most vets think your dog will be fine drinking tap water in U.S. cities.

Bone Appetite

In many European countries, dogs enter restaurants and dine alongside their folks as if they were people, too. (Or at least they sit and watch and drool while their people dine.) Not so in the United States. Rightly or wrongly, dogs are considered a health threat here. Health inspectors who say they see no reason clean, well-behaved dogs shouldn't be permitted inside a restaurant or on a patio are the exception rather than the rule.

Fortunately, you don't have to take your dog to a foreign country in order to eat together. Despite a drippy sky, the Pacific Northwest has restaurants with seasonal outdoor tables and many of them welcome dogs to join their people for an alfresco experience. The law on outdoor dining is somewhat vague, and you'll encounter many different interpretations of it. In general, as long as your dog doesn't have to go inside to get to outdoor tables and isn't near the food preparation areas, it's probably legal. The decision is then up to the local inspector and/or restaurant proprietor. The most common rule of thumb we find is that if the patio is fully enclosed, dogs are discouraged from dining. Coop 'n' Isis have included restaurants with good takeout for those times when outdoor tables are stacked and tucked away.

The restaurants listed in this book have given us permission to tout them as dog-friendly eateries. But keep in mind that rules change and restaurants close, so we highly recommend phoning before you set your stomach on a particular kind of cuisine. Since you can safely assume the outdoor tables will move indoors for a while each year, and some restaurants close during colder months or limit their hours, phoning ahead is a doubly wise thing to do. Even for eateries listed in this book, it never hurts to politely ask the manager if your dog may join you before you sit down with your sidekick. Remember, it's the restaurant proprietor, not you, who will be in trouble if someone complains to the health department.

Now, we all know that the "five-second rule" for dropped food does not apply in most dog households. You're lucky if you get two seconds after uttering "Oops!" before the downed morsels become the property of your dog's maw. However, we're aiming for some better behavior when eating out. Some fundamental rules of restaurant etiquette: Dogs shouldn't beg from other diners, no matter how delicious the steak looks. They should not attempt to get their snouts (or their entire bodies) up on the table. They should be clean, quiet, and as unobtrusive as possible. If your dog leaves a good impression with the management and other customers, it will help pave the way for all the other dogs who want to dine alongside their best friends in the future.

A Room at the Inn

Good dogs make great hotel guests. They don't steal towels, burn cigarette holes in the bedding, or get drunk and keep the neighbors up all night. In the Pacific Northwest, we've seen a positive trend in the number of places that allow pets. This book lists dog-friendly accommodations of all types, from affordable motels to bed-and-breakfast inns to elegant hotels, and even a few favorite campgrounds—but the basic dog etiquette rules apply everywhere.

Our stance is that dogs should never be left alone in your room, even if crated. Leaving a dog alone in a strange place invites serious trouble. Scared, nervous dogs may tear apart drapes, carpeting, and furniture. They may even injure themselves. They might bark nonstop or scare the daylights out of the housekeeper. If you do leave your dog, tell someone at the front desk.

Bring only a house-trained dog to a lodging. How would you like a houseguest to relieve himself in the middle of your bedroom?

One of the hosts we met recommended always entering a new place with your dog on a short leash or crated, unless you've inquired ahead otherwise. We think that's a splendid idea. There are too many factors beyond your control.

Make sure your pooch is flea-free. Otherwise, future guests will be itching to leave. And, while cleanliness is not naturally next to dogliness, matted hair is not going to win you any favors. Scrub your pup elsewhere, though; don't bathe your dog in a lodging's bathroom.

It helps to bring your dog's bed or blanket along for the night. Your dog will feel more at home having a familiar smell in an unfamiliar place, and will be less tempted to jump on the hotel bed. If your dog sleeps on the bed with you at home, bring a sheet or towel and put it on top of the bed so the hotel's bedspread won't get furry or dirty.

After a few days in a hotel, some dogs come to think of it as home. They get territorial. When another hotel guest walks by, it's "Bark! Bark!" When the housekeeper knocks, it's "Bark! Snarl! Bark! Gnash!" Keep your dog quiet, or you'll find yourselves looking for a new home away from home.

For some strange reason, many lodgings prefer small dogs as guests. All we can say is, "Yip! Yap!" It's ridiculous. Isis, bless her excitable little heart, is living proof that large dogs are often much calmer and quieter than their tiny, high-energy cousins.

If you're in a location where you can't find a hotel that will accept your big brute, it's time to try a sell job. Let the manager know how good and quiet your dog is (if he is). Promise he won't eat the bathtub or run around and shake all over the hotel. Offer a deposit or sign a waiver, even if they're not required. It helps if your sweet, immaculate, soppy-eyed pooch sits patiently at your side to convince the decision-maker.

We simply cannot recommend sneaking dogs into hotels. Accommodations have reasons for their rules. It's no fun to feel as if you're going to be caught and thrown out on your hindquarters or charged an arm and a leg and a tail if discovered. You race in and out of your room with your dog as if ducking the dogcatcher. It's better to avoid feeling like a criminal and move on to a more dog-friendly location. The good news is that many hotel chains are realizing the benefits of courting canine travelers. For sure bets, see *Hotel Chains* in the *Resources* chapter of this book.

Unless you know it's a large facility with plenty of availability, call ahead to reserve a dog room and always get prior approval to bring your pets to bed-and-breakfasts and private inns. Listed rates for accommodations are for double rooms, unless otherwise noted. They do not include AARP, AAA, or other discounts you may be entitled to. Always ask about discounts and specials. Likewise, pet fees listed are nonrefundable, per pet, per night unless we say otherwise. The places that don't charge a pet fee are few and far between, but where we haven't listed one, you can assume there's no canine upcharge unless damage is done.

Natural Troubles

Chances are your adventuring will go without a hitch, but you should always be prepared to deal with trouble. Know the basics of animal first aid before you embark on a long journey with your dog.

The more common woes—ticks, burrs, poison oak and ivy, and skunks—can make life with a traveling dog a somewhat trying experience. Ticks are hard to avoid in parts of the Pacific Northwest. Although Lyme disease is rarely reported here, you should check yourself and your dog all over after a day in the country. Don't forget to check ears and between the toes. If you see an attached tick, grasp it with tweezers as close to your dog's skin as possible and pull straight out, gently but steadily, or twist counterclockwise as you pull. Disinfect before and after removing the pest.

The tiny deer ticks that carry Lyme disease are difficult to find. Consult your veterinarian if your dog is lethargic for a few days, has a fever, loses her appetite, or becomes lame. These symptoms could indicate Lyme disease. Some vets recommend a vaccine that is supposed to prevent the onset of the disease. If you spend serious time in the woods, we suggest you carry a tick collar and have your dog vaccinated.

As for mosquitoes, although a few cases of the West Nile virus have been reported in Washington and Oregon since 2006, it is very rare for humans to get infected in our area and scientists at Washington State University's animal disease lab have no confirmed cases in dogs. Your best bet is a good deet repellant for yourself.

Burrs and seeds—those pieces of nature that attach to your socks, your sweater, and your dog—are an everyday annoyance. In rare cases, they can be lethal. They may stick in your dog's eyes, nose, ears, or mouth and work their way in. Check every nook and cranny of your dog after a walk in dry fields.

Poison oak and ivy are very common menaces in our woods. Get familiar with them through a friend who knows nature or through a guided walk. Dogs don't generally have reactions, but they easily pass the oils on to people. If you think your dog has made contact with some poison plant, avoid petting her until you can get home and bathe her (preferably with rubber gloves). If you do pet her before you can wash her, don't touch your eyes and be sure to wash your hands immediately. There are several good products on the market specifically for removing poison oak and ivy oils.

If your dog loses a contest with a skunk (and he always will), rinse his eyes first with plain warm water, then bathe him with dog shampoo. Towel him

off, then apply tomato juice. If you can't get tomato juice, try using a solution of one pint of vinegar per gallon of water to decrease the stink instead.

Sea water may not seem sinister, but a dog who isn't accustomed to it may not restrain himself from gulping down a few gallons, which makes him sick as a dog, usually all over your car. Keep him hydrated to avoid temptation, and when you arrive at the beach, don't let him race to the sea and drink.

The Price of Freedom

Few dog parks in the Pacific Northwest have picked up on the trend of paying for off-leash play, but most state parks and national forests require daily parking fees unless you are also camping overnight. A $30 annual Northwest Forest Pass is good for all United States Forest Service (USFS) sites except a few with private concessions. They are available online at www.discovernw .org or at ranger stations. As of 2006, Washington State Parks eliminated all daily parking fees. Only 26 of Oregon's nearly 200 parks charge a $3 day-use fee. Oregon's annual pass is $25 ($40 for a two-year pass), available with a credit card by phone at 800/551-6949. Various Army Corps of Engineers sites, Bureau of Land Management (BLM) sites, and Fish and Wildlife locations may charge $1 to $10 per day for parking and/or camping.

Washington fishing, shellfish harvesting, and hunting licenses can be purchased online at www.greatlodge.com. You can also find a store near your destination that sells permits using the Washington Department of Fish and Wildlife's online search engine at www.wdfw.wa.gov. For Oregon, go to www .dfw.state.or.us and click the Licensing and Regulations link.

A Dog in Need

If you don't currently have a dog but could provide a good home for one, we'd like to make a plea on behalf of all the unwanted dogs who will be euthanized tomorrow—and the day after that and the day after that. Cooper came from a rescue organization and Isis from previous owners who knew they couldn't give her the personal attention she deserved. In their extended family, Coop 'n' Isis have a grandmother with two more dachshunds and a terrier, an uncle with a boxer, and an aunt with a corgi mix, all rescued. Animal shelters and humane organizations are overflowing with dogs who would devote their lives to being your best buddy, your faithful traveling companion, and a dedicated listener to all your tales. We also strongly support efforts to control the existing dog population—spay or neuter your dogs! In the immortal words of *Nike*, just do it.

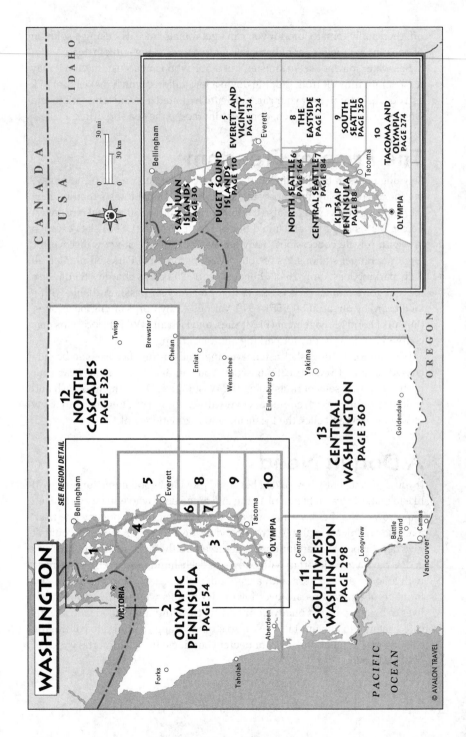

Washington

Washington is nicknamed the Evergreen State, not because of the greenbacks that line the pockets of billionaire Bill Gates, but because of the abundance of majestic conifers, nurtured by its infamous rains. While money may not grow on trees, fun sure does—and on the state's beaches, in city and county parks, national forests, and more than 125 state parks. In the Emerald City of Seattle and its suburbs alone, there are a dozen off-leash parks that make other cities' dogs green with envy. Speaking of green, as in money, the Washington State Park system eliminated the $5 parking fee for state parks in 2006, to make them more accessible to all visitors.

For a little money state residents can now get a specialized "We Love Our Pets" Washington State license plate. They are adorable, featuring a design created by cartoonist Brian Bassett of "Red and Rover" fame. The additional $40 per plate ($30 per renewal) goes to organizations and individuals dedicated to the humane treatment of animals, including animal rescue and spay/neuter education programs. Get yours at www.dol.wa.gov.

Washingtonian dogs are happy to let the world at large think of the state for its famous, high-ticket exports—Microsoft software, Google and Amazon, Boeing airliner jets, and Starbucks coffee, to name a few—while they go about enjoying the natural riches of the region that can't be exported, bought, or sold.

For starters, you can't get very far in Washington without running into a mountain and all the great outdoor activity that implies. The Olympic Mountain Range dominates the western skyline, and the Cascades line the east. Mt. Rainier, Mt. Adams, and Mount St. Helens tower to the south, and Mt. Baker to the north. As you take a ferry to the islands, cross Puget Sound bridges to the peninsulas, or walk a remote beach on the Pacific Ocean, you realize how much water shapes the landscape, and not just the gray stuff from above. While many people wait out the drizzle in more bookstores, movie theaters, and coffeehouses per capita than anywhere else in the country, there are as many who

put on microfiber, grow webbed feet, and get out 24/7/365. You'll find these people and their dogs in the best places, on, say, the Mountains to Sound Bicycling Greenway, or kayaking and canoeing the Cascade Marine Highway, or on extensive Rails-to-Trails multi-use pathways.

While you're at it, Washington's 24 scenic byways prove the theory that getting there is half the fun. A Department of Transportation Scenic Byway Map, free at visitors centers, shows you how to make your journey as worthwhile as your destination.

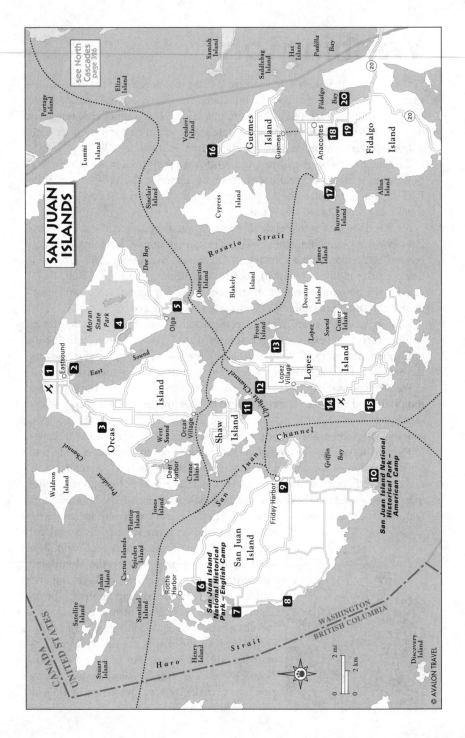

CHAPTER 1

San Juan Islands

There's nothing quite like an island to give you the feeling that you're getting away from it all, and if you believe some of the tourist literature, the San Juan Archipelago, or group of islands, has 743 of them at low tide. That number sinks to 428 at high tide; only 60 of those rocks are inhabitable. Unless you own or charter a boat, you can get to only four of them by regular ferry service: Orcas, San Juan, Shaw, and Lopez.

The San Juans sit in the rain shadow of Vancouver Island. All the rain dumps on Vancouver, leaving the islands typically sunny and dry. It is a welcome change from Portland or Seattle in the winter, but can cause droughts and water restrictions come summer. Fortunately, dog water bowls never seem to run dry on these dog-loving isles, and free treats are easy to score at drive-through bank tellers and latte stands.

The key to enjoying a trip to the islands is to plan ahead. Two things come in very handy: a Washington State ferry schedule and a tide table. The San

PICK OF THE LITTER—SAN JUAN ISLANDS

BEST PARK
Moran State Park, Orcas Island (page 35)

BEST DOG PARK
Eddie & Friends Dog Park, San Juan Island (page 41)

BEST BEACH
Young's Park, Guemes Island (page 48)

BEST HIKE
Turtleback Mountain Preserve, Orcas Island (page 34)

BEST PLACES TO EAT
Backdoor Kitchen, San Juan Island (page 42)
Love Dog Café, Lopez Island (page 47)

BEST PLACES TO STAY
Blue Heron B&B, Orcas Island (page 36)
Pebble Cove Farm, Orcas Island (page 37)
Earthbox Motel and Spa, San Juan Island (page 43)

Juans are accessible only by boat, plane, or a Washington State Ferry that leaves from Anacortes. Ferry schedules limit when you can come and go from the islands, and lines of waiting cars can be brutally long on summer weekends. Plan to travel at off-peak times or park your car in line early and leave it there while you sightsee nearby. Dogs are welcome on ferries but must stay in the car or on car decks.

For camping and lodging in the high season, May 15–September 15, make reservations well in advance to score your favorite site or room. Many of the restaurants and services on the islands are closed or have limited hours in the off-season. Call ahead for availability. For all state parks, the contact phone number is 888/CAMPOUT (888/226-7688). Windermere real estate has pet-friendly vacation rental properties available for longer stays on all of the San Juan Islands; call 800/391-8190 or check www.windermerevacationrentals.com.

Whale-watching, sailing, kayaking and cycling are the most popular island pastimes. You can rent bicycles and kayaks, charter boats, and book whale-watching tours on all the islands except Shaw. Most importantly, relax, you're on island time.

Orcas Island

At 60 square miles, Orcas is the largest and the hilliest of the San Juans. Its beautiful state park, Moran, takes full advantage of both of these features, including the towering Mt. Constitution with a viewpoint many would say is the best in the state. There are more acres in Moran than there are total residents on the island—how's that for a standout statistic? You'll find those people in pockets of activity centered around the small hamlets of Deer Harbor, Olga, Doe Bay, and the Orcas ferry landing. The center of commerce is Eastsound Village, with good restaurants and shops highlighting local artists. The *Island Sounder* is the Orcas newspaper and Pawki's is the name of the dog store in Eastsound (199 Main St.; 360/376-3648; www.pawkis.com). You'll want to find both, as they are great sources of information for all things island and all things island dog, respectively.

PARKS, BEACHES, AND RECREATION AREAS

1 Eastsound Off-Leash Area–Port of Orcas Day Park

🐾🐾🐕 (See San Juan Islands map on page 30)

Orcas Island dogs can see which way the wind is blowing, watching the orange windsock of the island airport next to their off-leash area. It's blowing in their favor. First, a dog park opened next to the animal shelter in November 2006. When it closed, a bigger, better space opened up in 2008, thanks to the Port of Orcas. It's "more dogs, more people, more fun," said one of the dog park's four committee members. For people, it's fun to watch the biplanes land next door.

This basic acre is beautiful in the eye of the beholder, especially if that eye is on the ball being chucked. The gently sloping field is perfect for those doing the chucking, for balls will bounce downhill, providing more bang for each chuck. Perhaps the best feature of the park is the toy box, kept full of tennis balls and chuckers. You'll make some fast friends by bringing extra tennis balls to restock the box when you visit.

The OLA is fully enclosed with field fencing, and entered through a double-gated entry. The observant Dachsie Twins noticed two picnic tables, three bag dispensers, pooper scoopers and a garbage can, a fire hydrant for effect, and about a dozen gallons of water on hand, brought in by regular park attendees. Someone had left a bottle of hand sanitizer on the fence.

When you get off the ferry, you'll be on Orcas Road, affectionately known as Horseshoe Highway for the shape of the island. As you enter Eastsound, turn right on Main Street. Turn left and go north on Prune Alley, go straight through the stop sign at the end of town onto North Beach Road. After 0.6 miles, turn left into the parking area, immediately after the intersection with Mt. Baker Road. The park will be on your left, before the pea patch.

2 Eastsound Waterfront Park

😺😺 (See San Juan Islands map on page 30)

You've been on the ferry for an hour, and, as you follow the trail of cars off the boat into the center of town, you realize that a pit stop for your pit bull would be a really good idea right about now. Eastsound Waterfront Park is your first, best bet for a potty break and provides the bonus of a decent bay view. A lawn with a few picnic tables and a bike rack are about it for niceties. Its sliver of beach isn't passable due to the amount of driftwood piled up.

You'll be on Orcas Road from the ferry headed into Eastsound until you turn right on Main Street, where you'll immediately find the half-dozen parking spaces and the park on your right, but no signs. 360/378-8420.

3 Turtleback Mountain Preserve

😺😺😺😺 (See San Juan Islands map on page 30)

More than 2,000 donors from all over the islands, led by the San Juan County Land Bank, contributed 10 million dollars to buy these 1,576 acres. Another 8.5 million came from the Trust for Public Land and the San Juan Preservation Trust, and a conservation easement protects the land in perpetuity. The deal was sealed in November 2006, and the trails were dedicated in July 2007. The Wonder Wieners are grateful for this place. It is efforts such as these that restore their faith in humanity and give them hope for the planet's future. You've got to forgive them for being so melodramatic, and you simply must experience the preserve for yourself.

It's gorgeous up here. That's all there is to it. Rarely is so beautiful a forest so readily accessible. You have your choice between narrow, winding trails or a wide, level dirt road to take you up and around the mountain. The trails are steadily steep, leading up to 1,519 feet above sea level at the top, but they're doable by a dachshund, so it should be easy pickings for most any body. The entire park is reserved for pedestrian access only—no bikes, motorized or otherwise; no horses; no fires, camping, or hunting—it's just you and the sound of your own breath mingling with the sigh of the woods and its natural inhabitants. Breezy sloped meadows and oak woods dominate the southern end. On the northern slope, especially as you near the top, rocky ledges and high meadows break through the conifer forest, giving you unmatched views of the San Juan and Canadian Gulf Islands.

If you're ready to run like a rabbit, take the South Trailhead to get to the curvier trail sooner. From the south end, it's a mile to the West Overlook, and 1.3 miles to Ship Rock. To follow in the footsteps of the tortoise, start at the North Trailhead to ramble up the slow and steady incline of a former dirt road.

South Trailhead Directions: From the ferry landing, turn left and take Orcas Road north toward Eastsound for 2.4 miles. Turn left and travel west on Deer Harbor Road, through West Sound, for 2.4 miles. Turn right on Wild Rose Lane to parking on the right at the top of the field.

North Trailhead Directions: From the ferry landing, take Orcas Road north for 3.4 miles. Turn left and travel west on Nordstrom lane. Turn right on Crow Valley Road, and travel north 1.7 miles. The entrance is a gravel road on the left, one driveway before the historic Crow Valley Schoolhouse.

Each trailhead has a nice gravel parking lot, bike rack, bulletin board with extra leashes, and a portable potty. Noticeably absent were garbage cans for poop. San Juan County Land Bank; 360/378-4402; www.sjclandbank.org.

🖪 Moran State Park

🐾🐾🐾🐾 🐾➔ (See San Juan Islands map on page 30)

Moran is a four-paw park all the way, with something for everyone. Driving into the park, a grand stone archway welcomes you to more than 5,000 acres of forest, five freshwater lakes, a couple of waterfalls, majestic old-growth trees, and 30 miles of hiking trails. Shipbuilder and one-time mayor of Seattle Robert Moran and his wife Millie donated the first 2,700 acres to the state to open the park in 1921, adding another 1,000 acres to their gift in 1928. It has gradually grown over the years to become Washington's fourth largest park.

The first thing you'll see is the day-use area along the shores of Cascade Lake, which features a designated swimming beach. Dogs are not allowed in the roped-off area. No visit to the park is complete without a drive or hike up to the 2,409-foot peak of Mt. Constitution. From the sandstone observation tower built by the Civilian Conservation Corps in 1936, the view extends easily 100 miles in every direction.

Trail maps, available at the ranger station, identify 15 separate trails rated as easy, challenging, or difficult depending on elevation gain. Cooper and Isis adored the flat Cascade Loop and Mountain Lake Loop. The ranger also recommended the Cold Springs Trail, with its 2,000-foot elevation gain, perhaps for pets with less vertically challenged legs.

Getting there is easy. Turn left when you get off the ferry and follow the signs 14 miles to the park entrance. Hours are 6:30 A.M.–10 P.M. in the summer, 8 A.M.–dusk in winter. 360/376-2326.

🖥 Obstruction Pass

🐾🐾🐾 (See San Juan Islands map on page 30)

This remote, primitive area was acquired by the State Parks and Recreation department in April 2003. After a moderate half-mile hike, you'll come upon 11 rough campsites, distinguishable from the thick woods only by tiny markers, picnic tables, and fire pits. It's rugged and unkempt, which adds to its unspoiled, natural beauty. There is a rock worthy of note here, a sitting rock, on a promontory overlooking the water and at least a dozen other islands. On each side of the bluff are two tiny coves, and around to the east are stairs leading down to a wider beach, covered in tiny pebbles. In crystal-clear waters,

Isis saw a starfish hanging out at low tide. Other than a latrine, there are no amenities. Camping is on a first-come, first-served basis for $11 per night, payable by check or cash at the self-pay station at the trailhead. Pack out what you pack in.

To find this out-of-the-way wonder, follow Olga Road through Moran State Park, turn left on Point Lawrence Road, right on Obstruction Pass Road, and right on Trailhead Road.

PLACES TO EAT

Bilbo's Festivo: If your dog can wait for you calmly just outside the wall, you owe it to yourself to sit on the patio and cool off with a marionberry margarita while you spice it up with chicken molé or another fabulous authentic Mexican dish for lunch or dinner. The carved wooden tables and knickknacks were inspired by the restaurant's Hobbit namesake, 20 years before the *Lord of the Rings* movie craze. 310 A St., Eastsound; 360/376-4728.

Portofino Pizzeria: Its claim to being "the best pizza on the island" is akin to you telling your only sibling he's your favorite brother. Fortunately, the only pizza available on the island is really good, and the salad bar's not half bad either. It's unbelievably busy on weekend nights; order for takeout or delivery an hour before you get hungry. 274 A St., Eastsound; 360/376-2085; www .portofinopizzeria.com.

The Sunflower Café: Cooper and Isis are all for supporting this establishment, knowing that the owners donated $500 toward the dog park on the island. It certainly doesn't hurt that the food is fresh and delicious; there was every kind of green imaginable in our balsamic vinaigrette salad and, if you want the crab cakes, you better show up early for lunch. Outdoor seating is ideal for pets, with a wraparound deck and picnic tables in a garden courtyard. Corner of Main Street and North Beach Road; 360/376-5435; www.the sunflowercafe.com.

PLACES TO STAY

Blue Heron B&B: "Pets welcome and pampered!" states their website, right on the front page, alongside the grinning mug of their black lab Pulaski, who hopes your pet will play with him the whole time you're there. The Blue Heron is a historic 1910 home with not one, but two fenced yards for pup play, as well as a private beach across the street. The three attractive rooms are upstairs, the Pelican and Egret have private decks and the Walrus is smaller, with a private bath across the hall (spring for the rooms with the decks!). Everybody gets cookies—Carole puts out her special recipes for the humans each afternoon, and the treat jar is always on the porch. Open May through October. Rates range $95–160, plus a $15 pet fee. 982 Deer Harbor Rd.; 360/376-4198; www .orcasblueheron.com.

Cottages at Cayou Cove: These three free-standing cottages are cozy and perfect in every detail. How do we love them? Let us count the ways: wood fireplaces, down duvets, fully equipped kitchens, decks with hot tubs with views of Deer Harbor marina, DVD/VCR/CD/satellite cable, clawfoot tubs and two-person showers, antique furnishings, continental breakfast delivered to your door, and an organic garden that guests are welcome to raid for their meals. Resident pooches Bruno and Hoshi live in the inn next door. Owner Valerie welcomes dogs with biscuits, bowls, bags, and blankets and asks only that they be kept off of the furniture. They are welcome to wander the property unleashed as long as they don't bother other guests and are under voice control. Rates range $195–510 plus $25 for one pet, $40 for two. Closed December through Valentine's Day. Call for directions; there's no sign. Deer Harbor; 888/596-7222; www.cayoucove.com.

Doe Bay Village: Pets are welcome in the campsites ($35–50) and in the yurts and domes ($85–110) for no extra fee. They are also allowed in the upper field cabins ($115–170) for an additional fee of $20 per pet per night. Accommodations are simple, without TVs, phones, or Internet. To further help you unplug and unwind, relax in the mineral springs pools and in a huge sauna, where everyone hangs out in the buff. Very refreshing. Doe Bay Café, serving vegetarian fare, is open all summer and winter weekends. 107 Doe Bay Rd., Olga; 360/376-2291; www.doebay.com.

North Shore Cottages: The same family has owned and operated this property for 17 years, and it's obvious they love animals. Each unique cottage is named for a totem creature: Eagle, Salmon, Heron, Orca, and Seal. Dog owners themselves, they're thrilled to have pet visitors, especially in the off-season, when its easier to find space. The cottages are full of unique artifacts and art, stained glass and rock walls, custom-made furniture, metal sculptures, mosaics, and knick-knacks. The spaces have lots of personality, without being overwhelming. The views are overwhelmingly excellent, looking out at Saturna, Patos, and Sucia Islands. The deck hot tubs and saunas, trails to the beach, TV/DVD/surround-sound systems, and "Sleep by Number" beds add to the allure. Rates vary $205–355, depending on the unit. "Your furry family members are free," says owner Elizabeth. All she asks is that you pick up after your pets on the grounds. 271 Sunset Lane; 360/376-5131; www.northshore4kiss.com.

Pebble Cove Farm: All things organic and natural, that's what matters to this environmentally sensitive lodging alternative. The setting is awesome, looking out through glass doors onto a wide deck, an even wider lawn, then onto a private beach on Massacre Bay. Two refreshing and spare studio suites ($125 winter/$175 summer) sleep couples, and a master suite ($175/$225) above the garage can sleep four. Good food is another perk of your stay here. Each suite is stocked with organic granola, milk, coffee, and a healthy snack basket. You are welcome to organic eggs from the chickens and your pick of veggies from the organic garden. The pet fee is $15 per stay. 3341 Deer Harbor Road; 360/376-6161; www.pebblecovefarm.com.

Moran State Park Campground: Tent camping is available at three sites in the woods, one on the shores of Cascade Lake, and one at Mountain Lake, for a total of 150 available spaces. Fees are $17 per night for a standard site. May 15–September 15, reserve a space in advance by calling 888/226-7688 or online at www.camis.com/wa. Limited campsites are available in the off-season; reservations not required.

San Juan Island

San Juan, the largest of the islands, has the most developed tourist facilities in its main town of Friday Harbor, good shopping, and, to our delight, the best-maintained parks. The island is most famous for its role in history as the location of The Pig War, a conflict between the United States and Britain over the Oregon Territories, which included parts of Oregon, Washington, Idaho, Wyoming, and Montana. In 1859, as the two countries haggled over the San Juans, the last bits of real estate to be divvied up, an American farmer killed a British pig. It was the final straw that nearly plunged the two countries into war. Troops of the two nations were sent to opposite ends of the island for a time out to await the decision over territorial rights. The United States was awarded ownership of the islands in 1872. The former garrisons of the two armies, English Camp and American Camp, were brought together to form the San Juan National Historical Park. Armed with this little bit of history, you and your Havanese may better appreciate the legacy of the parks all this activity left behind.

PARKS, BEACHES, AND RECREATION AREAS

◢ English Camp

🐾🐾 (See San Juan Islands map on page 30)

When the Americans were awarded ownership of the San Juans by peaceful arbitration, the British abandoned their garrison on the northwest side of the island, and James Crook and his family settled on the property. He lived on the island for 93 years and maintained the buildings, gardens, and parade grounds in excellent condition, preserving the area's history for us to enjoy.

Pick up a historical interpretive guide at the parking lot, which will provide detailed background on the log house, barracks, commandant's house, and formal gardens on the wide field that served as the parade grounds. It's a nice area for bird-watching, flying a kite, and gazing across Garrison Bay to Vancouver Island. There are two trails to hike, a 1.25-mile hill climb past the cemetery and up to Young Hill (at 650 feet, the highest elevation on the island) and a loop of similar length that leads to a bluff viewpoint.

Turn right on Blair Avenue from Spring Street, left on Guard Street, and

DIVERSIONS

Just because you want to bring your sweet pea with you doesn't mean you want to spend every waking moment with her. Give yourselves both a break by packing your slobbering sweetheart off to **Downtown Dog** for the day. Not only do they have fenced yards for supervised pack play, they have the **Bow Wow Bus to the Beach,** which carts your canine to the choicest spots on the island for a couple of hours, and returns her tired, happy, and, if you so desire, bathed, groomed, and better behaved. D-Town dogs run, swim, and hike together. D-Town dogs rule! Psssst, D-Town also does overnights, Zzzzzz. 1021 Guard St.; 360/378-0981; www.dtowndog.com.

Friday Harbor Pet Supplies is full of creature comforts, most memorably what the Wieners call the "Wall of Treats," where you can buy your biscuits by the pound out of buckets. 50 Malcolm St., #605; 360/378-0978.

right on Beaverton Valley Road, which will become West Valley Road leading into the park. Park hours are dawn–11 P.M. 360/378-2902; www.nps.gov/sajh.

7 San Juan Island County Park

🐾🐾🐾 (See San Juan Islands map on page 30)

Bring your binoculars, because this is prime whale-watching territory. Unofficially called West Side Park, this pretty, pint-sized 12-acre county property on the sunny side of the island includes a beach, rocky bluff, and a campground with unobstructed water views of the migratory path of orca whale pods. From the gravel beach, you can walk a path up and over the bluff that leads to strategically paced picnic benches for maximum views, and onto a soft, grassy slope for picnicking and even more ocean lookouts.

From West Valley Road, turn onto Mitchell Bay Road, and then left on West Side Road. Hours are 7 A.M.–10 P.M. 360/378-1842; www.sanjuanco .com/parks.

8 Limekiln Point

🐾🐾🐾 (See San Juan Islands map on page 30)

This is such a choice location for whale-watching, overlooking Haro Strait where orcas and minke whales travel May–October, that this state park is plainly called Whale Watch Park by the locals.

Much of the island's wealth came from a hundred years of mining lime from rich limestone deposits for use in steel production, paper, cement, and plaster.

NATURE HIKES AND URBAN WALKS

Which came first, the nature preserve or the sculpture garden? No matter, your dog will think you're treating him to a walk through the forest, meadows, ponds, and wetlands of **Wescott Bay Reserve** on San Juan Island, while you enjoy more than 100 works of art by Pacific Northwest sculptors. Discovering the sculptures in a 19-acre natural setting adds to their appeal, and each piece created in bronze, wood, stone, metal, glass, or ceramic is placed for maximum effect. The reserve is maintained using only native plant landscaping designed to attract more than 120 bird species. It is an excellent pairing that makes for a special treat.

The area is fenced, although dogs should be kept on leash to protect the art and natural habitats. There is a suggested $3 donation at the entrance and maps to guide you through the maze of artwork. In case you find something you can't live without, most of the pieces are for sale. Open dawn–dusk. 360/370-5050; www.wbay.org.

Left behind is yet another interesting historical island park with the best interpretive trail we've hiked. It's a one-mile loop that leads to the lighthouse (built in 1919) and an interesting reproduction of a lime kiln operation. On the way, you'll pass large groves of madrona and Douglas fir trees. A steep wooden staircase leads down to the kiln for a closer look.

To the east, and stretching north along Westside Road, are two more miles of trails in the 176-acre Limekiln Preserve. When the park is often filled with picnickers hoping to spot an orca, hikers seeking solace will find it here. Some sections are a bit steep, and that's how you get the rewarding views of Haro Straight. About 0.1 mile before the state park entrance is a gravel pullout with room for only two cars. Across the road is the trailhead, marked with a Land Bank "Day Use and Pedestrian Access Only" sign.

Getting to Limekiln is almost as much fun as the park itself, winding along the coast on the scenic West Side Road. From the parking area, an ADA-accessible trail leads 300 yards down to a viewing platform. A dozen picnic tables are scattered through the park. Along the park's 2,500 feet of coastline is a 0.3-mile hike to Deadman Bay. It's steep, narrow, and on the edge of a cliff—not for those who get woozy at the sight of heights. The reward is a rocky beach with exciting surf and more amazing views.

From Spring Street at the ferry, take San Juan Valley Road, turn left on Douglas Road, and right on Bailer Hill Road, which becomes West Side Road. Park hours are 8 A.M.–dusk. 360/378-4402; www.sjclandbank.org.

9 Eddie & Friends Dog Park

🐾🐾🐾🐕 (See San Juan Islands map on page 30)

Two acres of freedom costs about $20,000 these days, and more power to the good people of San Juan Island for making it happen on their rock. The grand opening of their off-leash park happened on September 6, 2008.

A mostly level playing field is completely enclosed with six-foot-high field fencing, each 10-foot section of which is marked by a plaque honoring a dear departed dog, or a person or business who paid for that section of security. Many of them are hand drawn and painted, a sweet remembrance. Isis was particularly taken by one for "Sir Rufus the Bold," a dachshund who "served his family fearlessly for over sixteen years." Island Rotary matched fence funds, other participants donated beautiful log benches and a classy gazebo for shade, JW Design contributed the storm-water drainage design, Island Rec is kicking in for liability insurance—and let's not forget the family of Browne's Home Center, who are leasing the land to the dog park steering committee for $1 a year. In gratitude, the park is named for their mascot Eddie.

Within the larger fence is a small and elderly dog area, each with its own double-gated entrance. The landscape is mainly tamped-down field grass, dotted with a few tall pines. We saw cans, bags, bottled water, and a bucket of balls, but it wouldn't hurt to bring extras of everything.

From the ferry, stay on Spring Street through the first few blocks of town. Take a left on Mullis Street, go 0.5 miles, and turn left into the gravel lot for the dog park, between Browne's Home Center and the Fire Station. Open 7:30 A.M. to dusk.

10 American Camp

🐾🐾🐾🐾 (See San Juan Islands map on page 30)

Somewhat in parallel to the two countries themselves, English Camp is small, green, and tidy while American Camp is large and more untamed, with wide plains, grandiose forests, and long beaches, totaling 1,223 acres occupying the entire southeast tip of the island.

There's so much to see and do here, you might want to start at the visitors center to put together your game plan. Meanwhile, the following are some of our top recommendations: Drive the length of Cattle Point Road through the park to take in the views and see the lay of the land. Build a bonfire on Fourth of July Beach, on the quiet side of the bay. Take a walk on the wild and windy side, for miles and miles and miles, along South Beach, the longest public beach on the island. Not tired yet? Hike the old dirt road trail, covered by a forested canopy of fir, cedar, and maple to Jakle's Lagoon and Mount Finlayson. Finally, wade through the grasslands to the Redoubt, a buried gun battery.

If you and your pup enjoy a dose of education with your exercise, there are exhibits featuring the American-British boundary dispute, archaeology, and camp life. Historical tour guidebooks are available to borrow in boxes at the top of each trailhead. One-mile self-guided walks start at the visitors center and Jakle's Lagoon parking lot.

From Spring Street off the ferry, turn left on Mullis Street. Mullis becomes Cattle Point Road, and you can follow the road's twists and turns and the signs directly to the park entrance. Park hours are dawn–11 P.M. 360/378-2902; www.nps.gov/sajh.

PLACES TO EAT

Backdoor Kitchen: A local favorite with a heated patio in a garden setting, the Backdoor is front and center on our list of must-dos for dinner or late-night cocktails. While only two blocks from the ferry, it's tastefully hidden, so ask for directions. The menu changes regularly to feature island farms, with especially artful fresh vegetable dishes. Admittedly, Coop 'n' Isis's mom is a pushover for any drink in a martini glass with a fresh fruit slice in it. 400 A Street; 360/378-9540; www.backdoorkitchen.com.

The Doctor's Office: Walk off the ferry and across the street into this self-proclaimed "treatment café" and treat yourself to espresso, homemade hard-pack ice cream, a juice bar, daily pastries, sandwiches, and breakfast burritos. A convenient walk-up window makes it easy, just what the doctor ordered. 85 Front Street, Friday Harbor; 360/378-8865.

Garden Path Café: Garden salads, deli salads, salmon and Cobb—if you like your lunch tossed and eaten with a fork, the Garden has got your number. It's a tiny storefront with a single picnic table. Go to the counter, point at the pre-made deli salads in the case or order a made-to-order green salad, and pay. It's that easy to be healthy. 135 Second St.; 360/278-6255; www .gardenpathcafe.com.

Golden Triangle: Affordable, filling, and tasty—could these be the three legs of the aforementioned triangle? Or is it the triumvirate of Vietnamese, Thai, and Laotian specialties served at this popular spot? No, wait, perhaps it's the three choices you get from the hot lunch bar to make your meal. Lastly, is it a coincidence that there are three tables under the sidewalk patio trellis? We'll never know, and if we did, we don't eat and tell. 140 1st St.; 360/378-1917.

PLACES TO STAY

Argyle House: This relaxing B&B is ideally situated a couple blocks from the center of Friday Harbor and right across the street from a small city park called Cahail. Toby the golden retriever will wag you a warm welcome, and promptly request to play with your pals. Upstairs in the main house, the Robyn's Nest and Sunflower Rooms are $145. Each has a private shower bath, a queen bed, and a full bed or sitting area. Isis thinks you should spring for the Honeymoon Cottage ($175), in the back yard with its own front porch. New owners in 2008 haven't set any pet restrictions or fees yet; let's hope responsible visitors allow them to continue this generosity. 685 Argyle Ave.; 800/624-3459; www.argylehouse.net.

Earthbox Motel and Spa: The Friday Harbor Inn in a previous life, the Earthbox has gone upscale, with a remodel done in very good taste, completed in 2008. The stylish rooms are subtly themed Earth, Sky, Sun, and Water, starting at $140 and ranging up to $230 depending on size and season. It's got the kind of flair we'd expect in a more urban setting, say, L.A. or New York, with the likes of leather chairs, Pergo floors, and brushed aluminum countertops. Extra touches include a pet goodie basket and a little dog lawn. Its location is ideal, but book early, as they designate only a half dozen rooms for dogs. The pet fee is $15. 410 Spring St., Friday Harbor; 360/378-4000; www.earthboxmotel.com.

Lakedale Resort: This private, 82-acre property is a vacation unto itself, with camping, cabins, a grand lodge and dining room, a general store, and three lakes stocked with rainbow trout and wide-mouth bass. Campsites on Dream Lake and Neva Lake are $30–60 per night (available May–Sept. only). Pets are also welcome in the six cabins featuring two bedrooms, two baths, fireplaces, lakeside decks, full kitchen, linens, and cookware. It looks like L. L. Bean or Eddie Bauer had a hand in decorating. Take a dip in the lake or grab a pole and catch some dinner. Rates are typically $250–340, plus a $25 cleaning fee per pet per visit, but call for great off-season specials. 4313 Roche Harbor Rd.; 800/617-2267; www.earthboxmotel.com.

Snug Harbor Resort & Marina: Modern, waterfront cabins are tucked into Mitchell Bay on the northwest side of the island. They include queen-size beds, kitchens, and view decks, and some have fireplaces. Pets are $20, in addition to the regular rates of $155–230. Snug Harbor is also a popular marina, with a gift shop/general store and kayak and whale-watching tours. 1997 Mitchell Bay Rd.; 360/378-4762; www.snugresort.com.

San Juan County Park Campground: The campsites are all together on an open slope, and because they are placed for 360-degree views, there's nothing to stop anyone from looking in your tent, either. Advance reservations are your only hope of getting one of the 23 sites in the summer. Water, real flushing toilets, picnic tables, fire rings, and firewood are available. Cost is $28–39 per night, plus an $8 reservation fee. West Side Road; 360/378-1842; www.sanjuanco.com/parks.

Shaw Island

This tiny island of 7.7 square miles, with a population of about 150, has one general store at the ferry landing, a library, and a county park with camping and a lovely sandy beach as its only public amenities. It often gets overlooked by the hordes of summer island tourists, meaning you stand a good chance of being one of only a handful of people enjoying gorgeous views and peaceful country roads.

PARKS, BEACHES, AND RECREATION AREAS

11 Shaw Island County Park

🐾🐾🐾 (See San Juan Islands map on page 30)

You'll hear the locals call this South Beach, a beautiful spot that meets our every requirement for a perfect beach. It is secluded, with great views of Canoe and Lopez Islands. The sand is soft for squishing between paws and toes, and there are comfortable observation rocks and driftwood logs to sit upon and watch the waves. The beach is accessed by two steep wooden staircases that descend from the campground and day-use area. A picnic shelter, some tire swings, and a small lawn make up the area above the beach.

From the ferry landing, Gratzer Road will lead you to Blind Bay Road. From there, it's less than a mile before you turn left on Squaw Bay Road, then right on Indian Cove Road and the park to your right. 360/378-8420.

PLACES TO STAY

Shaw Island County Park Campground: There are 11 campsites, numbers 1–6 have water views for $18 per night, and numbers 7–11 are on the hillside for $14 per night. Each site has a picnic table and a fire pit, and some privacy is provided by tree cover. Camping is by reservation only April–October, for an additional $8 per reservation. Call 360/378-1842 up to 90 days in advance, and pay by VISA or MasterCard. Campsites are first come, first served the rest of the year, and you pay by cash or check at self-pay stations in the park. There's one vault toilet and running water, but no shower facilities. 360/378-1842; www.sanjuanco.com/parks.

Lopez Island

Lopez is the friendliest and most casual of the San Juans. The flat, mostly agricultural island is open and pastoral. We knew a dog named Lucia who barked only at cows and bicycles; she would have been hoarse and happy here. There is a tradition to greet everyone you pass in the car with a wave. It's easy enough to hop a quick ferry from Orcas or San Juan to come for the day. Lopez Village is the town center, with shops, restaurants, a good-sized grocery, and the only public showers available on the island.

PARKS, BEACHES, AND RECREATION AREAS

12 Odlin

🐾 🐾 (See San Juan Islands map on page 30)

This county park offers 80 acres of near-instant gratification, only one mile south of the ferry landing. You can park your car on the beach and step out onto the sand. Picnic tables are lined up along the waterfront, with views across Upright Channel to Shaw Island. When you've had your fill of the beach, you can hike the dense, narrow, winding Little Bird Trail, accessible from behind a small meadow. Be prepared to get muddy in the rainy season; some puddles were deep enough for Cooper to swim through! We discovered our first beachfront baseball field here and wondered how many foul balls have been retrieved from the surf over the years.

Odlin is to your right, off Center Road, about a mile after you get off the ferry. 360/378-1842; www.sanjuanco.com/parks.

DIVERSION

It's a rare and special place where literature and dogs get equal billing, as they do at **Islehaven Books & Borzoi** in Lopez Island Village. At any given time, shop owner Phyllis has about a half dozen of these Russian beauties, who alternate coming with her to the shop every day. As you browse for literature, you might also ask about the dogs' show names and see their winning ribbons on the wall behind the counter. Please leave your pets to bask in the sun on the deck out front while you shop, to avoid any potential conflicts of interest. #2 Village Center, Lopez Village; 360/468-2132.

13 Spencer Spit

🐾🐾🐾 (See San Juan Islands map on page 30)

The spit is a symmetrical triangular sandbar, created by the action of waves eroding sand from cliffs to the north and south and transporting sand along the shoreline. In the middle of the spit is a protected saltwater lagoon. This unique land feature is named for Theodore Spencer, who built a house for his family on the hillside and a log cabin at the tip of the spit for guests sometime between 1913 and 1920.

The first parking you see is a view lot with a 10-minute limit. Past the restrooms to the second parking area is a short hike down and onto the spit itself. You'll want a sweater or jacket, even in good weather, to defend you against the brisk winds. It's fun to check out the replica of Spencer's cabin, built in 1978 from materials washed up on the shore. Picnic benches and fire pits are lined up along the north edge of the sandbar. You're welcome to swim if you have the fortitude. You can go crabbing and clamming for your sustenance as did the island's first Native American inhabitants, but you must have a state license to do so.

To make your way to Spencer Spit, follow the signs from Center Road to Cross Road, turning right on Port Stanley Road and left on Bakerview Road.

14 Otis Perkins Park

🐾🐾 (See San Juan Islands map on page 30)

Our friend Daniel, though dogless, is a dog person at heart. He is also a sailor who knows the islands well, and when we mentioned the dog book, he started rattling off a list of places we should visit. He particularly thought this spit of land on Fisherman Bay would be interesting for dogs for the curiosity factor. This beach walk offers a first-rate olfactory marine biology lesson for those whose sinus senses are more finely tuned than ours. Meanwhile, you can enjoy the views across the water to San Juan and Shaw islands, a simple pleasure.

From the ferry, follow Ferry Road and Fisherman Bay Road toward Lopez Village. Continue on Fisherman Bay Road past the village for a couple of miles, and turn right on Bayshore Road. Park at the end of the spit off to the left, by the single picnic table and can. Stay down on the beach, as the road above is heavily traveled.

15 Shark Reef Sanctuary

🐾🐾🐾 (See San Juan Islands map on page 30)

At Shark Reef, it is absolutely vital that you respect the signs cautioning you to keep dogs on leash and stay on the trails. After a quick, half-mile trot through the woods, the trail ends abruptly on a cliff, high above big waves crashing against the rocks. It would be way too easy for your English setter to run right over the edge in his enthusiasm. Shark Reef gets its name from rocks as chiseled as a shark's teeth. It is dangerous, dramatic, and stunning. Once you arrive at that first arresting viewpoint, the trail continues along the cliff's edge, presenting you with viewpoint after viewpoint of islands with equally dangerous names such as Mummy Rocks and Deadman Island, and just when you think you've passed the last good view, you come upon another. There are plenty of opportunities to put down a blanket, perhaps to enjoy a picnic, and be inspired by the views of the surrounding islands and the Strait of San Juan de Fuca. This gorgeous, wild sanctuary is preserved by the joint efforts of the Department of Natural Resources and the San Juan County Parks department. Take the proper precautions to fully enjoy the drama it presents.

When you reach the southern boundary at the end of the cliff trail, Cooper recommends retracing your steps back to the main trail. The rest of the paths through the park are barely discernable through the brush, and it is easy to get lost (or so he heard, not willing to admit that as a hound, he couldn't pick up the scent of the track).

To reach the park, take the right fork in the road from Ferry Road to Fisherman Bay Road, turn right on Airport Road, and then left on Shark Reef Road to the end, where you'll see a trailhead with room for about four cars, a latrine, and a trash can. The trail to the bluff is right at the park sign.

PLACES TO EAT

Lopez Islander Restaurant: The Islander caters to boaters, with a huge deck out back and covered umbrella tables overlooking the marina. Bring your pet to hang out with the sea dogs, while you order drinks from the Tiki Lounge. "The prime rib is good stuff," says one staffer, and another saves her tips for the macadamia-crusted halibut. Open for breakfast and lunch year-round, dinner only in the summer. 2864 Fisherman Bay Rd.; 360/468-2233.

Love Dog Café: Owner and chef White Bear Woman believes in the power of good food to comfort and soothe the soul, and she certainly made believers out of us. A grilled cheese sandwich with tomatoes and onions was doggone good, and the homemade desserts all looked lovely. Buy a bag of the homemade, heart-shaped peanut butter dog treats for the road. #1 Village Center, Lopez Village; 360/468-2150.

Vita's Wildly Delicious: Vita is a caterer with a fancy shop that caters to picnickers who want to put together a gourmet spread of wine, cheese, and lovingly made delicacies to take on the road or home for a patio supper. Vita has wildly good taste and high style. She might close the kitchen for several weeks in February, so plan your trip to Lopez any other month of the year. She's that good. 77 Village Road, Lopez Village; 360/468-4268.

PLACES TO STAY

Bay House & Garden Cottages: Our highest recommendation for where to stay on Lopez, these two Garden Cottages are tucked into a landscaped retreat in the heart of Lopez Village. They are petite and sweet, sunny and charming. They feel very private, with a sunny courtyard, goldfish pond, and patio table shared between the two. The Bay House has two bedrooms, a full kitchen, woodstove, and an unbeatable deck view across Fisherman Bay. The house also features beautiful landscaping. Cottages $150/Bay House $200. The pet fee is $35 per stay. Call for locations. 360/468-4889; www.interisland.net/cc.

Spencer Spit State Park Campground: Sites at this 138-acre park are available March 5–October 26, and they are some of the best we've encountered. They are spacious, level, paved with gravel, and spaced much farther apart than usual, offering complete privacy. In addition, there are seven walk-in sites right on the beach just south of the spit, with the ocean just outside your tent flap. There are no showers or utility hookups. Camping is $17 per night. 521A Bakerview Rd.; 888/226-7688.

Guemes Island

Cooper and Isis felt the spirits of distant ancestors here on "Dog Island," nicknamed for the companions raised by the Samish Indian Nation whose fur was used to weave blankets when goat hair was sparse. Guemes (GOO-eh-mus) Island, a tiny oasis reached by a seven-minute ferry ride from Anacortes, is the place to go to get your island fix if you don't have the time or money to head to the San Juans. The county ferry leaves from the intersection of 6th and I streets in Anacortes and costs $9 round-trip. The island retains its character of peace and quiet; at only four miles from bottom to top, it's too small to draw much attention. You have one choice for lodging, one for food, and two public beaches. In short, Dog Island is perfect for a dog's day out.

PARKS, BEACHES, AND RECREATION AREAS

16 Young's Park

🐾🐾🐾🐾 (See San Juan Islands map on page 30)

Generations of people have enjoyed this plot of land since 1925. It is the place to go for fishing, crabbing, clamming, beachcombing, stick throwing, swimming, sunbathing, kite flying, boating, exploring, sniffing… we could go on, but you get the idea. You and your pooch can pick your pleasure on land and in the waters around the island.

The area immediately south of the park is private, but you can walk around the island to the north just about as far as you want. You'll pass in front of the Guemes Island Resort and a group camp; they don't mind sharing. The beach is a combination of sand and gravel, easy on the paws. Views to the north are prettier than those on the island's south side, looking out on Canada, with snow-capped Mt. Baker hogging center stage.

The county has maintained the park since 1977, providing a comfortable lawn, a few picnic tables, trash receptacles, and a portable potty. There is one more county park in the center of the island, Schoolhouse Park, but we've left it off the list because there's nothing there of interest to a dog other than soft grass in an emergency.

The way to Young's Park is idiot-proof. From the ferry, drive four miles, go straight past the park sign to the end of the road, bear right, and park in the gravel parking lot. Day use only. 4243 Guemes Island Rd.; 360/336-9414; www.skagitparksfoundation.org/youngs.htm.

PLACES TO EAT

Anderson's General Store and Kitchen: The kitchen serves up huevos rancheros, omelets, yogurt parfaits, and legendary cinnamon rolls for breakfast. Burgers, hot dogs, Greek salad, and pesto chicken sandwiches dominate the lunch and dinner menus. The Andersons also offer ice cream, espresso, and, as they say, free advice. Outdoor seating is on a wraparound porch overlooking the ferry terminal. The general store shelves are well stocked with unusual treats. This is your only choice for island groceries. Their tongue-in-cheek motto is "If we don't have it, we'll explain how to get along without it." 7885 Guemes Island Rd.; 360/293-4548; www.guemesislandstore.com.

PLACES TO STAY

Guemes Island Resort: It seems as though every place is called a resort on the islands, harkening back to quainter days when people were in the habit of summering here. These five simple, cozy cabins and a house share the driveway that leads to Young's Park and a stretch of sandy beach. The cabins are heated by woodstove only. The Mt. Baker house has furnace heat and is wheelchair accessible. They do not provide TV, phones, or radio. Who needs them when every window frames a view of Mt. Baker and the islands? Cabins are $125–150 per night, and the house is $150–170. Barbecues, kayaks and rowboats are provided to guests at no charge. Pets are $10 per night. 4268 Guemes Island Rd.; 800/965-6643; www.guemesislandresort.com.

Anacortes

The channel of water separating Fidalgo Island from the mainland is so narrow that most people don't even realize that the city of Anacortes is on an island. Recreational opportunities are overshadowed by the city's blue-collar reputation and people rushing through town to get on the next ferry to the San Juans. Good thing dogs don't discriminate. In town, all retail activity centers, appropriately, on Commercial Avenue.

PARKS, BEACHES, AND RECREATION AREAS

17 Washington Park

🐾 🐾 🐾 (See San Juan Islands map on page 30)

Everyone we talked to in Anacortes said, "Have you been to the loop yet? Isn't it great?" We quickly learned that the loop is a two-mile paved trail around the beachhead of Fidalgo Island in Washington Park. And, sure enough, it is great. It is the social circle for high-paw society in Anacortes, and debutante dogs happily drag their humans on leashes behind them as they meet and greet. Let's just say there's a whole lot of sniffing going on.

Peek-a-boo views of Rosario Strait, Fidalgo Head, Burrows Bay, and the surrounding islands through the trees keep you occupied while your dog works the crowd. At several points along the loop, unpaved 0.1-mile spurs stick out to take you to little beach spots, tide pools, and less obstructed views, particularly at Green Point. The rest of the 220-acre park includes a campground, playground, 24-hour boat launch, and waterfront picnic tables off to the right at the entrance to the loop. The loop is restricted to walkers 6 A.M.–10 A.M., after which it is open to cars until the park closes at 10 P.M. However, dogs looked down their noses at us and walkers gave us the big stink eye when we tried to drive around; it is obviously local custom to walk.

Take the Highway 20 spur all the way through town and out Oakes Avenue. At the fork in the road where all the cars go right to get on the ferry, take the left fork instead onto Sunset Avenue and straight into the park. 6300 Sunset Ave.

18 Ace of Hearts Dog Park

🐾 🐾 🐾 🐕 (See San Juan Islands map on page 30)

The city of Anacortes is mapped on an alphanumeric grid (east–west streets numbered 1–41 and north–south avenues A–Z), which is why you'll hear this

park called the "H & 38th." As Coop and Isis set about doing their research, the local dog organization Fidalgo Islanders for Dogs Off-leash (FIDO), was busy getting their dog park ready for a late 2008/early 2009 opening. It's a 1.5-acre space, with some rolling topography and a tiny triangle fenced separately for the little dogs (the little guys got gypped).

When we stopped by in September 2008, the parking lot had been leveled, and gravel had been laid down. The tall chain link fence, with double-gated entries, was installed. A thick layer of wood chips had been spread around the infield. Hydro-seeding of ground cover was scheduled for the following week.

We spoke to FIDO leader Amy, who was confident they'd have a gazebo by spring, as well as trees, shrubs, and landscaping. The watering station, wash-off station, and a brick pathway of donated and engraved pavers will be built. They clearly have their act together, and funds in the bank, so we expect all the trimmings to be there for a grand opening in early 2009. Stay tuned by going to www.anacortesdogpark.com.

From Commercial Avenue, turn west onto 32nd Street, and left onto I Avenue, which curves to become H Avenue a block later. At 0.4 miles, just south of 38th, you'll see a dirt road on the left, across from the sign for Cedar Springs.

19 Anacortes Community Forest Lands

🐾🐾🐾 (See San Juan Islands map on page 30)

We were pleasantly surprised to learn of an extensive network of trails (50-ish miles) on protected land managed through the ACFL program. Unless you're lucky enough to stumble upon trail markers for the 2,800 acres of ACFL lands, your best bet is to buy a set of water-resistant maps at the visitors center for $10 (corner of 9th Street and Commercial Avenue; 360/293-3832). You'll find out where to park and where main trail access points are located. Other handy map information includes elevation gain, mileage, trail usage restrictions, and difficulty ratings. Map-loving geeks, like Cooper's dad Steve, will be in heaven.

It's a big, messy maze of sparsely used lakes, forests, ponds, wetlands, forests, and mountains, but don't let that scare you off. Trails are short, less than two miles, and you can't get lost for long without bumping into civilization or the water. Speaking of water, in attempt to put some kind of framework around ACFL lands, trails are grouped around the three biggest inland bodies of it: Cranberry Lake, Heart Lake, and Whistle Lake. What the locals call Little

DOG-EAR YOUR CALENDAR

Anacortes Bark in the Park happens on the second or third Saturday in June, depending on when the kids get out of school. They celebrated their fourth year in 2008 at John Storvick Park. And, get this: They met their fundraising goals to build the dog park (which will be opening in 2009), so future events will also raise money for local dog rescue organizations and charities. Help them keep up the good work—dress up for the parade, show off in the demos and contests, peruse the vendor booths. Try agility! Try flyball! Or, just root around in your goodie bag. For schedule and information, go to www.anacortesdogpark.com or call 360/588-8749.

Cranberry Lake (not to be confused with Big Cranberry Lake in Deception Pass State Park) is the perennial favorite. Another highlight is the summit of Mt. Erie at 1270 feet, which can be reached from either Heart Lake or Whistle Lake. Some trails are open to horses and mountain bikes, and a few are open even to off-road motorbikes. We didn't encounter anyone in the winter, and hopefully everyone will share and share alike. 360/299-1953.

20 Tommy Thompson Parkway

🐾🐾 (See San Juan Islands map on page 30)

This is an urban trail through the working heart and history of Anacortes. The asphalt, multi-use pathway gets more interesting the farther away you get from the center of town. It starts, paralleling a road, at the Cap Sante Boat Haven, at the corner of 11th Street and R Avenue. You'll pass marinas, industrial warehouses, and boat dry docks. Additional parking is available in a gravel lot at the corner of 22nd Street and R Avenue. From there, the trail separates from the road, passing through more of the working guts of a maritime town. The best parking is at 30th Street and U Avenue, where the Soroptomists built the lot, and heading south from here the trail becomes less commercial and more scenic. Each trail segment is less than a mile between lots. Finally, parking is available at the Fidalgo Bay RV Park, off Fidalgo Bay Road, for a final mile of trail around the inner bend of the bay to March Point Road. The pathway is easy to find throughout, marked by bright yellow posts. Coop's favorite part was popping across the street for an espresso at Strawberry Bay Coffee Company at 21st and R. Hours are dawn to 10 P.M. 360/293-1918; www.cityofanacortes.com/parks/tommy_thompson.htm.

PLACES TO EAT

Brown Lantern Alehouse: The Brown's been around since 1933, and lately they've been winning a lot of awards: for best burger, best tavern, and best lounge out in back, to name a few. It's nothing much to look at, but looks can be deceiving, ask any lovable bulldog. 360/293-2544; 412 Commercial Ave.; www.brownlantern.com.

Rockfish Grill: The pub grub pleases and the Anacortes ales and lagers go down nice and easy on the side patio. Nachos, tostadas, fish and chips, vegetarian specialties, and wood-fired brick-oven pizzas are the biggest crowd-pleasers for lunch and dinner. 320 Commercial Ave.; 360/588-1720; www.anacortesrockfish.com.

PLACES TO STAY

Fidalgo Country Inn: Pine furniture and French country patterns soften the look of an otherwise standard motel. Freshly baked cookies and a gas fireplace in the lobby don't hurt either. It's ideally located halfway between the Anacortes ferry and Deception Pass State Park. Standard room rates range $60–140; suites $200–400; $20 per pet per night. 7645 SR 20; 360/293-3494; www.fidalgocountryinn.com.

Ship Harbor Inn: Every one of the inn's 28 rooms has a view of the ferry harbor, Guemes Channel, and the San Juans. Situated in a couple of buildings on a hillside, the inn is surrounded by six choice acres of mature trees. It's a much nicer setting than the motels in town. Rooms are casual, comfortable, and reasonably priced, starting at $110, plus a $10 pet fee. 5316 Ferry Terminal Rd.; 800/852-8568; www.shipharborinn.com.

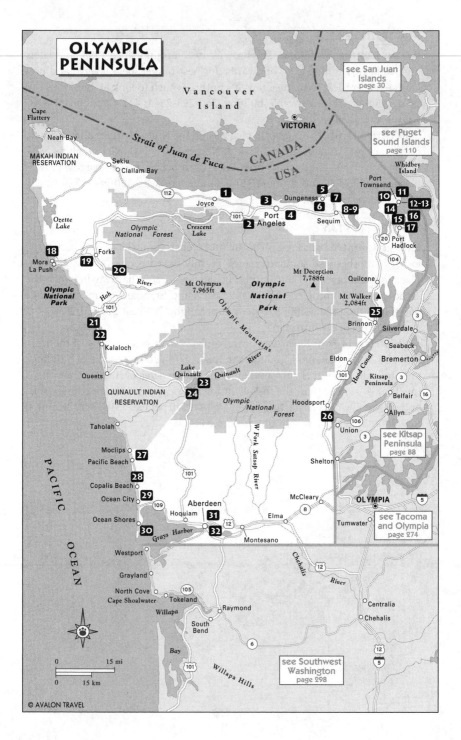

OLYMPIC PENINSULA

CHAPTER 2

Olympic Peninsula

First, the bad news. The core of the Olympic Peninsula, and about half of its coastline, consists of 922,651 acres of wilderness where dogs are forbidden on trails, in buildings, or anywhere in the backcountry. This is the **Olympic National *Park*** (ONP). Dogs are allowed in national park campgrounds and they may stay in the car if you travel up to Hurricane Ridge or into the Hoh Rainforest.

Now for the good news. That still leaves 632,324 acres of **Olympic National *Forest*** (ONF) surrounding the national park where your dog is allowed, on leash. The ONF offers countless recreation opportunities for pups with boundless energy. In many cases, the only things that restrict a dog's life, other than an eight-foot tether, are high tides that limit the amount of beachfront real estate at seaside parks. You may want to consult a tide table before you head out, available for a few bucks at most convenience stores.

It gets better. In addition to state, county, and city parks that are lively, beautiful, and dog-friendly, the peninsula is host to 101 campgrounds; a few of the

PICK OF THE LITTER—OLYMPIC PENINSULA

BEST PARKS
Chetzemoka, Port Townsend (page 66)
Fort Flagler, Marrowstone Island (page 69)

BEST DOG PARK
Sequim Dog Park, Sequim–Dungeness Valley (page 62)

BEST BEACHES
North Beach, Port Townsend (page 64)
Rialto Beach, La Push (page 71)

BEST TRAIL
South Shore Trails, Lake Quinault (page 76)

BEST PLACES TO EAT
Bella Italia, Port Angeles (page 60)
Dos Okies, Port Townsend (page 68)
Front Street Café, Pacific Beach (page 80)

BEST PLACES TO STAY
Chevy Chase Beach Cabins, Port Townsend (page 68)
Manitou Lodge, Forks (page 73)
Sunset Marine Resort, Sequim–Dungeness Valley (page 64)

BEST CAMPING
Ocean City State Park, Ocean City (page 82)

best are listed here. Lest this paint too rosy a picture, you will have to prepare yourself and your sad-eyed basset hound for the sight of clear-cut forests in some areas. Forestry is the area's largest industry and the majority of land not protected by the federal government belongs to logging companies.

NATIONAL FORESTS AND EXTENDED TRAILS

Olympic National Forest
🐾🐾

ONF is divided into two ranger districts, Hood Canal and Pacific, with three offices around the Olympic Peninsula. At each ranger station, you can get current information about campground listings, weather, and road conditions. Trail descriptions include trailhead directions, highlights, length, elevation gain, and latest reported conditions. If the office is closed, pertinent information is posted on a bulletin board and online. Even if you've been to a specific destination before, stop by or call ahead, as frequent closures and restrictions are reported due to fallen trees, landslides, spring floods, and other whims of Mother Nature. ONF trails are serious business. All of them can be described as back-country; know your limits, register at trailheads, and take the essentials. Forks: 437 Tillicum Ln.; 360/374-6522; Quilcene: 295142 Hwy. 101 S.; 360/765-2200; Quinault: 353 Southshore Rd.; 360/288-2525. www.fs.fed.us/r6/olympic.

Olympic Discovery Trail
🐾🐾🐾

The main parts of the Olympic Discovery Trail run through Sequim on the way west to Port Angeles and east to Port Townsend. It's a great trail to hike/bike/geocache/walk dogs on leash. The route is paved between Port Angeles and Sequim. The Adventure Route, finished in 2007, is a combo of gravel, dirt, and forest roads heading west from the Elwha River to Lake Crescent. The lofty ultimate goal is to connect Port Townsend to the ocean at La Push. There are excellent maps of every section at www.olympicdiscoverytrail.com.

Joyce

The town is tiny, the views huge. The Strait of Juan de Fuca Highway, Highway 112, is an American Scenic Byway that hugs the jagged cliffs and cedar forests on one side and the ocean on the other. It winds 60 miles from west of Port Angeles to the Makah Indian Reservation at Neah Bay. Across the water is Vancouver Island, British Columbia.

PARKS, BEACHES, AND RECREATION AREAS

1 Salt Creek Recreation Area
🐾🐾🐾 (See Olympic Peninsula map on page 54)

Salt Creek/Tongue Point/Crescent Beach/Fort Hayden is known by four names, with three paws, and two campgrounds, for one park. Salt Creek Recreation Area is the name you'll see on the signs. There's a playground and immense fields designed for RV camping that also happen to be a blast for dogs to run around on. There are fun trails; the shortest follows the bluff past two heavily camouflaged concrete bunkers that are simultaneously creepy and cool, built before World War II for the Fort Hayden military reservation. Just behind the main gate to the right are more trails: a 1.1-mile jaunt to a cove, and a longer, rockier, narrower 2.4-mile path to the vista at Striped Peak nearby (that makes five names, doesn't it?).

Isis feels they use the term "beach access" too liberally. Out of the five "walkways," four are concrete stairs that end in the sky over rocky, slippery, dangerous cliffs. Not very inviting. The only practical way is to drive out the main entrance to the west and pay to hang out for the day at the private Crescent Beach RV Park for all-day access to the most pristine section of sand. Once there, you can walk around Tongue Point to study the tide pools.

Turn north on Camp Hayden Road, 13 miles west of Port Angeles on State Route 112. 3506 Camp Hayden Rd.; 360/928-3441; www.clallam.net/countyparks.

PLACES TO STAY

Crescent Beach RV Park: Cooper doesn't often recommend RV parks, but this one is neat. The fine folks here own a half mile of pristine beachfront, where you can hang out for the day for $5 a head. The lot is a field, shaded by large trees with nearby deer and bald eagles, and every site has an ocean view. It costs $35 a night for a tent site, plus $5 per pet. 2860 Crescent Beach Rd.; 360/928-3344; www.olypen.com/crescent.

Port Angeles

While it's true that dogs are not allowed in the greater Olympic National Park, you'd deserve a "bad human" scolding if you left out a drive up to Hurricane Ridge. Starting in Port Angeles, it takes about 45 minutes to drive up the cliff-hanging, gasp-at-every-turn road to the top of the Northwestern world. The bird's-eye panorama of the wilderness and mountains elicits the kind of "ooohs" and "aaahs" normally reserved for Fourth of July fireworks. The friendly park ranger said that no one will hassle you if you let your dog out at the top, on leash, as long as you don't go in the building with him or on the trails. Your pup will spend some quality hang time with his head out the car window.

PARKS, BEACHES, AND RECREATION AREAS

🛐 Peabody Creek Nature Trail

🐾🐾 (See Olympic Peninsula map on page 54)

In an exception to the rule in Olympic National Park, dogs are allowed on this 0.5-mile interpretive loop, a microcosm of what they're missing in the wilderness. It's a dandy post-lunch meander through the forest, complete with two wooden-bridge stream crossings and a few wooden steps to help you navigate easy hills.

There is a longer, 2.1-mile extension to the loop, but according to the park ranger, it's a buffer on the boundary of the National Park and the City of Port Angeles, and isn't maintained by either party. There are often obstacles that may prevent you and yours from a longer jaunt.

From downtown Port Angeles, turn south on Race Street to head up Hurricane Ridge Road. At 1.4 miles, turn right into the visitors center. The trail is marked, starting at the picnic area behind the center.

3 Waterfront Trail

🐾🐾 (See Olympic Peninsula map on page 54)

From the Coast Guard station entrance on a spit of land called Ediz Hook to just west of the old Rayonier mill site, the city maintains a five-mile waterfront walk. The eastern half is more developed; alongside the asphalt are lawn plots with picnic tables and viewing benches. The western section is more scenic, passing through a lagoon and circling the inner harbor. Through the center of town, the path switches to sidewalk. Check out the octopus sculpture of rocks, shells, and clay at the Art Fiero Marine Life Center before returning to the wider trail.

We prefer to access the paved walkway at Francis Street Park, in about the middle of the mileage, where there's good parking and a covered viewing platform on a hilly overlook. From Highway 101 in town, which is Front Street westbound and 1st Street eastbound, turn toward the water on Francis Street to the end.

4 Jesse Webster Park

🐾🐾🐾 (See Olympic Peninsula map on page 54)

There's nothing here except lush green grass and really tall trees for two whole city blocks—the doggie definition of just fine. Okay, there is a dirt trail cutting diagonally across and a bench or table or two, but your field spaniel will be too busy noticing the forest for the trees. Bordered on all sides by residential homes, this refuge is quiet and shady.

From U.S. Highway 101, go west on Eunice for two blocks and turn right onto 2nd Street for streetside parking. Open 5 A.M.–11 P.M.

PLACES TO EAT

Bella Italia: It's so difficult to find a superior place to eat dinner with your dogs. Which is why you should talk to Neil, the owner of this elegant establishment, and see if he'll set out a spread for you at one of his sidewalk tables for two. If the moon hits your eye like a big pizza pie, it'll probably be amore over his di Mare, with prawns, spinach, herbs, and parmesan. The smoked salmon ravioli, in a sun dried tomato and dill sauce, might also send you over the moon. 118 E. 1st Street; 360/457-5442; www.bellaitaliapa.com.

Spicers Delicatessen: They say they've got the best sandwich in Port Angeles. You can't take their word for it, so, guess you'll have to try one for yourself. Colorful jars filled with sugars, spices, and teas line the shelves like an old-fashioned general store. Two pretty tile-topped sidewalk tables add more color out on the sidewalk. It's a lunch-only deal, 11 A.M.–4 P.M. weekdays, to 3 P.M. Saturday and 2 P.M. Sunday. 222 N. Lincoln St.; 360/417-0909.

Van Goes: Maybe it takes a crazy person to put pizza and Mexican food together in one takeout joint, but his pies and burritos are works of art. Your choice of pizza sauces includes red, ranch, pesto, curry, BBQ, and teriyaki. Toppings can be equally unusual, or not; it's up to you. Burritos, nachos, quesadillas, and huge tacos are more traditional, enjoyed at the table out front or to go. 814 S. C St.; 360/417-5600.

PLACES TO STAY

Riviera Inn: This is a passable motel on the downtown drag. They are very good about providing all the regular amenities (fridge, micro, Wi-Fi, cable, etc.). It'll do ya, and there are no pet restrictions. Rates range $40–130; $15 pet fee. 535 E. Front St.; 877/766-8350, www.rivierainn.net.

More Accommodations: Please look under *Chain Hotels* in the *Resources* section for additional places to stay in this area.

Sequim–Dungeness Valley

Sequim sits in the Banana Belt, a crescent of land in the shape of the fruit that escapes the soggy fate of the Pacific Northwest, averaging 300 sunny days each year (see its website at www.visitsun.com). The biggest deal each year is the Irrigation Festival, celebrating its 114th annual in 2009. Sequim reuses 100 percent of reclaimed water in upland areas to grow its famed lavender, strawberry, and raspberry crops. The region is also home to a migrating herd of elk, which gives the city no small share of headaches when it wanders through town.

Dungeness is home to the Dungeness crab, a tasty delicacy you should try at the famous **Three Crabs** restaurant (alas, no patio seating). If you're looking for a nice scenic drive, but your dog whines about being trapped in the car all day, the Dungeness Scenic Loop is a perfect compromise. It's short, you get to see the scenery, and there are pet-worthy parks to stop at along the way.

PARKS, BEACHES, AND RECREATION AREAS

5 Dungeness Recreation Area

🐾🐾🐾 (See Olympic Peninsula map on page 54)

This is another place where a technicality could get you into trouble. Dogs *are* allowed in the 216-acre Dungeness Recreation Area, which consists of marshland, sand dunes, and cliffs leading up to the Dungeness Spit. Dogs *are not* allowed in the **Dungeness National Wildlife Refuge,** the land that makes up the seven-mile spit itself, the longest natural spit in the United States.

The mile-long scenic bluff trail offers phenomenal vistas that will give even your dog goose bumps. You'll come upon them suddenly as you make your way through tall dune grasses. Keep dogs on leash and stay behind the fence to avoid tumbling hundreds of feet to the beach below; go over that ledge and Lassie herself won't be able to rescue you.

In season, hunting dogs can strut their stuff as they flush out and retrieve quail and other migratory birds on Wednesday, Saturday, Sunday, and holidays. Camping is available year-round.

From U.S. Highway 101, turn north on Kitchen-Dick Road, turn left on Lotzgesell Road, and left again on Voice of America Road leading into the park. Open 7 A.M.–7 P.M. or dusk. 360/683-5847; www.clallam.net/countyparks.

6 Robin Hill Farm

🐾🐾🐾 (See Olympic Peninsula map on page 54)

It would be enough if this county park had only its six miles of trails winding through 150 acres of managed forest. The 20 acres of open grass fields would be satisfactory. The five acres of wetlands are fine. Put it all together, and add in experimental gardens, pastures, crops, an orchard, and the occasional farm animal, and you've got the wonder known as Robin Hill Farm. About 3.5 miles of trails are level, gravel footpaths; the rest, designated as equestrian trails, are narrower and have a wood chip or dirt surface and a greater variety of elevation changes. Although the humans found it disconcerting, Cooper and Isis didn't mind the "pop, pop, pop" sound of rifles from the nearby shooting range.

From U.S. Highway 101, turn north on Kitchen-Dick Road, west on Old Olympic Highway, left on Vautier Road, and right on Pinnell Road. There you'll find the parking lot and a garbage can. Clallam County Parks: 360/417-2291, www.clallam.net/countyparks.

7 Port Williams Beach

😺😺😺 (See Olympic Peninsula map on page 54)

Its real name is Marlyn Nelson County Park at Port Williams, named after a memorial of a WWII soldier killed aboard the U.S.S. *California* at Pearl Harbor. At first, you might see only the boat ramp, a vault toilet, and a picnic table. Then you might notice the great view of the Strait of Juan de Fuca, with Protection Island and Miller Peninsula up close. For your dog's sake, keep going. Down below, within easy reach, is a narrow strip of beach strewn with sea vegetables, so enticing to sniff. According to one dog-endowed local, you can run at least three-quarters of a mile in either direction from the boat launch. A tall sandstone cliff behind you blocks any exit and driftwood provides resting places along the way. Officially, the state owns the tidelands to the north, the county's got 1,000 feet, and the private tidelands start at Graysmarsh Farm.

Take the Sequim Avenue exit off Highway 101 and go straight through town to the roundabout. Take a right on Port Williams Road and go 2.7 miles to the road's end. Clallam County Parks: 360/417-2291.

8 Carrie Blake Park

😺😺 (See Olympic Peninsula map on page 54)

Like pearls before swine, or shelties for that matter, much of the beauty and functionality of this park may be lost on your pet. She can still enjoy walking the paved paths with you around the impeccably landscaped gardens, ponds, fields, streams, and recreation areas. City planners recognized this fact and conveniently placed a few garbage cans and doggie bag dispensers.

While your dog is getting her daily exercise, you'll view the Zen rock garden and a native wetland plants display. Most beautiful is the Friendship Garden and Lantern, donated by Yamasaki, Japan, Sequim's sister city. You'll see sculpture, totems, and the bronze bust of local-boy-made-good Matt Dryke, 1984 Olympic gold medalist and international skeet shooting champion. The winding walkways take you past water features, including bridges over streams, waterfalls, and ponds—parts of the park's progressive water reclamation program. You can watch the kids perform their "sick" tricks at the skate park and on the BMX track. It's a good place to meet locals who are deservedly proud of their park and visit it often.

Take the Washington Avenue exit from U.S. Highway 101, go a mile, and take a right on North Blake Street.

9 Sequim Dog Park

😺😺😺😺🐕 (See Olympic Peninsula map on page 54)

Seems like everybody's getting in the dog park game, and the wieners couldn't be happier about it. "Unleash me!" proclaims the snappy slogan at this designated off-leash area, opened in May 2007. Two chain-link-fenced plots break off from the main gate, one for the big boys and another for the little guys.

Each has all the necessities: level fields of open grass, huge shade cottonwood trees, sturdy green metal benches, water pumps, and poop disposal bags and cans. We couldn't find the stats, but there's got to be at least three acres of room to run here. Nice touches include commemorative bricks in the leash-up area and a sculpted metal entry gate. It's easy to find, really popular, and simply thrilling.

The OLA is in Carrie Blake Park, toward the back of the parking lot, just past the Guy Cole mini-convention center. 202 N. Blake Rd.; www.sequim dogparks.org.

PLACES TO EAT

Buzz: If the coffee doesn't get you humming, the gooey, frosted brownies will. When the car veered into this establishment offering ice cream, coffee, and sweets, the dogs thought the only thing that would make it perfect would be an outdoor patio; and, lo and behold, one appeared out back. Keep on the sunny side or sit in the shade. 128 N. Sequim Ave.; 360/683-2503.

Cone Heads: Order at the window for free dog biscuits, gourmet ice cream, espresso, and signature sausage dogs. The breakfast wrap is so good it'll make you howl, with sausage, eggs, onions, cheese, garlic, and mild peppers wrapped in a tortilla. 291 Washington Ave.; 360/683-1232.

Tarcisio's: That's-a some big Italian place, with a patio larger than a manicotti shell. Dogs are welcomed as part of the happy extended family. Unless you share with your dog, you might need an extra hole punched in your belt after their heaping plates of pasta, slabs of steak, and seafood swimming in rich sauces. 609 W. Washington; 360/683-5809.

PLACES TO STAY

Dungeness Beach Retreat: Doug doesn't say anything about pets on his website, but if you call and talk to him, he's easily persuaded to allow renters with nice dogs (he's allergic to cats) at this fully equipped vacation home. There is a little fenced yard along the front, following around the east side. From the backyard steps, it's about 20 feet to the breakwater rocks, up and over onto an extensive beach. Rates are $175 in the lowest season, $300 in the highest. Call for directions; 888/409-7760; www.dungenessbeachretreat.com.

Groveland Cottage: The Secret Room behind this 115-year-old bed-and-breakfast is open to traveling pets and their weary companions. The kitchen-and-bath unit is tucked away on grounds featuring lovely gardens where a dog can get out and smell the roses. It rents for $85–95 per night plus $10/day for pets. Owner Simone is a realtor who can hook you up with dog-friendly vacation rental properties in the area as well. 4861 Sequim-Dungeness Way; 360/683-3565; www.sequimvalley.com.

Juan de Fuca Cottages: These charming cottages are bright blue, shining in Sequim's frequent sun, with a seahorse motif throughout. Adirondack chairs, soft green grass, and an enclosed ocean-view gazebo invite you to sit and stay awhile. In July and August only one cottage is kept as a pet-friendly rental; several more open up to pets for the remainder of year. All have water views to one degree or another. Rates range $110–240; the pet fee is $20. 182 Marine Dr.; 866/683-4433; www.juandefuca.com.

Sunset Marine Resort: The resort has been around since the 1930s and some of the regulars have been coming since then. The property's cabins, ancient boat sheds, and rickety docks have that priceless weathered look that can't be faked, whereas cottage interiors are bright and perky. You'll feel right at home, except that this home includes waterfront cabins on a private beach. The Clam Cottage, Boat House, Landing, and Eagle's Nest allow pets. Rates are $115–250, plus $20 per pet. 40 Buzzard Ridge Rd.; 360/681-4166; www.sunsetmarineresort.com.

Dungeness Recreation Area Camping: There are 67 campsites in two loops, each loop with bathroom and shower facilities. All sites are on hard-packed sand with picnic tables and fire pots. There are no electric or water hookups, but water is provided at the campground. Fees are $16 for non-county residents, $14 for residents, available on a first-come, first-served basis. 554 Voice of America Rd. W.; 360/683-5847.

More Accommodations: Please look under *Chain Hotels* in the *Resources* section for additional places to stay in this area.

Port Townsend

Port Townsend wins the award for the dog-friendliest downtown in Washington. The sheer number of dogs walking the historic district will tell you they are welcome here, then there are the dog bowls outside nearly every shop and plenty of outdoor places to eat, sit, and relax. Several stores, including April Fool's and Ancestral Spirits Gallery, have resident canines.

The buildings of the core shopping and hotel district, along Water Street, feature restored Victorian and Romanesque architecture. It's a pretty maritime town, perched on the northeast tip of the peninsula. As a dog lover, you can appreciate it all the more knowing that your pets can enjoy so much of it with you. For a complete list of parks in the area—more than 25—check out www.ptguide.com/recreation.

PARKS, BEACHES, AND RECREATION AREAS

10 North Beach
🐾🐾🐾🐾 (See Olympic Peninsula map on page 54)
North Beach County Park is technically only an acre, but you'd never know it, because once you're on the sand, you can walk and beach comb for miles in either direction. The beach at this county park connects to Fort Worden, which

THINK GLOBALLY—BARK LOCALLY

Buy the cookbook from **Olympic Mountain Pet Pals** to support the many programs of this animal welfare organization in the Port Townsend area. **Palate Pleasers** has a couple hundred vegetarian recipes, including the all-important homemade treats section. Some of the recipes come from local restaurants and bed-and-breakfast kitchens. Eat right and help end animal homelessness with every bite! You can get the book for $20 at the local food co-op, or order it online at www.olympus.net/community/ompetpals.

connects to Chetzemoka, to create an extensive swath of coastline. An upland trail through waist-high dune grass and eventually into the woods also connects North Beach to Fort Worden. Above the beach, there's a mowed lawn area, picnic shelter, water, and restrooms.

From Sims Way, take a left on Kearney Street, left on Blaine Street, and a sharp right on San Juan Avenue. Stay on San Juan past Admiralty Avenue to turn left on 49th Street and right on Kuhn Street to the end. Parking is free. www.ptguide.com/recreation/county.html

11 Fort Worden

🐾🐾🐾 (See Olympic Peninsula map on page 54)

White clapboard buildings lined in soldierly order on a high bluff offer clues to the past of this former military installation. Fort Worden, along with Fort Flagler on Marrowstone Island and Fort Casey on Whidbey Island, formed a three-fort defense system dubbed "The Triangle of Death," designed to protect the entrance to Puget Sound. The main asset to protect was the shipbuilding yard at Bremerton, but the potential enemy changed, from 1898, through two world wars, up to the mid-1950s. In the end, all the defense buildup proved unnecessary. Twelve massive gun batteries never fired shots in battle, and all such fortifications have since been decommissioned and transformed into state parks.

The park is huge, encompassing everything from forested hiking trails to sand dunes. The excellent beach curves around a point from the north to the east and connects to other beaches north and south. Peace Mile Trail, Artillery Hill, and other headland trails keep hike-minded dogs busy. The parade grounds, five blocks long, is perfect for games of Red Rover, and an entire scout troop can play a thrilling game of Capture the Flag in and around the overgrown remains of the batteries.

From Sims Way, turn left up the hill on Washington Street, and immediately left again on Walker Street. Walker takes a sharp bend to the right and becomes

Cherry Street, which leads straight into the park entrance. 360/344-4400; www.parks.wa.gov/fortworden.

12 Chetzemoka

🐾🐾🐾 (See Olympic Peninsula map on page 54)

This community gathering place is named for a Native American who befriended European settlers. The bandstand, a replica of the first in 1904, regularly features barbershop quartets, brass brands, and weddings to be enjoyed on the wide lawns that slope down to the water. The beach and extensive tidelands connect northward to Fort Worden's stretch of sand.

Go all the way into town along Water Street until one block before it ends. Turn left on Monroe Street, go up the hill eight blocks, and turn right on Blaine Street. It's one block to the park entrance and angled parking. 360/344-3055.

13 Golden Age Club Dog Park

🐾 🐕 (See Olympic Peninsula map on page 54)

Yes, well-mannered dogs may be off leash in the city park and on many local beaches. Still, there are those who won't behave themselves if let loose. Good news for these less-than-angelic angels that there is a fenced off-leash area, however puny, in PT.

It's next to a decrepit building which once housed the Golden Age Club, hence the name. The OLA is an overgrown sandbox, entered through a single gate. Heavy brambles and fencing enclose the sand, and there's a water pump, bag dispenser, garbage, a couple of picnic tables, and some faded shuffleboard courts. If you peek over the bushes, you can see the water.

From State Route 20 into town, turn left at the light on Kearney. Turn right on Blaine Street and follow it to the T-intersection at the entrance to Chetzemoka Park. Turn left on Jackson, immediately right on Roosevelt, cross Clallam

Street, and follow the road around the bend. The park will be on your right, northwest of Chetzemoka. It is not marked.

🐾 Larry Scott Memorial Trail

🐾 🐾 (See Olympic Peninsula map on page 54)

Built by the paper mill, which also built a water pipeline for the city in 1928, this 3.5-mile-and-growing trail wanders through fields along the highway until it breaks out and hugs the hill around the bay to end up at the boat haven in downtown Port Townsend. The trail is gravel, and it was created from forest service roads and railroad beds, so it is comfy, wide, and level. Plus, there's a good variety of flora and fauna to hold a dog's interest for the duration.

Along the way, you'll pass the mill, which is still in operation making brown paper grocery bags out of scrap sawmill dust and recycled corrugated boxes. Even though you'll see steam billowing out of its stacks and strange pools of milky water, this mill is on the cutting edge of environmental protection. North of the mill is the best section of trail, with views of Admiralty Inlet and Port Townsend Bay.

To reach the southern end, turn right on Frederick Street from State Route 19 northbound, and right again onto Otto Street. There is limited roadside parking. Other trailhead options are on Mill Road and Thomas Street, both right turns off of S.R. 19.

🐾 Old Fort Townsend

🐾 🐾 🐾 (See Olympic Peninsula map on page 54)

Fort Townsend was built in 1853 to protect Port Townsend from a Native American uprising, but it was such a poorly planned effort that, should a battle ever have occurred, the Port would have had to protect the Fort. Guess no one told them a couple of well-trained German shepherds would've done the trick.

Although the half-mile beach is okay, it's the 6.5 miles of trails through wooded glades that perk up shaggy ears. The main road bisects the park, with trailheads snaking out in either direction. At the end of the road, the spacious fields of the former encampment are good for a roll in the grass, a game of fetch, or the toss of a Frisbee. Two of the trails that start at the beach have self-guided interpretive markers, one for nature, the other for historic highlights. If you can score one of four impromptu parking spaces at the entrance, you'll be closer to the rest of the hiking paths.

From State Route 20, turn east on Old Fort Townsend Road approximately two miles south of Port Townsend. Open 8 A.M.–dusk. In the summer, 40 campsites are available on a first-come, first-served basis. 360/902-8844.

PLACES TO EAT

Waterfront Pizza: If you're wondering what that great smell is, as you wander down the main shopping and dining street in town, it's the pizza pies at Waterfront, voted best around for 20 years running. Grab a slice or two (you'd better make that two) to go and sit outside on one of several nearby benches, or keep strolling, hopefully dropping toppings as you go. 951 Water St.; 360/385-6629.

Dos Okies: Two good ole boys from Oklahoma create phenomenal, mouth-watering, pit-barbecued ribs, chicken, and salmon. Their zippy sauce will make your lips buzz; mild sauce is available in case you forgot your antacids. It almost made Isis miss Texas. Almost. Okie Uno is Larry and Okie Dos is Ron; true to form, they advise you never to buy barbecue from a skinny man. Eat out on the covered patio or take it to go. 2310 Washington St.; 360/385-7669; www.dosoakiesbarbeque.com.

Lehani's Café & Coffee: It is refreshing to find a place that emphasizes light, healthy, all natural fare, well that and locally made chocolates. Lehani's makes daily salads, vegetarian dishes, couscous, and "live" fresh veggie pizza, all necessary to balance out their rich, thick cakes, pastries, and coffee. 221 Taylor St.; 360/385-3961.

PLACES TO STAY

Aladdin Motor Inn: By far the best deal in town, this motel's rooms go for $100–120, lower in the winter, plus a $10 per pet daily fee. It is outside the hustle and bustle of the historic district and thankfully quieter. The beach is practically yours, with a waterside picnic table. The rooms are decent and continental breakfast is included. 2333 Washington St.; 360/385-3747.

Big Red Barn: This romantic retreat is perfectly located, one block from the wonders of Fort Worden State Park. Every detail is perfect, such as warm wood walls and floors, a gas fireplace, jetted tub for two, fluffy bed, garden patio, and coffee, muffins, and fresh fruit delivered to your barn door for breakfast. The pet fee is $35 per stay. The nightly rate of $145 is more reasonable considering the amount of pampering your hosts provide. They also have a couple of beach units called Adelma Beach Properties that are dog-friendly. 309 V St.; 360/301-1271; www.bigredbarngetaway.com and www.accommodationsandmore.com.

Bishop Hotel: All the rooms in this boutique are non-smoking, and all are suites with kitchenettes, private baths, and separate bedrooms. For character, some rooms have the original brick walls and all are decorated in antiques, which are for sale in case you get the itch. Formal gardens and an open field surround the property. A cottage and studio at the jointly managed Swan Hotel are also available, closer to the water. Rates range $110–265; the pet fee is $20 per stay. 714 Washington St.; 360/385-6122; www.bishopvictorian.com.

Chevy Chase Beach Cabins: This resort is a class act, a treasure, perhaps inspired by actual buried treasure in gold coins somewhere on the grounds. The Chevy Chase has been a resort, off and on, since 1897. Guests rave about the water views, wide lawns, and sparkling individual cottages on a bluff overlooking Discovery Bay. Come to stay, and you won't want or need to leave. On-site there are tennis courts, a pool, shuffleboard, horseshoe pits, a trail to the beach, a DVD collection, bocce ball, tetherball, a tree swing, and the list goes on. All seven cottages, of varying sizes, allow pets for $20 per pet per night. Their yellow lab/sheltie mix Scout is very friendly and would love to play tetherball with your dogs. Rates are $95–290 based on season and capacity. 3710 S. Discovery Rd.; 360/385-1270; www.chevychasebeachcabins.com.

Palace Hotel: This gorgeous Richardson Romanesque building with 14-foot ceilings and soaring windows has a colorful history as a brothel, 1925–1933, among other things. Each room is extensively decorated with antiques, each different, named after a girl who worked in The Palace of Sweets, as it was known. The Madam's Room, restored with red velvet wallpaper and deep green woodwork, is the favorite. Doggie bags in each room include a blanket, bowl, and some treats. Rates range $60–140 by size and season, plus $10 per pet per night. The lowest-priced rooms share a hall bath. 1004 Water St.; 360/385-0773; www.palacehotelpt.com.

Port Hadlock and Marrowstone Island

Archaeological digs establish this area as one of the oldest continuously occupied areas of Washington, with evidence of Coastal Salish inhabitants dating back at least 12,000 years. Three dominant tribes, S'Klallam, Duwamish, and Suquamish, shared the area in relative harmony only after they had removed members of the Chemakum tribe, an effort led by Chief Sealth, after whom Seattle is named. Tribes would gather from the entire region for Potlach (share the wealth) celebrations of competition and feasting.

PARKS, BEACHES, AND RECREATION AREAS

16 Fort Flagler
🐾🐾🐾🐾 (See Olympic Peninsula map on page 54)

Even wet-nosed visitors have trouble knowing where to begin when describing all the wonders of this former military installation turned state park. There is so much to do and see, they won't even notice that they're not allowed in the environmental learning center, interpretive museum, hostel, vacation homes, or dorm-style camps.

Starting with the beaches, there are almost four miles of saltwater shoreline with three access points. Turn right and drive past the gun emplacement when you first enter the park to hit the south beach, favored by Isis. The second beach curves around the Western Fisheries Research Center at Marrowstone

Point. It's got the best views, including Mt. Baker, Mt. Rainier, and the Cascades. Here, a map shows where the nine gun emplacements are located and gives a little history lesson. Short climbs to the top of cannon embankments provide choice vistas.

The third beach is the windiest, where you'll find the kite-flying fanatics. It's also the most crowded, with RV camping right on the sand. A concession stand operates in the summer, thank goodness, because the Popsicles and ice cream won't keep in a cooler. People are busy water skiing, fishing, and power boating, or not so busy with their butts parked in lawn chairs. It's one enormous block party from Memorial Day straight on through to Labor Day. A forest trail loops the 784-acre park, with three shortcuts across to the beaches, for five miles of trails altogether.

Take State Route 19 to the four-way stop in Chimacum, turn right onto Chimacum-Center Road, right on Oak Bay Road in Port Hadlock, and left onto State Route 116. Fort Flagler is at the end of Route 116 on Marrowstone Island. Open 6:30 A.M.–10 P.M. 360/385-3701.

🔟 South Indian Island Parks

🐾🐾🐾 (See Olympic Peninsula map on page 54)

This is the local moniker for two waterfront parks connected by a quarter-mile headland trail. The first park you come upon is also called Lloyd L. Good Memorial Park. This meadow on a slope recalls those fond memories of when you were a kid and found that perfect hill to roll down, getting so dizzy that you couldn't stand up. With a view across the water to Old Fort Townsend, it's brilliant for picnics.

The second stop's official name is the Jefferson County Day-Use Park. A dirt road leads down to parking and picnicking on a wide, flat beach. You can take the trail between the two, or, when the tide is low, walk along the oyster shell beach.

The first park entrance is immediately to your right as you cross the first bridge on State Route 116 to Indian Island; the second is a couple hundred yards farther. Parks close at dusk.

PLACES TO STAY

Inn at Port Hadlock: Glass sconces, marble fireplaces, period furniture, oil paintings—art, in all its forms, graces this marina property. The lobby doubles as a gallery, and there is a shop, where some of the former owner and curator's large collection is available for sale. Even the windows act as pictures, framing bay views. If you're into art, this is the place to start, using the inn as a home base to explore nearby Port Townsend's galleries. Rates tend toward the higher end of $120–360; $25 pet fee; 310 Hadlock Bay Road; 360/385-7030; www .innatporthadlock.com.

Fort Flagler State Park: Camping is available March–October. There are 47 campsites, suited only for tents, in the woods. Some have water views through the trees, and 54 sites are on the open beach, with easy water access and full views, populated mainly by RV users. Cost is $17 for non-utility sites, $24 for hookup sites. Reserve a space up to 90 days in advance at 888/CAMPOUT (888/226-7688) or www.camis.com/wa. 10541 Flagler Rd., Nordland.

La Push

The Pacific Ocean is only 12 miles from Forks, near La Push. The land is the home of the Quileute First Nations people. The water is home to migrating gray whales, seals, and harbor porpoises, all frequently sighted from the beaches. Dogs will be ecstatic to learn that the abundant wildlife in the region includes an overabundance of squirrels, chipmunks, seagulls, and crows. People will appreciate the remote location, which does not include an abundance of civilization.

PARKS, BEACHES, AND RECREATION AREAS

18 Rialto Beach

🐾🐾🐾🐾 🐾 (See Olympic Peninsula map on page 54)

In a glorious exception to the Olympic National Park rule, dogs are allowed on Rialto Beach to the north for 0.5 miles, bordered by Ellen Creek. If you get to only one beach in Washington, this is the one you should see. Photographers pilgrimage to its shores, the definition of dramatic, pounding waves on a windswept coast.

Trails of river rock lead you through the driftwood, and as you approach the beach, the stones get smaller, turning into pebbles, and finally the smoothest of sand. Intense storms carve and shape a unique landscape, with sea-stack rock formations offshore and driftwood sculptures on the beach. Hole-in-the-Wall is perhaps the most famous feature, a tunnel carved out of the cliffside big enough to walk through.

While the humans blather on about beauty, Isis says the seashore is long enough to give even big dogs a workout and the sniffscape is excellent, even if the surf is too heavy for swimming. Warning: The local ranger is a Dudley Do-Right type with a reputation for throwing the book at dogs caught off-leash.

Signs to the beach are easy to follow from U.S. Highway 101; simply head toward Mora/La Push.

PLACES TO EAT

River's Edge: It's likely that the halibut, cod, salmon, oysters, and crab are caught the same day they are served at this dockside restaurant on the Quileute Reservation. Excellent breakfast, lunch, and dinner are served at outdoor tables at a remodeled boat launch building on First Beach. You may be serenaded by seals and soared over by eagles as you dine. The pie slices are gargantuan and so fine. 41 Main St.; 360/374-6163.

Forks

On U.S. Highway 101 from Port Angeles to Forks, you'll drive a spectacular 12-mile road that skirts the southern coast of glacier-carved Lake Crescent, where dogs are allowed only at Bovee's Meadow. Forks is the only true commercial center on the coast, with the honor of having the only stoplight on a 160-mile stretch of highway. If you don't stop here for groceries at the **Thriftway,** you're at the mercy of a few scattered trading posts and mercantile stores for more than a hundred miles. It's also the best place to stay if you prefer the reliability of a modern motel to the quirks of historic lodges and backwoods cabins. The Forks Timber Museum and Loggers Memorial give you an excellent perspective on the industry that shaped this entire region.

After quietly living in obscurity since the end of heavy logging, Forks is recently famous—and therefore often crowded with tourists—as the setting for Stephenie Meyer's *Twilight* novel series, the tale of a teenage vampire-human-werewolf love triangle played out in the appropriately angst and gloom-ridden world of the rainforest.

PARKS, BEACHES, AND RECREATION AREAS

19 Tillicum Park

😾 😾 😾 (See Olympic Peninsula map on page 54)

The City of Forks maintains this 15-acre park, which features two tennis courts, three ball fields, a playground, horseshoe pits, a covered picnic area, and natural turf open spaces. It's that last one, open spaces, that particularly appeals to Isis. Her favorite sport is soccer, which she plays by alternately biting, nudging, and dribbling on the ball in frenzied circles until she collapses, panting with glee. Kids get a kick out of the playground and looking at the real Shay steam engine train and Vietnam-era tank on display behind safety fences.

The city park is on the east side of N. Forks Avenue, which is also U.S. Highway 101, on the north end of town. 360/374-2531.

20 Bogachiel River Trail

😾 😾 😾 (See Olympic Peninsula map on page 54)

The hosts at Miller Tree Inn raved about this 1.5-mile section of moderately difficult hiking. It's pretty much the only place where dogs are allowed to experience the Hoh, the world's sole coniferous rainforest. It is an otherworldly trip through a deep and mysterious river valley, dripping with vegetation. Cooper believes that scat sniffing along this trail is far more exotic than the run-of-the-mill fare he's used to on his usual around-the-neighborhood walks. There

is a colloquialism about this remote region: "This isn't the end of the world, but you can see it from here." World's end looks good from a dog's-eye view.

You'll feel like you're going to the ends of the earth to get there. Go south on U.S. Highway 101 from Forks for five miles, look for mile marker #188, then immediately turn east on Undie Road. Travel another five miles to the trailhead, where there is plenty of parking.

PLACES TO EAT

Pacific Pizza: The grilled panini sandwiches and gourmet pizzas are just about the only things you can get to go in this town, made from "Monteleone Family Recipes." 870 S. Forks Ave.; 360/374-2626.

PLACES TO STAY

Dew Drop Inn: Dogs may join you at this motel, so clean that your bichon frise will stay winter white. Rooms are extra large, and there's a huge lawn for morning ablutions, rolling around in the previous night's dew drops. Pets are $10 per night. The most you'll pay is $90 a night in the high season. 100 Fern Hill Rd.; 360/374-4055; www.dewdropinnmotel.com.

Manitou Lodge: You and your pup are welcome to stay at either the Eagle ($100–140 per night) or Owl ($120–160 per night) cottages next to the main building. The lodge is an oasis of luxury in thick, primal rainforest. It is absolutely the Wieners' favorite place to stay on the peninsula, six miles from Rialto Beach. The pet fee is $10 per night. 813 Kilmer Rd.; 360/374-6295; www.manitoulodge.com.

Miller Tree Inn: An 80-year old cherry tree towers several stories high outside the window of the Orchard Suite, where dogs are welcome as long as they don't chase the cat. The bed-and-breakfast is nicely situated away from the center of town in an apple orchard. A whirlpool tub and a gas fireplace await you, along with a king-size bed, queen hide-a-bed, full bath, and kitchenette. Hearty breakfasts feature treats such as blueberry French toast or gingerbread pancakes. Rates are $155–185 plus a total of $10 per night for pets. 654 E. Division St.; 360/374-6806 or 800/943-6563; www.millertreeinn.com.

Kalaloch

It's wild, wet, wonderful Pacific Ocean as far as a dog can smell, and that's pretty far. In one more rule-breaking bonanza, dogs are allowed on all Olympic National Park beaches between the Quinault and Hoh Indian Reservations. That's 33 miles of smooth sand, sun, and surf. There are a handful of beach access points, simply called Beach 1, Beach 2, Beach 3, and so on, up to Beach 6. The fifth is difficult to find, and the sixth is only a viewpoint, so most people stick to the first four.

PARKS, BEACHES, AND RECREATION AREAS

21 Ruby Beach

🐾🐾🐾 🐾 (See Olympic Peninsula map on page 54)

This is one of those jaw-dropping ocean vistas complete with crashing waves, haystack rocks formed by water erosion, and trees clinging to cliffs above. In the distance, you can see the lighthouse perched on Destruction Island, named for the massacre of British explorers nearby by natives in 1787. In March, you can also catch glimpses of migrating gray whales spouting offshore.

This beach escapes the numbering convention, named instead for tiny garnets that can be found in the sand. It could just as easily refer to the jewel-colored evening sky; locals recommend it as the best place on the entire coast to experience an ocean sunset. Winter storms are equally dramatic, as the wind whips the waves into frenzied peaks.

After an easy trail, you'll have to cross those pesky driftwood logs again to get to the sand. If you love sparkly things as much as Isis does, you'll be glad you did. Ruby Beach is on U.S. Highway 101 at milepost 164.

22 Beaches 1–4

🐾🐾🐾 (See Olympic Peninsula map on page 54)

This stretch of ocean is so gorgeous it leaves people at a loss for words, which may explain why the access points are simply numbered. All in all, the beaches look about the same and you can walk the miles between them. Just remember where you started, because there are no markers on the beach to remind you how to get back up! Isis recommends you pick one, get to the bottom, and camp out all day, engaging in her favorite activities: running from surf foam and chasing seagulls until you collapse, panting and spent, for a nap.

All access points are along U.S. Highway 101, and some are hard to find. Your best marker is Kalaloch, two are south of this point and two north. For Beaches 1–3 access points, parking is a roadside pullout affair. The cars are easier to see than the signs, so follow their lead. Each access has about a half-mile trail leading to the sand, at the bottom of which is a minefield of drift-wood logs you'll have to navigate to reach the water. Isis will tell you this is no mean feat for miniature Dachsie legs.

Beach 4 is easier to get to, if only by a little bit. This is the only one of the four to have a parking lot, a latrine, and a bridge at the bottom of the trail. The bridge doesn't quite get you to the beach, but you can climb down a manage-able rocky ridge to do that. None of the areas are wheelchair-accessible, but Beach 4 does have a viewing platform that wheelchairs can reasonably reach. Of the four, this one is reputed to have the best tidepools at low tide for sniffing out the starfish, hermit crabs, clams, etc., that live in the shallows.

PLACES TO STAY

Kalaloch Lodge: Dogs are not allowed in the lodge, but they are welcome in the cabins on the cliffs overlooking the ocean for $13 per pet per night. They're real log cabins with wood stoves, showers, and kitchenettes. From $115–280 per night buys comfort, instant beach access, and the best ocean views in the state (no phones, TVs, or Internet). The Lodge's restaurant and mercantile are your only options for food; fortunately, they're good. Cooper says their chowder is the clammiest! 157151 Hwy. 101; 866/525-2562; www.visitkalaloch.com.

Kalaloch Campground: In summer, availability at 175 campsites disap-pears faster than Jack Russells after a lure. There are six loops of sites, some on the cliffs with ocean views, some hidden in groves of moss-covered trees spooky enough to inspire campfire stories. There are two 1.25-mile forest hikes along the Kalaloch River and an easy climb down to the beach from the day-use area. No water or electric hookups are available. Cost is $14–18 per night. On Highway 101, 35 miles south of Forks. Park information: 360/565-3000. Make reservations at 800/365-2267 or www.recreation.gov.

Lake Quinault

More than 65 percent of the world's temperate rainforests line the coasts of Washington, British Columbia, and Alaska. On the southern end is the Quinault Rainforest, where 140 inches of rain can fall in an average year. Lake Quinault is a glacier-fed oasis nestled among the evergreens and old-growth cedars. It's a long way from anywhere, a perfect antidote for city-weary canines. The northern shore of the lake is a national park boundary, off-limits to dogs. The south shore is A-OK, so look for the Lake Quinault South Shore Recreation Area sign.

PARKS, BEACHES, AND RECREATION AREAS

23 South Shore Trails

🐾🐾🐾🐾 🐾 (See Olympic Peninsula map on page 54)

Four miles of trails start across the street from your boathouse room at Lake Quinault Lodge. Along the Trail of the Giants and the Falls Creek Loop, and on short spurs that intersect, you'll encounter cascading waterfalls, Douglas firs that grow 200 feet tall, ferns and mushrooms of *Alice in Wonderland* proportions, and blankets of moss, lichen, and mold rivaling the shag carpets of the 1970s. It is a magical place. Isis wouldn't have been surprised if a unicorn had stepped out of the forest. At the very least, you have a good chance of seeing a Roosevelt elk or a black-tailed deer. Keep watch for river otters as well, and osprey that dive more than 80 feet from treetop nests to grab fish from the lake.

Take the 0.3-mile jaunt off the main trail to see the giant Sitka spruce tree, a magnificent specimen estimated to be at least 1,000 years old. Talk about your old-age spread, the base of the trunk is 58 feet in diameter.

The loop is accessible from several points along the South Shore Road. Signs are posted along the trail. Click the Hiking link at www.quinaultrainforest .com for a map or stop in at the information station next to the lodge if you don't want to wing it.

24 Rainforest Nature Trail

🐾🐾 (See Olympic Peninsula map on page 54)

This is a miniaturized half-mile trail, a highlights reel of all that is amazing about the topography of the region. It connects to the larger network of South Shore Trails if your dog is still dragging you on after the quick loop. You may have that extra burst of energy to manage it, thanks to the oxygen-enriched air of the jungle. Head rushes, rosy cheeks, excessive tail wagging, and nose twitches in overdrive are common side effects of a walk through this forest primeval. It feels like time travel; the world of dinosaurs is easy to imagine.

Follow the Olympic National Forest signs, 1.5 miles to the park from U.S. Highway 101 on the South Shore Road. Paved parking, picnic tables, and restrooms are available at the trailhead. Parking is $5 per day.

PLACES TO STAY

Lake Quinault Historic Lodge: Teddy Roosevelt loved it here when he visited in 1937 to talk about creating a national park on the peninsula. We don't know if his dogs Pete or Sailor Boy joined him on this visit. The lodge retains its 1926 character and charm, lent by designer Robert Reamer, who also built Old Faithful Inn in Yellowstone. Rustic rooms with private baths are available in the adjacent boathouse for travelers with pets. View rooms run $100–175 seasonally. 345 South Shore Rd.; 360/288-2900; www.visitlakequinault.com.

West Hood Canal

Slivers of human habitation are lean on the west side of the canal, sandwiched in between the water and the Olympic National Forest. There's only one road, and if it's blocked, you're not going anywhere. Land, rock, and mudslides happen infrequently, and when they do, the Department of Transportation will put up signs to let you know exactly how far you can get before you have to turn around. Oysters are the regional delicacy, and the waters of the canal are also home to the largest recorded octopus species in the world.

At the southern end of the canal, Hoodsport is the modern equivalent of a frontier town. The Olympic forest ranger station here (150 N. Lake Cushman Rd.; 360/877-5254) gave us maps for these recommended hikes: Mt. Rose (#814), Dry Creek Trail (#872), and the Upper Big Creek Loop Trails (#827.1 and #827.2). Hoodsport is your last big opportunity to gear up and lay in provisions for your adventures in the forest or along the canal. Divers, campers, and fisherfolk stop in for vital supplies: sunscreen and bug spray, batteries, stove fuel, ice cream.

PARKS, BEACHES, AND RECREATION AREAS

25 Dosewallips State Park

🐾🐾 (See Olympic Peninsula map on page 54)

Fishing and shellfish harvesting are popular pastimes at this unique park that offers both 5,500 feet of saltwater shoreline along the Hood Canal and 5,400 feet of freshwater fun along the Dosewallips River. The campgrounds are huge, a series of meadows with good shade trees to host the hundreds of people who come in the pursuit of edible things that live in shells. A popular pastime for the kids is riding their bikes on the paved roads through camp. This particular park is more popular with the RV crowd, as tent campers usually go into the Olympic National Forest nearby.

The campground is on the west side of the highway, day-use areas are on the east. To reach the beach trail, park at the northernmost day-use area. The beach is a marsh, the Dosewallips River Delta, very popular with dogs for the waterfowl sightings and fowl smells. An elevated pea gravel walkway winds through the grass, leading to a viewing platform and to the water. There are up to five miles of rough beach hiking and biking, but only if the tide is all the way out. Another trail leads through the woods above the main camp, where you can see evidence of rail beds where logs were hauled down from the forest to be floated to sawmills or ships.

Dosewallips is 20 miles south of the State Route 104 intersection on U.S. Highway 101. There are three separate entrances to the park, two to

DIVERSION

The western shores of the Hood Canal have the best spots in the state for digging for your dinner, and we've met many a dog who loves to dig. Salty dogs might consider giving up their bones in exchange for oysters, razor clams, geoducks, and mussels buried in the sand, waiting to be shucked and slurped. If mollusks don't move you, then how about the fishing? Both freshwater and saltwater fishing is in abundance throughout the Olympic Peninsula, some of the best in the country.

There are a few things that you have to keep in mind to enjoy food found in the wild: permits, limits, and toxicity warnings. The **Washington Department of Fish and Wildlife** issues permits and sets limits for shellfish harvesting and fishing. You can get information at 360/902-2200 or www.wdfw.wa.gov. They have a search engine you can use to find a store near your vacation spot that will sell licenses, or you can buy them ahead of time at www.fishhunt.dfw. wa.gov. Limits and toxicity warnings will be posted at each fishing or shellfishing location.

day-use areas and one to the main campground. Hours are 8 A.M.–dusk. 360/902-8844.

26 Potlach State Park

🐾🐾 (See Olympic Peninsula map on page 54)

The day-use area is a bump-out from the highway on the water. Sunny days and low tides bring out the people for oyster harvesting, clam digging, crabbing, and fishing. High tides bring out the divers, and the winds pull in the kite flyers. The rocky beach is accessed easily from the long north/south manicured grounds, where the Skokomish Native Americans set their winter villages and held gift-giving ceremonies called Potlaches. Oysters must be shucked on the beach, and their shells left for future generations of baby oysters to occupy. This leaves natural beach debris of high merit for the explorations of curious wet noses.

The campground and hiking trails are on the opposite side of the highway. The shorter hike, the half-mile Lower Loop, has a great viewpoint from which you can almost see the whole canal spreading north. The Upper Loop is a bit longer, 0.75 miles, winding through the forest.

Potlach is on U.S. Highway 101, south of Hoodsport. 360/902-8844.

PLACES TO EAT

Longshore's Drive In: French fries. If nothing else, go for the French fries. 21391 N. Hwy. 101, Potlatch; 360/877-0210.

PLACES TO STAY

Mike's Beach Resort: Mike's has mastered the laidback, seaside, summer camp vibe. There's a private gravel beach, kayak and paddleboat rentals, boat launch, playground, laundry room, and beachside showers. You and your hound can hang with the PADI people; dive instructors from all over the region bring trainees to Mike's for open water certification. Rates and amenities range widely, from $70 for budget rooms in the main building (think very budget) to $130 for a swank waterfront cabin with kitchen, hot tub, fireplace, and picture window on the water. The pet fee is $5. Campground sites also available for $25 per night. N 38470 Hwy. 101, Lilliwaup; 800/231-5324; www.mikesbeachresort.com.

    Mount Walker Inn: "Bring your family (pets too)" says the management, right on the front of their brochure. Tasteful standard and kitchenette rooms sit on a peaceful plot of land just off the highway within walking distance of the Quilcene River. Very relaxing. Rates range $55–95, plus $10 per pet, per night. Highway 101, Quilcene; 360/765-3410; www.mountwalkerinn.com.

Pacific Beach

The towns that include Pacific Beach, Moclips, Copalis Beach, and Ocean City are known as the North Beaches, heading north on State Route 109, not to be confused with the beaches at Kalaloch and La Push farther north. This strip of sand travels 30 miles before reaching the Quinault Indian Reservation, which is off-limits to any public access. These shores are more accessible and inviting, if not as dramatic as their northerly neighbors.

There are bunches of funky, destination beach resorts that are dog- and kid-friendly up and down this coast. They have more personality, but more variation in quality, than the resort hotels on Ocean Shores.

PARKS, BEACHES, AND RECREATION AREAS

27 Pacific Beach

🐾🐾 (See Olympic Peninsula map on page 54)

This waterfront state park doesn't waste real estate on nonessentials. There's a small parking-lot-style campground and an even smaller day-use area, both of which are situated for one purpose: to get you onto the beach ASAP. Once up and over a tiny hill, you and your dog can travel all 30 miles of coastline from this one access point. The sand is brilliant for castle building, fine and soft and moist enough to hold together for hours.

In Pacific Beach, turn west on Main Street and south on Second Street to enter the park. 360/276-4297.

PLACES TO EAT

Falcon's Nest: This drive-in with a half-dozen picnic tables has summer food down pat. The selection includes burgers, be they salmon, bacon, chicken, or fish, and chili, fries, onion rings, tuna sandwiches, grilled cheese, and don't forget pizza. Treats outnumber meals two to one: hot fudge sundaes, banana splits, Italian sodas, lattes, soft and hard cones, malts, and shakes. 28 Main St., Pacific Beach; 360/276-4755.

Front Street Café: It's a pleasant surprise to find such a perfect combination of excellent food and friendly outdoor seating on this lonely stretch of coastline. The menus for all three meals of the day, plus a kid's menu, are a single page each of carefully selected seafood and bistro fare. Even if you don't get any farther than the pommes frites, you'll be happy. Wall shelves bursting with bottles of vino are all available by the glass, for two or more glasses. The pet-guest water bowl was thoughtfully provided by resident dogs Daisy and Dexter. We'll drink to that! 5 West Myrtle Lane, Seabrook; 360/276-4884; www.seabrookwd.com.

PLACES TO STAY

Sandpiper: This beach resort wins the vote for the best ocean views from every room, the coolest gift and kite shop crammed with stuff, and the fastest access to a private beach. Suites are huge and newer than many on this piece of coast, with fully equipped kitchens and fireplaces. They provide pick-up bags and a wash station for dogs at the beach. Pets are $13 each per day; rates range $75–145. 4159 Rte. 109; 360/276-4580; www.sandpiper-resort.com.

Seabrook: An instant community that sprung to life in 2004, Seabrook's bright white and rainbow-hued buildings are a bit startling in an area that's weathered some harsh weather and tough economic conditions. With so little else out this way, they're building services to support themselves, including a café, market, and meeting place. There are about 20 pet-friendly cottage and house rentals in town, sleeping 2–14 people, that are in beautiful shape. Two-night minimums apply, as does a two-dog limit, with a $50 fee per dog per reservation. Rates start around $100, and go up to about $465 for larger homes (877/779-9990; www.seabrookwa.com).

Copalis Beach

What's cool about this shoreline is that when the signs say Beach Access, they're not fooling around. You turn off the main road and drive your car right onto the hard-packed sand. One of these spots is at Roosevelt Beach Road, with a vault toilet and a bit of parking. Areas of motorized beach alternate with strips that are pedestrian only, marked clearly with signs. In Ocean City, the terrain is fairly flat; when you get to this area, you'll see pine and cedar trees clinging to wind-carved sandstone cliffs.

PARKS, BEACHES, AND RECREATION AREAS

28 Griffiths-Priday

🐾🐾🐾 (See Olympic Peninsula map on page 54)

While it is much easier to get to the beach at Ocean City or Pacific Beach, dogs will give you several reasons why this state park is more fun. Cars are not allowed, it's not as crowded, and, best of all, you have to hike through the tall grasses and along the cliffs of sand dunes to reach the beach. Following the paths carved by foot traffic through the dunes leads to all kinds of adventures, including thorough inspection of the smells and textures that nesting birds have left behind.

If it looks like you may never reach the beach, don't lose hope! Keep going to the point of land, past where the Copalis River curves out to empty into the ocean, over a pile of driftwood, and there you are. Watch for aggressive geese protecting their fledglings in the spring. They'll eat your dog alive. Turn west on Roosevelt Beach Road from Highway 109 in Copalis Beach. 360/289-3553.

PLACES TO STAY

Iron Springs Ocean Resort: Mention this part of the coast, and dog lovers will tell you to stay at Iron Springs. Although the resort seems ramshackle and run down to us, its popularity could be due to a central location, 60 years of low-key friendliness, and instant private beach access. Twenty-eight cottages, dotted throughout the woods, have ocean views, kitchenettes, baths, and fireplaces or stoves. Prices range $70–170, most $130 and $140, plus a $20 charge per pet. Three miles north of Copalis Beach on Highway 109; 360/276-4230; ironspringsresort.tripod.com.

Ocean City

The farther north you go on this road, the quieter it gets. It's great for uninterrupted recreation, but you might want to eat down in Ocean Shores, as there isn't much else out here.

PARKS, BEACHES, AND RECREATION AREAS

29 Ocean City

🐾🐾🐾 (See Olympic Peninsula map on page 54)

Ocean City is the most popular park on the strip, with the best combination of beach access and secluded camping. To reach the beach, you drive over an estuary, past the ranger's house and four camping loops to the right fork in the road. A gravel beach trail transitions to sand, through the dunes and shore pines across a little stream to the beach. For canine entertainment, there are scented treasures to be found: crab and mollusk shells and stranded seaweed and kelp strands, not to mention hundreds of sandpipers! The dogs were no match for these tiny, long-legged birds that sprint along the leading edge of the waves. There are covered picnic shelters in clearings in the trees, not on the beach. Restrooms are located in the center of the camping loops.

From State Route 109, turn south on State Route 115. Farther south, on Chance a la Mer Street in Ocean Shores, there is a parking lot with restrooms and drive-on beach access that is technically a part of this state park. 360/289-3553.

PLACES TO STAY

Ocean City State Park: Four loops separate the tents from the RVs (three for tents, one for RVs), and everyone has good tree cover for privacy. There are trails to the beach from the two closest loops. The site's 178 spaces go unbelievably fast in the summer, so reserve ahead. 888/226-7688; www.camis.com/wa.

Ocean Shores

Ocean Shores' 6,000 acres are Washington's most popular seaside destination. The entire peninsula is incorporated as a resort city, made popular in the 1960s as the location of Pat Boone celebrity golf tournaments. The beach itself is a public highway, with a posted speed limit of 25 mph, and unlimited travel from

Labor Day through April 15. In the summer, parts of the beach are limited to foot, horse hoof, and dog paw traffic only.

However, Ocean Shores isn't for every dog. They'll have to compete with cars, mopeds, and horse riders on the long, flat beaches. Big hotels and resort homes are tightly stacked together on the dunes, limiting unspoiled views. And, as inviting as the ocean may be, the rip tides and undercurrents may be too strong for swimming in all but the shallowest places. That said, you can walk, beach comb, rock hound, dig for clams, fly kites, and so on for six miles on uninterrupted sand beaches with endless ocean horizons. Many hotels, condos, and private home rentals take pets, so we've limited our list to a few word-of-mouth favorites. You can find the rest of them, and more information, at www.oceanshores.com. For the mutt lover, **Go Dog Go Espresso** (360/289-4291), and **Kool Katz and Dawgz** pet store (360/289-0204) are worthy distractions.

PARKS, BEACHES, AND RECREATION AREAS

30 Damon Point/Protection Island

🐾🐾 (See Olympic Peninsula map on page 54)

Damon Point is a half-mile-wide, mile-long example of accreted land, where sand has piled up over the years to create walkable earth where once there was none. The spit is also called Protection Island, a fitting name now applied to protecting the endangered bird species the snowy plover. The park is limited to select pedestrian use only March 15–August 31. The trail to the beach is always open, as is the moist sand along the shore. There are excellent views of shipping lanes, Westport across the bay, and windswept land that is beautiful, stark, and quiet. People are serious about surf fishing here, even though they have to don heavy cold weather gear to do it. Dogs must always be leashed to prevent them from plundering plover nests.

Take Point Brown Avenue to the end, and take the right fork in the road onto Marine View Drive. Turn left onto Protection Island Road. There are six parking spaces at a circular driveway; the rest of the parking has been cutoff by a road washout. Open 8 A.M.–5 P.M. 360/902-8844.

PLACES TO EAT

Bagel Deli Bakery: Build-your-own bagel sandwiches and yogurt smoothies make for a great quickie picnic solution when all your border collie cares about is getting to the beach to chase sandpipers and seagulls. The bagel maker stops long enough to put together a few pans of dessert bars to add to the deli case. 821 Point Brown Ave.; 360/289-3164.

Peppermint Parlor: It's a common sight at the parlor, a dog with bated breath, attached to the hip of a child, waiting for a scoop to fall from a teetering cone into his open maw. So common, in fact, there is a sign, next to the

NATURE HIKES AND URBAN WALKS

In Ocean Shores, there are nine **Public Beach Access Points**, including the state parks, to get you onto six miles of uninterrupted shoreline. Dogs are allowed on these beaches off leash, unless stated otherwise below. Some roads lead right onto the sand, making it as easy as stepping out of your car onto the beach. Other spots are walk-on only, over a dune or two. A few have parking lots and restrooms, and some are nothing more than trails through the grass. Here's the list, in order from north to south.

Damon Road: drive-on, paved parking

Chance a la Mer: drive-on, restrooms, paved parking

Pacific Boulevard: drive-on

Ocean Lake Way: drive-on, paved parking, restroom

Taurus Boulevard: drive-on, no amenities

Butter Clam Street: walk-on, gravel parking, protected dune, dogs on leash

Marine View Drive: walk-on, protected dune, dogs on leash

Driftwood Street: walk-on, roadside parking, protected dune, dogs on leash

South Jetty: walk-on, paved parking, latrine

one advertising 53 ice cream flavors, that says replacement scoops are $2 each. They serve bagels also, and if there's enough demand, they'll fire up a cotton candy machine. Oh, sugar-induced bliss! 748 Point Brown; 360/289-0572.

Sand Castle Drive-In: Local seafood doesn't get any more authentic than the Castle's razor clam chowder in a sourdough bread bowl. Because not everyone appreciates the salty, chewy texture of a cooked clam, this joint is equally well known for its burgers and fries. 788 Point Brown Ave.; 360/289-2777.

PLACES TO STAY

Grey Gull: The gull is a big favorite of dog owners. Individually owned condos are tastefully furnished and include gas fireplaces and dune- and ocean-view patios. Rates range $130–250. The pet fee is $10; maximum of two pets per room. The building is an unmistakable landmark, a gray building in two wings that does indeed look like it could take off. 651 Ocean Shores Blvd. N.W.; 360/289-3381; www.thegreygull.com.

The Polynesian Resort: Our smart buddies Noel and Huxley recommended these digs, and boy, aren't we glad they did. Within a large building, each unit is a privately owned condo. Pride of ownership is apparent at the well-kept Polynesian. Grab a ground-floor room with a fireplace, kitchen, and sliding doors right onto the lawn. Past the lawn are trails winding through the dunes to the beach. Poly Park, for guests only, has a volleyball net, playground equipment, and a picnic area. Rates range $110–180 (double occupancy; up to $300 for six-person units) and the pet fee is $15. 615 Ocean Shores Blvd. N.W.; 360/289-3361; www.thepolynesian.com.

Aberdeen-Hoquiam

Aberdeen and Hoquiam are sister cities on either side of a river, like Minneapolis-St. Paul. They make up the biggest pocket of civilization on the way to Washington's lower ocean beaches. The main highways through town are complicated with twists and turns and are all one-way, which makes navigating especially interesting.

The deep-water port at Aberdeen is the largest on the Washington coast. The tall ship the **Lady Washington** is moored here, the only real vessel used in making the films *Star Trek Generations* and *Pirates of the Caribbean*. Recreation centers on area lakes and rivers, as do scores of migrating birds. These

inland river towns struggle economically, supported mainly by logging, fishing, and a growing boat building industry.

PARKS, BEACHES, AND RECREATION AREAS

31 Joseph Stewart Park

😺😺😺 (See Olympic Peninsula map on page 54)

Coop 'n' Isis butted in on a game of ring toss with a couple of dogs on the lawn at Stewart's Memorial Park. Just when they thought things couldn't get any better, they discovered a wooden bridge on the north side of the picnic area and playground leading to an elaborate one-mile trail. Within a few steps, you are deep in the forest, and the city instantly disappears. It's a miniature great escape, with bridges over streams, wooden staircases up and down hills, and an elevated boardwalk over the lush vegetation of the valley floor. Stumps of giant trees show logging activity of a century before. Isis especially liked the bird-watching in the Stewart forest. It definitely gets muddy after a good rain.

From U.S. Highway 101 westbound, turn right on F Street, immediately right on Market Street, and left on B Street. Follow B Street as it turns and take the left fork in the road to enter the park. Eastbound, turn left on G Street, right on Market Street, and left on B Street.

32 Morrison Riverfront Park and Walkway

😺 (See Olympic Peninsula map on page 54)

This convenient park and pathway is the perfect potty stop, and we mean that as a compliment. It's so easy to get to, and comes at just the right time on a drive out to coast beaches, that we stop here every trip. The north side of the paved, 1.6-mile path is dominated by the backside of a mall and the highway, but if you keep your gaze firmly fixed to the south, you'll see the more scenic river boat traffic and the workings of the Weyerhaeuser saw mill.

Halfway along, at mile marker 0.8, is 11.5-acre Morrison Park, with an open lawn, viewing dock, picnic tables, and benches. There's playground equipment, including three great slides, plastic ones that spiral around and make your hair stand on end with static. This is where we like to get out of the car to stretch legs and take a peek at the cool logging sculpture.

Immediately as you enter Aberdeen, you'll be on Wishkah Street. Turn left on Fleet Street into the Olympic Gateway Mall in front of Top Food and Drug. Immediately turn left again to enter the parking lot for Morrison Riverfront Park. This will put you in the middle of the trail. Closes at 10 P.M.

PLACES TO EAT

Anne Marie's: This downtown stop is the place for full breakfasts and lunches to go. A long list of omelets and pancakes tempts your palate, and an equally lengthy lunch list includes sandwiches named after the owner's handsome, grown sons. Of the daily specials, the taco soup is all the rage. 110 South I St., Aberdeen; 360/538-0141.

Deidra's Deli: Deidra runs an excellent sandwich place that's located in the same building as the farmer's market, so you can stock up on the best fruits and veggies while you lunch. There's a picnic table outside and a piece of play equipment to keep the kids busy while you squeeze the pears and sniff the melons. 1956 Riverside Ave., Hoquiam; 360/538-9747.

Huckle Bearies: If baked goods and espresso drinks with free whipped cream can't tempt you to blow your diet, you'll be in luck at this drive-up window with healthy, daily soups and Yoguccinos, a nonfat dessert with only 130 calories. Better yet, kick your metabolism into high gear with Jet Tea, a mixture of real fruit puree, green tea, ginseng, and gingko biloba. It's conveniently located on the main drag to the ocean. 2400 Sumner Ave., Aberdeen; 360/537-1170.

PLACES TO STAY

Guesthouse International Inn and Suites: Without question, this is the only upscale choice for lodging between Olympia and the ocean. They've scored a great location along the Riverfront Walkway downtown, sweetening the deal with good-looking rooms and an excellent list of services and amenities. A standard queen double goes for $80, plus $10 per pet, plus a $50 refundable deposit. 701 E. Heron St., Aberdeen; 360/537-7460.

More Accommodations: Please look under *Chain Hotels* in the *Resources* section for additional places to stay in this area.

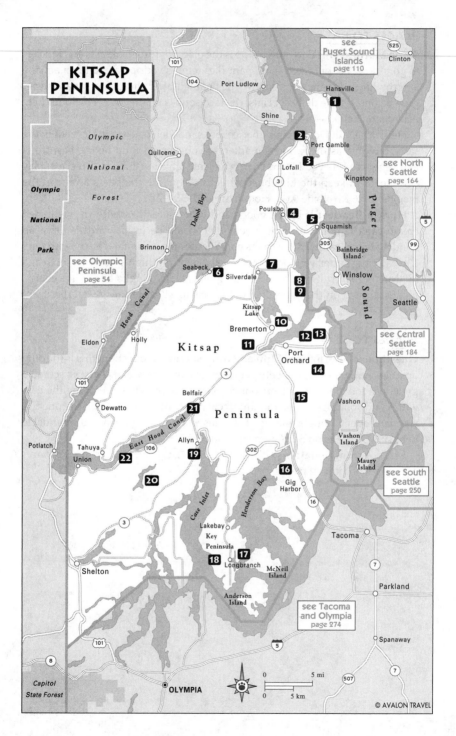

CHAPTER 3

Kitsap Peninsula

The Kitsap Peninsula has the largest accessible coastline in the state—not as dramatic and remote as the ocean, but fun to frolic on. The south end of the peninsula is accessed from Tacoma, across the Tacoma Narrows Bridge. There's a $4 toll for cars, southbound only. The upper end of the peninsula is reached by ferry from Edmonds (just north of Seattle) to Kingston.

The bottom half is dominated by the Hood Canal, an 80-mile stretch of saltwater that divides the Kitsap and Olympic Peninsulas. Mounds of white shells are piled at the side of the road, used as seedbeds for oyster farms cultivated in the canal's tideland basins. The canal is a playground for boating, scuba diving, and shellfish digging.

The center retains a strong military presence with the Naval Undersea Warfare Center in Keyport (a.k.a. Torpedo Town, U.S.A.), the Puget Sound Navel Shipyard in Bremerton, and the Bangor Trident Submarine Base outside of Silverdale. In the upper peninsula, most of the lumber mills are gone and the land is returning to nature, with plenty of perk-up-your-ears opportunities.

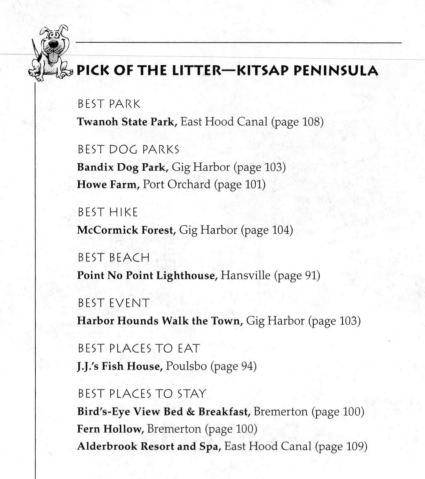

PICK OF THE LITTER—KITSAP PENINSULA

BEST PARK
Twanoh State Park, East Hood Canal (page 108)

BEST DOG PARKS
Bandix Dog Park, Gig Harbor (page 103)
Howe Farm, Port Orchard (page 101)

BEST HIKE
McCormick Forest, Gig Harbor (page 104)

BEST BEACH
Point No Point Lighthouse, Hansville (page 91)

BEST EVENT
Harbor Hounds Walk the Town, Gig Harbor (page 103)

BEST PLACES TO EAT
J.J.'s Fish House, Poulsbo (page 94)

BEST PLACES TO STAY
Bird's-Eye View Bed & Breakfast, Bremerton (page 100)
Fern Hollow, Bremerton (page 100)
Alderbrook Resort and Spa, East Hood Canal (page 109)

Kingston, Hansville, and Port Gamble

Kingston, a rip-roaring lumber town a hundred years ago, is a more mild-mannered ferry town today, built around commuters and visitors who travel back and forth from Edmonds on the mainland. There are a bunch of good places to eat here; the farther you go out onto the peninsula, the leaner the pickings get. Anglers come from the world over to Hansville to net salmon around this thumb of a peninsula that sticks straight north.

PARKS, BEACHES, AND RECREATION AREAS

1 Point No Point Lighthouse

🐾🐾🐾🐾🐾 🐾 (See Kitsap Peninsula map on page 88)

There's no point denying that we love walking the point at Point No Point. The sound of the water lapping against the shore, the silky sand extending for a couple of miles, and the sight of fishing boats trolling just offshore soothe the souls of human and hound. Views extend 180 degrees west to east, from the Olympics across Whidbey Island to Everett. The Native Americans call this low sand spit *Hahd-skus,* which means Long Nose. Isis and Cooper's long noses had a field day on the beach.

Onshore, the little whitewashed building with the red roof is the oldest operating lighthouse in Puget Sound. When the Fresnel lens and glass panes for the lantern failed to arrive in time for the scheduled exhibit on New Year's Eve in 1879, the first keeper hung a kerosene lamp in the dome.

Cooper wants to clue you in to a secret: There's a back entrance with better parking, a half-mile forest trail, and railroad tie steps down to the beach. Turn north on Hansville Road (about two miles from the ferry terminal on State Route 104). Drive 6.4 miles and turn right on Gust Halvor Road, then left at the T intersection onto Thors Road to the end. Open daylight hours only. You can tour the lighthouse (without food, drink, or your dog) noon–4 P.M., Saturday and Sunday, April 15–September 29; 360/337-5350.

2 Salsbury Point

🐾🐾 (See Kitsap Peninsula map on page 88)

Although the beach may be too rocky to enjoy, this tidy county park is good for families, with clean restrooms, public showers, a lively playground, a boat launch, and the ever-present picnic tables. The lawn is a lovely spot from which to dream of chasing the cars crossing the Hood Canal Bridge looming to the left, the best view of the bridge you'll find.

From State Route 104, turn right on Wheeler Street, then right on Whitford Road, 360/337-5350.

3 Port Gamble Trails

🐾🐾🐾 (See Kitsap Peninsula map on page 88)

Recreation is easy pickings on these wide trails—easy to get to, effortless to walk, possible to go for miles without being disturbed by anyone. Pope Resources lumber company has made more than 4,000 acres of timber management land available to the public for non-motorized use. Most of the time, you'll be walking former logging roads through quiet woods; occasionally there are foot trails that crisscross the roads, shortcuts that have developed over time. It's underused, except for the occasional bear—so leashes are safer than not. Please pack out what you pack in to keep this private property around for public enjoyment.

NATURE HIKES AND URBAN WALKS

Port Gamble is a preserved mill town that dates back to the 1853 site of the Pope & Talbot Mill. Pick up a brochure at the Kitsap Peninsula Visitor Center in town and head out on a self-guided tour of the restored New England Victorian buildings and grounds, cemetery, general store, and shops with your pup. Each 150-year-old building has a sign with pertinent names and dates. The buildings don't languish in antiquity, however. Today, one might be a chocolate shop, another a bed-and-breakfast; many are private residences. If your border collie gets bored with this stroll through history, there are shorefront picnic tables and large manicured lawns to give him a break. Dogs need to stay on leash. When you take Highway 104 toward the Hood Canal Bridge—which leads to the Olympic Peninsula—the road will take you through Port Gamble. Hop out and gambol about.

In Port Gamble, next to the espresso stand, there is a kiosk with a map of the trails, as well as restrooms, picnic tables, and other facilities. Printed maps are available at the visitors' center, and you can find one online at www.port gamble.com. Look for the orange gates to know you're in the right place. The gates with available parking areas are located as follows:

Gate 1: This is the largest parking area, on your left, 2.7 miles up State Route 104 after it splits off to the right at the intersection with State Route 307.

Gate 2: Take a hard left onto Port Gamble Road, 0.8 miles after State Route 104 splits off to the right at the intersection with State Route 307. Parking will be on your right, 0.1 miles after your turn.

Gate 4: Take the left fork in the road onto State Route 307 (Bond Road) at the intersection with State Route 104. Go a mile, take a right on Stottlemeyer Road, and go another 0.5 miles to find the gate on your right.

PLACES TO EAT

The Coffee Exchange: When all else fails, you can always count on a coffee shop in the Northwest to satisfy the grumblings of a hungry tummy. This Kingston grinder has milkshakes, soup, sandwiches, espresso, and baked goods. There's one lone table out front covered by an umbrella, and a deck for about a dozen people, pets welcome, out back. It's right on the main avenue to the ferry terminal, for that last cup o' joe before you go. 11229 Hwy. 104, Kingston; 360/297-7817.

J'aime les Crêpes: This is a growing trend in Northwest fast food, although the light, fluffy pancakes themselves date back to 16th-century France. Savory crêpes have fillings like smoked salmon, ham and Swiss, or veggies, and sweet ones drip with fruit, chocolate, butter, sugar, and whipped cream. Order at the window and relax at one of many outdoor tables. Espresso, ice cream, and Italian sodas are available, too. 11264 Hwy. 104, Kingston; 360/297-5886.

Port Gamble General Store: There's a gift shop and deli in the original 1853 historic building, serving a short menu of sandwiches, burgers, and salads; try the tomato stuffed with tuna. Your dogs can lay about the picnic tables and the kids can go crazy in the candy jar isle while you check out the internationally famous seashell museum upstairs (free admission). 32400 Rainier Ave. #3, Port Gamble; 360/297-7636.

PLACES TO STAY

Port Gamble Guest Houses: Contemporary furnishings and modern style update these graceful old homes, situated on large plots with front lawns and uninterrupted views of the bay behind them. Whole house rentals only are available for people with pets. A weekend escape from the city will run you $325 in the smaller house, which sleeps up to eight, or $500 in the larger house, which sleeps up to 12. Rates lower for weeklong stays, and there are no pet fees or restrictions, other than to keep grubby paws off the furniture. 32440 Puget Ave. N.E.; 360/297-5114; www.portgambleguesthouse.com.

Poulsbo

Dogs, please pardon us for a moment while we get carried away with a strictly human pursuit, enjoying the downtown shopping in the historic district of this Scandinavian town known as Little Norway. From window shopping to serious retail therapy, boutiques of enticing clothes, gifts, and knickknacks pack a few short streets. Now that we've got that out of our systems, you'll be pleased to know that this hamlet has its own tiny dog park. Besides, it's on the way to almost anywhere you want to get on both of the peninsulas.

PARKS, BEACHES, AND RECREATION AREAS

4 Bark Park at Frank Raab Municipal Park

🐾🐾🐕 (See Kitsap Peninsula map on page 88)

When you get to Frank Raab, you'll wind up the hill to the parking lot. With your dog on leash, take the exercise trail around the main field past the half court basketball blacktop, skateboard park, fire pit, horseshoe pits, sand volleyball, picnic shelter, swing set, and jungle gym. Just before you get to the amphitheater and the P-patch, you'll see the fenced off-leash area to your left.

They call this strip of wood chip–covered ground the Bark Park. It is fenced on one side and the rest is surrounded by thick blackberry and thistle bushes that cover a steep hill. You don't want any dog that's even vaguely fluffy to get into those brambles. Amenities include picnic benches, a water pump, and doggie bag dispensers. There are restrooms in the park for you, and decent views of Liberty Bay and the Olympic Mountains.

From State Route 305, turn east (up the hill) on N.E. Hostmark Street, and turn right on Caldart Avenue. The park is farther up the hill and around to the right. Open dawn–dusk. 18349 Caldart Ave. N.E.

5 Old Man House

😺 😺 (See Kitsap Peninsula map on page 88)

The old man lending his name to this park is Chief Sealth, the same whose roughly translated moniker is the name of Washington's largest city, Seattle. This is the ancestral home and communal gathering place of one of the most influential Native Americans in the Pacific Northwest. About an acre of his land is now yours to enjoy, from the shady hillsides to the sunny beach.

It is a teeny swath of beach that is particularly pleasant, looking out on Bainbridge Island across Agate Pass. The sand is bright white and silky soft, unusual for this area. A display board gives you some history of the cedar longhouse, and a log bench under a canopy provides respite. The park is relatively unknown, giving you a quiet place to play.

Immediately west of the bridge to the peninsula, turn north on Suquamish from State Route 305, go 1.8 miles and turn right on Division Street, which dead-ends into the park. There are only two parking spaces.

PLACES TO EAT

Jak's Café: Julie Ann Krucek is the force behind Jak's (notice the initials), on a sunny plaza where, for once, there is far more seating outside than in, and where the treat jar and water bowl are always full. Her shop is known for organic food, Boar's Head meats in all sandwiches, and whole meal salads. It's a tough choice between the Chinese almond chicken salad and the pastrami on marbled rye. 19355 Jensen Way N.E.; 360/394-5257; www.jakscafeand espresso.com.

J.J.'s Fish House: J.J.'s is immensely popular, with a packed patio of umbrella-shaded tables facing the marina, packed not just with people. "There always seem to be dogs out there," says one local. What stands out in our minds from the menu are the cioppino, chowder, shrimp on the barbecue, and crab cakes. 18881 Front St. N.E.; 360/779-6609.

Liberty Bay Bakery and Café: Choose from a yummy array of baked goods, soups, and sandwiches at the counter and then park your buns on the bench-booth outside. Sandwich specials come with a salad and your choice of a drink or a piece of pie (apple, cherry, blackberry, or strawberry-rhubarb). Guess you'll be thirsty. 18996 Front St. N.E.; 360/779-2828.

Sluy's Poulsbo Bakery: This Norwegian bakery has one of those window-front pastry displays that will have your tongues flapping before you enter the store. They are most famous for a traditional potato flatbread called *lefse* (looks like a tortilla, tastes like a 'tater). Isis is fond of the elephant ears, a flat sugary cinnamon confection that's bigger than her head. Cooper'll take the cheese sticks any day. 18924 Front St. N.E.; 360/779-2798.

PLACES TO STAY

Brauer Cove Guest House: The entire lower floor of this farmhouse is yours and your dog's, including the grill on the back patio over the water, a California king–size bed, jetted tub, wood stove, and bay windows that give you an actual bay view of the Poulsbo marina. Historic Poulsbo is a mile away by car or a half hour by paddle-powered canoe. $125 per night (no pet fees!). 16709 Brauer Rd.; 360/779-4153; www.brauercove.com.

Poulsbo Inn: This motel is a practical, reasonably priced roadside place to stay for pup lovers visiting the peninsula. Fees are $10 per pet, per night, and rates range $85–125. Limit of two pups. 18680 Hwy. 305; 800/597-5151; www.poulsboinn.com.

More Accommodations: Please look under *Chain Hotels* in the *Resources* section for additional places to stay in this area.

Silverdale and Seabeck

Since the 1970s, Silverdale has been the West Coast's Trident Submarine base, where scenes from the movie *Hunt for Red October* were filmed. The subs continue to go out on 60- to 90-day deterrent patrols; you may sight them coming and going in the Hood Canal. In the 1850s, Seabeck was a logging town with a bigger population than Seattle. Now it's a mere shadow of its former self; the only reminders are a general store, a post office, and Scenic Beach, a gorgeous state park.

PARKS, BEACHES, AND RECREATION AREAS

6 Scenic Beach

🐾🐾🐾 (See Kitsap Peninsula map on page 88)

While it's true that you can see the Olympic Mountains from many vantage points in the Northwest, at this state park they are right there, up close and personal, larger than life, take-your-breath-away huge. They take you by surprise as you come out of the dense trees onto the gravel beach littered with oyster shells. On the shore, the shipwrecked remains of a dinghy with a tree growing through its middle marks the southern boundary of the park.

Every distinct area of the park is a discovery, hidden from the others by dense forest canopy. In 1911, Joe Emel opened his homestead as a scenic resort. The restored Emel house has ADA-accessible wild rhododendron gardens, with a quaint bridge and gazebo with water views along the path. In another area is the deserted cabin and picnic grounds of the Frank Dupar family, who built a summer camp here that has grown into the state park.

One of the nicest features of the park is its bulletin board, no kidding. The park ranger has gone out of his way to make it educational, posting information about everything you could possibly want to know: guides to Pacific Northwest trees, Northwest Coastal invertebrates, and parks and backyard birds; maps of the Olympics marked with the peaks you can see from the park; stories of the local bald eagles, the salmon life cycle, and more.

The signs to Scenic Beach are easy to follow from State Route 3 to Anderson Hill Road, which becomes the Seabeck Highway. Open 8 A.M.–9 P.M. in the summer, until 5 P.M. in winter. 360/830-5079.

7 Island Lake

🐾🐾 (See Kitsap Peninsula map on page 88)

The phrase "to while away an afternoon" could very well have been coined at Island Lake. It's all very civilized, from the long, paved walkway along the western shores to the dock lookout over the water. It is the only lakefront park in the county that allows dogs. Although it is primarily used for fishing, there is a designated swimming beach and a couple of playgrounds, and for once, we didn't see any signs saying that dogs have to stay out. Of course, your dog may prefer to play on the sloping lawns; it's up to her.

Take Highway 3 and turn east on Wilcox Road, then south on Central Valley Road, which becomes Hillcrest Street. From there, you'll see the signs to the park from Island Lake Road. Open 9 A.M.–9 P.M.

PLACES TO EAT

Barbie's Seabeck Café: Jim, Charlotte, and our fearless dachshund playmate Toby found this nautically-themed restaurant where you can order items with names like P-nut Butter and Jellyfish, Fishwich, and The Pearl (an oyster omelet). Barbie's got a reputation for her biscuits and gravy, chili, and clam chowder. Your dog is welcome to join you on the deck out back, overlooking a small marina and the bay. Their restroom is a portable potty, but you can wash your hands in the general store out front. Barbie's menu is a newspaper that also gives you interesting tidbits of Seabeck history. 15384 Seabeck Hwy. N.W., Seabeck; 360/830-5532.

Monica's Waterfront Bakery and Café: Across the street from Silverdale's Waterfront Park in Old Town, and at the self-professed center of the known universe, is this spot for coffee and comfort. Our world revolves around the panini and focaccia sandwiches, daily wraps, and frosted fruit bars. The gourmet box lunches include a half sandwich, salad, fruit, chips, drink, and dessert. 3472 Byron St., Silverdale; 360/698-2991.

PLACES TO STAY

Forest Enchantment Cottage: Nestled in the woods, with fantastic Hood Canal views, this cottage home gets much of its enchanted feeling from the hand-carved log furniture in otherwise simple surroundings. The upstairs suite, complete with kitchen and wood stove, can sleep a family at the reasonable rate of $100 for two people, plus $10 per person or dog per night. They have beach access, plus a 153-acre tree farm where your four-legged friend is free to roam. You'll have to ask Helen about the 1,000 frogs that stayed here once. 7448 N.W. Ioka Dr., Silverdale; 360/692-5148; www.forestenchantment cottage.com.

Silverdale Beach Hotel: This hotel has suffered through several management changes, coming out in pretty good shape this round. Rooms are simply decorated in neutral colors with wicker bed headboards. A ground floor room on the water side is best, with sliding doors out to the lawn. There's a bonfire out back on non-rainy nights, and the hotel is on the six-mile Clear Creek Trail, a decent urban walk. Rates range $90–140, with a $20 pet fee per night; 3073 Bucklin Hill Rd., Silverdale; 360/698-1000; www.silverdalebeachhotel.com.

Bremerton

Bremerton was chosen as the site for a naval shipyard in 1889, a decision that led to significant military buildup in the region that continued through World War II. This, in turn, led to a large number of seaside state parks in the latter half of the century when all of those ports were decommissioned. President Truman gave his famous "Give 'em Hell Harry" speech here on the docks. The Puget Sound Naval Shipyard serves as moorage for the Navy's Inactive Mothball Fleet, including the Vietnam-era destroyer U.S.S. *Turner Joy*, which is open for public tours. There is a 45-minute ferry crossing to Bremerton from Seattle that is a beautiful trip through Sinclair Inlet and Rich Passage. Dogs will experience as much headwind sticking their noses out the car window on the ferry deck as they would if the car was moving. Now that's cool.

PARKS, BEACHES, AND RECREATION AREAS

⑧ Illahee Preserve Heritage Park

😾😾😾 (See Kitsap Peninsula map on page 88)

In 2001, the county purchased this 350-acre property to protect it as a largely undeveloped park. Over the next two years, work crews removed "85,000 pounds of garbage; 21 junked cars; nine engine blocks; 17 large appliances; and one telephone booth." Then, in 2005, the county Rotary built trails through a section of the preserve, with a stewardship plan to guide future generations.

This forested walk is a treat, even though you can still hear traffic for some

DOG-EAR YOUR CALENDAR

When 'tis the season to be jolly, get your jollies **Posing Pets with Santa** at various locations throughout Kitsap County. You know your family loves to get the holiday cards with your adorable dog on the cover! Kitsap Humane Society maintains this holiday tradition, where not only dogs, but cats, gerbils, rats, ferrets, ducks, llamas, horses, and everything in between are welcome to sit on Santa's lap. Poor Santa.

Yes, you can pose with your pets, too. Dates and times are announced on flyers posted at locations throughout the peninsula, and on the website at www.kitsap-humane.org. Call 360/692-6977, ext. 113.

of the route. What Native Americans called "a place to rest" offers a restful stroll through diverse trees including ancient conifers nearly 300 years old, red alder nearing 100 years old, Pacific madrona, western cedar, big leaf maple, white pine, and hemlock. Undergrowth includes heady swordferns and salmonberry, huckleberry, and Oregon grape. Off-street parking is the only amenity at the site.

From State Route 3, take the State Route 303 exit, Waaga Way, and follow it as it turns south to become Wheaton Way. Turn east on Riddell Road, and go 0.5 miles to the preserve entrance on your left. Open daylight hours only. 3200 N.E. Riddell Rd.; www.illaheepreserve.org.

🐾 Illahee State Park

🐾🐾 (See Kitsap Peninsula map on page 88)

Illahee gives you a bittersweet glimpse of what the entire peninsula was like, once upon a time, as the only remaining stand of old growth forest on Kitsap. One of the largest yew trees in the nation grows here. The road through the trees takes a series of curves, down a steep hill to the beach, with sweeping vistas of Port Orchard Passage and Bainbridge Island on the way down. From the beach, you can hike a half mile straight up the hill to the campgrounds and the playground for a serious aerobic workout. Huff, puff up; pell-mell down. Illahee is a popular park for shellfish harvesting and crabbing; rules and limits are posted at the dock.

From the ferry, turn left on Burwell Street and right on Warren Avenue. Shortly after you cross the bridge, the road becomes Wheaton Way, and you'll see the signs to turn right on Sylvan Way. There are view parking spaces down by the beach. Open 8 A.M.–dusk. 360/478-6460.

10 Evergreen Rotary Park

😊😊😊 (See Kitsap Peninsula map on page 88)

Whether you're a sun worshipper or break out in hives with anything less than SPF 50 on, Evergreen has got you covered. The north half of the park is forested with old evergreens, lending cool shade on hot days. The treed half has the playground, volleyball court, horseshoe pits, and restrooms. The south half is wide open, where they've planted small trees that won't block the sun for at least 10 years and a couple of picnic shelters thrown in for good measure. The views of the Washington Narrows and the Manette and Warren Bridges are only slightly marred by a hulking power tower.

From the ferry, turn left on Burwell Street, and almost immediately right on Pacific Avenue, which will lead you to the southern parking lot on the sunny side. Another, larger parking lot is accessible on Park Avenue between 14th and 16th Streets. A leash law is in effect and they're known for being sticklers about enforcing it. 360/478-5305.

11 Bremerton Bark Park

😊 🐕 (See Kitsap Peninsula map on page 88)

Although they felt obliged to include it as an off-leash area, the dachshunds have gotta say that Bremerton's designated dog park is pretty boring. A double gate allows entrance to an acre-ish flat patch of gravel and dry scrub, secured by chicken wire fencing. That's about the sum of it. A single picnic table, running water to fill a plastic pool, a non-functioning fire hydrant, and an empty bag dispenser were thrown in. There's a vault toilet outside the fence. After the spoiled wieners stopped whining, though, they noticed two pups having a screaming good time, playing chase and pouncing on each other in the wading pool.

From State Route 3, take the Loxie Eagans Boulevard Exit, and head west onto Werner Road. Turn left on Union Street. Go 0.3 miles and turn right on Sinclair Way into Pendergast Park. Turn right on Pendergast Parkway, right into the parking lot, and past the indoor soccer park. Entrance will be 0.5 mile on the right. 1199 Union Ave.

PLACES TO EAT

Boston's Deli.: The owner's accent will leave you with no doubts as to the authenticity of this deli's origins. Boston's serves up calzones, pizza, subs, soups, salads, and a little bit of everything. Pizza by the slice is subject to the whims of the cook of the day. 206 Burwell; 360/377-3595.

Second Park Lounge: This restaurant was too rough around the edges when we visited, having only been open about a week, but we're excited for its future, because their patio faces Evergreen park. Park-side sandwiches, wraps, pasta, pizza, and coffee are all winners in our book. 1223 Mckenzie St.; 360/479-3396.

PLACES TO STAY

Bird's-Eye View Bed & Breakfast: With a bird's P.O.V., you've got forest and Olympic mountain views from upstairs bedroom balconies at this impeccable B&B. The outside looks like a castle, and the three rooms are themed Victorian, Spring, and Americana, but not overly so. Pleasing details include claw foot tubs, gas fireplaces, and fresh flowers. This home is located in a comfortable neighborhood for walking your dog. Rates are $115–150, with a possible $15 pet fee for shedders. 8226 Kaster Dr. N.E.; 360/698-2448; www .bremertonbb.com.

Fern Hollow: This vacation rental has got the goods, from a utility room that can be left open to a fully-fenced backyard for the dog to widescreen flat-panel TVs with 200-plus channels in all three bedrooms. A stocked kitchen, granite countertops, master suite spa tub, plush wall-to-wall carpeting…the list goes on. If you ever need to spend any length of time on the peninsula and want to bring your pet, this is the place you'll want to call your temporary home. $150–195 a night; two-night minimum; $75 pet fee per week, negotiable for shorter stays; 440 N.W. Solnae Pl.; 360/308-8130; www.vacationrentals.com.

Flagship Inn: If you're not too fussy about the latest fashions, this motel is a respectable downtown choice. The pet fee is only $6, and rooms top out at $65–85. 4320 Kitsap Way; 360/479-6566; www.flagship-inn.com.

Illahee State Park Campground: There are 24 discreet, wooded tent sites way up on the hill above the beach with a slide, swings, and a baseball field nearby for family fun. All sites are available on a first-come, first-served basis for $16 per night. www.parks.wa.gov.

More Accommodations: Please look under *Chain Hotels* in the *Resources* section for additional places to stay in this area.

Port Orchard

Where Bremerton seems to be all business, Port Orchard across the bay is all play. The marina is bigger than the town, filled with boats mostly under sail power. The contrast is interesting as you look across the inlet to the hulking gray battleships of the naval yard. Port Orchard embraces the spirit of play for pets with a great dog park, sea legs not required.

PARKS, BEACHES, AND RECREATION AREAS

12 South Kitsap Community Park

🐾🐾 (See Kitsap Peninsula map on page 88)

If you ask locals for this park by name, fuggedaboudit, all you'll get are quizzical looks. Around these parts it's called Jackson Park, for the street it's on. Gone are the days when leash laws were not enforced here; so, round 'em up and tie 'em off. There are plenty of clearly marked areas where dogs aren't allowed at all. As for the rest, you and your Lhasa Apso are left with an unfenced field to roam alongside the playground, ringed with picnic shelters and an informal walkway. You can also wander those small trails through the woods at Camp Sinclair across from the field.

Of special interest to the kids, the Kitsap Live Steamers runs a model railroad train ride every second and fourth Saturday, 10 A.M.–4 P.M., April–October. Call 360/871-6414 or visit www.kitsaplivesteamers.org.

The park is at the corner of Jackson and Lund. From Highway 16, take Tremont Street east until it curves south to become Lund Avenue. Shortly thereafter, turn north on Jackson. The parking lot will be to your left.

13 Howe Farm

🐾🐾🐾🐕 (See Kitsap Peninsula map on page 88)

Every day, dogs romped happily through the fields of Howe Farm, oblivious to the hullabaloo swirling around them. For years, the county allowed dog owners free rein with their dogs on historic farmland. In 2004, they put up signs declaring that dogs had to be leashed, which caused a great uprising among the people and pets of the land. After much haggling, the parks commissioner approved a designated off-leash area of 11 acres. In 2007, fencing and facilities were installed.

The OLA at Howe Farm is huge, 5.5 acres of partially mown fields and the same of woods, with a half mile of forested trails, although everyone seemed to be congregating on the open plateau near the entrance. The front gates are tall chain link; the rest is effectively hemmed in with chicken wire and dense undergrowth. You can sit on some logs or scattered plastic chairs. There's a vault toilet, a dumpster, and very good paved parking, lacking only running water and perhaps some turf.

Turn south on Long Lake Road at the intersection with Mile Hill Road. Travel 0.2 mile and turn left on Natchez Street into the park. Check www .kitsapdogparks.org for the park's status before you visit.

14 Banner Forest

🐾🐾🐕 (See Kitsap Peninsula map on page 88)

Although used primarily for an equine clientele, canines will find this 643-acre open space to be a great place to take a hike. According to county regulations, you may take your dog off leash, but Cooper can only condone such behavior if you know exactly how your hound will behave around horses. Stick to the main trail, an old forest service road, or be adventurous and wind through the maze of unmarked trails that lead hither and thither.

Isis is so proud that a group of concerned citizens saved this old growth forest from development hell in 1991, and in 2000, the county purchased it with a 30-year protection ban from any use other than recreational. A stewardship committee plans to put up trail markers and signs eventually, but don't hold your breath as you enjoy it in its natural state.

From State Route 16, take the Sedgwick Road Exit, State Route 160, going east toward the Southworth Ferry. Turn right (south) on Banner Road, and go one mile to the parking area on your right, just north of Half Moon Drive. 253/337-5350.

PLACES TO EAT

Hideaway Café: Dogs are enthusiastically welcomed on the deck out back behind all the activity along the main street of old town Port Orchard. The menu doesn't hold any surprises, simply low-key breakfasts of eggs, bacon, and pancakes and stress-free lunches of soup, salad, sandwiches, and burgers. 807 Bay St.; 360/895-4418.

PLACES TO STAY

Manchester State Park Campground: Reserve one of Manchester's 50 forested campsites in the summer, or occupy one in the off-season on a first-come, first-served basis. The restroom and shower facility on the beach is especially nice. We changed clothes in there after falling into a lake at a different park, but that's a story for another time. 888/226-7688; www.camis.com/wa.

More Accommodations: Please look under *Chain Hotels* in the *Resources* section for additional places to stay in this area.

Gig Harbor

A maritime city that retains its fishing-village character, Gig Harbor is a place to boat, sight-see, people-watch, and window shop for antiques, crafts, and gifts. Sorry, dogs—make that seagull sight-see, squirrel-watch, and shrubbery shop for the latest in designer fragrances. Stroll along the town's two miles of waterfront walkways to take it all in, then grab some pup grub, toys, and treats at **Green Cottage Pets** (3024-A Harborview Dr.; 253/851-8806). Isis talked her mom into buying her a collar with daisies on it.

PARKS, BEACHES, AND RECREATION AREAS

15 Bandix Dog Park

🐾🐾🐾🐾🐕 (See Kitsap Peninsula map on page 88)

The organization that created this dedicated off-leash park, Kitsap Dog Parks, Inc. (KDP), was formed when the city of Tacoma closed access to the Tacoma Narrows Airport Landing Buffer, an unofficial off-leash area for more than 10 years. KDP immediately set out to create an official dog park, and boy oh boy have they succeeded masterfully!

Called a canine country club by some, Bandix is a full 33 acres devoted entirely to life as an unleashed dog, worth the ferry trip over if only to come

DOG-EAR YOUR CALENDAR

The **Harbor Hounds Walk the Town** charity event is a huge hit on the peninsula each September. Dogs of every persuasion take a collective two-mile stroll along Gig Harbor's scenic waterfront to raise money for the Prison Pet Partnership program, spay/neuter initiatives, and the rotary club. Event bandanas and T-shirts are must-have fashion accessories for the walk, along with the occasional costume, stroller, and red wagon brigade. There are tons of vendor booths set up in Donkey Creek and Skansie Brothers parks on either end of the trail, getting bigger and better every year. Contests, demonstrations, and giveaways add to the excitement. This is one you don't want to miss! Registration is $10–30, depending on the level of goodies you choose, and trust us, you'll want the goodies. Go to www.harborhounds.com for pictures and information.

and play for the day. There are a couple of quickie wooded trails and at least three open play areas, called the landing strip, the old log clearing, and the meadow, linked by other trails. Six-foot fences and gates protect the front entrance; maps on the bulletin board show the different open areas and trails in the park. There is a portable potty in the parking lot, a picnic table, and bag dispensers throughout. You are required to carry a leash in the park at all times, to leash up if necessary.

Feel free to patronize the businesses that advertise at the park, to support its ongoing success and to help build other OLAs. While you don't have to pay membership dues to use the park, an individual membership to KDP is only $10 a year. Visit www.kitsapdogparks.org.

Bandix is in a prime location, easy to reach from Bremerton, Port Orchard, and Gig Harbor. From State Route 16 at milepost 20, turn east on S.E. Olalla Road, travel 0.6 mile, turn right on Bandix Road S.E., and continue 0.3 mile to the entrance on your right. Open 8 A.M.–dark.

16 McCormick Forest

🐾🐾🐾🐾 (See Kitsap Peninsula map on page 88)

The Dachsie Twins have been able to spend more time on the peninsula since the first edition, and they are pleased to report new discoveries, most notably this quiet, well-maintained three-mile trail system. It's managed by PenMet Parks, formed in 2004 basically to get everybody outdoors. Good idea.

On 122 peaceful acres of old-growth trees, you can mix and match dozens of short spurs to create a different hike every day of the month. Each lettered trail (A to Z) is marked by a post, with the whole map on each, to get your bearings. Happily, we still got lost in the woods, managing to stumble upon a picnic meadow with tables, bag dispensers, and garbage cans. There are hiking-only trails and wider hiking-biking trails. Somewhere in the middle, down a canyon you can't really get to, is McCormick Creek. Due to recent bear sightings, dogs must be on leash at all times.

Take the Burnham Drive exit off State Route 16, going through the roundabouts to head east on Sehmel Drive. After a scant 0.5 mile, turn left on Bujacich Road. Roadside parking will be immediately on your left. Open dawn to dusk. 10301 Bujacich Rd. N.W.; 253/858-3400; www.penmetparks.org.

PLACES TO EAT

Kelly's Café: Kelly's makes great, fat deli sandwiches with fresh-cut meats and cheeses to devour at sidewalk tables. The hot sandwiches, burgers, and fish 'n' chips come with fries in a basket, and you can top it off with ice cream or intensely flavored handmade chocolates. They have a carousel horse, pinball machine, and jukebox to keep the restless natives happy while you relax under the red-and-white striped awning. 7806 Pioneer Way; 253/851-8697.

The Harbor Kitchen: This kitchen has outdoor seating front and back, dogs allowed in front only, where there's usually a water bowl and a kindly server willing to bring out a couple of biscuits while you settle for wraps, salads, quiche, and reputedly famous lasagna. Of the many baked goods, the scones are standouts. 8809 N. Harborview Dr.; 253/853-6040.

PLACES TO STAY

Inn at Gig Harbor: Isis feels right at home at this contemporary hotel with cherry wood furniture, a fitness room, and excellent restaurant on site. Standard rooms are $110–195, plus a $25 one-time pet fee. 3211 56th St. N.W.; 253/858-1111; www.innatgigharbor.com.

No Cabbages Bed-and-Breakfast: Jamee and her dog Trout have created a spare and serene place where they hope you will relax and renew. Her three acres, including a labyrinth and backyard deck, connect to 80 acres of county park land. The suite, done in neutral colors, is $135 per night and the rooms in the main house that share a bath are $80 per night, including breakfast. There is no extra charge for the privilege of bringing your dog with you. 10319 Sunrise Beach Dr. N.W.; 253/858-7797; www.nocabbages.com.

More Accommodations: Please look under *Chain Hotels* in the *Resources* section for additional places to stay in this area.

Key Peninsula

You are welcome to camp, but there's no place to lodge out here "in the sticks," as residents self-effacingly say. Your best bet is in town, meaning nearby Gig Harbor.

PARKS, BEACHES, AND RECREATION AREAS

17 Penrose Point

😃 😃 (See Kitsap Peninsula map on page 88)

Dare the dogs say it's just another beach, with just another great view? Forgive them for getting jaded; it's hard not to, with so many to choose from. The large picnic area is barely reclaimed from the swamp, a bit squishy in the rainy season. Doesn't matter much, because your dog has probably just come from a splendid romp in the mud along the tidal flats. Your only hope of staying dry is a grass bluff walk above a breakwater wall, where there are more picnic tables and a short trail down to the boat moorage and campground. Benches line the slope, facing the water to take in the views of Tacoma and nearby islands.

From the Key Peninsula Highway, turn left on Cornwall Road, right on Delano Road, and left on 158th Avenue. Open 8 A.M.–dusk. 360/902-8844.

18 Joemma Beach

😃 😃 😃 (See Kitsap Peninsula map on page 88)

Even though it was named after Robert Kennedy at its 1968 dedication, this state park is now diplomatically named after Joe and Emma Smith, regional renaissance merchants who operated a trading store, newspaper, flower bulb business, and impromptu beach resort on the land from 1917 to 1932. They started the tradition of coming to enjoy the broad sand and gravel beach on Puget Sound.

The Seattle Shellfish Company owns the right to farm the mollusks that live on the beach, and you have the right to walk among them and smell them to your doggie heart's content. A grassy picnic hill leads to a long pier, which is the extent of the park at high tide. When the tide is out, the beach goes on a ways, down to YMCA's Camp Coleman, and they'll share their beach with you, should you want to go farther.

From the Key Peninsula Highway, turn right on Whiteman Road, and follow the little brown signs. Take the left fork of the road, turn right on Bay Road, and you'll see the sign for Camp Coleman next door. Hours are 8 A.M.–dusk. 360/902-8844.

PLACES TO EAT

On the Way Deli: Make a run through the drive-through on your way to Penrose Point or Joemma Beach. Watch for daily specials, including pulled-pork barbecue subs, chicken cordon bleu, and good-looking, good-tasting pasta salads. 5501 N.W. 38th St.; 253/884-3354.

PLACES TO STAY

Penrose Point State Park Campground: With 82 tent spaces in the woods, all shaded or partially shady, Penrose Point has reliable availability. Tent sites are steps away from the beach. Reserve yours, for $17 per night, at 888/226-7688 or www.camis.com/wa.

East Hood Canal

Small towns—Belfair, Sunset Beach, Allyn, and Union—line scenic State Route 106 along the east side of the Hood Canal. Technically, it's not a canal at all, it's a fjord, a long, narrow body of water open to the ocean and bordered by steep cliffs or hills. The native tribes who lived here were considered some of the world's wealthiest. The area's abundant wildlife produced more than they could use, which they traded for goods up and down the coast. For domesticated dogs who visit, the wealth comes in the form of beaches, lakes, rivers, and trails to explore.

PARKS, BEACHES, AND RECREATION AREAS

19 Allyn Waterfront Park

🐾🐾 (See Kitsap Peninsula map on page 88)

The nicest feature of this community park is a tall link fence that protects the people and dogs enjoying it from the busy highway (even so, pets are supposed to be on leash). The boat launch, dock, and play area didn't warrant a glance from the wieners, who were drawn to the arbors, lawn, and picnic rotunda while visions of lunch, play, and naps danced in their heads. Puzzled by a topiary gone wild, Isis quizzed the park's gardener, who wished for someone practiced in the art of trimming to return the ivy beast to its former glory as a giraffe.

The park is on the water, to your left as soon as you come into town on State Route 3, with views of Case Bay.

20 Mason Lake

🐾🐾 (See Kitsap Peninsula map on page 88)

Cooper wasn't sure if he should include this county park at first. It's out of the way and really small. The deal was sealed when he saw Riley, the chocolate Lab, take a flying leap off the dock into the cool water. According to Riley's human, the park is well kept, quiet, and a good place for dogs to come take a bath because no one will bother them about being off-leash. The restroom is almost bigger than the lawn, with showers for humans to bathe as well. Most importantly, the beach is good for retrieving—clean, smooth, and no water hazards.

From State Route 3, go west on the Mason-Benson Road and follow the signs to the park. Parking is across the road from the lake.

21 Belfair State Park

🐾 🐾 (See Kitsap Peninsula map on page 88)

This is supreme, windblown, kite-flying territory at the tip of the inner hook where the canal begins. The day-use area is a field of tall marsh grasses with a playground and a swimming lagoon formed by a natural inlet that the kids love. The water is relatively warm; canal waters are the warmest saltwater bodies in the state. A dirt trail follows along 3,700 feet of saltwater shoreline through the fields, or you can pick your way along the sometimes-rocky beach. The view of the canal to the south, framed by forested hills, is excellent.

From State Route 3 in Belfair, turn west at the Safeway onto State Route 300, North Shore Road, and travel about three miles to the park. 360/902-8844.

22 Twanoh State Park

🐾 🐾 🐾 🐾 (See Kitsap Peninsula map on page 88)

Twanoh enjoys a choice waterfront location, with 3,200 feet of beachfront real estate along the canal. Its two parking lots are long, to hold the truck trailers of boaters who put in at Twanoh's launch. Picnic tables are everywhere; some of them are covered by shelters, with kitchens, fireplaces, and sinks in handsome brick, stone, and log shelters crafted by the Civilian Conservation Corps in the 1930s. Cooper met a man who has been coming here since then, as a child of six when his Dad worked in the corps. When asked if anything was different, the man said, "Yes. The trees are bigger."

The gravel beach is split by a creek that filters down from rainforest lakes. Berms create natural wading tide pools for youngsters to explore and swim. The water here is probably warmer than anyplace else in the state, so get your fins out and start dog paddling! The campground is on the opposite side of the highway from the beach, and it leads deep into an old growth forest. The park continues farther into the woods with a two-mile loop trail. The northern part of the trail is the prettiest, winding along the creek and up the side of a canyon through huge trees dripping with moss.

Twanoh is on State Route 106, about 10 miles south of Belfair. It's technically closed from mid-October through March, but you can still pull off the highway and enjoy the beach. 360/902-8844.

PLACES TO EAT

Big Bubba's Burgers: From the size of these whoppers, it oughta be called Bubba's Big Burgers. Big Bubba's Attack (could that be heart attack?) is a double burger with double cheese, large fries, and an extra large soda. A family of four, kids and dogs, can chow down for the price of a $23 Family Pack, and that includes soft dip ice cream cones. Garden burgers, onion rings, and BLTs are also available; cash only. Right across the street from Allyn Waterfront Park. 18471 E. State Route 3, Allyn; 360/275-6000.

PLACES TO STAY

Alderbrook Resort and Spa: This stunning spa, dining, and relaxation lodge in the grand Northwest style would be the toast of the town, if there were a town. You won't mind that there isn't, being too busy kayaking, or getting body treatments, or absorbing the Hood Canal and Olympic Mountain views to bother with civilization. Pets are welcomed with special amenities in all but the Cottages. May we suggest Garden View ground floor rooms with private access to a grass courtyard? Rates range widely from $110–550 per night (check for online specials), plus a $25 per dog fee. 10 East Alderbrook Drive, Union; 360/898-2200; www.alderbrookresort.com.

    Robin Hood Village: Most of these funky cottages have been around since 1934, and their historically preserved exteriors look straight out of Sherwood Forest. The interiors, however, have been constantly upgraded, and they're great. Fireplaces, big beds, private hot tubs, kitchens, entertainment centers, and lofts are among the amenities that make them regular favorites. The private beach and liquor store (aptly named Friar Tuck's Grog Shoppe) help, too. Rates are $135–195 with a $20 pet fee. 6780 E. Hwy. 106, Union; 360/898-2163; www.robinhoodvillage.com.

    Twanoh State Park Campground: Twanoh has 25 beautiful tent spaces and 22 RV sites nestled under huge trees, some along the winding creek that will sing you to sleep. Camping is on a first-come, first-served basis and is available only Aprl1–October 12 for $17–21 per night. East Hwy. 106, eight miles southwest of Belfair; 888/226-7688.

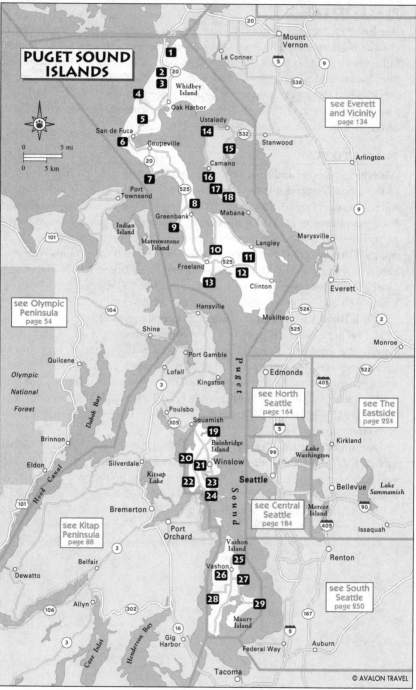

CHAPTER 4

Puget Sound Islands

Four islands of fun—Whidbey, Camano, Bainbridge, and Vashon—are all within easy reach of the Greater Seattle area. Camano, the smallest, is accessible by bridge, about an hour's drive north of Seattle. It boasts Washington's newest state park, Cama Beach, opened June 2008.

Bainbridge is the closest, a half hour's ferry ride, direct from downtown. Though most of the coastline is private property, more than 10 percent of the island's 28 square miles are public parks lands and forests and preserves protected by conservation easements.

Vashon is the least developed, a haven for artists and organic farmers. At 13 miles long and eight miles wide, it is accessible only by ferry, from West Seattle at Fauntleroy, Tacoma at Point Defiance, or the Kitsap Peninsula at Southworth. At wintertime crossings, you might glimpse an orca whale or harbor seal. By the way, it's actually two islands, Vashon and Maury, connected by a narrow causeway, but everyone refers to them collectively as Vashon.

When you add in Whidbey, the second longest island in the United States

PICK OF THE LITTER—PUGET SOUND ISLANDS

BEST PARK
Battle Point Park, Bainbridge Island (page 126)

BEST DOG PARKS
Marguerite Brons Memorial Dog Park, South Whidbey
(page 120)
Double Bluff Beach Access, South Whidbey (page 121)

BEST HIKE
Gazzam Lake and Wildlife Preserve, Bainbridge Island
(page 127)

BEST EVENT
Wine Tasting Walkabout, South Whidbey (page 120)

BEST GROOMING EXPERIENCE
Laurie's Warm Fuzzies, South Whidbey (page 116)

BEST PLACE TO EAT
Christopher's, Central Whidbey (page 118)

BEST PLACES TO STAY
Morris Farmhouse, Central Whidbey (page 118)
Ashton Woods Retreat, Bainbridge Island (page 130)

(after Manhattan), you have more recreational opportunities than you and your pup can, well, shake a stick at. The top of Whidbey Island is reached via the Deception Pass Bridge, the most photographed span in the state. The bottom of the island, 45 linear miles later, can be reached by the Clinton/Mukilteo ferry just north of Seattle. We've divided the island into its three commonly used regions: North–Oak Harbor area, Central–Coupeville area, and South, including the towns of Freeland and Langley.

North Whidbey

The island has an extensive naval military history evident in retired bases that have been given second lives as state parks (hooray!), and the Naval Air Station remains the island's largest employer today. A high ratio of soldiers on the island must be what lends it an air of strict discipline, extending to the

enforcement of leash laws, to the tune of a $500 fine if you're caught running free where you're not supposed to be. Fortunately, the island also has six good off-leash areas.

PARKS, BEACHES, AND RECREATION AREAS

1 Deception Pass State Park

🐾🐾🐾 🥾 (See Puget Sound Islands map on page 110)

Based on the number of annual visitors, Deception Pass consistently ranks as the most popular state park in Washington. From a dog's point of view, that's a deceiving statistic, because the majority of people are merely driving through, stopping for a snapshot at the famous bridge and to take in the views. Isis doesn't mind if they leave the shocking 77,000 feet of saltwater shoreline and 38 miles of hiking trails to her.

The park straddles the bridge from Fidalgo to Whidbey, but most activity is on the Whidbey side. One thing worth checking out on the north side is the Maiden of Deception Pass totem at Rosario Beach, depicting the lives of the Samish Indian Nation. On the south side, the main beach and picnic area cover a spit of land between the ocean and the lake. Foggy mornings are quite something as the mists lift over the lake and get swept out to sea. On the trails, really ambitious hikers can cover cliffs, forests, sand dunes, and wetlands in one day. The Park starts 10 miles north of Oak Harbor on Highway 20.

2 Clover Valley Dog Park

🐾🐾 🐕 (See Puget Sound Islands map on page 110)

This dog park is a popular hangout for local dogs, and visiting pooches are welcome to join in the fun. About two acres of the off-leash area is a rocky open field, basic for ball tossing and retrieving and generally chasing each other

THINK GLOBALLY, BARK LOCALLY

The local pro-pup organization on Whidbey Island is called **FETCH!**, Free Exercise Time for Canines and their Humans. The island rescue organization is called **WAIF**, for Whidbey Animals' Improvement Foundation. Together, the organizations have published a cookbook to raise money. If your dog could speak, he would tell you to buy a copy of *Culinary Tails: Recipes and Whimsy from Whidbey Island*, available for $19.95 at select island merchants or online at www.waifanimals.org.

around. Another third is a wooded area off to the east side, good for a quick walk and sniff. The area is fully fenced with a single wooden gate. One side borders along a busy street—fortunately the park has its own private driveway and parking away from the hustle and bustle.

There's a portable potty for human comfort and a single picnic table under a covered awning in center field, but it's B.Y.O. water and waste bags. There are other truly amazing off-leash areas on the island by comparison, so Cooper rates this one as just okay.

Getting here is a simple matter and the sign to the driveway is easy to see. Just take Highway 20 to Ault Field Road going west, and you'll see the park off to your right just past the Clover Valley Baseball Park. 360/321-4049; www .fetchparks.org.

🖪 Oak Harbor Dog Park

🐾 🦴 (See Puget Sound Islands map on page 110)

This little one-acre, off-leash area is literally down the street from Clover Valley and is not used as frequently, so it's an ideal park for small or timid dogs to enjoy some off-leash time without getting bowled over by the rowdier pups at the "big" park. It is a bit rough around the edges, with some uneven, rocky ground and a couple of scrawny trees. The park is next to a noisy welding warehouse, too.

On the plus side, the park is fully fenced and gated at the end of a cul de sac with a half dozen parking spots. Concrete pipes are laid out to run through; rock landscaping, a covered picnic bench, and running water add to the niceties.

Take Highway 20 to Ault Field Road, go west on Ault Field Road and turn left on Goldie Road. Pay close attention to find Technical Drive on your left a couple of blocks down the road, and go to the end of the lane to get to the park, past a small industrial area. 360/321-4049; www.fetchparks.org.

❹ Joseph Whidbey State Park

🐾🐾🐾 (See Puget Sound Islands map on page 110)

The park, like the island, is named for a nautical figure, Master Joseph Whidbey, the first mate of the *Discovery* sailed by explorer George Vancouver in 1792 to chart the Pacific Northwest for Britain. It's got what other island parks have, namely a good beach on 3,100 feet of shoreline, views of the Strait of San Juan de Fuca, and 112 acres of general picnic stuff. It's not one of the state parks in highest demand by the general public, which makes it all the better for its unofficial purpose, a regular coffee klatch for the canine set. Dog people from the Oak Harbor area take their dogs to the lower level of the park, down by the pebbly beach, and on a couple of miles of okay trails.

Take State Route 20 south through Oak Harbor and, just past town, turn right on Swanton Road for three miles. The park is officially closed October–April, which only means you'll have to improvise on parking when the gates are closed.

PLACES TO STAY

The Coachman Inn: Voted "Best of Whidbey," this motor lodge has standard rooms, but Isis prefers the bigger rooms with kitchenettes, which are also quieter, farther away from the highway, and closer to the pet area out back. Rates are $100–150, and the pet fee is $8. Ask for the Fleet Room, it's the best. Insurance requires them to exclude pit bulls and pit mixes. 32959 S.R. 20; 360/675-0727; www.thecoachmaninn.com.

Deception Pass State Park Campground: There are 251 campsites, most of them located near Cranberry Lake, which, by the way, is a *different* Cranberry Lake than the one in Anacortes, and a different Cranberry Lake than the one on Camano Island. Seven restrooms and six showers are sprinkled throughout. Call for reservations. Cost is $17–23 for overnight camping. 888/226-7688; www.camis.com/wa.

More Accommodations: Please look under *Chain Hotels* in the *Resources* section for additional places to stay in this area.

Central Whidbey

South of Oak Harbor, the island immediately becomes more scenic, with farms, views, and quaint towns such as Coupeville, the second-oldest town in the state, with more than 100 buildings on the National Historic Register.

PARKS, BEACHES, AND RECREATION AREAS

5 Patmore Pit

🐾🐾🐾🐕 (See Puget Sound Islands map on page 110)

As Pavlov's bell suggested to his dog that it was time to eat, the front fence and gate at Patmore Pit suggest to yours that he shouldn't go too far. The rest of the park is only partially fenced, and it's not exactly clear how much of the 40-acre parcel is officially off-leash, but suffice it to say that it's big enough not to have to worry about it. There's plenty of scrubby brush, trees, and crab grass for everybody in a field wide enough to stretch all four legs.

In addition to land, lots of land, under starry skies above, Patmore Pit features an agility course, with a few pieces of equipment to set up in the desired configuration. This smaller area is completely fenced, and a nearby sign suggests this secured spot for dogs in training, young and foolish dogs, and dogs new to the whole off-leash idea. We're not sure how practical that is, because you have to walk the gauntlet of off-leash dogs all the way across the wide field

DIVERSIONS

You're on island, you've checked the ferry schedule, and you've got an hour to spare before the next boat. What's a dog to do with all that spare time on her paws? In Freeland, head to **The Healthy Pet** (1801 Scott Rd., Freeland; 360/331-1808; www.thehealthypet.net), a large pet store and do-it-yourself dog wash, for a quick spin in the tub and some treats to go. In Langley, the shop to stop at is **Myken's** (212 First St., Langley; 360/221-4787; www.mykens.com) for designer dog toys, countless accessories, and more gourmet treats.

Pups, if you're on island for a few days, and you're looking a little shaggy, have your folks make a spa appointment for you with **Laurie's Warm Fuzzies** (360/579-2207; www.laurieswarmfuzzies.com). She pulls up in a big white van, plastered with colorful paw prints, and in you go. She doesn't just make you look good, she makes you feel good. She loves you up and down. Parents, we swear we've seen dogs, even shy ones, come out of Laurie's van strutting like John Travolta in *Staying Alive.*

and down a short road before you can even reach the fenced area. Other than a portable potty and some water in gallon jugs, we didn't see any facilities at the park, just room to roam.

To reach the pit from Highway 20, turn left on Patmore Road, and follow it just past Keystone Hill Road. 360/321-4049; www.fetchparks.org.

6 Fort Ebey and Kettles Park

🐾🐾🐾 (See Puget Sound Islands map on page 110)

If you're willing to share the trails with mountain bikers and the bluffs with model glider enthusiasts, Fort Ebey State Park is another one of many options on Whidbey created from former military defense posts.

A winding road into the 645-acre park forks to the right for access to the beach and Lake Pondilla and to the left for the campground and remains of the gun battery. A mile-long walking trail along a ridge leads between the two. The beach is unremarkable, too rocky and rough on the paws for walking and too much kelp growing in the water to swim. However, if you park at the gun battery, you can walk out onto a series of wide, grassy steppes with commanding views. This is where you'll see the warning signs—Caution: Model Glider Low Approach. Picnic tables are available at the beach and on the slopes.

Adjacent to Fort Ebey is access to Kettles Park, named for a geological formation visible in the area. The kettles are large indentations left in the ground from melting ice as the glaciers retreated and shaped the landscape 15,000 or so years ago. The labyrinth of 30 miles of trails is most frequently used by mountain bikers, maybe too rattling on the nerves for some dogs. Otherwise, the trails are fairly wide, well marked, short, hilly, and well kept. There's a worn map posted on the board at Fort Ebey.

From Highway 20, two miles north of Coupeville, turn left on Libbey Road, and then left on Hill Valley Drive to enter the park.

7 Fort Casey

🐾🐾🐾 (See Puget Sound Islands map on page 110)

The park is part three of the "Triangle of Death," along with Fort Worden on the Olympic Peninsula and Fort Flagler on Marrowstone Island (both in the first chapter). Of the three, this state park has the best-preserved display of firepower, of definite interest to history buffs. The concrete platforms of the William Worth Battery are a restored exhibit featuring four guns, that's guns as in cannons, that were operational from 1898 to 1942. Nearby, the Admiralty Head Lighthouse now houses an interpretive center; call 360/240-5584 for tours; pets are not allowed inside. Dogs are also not likely to join divers at the underwater scuba park. Cooper and Isis preferred chasing each other across the parade grounds and lying in the sun by the picnic tables, watching the ferries go back and forth to Port Townsend.

Highway 20 West, one of the island's main roads, leads directly to the park. Open 8 A.M.–dusk.

8 Greenbank Farm Trails

🐾🐾🐕 (See Puget Sound Islands map on page 110)

At the skinny waistline of Whidbey Island, Greenbank Farm has been known for its loganberries since the 1930s. What's a loganberry? It's a cross between a blackberry and a raspberry. After a 700-home development threatened the future of the farm in 1995, concerned citizens and conservancy groups rallied to save it as a living-history farm, cultural community center, and scenic recreation site. It is the latter that should interest your shiba inu most, because the recreation on Greenbank Farm is approved for off-leash fun! A 20-minute trail takes you through the fields and joins up with the Island County Woodland Loop Trail. One spur leads to the Lake Hancock Viewpoint, high enough to see the Olympic Mountains to the west, and Mount Baker and Mount Rainier to the east. It'll take you past the alpacas—who love loganberries, don't you know—the duck pond and benches, the picnic tables, and the historic barns and stables.

Hold up. Let's be honest, the real reason to come here is for the loganberry wine, the loganberry liqueur-filled chocolates, the cheese shop, and the art galleries that have moved into the big, red restored buildings. Get a map of the OLA at any one of the stores, also posted at several trailheads. The farm is right off the mainline of Highway 525, about 14 miles north of the ferry. Turn east on Wonn Road, just north of Coupe's Greenbank Store. 765 Wonn Rd., Greenbank; 360/678-7700; www.greenbankfarm.com.

PLACES TO EAT

Christopher's: From gourmet pizza to salmon in raspberry sauce, this restaurant has the seafood, steaks, soups, and salads for an excellent dinner at a good price. It comes highly recommended by the gals at Morris Farm. Pray for sun, so that they'll open up the patio. 103 N.W. Coveland St., Coupeville; 360/678-5480; www.christophersonwhidbey.com.

Kapaw's Iskreme: Spelling challenges aside, you have to love a place that gives away ice cream. When they close the store for the season the first weekend in December, they give away cones until it's all gone. Be one of the first to get your homemade waffle cone filled when they open again for the summer in March. 21 N.W. Front St., Coupeville; 360/678-7741; www.kapaws.com.

PLACES TO STAY

Morris Farmhouse: This relaxed B&B offers six rooms in a restored 1908 Colonial home set back in a garden. They provide towels for muddy paws, which there will be, because the Farmhouse sits on just shy of 10 acres of trails and meadows. Margaret and Katherine's only rules are that pets should be housebroken—we should hope so—and that they not be left unattended in rooms. Isis liked the beds, a sleigh bed in one room, a four-poster in another, Mission-style in a third. Cooper loved the low-key vibe, down to getting bitten playfully on the butt by resident standard poodle Hailey. Note: Hailey only bites the butts of guest dogs, not guests, and only gently, at that. Rates are $95 for rooms with a private bath, $200 for the family suite; with a $7 pet fee. 105 W. Morris Rd., Coupeville; 360/678-0939; www.morrisfarmhouse.com.

South Whidbey

For dogs, the farther south you go on the island, the better things get. The southern end of the island is prettier than the north, with better off-leash parks and outdoor dining opportunities. For $15, you can buy a copy of **Whidbey Walks the Dog,** a waterproof, pocket-size bound booklet with directions to 10 island trails, parks, and beaches; go to www.whidbeywalks.com. Whidbey and Camano Islands have a joint motto that is immortalized in the URL of their official website, www.donothinghere.com. It's amazing how tired you can get doing nothing, especially when there's so much of nothing to do. In Langley, check out the statue in Boy and Dog Park on 1st Avenue.

PARKS, BEACHES, AND RECREATION AREAS

9 South Whidbey State Park

🐾🐾 (See Puget Sound Islands map on page 110)

With names like Mutiny Bay and Smuggler's Cove, the roads to South Whidbey make you think the island was dominated by pirates, not farmers and the Navy. The park covers 347 acres of old-growth forest down to a 4,500-foot shoreline on Admiralty Inlet. A relaxing 0.8-mile trail leads through the woods to an ancient cedar tree. Unfortunately, as of 2007, the beach was closed permanently due to bluff erosion.

To reach South Whidbey by land, turn west on Bush Point Road from Highway 525, which becomes Smugglers Cove Road as it heads toward the park. Follow the signs from there.

10 Keller Trails

🐾🐾🐾 (See Puget Sound Islands map on page 110)

They're everywhere, they're everywhere! This prolific Department of Natural Resource trail system has several subsets, including the Saratoga Woods Complex, Goose Lake Woods, and Metcalf Trust Trails, but locals simply refer to them collectively as the Keller Trails. The 818 acres include woods, wetlands, waterfront, and a huge glacial erratic stone somewhere in the middle. It's a favored haunt of mountain bikers, who've given the trails goofy names like Wile E. Coyote, Wuthering Heights, and Rocky Road. Pick up a map at Half

DOG-EAR YOUR CALENDAR

It's no whine, all vine at the annual **Wine Tasting Walkabout,** at the Buchanan Vineyard in South Whidbey on the second Saturday in August. This fine FETCH! fundraiser to benefit island off-leash areas costs $25 per person, pets welcome for free, for an afternoon of wine, gourmet nibbles, good music, and fun conversation with fellow enthusiasts. It's a puppy play date with perks. Get the latest information at www.fetchparks.org.

Link Bicycle Shop in Bayview Corner (5603 Bayview Rd.; 360/331-7980). Bike or no bike, it's good, not-so-clean fun. No facilities.

We tried, and liked, the trails at Goose Lake Woods. From State Route 525, turn north on Bayview Road, left on Andreason, and right on Lone Lake Road to the trailhead parking area on your right.

11 South Whidbey Community Park

🐾 🐾 🐾 (See Puget Sound Islands map on page 110)

Okay, we know that many of you think of your pets as kids. If you happen to have children of the two-legged variety, this park is a must. It has the coolest playground we've ever encountered, with a huge castle like something straight out of Disneyland. A maze of corridors, towers, slides, bridges, turrets, and dungeons carved of wood provide countless hours of climbing, sliding, and hide-and-seeking opportunities. Each piece is marked with the names of the people and organizations in the community who donated time and money to make the play kingdom possible.

Pets are not allowed on the playground itself, but while the kids are releasing their pent-up energies, dogs can enjoy some beautifully maintained grass. Or, grab a map on-site and walk a mile and a half of short trails around the park and between various playing fields.

South Whidbey is halfway between Langley and the ferry terminal on Maxwelton Road, right off of Highway 525, just past South Whidbey High School. 5495 Maxwelton Rd.; 360/221-5484; www.swparks.org.

12 Marguerite Brons Memorial Dog Park

🐾 🐾 🐾 🐾 🐕 (See Puget Sound Islands map on page 110)

This park is really two parks in one, offering the best of both worlds. At the center of the plot of land is a fully fenced, two-acre field, with a couple of entry gates. It's a wide, open square tailor-made for running, tussling, and tossing the soft flying disks provided for you in a nearby bucket. Mud management is well handled, with plenty of gravel and grass. Then, surrounding the field, accessible from two separate gates, are 13 additional acres of fenced leash-free forest. The woods are dense, with trails winding through them, giving you the sensation of leaving civilization behind completely within a few feet. Word on the street is that it is typically less crowded here than at Double Bluff.

The park is pretty well stocked with the basics, including a covered picnic area, waste bags, shovel, portable potty, and garbage. Water is carried in and may not be reliable. Stop by the community bulletin board to see a picture of Dr. Alvin Brons, who donated this land in honor of his late wife, and his adorable dog Tuffy. To get to the Brons, turn south onto Bayview Road from Highway 525; the driveway is about a block past the cemetery on the left. The sealed gravel parking lot has room for about 20 cars. 360/321-4049; www .fetchparks.org.

13 Double Bluff Beach Access

🐾🐾🐾🐾🐕 (See Puget Sound Islands map on page 110)

Isis couldn't help but hum the tune to *Born Free* as she ran along the beach at Double Bluff, with her ears flapping in the breeze and no leash to tie her down. While most dog parks are finite, fenced-in areas by necessity, this strip of soft sand goes on for at least two miles. What a joy! On one side is a cliff too steep to climb, and on the other, the water, keeping the area naturally protected for off-leash beachcombing. Views from the beach look out onto the shipping

channel of Admiralty Inlet and across to the Kitsap and Olympic Peninsulas. We raise our paws in salute to the people responsible for designating this great beach an off-leash area. Of course, everybody loves it here, so it gets really crowded and parking is a pain in the tail. You're allowed to park on Double Bluff Road as long as your car is completely outside of the white border line.

You must keep your dogs on leash, strain as they might, from the parking area until you pass the first 500 feet of beach. Remember, the $500 fine applies if you're caught off guard and off leash (that's $1 a foot). There are signs and a big windsock on a pole that mark the start of the free-roam sand. Après-surf, there is a dog-rinse station with fresh water against the wall, near the park entrance. For fun in the sun, head south on Double Bluff Road from Highway 525. 360/321-4049; www.fetchparks.org.

PLACES TO EAT

Basil Café: Call ahead for take out, or sit nearby at one of several picnic tables on the lawns of Bayview Corner, a small shopping area north of Langley. Basil is an Asian grill and noodle house, with excellent Pho, tofu curries, and chow mein. 5603 Bayview Rd.; 360/321-7898.

The Beach Cabin: While not a cabin, nor on the beach, this is the best gourmet takeout on the island, with picnic tables on the front lawn, and artfully selected beach-life gifts and home brick-a-brack. Look for the water dish. 1594 Main St., Freeland; 360/331-1929; www.thebeachcabin.com.

Langley Village Bakery: This bake shop serves grilled panini sandwiches, soup, quiche, and vast shelves full of baked goods. Homemade dog bones in three sizes are a hit with the critters, and people rave about the *trés leches*, a three-milk cake. Courtyard tables offer seating for you near your pooch. 221 2nd St., Langley; 360/221-3525.

PLACES TO STAY

Barn Guesthouse: You'd be proud to say you were born in this barn. It's an elegant, modern, light-filled retreat perfect for pets, sitting away from the road on 20 acres of pasture and another 20 of woods. A one-mile loop trail is out the front door. We love the kitchen, vintage tub, and sunny deck. "Pets crated if left alone, no pets on the furniture, and no digging in the flowerbed," says owner Sheila. Two people and a dog are a steal at $140 per night (two-night minimum in the busy season). 3390 Craw Rd., Langley; 360/321-5875; www.barnguesthouse.com.

Country Cottage of Langley: Welcome to the Captain's Cove Cottage, with a spa tub and view of the water from the queen bed, allowing one pet for a $25 charge per night, plus $180 per night for the human inhabitants. Enjoy your gourmet breakfast al fresco on your private deck, then adjourn to the back lawn to throw some balls. 215 6th St., Langley; 360/221-8709; www.acountrycottage.com.

Harbour Inn: This very reasonable and tidy motel has the most dog-friendly rooms on the island, 10 good-sized ones, plus a lawn with picnic tables next to its parking lot. Its Freeland location is a perfect starting point for all your island activities. Rooms will cost you $90–115 a night, plus a $15 pup upcharge, and a two-pet limit. 1606 E. Main St., Freeland; 360/331-6900; www.harbour innmotel.com.

South Whidbey State Park Campground: Secluded in the forest, the 54 sites are close together, with enough forest cover to provide modest privacy. Closed December and January. Rates are $17–24; reserve ahead in summer; first-come, first-served in the winter. 888/226-7688; www.camis.com/wa.

Camano Island

The fishing, logging, and trading industries have been replaced by beach homes, art galleries, boat launches, and driftwood-strewn beaches. It's an island you can drive to, which means no inconvenient ferry schedules or fees. Take Highway 532 from I-5 over the General Mark Clarke Bridge. Stop by the Camano Gateway Information Center or go to www.donothinghere.com to find out the latest happenings. Places to eat out are rare on the island, but there are plenty of great spots in Stanwood, before the bridge. Your experience at many waterfront parks will depend on how high the tide, and how muddy and wet you're willing to get. Bring waders if you've got 'em!

PARKS, BEACHES, AND RECREATION AREAS

🔢 Utsalady Point Vista

🐾🐾 (See Puget Sound Islands map on page 110)

This tiny gem is a vest-pocket-sized park with three gravel parking spots, two picnic tables, and one barbecue grill. But, oh, the views! To the north, it is islands, bays, and the Skagit Valley as far as the eye can see. This park is cute—there's no better way to describe it. It's been carefully landscaped, and a tall, chain-link fence protects you and your dogs from going over the cliff down to the sea. You have a reasonably good chance of getting the whole place to yourself for a picnic.

When you reach the island, take the right fork in the road to North Camano Drive, turn right on Utsalady Point Road, and go about 150 feet to the bluff.

🔢 Iverson Spit Waterfront Preserve

🐾🐾 (See Puget Sound Islands map on page 110)

Washington's Audubon Society says it's one of the best birding areas in the state, a wildlife preservation and bird-watching area open to the public and dogs able to show restraint. Unmarked trails and overgrown dirt roads meander through marsh grasses, out onto the tidelands and driftwood beach, and then into the woods a ways. In addition to the many varieties of marsh dwellers, you may catch a glimpse of the common Birdwatcher with Binoculars species that frequents the area. There are nice views looking back toward the mainland across Port Susan.

There are no amenities other than a gravel turnaround where you can park, so plan to pack out whatever your pooch would be tempted to leave behind and keep him from harassing any seals and sea lions, lest he get squished.

Turn east on Russell Road from E. Camano Drive, then right on Sunrise Boulevard, left on Iverson Beach Road, and left on Iverson Road to the end. N.E. Iverson Rd.

16 Cama Beach State Park

🐾🐾🐾 (See Puget Sound Islands map on page 110)

On the National Register, this historic fishing village has been revived as a state park, opened in June 2008, with 31 restored resort cabins perched onshore. To preserve the character of the area, no cars are allowed down on the beach, making for a tranquil setting. Sadly, pets are currently allowed to overnight only in kennels on the cabins' covered porches. A 2008 pilot program to allow pets in state park cabins may change this policy in the near future.

While we wait with dew claws crossed for luck, the park is a jumping off point for picnicking, hiking, clamming, crabbing, bird-watching, and saltwater fishing along a mile of coastline.

The park's wooded 433 acres also connect to the Cross Island Trail system. The Bluff Trail and Waterfront Trail alone are spiffy walks; longer legs will enjoy connections to Ivy Lane and Cranberry Lake. The Center for Wooden Boats will offer programs from the restored boathouse and welcome center, open 9 A.M.–5 P.M.

From East Camano Drive, turn right on Monticello Road and left onto West Camano Drive. Keep an eye out for the park entrance on the right. 1880 S. West Camano Dr.; 360/755-9231; www.parks.wa.gov/camabeach.

17 Cross Island Trail

🐾🐾🐾 (See Puget Sound Islands map on page 110)

Ready for a hike? Starting at Camano Island State Park, you can hike a mile southbound to South Beach and back, or a mile northbound to Cama Beach State Park and back. At Cama Beach, the main trail continues another .5-mile north to Ivy Road and the Dry Lake Wetland Preserve, and a separate spur trail takes you .75-mile up to Cranberry Lake. The climb up to Cranberry Lake and the section between the two state parks are the best maintained portions of the trail system.

There's plentiful parking and easy trail access at either Cama Beach State Park, or Camano Island State Park.

18 Camano Island State Park

🐾🐾🐾🐾 (See Puget Sound Islands map on page 110)

This stunning park has an amazing history. The original 93 acres came into being in a single day, on July 27, 1949, when 900 volunteers showed up with trucks, tractors, hoes, rakes, spades, saws, and digging equipment to make trails, build roads, develop campsites, set up picnic areas, clear and level parking lots, construct buildings, and reach a spring for a water source.

It's grown into 134 acres with 6,700 feet of beachfront along the Saratoga Passage, looking out on Whidbey Island and the peaks of the Olympic Mountains. The North Beach day-use area has picnic tables on a grassy, sheltered bluff, with parking, restrooms, fire pits, and sheltered picnic areas. Lowell Point is a second day-use area, where the picnic benches are right on the rocky, windy beach just inches from the water.

If you can tear yourself away from the water, a 2.5-mile Park Perimeter loop trail leads along the beach for about a mile, then up through some steep sections that reward your efforts with tantalizing water views, and finally into deep, quiet woods. We saw two bald eagles on the day we visited, although Cooper thought they might be eyeing him as a potential snack.

From I-5, take Highway 532 through Stanwood. Once on the island, take the left fork onto East Camano Drive, keep going straight when it becomes Elger Bay Road, turn right on Mountain View Road, and then left on Lowell Point Road, which dead-ends into the park. Open 8 A.M.–dusk.

PLACES TO EAT

Brindle's Bistro: Chubby cinnamon rolls and donuts are the lure, and once reeled in for breakfast, you'll have to come back for lunch. Although Bonnie Brindle's breakfast-lunch-dinner menu is five pages long, the catch of the day is her award-winning fish and chips, enjoyed casually at a couple of plastic picnic tables. All hands on deck! 848 Sunrise Blvd.; 360/722-7480; www.brindlesmarket.com.

PLACES TO STAY

Camano Cliff Cabins: These two extravagant cottages on the waterfront include all the goodies: king-size beds, fireplaces, kitchens, TV/DVD/CD players, and view decks facing sunsets over the water, in a private, wooded setting. One is set up for two people, with a private hot tub and outdoor fireplace on the view deck. The second is the family cabin; it sleeps up to six and also has a wonderful view of the water. Both cabins have hard wood floors and wood beamed high ceilings. Owner Christina says she usually charges $10 extra for pets during flea season. To protect the privacy of the property, they don't publish the address; they'll give you directions when you make a reservation. Rates are $125–195. 360/387-4050; www.camanocliffcabins.com.

Camano Island State Park Campground: These 88 sites are surprisingly private thanks to the wooded canopy. Isis's shih tzu friend Sweetheart prefers Site #70 in the woods, while we liked #9 for its water view. Sites are first-come, first-served and range from $17 for a standard site to $24 for one with utility hookups. 888/226-7688; www.camis.com/wa.

Bainbridge Island

Bainbridge is packed with fun parks for pups, all with well-marked signs. There were dogs everywhere we looked—sitting by the side of the road, running up to greet us, tearing past us down hiking trials, galloping along beaches, and just a few heeling by their owners on leashes. They all seemed happy, as did their humans, perhaps because of an island philosophy we saw on a bumper sticker: Slow down, this isn't the mainland. Or, maybe it's because they've stopped and spent some time in the tasting room of dog-friendly Bainbridge Island Winery (8989 Day Road E.; 206/842-9463; www.bainbridge vineyards.com). The northwest access to Bainbridge is a drive across the Agate Passage from Poulsbo, and on the southeast from a Seattle ferry.

PARKS, BEACHES, AND RECREATION AREAS

19 Fay Bainbridge State Park
🐾🐾 (See Puget Sound Islands map on page 110)

Come with your lunch, or catch it while you're here. Dozens upon dozens of picnic tables parked on the beach offer water views, and a sign lists the seasons and limits for hauling in Dungeness crab, rock crab, oysters, steamer clams, Horse clams, mussels, and Geoducks (a giant local clam oddity counter-intuitively pronounced GOO-ee-duck).

When you're full, thread your way through the driftwood logs piled on the 1,420 feet of saltwater shoreline to a rocky beach with great skipping stones. Two prominent volcanoes, Mt. Baker to the north and Mt. Rainier to the south, are visible on clear days, with the entire Cascade Mountain Range in between. Of historical note, the Port Madison Bell is here, brought from San Francisco by Captain Jeremiah Farnum in 1883, and used to proclaim important events.

From either direction on State Route 305, you'll see the big brown signs to the park. Turn onto Day Road N.E., travel about two miles to a T-intersection and turn left onto Sunrise Drive N.E., then go another couple of miles to the park entrance. Open 8 A.M.–dusk. 15446 Sunrise Dr. N.E.; 206/842-3931.

20 Battle Point Park
🐾🐾🐾🐾 (See Puget Sound Islands map on page 110)

The center of this great city park is busy with kids playing every flavor of intramural sports. While parents go apoplectic over the ref's last call, Cooper recommends you sneak away to the fringes of the park. This is where things really go to the dogs. There's a 1.5-mile paved loop trail that circles the entire park, and from here, you can find wide fields, ponds with geese and ducks, hidden picnic tables and viewing benches, rolling hills, and rough trails winding through unkempt blackberry bushes, all pleasures dogs enjoy. Many of these areas are blocked from the supervised activities in the park's center by trees and clumps of tall vegetation. It is a versatile and popular park, much loved by the community.

From the north end of Highway 305, turn on West Day Road, and immediately look for the arrow to follow Miller Road. From the south, turn on Lovgren Road to Miller. From Miller, turn west on Arrow Point Drive, and you'll see the sign for the park. Open 7 A.M.–dusk.

21 Grand Forest

🐾🐾🐾 (See Puget Sound Islands map on page 110)

It's strictly follow your nose on the trails of Grand Forest. There's no development on the three parcels of land other than two trailhead signs and a bridge somewhere in the middle of the 240-acre old growth forest. One sign at Miller Road to Grand Forest West leads to a one-mile trail that parallels the road. The second at Mandus Olson Road, to Grand Forest East, marks a two-mile trail, which the Wonder Wieners liked even better. A river runs through it, providing atmosphere and navigation pointers. Trails are multi-use, designated for mountain bikes and horses as well as leashed pets and their people. Dogs and nature purists dig it.

Parking is equally ad hoc; simply pull over onto the side of the road. To find your way to Grand Forest, turn left on High School Road from I-305, turn right on Fletcher Bay Road and follow it until it becomes Miller Road. Watch for the sign on the right. To access the Mandus Olson section, take New Brooklyn Road to Mandus Olson Road and go north. Watch for the sign when the road makes a 90-degree turn. You're on your own finding your way through. 206/842-2306; www.biparks.org.

22 Gazzam Lake and Wildlife Preserve

🐾🐾🐾🐾 (See Puget Sound Islands map on page 110)

"Save, Don't Pave Gazzam Lake" read bumper stickers all over the island, trying to prevent developers from building a road that intersects park wetlands and habitats. The 313-acre preserve and 14-acre lake have no facilities, other than natural-surface trails, nice wide ones, for pure, natural enjoyment. Posted "ALERT!" signs warned of coyote, bear, and aggressive barred owl sightings, so be very alert and always stay leashed. Oh, and no swimming in the lake; it is rare for dogs to be allowed in nature preserves at all, so do your part to retain this privilege.

The directions to get here sound scarier than they really are. After exiting

the ferry, turn left at the first light onto Winslow Way. Take a right at Madison Avenue, and a left at Wyatt Way. Take a left at Eagle Harbor Drive N.E., then take the right fork in the road onto Bucklin Hill Road. Take the next right to stay on Bucklin Hill Road. At 2.5 miles after you've left the ferry, jog left on Fletcher, and turn right on Vincent Road. Travel 0.5-mile, take a left at N.E. Marshall Road and park to the left, 0.3-mile later. www.savegazzam.org.

23 Eagledale Park

🐾🐾🐕 (See Puget Sound Islands map on page 110)

Of the 6.7 acres at Eagledale, one acre is devoted off-leash area. A six-foot-high chain-link fence with a double gate protects the area, as much to keep deer out as dogs in. On the left is a playing field, stocked with tennis balls generously donated by the Island Racquet Club. On the right is a miniature forest with a winding trail. Plastic chairs and tables are strewn about and a couple of bag dispensers hang from the fence, but you're on your own for water. To reach the off-leash area, walk up the roped-off street to the top of the hill and around to the left.

In addition to the dog park, Eagledale has a meditation walking maze. At the top of the plateau is a design of concentric circles laid with stones in the grass. Following the path to the center leads you to a sitting rock, with a view of Mt. Rainier to the south framed by the trees. Restrooms are in the pottery studio building.

You'll travel over hill and dale to get to this park; it's well removed from the center of anything on the island. From Winslow Way, turn right on Madison

Avenue, then left on Wyatt Way, which becomes N.E. Eagle Harbor Drive when it turns to the south. Take the left fork in the road at the Eagledale sign, go 1.5 miles, and turn right on N.E. Rose Avenue. Residents kindly ask that you obey the 25 mph speed limit on your way to the park to protect their kids and dogs. 5055 Rose Ave. N.E.; 206/842-2306; www.biparks.org.

24 Fort Ward State Park

🐾🐾🐾 (See Puget Sound Islands map on page 110)

Three cheers, or paws, for another decommissioned military installation converted to a day-use state park. We thoroughly enjoyed walking the one-mile loop trail around Fort Ward, half on a paved road following the shoreline, half on gravel and dirt paths through the woods. You can hear seals barking in the harbor, watch the ferries headed to and from Seattle along Rich Passage, and check out the overgrown remains of two gun batteries. For kids, the upper gun battery in the woods along the trail is a really cool place to play hide-and-seek. The beach location is just right for swimming, walking, jogging, picnicking, and whatever other activities get your Pekinese panting for joy.

There are two entrances to this 137-acre park that lead to separate picnic areas. The upper picnic area and entrance are closed October–April, but the lower picnic grounds, on the beach, are open year-round. It's a short walk from the 25 parking spots to the tables, barbecue grills, and vault toilets.

The signs will direct you to turn west on High School Road from State Route 305, south on Grow Road to Wyatt Way W., then right at the fork in the road. Once you reach Pleasant Beach Drive N.E., follow the signs toward the boat launch entrance. It's the easier of the two to find and the only one open year-round. Open 8 A.M.–dusk.

PLACES TO EAT

Bainbridge Bakers: Travel through the center of town to the Winslow Green shopping area to find this casual eatery serving sandwiches on warm focaccia bread, soups, salads, and baked goodies. It's popular and crowded. With luck, you can find a place at one of a handful of benches, at a half-dozen tables under protected awnings on the broad flagstone patio, or on the nearby lawn. 140 Winslow Way W.; 206/842-1822.

Emmy's VegeHouse: It's really a veggie window, through which you order fabulous Vietnamese specialties for $5 a plate, with nothing over $8. Fried rice, spring rolls, stir-fry noodles, kabobs, golden tofu noodle salad, and more, all made without meat, eggs, fish, poultry, or MSG. Wash it down with hot green tea while sitting at a covered table warmed by an outdoor heater. 100 Winslow Way; 206/855-2996.

Treehouse Café: There's a soft spot in our hearts for this classic sidewalk café near Fort Ward because it offers a selection of bottled artisan beers and hand-dipped ice cream along with the hefty Plowman's lunch, Cobb salads, and fancy baguette sandwiches. 4569 Lynnwood Center Rd. N.E.; 206/842-2814.

PLACES TO STAY

Ashton Woods Retreat: How to choose between a river rock rainforest shower or a hydrotherapy spa tub? Between a stand-alone cottage in the woods or a suite above the Zen rock garden, listening to the music of the bubbling fountain? It's tough. Both of these pet- and gay-friendly retreats are decorated with exquisite taste by interior designer owners Steven and Christopher. Each features pet perks, including fleece blankets, treats, and a monogrammed A.W. tennis ball; the ball's yours to keep. It's set on a property with trails and romping meadows. The boys' four golden retriever ambassadors may be around to meet you; if not, you can admire the dogs' pictures on the walls. Each goes for $250 a night, with a $40 one-time pet-cleaning fee (it costs $38 to dry clean the gorgeous silk bedspreads). Sorry, we can't help you decide. Eeny, meeny, miny, moe? 5515 Tolo Rd. N.E.; 206/780-0100; www.ashtonwoodsretreat.com.

Boatel SV *Lille Danser:* Sail and sleep the night away on a 50-foot gaff cutter sailing vessel. This is a unique experience you'll rarely find. For $200, the all-gal crew will take up to six people, although four is more comfortable, on a two-hour sail, then bring you back to relax and spend the night on the boat, docked at Eagle Harbor Marina. It's not frilly or fancy; this is a working, wooden boat, a 1970s replica of a Danish boat common in the 1880s. It's like camping, only on the water. If you know dog lovers who're even remotely sailing buffs, this will rock their boat. Although the *Lille* has two heads (sailing terminology for toilet), additional full bathrooms, hot showers, and a gym are also at your disposal at the marina. In the morning, coffee and oatmeal perk you up. 206/855-4108; www.nwboatandbreakfast.com.

Island Country Inn: This one's a step above the norm, with pine furniture and pleasant decor that doesn't come out of the same catalog everyone else must use. It's smallish, offering only four rooms for dogs, and prefers smallish dogs (under 40 pounds). Rooms are $100–170, plus $10 per pet per night, maximum two furry friends. 920 Hildebrand Lane N.W.; 800/842-8429; www.islandcountryinn.com.

Waterfall Gardens Private Suites: Staying in these eco-friendly suites is akin to having your own shire. Susan and Robert have built the place from the studs, tucked into five forested acres. They've restored the riparian zone along their portion of Manzanita Creek and, in the process, have returned the most successful salmon spawning recovery on the island. Staying in this sanctuary of shady woods, sunny meadows, and spring-fed ponds is a balm to the spirit. It doesn't hurt that the suites are big and beautiful as well. Rates range $140–250 a night, with a one-time $25 pet fee. 7269 N.E. Bergman Rd.; 206/842-1434; www.waterfall-gardens.com.

Vashon Island

This contained community is dog-friendly and dog-smart. The Vashon Park District has installed pet waste disposal systems for your convenience, and many local businesses hand out treats, including the True Value Hardware store, Pandora's Box Pet Supplies, and the Fair Isle Animal Clinic. Karen at the Vashon Bookstore is especially pleased to welcome well-behaved pets and will dote on them while you browse.

PARKS, BEACHES, AND RECREATION AREAS

25 Ober Memorial Park

🐾 (See Puget Sound Islands map on page 110)

The main benefit of this destination is its convenient location, right on the main drag in the center of commerce for the island. Your dear will welcome the five acres of rolling hillsides after being trapped in the car for the ferry ride over. While she uncrosses her legs, you might take in the mosaic tile bas-relief map that gives you a bird's eye view of Vashon and Maury Islands, the metal sculptures, a fresh water drinking fountain, and a fun playground. Dogs aren't allowed on the playground, but there's plenty of room to hang out nearby. Pet waste bags are provided. Dogs must be leashed. The Vashon Park District building is right next door, a good place to stop for current island information, books, and maps. On Vashon Highway S.W. at S.W. 171st Street.

26 Fisher Pond DNR Trails

🐾🐾 (See Puget Sound Islands map on page 110)

At least once in every chapter, the Dachsies try to find a spot that is nothing more than a trail through the woods. On Vashon, the 90-acre Department of Natural Resources wildlife preserve is the place, and in the middle is the largest pond on the island. Longtime islanders also call it the Island Center Forest. Roadside parking is available. No facilities are available. That's about the sum of it.

From the ferry, head south on Vashon Highway S.W., and turn west on S.W. Bank Road. The trailhead will be to your right, before the 90-degree turn onto Thorsen Road.

27 KVI Beach

🐾🐾🐾🐕 (See Puget Sound Islands map on page 110)

As long as you don't mind a radio tower planted on *your* beach, Fisher Broadcasting Corporation doesn't mind you hanging out, in leash-free bliss, on theirs. It's privately held land, not on any map, nor is it marked, except for a tiny sign when you get to the path that says the public is welcome. So please enjoy the beach, but don't tell anyone else about this well-kept secret! The main path loops around a bog on the way to the sand, and many impromptu footpaths have been worked through the driftwood. When the tide is out, your dog can run for about four miles to the north, looking for the perfect fetch stick. Swim and dog paddle to your heart's content and take in the views of the tip of Rainier and the mainland south of Seattle. If there's no burn ban in effect and you get a permit in town before heading out, you can even build a beach bonfire below the high tide line.

Don't be intimidated by the directions; it's worth the journey. From Vashon Highway, turn left on Bank Road, right on Beall Road, left on 184th Street, and right on Ridge Road until just before it goes around the bend and becomes Chataqua Road. When you can see the red-and-white radio tower, you should be able to see the path to the beach.

28 Lisbuela Park

🐾🐾 (See Puget Sound Islands map on page 110)

This is a gem of a beach with a sign at the entrance: Dogs off leash ONLY if not disturbing others. Seems like a reasonable rule. Five and a half acres of sand and gravel beach lead to a sheltered bay of water. There's a rudimentary boat launch (meant for carry-in kayaks and canoes only) and some odd sculptures on the beach of wooden planks nailed to large pieces of driftwood.

It is quiet enough here to be unspoiled. We saw an otter run from the bushes into the water. Once he realized that Coop 'n' Isis wouldn't follow (water dogs they are not), he turned over on his back and taunted them as he floated along. Basic services include a gravel parking lot, recycling bins, a portable potty, and a couple of picnic tables on a patch of grass.

Take Vashon Highway to Cemetery Road, which winds around and becomes Westside Highway. Turn right onto 220th Street, which becomes Lisbuela Road, a windy, narrow, single lane leading directly into the park. Open from dawn to dusk.

29 Point Robinson Lighthouse

🐾🐾🐾 (See Puget Sound Islands map on page 110)

This 12-acre park is a perennial favorite, with good reason. The walk along the rocky beach was our favorite of the day, and if the number of paw prints in the sand is any indication, that of many others. The views across the water to Tacoma are great, and there's lots of boat traffic to watch. We saw a famous Foss tugboat chug along.

A tiny white lighthouse with a red roof and flashing light sits at an apex, kept for show. Nowadays, it's dwarfed by a massive radar tower, certainly more technically effective, if not as aesthetic.

There are two parking lots. From the upper lot, you can look out over the water while sitting on a grassy hillside with some picnic tables and a couple of fire pits. Follow the sign that says Trail (why mince words?) down a few stairs to the beach. Careful, they're slick when wet! The lower lot leads more directly to the beach and to the lighthouse, past the Keepers Quarters.

To get to Maury, you have to go through Vashon, with the only link being a single road along a narrow spit of land. To reach Point Robinson, take Vashon Highway to Quartermaster Drive, go east on Quartermaster Drive, and follow the left fork, which becomes Point Robinson Road, leading directly to the park.

PLACES TO EAT

Minglement: Outdoor seating has gotten scarce on Vashon, so get your salads, sandwiches, and coffee to go from this organic grocery/craft shop/tea and espresso bar on the main drag in town. 19529 Vashon Hwy. S.W.; 206/463-9672; www.minglement.net.

Sea Breeze La Boucherie: This organic farm has opened up a shop in town where they sell their eggs, goat milk, berries, and produce. They've done so well, they added a short menu of about five daily specials, served on an open patio. 17635 100th Ave. S.W.; 206/567-GOAT (206/567-4628); www.sea breezefarm.net.

PLACES TO STAY

Castle Hill: There are no fees or pet restrictions when you stay in Dockton on the south end of the island in Ron's suite with a full kitchen and bath with shower. It's light blue and bright, and the five acres of property benefit from the host's green thumb. Isis, with her tricky back, says the only disadvantage is that it's not handicapped accessible; it's above Ron's garage, reached by a long set of stairs. The reasonable rate is only $85 a night. 26734 94th Ave. S.W.; 206/463-5491.

Swallow's Nest Guest Cottages: The folks at Swallow's Nest have seven cottages in four separate island locations. Three small, rustic cottages near the golf course have fields for a dog run and are unequivocally dog friendly. The Edson House, with art by the photographer and artist Norman Edson, is a two-story Victorian in the Burton harbor, with a clawfoot tub and antiques. It, and "kids, pets, and the whole catastrophe" in the main house, are available for dogs with hair rather than fur, who are accustomed to town living. We recommend The Ladybug, a cozy place with unforgettable views of Mt. Rainier. Rates vary from $105–145. Pet fees are $15 each pet. 6030 S.W. 248th St.; 800/269-6378; www.vashonislandcottages.com.

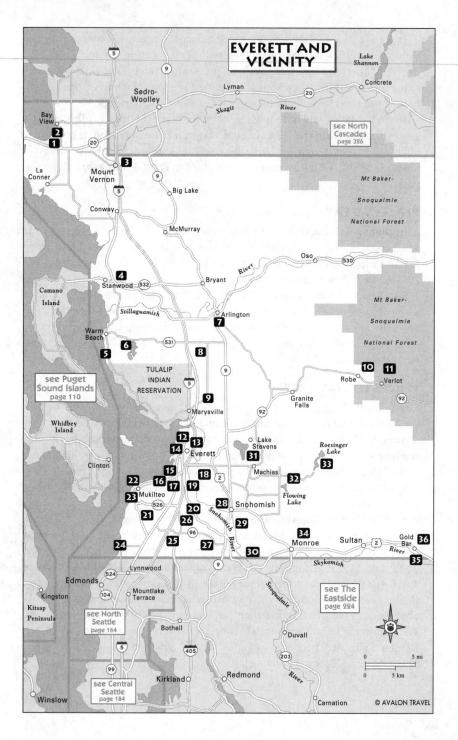

CHAPTER 5

Everett and Vicinity

Everett is the seat of the Snohomish county government, the second-largest freight port on the West Coast, and the home of Paine Field, the Boeing manufacturing facility building the world's largest 747, 767, 777, and now 787 airplanes. The city hosts Naval Station Everett, home of the aircraft carrier USS *Abraham Lincoln* when it returns from overseas deployment. Everett reflects the hardworking, patriotic, practical side of its inhabitants. In contrast, the parks of the region are showy, centered on the theme of water—lakes, rivers, creeks, streams, or the saltwater of Puget Sound. Two major intercity trails, the Interurban and the Centennial, can show you the region on bicycle, foot, and paw, following railroad and trolley lines long abandoned. Plan accordingly for the commuter slog through I-5 traffic between Seattle and Everett to make your escape with fewer headaches.

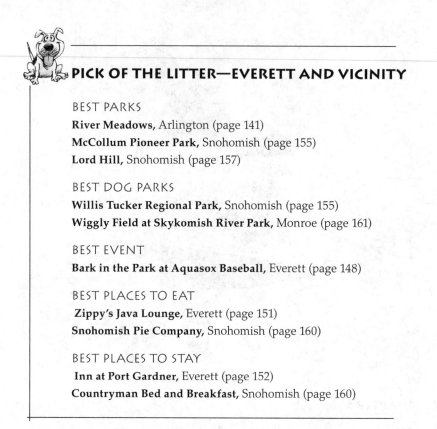

PICK OF THE LITTER—EVERETT AND VICINITY

BEST PARKS
River Meadows, Arlington (page 141)
McCollum Pioneer Park, Snohomish (page 155)
Lord Hill, Snohomish (page 157)

BEST DOG PARKS
Willis Tucker Regional Park, Snohomish (page 155)
Wiggly Field at Skykomish River Park, Monroe (page 161)

BEST EVENT
Bark in the Park at Aquasox Baseball, Everett (page 148)

BEST PLACES TO EAT
Zippy's Java Lounge, Everett (page 151)
Snohomish Pie Company, Snohomish (page 160)

BEST PLACES TO STAY
Inn at Port Gardner, Everett (page 152)
Countryman Bed and Breakfast, Snohomish (page 160)

Mount Vernon and La Conner

The Lower Skagit Valley is home to the largest fields of tulips outside of Holland. In April, visitors flock here from all parts of the globe to drive through the colorful fields during the Skagit Valley Tulip Festival. To avoid the crowds, you might enjoy coming earlier, in March, when the fields are full of bright yellow daffodils, or even in late February, when thousands of snow geese make a migratory pit stop in the valley. A bird dog might think she's died and gone to heaven when she sees thousands of geese take flight in waves, like noisy angels. Mount Vernon is the larger town, adjacent to the highway. Out on the sound, the smaller town of La Conner is known for its many art galleries and boutique shopping.

PARKS, BEACHES, AND RECREATION AREAS

❶ Bay View State Park

🐾🐾 (See Everett and Vicinity map on page 134)

Before it was a popular picnic meadow, the Skagit County Agricultural Association developed a racetrack and baseball diamond here to entertain the valley's hardworking farmers. Before that, it was a Native American village, home of Pat-Teh-Us, a prominent chief and one of the signers of the 1855 Point Elliott Treaty.

Down the hill and under the road is a picnic meadow and the Joe Hamel Beach. You have views of Fidalgo Island from the gravelly beach, a nice picnic stop on a tour of the valley. There are facilities for both species, in the form of vault toilets and bag dispensers.

From I-5, take Exit 226 west into Mount Vernon, follow the signs to stay on State Route 536 (Memorial Highway) for five miles, turn left on State Route 20, continue 1.7 miles, turn right on Bay View–Edison Road, continue 3.6 miles. Open 8 A.M.–dusk. 360/757-0227.

❷ Padilla Bay Shore Trail

🐾🐾🐾 (See Everett and Vicinity map on page 134)

Coop 'n' Isis don't think the views of the oil refinery towers across the bay on Fidalgo Island spoil this walk in the least. The wide, finely graded gravel trail

---

🐕 THINK GLOBALLY, BARK LOCALLY

The world would be a better place if all animal shelters were as loving and beautiful as the **Northwest Organization for Animal Health,** or NOAH, Center. It is a luxurious animal adoption center, a low-cost spay/neuter clinic, a training and grooming facility, and much more. You must come see the wonderful things they are doing here if you are in the vicinity. Besides, they've got two fully fenced potty stop areas you may use for a $1 suggested donation. Tours are free and take only about 15 minutes. There are many ways to give to NOAH. You can become a member, sponsor a dog or cat suite, place a tile on the friendship wall, and more.

The NOAH Center is at Exit 215 on I-5. Hours are 11 A.M.–6 P.M. Monday–Friday and 11 A.M.–5 P.M. Saturday and Sunday; 360/629-7055; www.thenoahcenter.org.

is 2.2 miles one-way, along the edge of the Padilla Bay Estuarine Reserve and a demonstration farm. It's a choice area for birders with binocs.

From I-5, take Exit 226 west, follow the signs to stay on State Route 536 for five miles, turn left and continue 1.7 miles west on State Route 20. Take a right on Bay View–Edison Trail and continue 0.8 mile to the south end, where there's room for a couple of cars. The north trailhead is 2.2 miles farther on Bay View–Edison Road, on the left. Parking for the north trailhead is in an overflow lot, 0.1 mile further, right on 2nd Street. Be extra careful crossing the road to get back to the trailhead. 360/428-1558; www.padillabay.gov.

🖪 Little Mountain City Park

🐾🐾🐾 (See Everett and Vicinity map on page 134)

You'll see said mountain off to your right as you drive toward the park. Once in the park, on the 934-foot drive to the top, there's a grab bag of parking pullouts and trails. The largest loop is 1.5 miles, so pick a direction and go for it. At the top, there are a few picnic tables perched on the lawn and two phenomenal viewpoint towers. And oh, what views there are. You can see the whole valley, and in April it looks like a patchwork quilt with all the colors of tulips in the fields. A dog bag dispenser is provided at the entrance.

From I-5, take Exit 226, turn west into Mount Vernon on Kincaid Street, turn left on 2nd Street, continue 0.7 mile, turn left on Blackburn Road and continue 1.4 miles, veer left on Little Mountain Road for 0.2 mile. Open 10 A.M.–dusk, weather permitting. 360/336-6215.

PLACES TO EAT

Conway Skagit Barn: The deli sandwiches and salads in the cold case are made daily, and our recommendations include the homemade fudge, teriyaki, salmon chowder, and generous scoops of ice cream, slurped on a wooden deck with a half dozen plastic patio tables. Discover the answer to the age-old question, "How many licks does it take a dog to get to the center of a waffle cone?" F.Y.I.: They sell hunting and fishing licenses also. 18729 Fir Island Rd., Exit 221 at Conway; 360/445-3006.

Rexville Grocery: You can smoke, drink, and sit with your dog on their patio, and they'll bring out a bowl and biscuits to soothe the savage beast while you devour generous sandwiches and homemade pie. Rexville is also a good bet for live crab, fresh oysters, and picnic goodies. 19271 Best Rd., Mount Vernon; 360/466-5522; www.rexvillegrocery.com.

PLACES TO STAY

Country Inn: The eight first-floor rooms of this cheerful inn are pet-friendly. They're cozy, gracious, and warm, each with a gas fireplace and flat-panel TVs. The $50 cleaning fee for pets is awfully steep, although it includes treats and use of a pet bed and bowls. We usually travel with our own dog beds and bowls, don't you? Anyway, rates range $120–180; 107 S. 2nd St., La Conner; 360/466-3101; www.laconnerlodging.com.

Katy's Inn: Dogs of all sizes with well-trained owners, says Katy, are welcome in the Captain John Peck Suite, downstairs with a private entrance. Small dogs willing to sleep in kennels are welcome in the additional three rooms upstairs. Private baths, a deck hot tub, free parking, and treats for people and dogs at bedtime are perks of staying at this B&B. The suite is $160 a night and there's a $25 one-time pet fee. 503 Third St., La Conner; 360/466-9909; www.katysinn.com.

Bay View Campground: The higher the number, the more secluded the site, with 46 tent spaces and 32 utility spaces. Rates are $15–22; 10905 Bay View–Edison Rd.; 888/226-7688; www.camis.com/wa.

More Accommodations: Please look under *Chain Hotels* in the *Resources* section for additional places to stay in this area.

Stanwood

The local greeting is *Vilkommen til Stanwood* (Welcome to Stanwood) in this Norwegian stronghold, where Lutheran churches, dairy farms, and bakeries carry on the traditions of their Viking ancestors. You'll love the farm country views, and your dog will go crazy for the smells, mostly manure, if you exit I-5 at Marysville and drive the Pioneer Highway through the valley north to town. For an intimate glimpse into Norwegian culture, stop at the **Uff Da Shoppe** ("Uff Da!" is the Norwegian equivalent of "Oy Vey!"; Viking Village; 360/629-3006). New traditions are being forged in art nearby at the internationally acclaimed Pilchuck Glass School, formed by Dale Chihuly. Stanwood is a good place to eat before heading across the bridge to Camano Island, where choices are limited.

PARKS, BEACHES, AND RECREATION AREAS

🐾 Church Creek Park
🐾🐾 (See Everett and Vicinity map on page 134)

This 16.5-acre city park is popular enough with the summertime picnicking crowd that parking in the lot is limited to 90 minutes. Tall trees and rolling hills are complemented by a smattering of tables, horseshoe pits, a basketball court, a cool rocket ship slide, and some rocking horses for the tots. Short trails lead to a picnic shelter, down to the creekside, and back to a little league field.

From I-5, take Exit 212 and go west on State Route 532. Turn north on 72nd Avenue N.W. for a couple of blocks. The park is on the right. Open 9 A.M.–dusk; only open weekends October–March.

5 Kayak Point

😺 😺 😺 (See Everett and Vicinity map on page 134)

This regional favorite used to be a private resort, and much of that refinement shines through the impeccably groomed 428-acre county park. Many sheltered picnic tables line up neatly along 3,300 feet of saltwater shoreline, offering ideal views of Port Susan. Clamming, fishing, crabbing, and windsurfing are popular pastimes for people, while pets probably prefer lounging or running on the huge beachfront lawn that leads right up to the water. We also wandered on the steep hiking trails up to and around the campsites and a little ways into the woods. The real star here is the beach, and that's where you'll probably want to spend most of your time soaking up the views, the sunshine, and the antics of the sailboarders. Dogs are not allowed on the fishing pier or playground.

From I-5, take Exit 206 and stay in the right lane to go west on State Route 531, Lakewood Road. Turn south onto Marine Drive, go two miles, and turn right on Kayak Point Road. The park is open 7 A.M.–dusk. There is a $5 combined fee for parking and launching a boat if you've got one. 15610 Marine Dr.; 360/652-7992.

6 Lake Goodwin Community Park

😺 (See Everett and Vicinity map on page 134)

When including the dog on a family outing, this lakefront park, dedicated in 2006, is a decent option. The 14-acre site has all the niceties of a newer park, including a covered picnic shelter, neat restrooms, and good parking. Picnic tables, viewing benches, and lawns all face a slice of lakefront, with a designated swimming area, playground, and fishing dock for the kids. For the dog, there's a woodchip path leading to a viewing platform and a few short trails through a stand of trees. Nearby homes, native growth protection areas, the closeness of the road, and Snohomish County park regulations all dictate leaving your pal on an eight-foot or shorter leash.

From I-5, Take Exit 206 and go west on State Route 531, Lakewood Road. After two miles, turn right at the stop sign to stay on Lakewood Road, and after five miles the park will be on the left. Open 7 A.M.–dusk. 4620 Lakewood Road.

PLACES TO EAT

Scandia Coffeehouse: In addition to making many breeds of cookies, they serve gourmet waffles, croissants, and smoothies for breakfast. Lunch includes a dozen salads and creative sandwiches. An awning protects a few outdoor tables, and there is a drive-through. 9808 S.R. 532; 360/629-2362; www.scandiacoffee.com.

Country Burger: When you've got a hankerin' for old-fashioned burgers and shakes, nothing else will do. If it's been a while since you've had a chili dog or a corn dog, fishwich or chicken strips, one or two won't hurt you. The dogs on board vote for the drive-through window. Across the parking lot is an espresso stand named Locals for your latte to wash down the last of the fries and onion rings. 3110 Lakewood Rd.; 360/652-8844; www.countryburger.com.

PLACES TO STAY

Kayak Point Park Campground: The campground is well situated up the hill from the water. This gives each of 30 tent sites wooded seclusion and privacy from the RV, bus, trailer, and boat parking. Sadly, dogs are not allowed in Yurt Village. The staffed office and information center includes a vending machine, hot drinks and snacks, and a pay phone (cell service here is spotty). Campsites are $20 in the summer and $10 October–March. 15610 Marine Dr.; 425/388-6600.

Arlington

More people probably know what Arlington looks like from the air than on the ground, because this town hosts the annual **Arlington Fly-In** around the Fourth of July, the third-largest exhibition of experimental aircraft in the United States. Much of the area's recreation focuses on "The Stilly," or the Stillaguamish River, including the Annual Duck Dash to determine the fastest floating rubber duck. Hey, don't laugh, the winner nets $5,000! Okay, go ahead and laugh anyway.

PARKS, BEACHES, AND RECREATION AREAS

7 River Meadows

🐾🐾🐾🐾 (See Everett and Vicinity map on page 134)

This county property merits the highest paw rating, with an extra tail wag thrown in during the off-season, when it's not crowded. Imagine 150 acres of pasture to bound through, without having to worry about those pesky cows or stepping in any cow pies. This former dairy farm is tucked into a bend of the Stillaguamish River, giving boaters water recreation opportunities, although the river runs too fast for dogs to swim during spring runoff.

When no one is camped out, people have been known to bring their dogs for hours of fun without being hassled. Unless your pooch is a champion sniffer-outer, you have to be willing to lose a tennis ball or two in the deep grass. Cooper and Isis literally disappear into the fields, what we call "going on safari." As if endless prairie isn't enough, there are six miles of trails winding along the river and around the meadows into nearby forests.

Take State Route 530 east through Arlington and turn right onto Arlington Heights Road. Bear right onto Jordan Road and go approximately three miles to the park entrance. Open 6 A.M.–dusk. 20416 Jordan Rd.; 360/435-3441.

PLACES TO STAY

Arlington Motor Inn: The staff is dog-neutral at this convenient, average-looking motel. The gal behind the counter giggled as she said that they tend to charge a one-time fee of $15–25, based on the "size and hairiness" of the dog or dogs joining you for your stay. Rates are in the $60–80 range. 2214 Rte 530; 360/652-9595.

Quality Inn–Airport: It's across the street from the Arlington airfield, so you may get the occasional overhead buzz noise at this motel. Cooper and Isis were too busy noticing how friendly and welcoming the staff were to pets, while we paid attention to nice touches like mini-fridges and microwaves in the rooms, and a spa tub in the workout room. Double rooms range $80–100, plus a $20 pet fee, discounted for more than one pet. 5200 172nd St. N.E.; 360/403-7222.

River Meadows Campground: It's every tent for itself out in the fields of this huge pasture. For $19 a night, you can pick a spot, designated by a fire pit, and lie under the stars, searching for Sirius by Orion's side as the burbling river lulls you to sleep (your dog's already snoring). No reservations, no showers, and no out-of-county checks. Come early, come clean, and bring cash. 20416 Jordan Rd.

Marysville

Many of the Native American reservations in Washington run casinos, and the Tulalip Casino across the highway from Marysville is one of the nicest, with a good reputation for being fun. Drop your dog off for a day or an overnight at the securely fenced, fully licensed, five-acre **Bone-a-Fide Dog Ranch** in Snohomish (7928 184th St.; 206/501-9247; www.bone-a-fide.com) and she'll romp while you roll the dice. When she's tired, she sleeps in their house, not a kennel, and when you've won the jackpot, you can buy her a diamond dog collar.

PARKS, BEACHES, AND RECREATION AREAS

8 Strawberry Fields Athletic Park

🐾🐾🐾 (See Everett and Vicinity map on page 134)

Like Marlin and Jim on old episodes of *Mutual of Omaha's Wild Kingdom*, naturalists Cooper and Isis are on the hunt for that most elusive of species: the Marysville off-leash area. After expeditions to Mother Nature's Window and Tambark Creek proved fruitless, our dachshund trackers caught scent of another possibility on the wind, that of an official dog park on six undeveloped acres of overgrown clover behind some of the city's soccer fields.

Whether or not it proves to be the great white hope of north-end canines, these fields that go on almost forever are full of four-legged fun in their current, untamed state. It's an ideal choice, effectively hemmed in by blackberry brambles, morning glory, and tall rush grasses.

DOG-EAR YOUR CALENDAR

On the last day of the Strawberry Festival in Marysville, the city goes to the dogs for **Poochapalooza,** on a Sunday in late June or early July. See flyball dogs in action, take a test run through the NOAH agility training course, and check out vendor booths. Enter your dogs in the non-pedigree pet show-case for wackiest pet, cutest ugly dog, best costume, best bark, among others. Donations net you an event bandana, with pro-ceeds going to develop Marysville's first off-leash dog park. www.poochapalooza.org.

At the park entrance, follow the sign to your left reading Strawberry Fields Trail System. This is the first of many helpful pointers, as the so-called trail is nothing more than a 10-foot-wide swath of loop-de-loops mown through the grass. You'll have excellent parking, restrooms, a bag dispenser, garbage cans, drinking fountains, and a covered picnic shelter available to you.

Take Exit 206 from I-5, heading east on State Route 531. Turn south on Smokey Point Boulevard and go 1.2 miles. Turn east on 152nd Street N.E. and head east, straight at the stop sign at 51st Avenue, a total of 1.5 miles to the entrance on your right. Open 6:30 A.M. to dusk. 6100 152nd St. N.E.

🐾 Jennings Memorial and Nature Park

🐾🐾🐾 (See Everett and Vicinity map on page 134)

The memorial part of the park is 51 acres of fun, the nature side is 17 acres of wetland observatory, and altogether it's an impressive city park. They've got picnic shelters with heavy-duty barbecue grills, and that's just the beginning.

The varied topography includes hills, dales, ponds, bridges and wetland observation platforms, grass slopes, and a creek, all of which you wander through on gravel and wood chip trails. It's enough to keep even the most attention-span-challenged puppy occupied for hours. Oh, and did Isis mention the trees? Big, beautiful trees, and ducks, and frogs, and so on, and so forth.

Kids rave about the display cannon, miniature steam engine, fishing pond, and, most frequently, Dinosaur Park, where they can crawl all over a 23-foot-long Stegosaurus, a 17-foot Salamander-saurus, a Pterodactyl swing, T-Rex, Triceratops, and a baby Brontosaurus.

You'd never know it's close to the highway. Take Exit 199 from I-5, go six blocks and turn left on 47th Avenue N.E., which bears to the right and becomes Armar Road. Shortly thereafter the park entrance is on your right at 6915 Armar Rd. 360/363-8400.

PLACES TO EAT

Oosterwyk's Dutch Bakery: You don't have to be able to pronounce it to enjoy it (even they just answer the phone "Dutch Bakery"). They were here long before the low-carb craze, and they'll likely be here long after. If it is sticky, sweet, or filling, you'll find it behind the long, tempting counter. Cash or check only. 1513 3rd St.; 360/653-3766.

PLACES TO STAY

Village Inn & Suites: At this super-squeaky-clean motel, one or two dogs, each under 15 pounds, are allowed in four of the rooms for a $15 dog fee (that's a buck per pound!). They're not terribly dog-friendly, but it's the only choice in town. Rooms are $95. 235 Beach Ave.; 877/659-0005; www.village innsuite.com.

Granite Falls

What used to be a provision town for miners and loggers is now the gateway to the recreation along the 55-mile Mountain Loop Highway. Most of it is paved, except for about 15 miles of gorgeous mountains, rivers, and valleys along the remote dirt section. It's not a loop in the winter, as they close the gate at Deer Creek, before Barlow Pass. You and your pal with his nose to the ground have access to the Big Four Ice Caves and the mining ghost town of Monte Cristo, plus dozens of campgrounds and hikes in the Mt. Baker–Snoqualmie National Forest. Road and trail conditions change frequently, so call ahead to the Darrington Ranger District at 360/436-1155.

PARKS, BEACHES, AND RECREATION AREAS

10 Robe Canyon Historical Park

😸 😸 😸 (See Everett and Vicinity map on page 134)

When you hike through Robe Canyon, your footsteps will follow the trail of the Monte Cristo, a narrow gauge railroad built in 1892, connecting the frontier town of Granite Falls to the mines. Hopeful prospectors found plenty of trouble, but little gold.

It's a mile from the road to the river, with inspiring canyon views on the way. After winding down some steep and narrow switchbacks to get to the valley floor, the trail levels out through a canopy of trees and along the sandy banks of the Stillaguamish river. It's definitely rough around the edges. Floods wiped out the railroad time and again; they'll do the same for the trail. It's a blast if you're willing to get your paws wet in errant streams and if you can jump over and under fallen logs. Isis noted that it's like agility trials, complete with tunnels at about 1.4 miles in, only these arches are carved through rock and big enough for a steam engine to travel through.

From the town of Granite Falls, follow the Mountain Loop Highway for seven miles. Look for a low brick wall with the sign Old Robe Trail across the street from Green Mountain Road. Parking is a roadside affair. There are a couple of picnic tables; you're on your own for everything else. Signs warn that the area is hazardous to unleashed dogs.

11 Mt. Pilchuck Road at Heather Lake Trailhead

🐾🐾🐾 (See Everett and Vicinity map on page 134)

The Heather Lake Trail is a pretty, popular, and mildly challenging four-mile round-trip hike through 30-foot-tall trees that have had plenty of time to grow since the last clear cut in the national forest. You'll climb steadily through sub-alpine forest to a flat meadow where the glacier-carved lake sits, waiting for a photo op, beneath the cliffs of Mt. Pilchuck. It's pretty enough to be pretty crowded on summer weekends. The rocky, boulder-strewn shore areas on the south side of the lake offer the best opportunity to get out your fishing pole, and pick wildflowers and berries.

In winter, the forest service road closes at the end of the paved section, and the 0.5-mile dirt road becomes an additional snow shoeing and cross-country skiing trail. The whole trail is a blast on snow shoes.

Go 12 miles east on the Mountain Loop Highway from Granite Falls, a mile east of the Verlot Public Service Center. Turn south on Forest Service Road #42, and go another 1.5-miles to the trailhead on your left. A $5 daily Forest Service Pass is required. 360/691-7791

PLACES TO EAT

Mountain View Restaurant, Cocktail Lounge, and Robe Store: People come from miles around for the trout (flown in from Idaho) and hand-cut steaks. The only big screen TV lounge within a 50-mile radius is another huge draw, as is Russia, the cat, who sits on a bar stool and checks IDs at the door. Outdoor dining at umbrella-covered tables is available in the summer. The store carries basic conveniences, and it's all run by the same hardworking folks at the Inn. 32005 Mountain Loop Highway; 360/691-6668.

PLACES TO STAY

Mountain View Inn: It's a tiny place, simple and spare, the only lodging between Marysville and Darrington, and it's a good 'un; hand-carved log furniture from Montana inside, view of Mt. Pilchuck outside, and less than a mile from the Snoqualmie–Mt. Baker National Forest. Hosts Vince and Diana have turned getting away from it all into an art form. Just $60 and a $25 refundable deposit covers you and your pets for the night. 32005 Mountain Loop Highway; 360/691-6668.

Everett

While the city itself is highly industrial and experiencing the uneven develop-ment that comes with economic growing pains, you've got to hand it to Everett for having the most parks with the best views. You can hit a bunch of them in one trip if you start at Mukilteo Lighthouse Park and drive north on Mukilteo Boulevard.

PARKS, BEACHES, AND RECREATION AREAS

12 American Legion Memorial

🐾🐾 (See Everett and Vicinity map on page 134)

Although much of the park is designated for specific uses that don't involve dogs, there's room to hang out, enjoy the view of Port Gardner Bay, and comb the grass for a beetle or spider to pester and then eat (one of Cooper's favorite activities). You could probably convince your pooch to walk the gravel trails of the Evergreen Arboretum and Gardens with you. This elaborate and educa-tional series of planted landscapes includes the fernery, conifer forest, dahlia garden, Japanese maples, and more. It's at the south end of the park, next to the golf course.

Follow Marine View Drive north around to the crest of the hill and turn on Alverson Boulevard. 145 Alverson Blvd.; www.evergreenarboretum.com.

🔟 Langus Riverfront Trail

🐾🐾🐾 (See Everett and Vicinity map on page 134)

As hard as it is to find this park, you'd think it would always be peaceful and uncrowded. However, when the salmon are running the river, usually in August and September, there are so many boaters and anglers it's hard to get a dog in edgewise. Stick to the rest of the year, and you'll have enough room to throw a stick for your pooch along this excellent riverfront pathway.

Three-ish miles of paved avenue wind along the mouth of the Snohomish River around the perimeter of Smith Island. Some of the trail is more interesting than picturesque, such as underneath the I-5 highway, past grain elevators and a sawmill, and around the sewage treatment plant. If the wind is blowing the wrong way, you might get a whiff. As far as your dog is concerned, that's probably akin to stepping into a French perfume boutique. The river is lovely for the rest of the trail and the picnic grounds are as well groomed as a New York Fifth Avenue poodle. Tall fencing protects you from the industrial areas. Bring a towel in case either of you decides to swim, and be prepared for muddy river banks or use the row boat launch as your entry point.

It's easier by far to access the Frontage Road from I-5 Southbound, exit 198, where you'll see the signs for Riverfront Park. Bear left onto 35th Avenue, left onto Ross Avenue, wind through Dagmars Marina and some industrial warehouses, keep going, and, finally, bear right onto Smith Island Road. As a side note, Dagmars has one of the largest collections of pleasure craft on the coast. You may be tempted to window shop, or even buy a Bayliner, if you've got a couple hundred thousand bucks lying around unused. 411 Smith Island Rd.

🔢 Grand Avenue Park

🐾🐾 (See Everett and Vicinity map on page 134)

The homes are grand, the immaculate grass grander, and the view grandest. At the turn of the 20th century, Everett was proud of its mill and shingle town status, when this park overlooked the factories of an industrial boomtown. The smokestacks are gone, replaced with one of the largest pleasure craft moorages on the Pacific Coast and Naval Station Everett. Bordering three city blocks, this park is befitting of the stately Colonial-style homes along the avenue. It's what Europeans would call formal gardens, with historic lighting fixtures, art installations, precise trees and flower beds, trimmed hedges, and strategically placed benches along a wide, ADA-accessible path. Ideal for a Sunday stroll, perhaps, rather than a place to let your tongue hang out. Isis lifts her nose and revels in her purebred, blue-blood lineage; Cooper straightens his collar and tries to look respectable.

The park extends three blocks on Grand Avenue between 16th and 19th Streets. 1800 Grand Ave.

DOG-EAR YOUR CALENDAR

It's dogs and frogs and a human-sized hot dog named Frank at **Bark in the Park** night at the Everett Aquasox, a class-A farm team for the Seattle Mariners baseball club. Webbly is the team mascot, a pop-fly catching toad. This ball club is the movie *Bull Durham* come to life. Your pet can enjoy America's pastime with you at Homer Porch, a lawn behind right field. Tickets are a steal at $7 per person, no charge for the dogs. The stadium has a policy of no outside food. Cooper had no problem polishing off the stadium's way-better-than-average concession food, including chowder or chili in sourdough bread bowls. All dogs' eyes will be riveted on Frank, who tosses free frankfurters into the crowd. To find out which night the ballpark goes to the dogs, call 800/GO FROGS (800/463-7647). Order tickets by phone or get them online at www.aquasox.com.

15 Howarth Park

(See Everett and Vicinity map on page 134)

This is one of three parks in Everett that's advertised as having an off-leash area. Isis gives it a lowly fire hydrant rating for many reasons. First of all, the north end of the beach is supposed to be off-leash, but she couldn't find any sign or boundary saying so. The unmarked OLA is the rockiest and least-accessible section of the park. Getting there requires navigating a rickety bridge over a muddy stream, dozens of flights of concrete stairs, and a high bridge over the railroad tracks. If that doesn't spook your dogs, the hurtling steel of trains rattling by will. Fencing is minimal and in many places there is nothing to separate the beach from the rails at all. At high tide, there is no beach. The park has a great water view, but there are better beaches nearby, preferable even if Lassie has to be leashed on them.

From Mukilteo Boulevard (41st Street) in Everett, turn right on Olympic Boulevard and follow it into Howarth Park. Leave your car in the first lot, a hard right turn at the bottom of the hill, to access the beach trail. The second parking lot is for the playground and other designated areas where dogs are not allowed. Open 6 A.M.–10 P.M. 1127 Olympic Blvd.; 425/257-8300.

16 Harborview

(See Everett and Vicinity map on page 134)

You can easily fool your pup into thinking that you are stopping for her because there is plenty of room to run around, when in fact you are coming here for the all-encompassing views of Port Gardner Bay, Possession Sound, and Everett. From the wide promontory, you can see Whidbey, Hat, Jetty, and Camano Islands; the port, naval station, and city of Everett; the Tulalip Indian Reservation; Mt. Baker; and Saratoga Passage leading to Deception Pass and the Pacific Ocean. While your darling putters around, you can watch ferries cross the water, trains roll by hugging the shoreline, and industrial ships being tugged out to sea. The park is on Mukilteo Boulevard at the intersection of Hardeson Road. 1621 Mukilteo Blvd.

17 Forest Park

😺 (See Everett and Vicinity map on page 134)

Cooper finds it ironic that what draws people to Forest Park isn't forest, but a pool, playground, animal farm, tournament-quality horseshoe field, tennis courts, day care, meeting hall, and classrooms. There are a few trails through a tall grove of trees, perhaps a half mile total. You can find them if you park at the top of the hill and walk just behind the playground to the west. Or, grab a map at the park office, clearly marked next to the parking lot.

From I-5, take Exit 192 and go west on Mukilteo Boulevard to the park on your left. Open 6 A.M.–10 P.M. 802 Mukilteo Blvd.; 425/257-8300.

18 Ebey Island Public Dog Park

😺😺🐕 (See Everett and Vicinity map on page 134)

Ebey Island is open, barely. Plastic orange fencing and a nice front gate surround the scrub. Some wonderful person with a powerful mower is keeping the fields and blackberries at bay. People have donated odds and ends patio furniture, and the City of Everett tossed in a couple of rain barrels for drinking water. About five total acres of wildly uneven ground is designated for the off-leash area. The small dog piece is kept closely cropped, and the large dog section has trails mown randomly through the fields. It's rough and tumble, a natural habitat to explore. Ball tossing might not be such a great idea though, as the object of your Old English sheepdog's desire is likely to get lost in the undergrowth.

Ultimately, with love, money, and hard work, local volunteers hope to turn Ebey Island into a canine sports park and regional community center, with agility equipment, shelters, and the works. Any and all help is welcome.

Take Exit 194 from I-5 onto State Route 2 eastbound. Take the Ebey Island/Homeacres Road Exit about halfway across the trestle. Go straight through the stop sign at the bottom of the exit and the next stop sign about 100 feet past that. Take a left at the next street that goes underneath the trestle, on 55th Street. The OLA is immediately to your left after you go under the bridge. Pull off to the side of the road. Open sunrise to sunset. www.ebeydog.org.

19 Lowell Park

🐾🐕 (See Everett and Vicinity map on page 134)

Poor Lowell Park. It's tiny, alternately hot and dusty or wet and slimy, and jam-packed. The back gates require two hands to operate, which is an exercise in frustration when you have two dogs with you and others trying to make a break for it. There's a bench and a garbage can. That's it. That said, local dogs will make their bid for freedom any way they can.

Regulars come here in shifts, nothing official, but patterns that have developed over time. It's small town life. Everybody knows, and has got their noses into, everybody else's business. People are busy chatting each other up, leaving the pup playground unsupervised in a state of mild chaos. It's a blast for any Maltese looking to see how much mischief she can get into before being called onto the carpet. Isis can recommend it only if you're not dogmatic about discipline and your canine can comport herself in a crowd.

Take Exit 192 from I-5, and go east at the bottom of the ramp instead of west toward town. Turn right onto 3rd Avenue and follow it down to 46th Street. You'll see the park on the left and angled parking in front of the tennis courts, with the off-leash area to the north. Open 6 A.M.–10 P.M. 46th St. and S. 3rd Ave.; 425/257-8300; www.everettwa.org/parks.

20 Lowell Riverfront Trail

🐾🐾🐾 (See Everett and Vicinity map on page 134)

The river you're fronting in this case is the Snohomish, nicely framed by a backdrop of Cascade Mountains and the remains of an 1880s frontier farmstead on the opposing bank of Ebey Island. From the ample parking lot, the paved boulevard travels 1.6 miles north, hugging the river. The level, smooth trail is a hugely popular spot for young families to go strolling, socializing, and tricycling or training-wheeling, with a few hard-core joggers whooshing by. Along the path are landscaped bump-outs, peppered with square picnic tables, barbecue stands, and garbage cans. Lowell is highly walk-worthy in Cooper's estimation. He fondly remembers chasing a remote-control car brought by a couple of teenagers and being mesmerized by a tiny garter snake slithering across his path.

Take exit 192 from I-5 going east. You'll be on S. 3rd Avenue, which curves around south and becomes 2nd Avenue. Turn left on Lenora and follow the signs to Lowell–Snohomish River Road. The parking lot will be on your left. Open 6 A.M.–10 P.M. 46th and S. 3rd Ave.

21 Loganberry Lane

🐾🐾🐾🐕 (See Everett and Vicinity map on page 134)

Finally, Loganberry wins best in show for Everett's off-leash areas. The lane offers a merry jaunt through a strip of woods sandwiched between the W. E. Hall golf course and playfields of Kasch Park. A couple of decent trails wind through cool shade trees, thick undergrowth, and brush for about a half mile. The entrance is not gated, but the remaining park borders are effectively secured by adjacent fences. It's a welcome contrast to the typical rectilinear, blockhead dog park.

There are a couple of parking spots available in a clearing laid with gravel. Don't be misled by the sign that says pets must be leashed. As soon as you pass the concrete barriers into the park, you are welcomed into the dog area by a sign and a baggie dispenser. Bring your own water to avoid a couple of brackish ponds in the park that look decidedly non-potable for pets.

From I-5, take Exit 189 to State Route 526 west, and turn left on Evergreen Way, right on 100th Street, and right on Loganberry Lane (18th Avenue W.). Drive until it dead-ends into the park. Open 6 A.M.–10 P.M. 425/257-8300; www.everettwa.org/parks.

PLACES TO EAT

Mermaid Market Café: The Mermaid's seasonal fruit salad is a magical concoction of mythic proportions, with mouth-watering chunks of watermelon, apples, grapes, and berries. Whatever the season, a tremendous amount of motherly love and elbow grease goes into the fresh daily soups and meal-size salads made at this mom-and-son operation. Even the two sidewalk tables, with colorful vinyl covers, make you feel right at home. 2932 Colby Ave.; 425/293-0347.

Meyer's: This half-bistro/half-bar is next to the Inn at Port Gardner and the Everett Marina, with outdoor tables on the pier, a dog biscuit jar on the counter, and several choice beers on tap. The light supper fare keeps hotel patrons happy, and they do decent breakfast and lunch business for the boaters docking for the day. 1700 W. Marine View Dr.; 425/259-3875.

Pavé Bakery: This is the home of the Cake Therapist, who will create tasty, artistic cakes for any dessert crisis. Even if your needs aren't urgent, or your tooth sweet, you'll love the quiches, soups, salads, sandwiches, and lunch specialties such as southwestern chicken chops and warm goat cheese salad. The sidewalk seating is on the most fashionable street in town. 2613 Colby Ave.; 425/252-0250.

Philly ya Belly: Everett-ites must have a thing for Philly cheese steaks, because Cooper saw lots of places that offer them. This is the home of the Belly Buster, with beef, chicken, pastrami, Portobello mushroom, and egg with gobs of green peppers and onions (hold the onions for the dogs, please). 12432 Hwy. 99; 425/710-0130.

Zippy's Java Lounge: Zippy is a Dalmatian, and for starters, he's a photogenic ham whose annual calendar benefits local charities. Then there's this wonderful place his owner Marilyn has created with an active summer outdoor scene. Her coffee café serves delicious food along the healthy spectrum from local organic and vegetarian to vegan and even raw. She's a force for positive change in the community, hosting green and sustainability seminars and recycling and composting all but 20 percent of waste. Zippy's provides an outlet for artists, hosting live music and open mike poetry nights. Wi-Fi, computers, and old-fashioned board games provide everyday distractions. 1804 Hewitt Ave.; 425/258-4940; www.myspace.com/zippysjava.

PLACES TO STAY

Days Inn: Tucked into a corner above the Everett Mall, this location of the chain is actually cute, with pretend period styling. Rates range $65–110, and a $20 pet fee covers your dogs without restriction. 1602 S.E. Everett Mall Way.; 425/355-1570.

Holiday Inn–Downtown Everett: This is a glammed-up Holiday Inn, the closest hotel to the Everett Events Center, convenient if you're going to see a show, such as Clifford the Big Red Dog on Ice, for example. They allow two dogs 40 pounds or under for a single $40 non-refundable pet fee. Rates range $100–160. 3105 Pine St.; 425/339-2000; www.hieverett.com.

Inn at Port Gardner: This boutique hotel is sleek and upscale, inside and out. Most rooms have marina views, and whirlpool tubs and fireplace suites are available, as are doggy biscuits at the front desk. Its choice location puts you right on the waterfront near the city's best dining, and that fact is reflected in the rates, $110–300 per night, plus a $15 per night pet fee; pets under 50 pounds only. Reservations are a must; the inn's 33 rooms go quickly. 1700 W. Marine View Dr.; 425/252-6779; www.innatportgardner.com.

Mukilteo

Old Town Mukilteo, as it is known locally, is tucked inside greater incorporated Everett. There are a few bistro-style eateries and lovely shops (for example, Rose Hill Chocolate Company) in this tiny waterfront village. It's the Eastern terminus of the Clinton/Mukilteo ferry, taking you and your pup to the wonders of Whidbey Island.

PARKS, BEACHES, AND RECREATION AREAS

22 Mukilteo Lighthouse Park

🐾🐾 (See Everett and Vicinity map on page 134)

This site has historic significance as the location of the signing of the Point Everett Treaty, where 2,000 members of dozens of regional tribes met with Isaac Stevens, Superintendent of Indian Affairs, in 1855. Picnic tables are lined in soldierly order along the beach, each with a huge fire pit and standing grill. Behind them, there is a field wide enough to roam, and in front, plenty of rocky beach to walk. From this site, you are looking out over Whidbey and Camano Islands across Port Gardner Bay.

The parking lot is bigger than the park to provide plenty of boat trailer parking, a disappointment at this prime waterfront location. Fortunately, that is changing. Beginning in 2007, a master plan is being put into action that will alter this park for the better, to include a waterfront promenade, soft-surface trails, and big lawns. Accordingly, be prepared to face construction when you visit.

Next door, the grounds of Light Station Mukilteo, the lighthouse built by the U.S. Army Corps of Engineers in 1905, are open noon–5 P.M. Saturday, Sunday, and holidays, April–September (no pets in the lighthouse). The rest of the park is open year-round.

Take the Mukilteo Speedway to the water, staying in the left lane, and turn left into the park at the ferry dock. Parking is limited to four hours. 609 Front St.

23 92nd Street Park

🐾🐾 (See Everett and Vicinity map on page 134)

It's like the putt-putt equivalent of a state park, without the camping, shrunk to city-size to fit in a crowded suburban area. There are a few ponds to sniff around, groomed grass to roll in, and a maze of miniature trails through the woods to walk. Probably the only ones who'll get any exercise are the kids, who can romp in two play areas. It is hilly, so you could run your dog up and down to mellow him out for the ride home. The park staff is determined you pick up after yourself, providing poop bag dispensers and garbage cans, seemingly every few feet.

At the intersection of 92nd Street and the Mukilteo Speedway, turn south on 92nd Street to enter the parking lot.

24 Picnic Point

🐾🐾 (See Everett and Vicinity map on page 134)

Picnic Point's got picnic tables, six of them, on a small green plot overlooking the water. They're nifty, but that's nothing compared to the beach below. At low tide, the sandy shore is a real winner, a huge expanse of salty tidal flats tailor-made for dog-day afternoons. Unlike Howarth Park, which Isis whined about earlier, the beach is wheelchair-accessible by means of a gentle ramp and pedestrian overpass over the railroad tracks.

The park is due north of Edmonds and can be reached by heading west on Shelby Road from State Route 99, then taking the right fork in the road onto Picnic Point Road. 13001 Picnic Point Rd.; 425/388-6600.

PLACES TO EAT

Ivar's: On Mukilteo Landing, at the ferry terminal, this local chain of the famous "Keep Clam!" slogan has a walk-up fish bar for all types of seafood that can be fried and served with fries, a couple of salads, plus slurpable clam chowder and lickable soft serve ice cream. 710 Front St.; 425/742-6180.

Weller's Speedway Café: Slow down on the Speedway to work your way through an omelet and hash browns at one of two front picnic tables. Or, if you're stuck in the ferry waiting line, pull out and plow through a Philadelphia steak sandwich instead. Generous portions of classic food will warm your stomach whether you're coming or going. 8490 Mukilteo Speedway; 425/353-4154.

Whidbey Coffee Company: Coffee tastes better when sipped at your table on the garden terrace, looking out over the bay. Oatmeal, granola, bagels, and croissants are featured for breakfast, along with fresh-squeezed juices and foamy lattes. Lunch is light, including salads, a few sandwiches, and hot specials. We luv it. 619 4th St.; 425/348-4825; www.whidbeycoffee.com.

PLACES TO STAY

Hogland House: This bed-and-breakfast is a classically styled and furnished romantic Victorian that's listed on the Register of Historic Places. There is a hot tub deck overlooking Puget Sound, and there are trails to the beach. Rates of $115 for the Rose Room and $125 for the Lilac Room include a hearty breakfast. Or, you can make your own meals—with in-room refrigerators, microwaves, and coffee—and save. There is a two-dog limit, and each dog is $10 per night. 917 Webster St.; 425/742-7639; www.hoglandhouse.com.

TownePlace Suites by Marriott: All-suite hotels are really handy when you're traveling with pets. The rooms are larger and have many of the comforts of home, without the embarrassing childhood family photos on the walls. These suites have everything, including the kitchen sink, in a personable setting at an affordable price. Limit two dogs under 75 pounds; rates of $80–100, plus a $15 pet fee; 8521 Mukilteo Speedway; 425/551-5900.

Snohomish

Snohomish is famous as the antiquing capital of the Northwest, the personification of an old town you hope to discover when traveling the countryside. Historic First Street is packed with shops bearing gifts, collectibles, furniture, and good food. There are several proposed off-leash areas in various stages of approval and creation in Snohomish County; Sno-Dogs can keep up-to-date with developments at www.sno-dog.org.

Only an hour from downtown Seattle, the Snohomish Valley is rural, with farm country scenery and prime lakeside parks. You're heading into country where you'll see Tractor Crossing signs, where pickup trucks rule the road, and nearly every car you pass has a dog with his head stuck out the window, tongue flapping in the breeze.

PARKS, BEACHES, AND RECREATION AREAS

25 McCollum Pioneer Park

🐾🐾🐾🐾 (See Everett and Vicinity map on page 134)

One man's dump is another dog's pleasure. In other words, what used to be a landfill is now a jam-packed, 78-acre, activity-oriented county park. In between the BMX track and the bus park-and-ride shelters, the heated outdoor swimming pool and the playground, it is possible to fit in some downtime with your dog.

To get the lay of the land, follow the landscaped, paved loop around the athletic fields and the picnic area. Better yet, like the first settlers who arrived in the 1920s, leave civilization behind and explore the wilds, where all the juicy stuff at McCollum Park happens. Coop recommends the Forest Loop, which starts from the first parking area on your right, northeast of the swimming pool, along and around and over North Creek, which is a critical salmon spawning habitat. It ends up being much farther than you think, and those well-tended lawns start to look mighty inviting after a while. This park is easy to get to, has something for everyone, and reveals a great trail. We were so glad we stopped by.

Take Exit 186 from I-5, and go east on 128th Street. The large park is 0.3 miles from the highway, visible immediately to your right. 600 128th St. S.E.

26 Green Lantern Trail

🐾 (See Everett and Vicinity map on page 134)

The Green Lantern Trail follows the Silver Lake shoreline for a mile from Hauge Homestead park, through Green Lantern Park, ending at Thornton A. Sullivan park. Sorry, no dogs allowed on the beach. It's not a trail, rather a busy sidewalk in shop-happy suburbia. Let's say you're out running errands in the minivan, the kids are strapped in booster seats, and the dog's in the cargo area. Everybody needs to get out and stretch their legs. This walk could save your sanity someday. Besides, **Dirty Dogs Bathhouse & Biscuits** is down the street (12902 Bothell-Everett Hwy.; 425/357-9921) and **Paddywhack,** a most excellent dog boutique, is right around the corner in Mill Creek (15415 Main St.; 425/357-6510).

From I-5, take Exit 186 east onto 128th Street, turn left on 19th Avenue, and left on Silver Lake Road to the parking lot immediately on your right. 1819 121st St. S.E.

27 Willis Tucker Regional Park

🐾🐾🐾🦮 (See Everett and Vicinity map on page 134)

Sno-DOG, the Snohomish Dog Off-leash Group, worked with Snohomish County to score 11 acres at Willis Tucker for the first off-leash area in the

DIVERSION

Do you have a dog like Isis, who is way too smart for her own good, a sociable but easily bored canine with too much time and undirected energy on her paws? You need to find a great activity, a bonding experience the two of you can do together. Welcome to the home base for the **Sno-King Agility Club,** one of the area's most active dog agility clubs. If you're reading this book, you're already someone willing to spend some face time with your pets. Take it a step further, grab your clicker and tiny treats, and register to take a six-week class for $80. Maybe your couch potato, or couch shredder as the case may be, is destined to pole weave with the pros. Check it out at www.snokingagility.com.

county, situated on the Seattle Hill plateau. A couple of fenced and gated acres opened in July 2007. By the official grand opening, November 1, 2008, a total of 4.5 acres were seeded, secured, and planted with young saplings and shrubs in an attempt to stabilize hillsides and stave off the wet-season mud. Don't count on it; bring plenty of towels. Another 3.5-acre Tree 'n' Trail section was completed in December 2008, with gravel walking paths, and a 0.5-acre OLA for shy dogs was receiving its fence and gate as we went to press. Not too shabby.

At Willis Tucker, there are hills and dales where you dog can play king of the mound. A few level strips of ground are perfect for practice runs, long enough for power chuckers. The remainder of the area includes agility equipment, varied topography, a wetland stream, and some steep ravines. Let the dog slobbering commence!

There are buckets for water and used bags hanging around, but we always recommend you BYO. Garbage cans are tucked away in the gray box outside the fence in the gravel parking area. The people potty is in the activity center at the main park entrance.

From I-5, take Exit 186 to 128th Street, following it east for four miles, as it becomes 132nd Street and 134th Place. Take a right onto Snohomish-Cascade Drive (65th Ave S.E.), and a left on Puget Park Drive. Travel 0.3 miles past the main entrance to the off-leash area. 6705 Puget Park Dr.; 425/388-6644.

28 Fields Riffles

🐾🐾🐕 (See Everett and Vicinity map on page 134)

At press time, this was an undeveloped area fronting the Snohomish River, much like Irving Lawson (described later in this section), but there's no official parking, no official park, no official anything. The sign on the gate reads: Future Park Site, Snohomish River Access and Trail. We wanted you to know where it is because an off-leash park is proposed for at least 10 acres of the site, whatever the uncertain future holds for the rest. The day the dogs visited, a lone farmer with his old dingo drove up in an ancient pickup and took a stroll down the woodchip covered lane to the riverbank and back; by the time you read this, it could be a bustling canine cosmopolis. Keep up on the news at www.sno-dog.org.

Fields Riffles is one mile west of Avenue D on Lowell–Snohomish River Road.

29 Irving Lawson Access Area

🐾🐾🐾🦮 (See Everett and Vicinity map on page 134)

While this area maintained by the Department of Wildlife is listed on the county's website as an off-leash area, it isn't set up as an official dog park. It's a large area of rough fields, with a long walk along the top of the dike keeping the Snohomish River in check. Owners have permission to let dogs off leash, but be aware that there is no fencing and steep slopes leading down to the river.

This is serious country. To get there, you will cross the railroad tracks, pass pygmy goats, and go through pumpkin farms and tree-nut orchards. On a winter weekday it can be a bucolic, peaceful walk along the riverbank, watching Peregrine falcons and snow geese. We encountered a bald eagle so big Cooper saw his life flash before his eyes as he imagined himself in the talons of America's national treasure. On the other hand, locals tell us it can get a bit too populated on nice weekends and evenings.

The area is marked by a big metal gate with a pass-through, and there is paved parking for a half dozen vehicles. There are no facilities, so bring your own poop bags and water. Pack it in, pack it out.

Go south on Avenue D to Airport Way (past the airport), bear to the left to continue on Springhetti Road. At 1.5 miles from town, turn left on 111th Street to the end of the road, to the dead end. Lawson is a good find for the price of the $10.95 quarterly Vehicle Use Permit (plus $2 processing fee) that is required, which can be purchased at most sporting goods stores or online at wdfw.wa.gov.; 360/563-2633.

30 Lord Hill

🐾🐾🐾🐾 (See Everett and Vicinity map on page 134)

This 1,400-acre upland nature preserve is a fantastic trail-dog destination, and dogs of the region probably lord that fact over others. Eleven miles of roughly groomed trails take you past ponds, marshes, several lakes, a couple of deserted rock quarries, rivers, and deep forests of evergreens. A couple of hikers-only trails lead to a series of viewpoints that give you a distinct feeling of being a lord or lady, surveying your kingdom and perhaps watching for invading foes. The origin of the park's name isn't quite so dramatic, just from some dude named Mitchell Lord who bought the land for a dairy farm in 1879.

To get to the bulk of the trails, you must cross a series of long boardwalks built over a swamp. Beavers are the ruling class of wildlife at Lord Hill; your dog might see one at work, or at least the evidence of their handiwork. You'll share the trail with quite a few horses, mountain bikes, and trail runners. Even so, it doesn't seem crowded, but use your horse sense.

To reach Lord Hill from 2nd Street in Snohomish, turn south on Lincoln Avenue, following it until it becomes Old Snohomish-Monroe Road. Go 2.5 miles, turn south on 127th Avenue S.E., and follow the signs another two miles to the entrance. 12921 150th St. S.E.; go to www.friendsoflordhill.org for a park map.

31 Centennial Trail

🐾🐾🐾 (See Everett and Vicinity map on page 134)

For almost a hundred years (hence the name) the S.L.& E. Railroad carried freight, mail, and passengers from Seattle to Canada. From 1889 to 1987, postal mail, lumber from the sawmills, and iron, copper, lead, silver, and gold from the Mt. Pilchuck and Monte Cristo mines were hauled on the rails. The same right-of-way that now provides for this popular trail has given us the beloved Burke-Gilman Trail in Seattle, as well as the Sammamish Trail on the Eastside. Someday, 44 miles will be joined together along original lines.

The six-foot-wide paved path winds through a country valley, generally following the Machias Road for seven miles from Snohomish in the south to Lake Stevens, then winding another seven miles north to Arlington for an even more scenic section.

Centennial is best for dogs trying to get their owners in shape with a long-distance jog, cycle, or in-line skate session, rather than a place to stop and sniff the bushes. It's often populated by training speed cyclists, so Coop and Isis recommend the smaller soft-surface trail that runs alongside, shared with the horses.

While there are seven formal and several informal trailheads along the path, Cooper's favorite place to hit the trail is outside Snohomish in the town of Machias. There's a replica of an 1890s railroad depot, expansive parking, a covered picnic shelter, restrooms, and a trail marker that lets you know just how far it is to each stop along the way. From Highway 2, take the 20th St. Exit (the middle of the three), then turn right on Williams Road when 20th ends. Take a right again on S. Machias Road, go straight at the stop sign, then left on Division street in town. 425/388-6600; www.snocoparks.org.

🐾 Flowing Lake

🐾🐾🐾 (See Everett and Vicinity map on page 134)

Once upon a time, the Leckie family operated a lakeside resort on this now-county-owned property. Once upon a summer's day, the Dachsie Twins got comfortable on a lawn blanket facing the water, and they thought they might never want to get up again. They were happily ever after, hypnotized by the boats making lazy circles on the water and the swish, click, and whir of anglers' fishing poles on the pier and shore. Summer also brings out the swimmers, water-skiers, volleyball players, and more kids for a rowdier atmosphere. There are too many expensive homes along the shores to get away from it all, yet it is forested and rural enough to induce a tranquil spell.

Take the Snohomish exit off I-5 onto Highway 2 and go toward Monroe. At milepost 10, turn left onto 100th Street S.E. (Westwick Road), which will eventually make a sharp turn to the north and become 171st Avenue S.E. Turn right onto 48th Avenue S.E. into the park. Parking is $5 for the day. Open 7 A.M.–dusk. 17900 48th S.E.; 360/568-2274.

🐾 Lake Roesinger

🐾 (See Everett and Vicinity map on page 134)

You wouldn't know by looking that Lake Roesinger is actually bigger than Flowing Lake. Roesinger's park is much smaller, and the lake goes around a steep bend out of sight. A sloped hillside leads to the beach access for boating, fishing, and swimming (for dogs, outside of the roped area). It's a fallback plan if Flowing Lake is too crowded or you don't want to shell out the $5 for parking there. Here, a dozen parking spots across the road from the park are free. A short trail across a few bridges and into a wooded area is bordered by Gemmer Road and the lake road.

Take the Snohomish exit off I-5 onto Highway 2 and go toward Monroe. At milepost 10, turn left onto 100th Street S.E. (Westwick Road), which will eventually make a sharp turn to the north and become 171st Avenue S.E. Turn right on Dubuque Road, travel six miles, and turn left onto Lake Roesinger Road. Stay to your right at the Y intersection, and go another mile to the park. 1608 S. Lake Roesinger Rd.

PLACES TO EAT

BBQ Shack: There's a strip of outdoor seating alongside this so-called "home of the naked pigs," where you can enjoy a strip of baby back ribs, or any number of other marinated meats, hopefully dripping juices all the way. 130 Avenue D, 360/568-7222; www.bbqshackonline.com.

Chuck's Seafood Grotto: The grotto took over an auto body shop; basically, when they roll up the garage doors, it's all outdoor seating. It's all seafood as well, the good, the fried, and the fresh. Try salmon, halibut cheeks, and catfish; seafood wraps; or shrimp and chips, scallops and chips, calamari and chips, fish and chips. . . well, you get the gist of it. 1229 1st St.; 360/568-0782.

Collector's Choice: This spot is definitely your best choice in town for breakfast or dinner, with a big menu of reliable American favorites. Large plates are served with a welcoming smile for your pet on the patio, which takes over the sidewalk and part of the parking area at the Star Center mall building. 120 Glen Ave.; 360/568-1277.

Snohomish Pie Company: Oh lordy, there are few stronger temptations than chocolate pecan pie á la mode. That's merely one of a dozen or so daily specialty pies you can order by the slice, or whole, and wolf down at the one sidewalk table. The combo—soup, half a sandwich on homemade bun, and slice o' pie—is $7.25. If you start with the garden or chef salad, you'll save more room for pie. Heck, go straight to the pie. 915 1st St.; 360/568-3589.

Spotted Cow Cream & Bean: It's refreshing to "stray from the herd," as the folks at this café say, and eat at a local, family-owned business. They really do make their ice cream, gelato, and sorbets on site, and their cream comes from a local dairy. It's even more refreshing that the menu includes grown up choices such as smoothies, wraps, and Washington wines and bottled beers. Sit a spell at a covered sidewalk table and watch the rest of the herd drive by, then head to nearby Willis Tucker OLA and run off the extra hot fudge you ordered. 3414 132nd St. S.E., #307, Thomas Lake Center; 425/337-8494.

PLACES TO STAY

Countryman Bed and Breakfast: Beautiful antiques and handmade quilts grace this 1896 restored Victorian home. Dogs are welcome without extra charge, as long as there's no extra wear and tear on the room. She prefers that dog lovers stay in the Tower Room, with a wood floor, but may also open up the Fireplace Room as needed. "But, please," says owner Sandy, "if you've got a big dog, just say so. I'd like to know." You get to pick the time and menu for breakfast! Rates are $115–125. 119 Cedar Ave.; 360/568-9622; www.countrymanbandb.com.

Inn at Snohomish: This motel on the edge of historic downtown is bright, sunny, and tidy. Rooms are named after famous local historical figures, with photographs and a short history lesson about that person in framed pictures on the walls, a unique touch that impressed us. Pet policies include not leaving dogs unattended and not bathing pets in the room. "It's hard on the tub drainage system," said the gal at the counter. Your $150 pet damage deposit is returned in full when you leave the room in good condition. Standard rooms are $80; suites with whirlpool tubs are $100. 323 2nd St.; 800/548-9993; www.snohomishinn.com.

La Quinta: This motel, opened in 2007, is hard to see at first, because it's hidden behind the Holiday Inn and about the same color. They have a two-dog limit, each under 30 pounds, and dogs are allowed on the third floor only. There's no pet fee, if you sign a contract not to leave your pet unattended; $80–105. 12619 4th Ave. W., off the 128th Street Exit; 425/347-9099.

Motel 6–Everett South: All Motel 6 properties accept dogs under 80 pounds, and there are no dog fees if you declare pets at check-in. This location of the chain is called South Everett, but it's in our definition of Snohomish for all intents and purposes, across the highway from McCollum Park. A reliable pocketbook pleaser, as always, at $45–60 per night, with a 10 percent discount for booking online. 224 128th St. S.W., I-5 exit #186 at 128th St.; 425/353-8120.

Flowing Lake Park Campground: There are 30 extra-wide campsites in the woods surrounding Flowing Lake, seven of which are handicapped-accessible. Ten are tent sites at $14 per night, and the rest are hookup sites for $20. For the ultimate in lakeside luxury, tidy cabin #4 is designated for pets and up to five owners, furnished with a bed, futon, lights, and a heater for $40 a night, plus $5 per pet. 17900 48th St. N.E.; 425/388-6600.

Monroe

On the outskirts of Everett, Monroe is the last substantial bastion of civilization before heading into the woods. As you continue toward Stevens Pass, a series of mining and logging towns straggle into the mountains, with quirky names such as Sultan, Start Up, Index, Gold Bar, and Grotto.

PARKS, BEACHES, AND RECREATION AREAS

🐾 Wiggly Field at Skykomish River Park

🐾🐾🐾🐕 (See Everett and Vicinity map on page 134)

Cooper and Isis were proud to be there the day after Opening Day, July 20, 2008, when this small community opened their three-acre pooch playground. It's open and level, with heavy-duty field grass and a few shade trees along one edge. There's a tall chain-link fence to separate the dog park from the ball fields along one long edge, but the rest is bordered by a split rail corral that'll be more effective when it's lined by chicken wire to keep wanderers in check.

Isis got a kick out of the hand-built agility equipment, which includes an A-frame, tunnel, steps, a jump, and some dog walks. It's impressive that this park was created by hard volunteer work and only $5,000 in donations. No city money was used, and further donations will add a water pump and message board. At the moment, amenities include a bag dispenser, garbage cans, and a couple of metal benches. For water dogs, there's a short path to the Skykomish River at the southeast corner of the OLA—hooray!

From Highway 2 in Monroe, turn south on Kelsey Street, right on Main Street, left on Village Way, and left into the park on Sky River Parkway. Drive as far as you can, past the Senior Center, Boys and Girls Club, and around the ball fields to reach the OLA parking area. 413 Sky River Parkway; www.sno-dog.org.

PLACES TO STAY

Best Western Sky Valley Inn: Tidy and roomy singles have a vaguely colonial theme at this roadside motel. They like to assign first-floor rooms near the hallway door to pet families, and ask that you avoid the lobby and walk your dogs in the back lot to the north. There are no pet restrictions, and the fee is $20. Rates range $100–120. 19233 Hwy. 2; 360/794-3111.

Gold Bar

Gold Bar was settled first by gold prospectors, then by laborers for the Great Northern Railroad. Don't forget to register your claim if Sparky digs up anything sparkly.

PARKS, BEACHES, AND RECREATION AREAS

35 Gold Bar Dog Park

🐾 🐕 (See Everett and Vicinity map on page 134)

Gold Bar's off-leash area is a smidgen of land between the railroad tracks and the highway. The only thing separating the grass from heavy traffic is a small ditch, so you must have control of your dog at all times, physically or verbally, for her safety. It has trees, dry grass, and blackberry bushes to sniff. For dogs, it ain't much, but it is all theirs. Bring your own everything; there are no services or amenities, but you can throw your poop bags in the trash can at the gas station across the street.

It's on the south side of U.S. Highway 2 at the intersection of 6th Street in Gold Bar. A couple of cars can park in a gravel lane bordering the OLA.

36 Wallace Falls State Park

🐾 🐾 🐾 🐾 (See Everett and Vicinity map on page 134)

The park's name is the Anglicized version of *Kwayaylsh*, for Skykomish Native Americans Jack and Sarah, the first homesteaders in the area. Wallace is a tremendously popular 4,735-acre park specifically for hiking and, through word of maw, has cultivated a dogmatic following of canine climbers. The main footpath is the Woody Trail, a moderately difficult trek, gradually climbing from 500 to 1700 feet in elevation, past nine falls of more than 50 feet each, the largest of which tumbles 265 feet through a narrow gorge. It's 1.8 miles to the Skykomish Valley Overlook and Picnic Shelter at the Lower Falls, 2.4 miles to the top of Middle Falls, and 2.7 miles to the Upper Falls. You'll cross several bridges and navigate stairs along the way.

The round-trip trek takes about three hours if you're going at a steady clip. We won't tell you how long it took Cooper. Cougars have been sighted near the falls, so leashes are a really good idea, even more important on summer weekends when large crowds have been sighted more often than big cats. Seven primitive walk-in tent sites are available, from 50 to 150 feet from the parking area, for $15 per night on a first-come, first-served basis.

From U.S. Highway 2 in Gold Bar, turn north on 1st Street, travel 0.5 mile, turn right on May Creek Road, follow the left fork when it becomes Ley Road, and the left fork again at Wallace Lake Road into the park. Open 8 A.M.–dusk.

PLACES TO EAT

Zeke's Drive In: Bigger and better than your average drive-up, Zeke's has about a dozen shiny red picnic tables scattered over a couple shady meadows. Manager Mike is a drill sergeant, keeping a corps of teenagers doing double-time in the kitchen, so even when it's crazy crowded, which is often, the lines move speedily. Try the ostrich burger, which Coop thought tasted better than beef, and the beer-battered onion rings. 43918 S.R. 2; 360/793-2287.

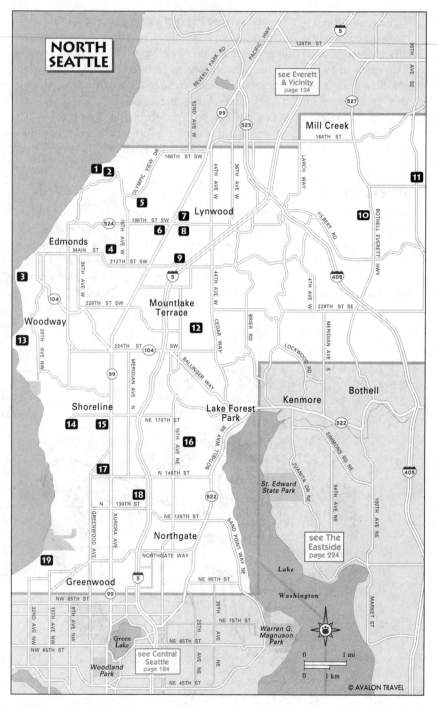

NORTH SEATTLE

see Everett & Vicinity
page 134

Mill Creek

Lynwood

Edmonds

Woodway

Mountlake Terrace

Shoreline

Lake Forest Park

Kenmore

Bothell

St. Edward State Park

Northgate

see The Eastside
page 224

Greenwood

Lake Washington

Warren G. Magnuson Park

Green Lake

see Central Seattle
page 184

Woodland Park

© AVALON TRAVEL

CHAPTER 6

North Seattle

The going gets a little rough for canines as you head north of the city. Big malls like Northgate and Alderwood chew up available real estate and suburban sprawl dominates the landscape. The city's longest and least attractive commercial strip, Aurora Avenue, cuts a wide swath diagonally through the housing developments west of the interstate. This human tendency to focus on commerce and industry is all the more reason for dogs to take it upon themselves to keep their owners from losing touch with all that is good and green in the heart of the concrete jungle.

In more tough news, to the north of King County, Snohomish County has a reputation for strictly enforcing its dangerous dog and potentially dangerous dog ordinances. In Edmonds, dogs are not allowed in city parks at all, except on fringe trails. At least there's hope in Shoreline, where the advocacy group ShoreDOG submitted an Off-Leash Dog Area study in September 2008 to the Parks, Recreation, and Cultural Services Board, recommending

PICK OF THE LITTER—NORTH SEATTLE

BEST PARKS
Meadowdale, Edmonds (page 167)
Richmond Beach Saltwater Park, Shoreline (page 176)

BEST DOG PARKS
Marina Beach Dog Park, Edmonds (page 168)
Northacres, Northgate (page 180)

BEST PLACES TO EAT
Red Twig, Edmonds (page 170)
Laughing Ladies Café, Shoreline (page 179)

BEST PLACES TO STAY
Best Western Edmonds Harbor Inn, Edmonds (page 170)
Residence Inn by Marriott, Lynnwood (page 174)

six potential sites for future dog parks. You can keep track of their progress at www.shoredog.org.

Amidst all this dog doom and gloom are bright spots, where leaping for joy is still legal. Marina Park in Edmonds has an awesome dog beach, and some undeveloped land in Mill Creek is a strong contender for a future off-leash park at Tambark Creek. Keep your paws crossed that things lighten up a little in North Seattle.

Edmonds

The city of Edmonds is an overgrown sea-side resort town that's not particularly Fido-friendly. The party line is that dogs are not allowed in city parks, except on trails. Fair enough. We discovered plenty of parks within the city limits that have trails, and some truly wonderful county parks that do allow pets. When you've exhausted the possibilities in Edmonds, catch the ferry over to Kingston, leading to all the wonders of the Kitsap and Olympic Peninsulas.

PARKS, BEACHES, AND RECREATION AREAS

▌ Meadowdale

🐾🐾🐾🐾 (See North Seattle map on page 164)

This awesome park on the northern border of Edmonds is a cheerful, mutt-like breeding of half-forest and half-beach that's pure fun. From the parking lot, a 1.25-mile trail leads down a moderate incline to the beach, wandering through groves of old-growth trees and alongside a bubbling stream. The gravel path is tidy and wide, manageable for everyone from toddlers to seniors. We could feel the tension melting away as we walked, and the wonder wiener twins had grins on their faces the whole time.

At the bottom of the trail is a loop surrounding the promised meadow and dale, dotted with covered and open picnic tables. Past that is a tunnel, maybe 15 feet long, that leads to the beach. What a beach! It's wide, flat, sandy, and long, broken only by the marine estuary formed by the stream as it empties into the ocean. More picnic tables are tossed in between the driftwood. Our only caution is that you remember to save some strength for the one-mile walk back to the car. We exhausted ourselves playing on the *playa del sol* and had to take advantage of every bench as a rest stop on the climb back up to the parking lot. Those with limited mobility can make prior arrangements with the Park Ranger to take the service road directly to the beach.

Exit onto 164th Street (#183) from I-5 and follow 164th Street, bearing right

DIVERSIONS

Firdale Village is a good place for dogs. In a tiny shopping center bordering Shoreline and Edmonds, there's The Poodle Place, Woof-N-Wiggles doggy daycare, Splashdog canine water therapy, and, last but definitely not least, The Dining Dog. **The Dining Dog Café and Bakery** is a four-paw gourmet restaurant designed exclusively for dogs. Chandeliers cast a warm glow over white linen tablecloths on tables low to the ground. Standing on these tables is encouraged while eating three-course healthy meals off paper plates lining gold chargers. Dinner might begin with a chicken broth cocktail stirred with a beef swizzle stick and end with the traditional bringing out of the three-tiered dessert treat tray. Meanwhile, humans need not go hungry; they are allowed to order food to go from the Colonial Pantry Restaurant upstairs. This is a very special place, a great spot for a canine birthday party. They are open Thursday–Saturday, 3–7 P.M., and reservations are highly recommended. 9635 Firdale Ave., Edmonds; 425/314-4612; www.diningdog.com.

to cross Highway 99. Turn right onto 52nd Avenue, left onto 160th Street, right onto 56th Avenue, and left onto 156th Avenue to the park entrance at the end of the road. 6026 156th S.W.; 425/388-6600; www.snocoparks.org.

2 Southwest County Park

🐾🐾🐾 (See North Seattle map on page 164)

The term "park" is used loosely in this case to describe 120 acres of open space on either side of Olympic View Drive. Old logging skid roads are now trails, grouped in concentric loops, with shortcuts in between. The outer loop is seven miles, following the road. The inner path is four miles, passing through ravines and along Perrinville Creek. You'll pass through time, seeing the history of second-growth forest and buckboard notches in old-growth stumps where loggers stood to muscle the mighty saws. Cooper will take a hilly trail in dense woods over a sidewalk walk any day.

Parking is at the corner of 180th Street S.W. and Olympic View Drive; www.snocoparks.org.

3 Marina Beach Dog Park

🐾🐾🐾🐕 (See North Seattle map on page 164)

It's smallish, hard to find, and surrounded by parks with cruel No Dogs Allowed signs, but none of that matters to aquatic-minded animals who just want to take a dip in cool ocean waters. It's a very popular dog park. As long as you keep your dog in the Marina Beach South off-leash area, south of the pier beyond the fence, he's free to roam the sand dunes and swim in the sound

with abandon. Go north of the fence, and McGruff the Crime Dog will be on your tail faster than you can say, "Take a bite out of crime."

When you should come depends on what you want to do. At high tide, there's more water for dog paddling and water retrieving exercises. Low tide expands the beach area for ball playing, digging, and sand castle building. Fences separate the dog park from the pier and the hillside railroad tracks, and a double-gated entry was added in September 2007 as a Scout project (thanks!). Saltwater is plentiful; but drinking water is iffy. Driftwood, a bench, and some plastic chairs serve as seating for weary toy tossers. Bag dispensers and cans are available.

Take Highway 104, Sunset Avenue, all the way to the ferry terminal at the Port of Edmonds, but instead of getting in the ferry lane, turn left onto Dayton Street at the light. Dayton curves right onto Admiral Way. You'll see signs to Marina Park. Turn left at the stop sign and continue to follow the signs all the way to the end of the marina. Parking is limited to three hours. Open 6 A.M.–10 P.M. 498 Admiral Way; www.olae.org.

🐾 Pine Ridge Park

🐾🐾 (See North Seattle map on page 164)

Pine Ridge is a rare Edmonds city park where dogs *are* allowed. The park centers around an old dirt road though a pizza-pocket-shaped patch of woods, with a few trail offshoots up and down the ridge. The road leads to Goodhope Pond, a highly active home for ducks and a raucous murder of crows. (Ever wanted to know how to refer to groups of different types of animals? Read "An Exultation of Larks" by James Lipton.) Only infrequently will you encounter anything other than trees, such as a garbage can, lone bench, or bicycle police officer taking a shortcut, who will enforce local leash and scoop laws.

From Highway 99, turn west on 196th St. S.W., also marked as State Route 524. Turn south on 81st Place, take a quick jog left at the stop sign to 81st Avenue, and follow it until it leads you to 204th and the clearing, to mark the park entrance on your right. 83rd Ave. W. and 204th St. S.W.; www.ci.edmonds .wa.us/parks.stm.

PLACES TO EAT

5th Avenue Grillhouse: At 5th Avenue, dogs are treated as first-class citizens, soaking up the sun on huge sidewalk dining patio with its own fountain pond. Humans are treated to generous double martinis. Steak, lobster, and pork chops from the grill are accented with fresh vegetables and healthy salads. They offer box lunches to go for $5 on weekdays. 610 5th Ave.; 425/776-1976; www.5thavenuegrillhouse.com.

The Loft: A social lounge first and café second, The Loft takes relaxation very seriously. People-watchers of the furry sort will want to tie up out front to watch the world walk by while their owners sip lovely libations and chat

amongst themselves. The menus for lunch and dinner are very short, allowing the chef to specialize seasonally in only the best, such as warm quinoa and stone fruit salad (think peaches) or pan-seared halibut. 515A Main St.; 425/640-5000; www.theloftlounge.com.

Olive's Café and Wine Bar: For lunch or dinner featuring Mediterranean-influenced salads and tapas, this intimate little restaurant will do take-out from their online menu. Friday and Saturday nights are ideal for indecisive types, when the chef chooses the evening's repast, and once in a while, on hot summer nights, the staff sets out a single sidewalk table. 107 5th Ave.; 422/771-5757; www.olivesgourmet.com.

Red Twig: While "majorly yummy" may not be proper English, it is the best way to describe this bistro's quiches, made in edible baskets shaped from savory crêpes. Cooper is also a big fan of their banana pancakes and other full breakfasts. Gourmet lunches lean toward soup, salad, and sandwich specials served with refreshing mixed greens. Doggy dears, please don't drink out of the water feature while you relax on the large patio out front. 117 5th Ave. S.; 425/771-1200; www.redtwig.com.

Waterfront Coffee Company: If you get stuck waiting for a ferry, wander over to Waterfront for daily soups, croissants, pastries, espresso, and ice cream. The store manager will serve your pooch a scoop of ice cream with a humongous dog bone for $1.50. It's much nicer to bask in the sun at the outdoor tables than bake in your car until the next boat arrives. 101 Main St.; 425/670-1400.

PLACES TO STAY

Best Western Edmonds Harbor Inn: With this one notable exception, motels in the immediate area are low on the respectability scale. This appealing hotel is down by the waterfront, near the ferry terminal, offering many types of rooms with an extensive list of niceties. Rates range $110–130; prefer small pets under 20 pounds; the pet fee is $20. 130 W. Dayton St.; 425/771-5021; www.bestwestern.com.

Travelodge Edmonds: Finding a decent hotel on Aurora is a hit or miss proposition, so we were happy to discover that this Travelodge's nicely updated rooms go for the very good rate of $75–100. You're limited to a couple of medium dogs for $25 per dog per stay. 23825 Hwy. 99; 425/771-8008.

Lynnwood

Edmonds is an attractive waterfront community, while neighbor Lynnwood got the short shrift, the northernmost Seattle suburb known primarily for its massive mall complex at the Alderwood Shopping Center. When retail therapy simply isn't cutting it anymore, heed the unspoken advice of your four-legged counselor, and look to the therapeutic benefits of Lynnwood's greenbelt for some stronger medicine.

PARKS, BEACHES, AND RECREATION AREAS

5 Lynndale Park

🐾🐾🐾 (See North Seattle map on page 164)

Cooper ignored the leaf blower guys; didn't pay much mind to the ball fields, amphitheater, or reserveable picnic shelters; and looked past the skate park at the bottom of the hill to the 22 acres of native forest with soft-surface hiking trails at this 40-acre city park. The section of park left largely in its natural state has the ideal mix of pocket lawns hemmed in by native forest to really get the boy's butt wagging in the happy trot. Posts with red and white tops mark the trails, both natural surface and lengthy asphalt walkways for folks who need better accessibility.

There's plenty of good parking and good restrooms down by the skate park and more parking at the top of the hill. We saw a few garbage cans, but bring your own bags.

From Highway 99, go west on 168th Street S.W. for a mile to the light, where you continue on Olympic View Drive for another 1.5 miles to the park on your left.

6 Golf Course Trail

🐾🐾 (See North Seattle map on page 164)

Skirting around the Lynnwood Municipal Golf Course on the west and the fences of Edmonds Community College on the east is a surprising 1.5-mile perimeter trail. Your path is heavily shaded by large pines that deposit their needles for soft footfalls underneath. Peek-a-boo views of mint green turf and sand traps frame your meanderings. Little known as much other than a shortcut for kids late to class, the only other people we encountered were a couple of joggers, some liplocked teen romancers, and other dog walkers out for a stroll.

There's an entrance and street parking in the middle of the trail at 202nd Street S.W. and 73rd Avenue W., but we preferred the overflow school parking lot on 208th Street S.W., just east of 76th Avenue W. Walk into the woods and go north for the best part of the trail.

Take Exit 181B from I-5 northbound and go west on 196th Street S.W. (State Route 524). Turn south on 76th Avenue W. and take a left on 202 Street or 208th Street.

7 Wilcox Park

🐾🐾 (See North Seattle map on page 164)

This is the civilized neighbor to Scriber Park across the street. While the huddled masses stick to viewing the flag pavilion and playing in the playground area, a.k.a. tot lot, you can enjoy seven acres of lush lawn bordered by a couple of tree groves. There's not much else to bark of, other than picnic tables, a clean restroom, and enough space to lay down a tablecloth and eat fried chicken from Ezell's just down the street.

The dogs like to sneak in the back entrance to avoid the crowds. Take 196th Street west from I-5 and turn right on 52nd Avenue, then left on 194th Street into the parking lot. Open dusk–dawn. 5215 196th St. SW.

8 Scriber Lake Park

🐾🐾🐾 (See North Seattle map on page 164)

If a dog were a landscape architect (a dogscaper?) and she were asked to design a park solely for the purposes of an ideal walkabout, Scriber would be the result. It is a simple place with 20 acres of trees surrounding a lake—no fuss, no frills, and as close to nature as you can get in an otherwise suburban, strip-mall environment.

A series of paved and soft-surface trails lead you on a magical mystery tour; one trail ends up at a viewing platform over Scriber Lake, another at a multi-trunked tree, a third to another park called Mini Park, and on it goes. The best part is a series of floating bridges on the lake itself, what the city calls observation nodes. Isis commented that it would be perfect if dogs were allowed to swim, but she's trying to understand the need to preserve such enjoyable natural habitats for future generations of dogs to enjoy. No chasing the waterfowl, please.

You'll pass the park on the left on 196th Street before turning left on Scriber Lake Road, then almost immediately left on 198th Street. It looks like you are entering a shopping mall; past that, you'll see the park entrance to your left.

🐾 Interurban Trail–Lynnwood Section

🐾🐾 (See North Seattle map on page 164)

Snohomish County's done their part to make the most of the routes once used by the Interurban Trolley, which operated between Ballard and Bellingham from 1910 until 1939. The corridor is under Public Utilities District ownership, and their power lines run overhead, but for the most part, the six-foot-wide asphalt path is separated from motorized traffic. Once in a while, signs will lead you to designated connections on bike routes along main roads. The trail is complete from Everett south for about 11 miles to Lynnwood. Mountlake Terrace is a weak link in the system, and then the trail takes up again nicely in Shoreline.

The north end is easiest to find. Take Everett Mall Way to West Mall Road to the end, and park in the fringes of the mall lot behind Sears. Along the route, parking and access is available at Thornton A. Sullivan Park at Silver Lake (11400 W. Silver Lake Dr.); McCollum County Park (600 128th St. S.E.); and Martha Lake Park (East of I-5 at Exit 183).

PLACES TO EAT

Corner Coffee Bar and Café: A drive-through and patio seating are available to you and your dog at this shop in Perrinville Village, where Olymic View Drive meets 76th Street. A water bowl and dog treats are on the house; good thing, because your pup will surely be parched and starved after exertions at nearby Southwest County or Lynndale parks. 18401 76th Ave. W.; 425/776-3616.

Ezell's Famous Chicken: Cooper says Ezell's is the best fried chicken in the solar system, including that 10th planet they just discovered named Pluto. This is the stuff Oprah had flown to Chicago. You can die and go to heaven content after eating their crisp, not-too-greasy, secret-recipe fried chicken; lumpy gravy and mashed potatoes; and crunchy, sugary, buttery peach cobbler. Don't forget a side order of liver and gizzards for the pups. Isis says go for the spicy recipe. 7531 196th Ave. S.W.; 425/673-4193.

PLACES TO STAY

Best Western Alderwood: This motel is located where I-5 and I-405 meet, nicely tucked into a grove of trees to shelter you from the madness of the mall. Isis detected a Roman motif among the furnishings and rich tapestry colors here, and she was completely taken with the friendly front desk staff. She tried to talk them into accepting her larger friends, but policy allows only lap dogs under 20 pounds. They restrict breeds due to Snohomish County's harsh insurance requirements on "potentially dangerous animals," so call ahead and talk to the management before your stay. Dogs are allowed on the first floor only, for $25 per visit. Rates range $100–145; 19332 36th Ave. W.; 425/775-7600.

La Quinta Lynnwood: On the plus side, La Quinta doesn't charge a pet fee. On the negative, they place dog patrons on the fourth floor only, which isn't terribly helpful for midnight potty runs (Isis blames a small bladder). Rates are decent, hovering right around $110–115. 4300 Alderwood Mall Blvd.; 425/775-7447.

Residence Inn by Marriott: The mini-apartments are so warm and homey, and the property looks so much like an apartment complex, it's easy to forget you're at a motel. Cooper was impressed by how important food is here: rooms have full kitchens, there's free breakfast every morning and an appetizer supper and drinks Monday–Thursday, they have a grocery shopping service and a van to take you to the supermarket, and glass-topped tables dot the property for outdoor eating. It's refreshing to find a north end motel without pet restrictions. Rates are $130–250 nightly, pro-rated for longer stays, and the pet fee is $15 per night up to a maximum of $75 for longer stays. 18200 Alderwood Mall Pkwy.; 425/771-1100.

Mill Creek

PARKS, BEACHES, AND RECREATION AREAS

🔟 North Creek Wetlands

🐾🐾 (See North Seattle map on page 164)

This county park's expansive wetland is a sniffalicious network of elevated boardwalks and gravel trails. It's a wildlife habitat. It's a flood control facility. It's heavy-duty, nose-twitching, snorfling fun. Enjoy it while you can, as it is almost impossible to preserve such places in the midst of urban expansion. Even now they are clearing 80 acres of forest just north of the park and planning for 220 more homes in six developments.

We visited on a barren and wintry day when everything was frozen over, strolling with binoculars and listening to the snap-crackle-pop of ice melting in the sun. (Careful, the boardwalks are slippery when wet; Cooper got dunked chasing a duck!) We bet it's even more luscious in the summer.

You should contribute to a "What did you see?" journal kept at the viewpoint. Isis's favorite entry was "two snakes, seven ducks, and five dogs." The park has a good parking ring, playground, and a couple of covered picnic shelters, but a Honey Bucket was the only potty and garbage cans were conspicuously absent.

Take Exit 183 from I-5, heading east on 164th Street S.W. Turn right on the Bothell-Everett Highway, State Route 527. Go one mile, turn right on 183rd Street S.E. to the parking lot on your right marked by stone pillars. Open 7 A.M.–dusk. 1011 183rd St. S.E.

🔟 Tambark Creek

🐾🐾 (See North Seattle map on page 164)

Is there an off-leash area in this park's destiny? It's "being evaluated," say reps from the county. Well, the Wonder Wieners are not ones for waiting, having decided to include Tambark in the hopes it'll already be a dog park before the next edition. Granted, it doesn't look like much now, a mere pull-off on the side of the road, with a single narrow trail leading into the 40-acre woods, marked by a couple of large boulders and a post with a temporary sign.

Bring your binoculars if you like bird-watching, listen to the crickets chirp in the grass, and go potty before you go, as there are no amenities here at all. Our exploration unearthed only three signs of humanity: a bridge over the crick, the wreckage of a tree fort between two massive tree trunks, and the burned-out stump of what must have been an ancient timber of staggering proportions. The path can't be more than a half mile.

Take Exit 183 off I-5, go east on 164th Street for 1.7 miles, turn right on the Bothell-Everett Highway, take a left on 180th Street S.E. and go a mile, take a left on 35th Avenue S.E. and go exactly 0.3 miles to the pullout on the right side of the road, across from the Mill Creek Meadows sign. Open 7 A.M. to dusk. 17217 35th Ave S.E.

PLACES TO EAT

Tony's Pea Patch Café: "Whisper those three little words of love to me," says Cooper. "All-day breakfast," says Isis. Create-an-omelet, corned beef hash, and potato scramble are the order of the day at Tony's on Saturday and Sunday. Come during the week and the tuna sandwich is a winner, with your choice of fresh fruit, chips, salad, or soup. The Pea Patch has a couple of outdoor tables, or pull up a spot on the grass under a couple of trees, which is what we did. It's close to Tambark Creek and North Creek Wetlands. 17917 Bothell-Everett Hwy.; 425/485-4562.

Mountlake Terrace

PARKS, BEACHES, AND RECREATION AREAS

🔟 Terrace Creek Park

🐾🐾🐾 (See North Seattle map on page 164)

There's a whole ecosystem going on down here in the ravine, and though you know there are houses up above, most of the time you can't see them or hear the people in them. You *can* hear and see the creek, which makes for a nice walk, although the water is too overgrown and stagnant to get into. After an open field and playground, a 0.75-mile, one-way trail leads through patches of alternating sun and shade. The track alternates between crumbling pavement, gravel, and dirt, heavily jungled with morning glory and blackberries (which you shouldn't eat, because they spray them with chemicals). Mountlake Terrace police keep the peace in the park so, a) don't speed, and b) mind your leashes and poop. Nearby Evergreen Playfield, off 56th Avenue, is your best bet for restrooms and picnic tables.

To get right to the trail, take Exit 178 from I-5, go east on 236th Street S.W., and take a left on 48th Avenue W. The main entrance on 228th Street S.W. leads to a huge recreation pavilion.

PLACES TO STAY

Motel 6 Studio Suites Mountlake Terrace: These bright, compact suites are quieter than your average Motel 6, especially if you ask for rooms on the side away from the highway. Wi-Fi is only $5 per stay, and rooms start at $60 per night, $250–320 weekly. The pet fee is $10 per night, up to a maximum $50 per stay. Motel 6 policy is to accept one dog under 80 pounds per room, but we've stayed with more than one, so don't be afraid to ask. There is a 10 percent discount for booking online. 6017 224th St. S.W.; 425/771-3139; www .motel6.com.

Shoreline/Lake Forest Park

This quiet residential area split from Seattle to incorporate in 1995. Canines can rest assured that city leadership has its priorities straight. Two of the largest projects in progress are finishing the section of the multi-use Interurban Trail to connect Seattle to Lynnwood, and adding greenery, landscaped medians, and wide sidewalk promenades to improve walking along Aurora Avenue, the main north-south commercial strip. There's an active group trying to convince Shoreline to add off-leash areas to city parks. Six potential sites were proposed to the city's Parks Board in September 2008. You can keep up with developments by joining the mailing list at www.shoredog.org.

PARKS, BEACHES, AND RECREATION AREAS

13 Richmond Beach Saltwater Park

🐾🐾🐾🐾 (See North Seattle map on page 164)

Isis and Coop's buddies Holly and Hailey "The Comet" Pengelly turned the dogs on to this city park on Puget Sound, which might be easy to miss if you don't live in the neighborhood. It is worth every minute of the 10-mile drive north from downtown for the views, without the masses of humanity you'll find on beaches closer in.

The park comes in layers, starting on the top of the bluff with a gravel trail that leads around the point. The water views from here are high enough to give you a good case of vertigo. Halfway down the hill is a covered picnic shelter, and closer to the bottom are a circular lawn with parking, a playground, and the basic handy stuff, including restrooms and water fountains.

Now, if your dog hasn't heard a word we've said up to this point, it's because he only cares about the bottom layer, the beach. Shoreline doesn't have the strict rule of prohibiting dogs from park beaches as Seattle does, merely the standard leash and scoop provisions. After crossing over the railroad tracks on a cement footbridge, thar she blows, with a berm built of river rock and gravel that gives way to sandier spots north and south.

From I-5, take Exit 176 and go west on N.W. 175th Street, turn right on Aurora Avenue (State Route 99), and turn left on N.W. 185th Street. You'll travel west on 185th Street for two miles, as it becomes N.W. Richmond Beach Road, and then N.W. 195th Street, then turn left on 20th Avenue N.W. into the park. 2021 N.W. 190th St.

14 Shoreview Park

🐾🐾🐾 (See North Seattle map on page 164)

The initial impression of Shoreview is all of ball fields and playgrounds, with the view, as hinted, across to Puget Sound capped by the Olympic Mountains. Yet, peeking out of the corner of the upper parking lot is a tiny Trail sign that looks intriguing and, sure enough, it leads to a impressively challenging short hike through several distinct habitats. It's an enchanting outing under any conditions. From the upper lot, you quickly descend into a deep, forested gully, following Boeing Creek. There are several log and stone water crossings (please don't ever tell anyone that the Dachsies had to be carried across). You'll happen upon Hidden Lake, then hike up some switchbacks onto a dry plain through gorse, madrona, butterfly bushes, and juniper trees. The trail emerges behind the soccer fields, and it's up the hill again to return to your car and the restrooms. We met lots of dogs of all types and sizes along the way: Violet, the 10-month-old dachshund; a springer spaniel; some terriers; and, where there is water, the labs.

Take Exit 175 from I-5, heading west on 145th Street. Turn right on Greenwood Avenue N., and immediately jog left to stay on Greenwood (instead of Westminster Way). Turn left on Innis Arden Way, pass Shoreline Community College, and go up around the bend, turning right on 9th Avenue N.W. into the park.

15 Ronald Bog

🐾 (See North Seattle map on page 164)

What can you say? It's a bog, a low, wet field with a pond and an overlook. Weeping willows and alders fringe the water, and plantings in 2008 may help to mitigate the present squishiness along the waterfront. It is easy to get to, it is close to the highway, maybe as a potty stop on the slog, or if everyone needs to get out and stretch their legs and take a look at the sculpture of the horses marking the entrance to the City of Shoreline.

Although the park is on N. 175th Street, at Exit 176 off I-5, road dividers prevent you from entering the park going eastbound on the street. You can find a place to turn around at the first light on Meridian Avenue. Or, take Exit 175 from I-5 onto N. 145th Street, turn right on Meridian Avenue N., and right again on N. 17th Street.

16 Hamlin Park

🐾🐾🐾 (See North Seattle map on page 164)

We're glad Becky and her pack mate Dante reminded us of this 80-acre forest, where dogs flock faster than ants to a picnic. White posts with black arrows mark trails that get a lot of use. Please respect cordoned-off areas and stick to the trail while the city undergoes revegitation and native plant studies during 2009–2010. This happy dogtown is quite hilly and heavily forested, the perfect place to go on a squirrel or rabbit hunt. We caught the first crisp scent of fall here on a September day.

Of mysterious historical interest, there are two cannons in the park, eight-inch, 30-caliber guns from the U.S.S. *Boston* and the Battle of Manila Bay in the Philippines on May 1, 1898. How and why they're here is not explained, and we weren't able to find out. They sit, silent and weighty, next to the playground, picnic tables, and restroom.

Take Exit 176 from I-5, go east on 175th Street to 15th Avenue N.W., take a right and go down to 160th, take a left into the park. 16006 15th Ave. N.E.

17 Interurban Trail–Shoreline Section

🐾🐾 (See North Seattle map on page 164)

Not all trails can be over the river and through the woods; some have to traverse the urban jungle. Thankfully for city dogs, the Interurban is one of these. From 2005–2008, Shoreline undertook major improvement projects on Aurora between 145th and 205th streets. Shabby old strip malls slowly disappeared, to be replaced by, uh, shiny new strip malls, but at least they added the Interurban in between them and the highway. Tree-lined medians separate north and southbound traffic, and sidewalk lighting has been improved everywhere. The young trees will grow, lawns will mature, and at least this strip of commercialism will age more gracefully.

Shoreline's section starts with a small parking area on 145th, just west of Highway 99 (Aurora Avenue). There, a map directs you to the 10-foot-wide, asphalt multi-use trail. Two pedestrian bridges were built, crossing 155th Street and Aurora—cool examples of modern architecture lit by moving colored lights at night. There are benches, drinking fountains, and periodic garbage cans along the route. The top of Echo Lake is a good rest stop with picnic tables and grass. The only piece we had difficulty finding was the section that goes onto the road behind Sky Nursery north of 185th.

From I-5, take Exit 175 and go west on 145th Street. Immediately past Aurora Avenue, turn right into the parking area.

PLACES TO EAT

Laughing Ladies Café: The ladies Angela, Miriam and Ali hope to tickle your tummy with a long list of sandwiches and plates, smoothies, low-carb wraps, salads, and donuts. They hope to make you smile with nearly nightly music, local art on the walls, $1 chair massages, and free wireless Internet. They wish to elicit giggles and wiggles with water bowls on the elevated sidewalk and a jar of biscuits inside. Take your food and chuckle all the way to nearby Hamlin Park and Ronald Bog. 17551 15th Ave. N.E; 206/362-2026; www.laughingladiescafe.com.

O Melon: This Asian nonfat frozen yogurt shop has been done up with space-age plastic furniture and namesake colors of honeydew and cantaloupe. The counter features two daily flavors: vanilla and a rotating fruit, which often seems to be mango. There are plenty of toppings, including sweet-sticky rice mochi, and a larger selection of loose-leaf teas. There's no outdoor seating; get it to go. 13242 Aurora Ave. N., #103; 206/420-4711.

Richmond Beach Coffee Company: Perhaps you'll forgive us for including so many espresso joints in our book, for this is yet another worthy one. It is at the heart of our culture in the Northwest to look to these establishments for our daily fix, made-to-order deli sandwiches, hot soup (as opposed to cold?), free Internet, and social interaction at sidewalk seating in front of big, open, picture windows. 1442 Richmond Beach Dr.; 206/542-0511; www.richmond beachcoffee.com.

Taqueria el Sabor: The *el sabor* refers to a pleasing taste or flavor, an honest brag for this taco house that is the real deal. English is a distant second language among patrons and staff alike. The ochre adobe building and patio invokes sunnier climes, serving as a good jumping off point for your travels on the adjacent Interurban Trail. That is, if you can move after ingesting who knows how many soft corn tacos filled with juicy meats. Spend some time at the fresh salsa bar, topping everything with pickles, radishes, carrots, onions, and tomatoes, and don't pass up the *horchata,* a cold rice-milk beverage with cinnamon and spices. 15221 Aurora Ave. N.; 206/417-3346.

PLACES TO STAY

Econolodge: This chain locale is respectable, and at $60–70 a night, a couple of pet-friendly rooms will do for some decent bed rest. $10 pet fee; 14817 Aurora Ave. N.; 206/367-7880.

Northgate

Northgate Mall has the distinction of being the first indoor shopping center in the United States to coin the term "mall" in 1950. It was also the first to have public restrooms, in 1954. While Cooper contemplates why people didn't feel peeing on bushes was sufficient, Isis wonders who coined the term "meanderthals," to describe those who wander endlessly without shopping at flagship stores Nordstrom, J.C. Penney, and Bon Marché (now Macy's). As dubious proof that there is life after Nordstrom's, dogs drag their owners to the Northacres off-leash area when their preoccupied people are finally finished shoe shopping.

PARKS, BEACHES, AND RECREATION AREAS

18 Northacres

🐾🐾🐾🐕 (See North Seattle map on page 164)

Northacres is the home of one of the city's off-leash areas, along with picnic tables and grills, baseball fields, a playground, wading pool, and groomed trails. Strict signs warn that dogs are not allowed in the children's play area or on the athletic fields, so keep your pals under control until you reach the

DIVERSIONS

The fabulously photogenic Wonder Wieners wanted to take a moment to mention their top picks for the area's best dog photographers, one for each leg.

B. Sparks Dog Photography: Bev Sparks is the ultimate pro. Dogs naturally gravitate toward her and put on their best faces for her camera lens. Much of her work specializes in black and white (206/723-8655, www.dogphotography.com).

Best Friend Photography: It's uncanny how perfectly Emily Rieman's sepia-toned photos distill the distinct personality of each individual dog (206/935-5624, www.bestfriendphoto.com).

Dane and Dane Photography: You don't have to be a big breed to appreciate J. Nicole Smith's eye for detail and the sense of humor that comes across in her colorful photography (888/201-3778, www.dane-dane.com).

Four Legs Photography: Isis likes Jen Flynn's documentary-style photography, which features interesting compositions and include elements from the environment for more dynamic portraits (206/890-8295, www.fourlegsphoto.com).

designated romping grounds. The OLA occupies a fraction (0.7) of the total park acreage (20), but it is a little jewel worth exploring in the middle of a forest of fir trees. Within the fenced area are smaller fenced-in Habitat Protection Areas, leaving the play space looking like an off-road rally course with plenty of sharp turns. Dogs like to chase each other around the figure eights, pick up sticks, and poke their noses into the ferns.

Northacres is very progressive when it comes to waste disposal, providing biodegradable pick-up mitts and a doggy latrine. No, your Pekinese doesn't sit on the potty, but you can use the pooper-scooper to toss the waste into a compost bin. Traditionalists will also find spare bags attached to the community bulletin board. No matter how much gravel and wood chips volunteers spread around, you're bound to encounter mud puddles here three seasons out of four. As far as Cooper is concerned, that's a bonus. Cooper will do anything for a tummy rub, and as a low rider, he gets treated to a warm washcloth rubbed over his dirty underbelly when we get home.

Take the 130th Street exit from I-5 North (145th Street exit if you're going south), then a left on 130th, a left on 1st, a left on 125th, and a left on 3rd to the end of the cul de sac. 12718 1st Ave. N.E.

PLACES TO EAT

Qdoba: We're cheating, because this is a chain, but it has the best outdoor seating in the vicinity, fresh make-your-own burritos, quesadillas, and *tres-queso* nachos the size of a Chihuahua. 10002 Aurora Ave. N.; 206/528-1335; www.qdoba.com.

PLACES TO STAY

Hotel Nexus: The Nexus is a bit funkier, a little hipper than your average chain, with a very good list of amenities, and soothing hues in the colors of the sea. It's an ideal locale for shopping at Northgate Mall, although their steep $50 one-time pet fee might cost you a pair of shoes or two at Ross Dress for Less. Rooms go for $120–150. 2140 N. Northgate Way; 206/365-0700; www.hotelnexusseattle.com.

Greenwood

PARKS, BEACHES, AND RECREATION AREAS

19 Carkeek Park

🐾🐾🐾 (See North Seattle map on page 164)

Coop 'n' Isis are embarrassed to admit they visited Carkeek a half dozen times before they realized that this city park provided more than glorified beach access and views. They didn't even include it in the last edition, because dogs are not allowed on city beaches. They had only vaguely remembered the wide open fields when you get to the bottom of the hill and the first big parking

area. They hadn't remembered the trails at all, past Piper's Creek with the baby salmon swimming in it, up the North Meadow Hill climb, huffing and puffing along the South Ridge Trail. It sure seems big. It only makes sense that you can hike through all of that tree cover. After finally getting curious enough, and printing out a map online, the dogs discovered that major trail improvements had been completed in 2006, opening up a brave new world to them. The only drawback Isis discovered is that the grating on a couple of the bridges is so large that little paws fall right through. Talk about embarrassing. For the kids, the playground has a cool salmon slide, where you can slip through the belly of a fish.

Directions to the park are a bit exotic, so bear with us. Take the Northgate exit from I-5, Exit #173, and go west on N. Northgate Way. Past Aurora Ave. N (Highway 99), Northgate becomes N. 105th Street. Turn right on Greenwood Avenue N. Turn left on N.W. 110th Street (look for the crosswalk lights above the street). After six blocks, 110th becomes N.W. Carkeek Park Road. Carkeek Park Road winds down into the valley for 0.5 mile to the park entrance. Watch for the Park Department rainbow sign on your left. Open 6 A.M.–10 P.M. 950 N.E. Carkeek Park Rd.

PLACES TO EAT

Kort Haus: If you think a burger is a burger, then you haven't tried ostrich, buffalo, wild boar, kangaroo, elk, venison, alligator, black bear, or black bean veggie patties on your bun. Come to the Kort for your beer and an exotic burger with your bud on the back deck. Slip your sweetie a tater tot or fry, and you'll reinforce that loving bond you two share. 6732 Greenwood Ave. N.; 206/782-3575.

Wayward Coffee House: The owners here are sci-fi fans who obviously believe that we should take care of the earth before we take to the stars. The coffee served here is 100 percent organic, fare trade, and shade grown. Vegan and veggie sandwiches are prominent on the menu, and even the cold drink cups—for frozen, blended beverages they call Eskies—are biodegradable. Wayward's outdoor seating is under a covered overhang, oh so essential in our clime's many drippy days. Parking in this neighborhood is a pisser; may we suggest public transportation as a green alternative? 8570 Greenwood Ave. N.; 206/706-3240; www.waywardcoffee.com.

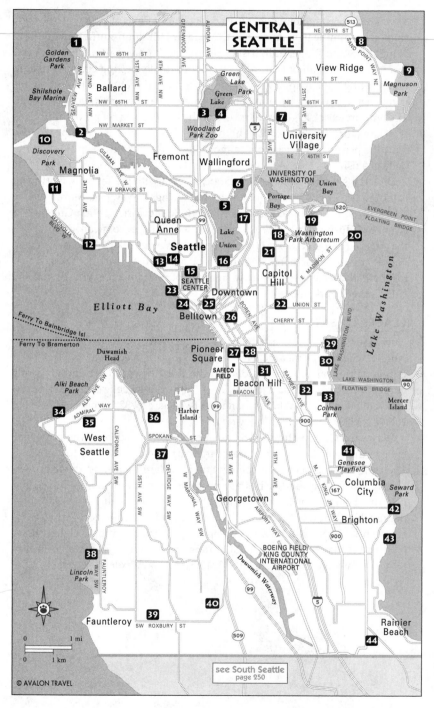

CENTRAL SEATTLE

Golden Gardens Park

Shilshole Bay Marina

NW 85TH ST

Ballard

NW 65TH ST

NW MARKET ST

Green Lake Park

Green Lake

Woodland Park Zoo

View Ridge

NE 95TH ST

NE 75TH ST

NE 65TH ST

Magnuson Park

Discovery Park

Magnolia

University Village

NE 45TH ST

W DRAVUS ST

Fremont

Wallingford

UNIVERSITY OF WASHINGTON

Union Bay

Queen Anne

Seattle

Lake Union

Portage Bay

Washington Park Arboretum

Lake Washington

EVERGREEN POINT FLOATING BRIDGE

Downtown

Capitol Hill

SEATTLE CENTER

Elliott Bay

Belltown

UNION ST

CHERRY ST

Ferry To Bainbridge Isl

Ferry To Bremerton

Duwamish Head

Pioneer Square

SAFECO FIELD

Beacon Hill

BEACON

LAKE WASHINGTON FLOATING BRIDGE

Mercer Island

Alki Beach Park

ADMIRAL WAY

West Seattle

SPOKANE ST

Harbor Island

Colman Park

Genesee Playfield

Columbia City

Seward Park

Georgetown

Brighton

BOEING FIELD/ KING COUNTY INTERNATIONAL AIRPORT

Lincoln Park

Fauntleroy

SW ROXBURY ST

Rainier Beach

Duwamish Waterway

0   1 mi

0   1 km

© AVALON TRAVEL

see South Seattle page 250

CHAPTER 7

Central Seattle

The *Seattle Times* article "Our Dogs, Our Selves," May 14, 2006, reported a total of 125,000 licensed dogs in the City of Seattle, and only 90,000 children from the latest census. Pet boutiques have multiplied exponentially to meet the demands of discriminating dog lovers, and a dynamic new quarterly, *CityDog Magazine,* advises canines on how to navigate big city life. Clearly, it is a good time to be among the *Canis familiaris* in the Emerald City.

As for getting out and about in the city, dogs of Seattle owe much to John C. Olmsted and Frederick Olmsted Jr., sons of famed Central Park architect Frederick Law Olmsted. The Olmsted brothers are the master planners behind a connected string of 20 of Seattle's most beloved parks, and their work set the tone for a continued respect and priority for city greenery.

To experience the heart and soul of Seattle, walk with your dog through the Pike Place Market, the country's oldest continually operating open-air market, and in Pioneer Square, the core of early Seattle with its preserved Richardsonian-Romanesque buildings.

PICK OF THE LITTER—CENTRAL SEATTLE

BEST PARKS
Green Lake Park, Green Lake (page 189)
Discovery Park, Magnolia (page 196)

BEST DOG PARKS
Magnuson Park at Sand Point, View Ridge (page 195)
Westcrest Dog Park, West Seattle (page 219)

BEST EVENTS
Bark in the Park and PAWSwalk, View Ridge (page 195)
Dog-O-Ween, Columbia City (page 221)

BEST PLACES TO EAT
Norm's Eatery and Ale House, Fremont (page 192)
Madison Park Café, Montlake and Madison (page 204)
Le Pichet, Downtown Core (page 207)
Volunteer Park Café and Marketplace, Capitol Hill (page 205)
St. Clouds, Madrona (page 213)

BEST PLACES TO STAY
Edgewater Hotel, Belltown (page 208)
W Hotel, Downtown Core (page 210)

One note of restraint: In Seattle city parks, dogs are not allowed on beaches, in playgrounds, or on organized sports fields. For areas to call their own, the needs of dogs in the greater metro area are looked after by **Citizens for Off-Leash Areas (COLA),** www.coladog.org.

Ballard

Still fondly referred to as Little Scandinavia, this neighborhood struggles to retain the flavor of its mariner and millwork settlers, even as it becomes the next best place to open an art gallery, shop, or sidewalk bistro. Market Street is the one to stroll along for people-watching, and if you follow this arterial all the way around the point past yacht-packed Shilshole Marina, it leads to a popular beach with its own rowdy dog park.

PARKS, BEACHES, AND RECREATION AREAS

1 Golden Gardens

🐾🐾🐕 (See Central Seattle map on page 184)

The masses of Seattle flock to the beach at Golden Gardens to capture elusive sun rays and unbeatable views of Puget Sound and the Olympic Mountains. Dogs are not allowed on the beach or playground; leashed dogs are allowed on the paved beach trail and in the picnic areas; and, they have a place to call their own a little ways up the hill.

The Golden Gardens off-leash area is a rough and tumble four acres, with a bunch of rambunctious regulars who rule the turf. If you've got an outgoing pup with too much energy on your hands, this is the place to bring him, and he'll nap like a baby afterwards. Cooper thinks it's the WWE of the dog world; we think some owners could be in better control of their animals.

Two gates open into a wide, fenced enclosure, with a gently sloping hill with a few benches, a couple of tables, a water pump, and some dog bowls. A covered enclosure and lighting for dark evenings are particularly nice features. It's wood chips and mud with plenty of room for rompin' and stompin'.

From the south, take N.W. Market Street through downtown Ballard, which becomes 54th Street N.W. and then Seaview Avenue N.W. At the entrance to the park, turn right on Seaview Place N.W., go under the railroad trestle and up the hill to the dog park. Open 6 A.M.–11:30 P.M. 8498 Seaview Pl. N.W.

2 Carl S. English Jr. Botanical Gardens at the Locks

🐾🐾🐾👣 (See Central Seattle map on page 184)

More than 85,000 vessels pass through the two navigation locks each year, allowing passage between the saltwater of Puget Sound and the freshwater ship canal to Lake Union and Lake Washington. Opening day of boating season, May 1, is a sight not to be missed at the locks.

In the seven-acre park surrounding the locks, 500 species of plants and 1,500 varieties of flowers were planted to transform the mounds of dirt left over after locks construction in 1913. The gardens are separated into distinct beds with concrete pathways throughout. Dogs on leash are welcome as long as you pick up after them. The only areas dogs are not allowed are in the visitors center and underground in the fish-viewing windows. Hand your leash to a friend for a moment to see a rare glimpse of salmon migrating through the 22-step fish ladder.

On either side of the locks are stepped hills, designed for picnicking; you just have to watch out for goose droppings at migratory times of year.

From I-5, take Exit 166 westbound on Denny Way, which curves around to become Elliott Avenue, and then 15th Avenue N.W. Continue north across the Ballard Bridge, turn left on N.W. Market Street, and follow it through Ballard.

Take the left at the Y intersection onto N.W. 54th Street, and the locks are a hundred yards or so past that point. The grounds are open 7 A.M.–9 P.M.; the visitors center hours vary by season. 3015 N.W. 54th St.; 206/783-7059.

PLACES TO EAT

Lunchbox Laboratory: Designer burgers is what you get when a chef at a five-star restaurant decides he wants to chuck the "scene" and have a little fun. The blackboard-scribbled menu includes lamb, venison, Kobe beef, and dork patties (a rich duck/pork combo) and more toppings, custom creations, and sides than there are fleas on a junkyard dog. Outdoor seating is a combination of picnic tables and barstool tables on an asphalt lot. Cash only; custom combo platters are $14. Even the address is unconventional: 7302 1/2 15th Ave. N.W.; 206/706-3092; www.lunchboxlaboratory.com.

Mr. Spots Chai House: This tea parlor, herb and incense peddler, and DJ/open mike club is what you would call a fixture in the community. The cups of Morning Glory Chai runneth over, as does the beer after 10 P.M. A short menu of vegetarian-only consumables is highlighted by the hummus and veggie platter. Two outdoor benches teeter precariously on the sidewalk. Of no particular importance, Isis believes that Mr. Spots is a cat. 5463 Leary Ave. NW; 206/784-5415; www.chaihouse.com.

Purple Cow: Yup, this tiny shop attached to a marine supply secondhand store is shockingly purple, with a green awning, and the namesake lavender bovine sculpture mounted impossibly above the marquee. The litany of lusciousness on the sandwich board out front reads: bagels, cookies, smoothies, shakes, soup, sandwiches, and espresso. Isis sampled the Carmen Mooranda, a smoothie concocted of pineapple, banana, and OJ on the Cow's postage-stamp-sized wooden deck accented with flower boxes. 6301 Seaview Ave. N.W.; 206/784-1417.

Totem House: This seafood and chowder house by the locks has been around forever; its distinctive yellow and highly cheesy totem poles make it easy to spot. There are a few token chicken items for the non-seafood lovers and excellent Caesar salads. 3058 N.W. 54th St.; 206/784-2300.

Green Lake

All life in this neighborhood revolves around the 300-acre body of water named for the algae blooms that give it a characteristic jade color.

PARKS, BEACHES, AND RECREATION AREAS

🖪 Woodland Dog Park

🐾🐾🐾🐕 (See Central Seattle map on page 184)

In 1889, lumber baron Guy T. Phinney bought the land for his estate and an exotic animal menagerie, which he opened for public viewing. The city acquired his estate in 1899, and 90 acres of woods are now home to a certified rose test garden, a popular summer concert series, and the world-famous Seattle Zoo. Your dogs will undoubtedly enjoy indulging their animal instincts in the leash-free zone.

The one-acre off-leash area is swank, hilly, and thick with trees. It's surrounded by a six-foot, rubber-coated chain-link fence, with double gates at three entrances. Railroad-tie steps on two sides lead up to a plateau where everyone hangs out in a very well-behaved fashion. If you or your dog get bored, Green Lake Park's three-mile loop trail is right down the hill.

There is running water and a few picnic tables and benches. In addition to waste bag dispensers, a portable waste composter, and scoopers, there is a whimsical fire hydrant, painted yellow and blue with dog bones.

From I-5, take Exit 169 and go west on N.E. 50th Street for 0.7 miles. Turn right onto Green Lake Way, and take the next available left at 0.2 miles. Turn left in the next driveway at the sign for Woodland Park, and follow the road up the hill to the right of the tennis courts. Parking and the off-leash area will be on your left. 1000 N. 50th Street.

🖪 Green Lake Park

🐾🐾🐾🐾 (See Central Seattle map on page 184)

Without a doubt, the paths around this natural lake see more dog-walking action than anywhere else in the city. Brave souls never fear to tread the 2.8-mile paved inner pathway, flinching not an inch when in-line skaters and speed cyclists buzz by. The meek can inhabit the 3.2-mile outer ring, a soft-surface path preferred by the joggers. The lake is visible throughout, where you can watch scullers drill and ducks dawdle. There are wide expanses of lawn encircling the whole shebang, plus playgrounds, wading pools, a community center, and the list goes on. Dogs with masterful socialization skills will thrive in this canine cosmopolis. If your dog can handle Green Lake, she can probably pass the Canine Good Citizenship test without lifting a paw. Leashes are mandatory—don't leave home without them.

From I-5, take Exit 169 and go west on N.E. 50th Street for 0.7 miles. Turn right onto Green Lake Way. Go north on Green Lake Way and park along the street surrounding the lake or in one of several small, free parking lots. 7201 East Green Lake Drive.

PLACES TO EAT

Blu Water Bistro: At this open-air dining establishment, across the street from Green Lake, the summer menu fills up with salads, and come winter, meatloaf goes back on the menu along with heartier soups. Dogs tie up to a tree alongside your patio tables, and the staff will bring out a water bowl for them. 7900 E. Green Lake Dr. N.; 206/524-3985; www.bluwaterbistro.com.

Chocolati Café: Drinking chocolate, honey chocolate cakes the shape of the Swiss Matterhorn, and Aztec truffles of cinnamon and spice are just what you need to replenish all those lost calories burned off running or rowing on the lake. 7810 E. Green Lake Drive N.; 206/527-5467; www.chocolati.com.

Mae's Ice Cream Shoppe and Dessert Bar: If you're seeking places unique to Seattle that have been around awhile, as in, since the 1920s, Mae's certainly fits the bill. While Mae's diner only has a couple of two-tops outside, this adjacent walk-up-window wonderland of sweet sugar highs is open rain or shine, until dark in the summer, until 3 P.M. in the winter. 65th & Phinney; 206/782-1222; www.maescafe.com.

Mighty O Doughnuts: After a spin at the Woodland Park OLA, this is where Isis and Cooper rendezvous with their friend Blue, who goes for the hard-core cake doughnuts in all their gut-bomb glory. Take comfort in the fact that the Mighty O's are vegan and organic, which has to be better for you than trans fats, even if you do eat a dozen. 2110 N. 55th; 206/547-0335; www.mightyo.com

Fremont and Wallingford

Left-of-center and slightly off-kilter, Fremont is a free-spirited community with a high concentration of artists and a Google of software engineers thrown in for good measure, Adobe and Corbis, too. Even before it starts officially at Gas Works Park, you can pick up the Burke-Gilman trail anywhere along the waterfront to watch the boats going through the Montlake Cut. Street-corner art is everywhere. Walk your pup past *Waiting for the Interurban* at 34th Street and Fremont Avenue, the troll under the Aurora Bridge, a rocket that "takes off" every day at noon at 35th Street and Evanston Avenue, and an intimidating statue of Lenin rescued from a ditch in Poland and placed at 36th Street and Fremont Avenue.

East of Stone Way, Wallingford is toned down a bit, unless there's food involved at festivities such as Bite of Wallingford and the Wallingford Wurst Fest. Cooper's got a soft spot in his belly for this restaurant-heavy neighborhood.

PARKS, BEACHES, AND RECREATION AREAS

5 Gas Works Park

🐾🐾 (See Central Seattle map on page 184)

There is one day a year you should avoid bringing a dog to this city park at all costs. First and foremost, dogs typically despise and fear fireworks, and secondly, several hundred thousand people crawl all over the 20-acre hill on Independence Day to watch the Fourth of JulIvar's fireworks shot off a barge in Union Lake (Ivar's is a clam restaurant chain started by colorful historical figure Ivar Haglund).

Any other time, there are a bunch of reasons to visit Gas Works. Come to check out the hulking remnants of the pipelines that provided natural gas to early residents and give the park its name. Watch people fly kites on the breezy hill and take in choice views of downtown and the houseboats, including the one made famous as Tom Hank's pad in *Sleepless in Seattle*. This park is the official starting point for the Burke-Gilman multi-use trail and the best place to find free parking to get on the trail.

From I-5, take Exit 169, go east on N. 45th Street eight blocks, turn right on University, go seven long blocks and turn right on N. Pacific Street. As the road curves right, the park is on your left. The park is open 4 A.M.–11:30 P.M., the parking lot only from 6 A.M.–9 P.M. 2101 N. Northlake Way.

6 Burke-Gilman Trail

🐾🐾🐾🐾 (See Central Seattle map on page 184)

This paved, multi-use trail hugs the shores of Lake Washington after passing Lake Union and the University of Washington. Its 14 miles are heavily used by cyclists and inline skaters as well as walkers with leashed dogs. There are six park rest stops along the way. At the top of the lake, in Kenmore Logboom Park, the trail connects to the Sammamish River Trail.

Although it starts over in Ballard, behind maritime industrial warehouses, it's much easier to hop on at Gas Works Park. It was while walking this trail, one day in early April, that the Dachsies' Mom came to realize that Seattle was their forever home.

For an excellent interactive map, go to www.cityofseattle.net/parks/burkegilman/bgtrail.htm.

PLACES TO EAT

Irwin's: Dog biscuits in a mug and good grub under $10 are only two of the reasons this neighborhood hangout is so popular. Club sandwiches, pizza by the slice, and chicken pot pie are a few more. Isis was pleased to discover they donate 20 percent of profits to local non-profits on the third Tuesday of every month. Plastic lawn furniture is casually strewn about outside. It's a great place to lounge around. 2123 N. 40th St.; 206/675-1484.

Norm's Eatery and Ale House: Pictures of Norm and Polly the goldens are plastered on the walls, the drinks are named after them, and the dog theme is carried out in every aspect of the bar's decor. Norm and Polly welcome guest dogs and recommend the cumin-chipotle meatloaf, creamy tuna casserole, and steak sandwiches. If you sit quietly and don't beg, your pets may allow you to share. Ask any dog walker, dog sitter, dog groomer, or dog lover in town; they'll all vote for Norm's as the happiest hound hangout around. 460 N. 36th St.; 206/547-1417.

PCC Natural Market: This local, organic food co-op is the largest of its kind in the nation, with nine stores over the Greater Seattle area. The Fremont location has a tremendous amount of covered outdoor seating, in a sunken patio at the heart of the action. Their deli rivals any. PCC's hot oven pizza slices, fat cookies, and beer and wine selection will redefine your thoughts on health food. 600 N. 34th; 206/632-6811; www.pccnaturalmarkets.com.

RoRo BBQ & Grill: Good dogs get free brisket at RoRo's, hand-delivered by the waitress to a half dozen picnic tables on the extended sidewalk. Cooper likes to sit next to the bike lanes, eating tri-tip, licking sweet and smoky sauce off his paws. The pulled Portobello sandwich with smoked red peppers and sweet potato fries is brilliant for vegetarians. 3620 Stone Way N.; 206/954-1100.

Tutta Bella: Tutta Bella's applewood-smoked thin Neapolitan-style pizza is beloved by the Pope himself. Okay, maybe not, but it is the first pizzeria in the Northwest to receive the coveted VPN certification from the Associazione Verace Pizza Napoletana based in Naples, Italy. Their sidewalk seating takes up almost an entire block and their Caesar salad is bigger than a beagle. It's for you, too, Brutus! 4411 Stone Way N.; 206/633-3800; www.tuttabella pizza.com.

University District and Ravenna

Dogs will feel right at home in the home of the Dawgs, the University of Washington Huskies. About 40,000 students come to party—oops, we mean study—at U-Dub annually. The heart of the U-District is a good source for second-hand shopping and ethnic eats ordered through walk-up windows.

PARKS, BEACHES, AND RECREATION AREAS

🖪 Cowen and Ravenna Parks

🐾🐾🐾 (See Central Seattle map on page 184)

Seattle has an endearing habit of linking parks together, and this is one of many you'll find in this chapter. Cowen is the developed piece, with a playground, open lawns, picnic tables, and bathrooms. Ravenna is a neighborhood secret, although a pretty big one to try to hide. It is a deep, dark, and mysterious ravine, starting at Brooklyn and sheltering underneath a 15th Avenue N.E. bridge. Natural trails, bridges, and stairways take you through what is almost completely wooded and wild territory in an otherwise highly groomed residential area. Rumor has it that medieval re-enactment societies and Wiccans meet within these borders for ceremonies.

From Exit 170 off I-5, go east on 65th Street N.E. and turn right on Brooklyn Avenue. Go a couple of blocks south and park on the street for Cowen Park on the west side. For the east side of Ravenna Park, continue east on 65th Street, turn right on 20th Avenue and right on N.E. 62nd Street to find side-street parking on the north side of 62nd.

PLACES TO EAT

Agua Verde Paddle Club and Café: In addition to serving some of the best authentic tacos north of the Mexican border, this unique establishment in the University District rents sea kayaks by the hour. Munch on the renowned yam or portobello mushroom *tacos de la casa* with pineapple-jicama salsa, and work off the calories paddling past Seattle's famous houseboats on Lake Union. Kayak rentals are available March–October; the cafeteria-style restaurant is open year-round. Order at the counter or the to-go window and relax at the picnic tables in the waterfront park next door. 1303 N.E. Boat St.; 206/545-8570; www.aguaverde.com.

Cowen Park Grocery: It's half a gourmet grocery store and half a deli, serving lazy weekend breakfast and afternoon barbecue, and, every day, the best croissants in town from Le Fournil French bakery and coffee from local legend Zoka. CPG's wide sidewalk patio is across the street from Cowen Park. 1217 N.E. Ravenna Blvd.; 206/525-1117; www.cowenparkgrocery.com.

Dick's Famous Burgers: When dogs run in their sleep, they are heading to a place where they can walk up to a window through which come greasy burgers, thin fries, and milkshakes from early in the morning until 2 A.M. at night. The dream has been true at Dick's since 1954. Though not the first, Dick's is a Seattle icon, walkup window. 111 N.E. 45th St.; 206/632-5125; www.ddir.com.

PLACES TO STAY

University Inn: Legendary for the staff's quality of service, this hotel bills itself as the "hotel with a heart," which extends a warm welcome to pets under 75 pounds, as many as you like, for $10 per pet per night. Pets are allowed in 20 traditional rooms, much too modern and stylish to be called such. Rates are $125–165; the pet fee is $20. 4140 Roosevelt Way N.E.; 206/632-5055 or 800/733-3855; www.universityinnseattle.com.

View Ridge

PARKS, BEACHES, AND RECREATION AREAS

🖫 Matthews Beach Park

🐾🐾 (See Central Seattle map on page 184)

Pioneer John G. Matthews homesteaded on this site in the 1880s, and by the 1940s it was already a popular park, the site of Pan American World Airways' offices, and the dock for the clipper ships, the world's first amphibious commercial air transports over the ocean.

While dogs are not allowed on Seattle city beaches, the sand makes up a fraction of the acreage here. Coop 'n' Isis hardly noticed as they scampered about, chasing ducks, geese, squirrels, and crows over hill, over dale, and on the bridge over cloudy Thornton Creek. Old parks mean big trees, and there are plenty here, alternating with wide picnic and sunning lawns. It's a stopover for cyclists on the Burke-Gilman Trail, with restrooms and changing rooms in the bathhouse.

Take Exit 171 northbound from I-5, and stay to the left to continue on Lake City Way N.E. (Highway 522). Head northeast for 1.6 miles, turn right on N.E.

DOG-EAR YOUR CALENDAR

It's the biggest doggone party with a purpose every September at **Bark in the Park and PAWSwalk** at Sand Point in Seattle. The festivities include a 1K and a 5K walk, music, food (human and canine), and nearly a hundred booths of dog-related products and vendors. The point is to have a blast while raising money for PAWS. Coop 'n' Isis came home with enough treats and food samples to last a month. Upwards of 5,000 people plus pets attend. Pre-registration is $20 per person, $25 at the door. You get a T-shirt and your dogs wear sporty bandanas. 425/787-2500, ext. 833; www.barkinthepark.com.

Have a ball raising money for the Seattle/King County Humane Society at the annual **Tuxes and Tails** benefit, one of many events and activities sponsored by SHS. This dinner and auction brings out celebrities and high society in packs to promote a wonderful cause. For the highlight of the evening, dogs in the latest designer attire walk the runway in a Celebrity Pet Fashion Show. Tuxes and Tails is held annually in April, at different venues in downtown Seattle. Top Dog Tickets are $175 for front-row seats at this evening of superstars. 425/373-5384; www.seattlehumane.org.

95th Street and go 1.3 miles. Turn right on Sand Point Way N.E. and, almost immediately, bear left onto N.E. 93rd Street into the park. 9300 51st Ave. N.E.

◙ Magnuson Park at Sand Point

🐾🐾🐾🐾🐕 (See Central Seattle map on page 184)

This is the land that doggie dreams are made of, a nine-acre site with winding trails, several open areas, and the only paw-approved water access within city limits, along Lake Washington. Your canine will never lack for companionship at this dog park, between the puppy play dates, mutt meet-ups, dog-walker outings, and regulars who spend quality time in Seattle's largest pet playground. Cooper, who is both shy and small, is pleased to announce that Magnuson has a separate Small and Shy Dog Area. Despite the best efforts of the wood-chip patrol, the OLA's main field is often mud soup, so you'll be pleased to know that there is a dog wash station at the main entrance.

The OLA is completely fenced, with several double-gated entry points. To reach the beach, you have to leave the main fenced section and cross a trail to enter another gated area. Water is plentiful, but the bag supply is sporadic. Magnuson is Seattle's second-largest park, a 350-acre former Navy facility with many uses, but frankly, once you've seen the dog park, you've seen all there is to see.

The off-leash area is straight east from the 74th Street entrance. Open 4 A.M.–10 P.M. 7400 Sand Point Way N.E.; 206/684-4946.

PLACES TO EAT

60th Street Desserts and Delicatessen: This kitchen bakes the cakes for the pastry cases of the finer grocery stores in town. It's a quick stop for good take-out lunch foods, across the street from the entrance to Sand Point. 7401 Sand Point Way N.E.; 206/527-8560; www.60thstreetdesserts.com.

Magnolia

This old-money peninsula grew out of a summer home enclave. It stands out from other communities for the pruning, grooming, landscaping, and manicuring of its lawns and gardens. There are poodles who would give their canine teeth to be this tricked out. A sidewalk stroll around Magnolia Bluff gives your heeler a chance to hobnob with local purebreds, while you watch the ferry boats in Elliott Bay and snap a shot of the Space Needle with Mt. Rainier hulking in the background.

PARKS, BEACHES, AND RECREATION AREAS

10 Discovery Park

🐾🐾🐾🐾 (See Central Seattle map on page 184)

The young city of Seattle donated 500 acres to the federal government in 1894 for an army base on the tip of the Magnolia peninsula. More than a million troops were shipped out to Europe from Fort Lawton during World War I and World War II, with up to 10,000 a day headed to Korea in the early 1950s. Seventy years later, the land was returned to the city, and Discovery Park was born.

Every trip to these largely untamed woods is an adventure, with two miles of tidal beaches, grassy meadows, shifting sand dunes, forested groves, and plunging sea cliffs. The southwest entrance is closest to the former parade grounds, perfect for kite flying, picnics, picking blackberries in August, and taking in sweeping views of the Olympic Mountains and Elliott Bay. Down the trail to South Beach, you can harvest clams on 50 yards of mudflats at low tide and check out the lighthouse.

The east entrance leads to the visitors center and North Beach, a picnic spot with a birds-eye view of the yachts at Shilshole Bay Marina. Down a winding driveway is the Daybreak Star Indian Cultural Center, telling of the Duwamish people who fished here more than 4,000 years before Scandinavian settlers came for the region's gold, timber, and salmon.

The three-mile loop trail is a moderate hike that leads you through the park's highlights. Dogs must be leashed, and this is especially important on the bluffs, where entire hundred-yard sections of the hillside have been reclaimed by the sea.

No bones about it: We love this place. It's out of the way, and worth the effort. From downtown, take Denny Way, which becomes Elliott Avenue and then 15th Avenue. Take the Nickerson/Emerson exit and loop around onto W. Emerson Place past Fisherman's Terminal. Turn right onto Gilman Avenue, and follow it around until it becomes Government Way and leads directly into the park's east entrance. Park closes at dusk; 3801 W. Government Way; 206/386-4236.

11 Magnolia Manor Park

🐾🐾 (See Central Seattle map on page 184)

Sometimes life moves at a snail's pace, even in the big city, where the signs proposing an off-leash area at this city park have been up since 2006, with no official progress having been made, largely due to lack of funds, per usual. It is an ideal spot for a dog park, already fenced with very tall chain link topped with barbed wire. While there are two entrances without gates, the rest of the plateau is completely enclosed. Underneath you is a water reservoir, and surrounding you are city views, fragrant butterfly bushes, and a trim lawn with blackberries overtaking the edges. What minimal infrastructure there is consists of a couple of benches, a bag dispenser and a can, and some faded, illegible interpretive signs about water conservation.

Take the Dravus Street exit from 15th Avenue N.W., and go west on Dravus, through the light and up the 19 percent grade hill, a hill so brutal the sidewalk has steps. At the crest of the street, turn right on 28th Avenue W., and go a block and a half to the park on your right. Open 4 A.M. to 11:30 P.M., but there's no lighting, so you might want to stick to daylight hours.

12 Magnolia Park and Magnolia Bluff

🐾🐾 (See Central Seattle map on page 184)

When Cooper first saw green bark peeling off red Madrona trees, he thought they were wounded, but later discovered this is a normal function of these unique evergreens found throughout the Pacific Northwest. He's not the first to harbor a mistaken impression; the whole neighborhood was wrongfully identified by a Navy geographer who mistook Madronas for Magnolias, and the name stuck.

This 12-acre view park has plentiful misnomer trees, picnic tables, and lawns. Continuing northwest from the park is a fabulous drive on top of a bluff. On top of the hill is a small parking lot, allowing you to get out and walk the bluff on sidewalks.

On one side are stately homes with elaborate landscaping—you'll see what we mean when we say Magnolians take tree-trimming cues out of Dr. Seuss books—and on the other are wide views of Puget Sound and Elliott Bay.

It's a perfect perch from which to watch ferry traffic to and from Bainbridge Island and Bremerton, and container ships led by tugboats bound for parts unknown.

From downtown Seattle, take Denny Way west, curve right onto Elliott Avenue W., and follow it north as it becomes 15th Avenue N.W. Take the Magnolia Bridge exit and continue up and over the bridge, going straight as the road becomes W. Galer Street, and then Magnolia Boulevard. Turn left over the bridge at the stop sign to continue on Magnolia Boulevard and the park will be around the bend. 1461 Magnolia Blvd. W.

PLACES TO EAT

Little Chinooks: This seafood bar is located at Fisherman's Terminal, one of the largest working fishing ports on the west coast. Even fried, your fish will be very, very fresh. 1900 W. Nickerson St.; 206/283-4665.

Red Mill Burgers: There is a strict no-cell-phone policy at Red Mill, the owners are unrepentant Rolling Stones fans (closing the store to take all employees to the latest concert), and they accept only cash and local checks. They can afford to be picky because their bacon chili verde burgers have won the award for Best in Show 10 years in a row, at last count. Oprah voted them "one of the top 20 places to eat before you die." Two picnic tables provide less than scenic, but perfectly suitable, outdoor seating. 1613 Dravus St.; 206/284-6363.

Queen Anne/Uptown

This neighborhood comes in two flavors, Lower Queen Anne, also called Uptown for being north of downtown, and Top of Queen Anne, up the steepest street in the city, known as the Counterbalance. Dividing the plateau on one of Seattle's few remaining original hills is Queen Anne Avenue, a chic shopping and dining destination.

PARKS, BEACHES, AND RECREATION AREAS

13 Kinnear Park

😺😺 (See Central Seattle map on page 184)

Stop, drop, and roll down the hill is the drill at this pie-shaped, two-tiered hillside park that is larger and grassier than any of the tiny pocket parks in this snobby neighborhood. There, we said it, Queen Anne is snobby. As in Magnolia, an off-leash park has been approved for a section of this park since 2006, but don't bet your furry coat on it happening any time soon. Never mind, it remains cool to come take in the view of the grain elevator and Pier 86, watching the tankers get their cargoes through snaking tubes. From here, the joggers, cyclists, and skaters at Myrtle Edwards below looks like busy ants.

From Denny, turn north on 1st Avenue N., left on W. Mercer Street, right on

2nd Avenue, and left on W. Olympic Place. Street parking is available along the length of the park sidewalk. 899 Olympic Pl.

14 Kerry Park Viewpoint

🐾 🐾 (See Central Seattle map on page 184)

Sorry dogs, this one's for the humans, but we had to include it because it has the best view *of* the city, *in* the city, of the Seattle Skyline with Mount Rainier as a backdrop. For years, we didn't know the real name of this park, even as we brought out-of-town visitors here, simply calling it Overlook Park. The large sculpture in the park, "Changing Form" by Doris Chase, is a local landmark worth seeing.

From Denny, turn north on 1st Avenue N., left on Roy Street, and right on Queen Anne Avenue N. Continue up the steep hill, turning left on Highland Drive, to the park on your left.

15 Seattle Center Grounds

🐾 🐾 (See Central Seattle map on page 184)

Since it was created for the 1962 World's Fair, the 87-acre Seattle Center continues to house more cultural attractions per square foot than any other plot in the city. There are so many things for people to see: the Space Needle, the colorful blob of the Experience Music Project, the Monorail, and the spires of the Pacific Science Center, to name a few. Walking by all of these must-sees is good for a spot of exercise, and a tug of the leash in the right direction will lead to the center square of grass surrounding the International Fountain. The size of a small mountain, the dome spouts water-jet shows choreographed to classical music. Kids delight in being caught off-guard and getting drenched when the fountain bursts to life; dogs will have to settle for stray spray.

Seattle Center hosts the city's oldest and biggest event traditions, including the Northwest Folklife Festival, Bite of Seattle, and Bumbershoot. These are the times when being a dog in the park is a drag, and as a human, you may get dragged by the crowds in directions you had no intention of going.

From I-5, take Exit 167 and follow Mercer Street straight west. There are multiple paid parking lots around the center.

PLACES TO EAT

Chinoise: For pan-Asian specialties, this sushi bar consistently ranks in Seattle's top favorite polls. We swear, when Isis tried her first rainbow roll, we saw her eyes widen in delight. It's doubtful you'll suffer from the hungry-two-hours-later syndrome if you try the soup pots or noodle bowls. Patio dining is weather permitting, and there's always those little white to-go boxes. 12 Boston St.; 206/284-6671; www.chinoisecafe.com.

El Diablo Coffee Company: Every surface of this Cuban coffeehouse is painted with folk art depicting charming devils, tempting you with steaming mugs of Cubano coffee, sweet and sticky with caramelized sugar. We'd consider selling our souls for an eternity of their pulled pork sandwiches. Perhaps most amusing of all is that students from the local Christian college gather here for theological discussions. The Wieners thank heaven for the tile patio, dog biscuit jar, and water bowl. 1811 Queen Anne Ave. N., #101; 206/285-0693; www.eldiablocoffee.com.

South Lake Union and Eastlake

Microsoft billionaire Paul Allen and his company Vulcan owns this section of town, pretty much lock, stock, and barrel. He's put in a streetcar called the South Lake Union Transit (which spawned T-shirts reading "I rode the S.L.U.T.!"). His office buildings are going up, as are lots of condos. Following the money are hip shops, restaurants, and the young and sexy.

PARKS, BEACHES, AND RECREATION AREAS

16 South Lake Union Park

(See Central Seattle map on page 184)

The full development of all 12 acres of South Lake Union Park is slated for completion in 2010. In April 2008, the first 1.6 acres opened with terraced waterfront steps, a cedar plank boardwalk, a pedestrian bridge, and a little bit of green space. It's already a fun place to wander around, to watch the sailboats on Lake Union and the takeoffs and landings of Kenmore Air floatplanes. The park includes the Center for Wooden Boats, so extend your walks up and down the piers to gawk at the historic watercraft moored here.

From I-5, take the Mercer Street exit, and stay in the second to the right lane to turn right on Fairview Avenue N., and then left around the lake on Valley Street. 860 Terry Ave. N.

17 I-5 Colonnade Dog Park

(See Central Seattle map on page 184)

Like Clara barking "Where's the Beef?" Isis has a beef with this strange, 1.2-acre moonwalk of a park. "Where's the grass?" she cries. This dog park is all crushed gravel, a recent concept in easy maintenance and drainage, not so easy on tender little paws. Under the highway overpass, the OLA is long and skinny, in a series of terraced sections and stairs that step down the hillside. It's otherworldly, a strange, urban interpretation of a dog park. The remainder of I-5 Colonnade Park is a mountain bike trials course, and it is *sick*, as the kids say, meaning excellent. It's the only thing that's ever made Cooper wish, like Pinocchio, that he was a boy, showing off his mad skills on knobby tires.

This underworld park is located beneath I-5 in an area south of E. Howe Street between Lakeview Boulevard and Franklin Avenue E. It is impossible

DETOUR

Dogs are welcome to come on the **Sunday Ice Cream Cruise,** but no, that's not why they call it the poop deck. If your dog is calm and sea worthy, she's welcome, at the captain's discretion, to test her sea legs on board the MV *Fremont Avenue,* a small ferry plying the waters of Lake Union.

The tour cruises the inside passages of Seattle's canals and lakes for 45 minutes, giving you the best views of resident houseboats, glass artist Dale Chihuly's studio, and the city skyline. The captain keeps bacon-flavored treats on board, knowing that ice cream is not always the best for canine stomachs. Tours depart summer Sundays, on the hour 11 A.M.–5 P.M. Adults are $11, kids are $7, and four-leggeds are free. Ice cream treats are extra. The vessel departs from South Lake Union Park. Watch for the sandwich board signs, flags, and balloons. It's walk-on only. Contact Captain Larry Kezner; 206/713-8446; www.seattleferryservice.com.

to park on the west of the highway, so the easiest instructions to get here are as follows: from I-5 northbound, take Exit 168A, the Lakeview Boulevard exit. Take a left at the stop sign and, immediately, parking is in a pullout to your left, so pull a safe U-turn when you can. From the main steps of the park, the OLA is to your left, south and down the hill.

PLACES TO EAT

Grand Central Bakery: Boasting the biggest patio in Eastlake, this local bakery is a great lunch choice for sandwiches, salads, soups, and mouth-watering triple-chocolate cookies, strictly for the humans. 1616 Eastlake Ave. E.; 206/957-9505; www.grandcentralbakery.com.

Serafina's: Serafina's is an *osteria* and *enoteca,* which is a neighborhood place to eat delicious Italian food and drink good wine. The chef specializes in the cuisines of Tuscany and Umbria, leaning toward lighter sauces and more seafood. Its intimate atmosphere and traditional dishes have made it a local culinary landmark since it opened in 1991. When weather permits, service on the front patio is dog-friendly. 2043 Eastlake Ave. E.; 206/323-0807; www.serafinaseattle.com.

PLACES TO STAY

Pan Pacific: At a choice downtown address above Whole Foods Market, this Asian-inspired luxury hotel allows dogs on the third floor for a $50 fee per stay. Opened in 2007, it excels at providing all the latest technology and comforts available, including plasma screen TVs, high-thread-count Egyptian cotton sheets, Bose Wave radios, Herman Miller designer chairs and furniture, and coffee service by Torrefazione. When Isis has delusions of grandeur, she imagines the Pan Pacific to be her permanent home. Rates range $165–300; 2125 Terry Ave.; 206/264-8111; www.panpacific.com.

Residence Inn–Lake Union Seattle: As is typical of these long-term stay hotels, it looks more like a high-rise apartment than a motel. It's across the street from Lake Union Park, and within walking distance of much of downtown. Rates range $150–190, and there is a $10 pet fee per night; 800 Fairview Ave. N.; 206/624-6000.

Montlake and Madison

These two communities on Lake Washington are generally quiet, with an air of charm created by tree-lined boulevards and the old Seattle-style brick and wood-frame combination homes of the early 20th century, bought up and meticulously restored by baby boomers. To get the full flavor of the neighborhood, stop and smell the roses at Martha E. Harris flowers and gifts (4218 E. Madison St.; 206/568-0347).

PARKS, BEACHES, AND RECREATION AREAS

18 Boren Lookout/Interlaken Boulevard

🐾🐾🐾 (See Central Seattle map on page 184)

Get lost. Seriously. Hidden in a neighborhood with way too many one-way streets, this is not a park for the control freak or casual tourist. You have to be willing to lose your way a couple of times to find it, then be up for wandering in the park's maze of trails once there. Steep hillsides, thick woods, and surprises of public art and sculpture are the rewards for the willingness to let go and go with the flow.

Before you get too deep into the woods, take a moment to stop at the Luisa Boren Lookout, from which you can see Mount Baker, the Cascade Mountains, Lake Washington, and the Husky Football Stadium. For directions to the overlook, take Roanoke Street east of I-5, turn south on 10th Avenue E., then turn left on E. Aloha, and left on 15th Avenue E, heading back northbound. Turn right at the corner of Garfield and park there. The Overlook is on the northeast corner of Garfield Street and 15th Avenue.

To head into the heart of Interlaken Boulevard Park from I-5, take the Roanoke Street Exit, and go east on Roanoke. Bear right onto Delmar Drive. Turn right on Boyer Avenue, and right again onto 19th Avenue E. You'll find a few opportunities to park and a visible trail leading into the park at the intersection of 19th Avenue and E. Interlaken Boulevard.

19 Washington Park Arboretum

🐾🐾🐾 (See Central Seattle map on page 184)

To walk through the arboretum is to commune with nature as designed by man, for rarely will you find more than 5,500 varieties of trees together in one 230-acre living museum. Opened in 1934, the woodland was designed by James F. Dawson, of the Olmsted Brothers landscape architecture firm. Every one of the 40,000 trees and shrubs is deliberately placed and grouped by species. Money and manpower shortages have left the park overgrown, a bit like an overblown rose, which doesn't dampen your dog's enthusiasm for a walk through areas with quaint names like Honeysuckle Hill, Azalea Way, and Loderi Valley. During any given season, there are a half dozen species in full glory. Isis chooses fall, when Japanese maples and Chilean fire trees are ablaze with color. New in 2008 is the Pacific Connections garden, highlighting native xeriscaping and plants to attract wildlife.

You can do a drive-by through the park on Lake Washington Boulevard or Arboretum Drive East. Or stop by the visitors center to get a trail map for five or so miles of bark mulch trails and to find out which gardens are not to be missed when you visit. Dogs are not allowed in the Japanese garden.

From I-5, take Exit 168B onto State Route 520 and immediately take the first exit off S.R. 520 to Montlake Boulevard. Go straight across Montlake to E. Lake Washington Boulevard; at the next left, turn onto E. Foster Island Road to reach the Graham Visitors Center. Hours are 10 A.M.–4 P.M.; the park is open dawn–dusk. 2300 Arboretum Dr. E.; 206/543-8800; www.depts.washington.edu/wpa.

20 Madison Park

🐾 (See Central Seattle map on page 184)

Madison's current eight-acre grass hillock is a winner, even at a fraction of its former glory. In the late 19th century, a bigwig judge named McGilvra created the beach promenade that was once Seattle's most popular, replete with floating bandstands, a paddlewheel steamboat, beer and gambling halls, athletic fields, greenhouses, and ship piers. A cable car ran direct from Pioneer Square.

Today, one square holds a humble playground and tennis courts surrounded by precise landscaping. Across 43rd Street is a lawn sloping down to the bathing beach. No dogs are allowed on the beach.

We included this little city gem because we couldn't help but notice that Madison Park and the surrounding sidewalks always seem to be full of friendly pedestrians who are eager to hand out extra pats and love to pooches.

Take the Madison Street exit from I-5, traveling northeast on E. Madison until it ends, at the water, and at the park.

PLACES TO EAT

Essential Baking Company: This is an essential stop when you're in the neighborhood. The artisan bakers that supply bread to many local, upscale grocery stores also make luscious soups (Isis loves the ginger and carrot puree), pizza, salads, select sandwiches, and entrées. The pastries are works of art, and the coffee is superb. The patio is smallish, with four tables for two, but it captures the morning sun. 2719 E. Madison St.; 206/328-0078; www.essentialbaking.com.

Madison Park Café: There's little pleasure better in life than savoring your white bean cassoulet and chocolate pot de crème on a shaded patio with standing heaters, tucked in between two vintage homes, one of which is this superlative café. That you can enjoy this outstanding food and wine with your best friend at your side borders on the miraculous. 1807 42nd Ave E.; 206/324-2626; www.madisonparkcafe.citysearch.com.

Capitol Hill

Pioneers optimistically named this mound, hoping it would become the site of the state capital. Instead, it has become the city seat for counterculture, a thriving gay and lesbian community, and is still leading the pack in variety of tattoo and body piercings per capita. Broadway, the main drag, has lots of foot traffic, more than its fair share of homeless kids asking for change, and designer collars on dogs, cats, and a few humans. Leash up tight and keep an eye out for potential pet skirmishes at crowded sidewalk cafés and when window-shopping for vintage clothing and retro home furnishings.

PARKS, BEACHES, AND RECREATION AREAS

21 Volunteer Park

🐾 🐾 🐾 (See Central Seattle map on page 184)

Called City Park at its dedication in 1887, this 48-acre hilltop was renamed in 1901 to honor the volunteers in the Spanish-American War. The park is a landscape legacy of the Olmsted brothers, with a 106-step tower leading to views of Lake Union and an exhibit about the green-thumbed brothers. Sun worshipers dot the hillside, kids stay busy at a playground and summertime wading pool, and local musicians and Shakespeare productions regularly entertain park goers.

Your pal will be pleased to indulge in this highly cultured park with you, also home to the Seattle Asian Art Museum (sorry, no pets inside). In the summer, don't miss the local Dahlia Society's display of these tall flowers with their fat, colorful blooms. Management kindly asks that dogs observe the flowers from a respectful distance. Dogs are not allowed in the Conservatory. Directly north is the Lake View Cemetery, where Jimi Hendrix, Bruce Lee, and Seattle pioneers enjoy eternity in the sun.

From I-5, take Exit 166, east on E. Olive Way, which merges into E. John Street. At the T intersection, turn left on 15th Avenue E. The park entrance will be on your left after 0.75 miles. Open 6 A.M.–11 P.M. 1247 15th Ave. E.

22 Plymouth Pillars Dog Park

🐾🐾🦮 (See Central Seattle map on page 184)

The barking from Capitol Hill canines got so loud, the city had to find a way to release all the spit and vinegar. The solution killed two birds with one stone, getting rid of a burnt triangle of land adjacent to the highway and providing city dogs with a bit of freedom. At only 0.22 acres, it's actually many stones, tiny ones, in the form of pea gravel, that make up the surface of the long and narrow rectangle, with double-gated entries on either side. This good thing in a small package comes with a single tree, a combo human/dog water fountain, and the requisite bag-and-can poop-containment system. Due to previous incidents, no eating or feeding of either species is allowed in the park.

The easiest way to get there is to drive east up Pike Street from downtown, and turn left and park your car on Minor Avenue. Walk down to Pine Street, turn left, and look for the three pillars. On Boren Avenue, between Pike and Pine Streets.

PLACES TO EAT

Baguette Box: The sandwich gets sassy, inspired by Vietnamese *bahn mi*, where amazing concoctions of hot goodness are stuffed into a French roll. Combinations such as apricot and pork, crispy drunken chicken, and tuna niçoise can also be made into salads, to save the carbs for a glass of wine. Oh, and the ambiance—right around the corner from Plymouth Pillars dog park, framed photos of four-legged loved ones adorn the walls. P.S.: Love the truffle fries. 1203 Pine St.; 206/332-0220; www.baguettebox.com.

Volunteer Park Café and Marketplace: Two girlfriends, a baker and a chef, created their dream café together. Good thing it's hidden discretely in a residential area, or it would be even more swamped by admirers than it already is. We stumbled upon it by canine intervention, getting lost while looking for an entrance into Interlaken Boulevard Park. Dinners are divine, and Cooper'll tell you the Cracker Jack cupcakes are unlike anything he's ever seen. An impossible number of two-person tables in cheery white, green, and red sit helter-skelter on the wide sidewalk at the corner of Gaylor and 17th Avenue. 1501 17th Ave. E.; 206/328-3155; www.alwaysfreshgoodness.com.

Belltown

Belltown is the very definition of high-profile, urban living, where the almost unbearably hip, wealthy, and young urbanites take dining, shopping, and living the nightlife to high art.

The borders between Belltown and Downtown seem blurry, but according to the Belltown Walking Map they are Denny Way–North, Elliott Avenue–West, Sixth Avenue–East, and Virginia Street–South.

PARKS, BEACHES, AND RECREATION AREAS

23 Myrtle Edwards Park

🐾🐾 (See Central Seattle map on page 184)

This 4,100-foot strip of waterfront property is the largest green space close to the downtown core, with a 1.25-mile winding bike and pedestrian path bordered by rolling lawns and Puget Sound. Every step awards views of Mt. Rainier and the Olympics across Elliott Bay. You'll start at the skyscrapers of downtown, and end at working docks and fishing piers of the wharf in Interbay. You'll come close to the Port of Seattle's working grain elevators; hopefully, you'll get the chance to watch one load up with grain.

Your dog will find likely walking partners with the many downtown dogs who frequent the trails and lawns. Watch out for the inline skaters and cyclists who may provide some unintentional agility training for you and your dog.

To reach Myrtle Edwards, think right-left-right-left-right: From I-5 northbound, take the left Exit 165 onto Seneca Street. Turn right onto 1st Avenue, left onto Battery Street, right onto Western Avenue, left onto Wall Street, and right on Alaskan Way, 0.3 mile into a metered parking lot. Open 24 hours, with an afterglow provided by the city lights. 3103 Alaskan Way W.

24 SAM's Olympic Sculpture Park

🐾🐾 🐾 (See Central Seattle map on page 184)

Cooper wants to take a moment to hop up on his soapbox and state, in his humble opinion, that projects such as this one are what create world class cities. A pat on the back to the Seattle Art Museum. More, please! Opened in 2007 to much excitement, this $85 million project took Seattle's largest undeveloped waterfront property and turned it not into condos and retail, but into a stunning park for outdoor art.

Using the canvas of the Olympic Mountains and Puget Sound as a starting point, the Z-shaped park zigzags across nine acres, with 20 large-scale sculptures on display. Many of the sculptures show a great sense of humor and a mastery of space and proportion. Among the favorites are five gargantuan traffic cones and a Paul Bunyan–sized pencil eraser, the old-fashioned kind with the wheel and brush.

There's no charge to walk through this outdoor art gallery, and leashed pets are permitted to join you on the walkways. There's no touching the pieces, and certainly no lifting of legs on them.

The park is between Western Avenue and Alaskan Way, north of Broad Street. From I-5 northbound take Exit 165, on the left, and turn slightly left onto Seneca Street. Turn right onto 1st Avenue and left onto Broad Street. From I-5 southbound, take Exit 165A straight onto Union Street, then left on 1st and left on Broad. 2901 Western Ave.; 206/654-3100; www.seattleartmuseum.org/visit/osp.

25 Regrade Dog Park

🐾🐾🐕 (See Central Seattle map on page 184)

Rarely has so small a space (0.3 acres) generated such huge excitement. More than 100 dogs packed the quarter city block when this off-leash area opened. Not only is this park a sight for the sore eyes of downtown dogs trapped on the patios of high-rise condos and apartments, but it helped clear up a city eyesore of illegal activity.

The ground is alternating patches of concrete and wood mulch. Because it was converted from a former use, there's probably more cement than is desirable, but at least it's not mud! Though the rubber-coated chain link fence that surrounds the area is five feet tall, you'll still have to watch how far and high you throw balls and fetch toys to avoid hitting parked cars and pedestrians on adjacent city streets. City bicycle cops have also hinted that they'll be extra strict about enforcing the leash laws until you get your pet into the park. Two double-gated entrances on either side of the park provide extra room for leash maneuvers.

Regrade Park borders the ultra-hip and pricey Belltown neighborhood, the address of choice for up-and-coming urban professionals. This could be an interesting place to scout for a date while your Scout tries to mate. At the very least, a little extra grooming couldn't hurt. Open dawn–dusk. On the corner of Bell and 3rd Avenue. 2251 3rd Ave.

PLACES TO EAT

Boulangerie Nantaise: Isis would love to *parler Français*, particularly if it would help her order from this certified organic French bakery, *mais oui!* The croissants have never been flakier, the brioche spongier, and oh, the ham and Swiss on a baguette with Dijon mustard and those tiny, tangy little pickles! It's so good. There are tiny, tangy little picnic tables on the sidewalk. 2507 4th Ave.; 206/728-5999; www.boulangerienantaise.com.

Top Pot Doughnuts: Like Mighty O, these babies are homegrown, handmade rings of frosted love, made and spelled the old fashioned way. Sidewalk tables sit under the monorail, so you can watch a Seattle landmark glide to and fro. 2124 5th Ave.; 206/728-1966; toppotdoughnuts.com.

Le Pichet: This multi-award-winning gourmet French bistro takes the European approach by allowing dogs on the patio. They confess they'd let them belly up to the bar for a glass of house red if the health codes would allow it. This isn't small and fussy food; it's rich and hearty and moderately priced.

The chef believes that elegant dining should be an everyday experience. 1933 1st. Ave.; 206/256-1499.

Macrina Bakery and Café: This bake shop's breads and pastries are sold in high-falutin' grocery stores and touted all over the city. Equally heavenly vegetable dishes are available only at the restaurant, salads of baby spring greens in a light vinaigrette, and roasted vegetables with mascarpone cheese on flaky pie crusts. Small, perky, downtown dogs are frequently spotted at Macrina's sidewalk tables. 2408 1st Ave.; 206/448-4032.

PLACES TO STAY

Ace Hotel: The super-short name of this boutique hotel often goes to waste. People instead choose to describe it as "that futuristic, minimalist, all-white hotel down by the water." Standard rooms, which share a bath, are $75–100; deluxe rooms with their own baths are $150–200. Most rooms have water views. There are no dog restrictions or fees; Astro never had it so good. 2425 1st St.; 206/448-4721; www.theacehotel.com.

Edgewater Hotel: "No dog restrictions" is music to a dog's ears, especially when it applies to a premier waterfront hotel. The Edgewater is on a dock over Puget Sound, a mountain lodge as seen through the eyes of a modern designer from Milan. Every room has a guard teddy bear and bear ottomans, which Isis barked at. The hotel's Wagnificent (wish we'd thought of that one) Dog Lover's Package comes with a copy of CityDog Magazine, a folding water bowl, PB cracker treats, a rawhide ring, a rubber ball, an off-leash area map, a bottle of water, Chukar Cherries trail mix, and biodegradable bags. Rates range $190–360. 2411 Alaskan Way; 206/728-7000; www.edgewaterhotel.com.

Downtown Core

There were several sleepy decades in Seattle when people came downtown only to work, and the city was infamous for rolling up its sidewalks at 9 P.M. Things started to change when the grunge music scene took hold, and the dot-com boom of the 1990s gave the inner core another boost. The movement continues, as people and businesses move closer in to the city instead of out to the suburbs. The tide is reversed, and a courthouse, symphony hall, sculpture garden, luxury condos, and office buildings continue to rise. Of special note is Rem Koolhaas' Seattle Public Library, an architectural marvel equally interesting inside and out; take your dog for a walk along 4th and 5th Avenues at Madison Street to check it out.

For top designer boutiques, head to Pacific Place and Nordstrom, founded in Seattle. At lunchtime, Westlake Plaza is the place to be for free summertime concerts and absorbing the city. Seattle's waterfront piers are another good choice for a city walk, always bustling with a mix of tourist and working port activities.

PARKS, BEACHES, AND RECREATION AREAS

26 Central Freeway Park

🐾 (See Central Seattle map on page 184)

The center of commerce is a tough place to be a dog. Where do you go to, ahem, go? Follow in the footsteps of dog-walking bellhops from downtown hotels to this unusual city green space, built in cement boxes, over downtown I-5 interchanges. Trees and native landscaping are being refurbished in 2008, and the park's checkerboard lawns are being re-seeded.

Freeway Park is bounded on the north by Union Street and on the South by Spring Street, between 6th and 9th Avenues. Easy access is available at 7th and Seneca. 700 Seneca St.

PLACES TO EAT

Il Bistro: Quintessential Seattle for more than 30 years, Il Bistro is tucked into Post Alley in the Pike Place Market. It's crowded, lively, bustling, romantic, and intimate, all at the same time. It has a very Continental flair to it. Go for happy hour at café tables set on the cobblestones of the market. 93 Pike St., Suite A; 206/682-3049; www.ilbistro.net.

Uptown Espresso in the Courthouse: Any hardcore Seattleite will have at least one preferred coffeehouse in every neighborhood. The "Home of the Velvet Foam," has several locations, this spot around the corner from the garden courtyard of the courthouse on Virginia Street. 1933 7th Ave.; 206/728-8842; www.uptownespresso.com.

PLACES TO STAY

Alexis Hotel: This elite hotel is a member of the Kimpton group, a select few stylish urban hotels in desirable major metropolises. The Alexis is so dog-friendly that you may feel jealous at the quality of treatment your pet receives, including treats, doggie in-room dining menus, a designer pet bed, and a blackboard that greets them, by name, when they check in. If you can't stay at this hotel, which is on the National Register of Historic Places, go into the lobby to see the glass sculpture by Dale Chihuly. Rates start at $165 for standard guest rooms. The Alexis is unique in the number of specialty suites, which range $215–550. 1007 1st Ave.; 866/356-8894; www.alexishotel.com.

Hotel Max: Artsy, funky, and fun, Hotel Max gives the Seattle Art Museum a run for their money, with rotating art exhibits in the lobby and a permanent installation of more than 350 pieces of original artwork and photographs in the guest rooms and corridors. It's part of the chain that includes Hotel deLuxe in Portland and Hotel Murano in Tacoma, all of which welcome pets without restrictions. A pillow menu, and the press-anytime "you got it" button are a couple of the peculiar perks native to this group of upscale hotels. The pet fee

DIVERSION

Within seconds of its opening, well-to-do downtown dogs who'd had enough of high-rise loft living were crawling all over the **Downtown Dog Lounge.** Within its first year, this doggie daycare center was voted the best in Seattle and had to open two additional locations to handle the volume of dogs scratching at the door.

This hip spot has separate play pens for different sizes and temperaments of dogs. The dog lounge features play care, overnights, and adventures, and that's just the beginning. Walks, hiking trips, herbal baths, healing massages, pawdicures, obedience training, pooch parties, and a rush-hour doggie valet are among the services offered. Your four-legged loved ones are pampered and preened while you do the same at the spa, or go out for dinner or perhaps to a museum or movie. Lounges are conveniently located in Capitol Hill, on Elliott Avenue near Queen Anne and Magnolia, and in Belltown, right across the street from Regrade Dog Park. If that's not good enough, the lounge will come to you. The business has established relationships with the W Hotel, Hotel Monaco, and others for in-room pet sitting. Find your happy place at www.downtowndoglounge.com.

is $40 total per stay; pets get little beds, bowls, and treats in the room. Rates range $140–300. 620 Stewart St.; 866/986-8087; www.hotelmaxseattle.com.

Hotel Monaco: It is so hard to choose among Seattle's dog-friendly Kimpton hotels with their different vibes; the Monaco is on the edge of avant-garde. Hotel Monaco's list of dog amenities, packages, and services is longer than most hotels' lists for people. You'll be equally pampered, and this hotel will even lend you a pet goldfish for your stay if you fail to bring a pet of your own. No dog restrictions or fees. Rates are $215–315. 1101 4th Ave.; 206/624-8000 or 800/715-6513; www.monaco-seattle.com.

Hotel Vintage Park: Each room is dedicated to celebrating a different Washington winery and vineyard. This four-star hotel gives dogs the five-star treatment, above and beyond what any pooch can expect, with no fees or restrictions. Rates range $140–260. 1100 Fifth Ave.; 800/853-3914; www.hotelvintagepark.com.

Seattle Pacific Hotel: An affordable choice close to Seattle Center and the Space Needle, with an outdoor hot tub to boot. Rates average $120; the pet fee is $15 per pet per stay. 325 Aurora Ave. N.; 206/441-0400; www.seattle pacifichotel.com.

W Hotel: At this ultra-sleek hotel, the staff goes out of its way to make dogs feel like members of the family. "Dear Doggie," begins a letter addressed specifically to them, "Kick back and enjoy your visit!" The lobby is decked out in suede, leather, and polished aluminum; the rooms are subtle and tasteful. You might even rub noses with the mastiff named Lucius who's a regular bar hound. Rates are $250–400. Dogs are an additional $25 per pet per night, which barely covers all the wonderful things pets receive in their care package. 1112 4th Ave.; 800/W HOTELS (800/946-8357); www.whotels.com.

More Accommodations: Please look under *Chain Hotels* in the *Resources* section for additional places to stay in this area.

Pioneer Square

Pioneer Square, Seattle's first neighborhood, struggles under the weight of a sizable homeless population and a rowdy late-night reputation. However, the enduring character of Seattle's birthplace shines in beautifully restored Richardsonian Revival that house more than 30 art galleries. If you're around on the first Thursday of the month, First Thursday Artwalk is a tradition to be seen. For more events, go to www.pioneersquare.org.

PARKS, BEACHES, AND RECREATION AREAS

27 Waterfall Garden

😸 (See Central Seattle map on page 184)

Of human interest more than canine, this Zen rock and water garden provides a much needed urban respite. The 22-foot waterfall can refresh city-weary souls. It is a surprising find, crammed into a tiny space. It also marks the birthplace of the United Parcel Service. Who knew?

Look closely for the garden on 2nd Avenue S., south of Washington Street. Open 8 A.M.–6 P.M., with gates that lock after hours. 219 2nd Ave. S.

PLACES TO EAT

Armandino's Salumi: A legendary butcher shop and curer of meats, Salumi is where no one thinks twice about ordering a meat-stuffed meat sandwich. The trouble is, they give you samples while you're in line, and then you're a goner for the best hand-cured meats this side of Manhattan. We've never made it to the daily pasta and soup specials, most of which actually include vegetables. It made us think of the Turduckhen, the turkey stuffed with a duck stuffed with a chicken, stuffed with stuffing. A dog must have thought of that one. 309 3rd Ave. S., 206/621-8772; www.salumicuredmeats.com.

International District

The "I.D.," as locals call it, is a unified neighborhood of at least a dozen distinct Pan-Asian ethnic groups, reportedly the most varied of it's kind in the United States. At points called Chinatown and Nihonmachi (Japan Town), the mayor renamed it in 1951 to encompass all nationalities. Herbal pharmacies, import stores, temples, restaurants, and fortune cookie factories are a jumble. The glorified grocery store Uwajimaya boggles the mind with the largest selection of Asian products gathered together on the West Coast and an international food court (600 5th Ave. S.; 206/624-6248; www.uwajimaya.com).

PARKS, BEACHES, AND RECREATION AREAS

28 Kobe Terrace
🐾🐾 (See Central Seattle map on page 184)

A steep hike up 7th Avenue leads to Kobe Terrace Park, named in honor of Seattle's sister city of Kobe, Japan. The history of this acre of terraced hillside dates back to 1974, when Kobe gifted to Seattle a four-ton, 200-year-old *yukimi-doro* "snow viewing" stone lantern. In the spring, the "snow" is actually thousands of tiny petals from the park's Mt. Fuji cherry trees, floating in the breeze.

Kobe Terrace is easiest to access at 6th Avenue and Main Street. 221 6th Ave. S.

PLACES TO EAT

Seattle Deli: If you don't speak Vietnamese, Laotian, or Thai, your best bet is to grab a to-go box and fill it with anything and everything from the hot lunch buffet. Even unable to read any of the labels, we've never had a bad experience at this international grocery and deli. 225 12th Ave. S.; 206/328-0106.

Madrona and Leschi

In 1975, the Historic Seattle Preservation and Development Authority hired architectural expert Victor Steinbrueck to inventory the homes of these old Seattle neighborhoods. The report found Victorian, bungalow, colonial, Tudor cottage, California cottage, ranch house, medieval mansion, early northwest regional, and contemporary structures, which give you and your dog an interesting and varied neighborhood in which to take walks.

PARKS, BEACHES, AND RECREATION AREAS

29 Leschi and Frink Parks
🐾🐾🐾 (See Central Seattle map on page 184)

This is a tale of two parks, one wild, one tamed, a before and after picture, perhaps, of what much of Seattle looked like before settlement. The former, a well-manicured, rolling hillside that hugs the water, planted with a rose garden and exotic trees, facing a marina. The latter, higher up, 1.3 miles of steep trails through an overgrown ravine. The path upward leads first to a restroom, then splits: right to a tennis court, and left to a playground and sandbox, before the wilds take over altogether. Careful, as you'll have to cross Lake Washington Boulevard several times, which winds through the park and is very popular with Sunday drivers and cyclists. Local dogs are regulars, resting under lake willows, or hoofing it up the hills.

From downtown, take Yesler Way going east, all the way to a right on 32nd Avenue, and immediately left onto Washington Street, which becomes Frink Place. You'll drive through the park you'll soon be hiking through. Take a sharp left onto Lake Washington Boulevard, and a sharp right on Lakeside Avenue, to park in the lot at Leschi on your left. Two-hour parking is free 6 A.M.–midnight. Leschi: 201 Lakeside Ave. S.; Frink: 398 Lake Washington Blvd. S.

30 Lake Washington Boulevard

🐾🐾🐾 (See Central Seattle map on page 184)

The alternating gravel and sidewalk paths along scenic Lake Washington are populated with walkers in any weather and the winding road is a regular training ground for Seattle cyclists and pleasure cruisers. Starting all the way south in Seward Park, or at the Genesee Dog Park if you prefer, you can choose the length of your walk past Sayres Park, Park, and Day Street Park. The lakeside walking trails continue up to Leschi and Madrona parks. Views of Bellevue and the Cascades are reflected in the water. It's a lovely dog walk, one that goes on forever.

Lake Washington Boulevard trails parallel the road from Park on the north to Seward Park on the South, then becomes Lakeside Avenue north of U.S. Highway 90. Restrooms and parking are available at most parks along the way. You're on your own for pet supplies.

Access Lake Washington Boulevard from E. Madison Street or Madrona Drive. Park is between Madrona Drive to the north and E. Alder Street to the south, north of I-90. 853 Lake Washington Blvd.

PLACES TO EAT

Pert's Deli: At this family-owned, homespun deli, owner May actually shook her head, grinned, and said "Tsk! Tsk! Parking money," when we used quarters fished out of the car ashtray to buy a peanut butter and chocolate chip cookie. Pick a deli salad from the fresh case, grab a Hank's black cherry soda off the shelf, and relax at one of three sidewalk umbrella tables, without being scolded. 120 Lakeside Ave., Leschi, Suite B; 206/325-0277.

St. Clouds: This neighborhood bistro is named after the orphanage in John Irving's *The Cider House Rules*. An orphan himself, Cooper rates this spot as his #1 favorite in the entire book. He may be biased because he knows the owner. A gated courtyard allows you and your dog to enjoy full service outdoors for dinner or heavenly weekend brunch. The menu mixes comfy favorites like mac 'n' cheese, fried chicken and mashers, and burgers with more trendy fare such as seared Ahi tuna, goat cheese and pear bruschetta, and market fish of the day. The kids' menu was designed by kids for kids. Ever had a fluffernutter (a.k.a. Cloudy Day) sandwich? Kids, make your parents order you one. They regularly feature local bands and the bartender mixes a mean Metaxa sidecar. Doggone it, you simply can't pass up this place. 1131 34th Ave., Madrona; 206/726-1522; www.stclouds.com.

Verité Coffee: The skeptics among you may be saying, "Not another coffeehouse." Ah, but this is the home of the Cupcake Royale, gourmet buttercream-frosted cupcakes! Verité also serves gourmet grilled paninis, has outdoor sidewalk chairs, and is next to the Madrona playground. 1101 34th Ave.; 206/709-4497; www.cupcakeroyale.com.

Beacon Hill and Mount Baker

Headquarters of Amazon.com, Beacon Hill brings greater diversity to Seattle with Asians, African-Americans, and Latin Americans together making up 80 percent of the Hill's population. Mount Baker, closer to the water, has an architectural heritage as diverse as the ethnic and socioeconomic backgrounds of the people who reside there.

PARKS, BEACHES, AND RECREATION AREAS

31 Dr. Jose Rizal Park

🐾 😾 🐕 (See Central Seattle map on page 184)

Dr. Rizal was a Filipino Renaissance man who made lasting contributions to the fields of social and political reform, engineering, medicine, art, and literature before he was executed in 1896 for participating in the Philippine Revolution. During the 1900s, people of Filipino descent formed the second-largest minority population in Seattle, after the Chinese, and this 10-acre park is in their honor.

The off-leash area may be the only known dog park that's busier during workdays than evenings or weekends because it's right across the street from the headquarters of Amazon.com, an employer that allows people to bring their pooches into work with them. Rumor has it there are 90-plus dogs who are office regulars.

Four acres of open and wooded areas follow a short trail. Running water, pooper-scoopers, and a compost bin are provided. A full fence with a double gate surrounds the area, which is largely brush, although the city is working on landscaping it with native plants and trees and getting rid of the overgrown blackberry bushes.

From here, you have the most amazing views of the city from any Seattle dog park. You're close to Seahawks Stadium, SAFECO field, south downtown, and Elliott Bay. It's noisy because the park borders the I-90 highway interchange.

Take exit 165A toward James Street, stay straight onto 6th Avenue, then turn left onto Yesler Way. Turn right onto Boren Avenue, then bear right onto 12th Avenue South. After the Jose P. Rizal Bridge, immediately turn right onto Charles Street, which continues as 12th Avenue. You'll see the park off to your right up the hill. Park up the hill in the parking lot and walk back down to the off-leash area entrance. Parking is limited to two hours 6 A.M.–10 P.M. 1008 12th Ave. S.

32 Blue Dog Pond

🐾🐕 (See Central Seattle map on page 184)

Is it: a) a rainwater detention basin; b) a sculpture garden; c) an off-leash dog park? If you guessed d) all of the above, you would be correct. To say it is damp here occasionally would be an understatement. During storms this big hole in the ground is designed to hold water until the city's drainage system can handle it. But it doesn't always rain in Seattle, honest, and the area gets put to good use when it's not flooded. Who better than dogs to fully appreciate playing in the mud? The little 0.25-acre area is fully fenced and gated. It has a water pump, and a couple of benches.

The park, also known by the name Sam Smith Park, is on the northwest corner of S. Massachusetts Street and Martin Luther King Jr. Way S. You can leave your car along 26th Avenue S., a dead-end street alongside the park's west edge. Open 4 A.M.–11:30 P.M.

33 Colman Park and Mount Baker Bathing Beach

🐾🐾 (See Central Seattle map on page 184)

Once a year, the first weekend in August, Seattleites flock to these interconnected parks to get buzzed at the culminating weekend of the annual Seafair Celebration (www.seafair.com). They get buzzed by the roaring Blue Angels air show overhead, they get buzzed by the hydroplane boats, racing a triangular course on Lake Washington, and they likely get buzzed on illicit concoctions on ice in water coolers, despite city regulations against alcohol in parks.

While perhaps too crowded for pooches during this particular celebration, Colman Park is enjoyable the remainder of the year. It is a starting point for walks along Lake Washington or a spot for a lakeside picnic under ancient, drooping Willows.

From I-90, take Exit 3, going south on Rainier Avenue for a mile. Turn left onto S. McClellan Street and follow it east toward the water. You'll see the start of the park to your left. If you take a slight left on Lake Park Drive, you can drive alongside the park down to the lake, with several opportunities to park along the way. Open 6 A.M.–10 P.M. 1800 Lake Washington Blvd. S.

PLACES TO EAT

Mioposto Café and Pizzeria: Meaning "my place" in Italian, this place welcomes you to come on over for amazing olive-oil and lemon-drizzled asparagus, for starters, and crisp, thin-crust pizzas with fresh basil and sun-dried tomatoes. Come on down to relax in a tidy row of Adirondack chairs on the sidewalk, and they'll open up the window walls so you can watch people across the street at Colman Park. 3601 S. McClellan St.; 206/760-3400; www.chowfoods.com.

West Seattle

A peninsula unto itself, this community is Seattle's oldest. The Denny Party, Seattle's first settlers, landed on Alki prior to moving over to Elliott Bay. Incorporated in 1902, it was annexed into the young city in 1907. For shopping and dining, go to The Junction, at the intersection of Alaska Street and California Avenue. From the end of Fauntleroy, catch the ferry to Vashon Island and the Kitsap Peninsula.

PARKS, BEACHES, AND RECREATION AREAS

34 Alki Beach Walk

🐾🐾🐾 🐾 (See Central Seattle map on page 184)

Dogs are not allowed on the beach at Alki. This has never stopped them from being a part of the see, sea, and be seen scene along the two-mile sidewalk promenade. Join the inline skaters and cyclists, off-road baby strollers, joggers, and sightseers getting the lead out. Alki is Seattle's seasonal equivalent of a California beach community, with rare sunbathers and beach volleyball. Aside from people-watching, the 360 degree views are unequalled in town, starting with the Seattle skyline across Elliott Bay, then wrapping around the point to the snow-frosted Olympic Mountains.

To reach Alki from downtown, take the West Seattle Bridge and peel off at the Avalon Way/Harbor Avenue exit. Turn right at the end of the off-ramp onto Harbor Avenue, which becomes Alki Avenue around the point. Watch the signs for street parking. Most of the action is around the point on the west side of the peninsula.

35 Schmitz Preserve

🐾🐾🐾🐾 (See Central Seattle map on page 184)

This section of forest has remained largely unchanged by human intervention since it became a park in 1908. From a short, paved road and parking lot in the northwest corner, trails lead off in at least three directions, eventually all connecting together and looping back to the beginning. The trails lead through an old-growth forest, even though the largest trees were logged prior to the land's protected status. Gradually, more than 50 acres were put together to form the existing park. Streams and bridges, stairs, and old roads add interest to the hilly terrain. It is an excellent place to take any trail hound. Cooper assumes the role of Protectorate of the Realm from squirrel intruders the moment he enters. Schmitz makes his list of the top five city walks.

From the West Seattle Bridge, take the Admiral Way exit, all the way up the hill and down again past California, remaining on Admiral Way. Turn abruptly left on Stevens Street, for the park entrance on your right. Be kind to the neighbors as you park on the street. 5551 S.W. Admiral Way; www .schmitzpark.org.

36 Jack Block Public Shoreline Access

🐾🐾 (See Central Seattle map on page 184)

Created in 1998, and managed by the Port of Seattle, this 5.8-acre shoreline park is as much industrial as park. Through a railroad tie entrance and across the tracks are access to a pier, viewing platforms, and wide sidewalks, with bathrooms and picnic tables for convenience. For boat nuts, it's one of the best places to watch the maritime goings-on at Harbor Island and the Port of

Seattle. The nautical theme is continued and carried out well in the park. Flags fly from a stationary mast, and a sandbox area has tanker fenders to climb on, painted the colors of beach balls. Just tell your Toy Fox Terrier you're taking him for a walk, he won't care where.

From the West Seattle Bridge, take the Avalon Way/Harbor Avenue exit. Turn right at the bottom of the off ramp onto Harbor Avenue. The park will be to your right shortly thereafter. 2130 Harbor Ave. S.W.

37 Delridge Community Park

🐾 (See Central Seattle map on page 184)

This one's more for the kiddies than the doggies, but perhaps you've got some of both. The wading pool rocks, the playground is spiffy, and big lawns with deciduous shade trees allow level ground for picnic blanket placement. If your dog is one to enjoy simply being with the family, contemplating his fuzzy navel and watching the world go by, this is the place to bring him.

From the West Seattle Bridge, take the exit onto Delridge Way. Stay in the left lane, which will curve underneath the overpass in a sharp cloverleaf to head south on Delridge Way. The park is on the right, after the intersection with Genesee Street. 4501 Delridge Way S.W.

38 Lincoln Park

🐾🐾🐾🐾 (See Central Seattle map on page 184)

Put together by piecemeal acquisitions over the years since 1922, the park suitably reflects the varied nature of West Seattle residents, who take great pride in being perceived as eclectic. Rather than giving a laundry list of the park's features, Coop 'n' Isis direct you to the picnic areas, the wooded trail that defines the perimeter of the park, and the long beach walk on Puget Sound in this 135-acre park. The trail is refreshing, a level one-mile walk in and out of the forest and then along the water. It's a fine line between walking the waterfront trail and being on the beach in the water, one that dogs are not supposed to cross. If your dog stays on leash and generally behaves herself, you should be fine.

From I-5, take Exit 163A, the West Seattle Bridge exit. Stay in the second to the right-hand lane and follow the signs to Fauntleroy Way S.W. Stay on Fauntleroy, almost the length of the peninsula, until you come to the park on the right-hand side of the street. If you end up in line for the Vashon Ferry, you've gone too far. Open 6 A.M.–11 P.M. 8011 Fauntleroy Way S.W.

39 Roxhill Park

🐾🐾🐾 (See Central Seattle map on page 184)

This is an easy morning starter park, with several good things going for it, primarily in the northern half of the 13.5 acres, facing Barton Street, across from Westwood Village Mall. It's got a sedge bog to walk through on gravel trails and boardwalks, with scents ripe enough for a dog's nose without being offensive to a human's. There are fenced soccer practice fields, which make for good ball tossing when not in use. And, according to Cooper, there are almost always leftover tidbits in the grass from weekend birthday parties and barbeques. The park's large playground is very popular with the preschool and kindergarten set, and as any good scavenger will tell you, they leave behind a lot of oat cereal O's, fish-shaped cheddar crackers, and wafer cookie bits, if the squirrels don't get to them first.

After coming over the West Seattle Bridge, get in one of the two left lanes to turn south on 35th Avenue S.W. Travel three miles and turn left, traveling east on Barton Street. Turn right on 30th Avenue to the large parking lot on your left. Restrooms and garbage are available.

40 Westcrest Dog Park

🐾🐾🐾🐾🐕 (See Central Seattle map on page 184)

At Westcrest, all roads lead to the dog park. Eight gates lead from wooded trails to the fully enclosed off-leash area, including our favorite, the Greenbelt Trail, which can be enjoyed on leash. They make good use of the four-acre OLA, with it's own trails that lead to several open spaces, including a hillside. Often, dogs come in clumps, with an overseer from a dog-sitting or dog-walking service. It's obvious that some thought and money went into creating a quality dog park here in the bohemian West Seattle neighborhood. For the dogs, there is a drinking fountain, trees, and open space. For people, there are benches and chairs, a covered shelter, and restrooms nearby outside of the fence.

From I-5, take Exit 163A onto the West Seattle Bridge. Take the Delridge Way S.W. exit, and stay in the left lane on the exit ramp to get onto Delridge Way. Go south for 3.3 miles on Delridge, turn left on S.W. Trenton Street, go 0.6 miles, turn left on 9th Avenue S.W., and take the next right on S.W. Cloverdale Street. Go four blocks and turn right into the parking lot on 5th Avenue S.W. This is the main entrance into the dog park. Open 4 A.M.–11:30 P.M. 8806 8th Ave. S.W.

PLACES TO EAT

Bakery Nouveau: We double-dog-dare you to compare this bakery café with the finest you'd find in Europe. The owner is the 2005 *Champion du Monde de la Boulangerie;* in essence, he was elected the best bread and pastry maker in the world by an international panel of peers. Everything tastes as beautiful as it looks, which is why weekend lines are long, a good excuse to mingle and strike up a conversation with cute local dog owners. 4737 California Ave. S.W.; 206/923-0534; www.bakerynouveau.com.

Beveridge Place Pub: Stephanie, and her goldens Petunia and Moose, reminded us that we must include this major local hangout to make this guide complete. While no food is served here, they don't mind if you order delivery from the many local choices to bring over to the patio and enjoy with one of 22 brews on draught. We also met the "Bassets for Obama" here, and if you haven't seen that *YouTube* video yet, you must Google it. After a move to a new building in 2008, this old standby is looking mighty spiffy. "This is our *Cheers*," says Stephanie. 6413 California Ave. S.W.; 206/932-9906; beveridgeplacepub.com.

Endolyne Joe's: This was the end of the line for old Trolley #2 in West Seattle, and Joe was a ladies' man conductor with a penchant for high living. At Endolyne's, half of the menu stays the same all year, offering unbeatable comfort food; the other half changes quarterly to feature unique cuisines of the world. There is no outdoor eating, so the deck out front is reserved for the many canines who wait patiently for their owners to bring out a bite of meat-loaf or a smidgeon of honey buttermilk fried chicken. 9261 45th Ave. S.W.; 206/937-5637; www.chowfoods.com.

Husky Ice Cream and Deli: You can't go wrong at a place named for a dog. These DAWG fans make dozens of ice cream flavors, scooping generous globs of it into homemade waffle cones. Cold and grilled specialty sandwiches feature exotic flavors like marinated artichokes with turkey, cashew chicken, liverwurst and pickle, or olive loaf and cream cheese on dark rye. To top it all off, there's an eye-popping selection of imported gourmet foods, chocolates, and cookies. Order to go. 4721 California Ave S.W.; 206/937-2810; www.huskydeli.com.

Spuds Fish and Chips: Another Seattle institution, kids on break from school have eaten battered and fried fish in the bright blue and white building on Alki since 1934. Coop's advice: Skip the fries, pay $1 for the extra piece of hand-cut halibut or cod, and get the large tubs of tartar and cocktail sauce to take across the street to Alki Beach Park. 2666 Alki Ave.; 206/938-0606.

Georgetown and Columbia City

PARKS, BEACHES, AND RECREATION AREAS

41 Genesee Dog Park

🐾 🐾 🐾 🐕 (See Central Seattle map on page 184)

Genesee Park is a wide field that extends about five city blocks. To the south are kids' ball fields, with the off-leash area taking up the entire north end. Three acres of open space have been lovingly designed by landscape architects for maximum canine enjoyment. It all sits elevated on a slight plateau, created by a garbage landfill, which tends to keep it drier than many of its local counterparts. Small trees, rocks, benches, and sitting logs are strategically placed for maximum comfort around the gravel play area. A community bulletin board and doggie drinking fountain round out the details.

Two double-gated entrances give you places to deal with leashes, which are extremely important until you get into the fenced area, because roadside parking is along an extremely busy thoroughfare. Genesee is a popular area, conveniently located in South/Central Seattle. In October, pups strut their stuff in

DOG-EAR YOUR CALENDAR

You might wish you, too, had fur when running or walking the **Furry 5K** around Seward Park in Seattle. It can still be chilly when this race is run in June. Proceeds benefit the Help the Animals Fund, providing veterinary care to shelter animals. Register early for $20 to get your T-shirt, $15 if you want to get the lead out but don't need the shirt. One fee covers you and your dog, who must run on an eight-foot or shorter leash. This is seriously fun business—results are timed and winners posted. 206/386-7387; www.furry5k.com.

Calling all ghostbusters, ghouls, and ghost dogs to the annual **Dog-O-Ween** costume contest at South Seattle's Genesee off-leash area. While some dogs have been known to sulk when costumed, at least they'll get to mix and mingle with their friends while you raise money for COLA, Citizens for Off-Leash Areas, Seattle's pro-pup-park organization. The festive fundraiser is held, rain or rain, 11 A.M.–2 P.M., with food and fashion, door prizes, a silent auction, and vendor booths. The suggested donation for your pet to enter the costume contest is $5; bring your checkbook to bid on auction items. Call for event dates. 206/264-5573; www.coladog.org.

the annual Dog-O-Ween costume contest to benefit Seattle's off-leash areas. The park shares lakeside borders with Lake Washington Boulevard, making it a great launching point for a day's walk along the water.

Take Rainier Avenue South to Genesee Street, and go east to 46th Street. Open 4 A.M.–11:30 P.M. 4316 S. Genesee St.; www.coladog.org.

42 Seward Park

🐾🐾🐾 (See Central Seattle map on page 184)

Most of this city park's 300 acres are left in their natural state, an old-growth forest where eagles are frequently sighted in the tops of trees. The forest and fern canopy in the core of the park is so thick that hiking the internal trails of the park can be downright spooky. That's just one reason most park-goers stick to the 2.5-mile perimeter trail, a wide road suitable for wheelchair-users. The other main motivator for using that particular trail is the continuous view from all angles of the park, a thumb of a peninsula that sticks out into Lake Washington. And, if you haven't had your fill by the time you make it around, the trail continues north on Lake Washington Boulevard for many more miles.

From I-5 southbound from Seattle, take Exit 163A, and keep left at the fork in the ramp onto Columbian Way S. Follow the arterial road as it weaves, to the right on 15th Avenue S., to the left on S. Columbian Way, and to the right on S. Alaska Street. Turn right onto Rainier Avenue S (State Route 167), and left onto S. Orcas Street into the park. Open 4 A.M.–11:30 P.M. 206/684-4396.

43 Martha Washington Park

🐾🐾🐾 (See Central Seattle map on page 184)

A city park doesn't have to be elaborate to be appreciated, as Martha Washington proves. It is a beautiful expanse, a gradual slope of green lawn, with stately trees and a short trail to the waterfront on the lake of the same name. It is an ideal place to bring your picnic blanket and a flying disc-shaped object. Locals say the park can get packed with families on summer weekends, but during the week and the winter, there are often more dogs here than humans. Much smaller and harder to find than nearby Seward Park, your Heeler can head here, and while humanity is headed there, a dog can be free to be who she needs to be in this quiet neighborhood, if you catch our drift. Or, at least, watch the waves drift from two small beaches. Catch a glimpse of Mount Rainier as your Collie catches the edge of a disc and brings it back to you, again. Lounge under a tree and look out over Lake Washington, as your Labrador returns the slobbery tennis ball longingly to your feet, again.

To get here, follow the directions to Seward Park. Then, from Orcas Street, turn right on Seward Park Avenue S. and then right again on Oakhurst Avenue S. Go straight through the stop sign, where Oakhurst becomes 57th Avenue S. to the park on your left. Open 6 A.M.–sunset; 6612 57th Ave. S.

PLACES TO EAT

All City Coffee: Hanging out for a single morning, we never saw so many dogs in one place. Dogs arrived in baskets on motorcycles and bicycles, dogs walked up, with and without owners. There were pups sitting in, on, and around the plastic sidewalk furniture. There wasn't so much as a biscuit jar, and still, the canines kept coming. Their coffee's pretty good, and so are the pastries. We have no other explanation for it. 1205 S. Vale St., Georgetown; 206/767-7146; www.allcitycoffee.com.

Rainier Beach

PARKS, BEACHES, AND RECREATION AREAS

44 Kubota Garden

🐾🐾 🐾 (See Central Seattle map on page 184)

Our first thought upon visiting this park was, "We've lived here 15 years and haven't visited yet? What's wrong with us?" Beyond the surprise that this garden exists where it does, and that visiting it is free, the unexpected keeps popping up. Around every corner is another offshoot trail that leads to a waterfall, or a bridge, or a rock outcropping, or a secret bench, all in miniature. The German orderliness in the Dachsies' nature helps them appreciate the control exerted in Japanese gardening to keep every leaf, rock, and needle in its proper place. Humans probably enjoy it more, but most dogs we know would be happy to be outside taking a garden walk with their peeps, no matter what, no matter where.

From I-5 southbound, take Exit 158, and go left toward Martin Luther King Jr. Way. Continue up the hill on Ryan Way, and turn left on 51st Avenue S. Make two immediate rights (onto Roxbury, then Renton), to go south on Renton Avenue S. Turn right on 55th Avenue S. to the garden entrance. 9817 55th Avenue S.; www.kubota.org.

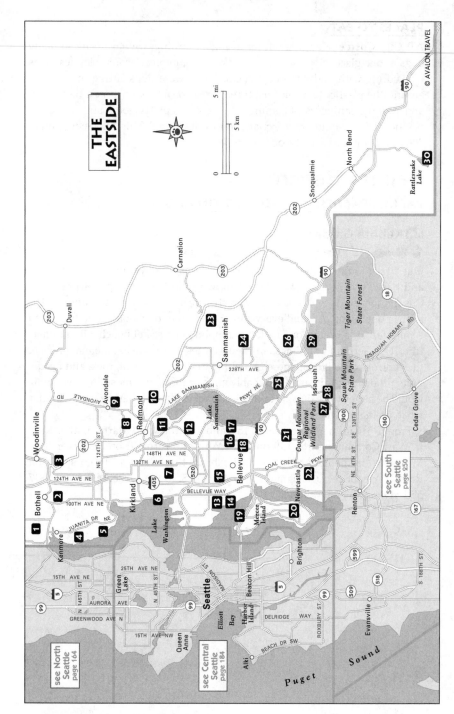

CHAPTER 8

The Eastside

Anything east of Lake Washington is the Eastside, the region's silicon for-est, led by giants including Microsoft and Nintendo. In the home of high technology, PDA-phone addicts and gamers might never get outside, and that would be a crime. From a dog's eye view, Seattle should have a serious case of green envy, for Eastside trees are bigger and more plentiful, lakes are larger, mountains loom, and valleys shine in the sun. Speed limits tend to be slow on the Eastside, averaging 25 to 30 m.p.h., so slow down and enjoy the scenery.

Cooper and Isis were impressed by the quality and clarity of trail mark-ers in both Redmond and Bellevue. They would like to see fairer policies in regards to dogs on city lakeside beaches; Kirkland prohibits them on beaches all year, and Bellevue allows them on the sand only when the sun's not out, September 16–May 31.

PICK OF THE LITTER–THE EASTSIDE

BEST DOG PARKS
Marymoor Dog Park, Redmond (page 235)
Beaver Lake Dog Park, Sammamish (page 243)

BEST HIKES
Cougar Mountain Regional Wildlands Preserve, Issaqauqh (page 245)
Tiger Mountain State Forest, Issaquah (page 246)

BEST PLACES TO EAT
The Purple Café, Woodinville (page 229)
Gilbert's Bagel and Deli, Bellevue (page 240)

BEST PLACES TO STAY
Willows Lodge, Woodinville (page 229)
Bellevue Club Hotel, Bellevue (page 240)

EXTENDED REGIONAL TRAILS

Sammamish River Trail
🐾🐾🐾

The transition between the Burke-Gilman Trail and this trail is so seamless, people often think they are one and the same. This segment adds about 11 miles through the valleys on the east side of Lake Washington, starting near Blyth Park in Bothell on the north end and ending at the dog equivalent of Disneyland, Marymoor Park. Soft-surface paths run parallel to the asphalt between Woodinville and Marymoor. The trail winds along the east side of the river, past Chateau Ste. Michelle and Columbia River Wineries and the Red Hook Brewery. In this chapter, we call out two offshoots from the trail, the Puget Power Trail and the Bridle Crest Trail. SRT got a facelift in 2008, with newly installed benches, picnic tables, and trash cans. Go to www.king county.gov for information.

Snoqualmie Valley Trail
🐾🐾🐾🐾

This crushed-rock and original ballast rail trail extends 36 miles through farms and forests, from Duvall down to North Bend. You'll pass over former railroad trestles, to which handmade decks and rails have been added. A long tunnel also remains, deep and dark enough that you'll definitely want to bring a flashlight. It is almost completely rural, offing excellent valley and Cascade Mountain views. Access and parking are available at McCormick Park in Duvall and at Rattlesnake Lake in North Bend, where the gravel trail begins across the road from the first parking lot. The trail also connects to the John Wayne Pioneer Trail at Rattlesnake Lake. 206/296-8687; www.kingcounty.gov.

Tolt Pipeline Trail
🐾🐾

This dirt and crushed rock surface trail travels 13.7 miles through a 100-foot wide swath of land north from the Snoqualmie River Valley to Bothell. There are the disadvantages of steep sections and busy road crossings, the advantages of being well maintained and easy to access from Blyth Park in Bothell, East Norway Hill Park in Woodinville, and along the Sammamish River Trail. It passes as many pastures and farms as residential areas. www.kingcounty.gov.

Bothell

Ah, the first signs of spring in Bothell: daffodils, crocuses, and white poop-bag dispensers restocked with pickup mitts in all the city parks. At the top of Lake Washington, Bothell serves as a buffer between Seattle and the Eastside.

PARKS, BEACHES, AND RECREATION AREAS

1 Wallace Swamp Creek
🐾🐾 (See Eastside map on page 224)

Managed by the city of Kenmore, this 17-acre wetland park pulls the pups in with rich, earthy smells and a 0.25-mile trail over a bridge and through spacious woods to a rocky beach around a bend in Swamp Creek. Paved and gravel paths converge at a picnic spot guarded by birch trees. Efforts to restore native vegetation and return spawning salmon to the site still allow some stream access. By the time you read this, the natural nature of the park may be diminished by baseball fields and a doubled parking lot. We suspect it will still have a leg to stand on as a dog destination.

From I-405, take Exit 23 and go west on State Route 522 for 3.5 miles. Turn right on 73rd Avenue N.E. and go another mile. Keep left at the fork; parking is on the left.

2 Blyth Park
🐾🐾 (See Eastside map on page 224)

Bothell's largest city park is your direct link to the Sammamish River Trail and the Tolt Pipeline Trail. Its 20 comfortable acres sit on a high bank over the

Sammamish River, with paved walking paths to circumnavigate restrooms and picnic shelters. Simple playgrounds are made of recycled materials, including a tire hill and former railroad tie steps, leading down a steep hill to the water, where Isis saw a chocolate lab swimming, no surprise there, intent on catching up with a couple of ducks who must have been laughing as they effortlessly paddled just out of his reach. The far-end of the park backs up against the Wayne Golf Course. Formerly a factory site, Blyth now serves in an olfactory capacity for your canine friends.

Take Exit 23 from I-405. Head west on State Route 522. Bear right onto Kaysner Way, turn left at Main Street, and turn left at 102nd Avenue N.E. Turn right at the intersection after the bridge, onto West Riverside Drive, which dead-ends into the park. Open 8 A.M.–dusk. 16950 W. Riverside Dr.; 425/486-7430.

PLACES TO EAT

Alexa's Café: "Dogs, frogs, whatever," says Leigh, owner of Alexa's and a high-demand catering business. Veggie breakfast burritos and chicken curry croissants, tomato basil soup and Bite Me brownies disappear quickly at a couple of sidewalk tables. Hang out at Alexa's if you want to meet the locals. 10115 Main St.; 425/402-1754; www.alexascafe.com.

Steve's Café: Of course they allow dogs, they said at Steve's down-to-earth diner. After all, the sidewalk furniture is no-nonsense plastic, where they serve, you know, "regular stuff" for breakfast, noontime soups and sand-wiches, and treats from the pastry case—meaning people treats. 10116 Main St.; 425/487-0481.

PLACES TO STAY

Extended Stay Deluxe: Come stay a while at studios with fully equipped kitchens and plenty of work space. Bring your dog, if you've got one (and no more than one) for $25 per night up to $150 per extended stay. Rates of $110–130 a night decrease the lon-ger the booking. 22122 17th Ave S.E.; 425/482-2900; www.extendedstay hotels.com.

Residence Inn by Marriott: This long-term stay hotel is smartly turned out, with a decent green setting in Can-yon Park. Two dogs, 50 pounds or less, are allowed for a $75 cleaning fee, charged once per stay. Rates range $100–195. 11920 N.E. 195th St.; 425/485-3030; www.residenceinnbothell.com.

Woodinville

Woodinville's 30 or more wineries are the big tourist draw, as is Molbak's famous garden nursery, founded in 1956, where dogs are always welcome.

PARKS, BEACHES, AND RECREATION AREAS

🐾 Wilmot Gateway Park

🐾🐾 (See Eastside map on page 224)

Upstanding citizen Jerry Wilmot—Woodinville founding father, Rotary member, and longtime general manager of Molbak's Nursery—is the namesake founder and funder of a key half-moon-shaped stopover on the Sammamish River Trail. A grand, ornate Pergola covers four square picnic tables on a plaza of commemorative tiles and bricks celebrating all who made the park possible through contributions.

A grass bowl of lawn is slathered with sunbathers on a bright day, and dotted with dogs people-watching as inline skaters, cyclists, and trail walkers bustle by. It's a hangout, for sure, with a playground on the north end. There is a restroom, and parking is across a very busy street. Thankfully, the triggered crosswalk light is very responsive, all the better to get you to your picnic blanket sooner.

From I-405, take Exit 23A going east on State Route 522. After a mile, take the State Route 202 exit to Woodinville/Redmond. Exit to the right and stay on State Route 522 as it becomes 131st Avenue N.E. The park is to the right, past 175th Street. Open dawn–dusk. 17301 131st Ave. N.E.; 425/398-9327.

PLACES TO EAT

The Purple Café: The buzz generated by a restaurant packed with happy people offers its own high. Add to that the glow in your cheeks from this wine bar's extensive list of vintages by the glass, and the contentment that comes from eating on the patio with your pet from a menu designed for the fine art of grazing, and you'll be practically apoplectic with Purple's infectious pleasure. 14459 Woodinville-Redmond Rd.; 425/483-7129; www.thepurplecafe.com.

Texas Smokehouse Bar-B-Q: Dine in, take out, or catered, Cooper can always tell if his ribs have been slow smoked over an open fire, the old-fashioned way. 14455 Woodinville-Redmond Rd.; 425/486-1957; www .texas-smokehouse.com.

PLACES TO STAY

Willows Lodge: The Willows combines Japanese influences, Native American art, and extravagant luxury into an appealing package. Speaking of packages, pet guests at Willows Lodge receive a full gift basket and doggie room service menu as part of the Willows' V.I.P. Program (Very Important Pet). Ruthie the

DOG-EAR YOUR CALENDAR

Watch for the **Dine Out with Your Dog** events, once each July and August, for the rare opportunity to eat together at the award-winning Barking Frog Restaurant at Willows Lodge. The bistro's northwest cuisine and wine list have garnered rave reviews from the press and public, and the courtyard seating is paw-approved for discriminating dogs. Three Dog Bakery prepares a three-course feast for the pets for $30; half of the proceeds go to the Seattle Animal Shelter. Check with Three Dog Bakery or Willows Lodge in early summer for more details (www.threedogbakery.com or www.willowslodge.com).

basset/rottie mix sits on her bed by the front desk to greet new pals at check-in. Rooms are rated nice ($240), nicer ($270), and nicest ($300); the pet fee is $25 per pet per stay. It's about 15 minutes north of Kirkland in the village of Woodinville. 14580 N.E. 145th St.; 425/424-3900; www.willowslodge.com.

Kirkland

Cows and canines are central to Kirkland, literally piled on top of each other in the Brad Rude sculpture at the main intersection of Lake Street and Central Way (okay, so it's really a coyote, close enough). Facing the eastern shore of Lake Washington, Kirkland keeps the feel of a waterfront resort town, even within spitting distance of mega-Microsoft. Dogs are allowed on leash in Kirkland's parks, which are largely waterfront, but not on the park beaches (Houghton, Waverly, Juanita) at any time during the year. Dogs are also not allowed in McAuliffe Park or Tot Lot Park, nor on the trails in Watershed Preserve, west of I-405 across from Bridle Trails State Park. The city's pet brochure says to call Kirkland Parks and Community Services at 425/587-3300 for more details.

PARKS, BEACHES, AND RECREATION AREAS

🐾 Saint Edward State Park

🐾🐾 (See Eastside map on page 224)

A Catholic seminary 1931–1977, 312-acre Saint Edward, just north of Kirkland, is a winner with local dog hiking aficionado Craig Romano. The stillness of reflecting on a higher power seems to be permanently infused into the park's 312 acres. Get a map of the hiker-only trails from the kiosk or park office, and work your way down the 0.75-mile trail to the undeveloped Lake Washington waterfront.

From Seattle, take Lake City Way, State Route 522, to Kenmore. Turn right onto 68th Avenue N.E. After a few blocks, 68th Avenue N.E. becomes Juanita Drive N.E. Proceed up Juanita Drive N.E. to Saint Edward State Park on the right. Drive into the park, bear right at the fork, then take the first right into a large parking area. Open 8 A.M.–dusk. 425/823-2992.

5 O. O. Denny Park

🐾🐾🐾 (See Eastside map on page 224)

Orion Denny, son of founder Arthur Denny, was the first white male whose birth was recorded in Seattle. It was his thoughtful widow who donated the land surrounding the Denny family's humble 1853 cabin to the city.

One of Denny's initials should stand for enjoying this park in the off-season. Your harrier might hope that the other O could stand for off-leash, but not since 2006, when the website began warning park patrons of increasing citations to manage the temptations.

The rough trails of Denny Park are not groomed, but that's okay, neither are quite a few of the dogs we've met there. The gentle lawns leading up to the shallow shoreline are the main draw at Denny, more peaceful than many beach parks because motorized watercraft are not allowed within a buffer zone 300 feet off the shoreline. Boardwalks and bridges cross the wettest of the wetlands, and Mount Rainier is visible to the south.

Follow I-405 north to the N.E. 116th Street exit, #20A (just north of Kirkland) and take a left at the stop light. Follow 116th Street two miles to the main intersection of Juanita, where it becomes Juanita Drive. From the intersection, go two miles and take a left on Holmes Point Drive. O. O. Denny is about two miles farther; the main parking area is on the left and the trail begins directly across the road. Open 6 A.M.–sunset. 12400 Holmes Point Dr. N.E..

6 Lake Washington Boulevard–Eastside

🐾 (See Eastside map on page 224)

Join the throngs of people walking the sidewalk of this waterfront promenade. It takes you past all of the prime real estate in town, the outdoor restaurants, galleries, and four beachfront city parks along its 1.2-mile length. If your dog wonders why you're making such a big deal about the views of Seattle and the lake, tell her you don't understand why she loves sniffing butts so much, but you don't give her grief about it.

Take the State Route 520 Bridge across the lake to Exit 14, follow the directions to Lake Washington Boulevard N.E., and stay in the left lane to continue straight on the boulevard. Free parking is available at the north end of the trail at the Kirkland Municipal Library parking garage.

7 Bridle Trails State Park and Bridle Crest Trail

🐾🐾 (See Eastside map on page 224)

Where equestrians and pedestrians meet, get along little doggie on 28 miles of trails through a lowland forest dominated by Douglas fir. There's little in the way of signage in this 482-acre wilderness in the city. If you've got the time, plunge into the heart of the park, or take the easy way out and follow the gravel perimeter trail.

The Bridle Crest Trail connects the state park to Marymoor Park to meet up with the Fido fanatics in Redmond, starting at the intersection of 132nd Avenue N.E. and paralleling N.E. 60th Street for a couple of miles. It's a corridor between suburban lots for a leisurely stroll along a soft surface path, although horses have right-of-way throughout. 800/233-0321.

Northbound: Take exit #17 off of I-405. At the end of the off-ramp, turn right and head south on 116th Avenue N.E. Continue straight through a four-way stop. The park entrance is located at the first opening in the trees on the left. 206/296-4281.

PLACES TO EAT

Cactus: Cactus' Mexican specialties have a Santa Fe style to them, with black beans and chipotle peppers making star appearances on the menu. The staff will put out water bowls on the sidewalk patio for the canine crowd, and they suggest that humans stick to the fresh-squeezed juice margaritas and Cuban mojitos. Southwest-inspired breakfast entrées have finally made this a three-meal-deal restaurant. 121 Park Ln.; 425/893-9799; www.cactus restaurants.com.

Grape Choice: We ask you, what better pairing is there than good friendships and fine wine? Downstairs from Planet Poochie is a wine bar with a pet-welcoming patio. See the beautiful golden retrievers on their website, for example. 7 Lakeshore Plaza; 425/827-7551; www.thegrapechoice.com.

Marina Park Grill: This marina cantina's popularity is of mastiff proportions. Reservations are recommended for this bistro in downtown Kirkland on the waterfront. To make room, your dog may have to sit just outside the fence next to your table. 89 Kirkland Ave.; 425/889-9000; www.marinaparkgrill.com.

Sasi's Café: Isis tried to talk them into letting dogs on the patio, but no go. Still, the food's good enough to get it to go to nearby Bridle Trails. Unusual sandwich combinations, such as pork loin with apricot chutney, and excellent green salads, soups, and cookies, make for a light lunch done right. 12630 N.E. 59th St.; 425/889-2411; www.sasiscafe.net.

PLACES TO STAY

Heathman Hotel Kirkland: When luxury knows no bounds, bring the hounds to the Heathman, for nightly stays ranging $200–800, plus a $200 refundable pet deposit. Pet people are housed in high style on the first floor of Kirkland's only luxury hotel. The world has been lavishing praise on Portland's original Heathman Hotel for years; it's time Washington got in on the action. 220 Kirkland Ave.; 425/284-5800; www.heathmankirkland.com.

La Quinta: When the pocketbook holds no pounds, the La Quinta's "No pet fees, no restrictions, no problem," policy is a perfect fit. Rates range $90–135. 10530 N.E. Northup Way; 425/828-6585.

More Accommodations: Please look under *Chain Hotels* in the *Resources* section for additional places to stay in this area.

Redmond

There are really only two words you need to know about Redmond: Microsoft and Marymoor, the software giant and the dog park by which all others are judged, respectively. Across the highway is the Redmond Town Center, an outdoor mall with abundant outdoor seating and a number of upscale food court options. All good dogs go first to the information center for a free biscuit.

PARKS, BEACHES, AND RECREATION AREAS

🟦 Jonathan Hartman

🐾🐾 (See Eastside map on page 224)

At this park, as in life, you have to look beyond the surface for true beauty. You'll see the welcome sign, bag dispenser, and trash can from the parking lot. Start on the paved trail, past the restrooms. Continue on the gravel trail, past the batting cages and football field. Find the woodchip trail past the meadow and playground, and, finally, you are among giant, towering evergreens on 40 acres. Take the quick forest loop, hop on the spur over to the tennis courts, walk out to 176th and down the street a bit to pick up another trail, over a stream to connect to the Ashford Trail, 0.85 mile to Avondale Road. All told, you can clock a couple of miles for the day round-trip.

Take State Route 520 to the end, as it becomes Avondale Road N.E., take the left fork to stay on Avondale at the intersection with Novelty Hill Road. Travel 0.4 mile and turn left on N.E. 104th Street. Drive another mile, past Redmond High School, the Redmond Pool, and the ball fields, and take a left on 172nd Avenue N.E., down to the second driveway on your left to the parking lot. 17300 N.E. 104th St.

🟦 Puget Power Trail–Farrel McWhirter Park

🐾🐾🐾 (See Eastside map on page 224)

Also called the P.S.E. Trail, for Puget Sound Energy, this three-mile run follows the power lines up switchbacks westward from the Sammamish River Trail to the north end of Farrel-McWhirter Park and on to Redmond Watershed Park and Trail. It crosses and jogs to the north a bit on Avondale Road at one

DIVERSION

No time to cook? Pop into **Paws Café** for home-cooked meals to thaw and heat up for dinner. Only, in this case, the top-quality custom meals are made strictly for animals, dogs and cats, by a certified pet nutritionist in close connection with sustainable, organic farmers and ranchers. Pasture-raised beef and lamb, free-range chicken and turkeys, and organic vegetables are the only ingredients in these meals. They are hide-savers for pets with allergies, joint trouble, or immune illnesses. Paws also stocks grain-free treats and yöghund probiotic yogurts for dogs with sensitive stomachs. While Shelly's cooking in the kitchen, low maintenance daycare dogs hang out in the Paws Corral, where training, nutrition counseling, and classes are also on offer. 16505 Redmond Way, Suite E; 425/256-2073; www.pawscafe.com.

point, but this detour is well marked. This well-maintained trail is good in almost all seasons, when many other places are too soggy to tolerate.

Amenities and multiple other trail connections are available at Farrell-McWhirter. A converted barn silo houses restrooms. Your dog may get worked up over the working farm animals at the park; stay on the fringe trails if your furry friend is unable to maintain her composure.

Directions to Farrel-McWhirter: Take 520 to the end, as it becomes Avondale Road N.E. Take a slight right at the fork in the road onto Novelty Hill Road. Travel 0.2 miles, take a left on Redmond Road, and follow the signs to turn left into the park. 19545 Redmond Rd.

10 Evans Creek Trail–Phase I

🐾🐾 (See Eastside map on page 224)

The Perrigo brothers were pioneers in Redmond, arriving by ship and rail to the wild territory of the Pacific Northwest in the late 1800s. Now it's your turn to blaze your way to Perrigo Park, opened in 2004, on the Evans Creek Trail. Dedicated in June 2006, this paved trail currently travels south from Perrigo Community Park (9011 196th Ave. N.E.) to the intersection of 196th and Union Hill Road, at a site designated for future development of Arthur Johnson Park (7901 196th Ave. N.E.). Funded by the Washington Wildlife and Recreation Program (WWRP), eventually it will link Novelty Hill Road to Redmond–Fall City Road.

From the parking lot, walk past the bathroom and covered shelter, around the Dream Turf playfields, and look for the bag dispenser, trash can, and picnic table to find the connection to the trail. From here, it's 0.7 miles south to Union

Hill Road. Part bucolic country lane over a marsh, part watch the big boy toys work at the Asphalt Paving Company Inc., the trail is not all ferns and roses, but it is a very interesting and impeccably maintained recreation corridor.

Take the State Route 520 Bridge to Avondale Road. Turn right on N.E. 95th Street and travel 0.7 mile. Take a sharp right onto 195th Avenue N.E. and the park will be on your right. Perrigo closes at 11 P.M.

11 Marymoor Dog Park

🐾🐾🐾🐾🐕 (See Eastside map on page 224)

If you get to visit only one dog park in the entire city (heaven forbid!), make Marymoor the one. Marymoor is massive and crowded, a live wire, the Big Apple for the doggie jet set. At last count, more than 650,000 carloads of dogs visit this 44-acre off-leash area each year, and that doesn't include the 3 million visitors to the 600 acres of the county park reserved for other uses.

The largest dog park in the state is naturally divided into many separate play spaces by the Sammamish River, as well as a long gravel promenade running the length of the southern edge of the dog park. Clumps of trees and dense blackberry bushes also break up the space, lining a multitude of bark-dust trails. Six bridges over marshes and wetlands, with names like Soggy Dog, Old Dog, and Swamp dog, move mutts from place to place. It's a mad, mad, mad, mad dog world, but even on the zaniest days, your dog should be able to find a territory to mark as his own for the day. There are five separate dog beaches, with steps leading down to them to prevent bank erosion, lined along the gravel trail.

There's no end to the things a dog can do at this off-leash area, from shaking a leg to sowing some wild oats. During salmon spawning season, mid-August through November, water activities are curtailed only slightly by fences that allow dogs into the river but restrict access to the main channel. The Memorial Pet Garden was added to Marymoor in 2007; call 206/205-3661 for more information. The Wash Spot opened in 2008, accepting only VISA, MasterCard, and Discover for an $8.75 Spot Wash or a $13.50 Max Wash, delivering herbal shampoos via a patent-pending wash-rinse-dry cycle in seven self-service cleaning tubs.

Every big city has its drawbacks, and here the downsides are water that gets stinky, hard to control canines, and cases of kennel cough that occasionally make the rounds. Otherwise, for the phenomenal usage it gets, Marymoor is kept in impeccable condition by people and dogs who take great pride in it, most of them volunteer members of Serve Our Dog Areas (www.soda.org). Marymoor is not fully fenced or gated. Dogs are expected to heed voice control and you are expected to exercise it.

Take State Route 520 east, turn right on West Lake Sammamish Parkway, and left onto N.E. Marymoor Way. To find the OLA, stay on Marymoor for 0.3 mile, turn right at the stop sign, and proceed to parking lot D. When you pass the community garden, you'll know you're almost there. Parking is $1 in self-pay automated stations, or buy annual parking passes from SODA for $100. 6046 W. Lake Sammamish Parkway. Open 8 A.M.–dusk. 206/205-3661; www.kingcounty.gov.

PLACES TO EAT

The Daily Bread: Not happy with the dozen daily special combos? Fill out the form to order your own custom sandwich made with Boar's Head meats. Don't want the carbs? Make your sandwich into a salad. Outdoors are a half dozen metal high-stool tables on a narrow sidewalk. 16717 Redmond Way; 425/882-0500.

PLACES TO STAY

In this area, *Chain Hotels,* listed in the *Resources* section offer the best choices for dogs and their people.

Bellevue

Sometimes dogs teach us to see things in a whole new light. People without pets may only perceive Bellevue as a place to shop, at Lincoln Square, Bellevue Square, and Bellevue Place, known as The Bellevue Collection (www .bellevuecollection.com). Those with pets can see another collection, of nine parks, strung together by the Lake-to-Lake Trail and Greenway, stretching from Lake Washington on the west to Lake Sammamish on the East.

Bellevue city beaches allow dogs only from September 15–May 31. They are Chesterfield, Chism, Clyde, Enatai, Meydenbauer, and Newcastle. Watershed Park is off-limits to pets, as a protected reserve. Kelsey Creek Farm Park is a no-no for dogs as well, maybe because of all those farm animals. Bellevue Park's website has excellent trail maps at www.bellevuewa.gov.

PARKS, BEACHES, AND RECREATION AREAS

12 Ardmore Trails

🐾🐾🐾 (See Eastside map on page 224)

Pulling up to Ardmore Park, you'll see putting-green perfect grass and a playground. Step onto the bark trail, and—BAM!—it's instant forest. Imposing Douglas firs and hemlocks, maples wearing moss sweaters, and an understory of classic northwest sword fern lend the forest a medieval air. There were so many nut-gatherers here that Cooper broke into song, "Heaven, I'm in Heaven…"

It's a quick 0.6-mile south on the trail to 24th Street. To double your pleasure, double your fun, walk 0.25 mile east when you come out of Ardmore on 24th, cross the street, and pick up the View Point Open Space Trail, a 1.5-miler, which leads to Tam O'Shanter Park, with another playground and half-court basketball.

From State Route 520, take the 148th Avenue N.E. exit, going south. Turn left on N.E. 24th Street, then left onto Bel-Red Road. Turn right on N.E. 30th Street, and the park will be on your right after 0.3 miles. Off-street parking only; no restrooms. 16833 N.E. 30th St.

🐾 Downtown Park

🐾🐾🐾 (See Eastside map on page 224)

A stroll through this gorgeous city park is a study in urban wildlife. You'll encounter Baby Gap–clad tots in strollers; power-walking, earpiece-talking execs on lunch break; MP3-player-equipped runners; and talented individuals who can juggle a latte, a leashed pet, a PDA, and their shopping bags from Bellevue Square next door. Even without the live visual stimuli, the park has unique architecture, sculpture, ponds, waterfalls, Kelly green lawns, and a ring of mature trees.

The walking path is wide with a sand-and-crushed-rock surface, dotted with benches every few feet and periodic bag dispensers. Dogs who are stuck downtown shopping with their people are happy to have the distraction.

From I-5, take Exit 13, go west on N.E. 8th Street, turn left on 100th Avenue N.E.; and left on 1st Street. Parking is in a lot in the center of the park on N.E. 1st Street. Open dawn–dusk.

🐾 Chism Beach

🐾🐾 (See Eastside map on page 224)

While not ignoring the fact that dogs are prohibited here June 1–September 15, we had to include at least one good beach park for your off-season pleasure. Stairs and accessible paths lead past two banked lawns down to a significant sand beach and natural rock breakwater. Views of Mercer Island and Seattle frame fishing piers and a swimming dock, with two picnic tables off to the side and the restrooms to the other. Look for the wood carving of the salmon.

Take Exit 13B from I-405, going west on 4th Street. Turn south on Bellevue Way, and turn right on 16th Street S.E. At the stop sign, turn right on 100th Avenue S.E., which becomes 97th Place S.W. as it rounds the bend. About 0.25 mile up the road, turn left on S.E. 11th Street, and bear left twice for the main parking lot. The entrance on 15th is for disabled parking and service vehicles only. Open dawn–dusk. 1175 96th Ave. S.E.

🐾 Wilburton Hill

🐾🐾🐾 (See Eastside map on page 224)

Wilburton's a bigun', at 105 acres. It's roly-poly, but you won't be, if you regularly hike its trails and romp on its lawns. The 3.4 miles of trails within park acreage form a major link in the Lake-to-Lake Trail system, from Lake

Washington to Lake Sammamish. The city says the park's primary purpose is to protect and enhance natural forests and wildlife habitats. Isis says the park's apparent purpose is to entertain dogs. She's the one who noticed that every car pulling up unloaded at least one dog. Her bark alarm triggered repeatedly.

From I-405, take the N.E. 8th Street exit, going east. Turn right onto 124th Avenue N.E. Get in the turn lane to turn left into the park at the intersection of 124th and Main Street. 12001 Main St.; 425/452-6914. From 124th Avenue N.E., turn east on N.E. 2nd Street to 128th Avenue N.E. for another trailhead entrance.

16 Lake Hills Greenbelt

🐾🐾 (See Eastside map on page 224)

It's far too easy to get overwhelmed on the über-achieving Eastside. The Greenbelt alone can be too much to take in all at once, so start with small bites. Start with blueberries, for example, they're small, from the U-Pick Larsen Lake Blueberry Farm (14812 S.E. 8th St.), one of the park's multiple working farms.

If you start at the visitors center (15416 S.E. 16th St.), you can go north on gravel paths to the blueberries, or south and west on paved trails to Phantom Lake. Three miles of flat gravel, bark, and paved pathways, with multiple wooden bridges, take you through 150 acres of wetlands, gardens, and agricultural history. Significant evidence of resident critters provides plenty of clues for your canine CSI wannabe while you study the interpretive displays. The Lake Hills Greenbelt forms the core of the Lake-to-Lake Trail.

From I-90, take Exit 11 to 156th Avenue S.E., traveling northbound to S.E. 16th Street. 15416 S.E. 16th St.; 425/452-6881.

17 Weowna Park

🐾🐾🐾 (See Eastside map on page 224)

There's gravel pullout parking for maybe seven cars for the entire 80 acres of this long and skinny open space park. Don't let that stop you from enjoying this ambitious and amazing oasis of old growth giants, with views of Lake Sammamish and the Cascade Mountains.

Trails ascend steeply from two entry points off W. Lake Sammamish Parkway. Stick to the South Loop for the short version, about a mile round-trip. Double that distance for the North Loop. Add them together and cut out the middle for a 2.5-mile total trek. The loops intersect at a third entry point on the eastside of the park, off 168th Avenue S.E. at 19th Street, where you'll find a picnic table and a viewpoint over Phantom Creek.

The creek's not natural, dug by a pioneer to drain what is now the Lake Hills Greenbelt to plant his crops, and restored by the city to improve drainage and lessen hillside erosion. If you've got miles to go before you sleep, this park marks the western end of the Lake-to-Lake Trail system.

From State Route 520, take the 148th Avenue N.E. Exit, going southbound.

Turn east on N.E. 20th Street, continuing on 20th as it crosses 156th Avenue to become Northup Way, all the way down the hill. Bear right onto W. Lake Sammamish Parkway. Travel 0.4 miles to the north pullout, and another 0.8 miles to the south pullout. Parking is limited to three hours. North: 529 W. Lake Sammamish Pkwy.; South: 2023 W. Lake Sammamish Pkwy.

18 Robinswood Community Park

🐾🐾🐕 (See Eastside map on page 224)

This city park full of after-school activities has two designated off-leash areas, former horse corrals with picket fences fortified with chain link. If a horse shows up, it has first priority, but in reality, these practice rings have gone completely to the dogs.

Together, the dog corrals add up to about an acre. Which one you saddle up to depends on your priority for the day. The southwest OLA has better security, not as many holes under the fence, and a double gate with a big leash-up area. Parking is close by, just a few yards north. What little grass there is won't save you from mud in the rainy season. The big boys like to congregate here.

Smaller dogs tend to socialize at the southeast OLA, which is funny, considering they're the ones who can squeeze under the fence, which doesn't quite reach the ground. Keep an extra eye out if you've got a Houdini dog. However, this area is more removed from the hustle of other park activities and the bustle of the main street. Parking is farther away, a walk of a hundred yards or so on leash, south past the tennis courts, before you reach the single, swinging gate. This lot has much better ground cover, at least during the season Cooper and Isis visited. Each area has a bag dispenser and garbage can right outside the gate. Bring your own water source, or fill 'er up from a park drinking fountain before you step into the ring. No spurs, please.

Take Exit 11 from I-90, and carefully follow the signs to go north on 148th Avenue S.E. Turn right on S.E. 24th Street, 0.8 mile from the beginning of your highway exit, to park for the Southwest OLA. Continue two more blocks on 148th to turn right on S.E. 22nd Street, and right again on 151st Place to park for the Southeast OLA. 2430 148th Ave. S.E.

PLACES TO EAT

Gilbert's Bagel and Deli: Owner Steve Gilbert is a funny guy who promises to treat dogs like royalty. He keeps milk bones on hand, provides water bowls "at no extra charge," and insists that if we were a civilized nation, dogs would be allowed inside and some of the customers would be required to sit on the sidewalk. This smart, urban deli has cheerful white Adirondack chairs and soda fountain tables. Go traditional, with matzo ball soup and corned beef on rye; or, step out with a salad of pears, toasted Stilton blue, lemon zest, and champagne vinaigrette. 10024 Main St.; 425/455-5650.

PLACES TO STAY

Bellevue Club Hotel: Isis knew she was right at home before she even entered the place, judging by all the Lexus, Infiniti, and BMW autos in the parking lot. A member of Small Luxury Hotels of the World, this class-act combines high style and high tech. Isis couldn't get over the fact that the lights come on automatically when you open the door to your room. The textures and colors of the rooms, and the private courtyard gardens, will win over the toughest critics. Rates range $285–350 weekdays. Primarily a business hotel, weekend rates are actually cheaper, at $165–240. One or two pets under 30 pounds; "old, quiet, bigger dogs okay," said the person at the reservation desk. $35 pet fee. 11200 S.E. 6th St.; 425/454-4424; www.bellevueclub.com.

More Accommodations: Please look under *Chain Hotels* in the *Resources* section for additional places to stay in this area.

Mercer Island

Upscale Mercer Island is a bastion for lawyers and doctors. It has the third-largest Sephardic Jewish community in the United States. The only island commerce is straight down Island Crest Way. It's fun to take twisty, curvy Mercer Way around the island and ogle all the fancy homes tucked in the trees.

PARKS, BEACHES, AND RECREATION AREAS

19 Luther Burbank Park

🐾🐾🐕 (See Eastside map on page 224)

The off-leash area of Luther Burbank is a small, soggy patch of ground, but it can be forgiven much because it has its own waterfront property. Dogs are welcome to wade right in, as long as they wait at least a half hour after eating (kidding!). The area is roughly designated by a couple of signs and a split-rail fence but is otherwise unsecured and has no other facilities or services. Railroad-tie steps lead down to the beach. There's a bit of grass and some tree cover, and everything is squishy this close to the water. This park should be rated for two rubber boots in addition to two paws.

A stroll on leash around the groomed trails of the park is enjoyable, with great views of Seattle, Bellevue, and Microsoft millionaires' homes across the water in Medina. Undeveloped areas of the 77-acre park foster wildlife, including beavers, muskrats, raccoons, rabbits, and loud tree frogs.

Take the 77th Avenue S.E. exit (#7A) from I-5. Turn left onto 77th, right at the stop sign onto N. Mercer Way, go through the light at 80th Avenue, immediately turn left on 81st Avenue S.E., and then right on S.E. 24th Street to the end. The dog park is at the north end; please walk your pets on leash until you reach the area. 2040 84th Ave. S.E.; 206/236-3545.

20 Pioneer Park

🐾🐾🐾 (See Eastside map on page 224)

Pioneer Park captures the feel of backcountry hiking in the midst of a dense population. The city divides the 113-acre park into three distinct areas called quadrants, containing 6.6 miles of trails. Cooper sees the illogic of lacking a true fourth to make up the quad, equating it to some three-legged quadrupeds he knows who get around quite well, thank you.

Cooper hiked the most popular Northwest Quadrant, which follows Island Crest Way down the center of the island for a while, then wanders off into the forest. The best parking for this park section is on 84th Avenue S.E., on the north end of the park off Island Crest Way.

The woods are denser in the Northeast Quadrant, with trails that skirt past a ravine, wetlands, and a stream, with a neat bridge suspended 15 feet over the water. Parking is on S.E. 68th Street in the middle of the block near a large maple tree.

The Southeast Quadrant is maintained specifically for equestrian use. Many of the Douglas firs in this area have root rot, and the fallen, decayed trees provide some extra padding underfoot, lending this forest a hushed quality.

Park on the east side of Island Crest Way, south of S.E. 68th Street. Open 6 A.M.–10 P.M. Island Crest Way and S.E. 68th St.; 206/236-3545.

Newcastle

As of 1872, 75–100 tons of coal was produced each day in Newcastle. By the time the mine closed for the last time in 1963, more than 13 million tons had been extracted. Its legacy remains ever-present in local place names such as Coal Creek Parkway. Normally, the three-mile Coal Creek Parkway open space is a great place to hike; however, the December 3, 2007, storm destroyed four bridges, closing the trail until they can be rebuilt. Trails are expected to re-open Spring 2009.

PARKS, BEACHES, AND RECREATION AREAS

21 Lewis Creek

🐾🐾🐾 (See Eastside map on page 224)

If your dog is waiting by the front door, leash in mouth, it could be Sunday, time for free Sunday Dog Walks in Lewis Creek park, led by a park ranger, rain or shine, May–September. Dogs must be on six-foot leashes; scoop bags are provided. Meet at the Lewis Creek Visitor Center—a cool place for a birthday party, by the way—at 2 P.M. Walks are approximately an hour, and no pre-registration is necessary. Call 425/452-6144 for more information.

Lewis Creek is good for a family outing any day of the week. At least 80 percent of this park's 55 acres are in their natural state, making it possible to disappear into the hinterlands, if only for a quiet moment. Park trails are varied, including paved, boardwalk, gravel, and soft surface, and they connect to the City of Bellevue Open Space Trail System.

From I-90, take Exit 13 south toward S.E. Newport Way. Turn right onto W. Lake Sammamish Parkway S.E./Lakemont Boulevard S.E. 5702 Lakemont Blvd. S.E.

22 Lake Boren

🐾🐾 (See Eastside map on page 224)

The city promotes pretty Lake Boren park as an ideal spot for outdoor events. Witness, the Seattle Humane Society was setting up for a huge volunteer appreciation picnic on the morning of the Wonder Wieners' visit, and they say "Amen" to that. People who rescue pets deserve picnics every day.

Gently rolling hills are the defining characteristic of the 22-acre park, with a restroom and tennis, basketball, and volleyball courts where it levels out. A series of paved, looped walking paths lead down a fishing pier on the lily-pad-decorated lake. At the far end, the paths join up with a one-mile trail over to Hazelwood Park. Whatever the occasion, feel free to stage your own event for the day.

Take Exit 10 from I-5, going south on the Coal Creek Parkway for 3.5 miles. Turn right on S.E. 84th Way, and right into the park.

PLACES TO EAT

Starbucks: It had to be done. Seattle is the official birthplace of the coffee company bent on world domination, and we simply couldn't let the whole book go by without including one Starbucks. Just one, for good coffee, good food, and great outdoor seating. 6977 Coal Creek Pkwy.; 425/603-9727.

Sammamish

On the eastern shore of Lake Sammamish, in between Redmond and Newcastle, Sammamish is a young city, incorporated in 1999. It is posh, from the estate homes to the international reputation of the golf course at Sahalee Country Club.

PARKS, BEACHES, AND RECREATION AREAS

23 Soaring Eagle Park

🐾🐾 (See Eastside map on page 224)

Which do you think is a better name for a park, Section 36 or Soaring Eagle? Known for the longest time by its legal platting designation, these 600 acres of serenity atop the Sammamish Plateau finally got a decent name in a contest held at a local elementary school.

There's no infrastructure here, aside from a large parking lot and a portable potty. According to the map found online, you and your Great Pyrenees can go gonzo on 26 trail segments in a million possible combinations. All combos will involve mud, ruts, and mountain bikers. The trails are not groomed, as far as we could see, other than for cutting of fallen logs and laying a few boards over the worst of the slop. Essentially, it's a good workout, especially if you include the do-it-yourself dog wash that'll be necessary afterwards.

From N.E. 228th Avenue in Sammamish, turn east on S.E. 8th Street and continue as it curves north and becomes 244th Avenue, for a total of 1.4 miles. Turn right on E. Main Drive and continue another mile to the end. Open 8 A.M.–dusk. 26015 E. Main Dr.

24 Beaver Lake Dog Park

🐾🐾🐾🐾🐾 (See Eastside map on page 224)

At Beaver Lake, it's not about the lake. Sure, you can get to it, see it, even get in it, without a lifeguard on duty. But it's not that attractive, and it's separated from most of the park.

Our journey took us first to the north entrance, where there is a lodge with bathrooms, a large totem pole, and a lakeside picnic shelter. We moseyed down the trail, no more than half a mile, to the south entrance, and stumbled upon … wait for it … a dog park we did not know about. "Inconceivable!" cried Isis.

Well, that explains all the happy heads hanging out of car windows we saw on the way there. Open since June 2008, the off-leash area had us seeing double. It's two acres, split down the middle into equal, level, rectangular plots. There are split-level water fountains (up human, down dog) on each well-fenced side, and pairs of benches, dispensers, and trash receptacles. Two signs, which can be switched at will, currently point 30 pounds and under to the right, everyone else to the left. The double-entry bullpen is sizable and paved.

To go straight to the OLA, take the south entrance: Exit 17 from I-90 onto E. Lake Sammamish Parkway heading north. Take a right on S.E. 43rd Way, which curves north to become 228th Avenue N.E., and go 2.5 miles. Turn right at S.E. 24th Street for a mile. Turn right and travel south on 244th Avenue to the park entrance on the left, 0.1 mile later. Walk past the restrooms, between baseball fields #2 and #3. Open 7 A.M.–dusk. S.E. 24th St. at 244th Ave. S.E.; 425/295-0500.

25 Lake Sammamish State Park

🐾🐾 (See Eastside map on page 224)

Dogs are denied the pleasure of swimming on the beaches in Washington's state parks. Smarty pants that she is, Isis hasn't figured out how to swim and be on leash at the same time anyway. That doesn't keep them from enjoying this park's two trails, along Issaquah Creek, 0.8-mile Meadow Trail following one side of the creek and 0.7-mile Homestead on the other. Both are level, effortless meanderings.

The picnic grounds, designed for large group gatherings, are also worth a tail wag when you have them to yourselves to wander around, chase rodents, and watch boaters and water skiers on the lake, which is a mile wide and 10 miles long. Restroom and concession stands are open only in summer.

From U.S. Highway 90, take exit 15 and go east on East Lake Sammamish Parkway N.E.; at the next light turn left onto N.W. Sammamish Road. Avoid the first entrance leading to soccer fields; take the second entrance on the right. To take the Boat Launch Trail to the Meadow Spur, stay on East Lake Sammamish Parkway to the boat launch. 20606 S.E. 56th St.; 425/455-7010.

PLACES TO EAT

Acapulco Fresh: No lard, no MSG, and no can openers were used in the creation of fresh-Mex food to go. Hungry appetites can call ahead to order taco ten packs and burrito bundles to stuff into your day pack. Talk about torture, making your trail hound walk beside you, smelling all that spicy goodness. 22830 N.E. 8th St.; 425/868-1447.

Issaquah

This desirable mountain town at the foot of the "Issaquah Alps" is growing faster than a Great Dane puppy, and suffering the growing pains of miserable traffic and encroaching commercialism. Fortunately, there's only so much it can grow before running into the base of those so-called alps, starting with Tiger, Cougar, and Squak Mountains. Together they provide more than 150 miles of hiking and biking trails within a half-hour drive from Seattle. Issaquah makes the Wonder Wieners wish for longer legs, because it has to be one of the best places on the planet to escape to for a day of righteous hooky with your recreational soul mate. It is time to head to the Outdoor and More cheap gear outlet for some trail running shoes and heavy-duty wool socks. In all seriousness, Issaquah recreation means being prepared for all conditions, a lack of amenities, and the likelihood of meeting non-domesticated animals of many types and sizes, even at the dog park.

PARKS, BEACHES, AND RECREATION AREAS

26 Issaquah Highlands Bark Park

😁😁😁🐕 (See Eastside map on page 224)

Dogs living in high-density housing are getting happy in the Highlands. This planned community didn't plan on a dog park until enough residents demanded it, a prime example of democracy in action. The two-acre result sits on top of the world, with great views for humans from a picnic table, a bench, and a protected gazebo for those drizzly days. In case the high, secured fence and bag dispensers didn't give it away, fun canine-centric quotes are posted outside the off-leash area. A single-gate entry leads to a rough and rocky plateau, with a steep drop-off down the far side. Isis suspects quite a few tennis balls end up at the bottom, lined up against the fence. At the back of the larger OLA is Mini-Mutt Meadows, a significantly smaller square for the tiny Totos.

Take Exit 18 from I-90, going up the hill on Highlands Drive N.E. Take a right on N.E. Federal Drive and another right on N.E. Park Drive. Go farther up the hill, take a left on 25th Avenue N.E. and another left on N.E. Natalie Way. The OLA is past Kirk Park on your right down the hill. Street parking is available for a couple of cars. Water and restrooms are next door at Kirk Park. Open dawn to dusk. Of note, pit bulls are not allowed in the Issaquah Highlands.

27 Cougar Mountain Regional Wildlands Preserve

😁😁😁😁 (See Eastside map on page 224)

It's nifty that, unlike Tiger, mountain bikes are not allowed on Cougar Mountain's 50 or so miles of trails. It's neat that trails designated for canines, in the company of humans, outweigh those designated for equines 3 to 1, or, more precisely, 36 miles to 12 miles. It's nice that the cougars, bears, deer, porcupines, bobcats, and weasels are willing to share the park with you. Honestly, we don't see big game when we hike, but then again, we sing Broadway show tunes as we take to the trails. It's difficult to know how else to sum up Cougar, except to say that its tight maze of trails are all wonderful. Even one of the Northwest's foremost conservationists, Harvey Manning, had a succinct way of putting it, calling Cougar "a great big green and quiet place." Quiet that is, until we start singing show tunes.

Try the Red Town Trailhead: Take Exit 13 from I-90, right on S.E. Newport Way, left on 164th Avenue, climb the hill for 1.7 miles, turn right on Lakemont Boulevard, 1.4 miles to trailhead on the left. 206/296-8687.

28 Squak Mountain Natural Area

🐾🐾🐾 (See Eastside map on page 224)

Cougar, Tiger, Squak... frankly, it's hard to tell them apart, weaving together as they do into one big, happy hiker's paradise. If you think a good day involves banana slugs, muddy paws, and more trees than your pooch can pee on in one lifetime, then these parks are your spiritual home. It's nitpicking to say Squak's the smallest; at a square mile, or about 2,500 acres, who's to notice?

Two things happen with frightening regularity on these 35 miles of trails less traveled: one, getting lost, and two, getting slimed (slugs). Try Green Trails Map #203S for the former, and let us know if you come up with a solution for the latter. The towering trees on this mountain are often older than on Cougar and Tiger, because its steeper sides made for less feasible logging. Please note that steeper sides also make for huff-puffier hiking.

There are multiple trailheads into Squak, many of them hidden down residential streets. Try this one: Take I-90 east to Exit 15, turn right onto Renton-Issaquah Road. Then turn left onto Maple Street, then right again onto 12th Avenue N.W. Drive uphill where 12th Avenue turns into Mount Olympus Drive. Stay right at the yield, then bear left on Mountain Park Boulevard. Turn right onto Mountainside Drive. Park at the end of the road, just before the switchback.

29 Tiger Mountain State Forest

🐾🐾🐾🐾 (See Eastside map on page 224)

When the Wonder Wieners discovered this mountain, they didn't hike anywhere else for a year. It is the golden child of the alps and the largest, at 13,000 acres and 80 miles of trails. There are three peaks, East, West, and South. West is favored by hikers, East by the mountain bikers, and South is the least frequented and most remote. You can tell immediately which trails are not frequently used, as the ferns and moss quickly claim the ground. Cooper's favorite trail starts at the High Point Way trailhead and goes up to Poo Poo Point, one of the country's top hang gliding and paragliding points. Isis growls about the weekend crowds on this, the most heavily trod of Issaquah's Alps. For more solitude, she suggests Taylor or Squak.

In September, Cooper nicknamed it Spider Mountain, for the plump arachnids weaving in the ferns, which he claims are a delicious protein supplement, once they stop tickling his nose. To avoid these world-wide-webs, try waving a stick in front of you in a cross pattern as you walk, as though you are blessing yourself.

For one of several trailheads, take Exit 20 from I-90, go south on 270th Avenue S.E., and turn right immediately onto S.E. 79th Street to High Point Way. You'll see multiple cars parked along this road, and there is a large parking area farther up a gravel road with restroom facilities and maps.

PLACES TO EAT

Issaquah Distillery and Public House: A brewpub and producer of Rogue beers, the Issaquah Public House has a permit for outdoor seating each year from May through September. If there is a scene in this foothills town, this is it. The food is reliable, and Rogue beers, originally from Oregon, go down nice and easy. 35 Sunset Way; 425/557-1911; www.rogue.com/locations-issaquah.html.

XXX Root Beer Drive-in: It is a doggone shame that a persnickety health inspector has declared this institution's patio off-limits to dogs. This XXX is the last of its kind in the world, and the homebrew, a smooth root beer produced with cane sugar rather than corn syrup, is named one of the Top 10 root beers in the U.S. of A. Get a burger, fries, and root beer float to go, or better yet, take a gallon jug home with you and have a kegger. Nothing here is good for you. We'll drink a float to that. 98 N.E. Gilman Blvd.; 425/392-1266; www.triplexrootbeer.com.

PLACES TO STAY

Motel 6: Tell you what, Motel 6 properties are reliably dog-friendly, they consistently offer the best prices in any market, and you know what to expect. Predictably, this location is conveniently situated to all things Issaquah. They allow two dogs, there is no pet fee if you declare the pets when you call or check in, rates are $55–75, and there's a 10 percent discount for booking online. 1885 15th Pl. N.W.; 425/392-8405; www.motel6.com.

Snoqualmie and North Bend

Stellar mountain recreation is within a half-hour drive from downtown Seattle out Interstate 90. You'll come first to Snoqualmie, where old railroad cars go to die in peace, displayed in all their glory at the **Northwest Railway Museum** (38625 S.E. King St.; 425/888-3030; www.trainmuseum.org) in an outdoor rail yard that you can explore together. Each rail car is labeled with make, model, year made, year acquired, and where it ran.

Fans of the TV show *Twin Peaks* will recognize Snoqualmie Falls and Salish Lodge, which sits perched above the cascade from the opening credits sequence. It's a shame that dogs are not allowed on the two-acre grounds of the falls nor at the lodge. You should make a quick stop to see the 270-foot waterfalls on your way to playing at the lake, or at least look at them online at www.snoqualmie falls.com. North Bend has some outlet shopping and a historic downtown main street, the last outpost before heading into the mountains proper.

PARKS, BEACHES, AND RECREATION AREAS

30 Rattlesnake Lake

🐾🐾🐾🐾 (See Eastside map on page 224)

When the kids are rattling your nerves, it's time to roll on over to the lake for some light hiking and swimming. Take to the Lake Trail, a 1.5-mile paved loop

along the southeast side of the lake that is level and easy for all abilities. The lake itself has a couple of good ball-throwing areas and, of course, the water.

Technically, there is no rule requiring a leash at Rattlesnake Lake. Reign in your dog, by leash or voice, when passing others on the trail, leash up on beach areas during summer weekends, and always walk with your dog on leash through the visitors center grounds. At the Cedar River Watershed Education Center, there is a fascinating drum garden, where the instruments are played by choreographed water droplets.

For not-so-light hiking, two heavy-duty trails are available for the very fit. As of 2007, the Rattlesnake Mountain Trail has been upgraded and extended to connect to Snoqualmie Point Promontory, an 11-mile, one-way trek. Ever more popular is the Rattlesnake Ledge Trail, a steep gravel path starting at Rattlesnake Lake and traversing switchbacks to the edge of the ridge. You might have to break out the paw booties for this one; at times, it's about as close as you can get to technical climbing without ropes. From the trail junction near the top, turn right to visit Rattlesnake Ledge, 2,079 feet above the

Snoqualmie Valley. Green Trails Map #205S, available at REI, is the reference you want for these hikes.

From U.S. Highway 90, take Exit 32, go south on 436th Avenue S.E. Continue on the road as it becomes Cedar Falls Road. The first parking lot on your right is at 2.8 miles for the Rattlesnake Ledge Trail. The Cedar River Watershed Education Center is at 3.5 miles. Gates to the center lot close at 6 P.M.; parking is limited to two hours. Other trailheads are open until dark.

PLACES TO EAT

George's Bakery: Folks at George's are super relaxed and friendly. It's been around forever in the old downtown strip, with a silly-looking chalet front and plastic checkered covers on rickety tables. Ignore the decor, and concentrate on the delicious donuts in the A.M. and vegetable-stuffed calzones for lunch. 127 W. North Bend Way; 425/888-0632.

PLACES TO STAY

Denny Creek Campground: Administratively, this campsite is in the North Bend Ranger District on the Mount Baker–Snoqualmie National Forest. Geographically, it's 17 miles east of North Bend, in a scenic mountain area where Denny Creek joins the South Fork of the Snoqualmie River. Level tent camping pads, good tree cover, and the soothing sounds of the water make this one a winner. There are 33 sites; 10 are on the river, 11 have electricity, and there are flush toilets. Rates are $17–24. 877/444-6777; www.recreation.gov.

DIVERSIONS

The water temperature is a balmy 94 degrees in the custom-designed pool, with terraced blue and white tiled steps and a hand-crafted wood enclosure. Lavender-scented towels and soothing background music set the tone. Water toys, life vests, and a state-of-the-art filtration system ensure a fur-free swim. Fur free? Yes, Virginia, there really is a **Heavenly Spa** for hounds in Fall City in the Snoqualmie Valley. It goes far beyond pampering, really, for aquatic bodywork at the spa is led by a state-certified practitioner in small animal massage. For infirm or injured dogs, it can be a lifesaver. For any human-animal bond, it can be precious quality time in a tropical environment on a dreary winter's day. Rates are comparable to fees for human massage, $45 for a half-hour, $85 for an hour. Self-swims are less, after you attend a session to learn how to swim safely together in the pool. 35022 S.E. Fall City–Snoqualmie Rd.; 425/222-7221; www.heavenlyspa.info.

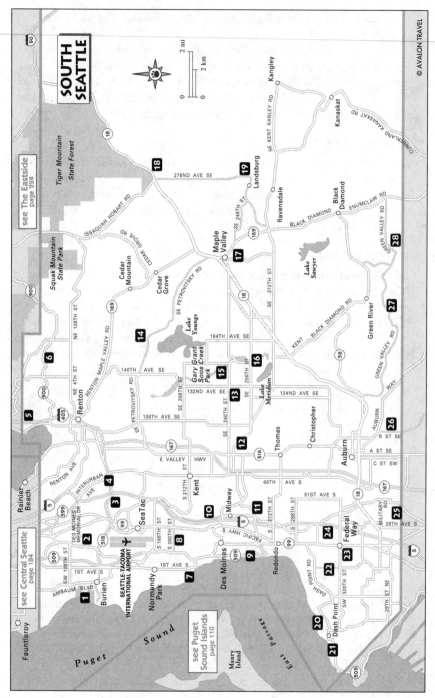

CHAPTER 9

South Seattle

Underappreciated. That is the single most descriptive word for this area of Seattle, particularly true when it comes to recreational activities. Perhaps it's because you have to wade through so much suburbia to get where you want to go, evidence of the growing pains of a popular and expanding metropolis. Pardon their dust, South Seattle is heavily under construction.

The Southcenter Mall Complex opened its new Westfield wing in August 2008, adding 75 stores, five restaurants, and a 16-screen movie theater. Says the mall's general manager, "We draw in 18 to 20 million shoppers annually." Across the highway, Sea-Tac Airport is in the final phases of constructing a third runway in 2008, to handle the 30 million passengers who pass through the country's 17th largest airport. More available ground and airspace south of the city is taken up by Boeing, the airplane and aerospace manufacturer, including their airstrip and the Museum of Flight (www.museumofflight.org). Lest we forget all the traffic that goes along with the infrastructure, most Seattle residents are thrilled about the opening of Sound Transit's Link light

PICK OF THE LITTER—SOUTH SEATTLE

BEST PARKS
Clark Lake Park, Kent (page 262)
Lake Wilderness Park, Maple Valley (page 265)
O'Grady County Park, Auburn (page 271)

BEST DOG PARKS
Grandview Dog Park, Kent (page 260)
Dog Park at French Lake, Federal Way (page 268)

BEST EVENT
Petapalooza, Auburn (page 271)

BEST PLACES TO EAT
Taco del Rey, Tukwila (page 256)
Famous Black Diamond Bakery and Deli, Black Diamond
(page 273)

rail system in 2009, connecting downtown to the airport (small pets in carriers allowed; www.soundtransit.org).

Ye dogs who live in the south metropolis, don't despair! Amidst all this hustle and bustle, the Dachsie Twins found a smattering of hidden treats. Along with riverside trails and open green space is one of the best off-leash parks in the region. For the first time in recreational history, eight cities and one county joined together to form a regional OLA, providing the fencing and capital improvements to open 37-acre Grandview. The park is in Kent, and the winning cities that ponied up for dogs are SeaTac, Kent, Auburn, Renton, Burien, Des Moines, Federal Way, and Tukwila, along with King County. The park is close to Sea-Tac International Airport, halfway between Seattle and Tacoma.

EXTENDED REGIONAL TRAILS

Green River Trail
🐾🐾🐾

The 19 miles of this commuter and recreation pathway is entirely paved, with a few roadway segments. As you go farther south, office buildings and warehouses eventually give way to open fields, hedgerows, and blackberries. We suggest you pick up the north end of the trail by parking at the Tukwila Community Center (12424 42nd Ave. S) or on the south end near Riverbend Golf Complex on Meeker Street west of State Route 167. Plans to extend the trail to Flaming Geyser State Park in the Green River Gorge may produce the prettiest part of the trail yet. For the best printed map of GRT, get a copy of King County's Bicycling Guide map, available at visitors centers or www.metrokc.gov/bike, or see it online at www.metrokc.gov/parks/trails/greenriver.html.

Interurban Trail–South
🐾

The Interurban is practical and tactical, 14.7 miles of arrow-straight asphalt following the historic BNSF rail line precisely north–south. Park at Fort Dent, off Southcenter Boulevard at Interurban Avenue (6800 Fort Dent Way; 206/768-2822), where the trail also intersects with the Green River Trail. The Interurban is not going to be green, but it is a way to see the local sights without burning any fuel other than your own. Get the King County's Bicycling Guide map, or visit www.metrokc.gov/parks/trails/interurban.html.

Burien

A revitalized small town Main Street and some pricey waterfront homes perk up an otherwise quiet suburb of about 30,000 people. Olde Burien's Farmers Market is worth a look, Thursdays 11 A.M.–6 P.M. on 10th Avenue S.W. between S.W. 150th and 152nd Streets.

PARKS, BEACHES, AND RECREATION AREAS

🔳 Seahurst Park
🐾 🐾 (See South Seattle map on page 250)

This 178-acre waterfront city property is all a bit unkempt and vague. Protectors of the mile-long waterfront and wetlands are trying to find a balance between human use and restoration of vital stream habitats. You can hike a gravel road that goes to the top of the hill, but for the most part, enjoyment of Seahurst comes from bringing a sandwich down to the small beach, sitting on the driftwood, and playing the "What does that cloud look like to you?" guessing game while your pal sniffs around the sand.

Take the S.W. 148th Street exit from State Route 509, going west on 148th. Take a right on Ambaum Boulevard S.W. (16th Avenue), turn left on S.W. 144th Street, and right onto 13th Avenue, which winds down into the park. There's a small parking lot on the water, and a larger overflow lot just a short trek up the hill. Opens at 8 A.M.; www.seahurstpark.org.

PLACES TO EAT

Geno's Coffee Shop and Bakery: A step into Geno's feels like a step back into a simpler time, when baked goods, pies, and potato and macaroni salads were stars at the potluck, instead of tofu and gluten-free rice crisps. Fill out the form to order sandwiches that are served on thick Texas-toast style slices of white bread. Remember white bread? Even with 2008 regulations prohibiting trans fats, Geno's is keeping it real. 11620 Ambaum Blvd. S.W.; 206/244-4303.

Hans' German Sausage and Deli: The meat case at Hans' would make any dog weep for joy, canines not being ones to worry about the cholesterol count of the variety of legitimate wursts, links, and bolognas arrayed before their bulging eyes. Fresh soft pretzels and rye breads are delivered on Tuesdays, Fridays, and Saturdays. This is also where Cooper's mom gets her fix of imported German liqueur-filled chocolates. Pick a pack of picnic goodies, or have them make a sandwich for you with mayo and pickles as the only condiments for meat, glorious meat. 717 S.W. 148th St.; 206/244-4978.

SeaTac

The inventive name for the halfway point between Seattle and Tacoma is primarily important as the location of the region's international airport.

PARKS, BEACHES, AND RECREATION AREAS

2 North SeaTac Park

🐾🐾🐾 (See South Seattle map on page 250)

This sizeable city park is 165-acres. The dogs like it best for the network of paved, gravel, and impromptu trails and periodic lawns surrounding the neatly fenced ball fields. The natural spaces are kept nicely unkempt, with pockets of blackberries, sweet peas, and buttercups poking through the brush. There's still plenty of room for a dog to get down and dirty in the spaces around and between the restrooms, basketball courts, community center, and playgrounds. Although you can't ignore the occasional jetliner streaming overhead from the airport due south, you might still find a few hiding spots to make the rest of the world go away for a while.

Take the S. 128th Street exit from State Route 509, going east on 128th. Turn right 20th Avenue S. into the large parking lot.

PLACES TO STAY

Red Roof Inn–Seattle Airport: Wi-Fi, a free shuttle within a mile radius, and fresh ground, whole bean coffee are yours, for rates that stay under $100, even for Thanksgiving. That red roof is starting to look mighty friendly. Up to two pets; no pet fee; $80–95. 16838 International Blvd.; 206/248-0901.

DIVERSION

The **AirPet Hotel** is a stroke of genius whose genesis comes from PDX in Portland. Now, quality dog day care and boarding services are available five minutes from Sea-Tac International Airport, with shuttle services to park-and-fly lots and the flight terminal. Board your dog, park your car, and board your flight—it's that easy.

For a reasonable $35 per day (20 percent discount for multiple dogs), your pet sleeps in a comfy indoor kennel overnight, and during the day she gets to play in a supervised indoor playpen with dogs of similar temperament and size, and she is taken outside for at least five 10-minute potty breaks. She'll fall asleep each night exhausted, well fed, and happy.

Although normal business hours are 7 A.M.–9 P.M., the facility is staffed 24 hours a day. You can arrange early or late drop-off and pickup times by appointment for those red-eye flights (19111 Des Moines Memorial Dr.; 206/788-4446; www.airpethotel.com).

More Accommodations: Please look under *Chain Hotels* in the *Resources* section for additional places to stay in this area.

Tukwila

The city of Tukwila is almost 100 percent commercially developed. With a couple of petite exceptions, it's office parks and industrial complexes all the way.

PARKS, BEACHES, AND RECREATION AREAS

3 Crystal Springs Park

🐾🐾 (See South Seattle map on page 250)

This 11-acre hillside woodland is steep and skinny and has many layers, like an onion, or a parfait. It begins at the bottom with groomed tennis courts, and the higher you go, the wilder it gets, so you know you're at the top when the paved pathway turns into a gravel trail. The lower portion contains the picnic shelter and restrooms. Up above and across 51st Avenue is the walking path and a little waterfall from a scummy water retention pond. Looks like it's a good thing the water is no longer used by valley residents as a drinking supply.

From State Route 518 eastbound, take the Southcenter Mall exit, also called 51st Avenue S., and go straight onto Klickitat Drive. Turn right on 53rd Avenue S., and right again onto 159th Street into the park. Crystal Springs closes at dusk. Restrooms are closed December–February. 15832 51st Ave. S.

4 Tukwila Park

😼 (See South Seattle map on page 250)

Established in 1934, this is the oldest of the city parks, created at a time when, dare we say, family time meant more than video games and ordering out for pizza. The city says the 6.5-acre site is "covered with mature vegetation," which translates to large fir trees and ancient rhododendrons overcome by holly, ferns, and English ivy. Facilities include a gazebo, swings, and a play place. A few picnic tables are tucked into private corners. A paved walkway ends abruptly at the top of the hill, and should your dog choose to take you bushwacking back to the car, watch out for face-level spider webs. Eewww.

From I-5 southbound, take Exit 154B onto Southcenter Boulevard. Go east, and take a left on 65th Avenue S. The park is on your right. Restrooms are closed December–February. 15460 65th Ave. S.

PLACES TO EAT

Taco del Rey: The food here is so authentic, the regulars who frequent this restaurant simply call it "Going to Mexico." Hispanic cooks at a taco chain to remain unnamed across the street sneak over here to eat. The chef-owner is from Acapulco, and he makes an unforgettable chicken molé from his Mama's recipe (think Olé! with an m). Even dogless, you'll probably want to sit at the couple of tables outside for lunch or dinner, to escape the throngs inside. 330 S.W. 43rd, Tukwila; 425/251-0100; www.tacodelrey.com.

PLACES TO STAY

Residence Inn: Spend the night, or several, with all the engineers, pilots, and mechanical types at this second home for Boeing Field employees and contractors. This is one of those dog-friendly Marriott properties, with rooms the size of a small apartment. The art on the walls might not be to your taste, but then again, how long has that *Star Wars* poster been up in your bedroom anyway? The pet fee is $25 for 1–3 days, $75 for longer stays. Nightly rates go lower the longer you stay, averaging $160–190. 16201 W. Valley Hwy.; 425/226-5500; www.residenceinntukwila.com.

More Accommodations: Please look under *Chain Hotels* in the *Resources* section for additional places to stay in this area.

Renton

Coop 'n' Isis are pleased to report that Renton appointed a task force in 2008 to review possible off-leash areas and make a recommendation to the city parks commissioner. They'll keep you posted in future editions as plans develop. They are not so pleased to inform you that Renton prohibits dogs in parks where swimming and boating occur, such as Gene Coulon Memorial Beach.

May Valley Road is an attractive route for a Sunday Drive, sharing the road with cyclists and horses.

PARKS, BEACHES, AND RECREATION AREAS

5 Honey Creek Trail

🐾🐾🐾🐾 (See South Seattle map on page 250)

Coop 'n' Isis cannot get enough of these kinds of discoveries, a taste of hidden forest sandwiched between suburban sprawl. The first 0.25 mile is an abandoned road down into a ravine. At the bottom, take the right fork onto a gravel path leading for another mile along the creek. A few times, you'll see storm drains and houses up on the ridge to remind you that you're still in the city; otherwise, it's easy to forget in this private place.

The dogs experienced a bittersweet moment here, coming upon a cairn marked with a small, white wooden cross bearing the single word "Molly." They can only imagine this must have been Molly's favorite spot in this life to walk with her human.

Take Exit 6 off I-405, and turn east on Kennewick Place N.E., which takes a sharp turn and becomes 27th Street N.E. When the road takes a 90-degree turn south, bear left at the No Outlet sign to stay on 27th Street. Park discreetly where the road ends. The trail begins after the gate. There are no services.

6 May Valley County Park

🐾🐾🐾 (See South Seattle map on page 250)

This 55-acre woods has one really good thing going for it: absolutely nothing. Talk about solitude, there is nothing here except for trees and trails, a winding maze of unmarked exploration known to few except for resident rodents and a couple of neighbors. There are three trailheads entering the forest, each marked by two boulders. The King County Park Boundary sign was almost completely overgrown. Only the first two have space for a single car to park on the shoulder, the third is down a private lane. We met a local, mowing his lawn, who gave us quizzical looks, and we were forced to confess to being city dogs out for a stroll in the country. There are no services. Bring what you need, and leave only side-by-side pairs of prints behind.

Take State Route 900 east out of Renton, past Duvall Avenue N.E., where it becomes S.E. Renton-Issaquah Road. Turn south on 148th Avenue S.E., and left on S.E. 112th Street. Watch closely for the boulders on your left past the last house.

PLACES TO EAT

Jay Berry's Café: Breakfast, lunch, dinner, each has its own three-page, take-out menu of respectable bar food, served in hearty portions to fill you up before you hit the trails at May Valley. The patio is sunny and dog-friendly, right outside the door to the sports bar. If you position yourself just right, you might be able to peak in and catch the big game, while keeping an eye on your BLT, to keep it out of the gaping maw of your malamute. 16341 Renton-Issaquah Rd.; 425/271-1817.

PLACES TO STAY

Larkspur Landing: This home-suite style hotel chain has properties in California and the Pacific Northwest. They feature Craftsman styling and fluffy comfort beds to differentiate themselves from the crowd. Pet guests stay on the first floor of the west wing, which has a side door to a small lawn. Studios go for about $150; suites with bedrooms more toward $180. The pet fee is a flat rate of $75 per visit. 1701 E. Valley Rd.; 425/235-1212; www.larkspur landing.com.

More Accommodations: Please look under *Chain Hotels* in the *Resources* section for additional places to stay in this area.

Des Moines

Des Moines coins itself the "Waterland City," encompassing six miles of Puget Sound shoreline, some of which is accessible along a popular boardwalk, a 900-slip marina, and a few parks saved for public access. If all that saltwater is putting too many kinks in your pet's coat, pop into The Soggy Doggy pet wash for a self-serve scrub. On a side note, you have to check out the Washmatic Hydromassage machine at the Soggy Doggy's Kent location; it's an automatic car wash for canines (21839 Marine View Dr. S.; 206/824-6600; www.the soggydoggy.com).

PARKS, BEACHES, AND RECREATION AREAS

7 Marine View Park

🐾🐾🐾 ✖ (See South Seattle map on page 250)

If a can and a can, a.k.a. a garbage and a portable potty, are all you need in life, then this city beach will get your pup doing the can-can, or at the very least, the happy trot. Marine View is proof that good things come in perfectly sized packages, in this instance, a 1,200-foot beach at the bottom of a primitive trail that's not much more than two dachshunds width across. "Use at your own risk," says the city, either on leash or under voice control. For trails, you've got your choice between the Valley Loop Road and the Beach Trail, each with enough ups and downs to get your blood pumping, winding steeply down the hillside, past a couple of peek-a-boo benches and one choice picnic table. Or, walk down a crumbling road and down a series of several dozen wooden steps to the beach, with views of Mount Rainier to the south and Vashon Island and the Olympics to the west.

Marine View is just north of Des Moines in Normandy Park. From the intersection of Des Moines Memorial Drive and S.W. 216th Place, take a left and go 0.8 miles, while the street winds north to become 1st Avenue S.W. Take a left on S.W. 208th Street, and another left onto Marine View Drive S.W. into the park marked with a homemade sign on the right.

🐾 Des Moines Creek Trail

🐾🐾 (See South Seattle map on page 250)

The scenery is tranquil, but the soundscape is not, at this park directly under the flight path for Sea-Tac Airport. Bring your MP3 player or some earplugs to enjoy a jog along the paved bike path and the natural-surface hiking trails that spin off from it. Otherwise, you'll get only about three to four minutes of peace in between each flyover. The paved route roughly traces the winding creek through nine acres in a natural gully.

Take Exit 151 off I-5, going west on S. 200th Street. Parking for about a half dozen cars is available on the south side of 200th, halfway between International Boulevard and Des Moines Memorial Drive (0.3 miles west of Highway 99). Open dawn–dusk.

🐾 Saltwater State Park

🐾🐾 (See South Seattle map on page 250)

Saltwater tells the tale of two cities, Seattle and Tacoma, whose mayors waged a bitter mud-slinging campaign against each other in the 1930s over whose city has the better quality of life. While no dirt was actually thrown, a hatchet is literally buried somewhere in the park in a symbolic gesture to end the feud. Good thing it wasn't a bone, or Cooper'd still be there trying to dig it up.

You can spend your time at 80-acre Saltwater on top of a breakwall, looking out on the water and Vashon Island, as long as you don't mind the 747s coming in on final approach at nearby Sea-Tac Airport. The lawn is good for kite flying, the picnic benches all have great views, and it's easy enough to generate an afternoon's entertainment by examining the sea life in the tide pools.

At the forefront is 1,445 feet of shoreline, cut neatly in half by a stream emptying into the sound. As you head inland, you'll pass picnic shelters and a campground tucked into the hillside. If you ever decide to get a s'mores support group together, they do have a really cool campfire ring, with benches built into a sheltering rock wall that faces the water. A concession stand operates in the summertime, specializing in corn and chili dogs, coffee and ice cream.

Take Exit 147 from I-5. Follow signs west on S. 272nd Street, and turn right on 16th Avenue S. past the Safeway store. Turn left on Woodmont Drive S., following signs to park. Turn right on Marine View Drive and left on S. 252nd Street into the park.

PLACES TO EAT

Des Moines Dog House: Anyplace with a neon wiener dog above the front door is a winner in Cooper's book. Add in beer and two big outdoor tables on a front deck, and this summertime spot can't be beat. Order from a list of at least a dozen types of dogs, from fancy andouille sausage and linquiça to plain old polish and beef. Dress it yourself at the condiment bar, with up to 20 toppings including neon nacho cheese and chili. 22302 Marine View Dr.; no phone.

The Reuben: This business has changed hands quite a bit in the last few years, but Cooper, for one, is hoping it sticks around in its current iteration as a build-your-own, New York–style sandwich shop. In any case, this spot's got coveted, covered patio seating, a warm welcome on soggy dog days. 21904 Marine View Dr.; 206/824-6672.

Salty's Fish Bar: What starts out as an espresso and pastry joint in the morning morphs into a fish and chips joint in the afternoon. The location is prime real estate, along the marina boardwalk at Redondo Beach and Waterfront Park, due south of Des Moines. Open Memorial Day–Labor Day. 28201 Redondo Beach Dr. S.; 253/946-0636; www.saltys.com.

Kent-Covington

Tell the city council of Kent that you want more off-leash pupportunities for your pets! Join the Kent Dog Owners and Supporters group and get involved. Go to www.kdogs.com for more information.

PARKS, BEACHES, AND RECREATION AREAS

10 Grandview Dog Park

😻 😻 😻 😻 🐕 (See South Seattle map on page 250)

This regional off-leash park is indeed grand, and the view of Mount Rainier and the Kent Valley is not half bad either. No afterthought carved out of an existing park, this is a stand-alone 40-acre masterpiece custom designed for dog revels. It's two plateaus: a grassy area for ruff-and-tumble play up top, and a trail down around to a lower playfield, the more dog-spectacular of the two. Level, smooth, sandy playgrounds are bordered by big logs where people sit and chat while their dogs chase each other into exhaustion. Most of the hillside has been cleared and seeded with grass, with steps leading between the main play areas. Even more greenery surrounds the sand pits. We're not grandstanding when we say that the place is immense.

The park is fully fenced, although the two entrances are not gated. The lower entrance leads down a long fenced pathway before it opens up to a secure area.

DIVERSIONS

Kent is home base for an active group of people who like to be pulled along by their dogs. **K9 Scooters Northwest** (www.k9scootersnw.com) is the name of the club sponsoring a monthly ride and other events to promote responsible dog scootering. If you're serious about getting outdoors with your dogs, they'll help you earn points toward titles and championships regulated by the International Federation of Sledding Sports.

Water therapy is a highly effective treatment for injured or aging dogs, and for anything larger than a small beagle, you can't just fill the bathtub. Luckily, down-on-their-haunches dogs have the **Aquadog Spa** (24317 172nd Ave S.E.; 253/630-3340; www.aquadogspa .com) canine hydrotherapy and massage center in Kent.

A former road serves as a trail into the upper park area. The parking lot is down a long driveway from the busy street.

Thick rolls of plastic bags, the same ones in the produce section of the grocery, are mounted onto five dispenser stations, next to trash cans. A covered shelter, benches, and picnic tables are placed for maximum views. The only water fountain is up top. The park, like Marymoor in Redmond, is managed by Serve Our Dog Areas (www.soda.org). SODA would like to remind you that car break-ins can be a problem in this area, so please lock your cars and keep all valuables out of sight or out of your car altogether.

Go to Grandview, and go often, by taking the Kent/Des Moines exit (#149) from I-5. Turn left at the bottom of the ramp, and take a left at the next light, Military Road. A couple of blocks up, past the Metro bus park-and-ride, you'll see the sign to your right at 228th Street. Open dawn–dusk.

11 Lake Fenwick

🐾🐾 (See South Seattle map on page 250)

There were dogs lounging everywhere the day we visited Lake Fenwick Park, happily watching people do all the work. A pooch sat in a canoe while his owner paddled around, as no power boats are allowed on the small lake. Dogs watched their owners thread fishing line with perfectly edible worms. Pups pranced on picnic blankets and tried to get up on picnic tables.

We passed dogs on the trail around the west side of the lake, hugging the shoreline and leading to a bridge and boardwalk over shallow wetlands, covered in lily pads (and, unfortunately, choked with milfoil). Yes, you guessed it, we sniffed a hello to a couple more canines on the east side of the lake, which winds up a hillside and into the woods, providing only a couple of lake views, but a little longer. Doing both trails provides a decent workout; either trail alone is too short. Seems like our dogs were the only ones doing something at the lazy lake on a summer afternoon. We're told this is an excellent place to bird-watch as well, but we were too busy watching the dogs.

From I-5, take Exit 149A, heading east on the Kent–Des Moines Road. Take a right at Reith Road, and shortly thereafter, a left onto Lake Fenwick Road. There are a couple of parking lots alongside the lake. 25828 Lake Fenwick Rd.

12 Mill Creek Canyon Earthworks Park

😼 (See South Seattle map on page 250)

The Mill Creek neighborhood is north of Seattle. Mill Creek Park, however, is south of Seattle in Kent, named for the site of a sawmill operated by Kent pioneer Peter Saar. Another trendsetter, landscape architect Herbert Bayer, designed the cool earthen dam and waterworks that filter neighborhood run-off into the creek. A trail of a mile or so wanders through the 107-acre park, although short boardwalks do little to manage the mud in the wet season.

From I-5, take Exit 149A, the Kent/Des Moines exit, and head east into Kent. Turn left onto Central Avenue and travel north for 0.5 mile. Turn right on Smith Street and travel east, turn right again onto E. Titus Street. Turn left at Reiten Road. The park entrance is on the left. 742 E. Titus.

13 Clark Lake Park

😼😼😼😼 (See South Seattle map on page 250)

From the moment we arrived, the song of the frogs on Clark Lake was nearly deafening, drowning out any residual traffic noise, and immersing us immediately in this city park's charm. Kent citizens call it their "Central Park," and it's easy to see why. We spent an hour wandering the many trails around the lake, and Coop's fairly sure we missed a few. Gravel and soft-surface trails, giant stone and wooden steps, boardwalks and bridges; they all take you through several habitats in the 124-acre open space. The official names for them—upland meadows, shrub/scrub wetlands, riparian corridors, coniferous forest—sound as impressive as the park really is. Isis met many of her feathered friends along the way, although she'd just as soon eat them as play with them.

The lake and streams that feed it are off-limits to swimming for all species. Everyone is trying to restore important salmon habitat, and snags and other submerged objects make water play unsafe in any case. It's so entertaining to walk around the lake that your Weimaraner won't miss not being able to go in. By the way, this is a good time to remind you never to let your dogs lick or eat salmon carcasses, as they contain bugs that cause Rickettsia, which can be fatal. Lately, they've been seeding the streams with the salmon to encourage Coho to return here to spawn.

Take the W. James Street exit from State Route 167, going east as it becomes S.E. 240th Street. The park will be to your right. www.clarklakepark.org.

14 Lake Youngs Trail and Petrovitsky Park

🐾🐾🐾 (See South Seattle map on page 250)

You won't lack for exercise or interest on this 9.5-mile loop trail around Lake Youngs, although the name is a bit of a misnomer, as you won't get to see the lake itself. The trail, at times packed dirt, wood chip, and gravel over a few old sections of pavement, encircles the fenced-off, protected watershed surrounding the reservoir. Tall chain link will be your guide through the native forest of big-leaf maples and firs, rhododendrons and roses. Even shared with mountain bikers and equestrians, you'll have plenty of time to yourselves, making for a peaceful and meditative walk.

Settled by Finns in the late 1880s, they farmed, logged, and mined coal on the site of nearby Petrovitsky Park, and used the lake to blow off steam from their hard lives.

The trailhead has a decent restroom, a single picnic table, a garbage receptacle, and plenty of gravel parking. Just around the corner, Petrovitsky has little place for a dog, taken up mainly by professional-grade playfields. However, if you've got kids, they'll want to spend serious playtime at the two custom-designed playgrounds with interactive, moving parts. There are more restroom and picnic facilities here as well. In tandem, the two parks are perfect, one providing rest and shade, the other the trail, where you can go as little or as long as you like.

Take Exit 4 from I-405 and go east on the Maple Valley Highway (Highway 169). Drive 2.2 miles, and turn right on 140th Way Southeast. Go south up the hill, and in two miles turn left on S.E. Petrovitsky Road. In another 1.6 miles, turn left on Parkside Way S.E. into Petrovitsky Park. For the trailhead, go another 0.1 mile and turn right on Old Petrovitsky Road. The parking lot is on the left, about a hundred yards in. 16400 Petrovitsky Park S.E.

15 Gary Grant–Soos Creek Parkway

🐾🐾 (See South Seattle map on page 250)

This extensive, eight-mile asphalt parkway is for athletes with four feets. For high-octane hounds who like to run alongside cycling or inline skating humans, the asphalt trail has enough ups and downs for a serious workout. This lesser-known multi-use corridor is tucked away from much of the cityscape, passing through wetlands and forest. Except for the occasional street crossing and short jaunts under power lines, it's pretty scenic. Even so, the Dachsie Twins got the feeling it's designed more for long-distance dogs, like their Bernese friends Naboo and Bella, who pull carts.

Gary Grant Park is a good starting point on the northern third of the trail. It offers parking, a bathroom, a covered shelter with a fireplace, and a small playground and lawn. Take a look at the posted map to see what habitats and wetlands you'll be traveling through. From I-405, take Exit 2 to South State Route 167. Take the S. 212th Street exit from State Route 167 going east, which curves slightly south to become S. 208th Street. Parking is on your left, three miles east, at the intersection of S.E. 208th and 137th Avenue S.E.

The Soos Creek South Trailhead is also easy to find, with all the amenities you could possibly want at Lake Meridian Park a block down the road. Take Highway 18 toward Auburn all the way to State Route 516, Kent-Kangley Road. Go west on Kent-Kangley Road for 0.7 miles, turn right onto 152nd Way S.E., and go 0.3 mile north, 0.1 mile past the boat ramp entrance to Lake Meridian Park, to the trailhead entrance on your right. 152nd Way S.E.

16 Lake Meridian Park

🐾🐾🐾 (See South Seattle map on page 250)

There is no better place to be on a sunny afternoon than on the undulating hills and sunning terraces of this lakeside retreat. Among its merits are lake views, picnic tables on pads, and a restroom and concessions building that looks like a Greek temple. There are No Swimming signs for the people, but nothing about sneaking a dog in; there are Don't Feed the Ducks signs, but nothing about eating them. Seriously, though, at least come sit on the mosaic bench and stare out at the water for a while, or walk the paved pathways in search of sunny spots. The Gary Grant–Soos Creek Parkway starts right around the corner, making Meridian the ideal before or after resting point to soak up the rays.

The main entrance to Lake Meridian is 0.8 miles west of Highway 18 on Kent Kangley Road, State Route 516. For the boat launch entrance and a secondary parking lot, turn right on 152nd Way S.E. and go 0.2 miles up and around the hill to the lot on your left. Open 7 A.M.–dusk. 14800 S.E. 272nd St.

PLACES TO EAT

Ghorm's Burgers and Teriyaki: Fact: One of Seattle's most famous burger chains is Dick's. Fact: One of Dick's founders was H. Warren "Ghorm" Ghormley. Coincidence? We don't think so. Like Dick's, Ghorm's burgers are sloppy, the fries soggy, and the shakes thick. It's a guilty pleasure for those with strong stomachs to handle the extra glop and grease. Devotees declare nothing less will do. On a lighter note, the rainbow trout sandwich is tasty, and although we didn't try the teriyaki, maybe you should. Special orders don't upset them, for example, a root beer and banana shake. Service is through a walk-up window, with no indoor or outdoor seating, so take your goods to go to nearby Earthworks Park. 10429 S.E. Kent Kangley Rd.; 253/852-0190.

Spiro's Greek Island: Is it possible to make dishes that are rich and light at the same time? The chef at Spiro's thinks so, also touting that his abundant plates of Mediterranean food are especially flavorful because he uses all-natural marinades made in-house. Sit on the patio in old downtown Kent. 215 1st Ave. S.; 253/854-1030.

Wild Wheat: The sandwiches at Wheat can't be beat, and they've got some stuff you might not expect to see on a deli menu, such as a grilled salmon tostada, or a lamb burger, or linguini with eggplant, butternut squash, and tomato. Never mind all the healthy stuff, it was hard to see past the dessert case filled with homemade pies and cakes. Wheat's sidewalk seating has a desirable covered awning. 202 1st Ave. S.; 253/856-8919.

PLACES TO STAY

KOA Campground: The catalog calls it the Seattle-Tacoma location, but that's because no one outside of Seattle knows what or where Kent is. This KOA has a nice location, backed up against a big greenbelt on the Green River, and next door to a bird sanctuary. Pancake breakfasts are served up all summer long for $3. Tent sites are $28–31; RVs $33–50. KOA's insurance provider prohibits pit bulls and pit bull mixes, rottweilers, and Doberman pinschers in their campgrounds. KOA does not charge pet fees. 5801 S. 212th St.; 253/872-8652; www.seattlekoa.com.

More Accommodations: Please look under *Chain Hotels* in the *Resources* section for additional places to stay in this area.

Maple Valley

PARKS, BEACHES, AND RECREATION AREAS

🐾 Lake Wilderness Park

🐾🐾🐾🐾 (See South Seattle map on page 250)

On your maiden voyage to this 117-acre city park, don't park at the first lot you see. Take the time to drive around and get the lay of the land before you decide where to stake your claim to the day's enjoyment. There is so much going on here, it's going to be a tough choice.

The arboretum is an option, a treasure trove of native plants, with one of the world's largest collections of Western Azalea (www.lakewildernessarboretum .org). You may want to take a moment to skirt around the amazing Lake Wilderness Lodge for an outdoor tour of its historic 1950s architecture, added to the state's heritage register in 2003 and renovated in 2008. Perhaps you'll want to take mini-hikes on the hill in the preserved forestland, or park and go long distance on the five-star, slow and easy Lake Wilderness Trail, which curves north to connect with the Cedar River Trail. All this is accessible from just the first of three parking areas.

If you make it to the second lot, this is the main access to the park's fantastic open lawns and beaches on the 67-acre lake. Isis settled here, watching impossibly fat dragonflies twitter about, and chatting with a couple of wetsuit-clad gals who were swimming the lake in training for a triathlon. Cooper licked his chops, wishing for picnic droppings, and mused on the benefits of opposable thumbs, eyeing anglers on the fishing pier and rowers in boats on the lake.

Past the golf course to the third lot, the dogs observed kids in the playground, someone getting spanked on a serve in a tennis game, and nonmotorized watercraft putting in at the boat launch. As for the three wetlands and Jenkins Creek, a tributary for Big Soos emptying in to the Green River, the dogs never saw them, but they're sure it's all in there somewhere.

From I-405, take Exit 4, the Maple Valley Highway exit. Drive south on State Route 169 for approximately 11 miles, and take a right onto Witte Road. Turn right at the light and drive to S.E. 248th Street. Turn left and follow 248th for 0.2 mile to the sharp curve. Turn left on Lake Wilderness Drive into the park. Open 7 A.M.–dusk. 425/413-8800.

18 Taylor Mountain Forest
🐾🐾🐾🐾 (See South Seattle map on page 250)

There's a thin line between being a glutton for punishment and a glutton for pleasure, and we're going to give you enough leash to let you figure out when you've crossed it. Endurance athletes, if a 100-mile trail run is what you need to spike your adrenaline, in comes 1,845-acre Taylor Mountain to save the day.

Massive trail clearing, bridge building over Carey and Holder Creeks, and trailhead parking improvements were completed in 2006–2008, to open up yet another 10 miles of mountain trails for seasonal use, April–October. Mountain Beaver, Carey Creek, and Boot Trail are the three named trails within the system. An additional nine miles of decommissioned gravel logging roads are open year-round. Deer and elk sightings are frequent; bear and cougar sightings are possible. Leashing up is highly advisable.

Trail maps are available at the new trailhead, opened May 2008, at 276th Avenue S.E., near the intersection of State Route 18 and the Issaquah-Hobart Road.

19 Cedar River Trail–Landsberg Trailhead
🐾🐾🐾🐾 (See South Seattle map on page 250)

How much fun you have on the Cedar River Trail depends on where you find yourself on it's 17.3 miles. For the first 12.3 miles, starting way up where the river enters Lake Washington in Renton, it is a multi-use, asphalt commuter pathway. Way down in Maple Valley, the last five miles are soft surface, through the much more secluded Rock Creek wilderness area, Big Bend open space, and down to connect with undeveloped Cedar Grove park in a prized, forested river valley. This is the section of the trail Cooper prefers, which is why he'll encourage you to drive all the way down, through the tiny town of Ravensdale, to Landsberg Trailhead Park. Trail hounds can see the whole hog on King County's Bicycling Guide map (www.metrokc.gov/bike).

Take Highway 169 from Renton to Maple Valley, turn left on Kent-Kangley Road, and, shortly thereafter, left on S.E. Summit-Landsburg Road. Take the right fork in the road when the opportunity arises, travel a total of 2.5 miles, and cross over the Cedar River. The trailhead is immediately on your left. No facilities are available.

PLACES TO EAT

Tasty Chef Café: Over the river and through the woods, to what looks like grandma's eating porch, people go. In the little red building, servers who have worked together for decades deliver generous breakfasts and, for lunch, their famous garlic burger, with homemade potato salad and root beer floats. The Wonder Wieners wish they were allowed on the back porch, but accepted with grace the news that they could order to go and pick up through the drive-through. 22607 S.E. 216th Way; 425/432-4795.

Federal Way

A trip out to Dash Point State Park in Federal Way often involves a quick dash into the Metropolitan Market shopping center for pet supplies at **Simply Paws** (1606A S.W. Dash Point Way; 253/874-5702), usually for squeak toys to replace the ones Cooper has gutted and de-fluffed. To re-fluff Isis's coat, the **Splish Splash Doggy Bath** (1606B S.W. Dash Point Way; 253/838-3109) self-serve dog wash is next door.

PARKS, BEACHES, AND RECREATION AREAS

20 Dumas Bay Wildlife Sanctuary

😺 (See South Seattle map on page 250)

Here's just one more reason to pick up after your pooch: According to a spokesman from the Ecology Department, pet waste could be contributing to the large blooms of sea lettuce on this Federal Way beach. When the sun hits the piles of ocean veggies on the beach, they decompose, giving off the smell of rotten eggs. The city says it'll cost about $100,000 to clean it up. Now, that's expensive poop.

At present, you can't even get down to said beach because the trail has been closed due to hillside failure, even though the city ripped up park sidewalks and replaced them with gravel paths that allow groundwater to absorb, instead of runoff eroding the hillside. Meanwhile, native plants and trees have been planted specifically to provide groundcover for birds and wildlife.

Where do dog walkers fit into all this? Well, behind the Dumas Bay Center and Knutsen Family Theater are great Puget Sound views, a rose garden and gazebo, interesting sculptures and interpretive markers, and a rock garden. That's about the sum of it.

For Dumas Bay, take Exit 147 off I-5, going west on 272nd Street. Turn south on Pacific Highway (State Route 99), and take a right onto Dash Point Road. Follow Dash Point Road as it winds toward the water, taking a right to stay on Dash Point at the intersection with 21st Avenue S.W., and a left to stay on Dash Point at the intersection with 30th Avenue S.W. The Dumas Bay Center and Knutsen Family Theater will be on your right. Open 7 A.M.–9 P.M. 30844 44th Ave. S.W.

☙ Dash Point State Park

😸😸 (See South Seattle map on page 250)

Dogs can make a run for the beach at this state park without going to the islands or all the way out to the Pacific. From the parking lot, a tunnel leads out onto the flat, quiet shoreline. The dogs engaged in a study of sea life, as the park brochure recommends, pestering a miniscule crab until it escaped safely under a tide pool rock.

If you want Cooper's two scents' worth, the 11 miles of trails here are the real draw. Heading north from the parking lot is a path that used to loop the entire 398-acres but now is stopped in the middle by a wrecked bridge over an impassable ravine. The state hasn't budgeted to fix the bridge anytime soon. That's okay; it takes a couple of miles just to get to the dead end, and four miles round-trip is plenty for us for one day. The little section of trail from the beach to the campground is steep enough to take your breath away. Dash Point is a quick getaway in Federal Way.

Take Exit 143 from I-5, going west on 320th Street S. Turn left onto 47th Avenue S.W. to enter the park. $5 per day for parking. Hours are 8 A.M.–dusk.

☙ Dog Park at French Lake

😸😸😸🐕 (See South Seattle map on page 250)

The rectangular off-leash area at French Lake Park is like the dog park equivalent of a fish tank. Think of the tall chain-link fence as the walls of the tank. The center of a sizable 10-acre plot is open, with a gently rolling topography, and toward the ends are large evergreens to hide behind if you're feeling solitary, looking a lot like the fake fronds fish use for hide-and-go-seek. Socializers tend to clump together on the high ground, circling each other in happy dances. There are sand pits for diggers, a nice touch, and even the classic arched bridge over a little pond that serves only to add visual interest. All they need is a treasure chest, which, when opened, produces tennis balls like bubbles.

That's where this stretched analogy ends, for this is terra firma, with the inevitable muddy spots entered through the industry-standard double gate. Benches and picnic tables have been thoughtfully placed, bags and cans are available, and humans can avail themselves of the portable potty outside the fence. In the end, since this isn't really a fish tank, you'll need to bring your own water.

From I-5, take Exit 143, going west on 320th Street S. Turn right on 1st Avenue S. Entrance is on the left (west side) of 1st Avenue, between 312th and 320th Streets. Plenty of parking is available. 31531 1st Ave. S.

23 BPA Trail

🐾🐾 (See South Seattle map on page 250)

As football dogs that fit in the crook of your arm, Cooper and Isis should also be able to sit comfortably in panniers on either side of a bicycle's back rack. This plan was hatched for the future, while taking a look at the neat 3.2-mile BPA trail, connecting several parks, schools, and open spaces in central Federal Way. Named for the Bonneville Power Administration, you'll be traversing the paved pathway along rights-of-way for the power lines, passing by the wetlands of Panther Lake and the soccer fields of Celebration Park. Cottonwoods and alders line the trail, which snakes gently back and forth, up and down, through town. A couple of short spurs reach the fringes of Panther Lake. Connect to the northeast end of the trail at Celebration Park, from a spur trail between soccer fields #7 and #8.

Take Exit 143 from I-5, going west on 320th Street S. Take a left on 11th Place S. Park near the main entrance to Celebration Park's field complex.

24 Steel Lake Park

🐾🐾 (See South Seattle map on page 250)

Steel Lake has what a lakeside park should have, namely a sand volleyball pit, a swimming beach Memorial Day–Labor Day, and a pier for fishing April–October. It's got picnic areas, bathrooms, and a boat launch for non-motorized watercraft. There are swings and a playground, and a concession stand that's rarely open. It's big enough to have hosted the U.S. Women's Triathlon for the last five years, which drew 700 women in 2008. If a family outing is in the works—whether or not swimming, running, or biking is part of the action—this city park will do nicely. Oh yeah, and there's a skate park at Steel Lake, if you've got a skateboarding bulldog you want to get on TV.

Take Exit 143 from I-5, going west on 320th Street. Turn right, going north on Highway 99, and turn right on 312th Street into the middle of the park. 2410 S. 312th St.

PLACES TO EAT

Big Apple Bagels: Even without outdoor seating, the Canine Caperers find themselves here for cream cheese with capers an awful lot, because it's at the same exit off I-5 that leads to Grandview Dog Park. There's good stuff stuffed into those soft yet chewy breads at Big Apple. We forgot to ask if it's named after New York, but if the pastrami bagel sandwich is any evidence, it's possible. 23321 Pacific Hwy.; 206/870-2604.

PLACES TO STAY

Quality Inn and Suites: Other than it being a little bit tricky to find the driveway (try through the Taco Bell parking lot, seriously), this hotel gets high marks all around. Rates are standardized around $90–120. The pet fee is $20 per pet per stay. 1400 S. 348th; 253/835-4141.

More Accommodations: Please look under *Chain Hotels* in the *Resources* section for additional places to stay in this area.

Auburn

The city of Auburn has four main claims to fame: Emerald Downs thoroughbred horseracing track, the Muckleshoot Casino, Pacific Raceways motor sports racetrack, and the White River Amphitheatre.

PARKS, BEACHES, AND RECREATION AREAS

25 Five Mile Lake

🐾🐾 (See South Seattle map on page 250)

King County has managed to preserve large deciduous and really tall evergreens at Five Mile Lake Park, even in the parking lot. In the thickly wooded south end at this popular 27-acre park, there are plenty of deadfall sticks, if you happen to know a fetch fiend. A 0.5-mile gravel trail takes in the whole perimeter, past a shallow beach, around a massive central lawn, up to a keen Observation Fort, and through the thicket of firs. It's not pristine by any means, as there are homes on the opposite shore. Still, it's a good place to grill out, and as long as they're on an eight-foot or shorter leash, there's nothing prohibiting dogs from the beach or the water.

Take Exit 143 off I-5, going east on S. 320th Street for 0.7 miles. Turn right on S. Military Road and follow it three miles to the park entrance on your right. Open 8 A.M.–dusk. 36429 44th Ave S.

26 White River Trail

🐾🐾🐾 (See South Seattle map on page 250)

It's hard to find a trail worthy of your time in these parts. Thankfully, this one's a beauty, and it wins high marks for accessibility. It's a good distance, 2.25 miles one-way, with parallel paved and soft-surface options. You can see, hear, and get down to the White River for much of the way, with a color akin to watery milk from glacial silt. It's especially fun for dogs to scramble around the dry riverbed rocks and sand. The White River Trail runs through and connects two parks, Roegner and Game Farm Wilderness.

Roegner is a 21-acre community park at the southwest end of the trail, next to and behind Auburn Riverside High School, dedicated in 1994 in honor of a council member and mayor named Bob (Roegner). The dog-friendly atmosphere includes open grass, a playground, restroom, and commissioned artwork. Handy garbage cans and bag dispensers are stationed along the path. Strategic viewing benches have excellent river views. Game Farm Wilderness is to the northeast. It is far less developed, tucked into native woodlands along the White River. It features 18 campground sites (with water and power hook-ups, available April 1–October 15), along with a day use area, picnic shelter, 18-hole disc golf course, play space, and bathroom. Between the two, the trail makes one main street crossing over Kersey Way.

To reach Roegner from State Route 167, exit onto Ellingson Road going east. Take a right on E. Valley Parkway, a left on Lakeland Hills Way, and left onto Oravetz Road. The park entrance is just past the high school. 601 Oravetz Rd.; 253/931-3043.

For Game Farm Wilderness Park, continue on Oravetz, turn left on Kersey Way, and right on Stuck River Road into the park. 2401 Stuck River Rd. For camping, click "Find a Park" at www.auburnwa.gov/parks..

27 O'Grady County Park

🐾🐾🐾🐾 (See South Seattle map on page 250)

O'Grady is gorgeous. The family that homesteaded and farmed here surely was able to appreciate the setting around a bend of the Green River. We were told you could find the foundations of an old silo, farmhouse, and barn near gnarled old apple and pear trees, but the grasses were waist high in the deep summer of our visit. The trail, though it's not fair to call it that, is a level gravel road, maintained better than any other we've seen. It starts up on the ridge, and winds down to the valley in gentle, swooping curves through a lush forest of big leaf maple and evergreens. After nearly a mile, you'll break out into the valley. After the bridge, take the right fork to the narrower trail to stroll at least another half mile along the river. Be very careful if you go straight out to the river after you've come out of the trees; there's a high, steep bank here that is eroding away.

This section of the river has the highest concentration of spawning Coho, Chinook, and chum salmon in the river system, and you might meet local elk on early morning walks. As a bonus, clear days will provide staggering views of Mount Rainier on the drive here. Besides disturbing the salmon, the river is wide and much too swift to allow swimming. Plenty of horse poop on the trail evidences its popularity with horseback riders. We met a family with two

DOG-EAR YOUR CALENDAR

Auburn's **Petapalooza** is turning out to be a well-received affair, typically held the last Saturday in May at Game Farm Park (330 R Street S.E.). A $15 early registration fee, $20 at the door, scores you a T-shirt and goodie bag. The Dog Trot fun run and walk starts at 9 A.M., followed by games, vendor booths, and contests 10 A.M.–2 P.M. Call 253/931-3043 or go to www.auburnwa.gov for information.

horses, two people, a Bernese mountain dog, a great Dane, and a wiener dog, who rode side saddle.

From Highway 18, take the State Route 164 exit, Auburn Way, southwest toward Enumclaw for 5.7 miles. Turn left on S.E. 380th Place and travel a total of two miles, following it around the bend to the right onto 160th Place S.E., and continuing as it becomes S.E. 384th Street. Turn left at 188th Avenue S.E. to the gravel road and parking at the end of the county road. There are no services or amenities.

PLACES TO EAT

Zola's: Panini sandwiches, salads, real fruit smoothies, and espresso specialty beverages—a guy could get by in life on these four food groups, insists Cooper. At least a dog could, given outdoor seating such as Zola's sunny sidewalk tables with afternoon's western exposure. 402 E. Main St., #120; 253/333-9652.

PLACES TO STAY

Best Western Peppertree Auburn Inn: At least lap dogs can find a place to sleep in Auburn. Dogs 10 pounds and under are allowed for $10 per night; even skinny Isis clocks in at 12 pounds. Tucked in behind the Supermall, at least it's a pretty decent location. Rates start around $135. 401 8th St. S.W.; 253/887-7600; www.peppertreeauburn.com.

More Accommodations: Please look under *Chain Hotels* in the *Resources* section for additional places to stay in this area.

Black Diamond

This tiny hamlet is one of the few remaining coal mining communities in the state.

PARKS, BEACHES, AND RECREATION AREAS

28 Flaming Geyser State Park

🐾🐾🐾🐾 (See South Seattle map on page 250)

One of the things Coop 'n' Isis like so much about the Pacific Northwest is that you get out in the country so quickly from the city. People escape to this park, less than 20 miles from the highway, for many reasons. With three miles of freshwater shoreline on the Green River, folks come to raft, kayak, float, and fish for steelhead and salmon. You and your companion can try flat meadow walks or steep forested hikes and spend some time in and around the river.

The park's featured attractions are fueled by methane gas seeping from 40 feet of an un-mined coal seam. In the 1960s, the Flaming Geyser regularly burned at 6–8 feet, now it manages about the same in inches. The Bubbling Geyser is a bit anticlimactic, popping bubbles not much more than Isis can

manage when she's eaten too much peanut butter or cheese. From this area, a moderate and muddy and kick-tail trail loops about three miles through the park's 480 acres of woods.

A smooth stone beach and the river are to the left when you enter the park. To the left is a remote control plane airport and a meadow trail, marked only with a dog bag dispenser, that parallels the river for about a half mile. The presence of bags confirms the suspicion that this trail, close to the water in many places, is a winner with the canines.

From I-5, take Exit 142 to State Route 18 toward Auburn, then take the exit for Auburn–Black Diamond Road. Take a right on 218th Avenue S.E., at 1.3 miles, take a left on Green Valley Road, travel another 0.5 mile, and turn right onto S.E. Flaming Geyser Road.

PLACES TO EAT

Famous Black Diamond Bakery and Deli: The brick oven for baking Black Diamond's bread was built in 1902. (How's that for a tongue teaser?) It has grown into a bone-a-fide tourist attraction. You can order from the full-service restaurant, a deli, an espresso stand, and the bakery. There are benches out front for you and your buddy. 32805 Railroad Ave.; bakery: 360/886-2741; restaurant: 360/886-2235; www.blackdiamondbakery.com.

PLACES TO STAY

Kanaskat-Palmer State Park Campground: This smallish campground has 31 tent spaces and 19 utility sites in a 320-acre camping park on a small, low plateau in a natural forest setting. The park sits on two miles of shoreline on the Green River. It is some of the closest camping to the city. Standard sites are $17, full utility spots are $24. Reserve at www.camis.com/wa or 888/226-7688.

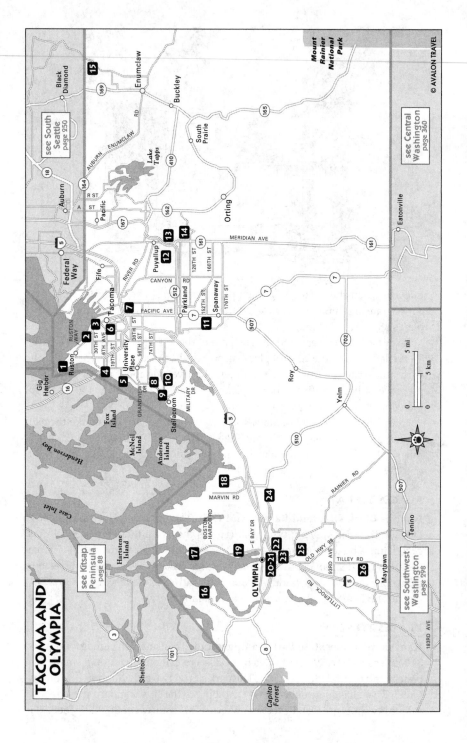

TACOMA AND OLYMPIA

© AVALON TRAVEL

CHAPTER 10

Tacoma and Olympia

The City of Tacoma has done a great job preserving its historic architecture and installing a tremendous amount of outdoor public art. We dare say they've done a much better job than Seattle! There's a thriving theatre district and stunning art and history museums, accented by brew pubs, hip eateries, and condos. City living is in vogue again.

The times, they are a changin' for dogs in Tacoma, decidedly for the better. The city's first neighborhood dog park opened in 2004, and then came a fabulous pair of dog parks at Fort Steilacoom in early 2006. Dogs are not allowed to enter water in the city proper: no lakes, ponds, fountains, wading pools, or water play areas. Never fear, there's plenty of that action if you get out a little ways to the county parks.

As you head south from Tacoma, you'll pass the Fort Lewis Army Base, which created and sent four Stryker Brigades to the fighting in Iraq. McChord Air Force Base is also on the way to the state capital of Olympia. Soon the scenery changes to old-growth and second-growth evergreen forests, butting right up against the capital.

PICK OF THE LITTER—TACOMA AND OLYMPIA

BEST PARKS
Point Defiance Park, Point Ruston (page 276)
Priest Point Park, Olympia (page 292)

BEST DOG PARK
Fort Steilacoom Park, Steilacoom (page 285)

BEST WALK
Ruston Way Waterfront, Old Town Tacoma (page 278)

BEST EVENT
Olympia Pet Parade, Olympia (page 282)

BEST PLACES TO EAT
Herban Café, Titlow Beach (page 281)
La Crème Brûlée, Steilacoom (page 285)

BEST PLACE TO STAY
Hotel Murano, Downtown Tacoma (page 283)

BEST CAMPING
Millersylvania State Park, Maytown (page 297)

Point Ruston

Incorporated in 1906 as a company town for ASARCO, a copper smelting plant on the waterfront, what was Ruston and Point Defiance is becoming Point Ruston. On the land tip of Tacoma, it is the entry point for a spectacular park.

PARKS, BEACHES, AND RECREATION AREAS

1 Point Defiance Park

🐾🐾🐾🐾 (See Tacoma and Olympia map on page 274)

We defy you to find a better urban park in any city in Washington. At 696 acres, it's just a shade under New York's Central Park's 843 acres and has been around almost as long, approved as a public park by President Grover Cleveland in 1880, whereas Central Park officially opened in 1878.

A five-mile drive around the perimeter includes five viewpoints, each with a few picnic spots. Our favorites are Owen Beach, with an unobstructed view of Mount Rainier, and the Bridge Viewpoint, looking at the Tacoma Narrows Bridge.

The diversity of this park keeps us coming back for more. A Japanese Garden with a pagoda, a rhododendron garden, and the lawn that looks out over the Talequah ferry terminal are some high points. A bunch of trails crisscross the park, each anywhere from 0.25 mile to four miles. There are two outdoor museums where your dog is allowed to join you: the Camp 6 Logging Museum and Fort Nisqually, a fur-trading post dating from the 1850s. Kids rave about Never Never Land, a playground and picnic area with a six-foot-tall, pre-fall Humpty Dumpty at the entrance. Finally, this park is home to the city's zoo and aquarium, which are not dog-friendly.

Take Exit 132 off I-5 to State Route 16 and turn north on 6th Avenue. Exit to State Route 163 (Pearl Street) and turn right, leading you directly into the park. Closes a half hour after sunset. 5400 N. Pearl St.

PLACES TO EAT

Antique Sandwich Company: This sandwich shop with a healthy bent is right on the way to Point Defiance Park. You can find salami or sardine sandwiches, hummus and pitas, spinach lasagna, and fresh juices. A daily selection of desserts features treats like huckleberry cheesecake and peanut butter fudge. Outside is the Garden of Eatin', a large, fenced garden with tables where dogs are welcome to bask in the sun with you. 5102 N. Pearl; 253/752-4069.

Tatanka Take Out: This wacky establishment claims that buffalo is "America's original health food." Two outdoor tables wear cowboy boots on their legs and counter seats are pulled off the nearest John Deere tractor. The menu includes bison burgers, bison burritos, bison chili, bison… well, you get the point. In keeping with the healthy theme, other selections include free-range chicken, tofu dishes, and yogurt shakes. Lest we forget, there are raw, frozen buffalo bones for dogs, with good meat still clinging to them. 4915 N. Pearl; 253/752-8778.

Old Town Tacoma and Waterfront

Where Tacoma began, Old Town has been around since 1869. It is a popular place for outdoor concerts and music festivals in Old Town Park (www.old towntacoma.org), and it is also the home of Tacoma's oldest Saloon, The Spar.

PARKS, BEACHES, AND RECREATION AREAS

◢ Ruston Way Waterfront

🐾🐾🐾🐾 🐕 (See Tacoma and Olympia map on page 274)

To appreciate Tacoma at its best, take a dog walk along any or all of this two-mile waterfront parkway. You'll pass pocket parks, piers, and public art. You'll encounter cyclists and the stroller brigade, divers in wetsuits and scuba gear, families and lovers, joggers and power walkers, and lots and lots of local dogs. You'll see tall ships, tankers, and speedboats on Commencement Bay, and behind you, across the street, freight trains will rumble by on clackety tracks. Mount Rainier stages sneak peeks and lower Vashon Island sulks in the mist.

There are at least a half dozen pocket parks along your route. On the northwest is Marine Park/Les Davies Pier, with bathrooms, picnic tables, and barbecue grills. The newest and largest park is Dickman Mill/Hamilton Park, with the ruins of an old mill and a firefighting boat in dry dock. More restrooms and parking are here. Cummings has a rock garden, and, finally, on the southeast end is the view from Jack Hyde Park. Walk a block up McCarver Street in Old Town for lunch. Tacoma's waterfront should not be missed by your canine exploration corps.

From I-5, take Exit 133 and stay on I-705 toward City Center. Keep right onto I-705 North/Schuster Parkway. Take the first left fork in the road to stay on Schuster (do not exit up onto Stadium Way). Travel a mile along the waterfront, then take another left fork in the road toward Ruston Way Waterfront. As you come up over the hill, the first thing you'll see on the right is Jack Hyde Park on Commencement Bay, the start of the walk. There are multiple parking areas, the first will be immediately to your left.

PLACES TO EAT

Café Divino Wine Bar: With a long list of wines by the glass, and a 3–6 P.M. happy hour, you'll need to balance your alcohol intake with food, for example, Italian sausage lasagna, ahi tuna, crab cakes, or blackened halibut tacos. Watch for the summertime tables to come out onto the sidewalk. 2112 N. 30th St.; 253/779-4226; www.cafedivinotacoma.com.

FishTales Bistro: The Northern Fish Company has been around since 1912. The Old Town Dock restaurant they've moved into was Johnny's for 70 years. That's old, tried and true. What's new, or, rather, fresh, are the seafood salads served from the case at a half dozen metal tables. The bistro shares the space with the take-home fish market; getting your smoked salmon spread to go is another great option. 2201 Ruston Way; 253/272-4104.

Spar Coffee Bar: Tacoma's oldest saloon has gone half-sies with the culture's newest obsession, coffeehouse on one side, pub on the other. Enjoy breakfast pastries at the espresso café and fishwiches or chicken and fries in the bar. Recycled fish buckets on the sidewalk read, "K-9 H2O." 2121 N. 30th St.; 253/627-8215; www.the-spar.com.

Proctor District

Proctor Street runs on the top of a ridge in a well-to-do district in town. The Proctor business district has 75 cool shops within three blocks between 25th and 27th Streets. The one shop for Spot is **Wag Pet Market** (2703 N. Proctor St.; 253/756-0924).

PARKS, BEACHES, AND RECREATION AREAS

🖪 Puget Gulch Nature Trail–Puget Park

🐾🐾🐾 (See Tacoma and Olympia map on page 274)

Puget Creek is one of Tacoma's remaining three salmon-bearing streams, hidden in a jagged ravine, tucked into a residential neighborhood of stately homes. Within the Puget Creek Habitat restoration area is a 0.7-mile trail, starting near the waterfront and climbing up to Puget Park at the top of the hill on Proctor Street. It's an easy hike under a forest canopy so thick that only dappled sunlight filters through. It's a steady climb, but the path is smooth, a wide and level gravel walkway. Natural surface spurs can add to your mileage. At the bottom is a hidden picnic meadow, with a giant metal fish sculpture to remind you not to go into the stream and disturb the baby salmon.

For Puget Gulch, follow the directions to Ruston Way Waterfront. Go straight through the light at McCarver, travel another 0.6 miles, turn left on Alder Way. There are a couple of parking spots in front of the trail entrance, 0.1 mile up the road on the left, where Alder takes a steep bend to become 36th Street. Continue up the hill on 36th Street and turn left on Proctor to 31st Street to reach Puget Park topside, with a playground, picnic tables, and a lawn. The trail hides at the back of the groomed park. Open 4 A.M.–10 P.M. 3505 N. Alder Way; www.pugetcreek.org.

PLACES TO EAT

Art and Soul: This pottery painting studio and coffee lounge has brick patio seating nestled under a few trees. More importantly, it's next door to Wag's Pet Market. 2701 N. Proctor St.; 253/756-0444.

Europa Bistro: At an intimate Italian restaurant with two outdoor tables, chef Alfredo (yes, real name), from Caivano near Naples, dishes up his pasta, pizza, panini, and *zuppa* for lovers who love dogs. 2515 N. Proctor St.; 253/761-5660; www.europabistro.net.

Titlow Beach

PARKS, BEACHES, AND RECREATION AREA

4 Scott Pierson Trail

🐾🐾 (See Tacoma and Olympia map on page 274)

Scott Pierson was a city landscape architect and urban planner who believed strongly in non-motorized transportation. He rode his bike to work every single day. This is his trail, in more than name, a five-mile, paved transportation corridor he traveled, that parallels State Route 16 from Gig Harbor to 25th and Sprague.

By far the most scenic section is across the Tacoma Narrows Bridge. In 1940, the original bridge wobbled, twisted, and collapsed due to wind-induced vibrations; the spectacular demise of Galloping Gertie was captured in a famous black-and-white silent video. There was one fatality, sadly: Tubby the dog.

To access the trail, park at the Park and Ride, at War Memorial Park (now, that's how to use the word park in a sentence in a spelling bee). As you enjoy the blustery scenery, you can spend a moment honoring all those commemorated here, including Tubby.

Bridge End: From I-5 southbound, take Exit 132 toward Gig Harbor/Bremerton, and merge onto State Route 16. From State Route 16, take Exit 4, the Jackson Avenue exit. Turn south on Jackson Avenue, and left on 6th Avenue, to the Park and Ride and War Memorial Park on your left.

5 Titlow Park

🐾🐾 (See Tacoma and Olympia map on page 274)

Titlow has a rich history, beginning as a campsite for gathering Puyallup and Nisqually tribes. By 1911, there was a tomato farm, silent movie studio, and the Hotel Hesperides on the property. The latter has been a lodge since the Works Progress Administration converted it in 1936. Ferry service originated here to Point Fosdick on the Kitsap Peninsula and Fox Island.

The saltwater pool opened in 1955, with a pancake feed, hosted by the real Aunt Jemima, and octopus wrestling championships. While dogs are denied the pleasure of the community pool, and everyone is denied beach access due to cleanup of arsenic and lead in the soil, there is enough here to keep them occupied. A rough walk leads around a marsh and through the picnic grounds.

A parcour fitness course, built in 1977 and revived in 2003 by the Boy Scouts, gives you a little extra run for your money. Restoration of Titlow is a high priority for Tacoma Parks in the next decade; hopefully, we'll have a bright future to report in addition to the history next time we visit.

From State Route 16, take the 6th Avenue exit and go west on the arterial for two miles to the park on your right. 8425 6th Ave.

PLACES TO EAT

Herban Café: This bistro is the open air division of Pinwheel Catering, run by a gal known in these parts as "the pink cookie lady." If Isis ever runs a café, it'll be like this one, where garage doors open up the whole front facade, allowing sidewalk eaters to feel as much a part of the action as those sitting inside. Come for the Sunday brunch buffet, and don't miss the *frites* with the potato skin still on, adorned with clumps of garlic and a killer fry sauce. 2602 6th Ave., Suite A; 253/572-0170; www.pinwheelcatering.com.

J. T.'s Original Louisiana Bar-B-Que: Though a longtime Seattle resident, the Dachsie's mom has lived in the south, and can attest that the closer you get to Louisiana, the better the barbecue. It's the sweet, followed by the heat, that makes those ribs and that brisket sing. You know J. T.'s legit 'cause he serves Southern sweet tea, which means you put sugar in iced tea until it just reaches crystallization. Said a recent reviewer, "Now I know why dogs smile" when they hear the word "bones." 7102 6th Ave.; 253/565-4587.

Downtown Tacoma

Revitalized downtown Tacoma has some attractions you should not miss, such as the Museum of Glass, Tacoma Art Museum, Pantages Theatre, and the Washington History Museum. So, pack the pups off to **Hound Hangout** (414 St. Helens Ave.; 253/573-0924; www.houndhangout.net) for the day and visit the dog park tomorrow.

PARKS, BEACHES, AND RECREATION AREAS

6 Wright

🐾 🐾 🐾 🐾 (See Tacoma and Olympia map on page 274)

In downtown Tacoma, squirrels are chasing each other around deciduous state-champion trees in this lovely city park, established in 1890. As a nod to the area's many Norwegian emigrants, a statue of playwright Henrik Ibsen, nineteenth century Norwegian playwright, scowls down from his pedestal.

Walking the crushed gravel walkways gives you the full tour of the greens and grounds, formed by the triangle of 6th and Division Streets. Leashed dogs are welcome, except in the W. W. Seymour Botanical Conservatory with its

DOG-EAR YOUR CALENDAR

The **Dugan Foundation's** mission is to end euthanasia of animals in Pierce County by sponsoring low cost spay/neuter clinics, working to establish a pet sanctuary, and educating the public. They host a series of annual fundraisers, including **Dog Day Afternoon** at the Tacoma farmer's market, **Happy Howlidays,** and their biggie, **The Fur Ball** black-tie gala each October. Attend them all, and remember, "It's hip to snip!" Go to www.duganfoundation.org for more information.

The annual **Olympia Pet Parade,** sponsored by the city's newspaper, the *Olympian,* draws about 1,000 kids in costume, pets in tow, to march through the Capitol, without politicking, every August. It's all free, there's no registration, a ton of prizes are awarded, and all the kids get free ice cream in Sylvester Park at the end of the route. Call 360/570-7790 and watch the paper for parade route and staging information.

distinctive 12-sided dome. The park does serve as a resting place for some of the city's transient population, so we can't recommend it after dark.

Take Exit 133 from I-5. First stay right to get onto I-705, then keep left on I-705 toward City Center. Then, stay in the left-most lane, toward A Street/City Center. Exit left at S. 15th Street/Pacific Avenue. Go up the hill on 15th Street, turn right on Tacoma Avenue. Drive 0.6 miles, turn left on 6th Street, turn right on G Street, and find street parking anywhere along the side of the park.

7 Rogers Dog Park

🐾🐾🐕 (See Tacoma and Olympia map on page 274)

The first of Tacoma's official dog parks is no less groundbreaking for its small one-acre size. The grass is green and level, the area is fully fenced, and there are two entry points with double-gates, one of which is wheelchair-accessible. There's a bag dispenser, garbage, and a functioning water source in the shape of a water hydrant with a stylin' flame paint job.

From I-5, take Exit 135 toward Portland Avenue. The ramp becomes E. 27th Street. Turn left on East L Street and go south the park, across from Wright Avenue. Park along the street. 3151 E. L St.

PLACES TO EAT

Dock Street Sandwich Company: For Jack Sprat, who could eat no fat, sandwich innards are available tucked into low-carb wraps. For his wife, who could eat no lean, the same and more are placed between herbed focaccia bread and grilled. For Sam I Am, there are green pesto eggs and ham. Relax at sidewalk or courtyard seating next door to Urban Dogs and the Museum of Glass, or order a boxed lunch with all the trimmings to go. 1701 Dock St.; 253/627-5882.

Harmon Brewing Co. and Restaurant: This is the place to meet friends after work, be they furry or fair, for a pint and a burger in the heart of Tacoma's museum and university district. When you're stuck at work, the "Real Fast" express lunch menu is just the ticket. 1938 Pacific Ave.; 253/383-2739; www .harmonbrewingco.com.

Hello Cupcake: Isis really hopes the cupcake craze isn't just another passing fad, for life is simply sweeter when topped with buttercream frosting. Wouldn't you know it, the cupcakes are cheaper by the dozen. 1740 Pacific Ave.; 253/383-7772; www.hello-cupcake.com.

Infinite Soups: At least a dozen homemade soups per day, both meaty and vegetarian, are infinitely pleasing to the palate. Sampling is encouraged; how else can you decide between the dozens of choices? When you've finally chosen your soup du jour, get it to go. 445 Tacoma Ave. S.; 253/274-0232; www.infinitesoups.com.

PLACES TO STAY

Days Inn Tacoma: Off I-5 before Tacoma, at Exit 129, the reliable Days Inn is convenient to the Tacoma Dome. They limit you to two dogs, each under 65 pounds. Rates range $70–110, plus a $10 pet fee. 6802 Tacoma Mall Blvd.; 253/475-5900.

Hotel Murano: The Dachsie Twins are occasionally prone to pronouncements, so you won't be surprised when they utter this one: If you stay in only one hotel in this entire guide, save up your pennies and make it this one. In fact, even if you can't stay here, come in to look at the glass art. Grab a guide from the Front Desk and walk through the building as though it were an art gallery, with the same hushed respect, because that's really what it is.

The original Murano is an archipelago of islands in Italy, where all glass-makers were forced to move to protect the city of Venice from the fires of their hot shops. The hotel does its namesake proud. Each floor is named for an artist, with pieces representing his or her work and an artist's statement describing the methodologies and artistic influences. Beyond all that, the beds are bliss-fully comfortable, the city views, from the fifth floor up, are unforgettable, and Murano has spared no expense on amenities. We could go on and on—just go! Rates are fairly reasonable, ranging $150–220; the pet fee is a flat $45 per stay. 1320 Broadway; 253/238-8000; www.hotelmuranotacoma.com.

La Quinta Tacoma: The La Quinta chain is wonderfully pet-friendly. As usual, there are no pet fees and no restrictions. Renovated in 2007, this location is especially spiffy. Rates range $120–210; 1425 E. 27th St.; 253/383-0146; www.lq.com.

More Accommodations: Please look under *Chain Hotels* in the *Resources* section for additional places to stay in this area.

Steilacoom

Incorporated in 1854, this waterfront community of about 6,000 residents was listed as a National Historic District in 1974. The fort nearby, now an excellent city park with a dog park, was built by the military in 1849, saw brief action during the 1855–1856 Indian War, and was already decommissioned by 1868.

PARKS, BEACHES, AND RECREATION AREAS

8 Chambers Creek Park

🐾🐾🐾 (See Tacoma and Olympia map on page 274)

At the headwaters of Chambers Creek there's a skim-boarding park, a local hangout for teens that's like a skateboard park, except it's in shallow waters, and the boards used are wider and have no wheels. It's hard to describe, so come watch.

Along the shoulder of the creek ravine is a moderately steep, 1.5-mile, well-traveled climb through a mature forest. It's a visual pleasure, leading first to a clearing by the bay, then to a high viewpoint over the clear, rushing creek. It's also an auditory journey, between the chattering squirrels, vocal birds, and the rustlings of rodents in the brush. On the olfactory front, you are within sniffing distance of a wastewater treatment plant, but we had to drive right up to the sewer gates to catch a whiff.

From I-5 southbound, take Exit 129, go west on 74th Street W. for 3.5 miles, which curves south to become Custer Road. Turn right on 88th Street S.W., which merges into Steilacoom Boulevard, and travel another three miles to downtown Steilacoom. Turn right on Main Street, right on Lafayette Street, and follow it another 1.5 miles after Sunnyside Park, as it becomes Chambers Creek Road. There will be a sign and limited parking off to your right, just south of where the road crosses Chambers Creek.

9 Sunnyside Beach

🐾🐾 (See Tacoma and Olympia map on page 274)

There's a song that talks about keeping on the sunny side, which we'd update to include beach volleyball, picnicking action, and open-water scuba diving lessons, where the outdoor shower has great views of Anderson Island and the Olympic Mountains.

Sunnyside is just north of downtown Steilacoom on Lafayette Street. Follow the same directions for Chambers Creek Park above to get here from the highway. Park closes at 10 P.M. Daily parking is $5 for non-residents.

🔟 Fort Steilacoom Park

🐾🐾🐾🐾🐕 (See Tacoma and Olympia map on page 274)

For more than a dozen years, dog lovers were using the unkempt fields of this 340-acre regional park as the last big land of the free for Greater Tacoma dogs. A leash-law crackdown starting in 2003 encouraged dog lovers to get busy. They got organized, got money together, and got a whopping 22 acres designated, fenced, and improved to create an excellent dog park. Even the little-dog zone is big; you'll come to it first from the parking area.

The fences are large wooden deer fencing, backed up by chicken wire that goes all the way to the ground. We're giving it the full four paws 'cause it's got everything a dog park really needs: cans and bags, double-entry gates, fresh water, separate small- and large-dog areas (the small-dog area is reserved for running greyhounds on Sunday mornings, by the way). There are trees and a covered shelter for shade and wide, open spaces for running and tossing. Benches, picnic tables, and covered seating are everywhere. Gravel trails wind through, to, and around the fences, to be walked on-leash as desired. The park has a huge, happy list of canine clientele. If your dog is really lucky, the local lady who makes organic dog treats may be on hand to ply her wares. Whooooee!

The only complaints we've heard are that park caretakers sometimes go too long between mowing, especially for, ahem, height-challenged dogs, and that the after-work happy hour can be a zoo. Waahooo!

From I-5, take Exit 129, go west on 74th Street W. for 3.5 miles, which curves south to become Custer Road. Turn right on 88th Street S.W., which merges into Steilacoom Boulevard, going another mile. Turn left on 87th Avenue S.W. and right on Waughop Lake Road. The OLA will be off to your left, almost another mile after you've entered the park. It sits in the triangle created between Angle Lane and Elwood Drive in the southeast section of the park. 8714 87th Ave. S.W.; www.parkdogs.com.

PLACES TO EAT

La Crème Brûlée: At this authentic French bistro, chef Bertrand serves a $10 crepe special for lunch and the classic, rich cuisine of his homeland for dinner. The savory crepes are themed after famous European towns; the sweet ones are more traditional and include Suzette with orange butter and Clichy with lemon butter and brown sugar. Covered sidewalk seating is very inviting, pulling you in at the very least for some French onion soup and a glass of wine. 1606 Lafayette St.; 253/589-3001; www.lacremebrulee.com.

PLACES TO STAY

La Quinta–Lakewood: Unlike most La Quintas, this hotel limits you to one pet per room, up to 50 pounds, but without a fee. Rates range $140–220; 11751 Pacific Hwy. S.W.; 253/582-7000.

Spanaway

PARKS, BEACHES, AND RECREATION AREAS

🟥 Spanaway Lake Park and North Bresemann Forest

🐾🐾🐾 (See Tacoma and Olympia map on page 274)

On a sunny Saturday, this 135-acre park is a massive, multi-cultural fiesta, party central for a multitude of ethnicities, many from the nearby Army and Air Force bases. It is tailor-made for a family outing, with something to please everyone. Three miles of accessible, paved trails wander through the developed park along the northeast side of the lake.

Across Military Road is another 70 acres, known as Bresemann Forest, with a system of nature trails along Morey Creek. Enter the forest through a wrought iron gate on the west side of the Harry Sprinker Recreation Center parking lot near Matterhorn-shaped SPIRE outdoor climbing rock.

From I-5, take Exit 127 and follow the Puyallup/Mount Rainier signs. Go east for two miles on State Route 512. Take the second exit to Parkland/Spanaway and turn right onto Pacific Avenue, State Route 7. Travel 2.5 miles and turn right on Old Military Road, also 152nd Street. Travel 0.5 mile to the park's main entrance on the left. Sprinker Center is 1 1/2 blocks east of the main entrance to Spanaway Park, across Old Military Road. Open 7 A.M.–dusk. 14905 Bresemann Rd. S.; 253/798-4176.

Puyallup

Think of the amorous French skunk Pepe Le Pew in those old cartoons to correctly pronounce the town's name (PEW-ahl-up). This is not, however, a reference to how the town smells, which as far as the dogs' adept noses could discern, smelled perfectly sweet.

PARKS, BEACHES, AND RECREATION AREAS

🟥 Clark's Creek Off-Leash

🐾🐾🐾🐕 (See Tacoma and Olympia map on page 274)

Were it only for the dog park, Clark's Creek would barely rate a paw, a 0.66-acre dirt patch with grass clinging for dear life to its fenced borders. As a package deal, it's the icing on a yummy cake, starting with the waterfowl pond across the street at DeCoursey Park. After playing duck-duck-goose, perambulate down a leisurely gravel trail around the pond to 7th Avenue. Carefully cross the street on the bridge over the creek, duck behind the tennis courts, and get goose bumps under your fur with a quick dip in the creek. Hike down the dirt road to the left, pass the yellow gate with the stop sign (meant to hinder only vehicles) and continue around the bend to find the OLA. It's no loss if you get

DOG-EAR YOUR CALENDAR

When you hear people say "Do the Puyallup," they're talking about the state fair at the Puyallup Fairgrounds in September. After the stampede has moved on, the dogs take over for **Canine Fest** at the fairgrounds, on a middle Saturday in October. This dog day is a family affair, where individuals with one dog each get in for $5, or the whole family and pack can come for $15. In addition to booths and a pet parade, the fair elects a Mr. and Mrs. Canine Fest canine king and queen, and some lucky, unkempt mutt gets a Mad Mutt Makeover. There are pet comedians, communicators, and trainers. You can also adopt a dog or get yours washed, microchipped, and blessed. Proceeds benefit the local 4-H Club and Pullayup Mainstreet. 253/840-2631; www.puyallupmainstreet.com.

distracted by the trails leading up the hill to the rest of the 55 acres on your way. Perhaps you'll pass right by the OLA and find yourself at the playground at the south entrance to Clark's Creek. Both parks have picnic tables, bathrooms, and trash receptacles. There are mutt-mitt dispensers everywhere, so take the hint.

From Tacoma, take State Route 167 into Puyallup. Turn south on Meridian, turn right on Pioneer Avenue, take a left on 18th Street, and a right on 7th Avenue S.W. Park at the north entrance to Clark's Creek or DeCoursey Park. 1700 12th Ave. S.W.

13 Wildwood Park

😛 😛 (See Tacoma and Olympia map on page 274)

In this park of 80 lush acres, 55 are forested, not bad odds for a species that likes to pee on trees. Primarily a gathering place, there are five covered picnic shelters, with fireplaces and grills, hidden in the woods. Once the site of a historic water reservoir, there is a shallow stream for both kids and dogs to cross and mess around in. Wildwood's fitness trail, the Jim Martinson Exercise Trail, is more fun than fitness. Built in 1980, and refurbished by free labor from overactive teens (a.k.a. the Boy Scouts), it winds up, down, and around the thick woods in roller coaster fashion. The dogs watched intently as we did our reps in the Beginner set. If we lived close to these exercise stations, we'd be skinny for sure.

Take State Route 167 from Tacoma to Puyallup and go south on Meridian Avenue, underneath State Route 512, and up the hill. Turn left on 23rd Avenue, and you'll see the entrance to your left, just past 9th Street. Take the right fork in the road when you enter the park to wind down to the more interesting

parts of the park, including the loop trail, the stream, and the playground. 1101 23rd Ave. S.E.

14 Bradley Lake

🐾🐾🐾 (See Tacoma and Olympia map on page 274)

Bradley Lake is positively pupular, as in popular with the pups. Word of the tri-level water fountain—adult, kid, dog—spread quickly when the park was dedicated in 2001, and the dogs have been migrating here to check it out ever since. The 0.8-mile paved lake loop may also be a draw, busy even on a rainy Sunday. Picnic stations, playgrounds, and restrooms cater to the species on the other end of the leashes of the many furry friends who hobnob at this lake rendezvous.

Take State Route 167 from Tacoma to Puyallup and go south on Meridian Avenue. Turn left on 31st Avenue, and left on 5th Street to the park entrance on your right. Open 6 A.M.–7 P.M. October–March; until 10 P.M. the rest of the year. 531 31st Ave. S.E.; www.cityofpuyallup.org.

PLACES TO EAT

Organic Comfort Food Café: This restaurant proves that it is possible to combine the terms "comfort food" and "vegetarian" in the same sentence. In addition to mounds of sidewalk seating, they have a $15 refundable borrow-a-picnic-blanket program, and—we love this part—casseroles of the day for dinner if you don't want to cook, in two-, four-, and six-person serving sizes. Opportunivores, never fear, there are full-on meat choices in addition to vegan, gluten-free, and vegetarian dishes. 210 W. Pioneer; 253/770-6147.

PLACES TO STAY

Best Western Puyallup–Park Plaza: Dogs hear in more frequencies than we do, perking up those talented ears when they hear of goodie bags at check-in containing poop bags, milk bones, and directions to the dog walking area at the hotel. Without limits or restrictions, pets cost a $25 flat fee per stay. Rates range $150–160. 620 S. Hill Park Dr.; 253/848-1500.

Holiday Inn Express–Puyallup: This hotel coughs up a few doggie treats at check in, and there's pet station out back, "which is really just a patch of grass," they confessed. Rates range $160–210, plus a $25 flat fee; 812 South Hill Park Dr.; 253/848-4900; www.hiexpress.com.

Northwest Motor Inn: This motel is tidy and cheap, with rates starting at $60 and a pet fee of $10, conveniently located near State Route 512 and downtown Puyallup. 1409 S. Meridian St.; 253/841-2600; www.nwmotorinn.com.

Enumclaw

The closer you get to Mount Rainier, the bigger it looks. That's logical, but there's no way to describe how profoundly large it is until you see it and it takes your breath away, which you can do from nearly any vantage point in this gateway town. If you really know your way around a compass and have a universal GPS and good orienteering and survival skills, you and your dog may enjoy trekking in some of the more remote areas of the Green River Gorge. Go to the website for the Middle Green River Coalition for recreation information at www.mgrc.org.

PARKS, BEACHES, AND RECREATION AREAS

15 Nolte State Park

🐾🐾 (See Tacoma and Olympia map on page 274)

A private resort until 1972, this 117-acre state park is named after the family that graciously donated the park for public use. This day-use only park centers around Deep Lake, with 7,174 surveyed feet of freshwater shoreline, and a one-mile, level, soft-surface trail around its perimeter. The 66-acre lake is well stocked with rainbow trout each year for anglers. The Dachsie Twins love it when they can take a lake walk and see nothing but the forest for the trees, no development other than a small RV park, no motors revving on the water. It's good for the soul of any species.

From State Route 410, turn north on 284th Avenue S.E., also called Farman Street at that intersection, and later Veazie-Cumberland Road. Look for the park sign, and continue approximately seven miles to park entrance. 360/825-4646.

PLACES TO EAT

Wally's White River Drive In: Your dog never even needs to get out of the back seat to enjoy a sample fry or two from you, as Wally's offers real, throwback, car hop service. Phone it in at the speaker, and a youngster will deliver your smeared burger, malt, and fries directly to your window tray. 282 Hwy. 410 N., Buckley; 360/829-0871.

DIVERSION

Ever heard of the B.A.R.F. diet? The Bones and Raw Food movement is gaining strength as people discover that their pets may have as many food allergies and sensitivities as humans. **Tonita Fernandez** has studied canine nutrition for more than a decade, and she is devoted to switching your dogs over to the diet nature intended. Tonita offers individual counseling by appointment if you are interested in exploring this alternative to better your loved one's health. An hour and a half session is $75, but she is such a passionate advocate, the sessions usually go much longer.

Tonita has also opened **The Pampered Paw,** a canine spa for the too many dogs who suffer from back and hip problems. In a purpose-built building, your fur-kids can come for rehabilitation, recovery, conditioning, or plain old pampering. Afterward, there are doggie videos to watch, a fireplace to dry in front of before going home, and gourmutt treats.

Call Tonita at 360/802-4888 to arrange for your private nutrition counseling and canine spa package.

PLACES TO STAY

Park Center Motel: Without being too disparaging of the other accommodations in town, the dogs would like to encourage you to stay here. The rooms are larger and cleaner, the pet fee lower at $10 per pet per night, and the rates reasonable at around $80 a night. 1000 Griffin Ave.; 360/825-4490.

Olympia

It's the state capital, guv'ner, and "Bowser is welcome," read the bag dispensers thoughtfully placed in all city parks. It goes on to say your dog can have fun, while keeping you on an eight-foot or shorter leash and requesting that you pick up after him.

PARKS, BEACHES, AND RECREATION AREAS

16 Frye Cove County Park

🐾 🐾 (See Tacoma and Olympia map on page 274)

Two miles of trails for nature walks, gently rolling lawns for good old-fashioned picnicking, and 1400-feet of prime shellfish gathering territory along Eld Inlet equals 86 acres of prime pup real estate with magnificent views of Mount Rainier thrown in for the human clientele. It's photogenic, often used as a backdrop for outdoor weddings. On the trail, informative signage helps you understand what you're looking at, which is typically big red cedars, Douglas firs, and a few big-leaf maples.

From I-5 in Olympia, take Exit 104 onto Highway 101 north, toward Aberdeen. Stay on U.S. 101 toward Shelton. Take the Steamboat Island Road exit. Go north on Steamboat Island Road for 5.8 miles and turn right onto Young Road N.W. Proceed about two miles and turn left on 61st Avenue N.W. into Frye Cove County Park. 4000 N.W. 61st St.

17 Burfoot County Park

🐾🐾🐾 (See Tacoma and Olympia map on page 274)

This county park is one of those out-of-the way places in a residential area where you often have the run of the place. Several easy trails connect a big picnic meadow with a 1,000-foot pebble beachfront on Budd Inlet. The Rhododendron Trail is the over-the-bridge-and-through-the-woods trail to the water. The Beach Trail is no-nonsense and gets you to the water in 0.25 mile or less; there's a set of railroad-tie steps and a boardwalk at the end. The 0.25-mile Horizon Trail is a wheelchair-accessible and Braille interpretive loop in the woods. Until you get to the beach, stay on the trails to avoid poison oak. Come out a ways to get some fresh air and watch a sunset.

From I-5, take Exit 105B, bear right onto Plum Street, stay on the road when it becomes East Bay Street and then Boston Harbor Road, seven miles from the highway to the park. Open 9 A.M.–dusk. 360/786-5595.

18 Tolmie State Park

🐾🐾 (See Tacoma and Olympia map on page 274)

This 105-acre park is named for Dr. William Frazer Tolmie, a surgeon, botanist, and fur trader who spent 16 years with the Hudson Bay Company at Fort Nisqually, which, by the way, you can tour with your dog at Point Defiance Park, described in this chapter. This multi-tasking Renaissance man also studied Native American languages during the Indian wars of 1855–1856 to improve communication and bring about peace.

Underwater enthusiasts have built a scuba park at Tolmie. Unless your dog can hold his breath for a good long time, he might prefer hiking the 1.25-mile Four Cedars or the 0.75-mile Twin Creeks Trails. Of course, there are always the simple pleasures of snooping around the tidal flats or selecting a driftwood fetch stick from the cobble and shell beach. Four Cedars climbs almost straight up from the lower parking lot, offering views of Anderson and McNeil Islands. Twin Creeks has fewer views, more trees, and little elevation changes.

From I-5, five miles north of Olympia, take Exit 111 onto Marvin Road N.E. and stay in the right lane to continue straight on Marvin through a series of roundabouts. Turn right on 56th Avenue N.E., left on Hill Street, and turn left down the hill at the sign into the park. 8 A.M.–dusk.

🔟 Priest Point Park

🐾 🐾 🐾 🐾 (See Tacoma and Olympia map on page 274)

At this centerpiece wooded city park, only two miles from downtown, you can glimpse what the area looked like before French Catholic missionaries came in 1848, when Native Americans gathered for *potlatch* feasts. The 320-acre park is wild and woody and woolly with moss, a jungle thick enough to provide secluded picnic spots. Bring your machete; even if you don't need it to hack through the brush, you could use it to open oyster shells from the mud flats.

On a hill to the east are short trails, picnic shelters, and the Samarkand Rose Garden. Ah, but go west, young dog, go west, to the Ellis Cove Trail along Budd Inlet. This 2.4-mile moderately easy path mixes boardwalks, steps, gravel, and dirt to take you past towering trees of nesting osprey, gravel beaches with water access, mud flats at low tide, and marshes before ending on the shore of south Puget Sound. It's for hikers only, and it couldn't be more fun.

From I-5, take Exit 105B, go straight onto Business 101, and bear to the right onto Plum Street through downtown, which becomes East Bay Drive leading to the park entrance, 2.5 miles from the highway. Start at the north trailhead to get to the gravel beaches faster. Pass up the main entrance into the park, continue north 0.5 mile, turn left on Flora Vista N.E., and parallel park along the side of the road. Open 7 A.M.–10 P.M. April–October, 7 A.M.–7 P.M. November–March. 2600 East Bay Dr. N.E.

🔟 Capitol Lake Park

🐾 🐾 (See Tacoma and Olympia map on page 274)

If you know someone who's begging to go for a walk, take her royal dogness to the 1.5-mile trail encircling the reflecting pond for the State Capitol Building. The six-foot-wide alternating gravel and concrete path is a favorite lunchtime stroll; maybe you'll meet your state representative and have the chance to make sure she's representing the constituency. In concentric circles around the pond are the trail, a ring of viewing benches, narrow lawns, and finally young cherry trees that show off in April.

From I-5, take Exit 105B west to Plum Street, left on Legion Way, continue nine blocks, and turn left on Water Street into the parking lot. Three-hour metered parking is available for $0.50 per hour. There's a dog bag dispenser a few feet from the parking lot. 5th and Water Streets.

🔟 Capitol Campus

🐾 🦴 (See Tacoma and Olympia map on page 274)

At the Washington State Capitol in Olympia, many of the attractions are outside, making a self-guided tour of the legislative heart of Washington and its groomed grounds a great walk for you and your dog. The buildings, outdoor art, gardens, memorials, and monuments cover 100 landscaped acres. The grounds were designed by the famed Olmsted Brothers architecture firm from New York, and the fountains include a replica of the famous Roman-style fountain located at Tivoli Park in Copenhagen, Denmark. Maps and information are available at the visitors center, which is in a handy location in a corner of the campus. 360/586-3460; www.ga.wa.gov/visitor.

To reach the campus, take Exit 105A from I-5 southbound, and follow 14th Avenue through the tunnel to the visitors center on your left. From I-5 northbound, take Exit 105 and the left fork in the road for the State Capitol/City Center route.

22 Olympia Woodland Trail

🐾🐾 (See Tacoma and Olympia map on page 274)

Make a day of it, and combine this 1.5-mile trial with Watershed, for a little on-road (Woodland), off-road (Watershed) combo. Woodland Trail is an asphalt path with a crushed rock sideline trail. Though parallel to I-5, it is enough removed from the highway to be enjoyable.

The Eastside Trailhead for the Woodland Trail has built-green bathrooms and a shelter with living roofs, solar tube lighting, and a rain garden that filters storm water. Stand at the shelter, look across Eastside Street, and you can see an entrance into Watershed Park, and its trail, the Eldon Marsh Trail.

From I-5 Southbound, take Exit 105B. As you exit, stay in the right lane toward City Center. Turn right on Union Avenue, then right again to go south on Eastside Street, crossing back over the highway. Park to your left, immediately past Wheeler Avenue. From I-5 northbound, take Exit 105, and then take the right fork in the road for the Port of Olympia route. 1600 Eastside St. S.E.

23 G. Eldon Marshall Trail in Watershed Park

🐾🐾🐾🐾 (See Tacoma and Olympia map on page 274)

At the turn of the last century, nearly every glass of water in Olympia came from wells in Watershed Park in the Moxlie Creek Springs Basin. The year 1955 was a watershed year for Watershed Park, when citizens went all the way to the Supreme Court to protect 153 acres slated to be sold and logged. Looping through the middle of it is the 1.4-mile G. Eldon Marshall Trail. Help yourself to the temperate rainforest canopy thanks to their efforts.

Although traffic is a dull murmur you can hear throughout the forest, it doesn't seem to matter. The trees are so large, and the vegetation so lush, it can't disturb the sense of peace. You feel like you can really breathe here. Chirping birds, gurgling Moxlie Creek, and the gentle thud of your hiking shoes on the boardwalks overdub highway noise, along with your Saluki's sighs of contentment. Moles, voles, mice, raccoons, black-tailed deer, and red-tailed fox dart through the undergrowth, creating endless distractions for the intensely curious. You'll cross over the creek on a bridge at one point, and can view it at another point. The many boardwalks are maintained in excellent

condition; even so, we imagine it could get slippery in wet weather. Signage is good, making it easy to track your progress.

There are two trailhead entrances on Henderson Boulevard, another at McCormick Court, and one at Harry Fain's Park on 22nd Avenue. Better yet, the Wonder Wieners recommend you follow the same directions for the Woodland Trail above, which leads you to their favorite trailhead of all on Eastside Street, across from the Woodland Trail, with paved parking and a spiffy restroom building. 360/753-8380.

PLACES TO EAT

Blue Heron Bakery: A hippie holdover, established in 1977, the Blue Heron has a tasty selection of bread and baked good and picnic tables on the lawn. What it doesn't have is a customer restroom. There's a portable potty, but the building is too close to the tidal flats to install sewer pipelines or a septic system. Pick up your sweet sustenance on the way to Frye Cove County Park. 4935 Mud Bay Rd.; 360/866-2253; www.blueheronbakery.com.

The Dockside Bistro: This deli adds deluxe hot meals—pizza, pasta, lasagna, and so on—to the traditional made-to-order sandwich and salad menu. Your canine will have the best seat in the house, dockside at the marina on Percival Landing. 501 Columbia St. N.W.; 360/956-1928; www .docksidebistro.com.

Traditions Café and World Folk Art: Tell your server there's no rush when making your light, healthy, and slightly exotic sandwich or salad. You'll want time to look through the connected shop of folk art products from more than 50 countries around the world. Everything is made available through equitable trade arrangements with low-income artisans and farmers. Traditions is also a center for concerts, public forums, and workshops promoting a worldwide community. The café's outdoor tables are across the street from Capitol Lake Park. 300 5th Ave. S.W.; 360/705-2819; www.traditionsfairtrade.com.

Wagner's European Bakery and Café: Like a good German deli should, Wagner's will make you a liverwurst and pickle sandwich or offer you a selection of knockwurst and kielbasa sausages. Save room for dessert from a pastry case filled with delicacies almost too beautiful to eat. Isis, being of German descent, reminds you that the "W" in Wagner's is pronounced like a "V" (VAHG-ners). 1013 Capitol Way S.; 360/357-7268.

PLACES TO STAY

Clarion Hotel: This business-oriented hotel is current and uncluttered. Two pets under 25 pounds each are permitted for a flat $25 fee per stay. The nightly rate averages $105. 900 Capitol Way S.; 360/352-7200; www.clarionhotel.com.

Millersylvania State Park Campground: This is an exceptional campground, quiet and sheltered, only 12 miles from Olympia. There are 128 tent spaces and 48 utility spaces. Rates are $15–22. Reserve sites May 15–September 15 at 888/CAMPOUT (888/226-7688) or www.camis.com/wa. A limited number of sites remain open on a first-come, first-served basis in the winter. 12245 Tilley Rd.

More Accommodations: Please look under *Chain Hotels* in the *Resources* section for additional places to stay in this area.

Lacey

Lacey is ahead of the environmental curve, as one of only a dozen cities in the United States recognized by the EPA for getting more than 5 percent of its total electrical power from green sources, including wind, solar, and biomass. Washington's current governor, Christine Gregoire, lives in Lacey.

PARKS, BEACHES, AND RECREATION AREAS

🐾 Woodland Creek Community Park

🐾🐾 (See Tacoma and Olympia map on page 274)

Granted, we saw dogs playing as soon as we passed the Community Center, where a wedding was being set up overlooking Long's Pond. It became a full-on canine social hour, however, when Coop 'n' Isis found the woodchip trail in the wetlands, where the city is in the middle of a revegetation project. The paved walkways are A Loop and B Loop, 0.3 mile each; what they call C Loop is A and B combined for a 0.5-mile walk around the lake where juvenile fishing is allowed (kids 14 and under, not juvie fish). The unpaved trail around the habitat restoration area is about 0.5 mile as well; look for the two yellow poles and the wooden footbridge over Woodland Creek to your right at the end of the parking lot for the habitat restoration area. Restrooms and picnic shelters are come one, come all.

Take Exit 107 from I-5 and go east on Pacific Avenue for not quite three miles to the park entrance on your right. 6749 Pacific Avenue S.E.; 360/491-0857.

PLACES TO STAY

La Quinta: Dogs like La Quinta's liberal pet policies; people are pleased that they rarely charge a pet fee. This location is no exception. Though a bit hard to find for something right off the highway (ask for directions), the hotel is backed by a wooded area, where they keep a doggie station with pick up bags. Two dogs under 50-ish pounds allowed; rates range $110–130. 4704 Park Center Ave. N.E.; 360/412-1200.

More Accommodations: Please look under *Chain Hotels* in the *Resources* section for additional places to stay in this area.

Tumwater

Tumwater Falls Park and Tumwater Historical Park meet at a cascading waterfall on the Deschutes River. The name is taken from the Chinook Native American name for the falls, *tumtum chuck,* meaning "heartbeat water." Although park grounds are privately owned, dogs are allowed on leash.

PARKS, BEACHES, AND RECREATION AREAS

25 Pioneer Park

🐾🐾 (See Tacoma and Olympia map on page 274)

Pioneer Park comes in two parts. The northern half is all soccer fields, where dogs are not allowed. The southern half is the sweet spot, with 0.8 mile of paved walkways and 1.25 miles of crushed rock trails leading you through open meadow, wetlands, and native woods to the Deschutes River. Now, that's what your best friend deserves. The trails lead to swimming holes at bends in the river. Riverside picnic tables have been placed so close to the water, we're surprised they aren't swept away during spring runoff. We saw one man standing in the river up to his armpits fishing, and another more reasonable one sitting on the banks doing the same. Cooper's only complaint is that the rock can be a little rough on the paws in some spots. He was going to give the park only two paws, but Isis reminded him he had to throw in an extra paw for water dogs.

Take Exit 102 from I-5, go east on Trosper Road to Capitol Boulevard. Go south on Capitol Boulevard and turn left on Tumwater Boulevard. Take another left on Henderson Boulevard and one last left on 58th Avenue S.E. into the park. Closes at dusk.

PLACES TO STAY

Guest House International: There's not much else going on at the exit where this hotel sits, it's a pleasant stop along the road. We wouldn't call it a dog destination, although there is a public green space behind the hotel, and a park down the street. You're limited to two dogs; each carries a $10 pet fee per night, capped at $50 for longer stays; rates range $90–135. The hotel has Wi-Fi, hot tub, gym, and a basic breakfast. 1600 74th Ave. S.W.; 360/943-5040; www.guesthouseintl.com.

More Accommodations: Please look under *Chain Hotels* in the *Resources* section for additional places to stay in this area.

Maytown

PARKS, BEACHES, AND RECREATION AREAS

26 Millersylvania State Park

😊 😊 😊 (See Tacoma and Olympia map on page 274)

It may sound like someplace vampires inhabit, but the only thing that'll want to suck your blood is a mosquito or two, and even those are pretty rare in these tall, cool fir trees on the shores of Deep Lake. This state park is considered one of the finest accomplishments of the Civilian Conservation Corps, formed to get Depression-era men back to work. An interesting pictorial history board tells of the 200 men living on the grounds 1933–1939 who created the park and built sturdy rock and log buildings used as restrooms, kitchen shelters, picnic areas, and a concession stand.

When we visited, a fat white duck was greeting everyone with loud quacks, and Cooper and Isis created a stir by responding. Several kids joined in, shouting "AFLAC" at the top of their lungs. The park brochure says it is an "842-acre hushed forest." So much for the hushed. For that, you'll have to hike the 8.6 miles of easy trails through the towering old growth. Dogs are not allowed between the buoys in the swimming areas or on the grounds of the environmental learning center.

From I-5, take Exit 95, turn right on Maytown Road S.W., travel three miles, and take a left on Tilley Road S. into the park.

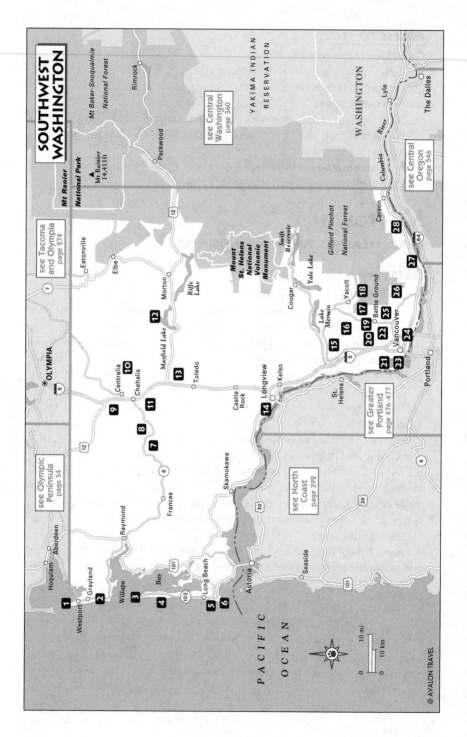

SOUTHWEST WASHINGTON

see Tacoma and Olympia
page 274

see Olympic Peninsula
page 54

see Central Washington page 360

Mt Ranier
National Park

Mt Rainier
14,411ft

YAKIMA INDIAN
RESERVATION

WASHINGTON

see Central
Oregon
page 546

Mt Baker-Snoqualmie
National Forest

Rimrock

Packwood

Mount
St. Helens
National
Volcanic
Monument

Swift
Reservoir

Gifford Pinchot

National Forest

Carson

The Dalles

Lyle

Columbia

River

Elbe

Eatonville

Morton

Riffe
Lake

Cougar

Yale Lake

Lake
Merwin

Yacolt

Battle
Ground

Vancouver

Portland

Mayfield Lake

Centralia

Chehalis

Toledo

Castle
Rock

Longview

Kelso

St.
Helens

Lake
Mason

OLYMPIA

see Greater Portland
page 476–477

see North
Coast
page 392

Hoquiam

Aberdeen

Westport

Grayland

Raymond

Frances

Willapa

Bay

Long Beach

Skamokawa

Astoria

Seaside

PACIFIC

OCEAN

Mt Rainier

PACIFIC

OCEAN

10 mi

10 km

© AVALON TRAVEL

CHAPTER 11

Southwest Washington

In Southwest Washington, you leave the volatile mountains behind and pass into old-growth and second-growth forests, butting right up against the state capitol in Olympia. It's sparsely populated until you get down to Vancouver, Washington, the state's fourth largest city and, whether they like it or not, often considered an extension of Portland that crosses state lines.

You'll skirt around the marshlands along the bottom of Puget Sound on your way out to Washington's lower beaches, flat stretches of unbroken sand, sea, and sky. On Long Beach Peninsula and Grays Harbor, the beaches are long and wide, without the power and drama of those farther north. On the other hand, you won't have to chase your tail in frustration trying to get to them, and they are more hospitable for playing on the sand and in the ocean.

Grays Harbor, including the towns of Raymond, Westport, Grayland, and Tokeland, is referred to as the Cranberry Coast, home to the world's largest cranberry bogs. It is especially pretty in the summer, when the bogs are blanketed with pale pink blossoms. The fields are flooded in the fall to make the

PICK OF THE LITTER— SOUTHWEST WASHINGTON

BEST PARKS

Seminary Hill Natural Area, Centralia (page 310)

Lake Sacajawea, Kelso-Longview (page 314)

BEST DOG PARKS

BPA Ross Dog Recreation Area, Vancouver (page 318)

Dakota Memorial Dog Park at Pacific Park, Vancouver (page 321)

BEST BEACHES

Grayland Beach, Grayland (page 302)

Cape Disappointment State Park, Long Beach Peninsula (page 305)

BEST PLACES TO EAT

Mermaid Deli, Westport (page 301)

Full Circle Café, Long Beach Peninsula (page 307)

BEST PLACES TO STAY

Inn at Discovery Coast, Long Beach Peninsula (page 308)

Columbia Gorge Riverside Lodge, Stevenson (page 325)

berries bob to the top for easy harvesting. You can see much of it along 50 miles of Scenic Highway 101 from Aberdeen to Westport and Raymond. Another interesting sight are metal sculptures that line the roadways, commissioned to portray the heritage of the area in and near downtown Raymond.

NATIONAL FORESTS

Gifford Pinchot National Forest
🐾 🐾

Gifford Pinchot is one of the oldest forests in the United States, starting with land set aside as early as 1897, now consisting of 1.3 million acres, including the 110,000-acre Mount St. Helens National Volcanic Monument. Mount St. Helens is a currently active volcano, experiencing regular steam and ash explosions, and oozing lava to rebuild its inner dome as recently as January 2008. This is definitely one of those areas you'll want to check out ahead of time for conditions and closures, online and at the Ranger Station in Randle. 10024 U.S. Hwy. 12; 360/497-1100; www.fs.fed.us/gpnf.

Westport

Although best known for deep-sea fishing, Westport is also gaining a reputation as the home of coldwater surfing. From the marina at the tip of the peninsula in Westport, you can watch, from an excellent viewing tower, the boats head out and return, walk past the docks of working boats, and check out the warehouses with stacks of crab traps.

PARKS, BEACHES, AND RECREATION AREAS

1 Westport Light State Park and Westhaven

🐾🐾🐾 (See Southwest Washington map on page 298)

It takes the smallest bit of effort to get to the beach at Westport. The trick is to pick an existing footpath that looks reliably worn through the dune grasses and walk a few hundred yards due west. You can also walk right up to the 107-foot-tall Westport Lighthouse at Grays Harbor, the tallest on the Washington Coast. For expansive views, walk some more, along the popular 1.3-mile paved dune trail and boardwalk that connects Westport Light with Westhaven, a popular surfers' beach. When your tootsies are tired of walking, the sand is soft and the water is cold and refreshing. Very refreshing. Bring your binoculars and watch for brown pelicans and gray whales.

From the sign in Westport on State Route 105, go west almost a mile on Ocean Avenue. There are restrooms and picnic tables and covered braziers sheltered by windbreak walls near the parking lot. Open 6 A.M.–10 P.M. summer; 8 A.M.–6 P.M. winter.

PLACES TO EAT

Mermaid Deli: Just north of the shipyards is a bright blue building painted with scenes of the sea. Out back is a patio, and beyond the fence is a partially enclosed lawn where your pooch can hang while you do your best to manage hot, gooey baguette stuffed with goodies of your choice. In the summer, they roll up the garage doors out back for a party by the bar. Owner Dave plans to build a dog run when he gets around to it. 200 E. Patterson; 360/612-0435; www.mermaiddeli.com.

Original House of Pizza: Cooper showed great restraint by not including a pizza place in every city in this book. He put his paw down for this one, insisting it be included, even though you'll have to order to go (no outside seating). If you've had enough delivery pizza to last a lifetime, there are other options: salads, seafood platters, and hot chicken, fish, or pastrami sandwiches. 1200 N. Montesano; 360/268-0901.

Whale of a Cone: The whale's got 31 flavors of ice cream and 50 flavors of nonfat yogurt, which ceases to be nonfat when you put it in a fresh-made waffle cone, but, hey, life is about balance, right? Kids will love the candy, corn dogs, and soda pop. Ice cream practically begs to be eaten outside, while walking the docks of the marina. 2435 Westhaven Dr.; 360/268-9261.

PLACES TO STAY

Beachy Day Vacation Rentals: This vacation rental agency shows all of its properties on the front page of the website, and at least half of them are pet-friendly. The pet fee is typically $10 per pet per night. Some homes have fenced yards for those of you with Houdini dogs. 360/267-3234; www.beachyday.com.

Breakers Boutique Inn: There's an on-site go-kart track at the Breakers (wahoo!). Other than an insurance-based bias against pit bulls and rottweilers, this motel allows two pets per room for $10 per pet per night; two-pet maximum. Standard room rates are $70–100. 971 N. Montesano St.; 360/268-0848; www.breakersmotel.com.

Grayland and Tokeland

Ahhhh, a dog can really breathe out here. A drive out here from the city can soothe jangled nerves and calm even the worst case of a multitasked mind. Despite glimpses of development, it remains largely a remote, sleepy area of the coast. If you are seeking solitude, not nightlife, come here for 18 miles of undisturbed beaches. The Grayland Community Hall, built by the Finnish community as a dance hall and meeting place in the 1930s, is still used for community events. Another Finnish dance hall doubles as a Cranberry Museum. Every so often, you'll see brown Beach signs with arrows. Pick one. You can't go wrong.

PARKS, BEACHES, AND RECREATION AREAS

🐾 Grayland Beach

🐾🐾🐾🐾 (See Southwest Washington map on page 298)

Captain Robert Gray is a pretty popular guy in these parts, one of the very first to explore the area by ship. As much as he could get away with it, he modestly named everything he discovered after himself. Isis is partial to simple beaches, and this one fits the bill perfectly. When you turn onto the beach road, it looks like you are driving straight into the sky, and you can, almost, drive straight onto the beach. Grayland has 7,500 feet of soft sand, light surf, and sun to greet you. The brave, stunted trees show you the direction of the wind, so you'll know which way to launch your kite.

Watch for the park signs on State Route 105 in Grayland. There's a restroom in the parking lot. 360/268-9717.

PLACES TO EAT

Local Bar and Grill: This bar and takeout window is the home of the Local Burger and juicy broiled chicken. It's on the only street in town, it's the only red building in town, and it's basically your only option until Westport. 2183 S.R. 105; 360/267-5071.

Nelson Crab: Stop by The Porch at the cannery to get the freshest crab you are ever likely to eat—whole cooked crab, crab meat, crab cocktail—plus shrimp, smoked Coho salmon, and gourmet canned seafood. It's on the main road in Tokeland, almost all the way to the end of the spit. Open daily, 9 A.M.–5 P.M. Can't wait? Order by phone or online. 800/262-0069; www.nelsoncrab.com.

PLACES TO STAY

Russell House Bed and Breakfast: The house is a Victorian confection, perched on the highest hill overlooking Willapa Harbor. Built in 1891 as an anniversary gift, it is listed on the National Register of Historic Places. If you appreciate the sheer opulence and romanticism of full-on Victorian style, it's worth your while to come to South Bend, about a half hour south of Tokeland. Dogs under 25 pounds are allowed in the Bay, Vista, and Turret Rooms. Rates are $100–125; the pet fee is $15. 902 E. Water St.; 360/875-6487 or 888/484-6907; www.russellhousebb.com.

Tokeland Hotel: This historic hotel was established in 1886, and it is an antique, with creaks and groans and crooked floors, and a bit of chipped paint here and there. By the same token, the antiques are originals, and staying here is an experience in the rich character and history of the community you won't find anywhere else. One dog is allowed, preferably under 15 pounds, larger if well-behaved. The 17 rooms share four bathrooms. Rates are $50–65, with no dog fee. 100 Hotel Rd.; 360/267-7006; www.tokelandhotel.com.

Tradewinds on the Bay: After a remodel to the studs in 2008, this small property went from outdated to outstanding. All rooms have water views of Shoalwater Bay, and the lawn out back is big and secluded. Pet-friendly rooms are #2, #3, and #4, and they are really well priced at $100 per night, which offsets the steep $50 one-time pet fee. Pets under 30 pounds only. 4305 Pomeroy Lane; 360/267-7500; www.tradewindsonthebay.com.

Long Beach Peninsula

Long Beach marks the most northwesterly point reached by the Lewis and Clark Expedition in 1805. The beach here is 28 miles long, flat and wide. It's ideal for family fun and absolute dog heaven. Be careful not to allow your pet to eat rotting fish on the beach, usually salmon, which give off toxins that can be harmful or deadly. In addition, cars are allowed on the beach with restrictions in the summer, so watch kids and pets around the autos.

If you decide to drive on the sand, stay on the hard pack, closer to the surf.

DOG-EAR YOUR CALENDAR

Long Beach is answering the question, "If dogs ran the world, what would the Olympics look like?" At the **Doggie Olympic Games,** competitions include dunking for hot dog pieces, a peanut butter lick-off, a shedding challenge, and the Rip Van Winkle sleep off, to name a few. It's held around the middle of June, the events begin at noon, and dogs in any physical condition may compete. Mutts of questionable parentage are encouraged to participate. Paw-shaped medals are awarded for human gratification. Bond, play, and laugh together in Long Beach at the Bolstad Beach Approach. The entry fee is $10 per dog and $10 per handler; handlers fees are waived if you pre-register. Call 800/451-2542 or go to www.funbeach.org for more information.

A popular pastime for locals is to bring a six-pack and a pickup with a winch to the beach to watch tourists who are unfamiliar with sand driving get stuck in the soft stuff. If they do have to haul you out, at least buy them more beer. We know this only through anecdotal evidence, of course.

There are many pet-friendly places to stay. Everyone we talked to had a different recommendation. For more lodging that there wasn't room to list here, go to www.funbeach.com. For a big pet boutique crammed with stuff, pop into **Unique Petique** while on the peninsula (2103 Pacific Ave. N.; 360/642-1202).

PARKS, BEACHES, AND RECREATION AREAS

3 Leadbetter Point

🐾🐾🐾 (See Southwest Washington map on page 298)

Bird dogs, look up! This state park is on the Pacific Flyway, the main thoroughfare for migrating waterfowl in spring and fall. While everyone, including the cars, crowds the main beaches on the peninsula, you and your dog can come out here to contemplate nature along marshy Willapa Bay, butting up against the Willapa National Wildlife Refuge. You really can't get much more away from it all.

Without going into the refuge, dogs can hike three trails. The two-mile Red Loop Trail is along the bay side, picking a path through a bog marsh flats. It will be muddy, smelly, and buggy. Oh, the joy! The 0.5-mile Green Trail follows the tree line along the beach, and the 1.3-mile southern route is the Blue Trail from the bay to the ocean. Once you've worked your way through the lowland forests and grass dunes, some serious beach romping is in order.

Getting away from it all and getting to Leadbetter requires some zigzag maneuvers. Take State Route 103 to Ocean Park. Turn east onto Bay Avenue and drive nearly a mile before turning left onto Peninsula Highway/Sandridge Road. Continue four miles, turn west onto Oysterville Road, and in 0.25 mile turn right onto Stackpole Road. Continue to the first parking pullout, about three miles.

🐾 Pacific Pines

🐾🐾🐾 (See Southwest Washington map on page 298)

Concerned citizens rescued this beach from development hell, ensuring that it would remain as permanent public beach access. Perhaps they named it after the proposed development as a reminder.

Unlike the public beach approaches, which are simply roads to the sand, this park has a nice lawn area with a restroom building and picnic tables within a grove of said pines, providing a protected windbreak. A short trail through the stubby trees and over the dunes leads to the beach.

Digging dogs, this beach is for you. The wind works the sand up into piles, not quite big enough to be called dunes, but certainly big enough to hide a dachshund. It's prime, smelly territory for your dog to excavate crab shells, kelp bits, or the perfect salty driftwood stick to use as leverage when pleading with you for a game of toss. It's much harder to resist those puppy dog eyes when he's got the stick already in his mouth, isn't it?

Take State Route 103 to Ocean Park. When State Route 103 turns right, continue straight onto Vernon Avenue, and turn left on 274th Place. Open 8 A.M.–dusk.

🐾 Long Beach

🐾🐾🐾 (See Southwest Washington map on page 298)

According to some, and as stated on a famous arch, this is the world's longest single beach. Of all the entry points to the water, the largest is Bolstad in downtown Long Beach, which offers decent restrooms and good parking. Cooper likes the boardwalk, which takes you up and over the dunes for better views and less sand in your paws. There's also a paved portion of the Discovery Trail here, leading past the wind-stripped bones of a gray whale.

North to south, the other approaches are Oysterville, Ocean Park, Klipsan, Cranberry, 10th Street, and Seaview. All are marked with small, brown Beach signs.

From the Highway 101 spur, turn left at Bolstad Street.

🐾 Cape Disappointment State Park

🐾🐾🐾🐾 (See Southwest Washington map on page 298)

When he failed to find inner passage to the Columbia River on a 1788 sailing exploration, Captain John Meares named this nearby headland. After life as an active military installation until 1957, this state park hasn't disappointed

anyone since. If you and your dog were to put your heads together and come up with a list of what you wanted in a beachfront park, 1,882-acre "Cape D" would likely fit the bill. It's got bluff views, access to 27 miles of beach to the north, hiking trials adding up to seven miles, and the Cape Disappointment and North Head Lighthouses.

Above all the other attractions, Beard's Hollow receives the most favorable puppy press. A level walking road leads to the beach through a marsh, with old-growth trees draped in moss, spooky enough to be interesting, not so much as to be scary. From the hollow, you can hike a naturally steep, muddy, and slippery trail 1.3 miles to the first lighthouse, 4.3 miles to the tip and the end.

From U.S Highway 101 into Ilwaco, turn left onto South Highway 101. At 1.8 miles, take a right on Spruce Street W., State Route 100, go another 1.8 miles to Beard's Hollow, or a total of three miles to the end of the park. Dogs are not allowed in the Lewis and Clark Interpretive Center.

PLACES TO EAT

Bailey's Bakery and Café: Sharing a building with the post office in the tiny outpost of Nahcotta, Bailey's short morning menu consists of granola, scones, and sticky Thunder Buns. Yes, those last are as good as they sound. The lunch menu branches out into a larger selection of sandwiches and baked goods. Outdoor seating includes a couple of tables on the porch and a picnic table under a tree. 26910 Sandridge Rd. Nahcotta; 360/665-4449.

Full Circle Café: If this great little daytime diner were any closer to the surf, you'd be in real danger of having saltwater spray on your food. As it is, you can peek at the beach from sidewalk tables while you and your schnauzer snarf a BST (that's bacon, sprouts, and tomato) or a Bog Chef Salad with homemade cranberry dressing, turkey, and avocado. It'll be tough, but try to save room for Colleen's pie or cobbler. 1024 Bay Ave., Ocean Park; 360/665-5385.

Scoopers: Cooper goes for Scoopers. It's ice cream, 48 flavors of it, a block from the beach. Need he say more? Highway 101 at Bolstad, Longbeach; 360/642-8388.

Surfer Sands: The three foods surfers seem to gravitate toward above all else are fruit smoothies, veggie sandwiches, and pizza. As soon as she saw the Carnivores' Corner on the menu, Isis gravitated right on over to the yellow-and-blue picnic tables. Order from the window, then relax under the awning. 113 Pacific Ave., Seaview; 360/642-7873.

PLACES TO STAY

Anchorage Cottages: This family-friendly getaway features sports courts, patios with barbecues, kitchens, and a private path straight to the beach. You quickly get the sense that you can let loose and get giggly here. Pets can get wiggly in 9 of the 10 casual cottages. Great rates range $70–120, plus a $10 pet fee; two-pet maximum. 2209 Blvd. North, Long Beach; 360/642-2351; www.theanchoragecottages.com.

Breakers: Of all the big hotel options in the area—not to be confused with the Breakers in Westport—this one has the best vibe, an indefinable combination of friendliness and comfyness, despite its larger size. Besides, it's got the biggest yard and three trails directly to the beach. Rates range $120–180; $10 pet fee, limit two pets. Hwy. 103 at 26th, Long Beach; 360/642-4414; www.breakerslongbeach.com.

Charles Nelson Guest House: You'd never guess that this stately home was originally purchased from a 1920s-era *Sears and Roebuck* catalog. Three elegant, elaborate rooms are set among pretty gardens with Willapa Bay views. Rates range $160–180; in the off-season, all additional nights are 50 percent off. There is a $25 fee per stay for pets, and one rule: no pets on the beds. You'll understand when you see host Ginger's quilt collection. 26205 Sandridge Rd., Nahcotta; 360/665-3016; www.charlesnelsonbandb.com.

Historic Sou'wester Lodge: Sou'westers are the winds that push treasures ashore during spring and winter storms. This collection of eclectic lodging options defines different, a treasure for those who can appreciate the owners' odd sense of humor and its quirky nature. You stay in cabins or 1950s trailers, bringing your own bedding. There are no dog restrictions or fees. It's an unusual getaway only for those who have a sense of adventure a motel can't tame. Rates range $80–160. Beach Access Rd. (38th Place) in Seaview, the first street on the left as you enter from U.S. Highway 101; 360/642-2542 or 800/269-6378; www.souwesterlodge.com.

Inn at Discovery Coast: This oceanfront property opened in 2004 and has been spoiling guests ever since with uninterrupted ocean views, jetted tubs, fireplaces, pine plank floors, and downy king beds. The rooms are small, yet they are among the most modern and upscale in the area. Pet lovers are placed in the three ground-floor rooms. For the same great taste in larger studios with kitchens, proprietors Brady and Tiffany also manage the spiffy Akari Bungalows. Rates range $95–195; $15 one-time pet fee. 421 11th St., Long Beach; 360/642-5265; www.innatdiscoverycoast.com and www.akaribungalows.com.

Moby Dick Hotel, Restaurant, and Oyster Farm: There are plenty of mega-motels on the beaches, so Coop 'n' Isis wanted you to have an option that exudes Bohemian charm. Moby Dick's manages a perfect balance between character and comfort. All rooms are colorful, each a little different, all allow two pets. A three-course breakfast is included, as is a Japanese sauna in the woods, and rambling grounds with forest paths along Willapa Bay to explore. All that, and a dog named Hoss to play with. Some of the less expensive rooms have shared baths. Rates range $90–150; the pet fee is $10. 25814 Sandridge Rd., Nahcotta; 360/665-4543; www.mobydickhotel.com.

Cape Disappointment Campground: Cape D has 152 standard sites, 83 utility sites, eight restrooms, and 14 showers. Reservations are absolutely necessary in the summer. Rates are $17–24. 888/226-7688; www.camis.com/wa.

More Accommodations: Please look under *Chain Hotels* in the *Resources* section for additional places to stay in this area.

Centralia and Chehalis

Lewis County is an antique-seeker's destination. In these two towns, and on the road between them, called the "miracle mile," there are close to 350 antique dealers in 20 shops and three specialty malls.

PARKS, BEACHES, AND RECREATION AREAS

7 Rainbow Falls State Park

😺😺😺 (See Southwest Washington map on page 298)

This park, Lewis and Clark, and Millersylvannia (in the Tacoma and Olympia chapter) were built between 1933 and 1942 by the Civilian Conservation

Corps. Each features old-growth and secondary-growth trees and the classic rock wall and timber-framed buildings that have withstood nature and time. Coop 'n' Isis are surprised at how empty many of these parks are, even in the summer. If you can manage weekday travel, you'll have quite a bit of freedom and privacy. In addition to the stands of old-growth forest and the Corps' log buildings, Rainbow Falls has 3,400 feet of freshwater shoreline on the Chehalis River, with the namesake falls, and a garden displaying 40 varieties of fuchsia flowers.

The park closed after a massive storm on December 3, 2007, and reopened in time for Memorial Day 2008. Although the main bridge accessing the hiking trails was destroyed, a park ranger let us know you can drive four miles from Rainbow on a forest service road to access the Hemlock, Woodpecker, and Deer Trails crossing Josh and Katie Creeks. They're all easy couple milers. Ask for directions from the campground host.

From I-5, take Exit 77, travel west on State Route 6 for 17 miles to the park entrance. 360/291-3767.

🐾 Willapa Hills Trail

🐾🐾 (See Southwest Washington map on page 298)

From Chehelis on the I-5 corridor to South Bend on the coast, the Willapa Hills Trail measures 56 miles, traversing diverse ecosystems from lowland forests and pastoral valleys to tidewater flats. Nature broke it into shorter, more manageable chunks, when three bridges were destroyed in the December 2007 storm. Several more bridges were barely navigable, even before Mother Nature got to them.

The trail is an old railroad grade, roughly paralleling State Route 6. Some sections are dirt, some paved, some improved by being leveled and coated with asphalt grindings used from highway construction projects. It's paved on the west end from the town of Raymond to South Bend and on the east end from Chehalis. The Dachshunds managed to enjoy a short portion of the gravel trail westward through wooded areas from Rainbow Falls.

Camping is available at Rainbow Falls on a first-come, first-served basis. State Parks reminds trail users to stay on the trail and off private property. Contact Rainbow Falls at 360/291-3767 for more information.

9 Fort Borst Park

🐾🐾 (See Southwest Washington map on page 298)

When the military fort built here in 1856 proved unnecessary to keep the peace with native Chehalis Indians, pioneer Joseph Borst bought the land to farm and mill grain. From a pooch's perspective, the main highlight of this county park is probably a stroll through the natural grounds around the historic schoolhouse, home, and granary left from that era. On your way, you'll discover a pond, soothing grass and shady tree cover, tiny fuchsia and rhododendron gardens, and a few rotting and overgrown picnic tables. There are poop bag dispensers everywhere. This rest stop is very convenient to the highway.

To bypass the rifle club, tennis club, athletic club, boat launch, wading pools, and playgrounds, the best entrance is to pass through the arches on Belmont Avenue. Take Exit 82 from I-5, go west on Harrison past the outlet mall and take a left on Johnson Road, another immediate left on Borst Avenue, and right into the park on Belmont. Open 7 A.M.–10 P.M., until 7 P.M. November 1–April 1.

10 Seminary Hill Natural Area

🐾🐾🐾🐾 (See Southwest Washington map on page 298)

At Seminary Hill, the emphasis is on the hill, giving even a greyhound a serious, if short, workout. If you add up all the mileages on the map, it's less than two miles. Never fret, you'll still work up a sweat, navigating quite a few railroad tie steps, up and down narrow trails through overgrown terrain.

We gave it four paws despite the fact that there are no amenities other than a picnic table, garbage can, and a bag dispenser in the gravel parking lot. Isis was impressed by the sweet Pets Welcome sign at the entrance. Cooper dug the slug life in the thick ferns. We found the heavy tree cover and chattering birds to be a balm to the spirit. Watch closely for the granite markers set into the ground. They're subtle, like a good Easter egg hunt.

Take Exit 82 from I-5 going east, following Harrison Avenue as it becomes Main Street going into town. Take a right on Pearl, the next left on Locust and follow it across the railroad tracks until you see the park entrance on the right. Open 7 A.M.–10 P.M.; until 7 P.M. November 1–April 1. There's a map at www.centraliaguide.com.

11 Robert E. Lintott/Alexander Park

🐾🐾 (See Southwest Washington map on page 298)

It's got two names and it's had two lives. Created in 1905, it fell into total disrepair and disrepute, thankfully to be revived and restored for the centennial in 2005.

Tucked into a bend of the Newaukum River, this city park is a peaceful place for a picnic and a romp in the field, where gentle summer afternoons make for family memories while the masses of humanity are using Stan Headwall Park to the south (not recommended for dog travelers). Here's how your afternoon might play out: You bring your wooden basket to the covered shelter and set a checkered blanket on the level lawn. After polishing off some fried chicken and watermelon, there's a quick game of fetch. You're refreshed by water from the tri-level drinking fountain (adult-kid-dog), ready for a walk around the park perimeter, ringed with commemorative benches. Perhaps your only fleeting regret as you look out over the river is that the bank is too steep and the water too swift for a swim. You choose to snooze under a tree instead.

Take Exit 77 from I-5, going west on Highway 6. At a 0.5 mile, take a left on Donahoe Road, which curves to the left to become Riverside Road, leading you through a gated entrance to the park on your right.

PLACES TO EAT

Market St. Bakery and Café: As a test of your willpower, the line at the counter is often long, passing by rows of treats in the pastry case and goodies in baskets on the way. Two tables share a partially enclosed, covered patio in the funky old town area of Chehelis. 492 N. Market; 360/748-0875.

Santa Lucia Coffee: Confess your addiction and be absolved in the form of a steaming cup worthy of your worship. To complete your religious experience, this homage to the bean is on the way to Seminary Hill. The paved patio is a comfortable hodgepodge of cement and wooden benches, rickety tables with gold umbrellas, planters and piped music. After realizing that this coffeehouse serves croissants and panini, *and* beer and wine, we felt positively blessed. 202 S. Tower, Centralia; 360/807-9600; www.santaluciaroasters.com.

PLACES TO STAY

In this area, chain hotels listed in the *Resources* section offer the best choices for dogs and their owners.

Mount Rainier

Although Mount Rainier National Park and Monument is off-limits to dogs, you can nibble around the edges, playing in and around pockets of civilization en route to the mount. The towns on the main westerly approaches to Mount Rainier—namely Eatonville on the north and Morton on the south—remain remote enough today; its hard to imagine what they must have been like for early fur trappers and loggers, who floated goods downriver to Kelso-Longview or packed them in and out on horseback.

PARKS, BEACHES, AND RECREATION AREAS

12 Ike Kinswa State Park

🐾🐾 (See Southwest Washington map on page 298)

Mayfield Lake has a lot of shoreline, 46,000 feet, and 454 acres spread out along that shoreline is slim, with just enough room for the 1.5-mile Mayfield Trail that follows the water's edge, and a 0.5-mile guided interpretive trail through the woods. The designated swimming beach and playground are off-limits to dogs. Let's see, that leaves about 45,400 feet of shoreline that's a-okay.

From I-5, take Exit 68 and drive east on U.S. Highway 12 for 14 miles. Turn north on State Route 122, which loops around Mayfield Lake, travel 1.9 miles, take a right at the fork in the road, and travel another 1.9 miles.

DIVERSIONS

Because so much of the nearby national park and monument land is off-limits to pets, it's nice to know that there's a place where they can go to be spoiled within inches of their lives. **The Mountain Dog Lodge** is, bar none, the coolest dog boarding facility we've ever encountered on our travels. Each dog gets his very own climate-controlled cabin, complete with fenced front and back yards and a covered porch. Your dog's favorite phrase from the website is guaranteed to be, "The evening cookie is served at 7 P.M." Rates start at $45 per night, plus $20 per each additional pet sharing a cabin; rates go down the longer your pet stays. Additional services, including door-to-door transportation, grooming, and photos, are available. The Dog Lodge is near the town of Ashford, just outside the National Park boundaries. 360/569-8833; www.mtdoglodge.com.

PLACES TO EAT

Country Lunch Box and Espresso: Sandwiches, homemade soup, and coffee; human and dog could survive quite nicely with this trio for sustenance, especially when you add stone-ground mustard to the sammie and put it on the Lunch Box's sunflower bread. 120 E. State St., Morton; 360/983-8090.

Truly Scrumptious: A café that does indeed live up to its name, Scrumptious excels in the daily soup department, and is generous with the sprouts on every sandwich. Outdoor seaters can be picky eaters, choosing between picnic tables on a lawn or covered glass tables on an elevated deck. 212 Washington Ave. N., Eatonville; 360/832-2233.

PLACES TO STAY

Mill Village Motel: Although the sign at the front desk reads Small Pets, the management translates "small" as "well-behaved," and won't fuss too much about your pet's size. The rooms are spotless and there's a spot of grass behind the building for business. Rates range $70–90, plus a one-time $10 pet fee. 210 Center St. E., Eatonville; 360/832-3200; www.whitepasstravel.com.

Seasons Motel: Part of the same group as the Mill Village, this big motel in the small town of Morton allows one pet per room if large, two if portable. The rooms are huge and very nice. Rates range $70–90. A nice continental breakfast is included. The pet fee is $10. 200 Westlake Ave., Morton; 360/496-6835; www.whitepasstravel.com.

Castle Rock and Mount St. Helens

From Castle Rock, the Spirit Lake Memorial Highway goes east for 53 miles to Washington's most famous and currently most active volcano, Mount St. Helens. Although much of the mount is on national park land off-limits to dogs, at least go five miles down the road to the visitors center across from Seaquest State Park for an incredible view on a clear day.

PARKS, BEACHES, AND RECREATION AREAS

13 Lewis and Clark State Park

😺 😺 😺 (See Southwest Washington map on page 298)

This CCC-legacy park focuses on the kids, teaching them about the forest with fun activities and displays. There is a forest life cycle exhibit, information about the Cowlitz Indians, an interesting story about the tallest flagpole in the world, and regular activities scheduled at the amphitheater, such as the Mount St. Helens Explosion movie and ever-popular slug races. On the way to the park, stop by the Jackson House, a homestead built in 1844, which became a famous resting stop for pioneers on the Oregon Trail.

For dogs who would rather blaze trails than read bulletin boards, there are eight miles of trails through the park's old-growth Douglas firs and red cedar. Although two-thirds of the trees (8.5 million board feet) were blown down in one tremendous storm in 1962, the remaining 5 million board feet are impressive enough. This storm wasn't the first time the big trees fell. Pioneers who traveled the Oregon Trail, which passed through the current site, had to build bridges over the logs because there were no saws big enough at the time to cut them. The Deer Trail is an easy walk through the hushed forest, starting from the far end of the parking area. Your dog needs to stay on leash to protect this game sanctuary.

From I-5, take Exit 68 and travel 3.6 miles east on U.S. Highway 12. Turn right on Jackson Highway, which will lead you directly into the park after another 2.8 miles. The park is closed for day use October–March. 360/864-2643.

Kelso-Longview

Situated at the confluence of three rivers, the Columbia, Cowlitz, and Toutle, this primarily industrial area is an international deep-water port with an active riverfront industry. If you want to get to the Oregon Coast from Washington, without the hassles of Portland traffic, the Lewis and Clark bridge from Longview crosses over to U.S. Highway 30 in Oregon, where it's a quick hour at most to Astoria.

PARKS, BEACHES, AND RECREATION AREAS

14 Lake Sacajawea

🐾 🐾 🐾 🐾 (See Southwest Washington map on page 298)

This city park is a stunning walkers' park. You know that every detail of this formal park was planned, yet it all looks so effortless. Around the long, thin lake is a wide, level, crushed-gravel trail surrounded by lawns good enough to eat and stately mature trees. The visual delights just keep coming: water fountains, an island Chinese garden over an arched bridge, and totem poles, all surrounded by handsome homes on quiet boulevards. Here and there are restrooms and playgrounds, benches, and picnic tables. At every long block, there is a bridge across the lake, so you can custom tailor the length of the loop you walk. The path is illuminated at night by antique-reproduction lampposts. It is the park city residents are most proud of, and you'll meet many of them and their canines jogging or walking the lake. Coop 'n' Isis spent such a relaxing afternoon here meeting the locals, they granted it four paws, even though swimmers of either species are not allowed to break the smooth water's surface.

From I-5, take Exit 39 onto State Route 4, and follow the road four miles as it crosses a bridge, zigs, and changes names to become Ocean Park. Turn south on Kessler or Nichols Boulevards and park along the street where signs allow.

PLACES TO STAY

Hudson Manor Inn and Suites: The sweet innkeepers have taken what could have been a very ordinary place and turned it into something special with deck chairs, tables, and potted trees outside every room, and elegant furnishings inside. As they say, only nice people get to stay, and two dogs under 40 pounds each may join you. Angus, the corgi of the manor, will greet you and request a scratch on the hind end. Fergie the cat will act as a paperweight on the register while you check in. Rates range $60–90, plus a $15 flat fee per room for pets. 1616 Hudson St.; 360/425-1100; www.hudsonmanorinn.com.

More Accommodations: Please look under *Chain Hotels* in the *Resources* section for additional places to stay in this area.

Battle Ground

This fast-growing community got its ironic name from a battle that never took place; disagreements between Native Americans and Fort Vancouver soldiers were settled peacefully in 1855.

PARKS, BEACHES, AND RECREATION AREAS

15 Paradise Point State Park

😺 (See Southwest Washington map on 298)

Coop 'n' Isis saw lots of people here with their dogs, perhaps because they can be left alone in peace to do their thing. Paradise Point is a strange, beautiful place on an offshoot of the Columbia River. It has what any state park would want, namely wooded campgrounds, open fields, big trees, and water access. The catch is that all of it parallels the noisy highway and the day-use fishing area is literally underneath it. You can't deny it's convenient, and perhaps if no one else is enjoying it, it can go to the dogs.

Take Exit 16 from I-5 at La Center, go east over the highway, and, immediately after the northbound freeway entrance, go north on Paradise Point Park Road for a mile.

16 Battle Ground Lake

😺😺 (See Southwest Washington map on page 298)

It'd be nice if this state park were a little easier to get to, but perhaps that's part of the charm, to be on and around a lake with no development on its shores. The natural body of water is a caldera, a basin formed with when the cone of a volcano collapses.

We were torn as to whether or not to include the park, which is not ideal for dogs because there's too much extracurricular activity going on. That said, it is possible to fit the family pets somewhere in between the swimmers, boaters, anglers, volleyball players, campers, and horseback riders.

Fortunately, among the extensive horse trails there are non-equine footpaths on the 279 acres of land. A 0.75-mile Lower Lake Trail along 4,100 feet of shoreline allows for a dip into the water if your pal can be polite enough not to disturb the fisher folk. Otherwise, a 1.5-mile Upper Lake Trail and its scenic overlooks might be more pleasant.

Take Exit 9 from I-5 northbound, and go north on N.E. 10th Avenue to State Route 502. Take N.E. 219th Street (State Route 502) through Battle Ground. Turn north on Grace Avenue. Turn right on N.E. 10th Street, which becomes 244th, and becomes N.E. Palmer Road. You'll feel like someone is playing a practical joke on you when, finally, 11 miles from the highway, you'll see a subtle entrance on your left. Open 6 A.M.–dusk. 18002 N.E. 249th St.; 360/687-4621.

17 Lucia and Moulton Falls

🐾🐾🐾 (See Southwest Washington map on page 298)

This 300-acre county complex has lots of bells and whistles, many of which are not readily apparent at the outset. At the joining of the East Fork of the Lewis River and Big Tree Creek, there are two waterfalls, Lucia and Moulton, and two bridges, one an arched wooden trestle three stories high over the Lewis, and the other a rare swinging bridge over Big Tree.

At the first pullout, for Lucia Falls, there's a 0.5-mile loop stroll along the river and through the woods that's level, wide, and shady. There's no getting in the water here, in order to protect salmon habitat.

Down the road are two pullouts, and, up the hill to the right, a parking area for Moulton Falls. It's very rudimentary here, with a maze of trails, rocky stairs leading to viewpoints, hidden picnic tables, multiple choice swimming holes, and rocks to sun oneself on, all with little or no signage. You might as well take your time sniffing around, since it took a while to get way the heck out here in the first place.

Take State Route 503 north from Battle Ground, called N.W. 10th Avenue in town. Turn right on N.E. Rock Creek Road, which becomes N.E. 152nd Avenue as it rounds the bend south. Follow it for five miles, taking the left fork in the road at the stop sign onto N.E. Lucia Falls Road. First on your right will be a parking area for Lucia Falls, then Moulton Falls three miles later. Open 7 A.M.–dusk. 27781 Lucia Falls Rd.; 360/696-8171.

18 Bells Mountain Trail

🐾🐾🐾 (See Southwest Washington map on page 298)

Serving hikers, mountain bikers, and equestrians, this four-foot wide primitive trail makes its way up to the 1,500-foot summit of Bells Mountain, allowing glimpses of Mount St. Helens and Mount Adams en route. After peaking early, the trail meanders through lower elevation fir and alder forests for a total of eight miles one way, south from the Moulton Falls area. You might be interested to know you'll pass volcanic rock formations from early lava flows and historic Indian meeting grounds. Your hiking partner will concern herself more with the Douglas firs and the riparian route, which Isis learned means "on the banks of a natural course of water."

For ADA access, there's a well-kept, two-mile paved trail from the Hantwick Road Trailhead that joins Bells Mountain Trail. To get right onto an earthier surface, start at Moulton Falls and find your way across the high trestle bridge, heading southeast to connect with the trail. We prefer to drive even further, to the DNR Rock Creek Campground. From there, a mile of the Tarbell Trail heading southwest connects you to Bells Mountain. Any or all of it is worthy of your time.

Follow the directions above to Lucia and Moulton Falls. Turn right on Hantwick Road to its end, 0.25 miles past Lucia Falls. Moulton Falls is three more miles down the road. For Rock Creek, go past Moulton Falls to where the road swings north toward Yacolt. Instead, at the T intersection, turn right on Sunset Falls Road. Go 2.1 miles to Dole Valley Road. Follow this south for five miles to Rock Creek Campground.

PLACES TO EAT

London Fish and Chips: "Pick one thing and do it well" might be the motto of this establishment, where generous portions of seafood in all shapes and sizes is dipped in a light batter and fried in trans-fat-free oil. We suggest the steamed rice instead of fries or slaw for a side, because the homemade teriyaki ginger sauce is fantastic. A wife, brother, husband, and baby daughter run the place, great people to meet. Outdoor seating is a long bench, with hopes for tables in the future. It's a choice find in a strip mall location. 2404 W. Main St., #101; 360/687-1751.

O'Brady's Drive In: Don't know how long it's been there, doesn't look like it's ever changed. Amaretto cherry milkshakes, strawberry lemonade, ham and swiss, and chili get top billing at this corner hangout. Order through the window and relax in a priceless bit of shade covering two side picnic tables. 7111 N.E. 219th St., Dollar's Corner; 360/666-4606.

Brush Prairie

PARKS, BEACHES AND RECREATION AREAS

19 Brush Prairie Dog Park

🐾🐾🐾 🐕 (See Southwest Washington map on page 298)

Clark County's off-leash advocacy group is doing a great job building dog parks in a hurry. The newest open space in their arsenal is this 7.5-acre field between Battle Ground and Vancouver, opened in November 2008. It's a rough, and roughly flat, unremarkable field, except for its hefty size. Fully fenced, with double-gated entries, it also includes a 1-acre small/shy dog area. This trend toward considering the little guys gives Cooper great joy! There's no telling what amenities might be added as the park matures; for now, it's best to bring what you need, including water, bags, and an umbrella to provide yourself with a rain shelter or summer shade.

To reach this new beauty, take Exit 30 off Highway 205 onto N.E. 117th Avenue (State Route 503) heading north. Take a left at NE 149th Street. Do not park or drive on NE 101st Place. Open 7 A.M. to dusk. www.clarkdogpaw.org.

Vancouver

Vancouver, Washington, is three hours south of Seattle, and Vancouver, British Columbia, is three hours north of Seattle. On the border of the Columbia River, within drooling distance from Portland, *this* Vancouver is the state's oldest and fourth-largest city. The website for Vancouver's parks, and greater Clark County parks in general, is an excellent resource (www.vanclarkparks-rec.org). The city tells a tale of two trails, one in town and one outside, allowing you and your dog to get up close and personal with the mighty Columbia River.

Since the last edition of this book, an ambitious advocacy group operating under the tidy acronym DOGPAW (which stands for the more unwieldy Dog Owners' Group for Park Access in Washington) has succeeded in opening two superb off-leash areas in the greater metropolis. They're working toward another estimated for fall 2009 at Hockinson Community Park, and five potential sites in neighboring towns. Keep up with the good times at www.clarkdogpaw.org.

PARKS, BEACHES, AND RECREATION AREAS

20 BPA Ross Dog Recreation Area

🐾🐾🐾🐾 🐕 (See Southwest Washington map on page 298)

The local dog advocacy group's first major success was to convince the Bonneville Power Administration (BPA) to allow free range canine activities on nearly eight acres of hilly terrain around the substation. Once you get over the ominous feeling of the electrical lines buzzing overhead, you can appreciate the varied topography of this excellent off-leash area.

At the topmost hill is a bench, shaded by a lovely tree. From this perch you can oversee most of your dog's activities. Toss games turn into hide and seek among the foliage and natural scrub of the bumpy landscape. For those among us with inaccurate throwing arms (like Isis and Coop's mom), avoiding the transformer tower in the middle of your field of vision may pose a challenge.

Ross is fully fenced, with a double-gated entry built by those charming and useful Boy Scouts. It looks like they assembled the garbage station as well, housed in plywood and painted turquoise blue. We'd lay bets they also created

DIVERSIONS

The **Beastie Boutique** in Salmon Creek Plaza shopping center has the choicest dog shopping in Vancouver. From the frivolous (pet perfume) to the serious (natural and holistic foods), and everything in between, Beastie Boutique is your best bet for pampering your pet. They said it; we agree. 13023 NE Hwy 99, Suite 8; 360/574-6400; www.beastieboutique.com.

the container holding the poop bag stockpile attached to the bulletin board. All are located near the entrance. Bring water. Rumor has it there's a small dog area in the works at Ross, but you know how long these things can take. Ross Park rivals any OLA in the greater Portland area, definitely worth checking out for dogs living on both sides of the state boundary.

Take Exit 3 from I-5, heading north on N.E. Highway 99. Turn right on Ross Street and immediately take another right, following the Ross Complex Deliveries signs. You'll skirt BPA facilities to the south for 0.6 miles and take a right on N.E. 18th Avenue to park. N.E. Ross St. and N.E. 18th Ave.

21 Frenchman's Bar Trail

🐾🐾🐾 (See Southwest Washington map on page 298)

This 2.5-mile riverfront trail is a 12-foot-wide asphalt path connecting Vancouver Lake to Frenchman's Bar on the Columbia River. A narrow wood-chip path, designed for equestrians, parallels the main trail. In tree clearings, you'll have close views of commercial ship traffic passing on the river.

Dogs of the land say pass on the pavement, and walk up over the berm to the mile-long sandy beach, yeah baby. Avoid the north end, too close for comfort to the volleyball courts and lawn chairs. Soggy dogs come grinning up over the hill from the south.

From I-5, take Exit 1D onto 4th Plain Boulevard, State Route 501, and follow it as it becomes N.W. Lower River Road out of town. Instead of paying for parking at the main entrance, we recommend the smaller lot at the south end of the trail system, 5.5 miles from the highway exit on the left side of the road. Caution: Nasty tire-slicing teeth are stuck in the road to prevent you from entering the wrong way. Go in the *first* entry point to your left. Open 7 A.M.–dusk. 9612 N.W. Lower River Road; 360/735-8838.

22 Discovery Loop Trail

🐾🐾🐾 (See Southwest Washington map on page 298)

You can walk forever and relax for hours on the seemingly endless grounds of the Vancouver National Historic Reserve and Vancouver Central Park. The only area that's off-limits to dogs is inside Fort Vancouver fences. A 2.3-mile loop begins on East Evergreen and winds through paved pathways of the site, past the historic homes of Officer's Row, around the runways of Pearson Air Museum, through the Barracks and eventually across the Land Bridge to join the Waterfront Trail. Sights along the way include parade grounds, gardens, elegant deciduous and fir trees, meadows, monuments, and memorials. The Land Bridge day-use trail, completed in 2008, is a 40-foot-wide earthen arch over the highway with scenic views and interpretive markers. It's a history buff's nirvana, once the headquarters for the British Hudson's Bay Company, and your dog will be thrilled simply to be along for the ride. Speaking of riding, you can drive most of the route if you'd rather. Free maps and multiple guidebooks are available at the visitors center.

Take Exit 1C from I-5, heading east on E. Mill Plain Boulevard. Take a left at the first main light after the highway onto Fort Vancouver Way. This is the North Entrance to the Historic Reserve. At the roundabout, continue east on Evergreen Boulevard to find the visitors center and the best parking opportunities.

23 Esther Short Park

🐾 🐾 (See Southwest Washington map on page 298)

Established way back in 1853, Propstra Square was Vancouver's town square, named for Esther in 1862. It's aged well. The bronze statue of The Pioneer Mother, unveiled in 1929, still graces the northeast corner. The southeast corner is dominated by the Salmon Run clock tower with melodious carillon bell chimes and glockenspiel clockworks. A playhouse, playground, and the riotous colors of the rose garden are along the western edge. A classic pergola adorns the center, where the brick pavilions and diagonal sidewalks meet. It's groomed in the formal European style, lending a sophisticated air to the city's social center. Get some ice cream down the street at Dolce Gelato and meet here on a bench in the shade of an old tree. It has public restrooms and some of the city's best shopping and dining clustered around it.

Take Exit 1C/1D. Metered street parking is available. Open 7 A.M.–dusk. Columbia and 8th Streets.

24 Columbia Renaissance Waterfront Trail

🐾 🐾 (See Southwest Washington map on page 298)

This four-mile-long, 14-foot-wide promenade is loving proof of Vancouver's extensive efforts to restore an industrial waterfront into an attractive public space. The sidewalk and boardwalk path hugs the river the entire way, allowing you to watch the active boat traffic on the Columbia. You'll pass other civic projects, including sculpture, fountains, the Renaissance Promenade, and Ilchee Plaza, plus some upscale condos, coffee shops, and a couple of brew pubs. Grass, trees, benches, picnic tables, and landscaping are available every few blocks. Come mid-morning to catch the mom-and-stroller crowd, watch downtown Vancouver escape cubicle life at lunch time, and spend time with the sunbathers in the afternoon.

From I-5, take Exit 1C onto Mill Plain Boulevard, travel five blocks, turn left on Columbia Street, and follow it to the water, under the highway and railroad trestle as it curves to the left. The first convenient parking is about a block beyond the Red Lion at Waterfront Park.

25 Dakota Memorial Dog Park at Pacific Park

🐾🐾🐾🐾 🐕 (See Southwest Washington map on page 298)

Named for a heroic police K9 who gave his life in the line of duty, this eight acre dog park is the largest and newest in the metro area that serves both Vancouver and pups from Portland. It is located within Pacific Community Park's larger scheme of things, including restroom buildings, a playground, skate park, paved pathways, and an amphitheater. But, seriously, the dog park takes up the majority of the territory.

Like Ross, this OLA is built around power towers, but that is where the similarity ends. Dakota's OLA is totally flat and largely unadorned by trees or other vegetation save for choppy grass and a tiny wooded area on the southern edge. There's a lengthy gravel path inside the perimeter of the chain-link fence. Dakota's got you seeing double, with two of everything: paved parking lots, double-gated entries, water fountains, garbage cans, and poop bag collections located on either side of the massive field. Hefty, hewn log benches provide a pair of resting points. Everything was new in 2008, so please keep your dog from digging to allow young vegetation to grow and thrive.

Take Exit 1A from I-5, heading east on State Route 14. Take Exit 6 and go north on Highway 205. Stay in the right lane to take the next exit, #28, and continue east on S.E. Mill Plain Boulevard. Take a left on N.E. 164th Avenue, which curves slightly to become N.E. 162nd. Take a right on N.E. 18th Street, and either right on 164th Avenue for the first entrance, or right on 172nd Avenue for the second.

PLACES TO EAT

Pepper's Taqueria: This colorful and festive restaurant has five hand-hewn picnic tables outside that are extra long, which is necessary because Pepper's is the home of the four-foot burrito. Standard-size dishes include Mexican standards, combo plates, and delicious tortilla soup. 800 Main St.; 360/737-0322.

Tiger's Garden Take-Out: There are almost as many Thai food places in the Pacific Northwest as there are coffee shops, yet this Laotian and Thai restaurant manages to stand out from the rest. The flavors are bolder, the ingredients fresher, and the stars hotter. 312 W. 8th St.; 360/693-9585.

Tommy O's Pacific Rim Bistro: The Hawaiian specialties at Tommy's will make you long for famous surfing and tropical beaches, the names of which grace the breakfast omelets and sandwiches. Slow-roasted kahlua pork quesadillas, crunchy coconut shrimp, and panko-crusted calamari top the list of tastes you should try. Tommy's has four sidewalk tables. 801 Washington St.; 360/694-5107.

PLACES TO STAY

Extended Stay America Efficiency Studios: Maggie the English cocker and her owner Mary prefer staying here for fully equipped kitchens, living areas, and full workspaces. Whether you end up working or playing is between you and your pet. Rates average $75–85 per night. One pet per room; $25 per night, not to exceed $75 per visit. 300 N.E. 115th Ave.; 360/604-8530; www.extendedstayamerica.com.

Homewood Suites: This Hilton-owned hotel allows two dogs over 80 pounds to a room, more if everybody but you weighs in at less than 80 pounds. In addition to impeccable rooms, there's a full breakfast bar for the humans and afternoon social with snacks. For the dogs, the hotel is couple of blocks from the waterfront trail. Rates range $140–170, plus a $35 first-night pet charge, $10 each night thereafter. 701 S.E. Columbia Shores Blvd.; 360/750-1100; www.homewoodsuites.com.

More Accommodations: Please look under *Chain Hotels* in the *Resources* section for additional places to stay in the area.

Camas and Washougal

The Columbia Gorge National Scenic Area starts in these small towns meandering along Highway 14. In Camas (named for an edible lily bulb), the Georgia Pacific paper mill looms over a tree-lined boulevard with a profusion of hanging flower baskets. Neighbor to Camas, Washougal is the second-largest wool-producing region in the states. At the factory store for the Genuine Pendleton Woolen Mill, you can buy rugs for your dog to sleep on and slippers for him to chew.

PARKS, BEACHES, AND RECREATION AREAS

26 Lacamas Lake Park

😾😾😾 (See Southwest Washington map on page 298)

From one parking spot and trailhead, you can walk four different trail systems through old-growth forests, along creeks and lakes, past fancy lakeside homes and golf courses, and alongside a water ditch, hand-dug by Chinese laborers in 1884 for paper mill production. Along the way, your dog's smart nose can pick up the distinctions between up to 100 different species of wildflowers.

The trail systems are Lacamas Park Trails, the Lacamas Creek Trail, the Heritage Trail, and the Mill Ditch Trail. All of the trails are unpaved, of three miles or less one-way. The best comprehensive trail map is the City of Camas Parks, Trails, and Open Space brochure, available in the rack at City Hall's lobby, at 606 N.E. 4th Avenue.

From I-5, take State Route 14 east to the Union Street/State Route 500 exit, a left exit. Go straight on Union and follow the signs to weave through town, staying on State Route 500/Everett Street for 2.5 miles. The parking lot and park entrance are immediately before you cross the bridge over the lake. The lot is open 7 A.M.–dusk. There's a $250 fine if you don't pick up after your pet or keep her on leash. Ouch.

Skamania

If you see Bigfoot picking huckleberries while you're hiking the backcountry trails, don't bug him. He's been granted official protected status by the Skamania County Board of Commissioners. He's allowed to harvest his annual allotment of three gallons of berries, like anybody else. Sasquatch sightings are rare, but according to the Bigfoot Field Researchers Organization, he's been seen in this county more than anywhere else in Washington.

PARKS, BEACHES, AND RECREATION AREAS

🐾 Sam's Walker Trail

🐾🐾🐾 (See Southwest Washington map on page 298)

Ahhh, for a trail even short legs can love, this 1.7-mile universal access walk has two loops through conifer forests and meadows. It's easy and level throughout, with peeks at wildflowers, wildlife, and Horsetail Falls across the Columbia River. It's not too heavily used, either, giving you and your dog the opportunity for some quiet, quality time together.

Turn south at the west end of Skamania Landing Road, a loop road, cross the railroad tracks and travel 0.3 mile to the parking lot on your right.

PLACES TO STAY

Skamania Lodge: This internationally esteemed golf course hotel often ranks on the Northwest's "most romantic" lists. The newest wing in the lodge allows pets in four rooms on the first floor, with outdoor exits that take you to three miles of trails on the property. A $50 nonrefundable pet fee per stay is non-negotiable, but the blow to your pocketbook is softened a bit by the big bag of goodies, including treats, a toy, bowl, towel, and leash that you are welcome to keep. A letter to the pet clarifies the lodge's expectations, including not running on the course or eating golf balls. Rates range $160–240. 1131 S.W. Skamania Lodge Way; 509/427-7700; www.skamania.com.

Stevenson

Sasquatch aside, the most frequently sighted form of wildlife in Stevenson are boardheads, the windsurfers and kiteboarders who come to Bob's Beach or Swell City or The Hatchery to ride the Columbia. The colorful patterns of their sails and boards are fun to watch on the water.

For those of you who find it hard to leave virtual reality behind, the entire town is a free wireless Internet hot spot. Pick up an instruction sheet with the user name and password at the visitors center. To leave Washington, the Bridge of the Gods in nearby Skamania is a $1 toll bridge to Cascade Locks in Oregon.

PARKS, BEACHES, AND RECREATION AREAS

🐾 Beacon Rock

🐾🐾 (See Southwest Washington map on page 298)

This 848-foot monolith is the core of an extinct volcano, named by Lewis in his journals as Beacon Rock or Beaten Rock, the latter probably after he climbed it. To make it possible for people to climb, a guy named Henry Biddle bought the rock and built the railings and rope ladders required to ascend. Sadly, dogs are not allowed on the rock itself, since they lack the opposable thumbs to hold on.

Across the highway from the rock lie 4,650 acres and 9,100 feet of riverfront shoreline, more than enough territory for a dog to chronicle in his personal scent journals. There's a hill you can drive or hike up and, overall, there are nine miles of trails. Or, your pal can sniff along the shore while you fish for sturgeon, salmon, and steelhead below the Bonneville Dam.

Beacon Rock and the park entrance are at milepost 36 on State Route 14. Coop can't recommend the campground. There's too much train and highway noise.

PLACES TO EAT

Crab Shack: Isis wishes her doghouse was as nice as this so-called shack, which serves all kinds of seafood in soups, salads, and sides for lunch, and surf, turf, and pasta for dinner. Sorry, no dogs on the deck; they'll have to settle for a spot on the lawn in the park next door, where you can keep an eye them. The Shack sometimes closes in deep winter, January–March. 130 S.W. Cascade Ave.; 509/427-4400.

Granny's Gedunk Ice Cream Parlor: Everybody asks, so Dorothy defines it on her menu: "Gedunk (GE dunk): A soda fountain or snack bar on U.S. Navy ships or snack bars on shore installations of the U.S. Navy and Marine Corps." Call it what you want, the Umpqua ice cream is cold and delicious and the mini donuts, made daily, are hot and scrumptious. 196 S.W. Second St.; 509/427-4091.

PLACES TO STAY

Columbia Gorge Riverside Lodge: Eight individual theme units share four modern log cabins on the banks of the river, in the middle of two popular parks. The rooms are decorated with authentic art and hand-carved furniture, and each has a gas fireplace, equipped kitchenette, and private or shared deck hot tubs. Your laid-back host Angus welcomes dogs and sailboarders and doesn't believe in unnecessary rules or high, variable room rates. His only request is no dogs on the furniture or beds. Units are $75 or $95, a phenomenal price for the quality and features; the largest unit is $170. The dog fee is $10. 200 S.W. Cascade Ave.; 509/427-5650; www.cgriversidelodge.com.

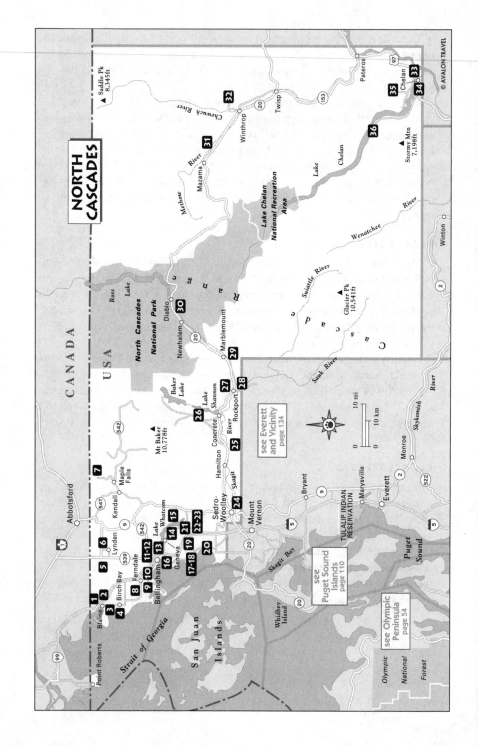

CHAPTER 12

North Cascades

The inroads are few and far between in the 10-million-acre core of the North Cascades protected ecosystem. Most dogs are not going to lose any sleep at night over the fact that they're not allowed in the North Cascades National Park Complex. At least 93 percent of the park is pure wilderness, with no accessible roads. Regarding the two exceptions, the Ross Lake and Lake Chelan Recreation Areas, the former can only be reached by a tiny inroad from British Columbia, and the latter only by boat, upriver from Chelan to Stehekin. There are many other wonderful opportunities in this extensive mountain range to keep your pooch busy during the day.

You can start a day on one of Bellingham's many off-leash trails and finish with a potty stop on the Canadian side of Peach Arch Park. Once in the mountains, your two corridors for recreation are U.S. Highway 2 and State Route 20. The northernmost of the two, State Route 20 takes you past the most glaciers outside of Alaska. It is one of Washington's most scenic byways, to be enjoyed fully in the summer. Parts of the road close for the winter due to the high danger of avalanches, rock slides, flooding, and washouts. Wintertime

PICK OF THE LITTER—NORTH CASCADES

BEST PARK
Rasar State Park, Concrete (page 347)

BEST DOG PARKS
Post Point Lagoon Dog Park, Old Fairhaven (page 342)
Lake Padden Dog Park, Old Fairhaven (page 344)

BEST TRAILS
North Lake Whatcom Park–Hertz Trail, Bellingham
(page 339)
North Fork 25-Mile Creek, Lake Chelan (page 358)

BEST EVENT
Dog Days of Summer Fun Run and Festival, Bellingham
(page 337)

BEST PLACES TO EAT
North Fork Brewery, Mount Baker (page 334)
Flats Tapas Bar, Old Fairhaven (page 345)

BEST PLACES TO STAY
Fairhaven Village Inn, Old Fairhaven (page 346)
Mazama Country Inn and Cabins, Mazama (page 354)
Uncle Tim's Cabins, Lake Chelan (page 359)

travel on the roads that remain open may necessitate traction tires and, over the passes, snow chains are sometimes required. Check mountain pass reports and conditions at www.wsdot.wa.gov/traffic for travel restrictions.

NATIONAL FORESTS AND RECREATION AREAS

Mount Baker–Snoqualmie National Forest
🐾🐾🐾🐾

At least 60 percent of the population of Washington is within 70 miles of the recreation opportunities in this massive forest, which extends 140 miles from the Canadian Border to Mount Rainier on the western slope of the Cascade Mountains. For recreation on the north side of the area, along Mount

Baker Highway, State Route 542, check with the Ranger Station at Glacier, 360/599-2714. Dogs are not allowed at Artist's Point, nor on the Table Mountain and Picture Lake Trails. For hiking and general recreating on the southern slope, along the North Cascades Scenic Byway, your best bet is the single-page Recreation Guide to State Route 20 Corridor Points of Interest, which has a good map and a list of trails and campgrounds. It's available at the Ranger District Office in Sedro Woolley, 810 S.R. 20; 360/856-5700; www.fs.fed.us/r6/mbs.

Blaine and Birch Bay

Blaine is the town on the American side of the most frequently used border crossing between Washington and British Columbia, Canada. Southerly neighbor Birch Bay is the epitome of a summer seaside retreat, with a great water slide park for the kids (sorry, no dogs).

PARKS, BEACHES, AND RECREATION AREAS

1 Peace Arch Park

🐾🐾 🐾 (See North Cascades map on page 326)

Half of this park is on U.S. soil as a state park; the other half is a Canadian provincial park. The arch, which straddles the two countries, was dedicated in 1921 to commemorate the lasting peace and friendship of the two nations. True to form, after September 11, Canadians gathered at the park to offer moral support and free coffee and food to traumatized Americans waiting in long lines to cross the border.

The grass is so perfect at this park, your dog may feel guilty using it as a restroom, but she may recover from her pee shyness once she realizes she can anoint two countries in one trip. The gardens are equally nifty, including Canadian and American flags done in flowers and colorful shrubs. Every year, the park hosts an International Sculpture Exhibition, May–September, adding to the things to see at this historically significant park. Your dog can dream of chasing cars across the international boundaries and contemplate whether or not the grass really is greener on the other side.

From I-5 take Exit 276. Don't miss the exit, or you'll automatically be in line for Canada! At the bottom of the exit ramp, go straight on 2nd Street into the park. Open 8 A.M.–dusk. 360/332-8221; www.peacearchpark.org.

2 Skallman Dog Park

🐾🐾 🐕 (See North Cascades map on page 326)

Skallman is unusual, an off-leash area where much of it is under large cedar trees and some of it is left uncleared of unruly vegetation. Skallman is small, yet they've managed to fit a separate little-dog area into the mix. The ground is uneven, and there's not a lot of ball tossing room without obstacles and the potential for loss in the brush. It's also hard to find the park, but all in all, we'll stick with the prevailing wisdom that it's better to have a dog park than nothing at all.

At the entry is a sign: PAWLEEZE Pick up Poop. They're begging you. Also interesting is a request to allow only one dog within the gated entry at a time; perhaps they mean only one group coming or going? The OLA is completely fenced, with a picnic table, bag dispenser, and can. They have plans to provide a drinking fountain for both dogs and their people.

To reach the park, heading northbound, take Exit 274 from I-5. After the off-ramp curves to the left, turn right on Peace Portal Drive. At the next four-way stop, turn right onto Bell Road. At the next stop, turn right onto Hughes, crossing back over the freeway. Immediately turn left at Yew Street in front of the power towers; this street is not clearly marked. The park is 0.7-miles later. Take a right at the sign for the public works department. The faded Skallman Park 1977 sign is easy to miss.

🔳 Semiahmoo Spit

🐾🐾 (See North Cascades map on page 326)

This natural landform was a site for canneries, warehouses, and a boat repair yard for the legendary Alaska Packers Association, which dominated the Puget Sound salmon industry from 1890 through the 1960s. The area has been completely transformed and reborn as a posh golf resort, with prime real estate, a boutique hotel, and a spa.

The spit trail is an easy-access paved path for users of all interests and abilities. It runs 0.8 mile on the skinny part of the 1.5-mile sand spit, dividing Semiahmoo Bay and Canada from Drayton Harbor. Walking the beach along both sides, for a loop of 1.6 miles, is prettier and more fun for your dog. Leashes are important; the paved trail closely parallels the roadway. Beachcombing, digging for clams, and bird-watching are hot tickets on the spit.

From I-5, take Exit 270 west on Birch Bay–Lynden Road, turn right on Harborview Road, and left on Lincoln Road, which becomes Semiahmoo Parkway. Limited parking is available in a lot next to the museum on the south end. 9261 Semiahmoo Pkwy.; 360/733-2900; www.whatcomcounty.us/parks.

🔳 Birch Bay

🐾🐾🐾 (See North Cascades map on page 326)

Cars on Birch Bay Drive have to share the road with the many dog walkers and bicyclists who come for views of the water on one side and the Cascades on the other. The state park features two miles of beach, a natural game sanctuary, and 14,000 feet of freshwater estuary of the Terrell Creek Marsh. Choose your pleasure: beachfront property for dog paddling and stick retrieving, a patch of lawn to call your own, or, when the headwinds are too cold, picnic tables up on the hill in the tree cover.

From I-5, take Exit 266, head west on State Route 548 for 6.8 miles, turn right on Jackson Road. After 0.7 mile, take a left on Helweg a final 0.4 mile.

PLACES TO EAT

Blackberry House: This coffeehouse is a warm and inviting place that focuses on light foods, bagels, wraps, and salads, until you get to the hearty daily soups and giant pumpkin cookies. Unobtrusive pets on leash may join you on the deck. 321 H St.; 360/332-5212.

The C Shop Summertime: This candy store posing as a café is straight out of a child's fantasy. The shop is open weekends mid-May–mid-June and daily mid-June–Labor Day, and closed the rest of the season. The litany of clapboard signs on the storefront say it all: bagels, muffins, pizza after 5 P.M., brownies, cookies, floats, sundaes, pop, espresso, baked goods, salads, soups, cinnamon rolls, breads, baked goods, candy, fudge, caramel, snow cones, cotton candy, ice cream, cheese corn, caramel corn, and chocolate. 4825 Alderson Rd.; 360/371-2070; www.thecshop.com.

Seaside Bakery Café: Cinnamon raisin French toast is a good lead in for breakfast, and a roasted eggplant sandwich on Seaside sourdough bread makes for a lovely lunch. Then there's dessert, perhaps a lemon bar or peanut butter square. Posted on the window are the daily soup and entrée specials, and there's always French Dip Fridays. The dog watering bowl out front attests to the Seaside's pet-friendliness. 477 Peace Portal Dr., #101; 360/332-9866.

PLACES TO STAY

Resort Semiahmoo: The emphasis is on the "ahhh" at this seaside golf resort, lodge, and spa, from ocean sunsets viewed on your patio or balcony to the warmth of your wood-burning, river-rock fireplace. If money is no object, the elegance and luxury of the hotel are unsurpassed. Small and medium-sized dogs are allowed at the manager's discretion for an additional $50 per pet per stay. Rates range $140–400. 9565 Semiahmoo Pkwy.; 800/770-7992; www.semiahmoo.com.

Smuggler's Inn: Motley, the golden retriever who runs this bed-and-breakfast, is a bona fide hero, internationally famous for informing the border patrol of kids sneaking pot across the border in backpacks. Five feet of the property's lawn is over the Canadian border, and Motley, with his keen nose, follows the suspicious kids around. The Mounties notice Motley away from home and know something must be up. Motley and co-host Sybel will walk your dogs along the cul de sac by the house and leave their toys in a line outside your room if they take a shine to your dog. The inn is a casual affair, where kids and pets feel comfortable and welcome, yet it also has extensive collections of art and antiques. Rates are $100 for rooms, up to $350 for suites. No pet fee. 2480 Canada View Dr.; 360/332-1749; www.smugglersinnblaine.com.

Birch Bay Campground: All campsites, 147 for tents and 20 with full utilities, are in the woods above the beach. Rates are $17–23; reserve at 888/ CAMPOUT (888/226-7688) or www.camis.com/wa.

Lynden

At least 50 percent of the population of this small community is of Dutch heritage, and historic downtown Lynden celebrates all things from Holland. Take your pup for a stroll past windmills, gardens, and bakeries to window-shop and sightsee along Front Street downtown, and then take a side trip to the excellent community park.

PARKS, BEACHES, AND RECREATION AREAS

5 Berthusen Park

🐾🐾 (See North Cascades map on page 326)

The Berthusens were an industrious family of homesteaders and farmers who emigrated from Norway, and patriarch Hans was an admired founder of the Lynden community. Hans kept 20 acres of virgin timber on his farm; when his children passed away, this old-growth forest and the 236 acres of farmland around it were willed as a memorial park for the benefit of future generations.

You can walk through the farm buildings and through the tractor club display, although your dog will likely prefer the trails in the old-growth and second-growth stands of trees. From the picnic area, cross the ball field to the fire road to reach a couple of miles of looped trails in addition to the developed areas of the park. The only bummer is that Bertrand Creek, which wiggles through the park, is too stagnant for a swim. In the old growth, a short interpretive trail is led with brochures created by the Girl Scout troop. The park manager is fond of hand-carved signs, including several stating that dogs must be on leash.

From I-5, take Exit 270, turn east on Lynden Road, travel eight miles, turn left on Guide Meridian for two miles, then left on Badger Road for one mile, and left on Berthusen Road for 0.2 mile. Closes at dusk. 8837 Berthusen Rd.; 360/354-6717.

6 Bender Field

🐾🐾 🐕 (See North Cascades map on page 326)

Bender is, first and foremost, a ball-field complex. Past all of that, you'll see a perfectly square, fenced area that you may suspect is a dog park. It is not; it is the bocce ball court. Past that is a short asphalt path called the Jim

Kaemingk Sr. Trail. Take to the trail, and just before it forks right to cross a wooden footbridge, look to the horizon and walk across a soccer practice field to finally get to the off-leash area. Cooper felt he'd exercised enough simply getting to the OLA.

The OLA is in the extreme southeast corner of the park. There are signs to it, but they don't help much. Look for a very tall chain-link fence to guide you. The two double-gated areas—one for entry and a separate one for exits—look like bull-riding corrals, to let your bronc into the ring. The maybe-an-acre OLA is level, with a long picnic table and four I-think-I-can-grow baby trees. A restroom building is available to you in the center of the ball fields.

From Guide Meridian, which is State Route 539, go east for two miles on Badger Road. Turn right and travel south on Bender Road for 0.3 miles. Closes at dusk.

PLACES TO EAT

Dutch Mothers: If you and your friend with the snout can score a tiny sidewalk table, you'll enjoy heaping plates of home cooking, served by waiters in traditional Dutch attire. Cooper considered changing nationalities after sampling *krenten brood met erwen soep,* a bun stuffed with ham and Gouda cheese and served with pea soup. 405 Front St.; 360/354-2174.

The Famous Lynden Dutch Bakery: If it's in the name, it must be so, and this must be the place for famous, authentic pastries, soups, sandwiches, salads, and more pastries. The folks behind the counter wear traditional garb and the shop's sidewalk tables are a nice spot to take off your clogs and rest awhile. 421 Front St.; 360/354-3911.

PLACES TO STAY

Windmill Inn: The owners of this tiny motel are not Dutch, but that hasn't stopped them from running away with the theme in the exterior decor. The rooms' interiors, where small pets are allowed, are more standard. Rates range $85–105. The pet fee is $7. 8022 Guide Meridian Rd.; 360/354-3424.

Mount Baker

In the winter of 1998–1999, Mount Baker set a world record for the highest seasonal snowfall, at 1,140 inches. This winter wonderland of a volcano, at 10,778 feet, is not the site of the actual ski resort, which is on an arm of adjacent 9,127-foot Mount Shuksan. When other ski areas were shunning snowboarders, Mount Baker welcomed them. By maintaining a funky, non-corporate style, the area continues to build an international reputation as the friendliest place for snowboarding and the burgeoning sport of snowshoeing. In the summertime, there are plentiful hiking opportunities and rafting and fishing on the Nooksack River. Pre-ski, the towns of Glacier and Maple Falls sprung up around gold- and coal-mining activities.

PARKS, BEACHES, AND RECREATION AREAS

7 Silver Lake

🐾🐾🐾 (See North Cascades map on page 326)

This 180-acre lake looks like a painting come to life, ringed with mountain peaks and complete with lily pads and cattails. Nearly every form of legal outdoor recreation is possible at this 411-acre county park, provided dogs are on leash and don't go in the water on the designated beach.

There's a campground, horse camps, picnic areas, swimming beaches, trails, and rentals of paddleboats, rowboats, and canoes. There are immaculate lawns and au naturel forests. There's a concession stand in the summer, a lodge, and family activities. One way or another, someone is going to see to it that you have a good time at this retreat. As you can imagine, it gets hectic on summer weekends.

The Black Mountain Trail is hip with the horse crowd. The one-mile Lookout Mountain Loop is reserved for hikers and bicyclists, no horse play. It can be reached near campsite #10, or from the park entrance.

From I-5, take Exit 255 and drive 28 miles east on the Mount Baker Highway, State Route 542, to Maple Falls. Turn left on Silver Lake Road and continue 3.4 miles to the park. Parking is $4 for non-county residents. 9006 Silver Lake Rd.; 360/599-2776.

PLACES TO EAT

Everybody's Store: There's something for everyone crammed into this tiny general store that's been around for more than 100 years. Try the famous Landjaeger, a dry sausage, or select from organic and gourmet goodies to put together a picnic. Grab an order form on top of the deli case and design your own sandwich. There are a couple of picnic tables out back, or you can walk across the highway to Josh Vander Yacht Memorial Park behind the Community Hall. 5465 Potter Rd., Hwy. 9, Van Zandt; 360/592-2297; www.everybodys.com.

North Fork Brewery: It's a brew pub, and a pizza place, and a beer shrine... oh, and the owner, Vicki, is an ordained minister licensed to perform wedding ceremonies. If the weather doesn't allow the lawn-chair seating to be set up for you and your dog, you must stop anyway at this local institution for pizza and a jug of the finest daily brew to go. 6186 Mount Baker Hwy.; 360/599-2337; www.northforkbrewery.com.

PLACES TO STAY

Mount Baker Lodging: If you're looking for a place to stay anywhere near Mount Baker, Dan Graham is your go-to guy. He has at least 25 different pet-friendly rental properties, including condos, cabins, and complete houses that sleep 2–8 people and up to two pets. Rates range $85–265 with a two-night minimum, three nights on holidays and during special events. There are no pet fees if you sign a rental contract and pay by credit card. The website shows the properties in all their glory and clearly states which ones allow pets. Office: 7463 Mount Baker Hwy.; 360/599-2453; www.mtbaker lodging.com.

Ferndale

This town of 10,000 or so keep busy at two oil refineries and the Alcoa Intalco Aluminum plant. Don't let all this heavy industry scare you away from some of the biggest, if least-developed, off-leash areas in the region. They are left in a natural state, intended primarily for the training of hunting dogs. A Washington Fish and Wildlife Access vehicle-use permit is required to park. Daily permits are free with the purchase of a fishing license, or quarterly permits are $10 at sporting goods stores. *Warning:* If you've got orange vests, wear 'em, and check hunting season dates at www.wdfw.wa.gov; 360/384-3444.

PARKS, BEACHES, AND RECREATION AREAS

🐾 F&W Boat Launch OLA

🐾🐾🐕 (See North Cascades map on page 326)

In the Tennant Lake Park complex, the smaller of the two off-leash areas is 28 acres, with a 0.3-mile section of the River Dike Trail and water access at the Nooksack River boat ramp. There's a garbage can, a mutt mitt dispenser, and a latrine.

From I-5, take Exit 262 west on Main Street for 0.5 mile. Turn left on Hovander Road under the railroad pass and immediately turn right at the Nooksack River Access sign. A Washington Fish and Wildlife Access vehicle-use permit is required to park. Daily permits are free with the purchase of a fishing license, or quarterly permits are $10 at any sporting goods store, Wal-Mart, Kmart, and Fred Meyer. Open dawn–dusk.

🐾 Hovander Homestead and Tennant Lake

🐾🐾🐾 (See North Cascades map on page 326)

This county park complex is a mixture of preserved farmlands and gardens on the National Register of Historic Places, plus a wild game reserve, river access, and hunting dog training grounds. As such, there's a complicated mix of on-leash and off-leash areas, as well as sections where pets are not allowed.

You can study the map at whatcomcounty.us/parks/hovander/dog_map.pdf. To make it easier on you, we've separated it into three distinct park listings: Hovander Homestead, the F&W Boat Launch, and Slater Road Access.

Hovander Homestead has carefully preserved an early 20th century farmhouse and big red barn, complete with barn animals. There's an enjoyable 2.2-mile one-way walk on the River Dike Trail, an old dirt road, although you can't see the Nooksack River much, if at all.

The Tennant Lake Loop is a 1.4-mile elevated boardwalk loop through a native marsh; it starts at the Tennant Lake Tower behind the Fragrance Garden.

The Fragrance Garden is a unique feature, created specifically for patrons without sight. The plants are meant to be touched and smelled, set in planters at a height convenient for wheelchair users, and there are detailed Braille descriptions of each plant species. All of these areas are to be enjoyed on leash.

From I-5, take Exit 262 west on Main Street, go 0.5 mile and turn left immediately under the railroad overpass on Hovander Road and turn right on Nielsen road and follow the signs. Open 8 A.M.–7 P.M. 5299 Nielsen Rd.; Hovander Homestead: 360/384-3444; Tennant Lake and Fragrance Garden: 360/384-3064.

🔟 Tennant Lake Wildlife Area–Slater Road Access

🐾 🐕 (See North Cascades map on page 326)

Approximately half of the total acreage the Hovander Homestead and Tennant Lake Wildlife Area allows pets off-leash. The only developed section of the fields and wetlands is a one-mile trail on an old road leading to Hovander Homestead Park. Going anywhere else requires waders, the ability to navigate through five-foot-tall native ground cover, and a keen sense of smell for retracing your footsteps to your car.

This section is 313 acres bordered by Slater Road, the Nooksack River, the railroad tracks, and the bottom fourth of Tennant Lake. There are no facilities.

From I-5, take Exit 260 and go west on Slater Road for 1.1 miles to the Public Access Area sign on the north side of the road.

Bellingham

The largest city in the region is slowly shedding its industrial maritime heritage, yet working ports, railways, and canneries still sit side by side with the fanciest boutique hotels and restaurants. The city has earned the designation of Trail Town USA from the American Hiking Society and the National Park Service for making excellent trails an integral part of its hardworking community. It is rumored that people move to Bellingham just because there are so many places to walk their dogs.

Bellingham certainly wins the blue ribbon for the largest number of off-leash hiking and walking opportunities in the region, *if* you know where to look. None of the city's off-leash trails are marked as such, but never fear! The Wonder Wieners will tell you where to go and what landmarks to watch for. Bellingham wins again for the most leash-free water frolicking. Again, hard to find and worth the hunt. Pets are welcome at the farmers market with their own water fountain at the corner of Maple Street and Railroad Avenue. For questions and updates, call the Bellingham Parks and Recreation office at 360/676-6985 or look on the web at www.gratefuldogs.org, Bellingham's group promoting off-leash opportunities. We took Little Squalicum Park off the list since the last edition, due to pollution concerns from a nearby superfund site.

Chuckanut Mountain Trail System: County, state, and DNR agencies jointly manage this labyrinth of more than 80 miles of interconnecting trails on 8,000 acres of public land. Larrabee State Park is the easiest access point for several hikes. By far, the Wiener's favorite map is called The Trails of the Chuckanut Mountains, produced by Skookum Peak Press (www.skookum peak.com), available at the Community Food Co-op.

Interurban Trails: This seven-mile walk is a finely crushed gravel bed on an old transit rail system pathway, connecting Fairhaven to Larrabee State Park and the Chuckanut Mountain System. It's wide enough for you and your

DOG-EAR YOUR CALENDAR

Dogs and the people who love them pound the pavement on the first Saturday in September to benefit the Whatcom Humane Society at Bellingham's **Dog Days of Summer Fun Run and Festival.** For those who would rather not run unless chased by an Animal Control Officer, pet-related booths and festivities pack pooches into the off-leash area of Lake Padden Park 10 A.M.–2 P.M. The festival is free, and the entry fee for the race is $25. 360/733-2080; www.whatcom humane.org.

People are talking about **Dog Weekends at Wildwood Resort** on the shores of Lake Whatcom near Sudden Valley, in the Bellingham area. Although not allowed in the cabins or yurts, pets in tents and RVs are thrilled to take over this camping haven one weekend per month in the summer, plus the entire month of September. The setting is idyllic, and this time you can bring the whole fam damily. Tents sites run about $20–30; RVers will have to pony up about $30–40. 990 Lake Whatcom Blvd.; 360/595-2311; www.wildwood-resort.net.

dog to walk abreast and leave room for the cyclists whizzing by. Convenient trailhead parking is located at the intersection of Old Fairhaven Parkway and 20th Street. Leashes must be worn on all sections of the Interurban.

PARKS, BEACHES, AND RECREATION AREAS

11 Cornwall Park

😺😺 (See North Cascades map on page 326)

Cornwall is a very old park, as indicated by a plaque, dedicated in 1948, honoring Pierre Barlow Cornwall, some dude who carried a charter a hundred years earlier to form some type of male-bonding Grand Lodge. Share a bonding moment of your own, strolling a deeply wooded gravel trail skirting the perimeter of the local horseshoe club courts, a disc golf course, and tennis courts. For longer jaunts, the trail connects to another, the Squalicum Parkway. Cornwall is a good place for a picnic, with shaded square tables, a playground, and a restroom.

Take Exit 255 from I-5, going west on E. Sunset Drive. Take a right on Illinois Street, and another right on Cornwall Avenue. Columns mark the entrance into the park to your left. Open 6 A.M.–10 P.M.

12 Sunset Pond Nature Area

😺😺😺🐕 (See North Cascades map on page 326)

Water dogs have got it made in the shade in B'Ham. Here's yet another spot for water training and exercise at Sunset Pond and Bug Lake, plus lots of trails, all free and clear to enjoy off leash. It starts out well groomed, with viewing benches and picnic tables, young maple and pine trees, and garbage cans and bag dispensers. The trail gets narrower and rougher the farther you go. A few wooden bridges and balance beams traverse the muddiest of the mud.

While it is theoretically possible to circle the entire lake on the trail, we got hopelessly lost doing so, and had to hike about a mile back to the car. You could go out and back on the trail starting clockwise around the lake, to the left. Or, hypothetically speaking, if you always take the right fork when the trail splits, you should come out parallel to Woodstock Avenue, on a trail marked by a brown and yellow painted post.

Take Exit 255 from I-5, going east on E. Sunset Drive, State Route 542, toward Mount Baker. At the first main light, turn left on James Road. At the three-way stop, take another left. It'll look like you're entering a shopping mall, but you'll actually skirt around it, a half mile to a gravel lot on your right.

13 Whatcom Falls Park

😺😺😺🐕 (See North Cascades map on page 326)

It's easy to figure out which trails are designated off-leash in this 209-acre city park; if you're north of Whatcom Creek, your dog is free and clear. Some pathways are level, wheelchair-accessible gravel, others are single-track hikes through the woods. Citizens are understandably proud of this treasure. From the main parking area, walk down to the falls, cross the bridge and view the water cascade, and as soon as you are on the other side, pick a direction and disconnect. The gal at the visitors center said this city park is gorgeous enough to be a state park, and that's about right.

From I-5, take Exit 253 east on Lakeway Drive for 1.5 miles and turn left on Silver Beach Road, then continue to the end. 1401 Electric Ave.

14 Bloedel-Donovan

🐾🐾🐾 (See North Cascades map on page 326)

There are some dogs for whom the call of the water pulls more strongly than a bowl of beef with gravy. For them, an off-leash beach is nirvana, even if it's one that exists only 6–10 A.M. May 15–September 15. Yes, water-frenzied canines, this city park on Lake Whatcom is another splashdown landing pad, allowing dogs off leash on the beach at certain times of the year. Dogs are limited to the sand between the marked swimming beach and the parking lot, on the north end of the park, plenty of the park's 18 acres for training water retrievers and ad hoc bathing. Bring the whole family, as there are picnic tables with standing grills, a playground, a volleyball pit in the area, and a marked people's beach. The lawn is wide enough to shake off the water and play fetch on land as well.

From the south side of Bloedel-Donovan's parking lot, you can take the gravel trail, cross the street, and continue over to Whatcom Falls Park. Once past the bridge over the creek, you can hike unleashed there.

From I-5, take Exit 253 east on Lakeway Drive and continue 1.6 miles, turn left to Electric Avenue, then go almost a mile to the entrance on the right. 2214 Electric Ave.

15 North Lake Whatcom Park–Hertz Trail

🐾🐾🐾🐾🐕 (See North Cascades map on page 326)

The Dachsie Twins can't say enough about this perfect hike. It begins with a pretty shore drive along Lake Whatcom to reach the county park. A vault toilet and bag dispensers are provided right up front, and then there's the sign that says, "If you don't have voice control of your dog, it will need to be on a leash." Thus, the converse is also true: Your dog may be off leash if you have voice control at all times. After a 0.25-mile connecting trail from the gravel parking lot through the woods and over a boardwalk, a grand entrance arch ushers you onto the main trail, and it keeps getting better from that point onward.

The wide, level, gravel path is fanatically maintained, smooth enough for easy wheelchair access. The trail is right on the shores of the sparkling lake, and there are many convenient areas for happy hounds to leap into the water. At the same time, humans are ogling the gorgeous mountain and lake views. It's 3.1 miles one-way, following the old Blue Canyon mine railroad, tucked between the lake and Stewart Mountain. On January 9, 2009, the last two miles of the trail were closed due to flooding and storm damage. They had not been re-opened as of press time, so call ahead for trail status if you'd like a longer hike.

Dogs are required to be on leash in Whatcom County parks, unless there is a sign allowing otherwise. When we spoke with the folks at the park office, they stressed that this policy could change, so if the sign isn't there when you visit, leash up.

From I-5, take Exit 254, go east on Iowa Street for 0.6 mile, take a soft left onto Yew Street (not the hard left onto Woburn). Continue 0.5 mile, take a right on Alabama, continue one mile and turn left at the T intersection onto North Shore Drive. Follow North Shore Drive seven miles, turn left at the sign for the trailhead and continue 0.5 mile. 360/733-2900.

16 Sehome Hill Arboretum

🐾🐾🐕 (See North Cascades map on page 326)

You and your dog can join Western Washington University kids crawling all over the 180-acre natural forest habitat on the hill, but the Dachshund Duo were at a loss to figure out which of the paths worn through the woods were technically part of the 5.9 miles of trails, and which were simply footpaths worn by students taking shortcuts to class. The official word is that dogs must be on leash on paved trails, along Jersey Street, and on the Arbor Walkway. Otherwise, you're good to go off leash. One suggestion is to drive to the top, walk on leash from the parking lot to your right toward the observation tower about a quarter mile, climb the stairs for fabulous views of the port, the city, and the marina, and call it good.

From I-5, take Exit 252 west on Samish Way, turn left at the second light on Bill McDonald Parkway (the first left puts you back on the highway south-bound), continue 0.8 mile, take a right on 25th into the Arboretum. Open 6 A.M.–sunset.

PLACES TO EAT

Little Cheerful: Probably the most popular breakfast spot in town, the Cheer-ful succeeds with a simple formula: great food and large portions. You might consider borrowing some friends' dogs to add to your own when you eat at Cheerful's sidewalk seating. You'll need lots of help polishing off legendary mountains of mixed hash browns. 133 Holly St.; 360/738-8824.

Mallard Ice Cream and Café: This parlor with sidewalk tables serves daily soups, fresh-pulled espresso, and unusual flavors of homemade ice cream in sizes small, medium, and "inner child." Have a brownie sundae with mocha brevé á la mode, for example, or an apricot ice. It's a crowded place, and every-one's happy to be there. 1323 Railroad Ave.; 360/734-3884.

Swan Café: This eatery, with a nice row of sidewalk tables, is the deli arm of the Community Food Co-op, so the food tends understandably toward the healthy, whole grain, and organic. 1220 N. Forest St.; 360/734-8158.

PLACES TO STAY

Hotel Bellwether: This marina-view hotel rivals the finest European boutique hotels, decked out in marble and granite and mahogany with imported Italian antiques, Hungarian and Austrian linens, and distinctly American decadence. After a stroll with your pet through the seaside rose garden, you should sit by your roaring fire or soak in a thermo-masseur jetted bathtub. Isis says it brings new meaning to the words lap of luxury, for those who can afford about $300–500 a night, plus a $65 nonrefundable fee per stay for one or two pets. For the lodging experience of a lifetime, save your pennies for the 900-square-foot Lighthouse Condominium, $450–725 per night, plus optional butler service, champagne, and caviar. One Bellwether Way; 360/392-3100; www.hotelbellwether.com.

Guesthouse Inn: This central motel is an excellent value. For rates of $80–125, plus a $10 pet fee, you get tidy, modern rooms and a good list of amenities including indoor hot tub, laundry facilities, continental breakfast, and high-speed wireless Internet. 805 Lakeway Dr.; 360/671-9600.

More Accommodations: Please look under *Chain Hotels* in the *Resources* section for additional places to stay in this area.

Old Fairhaven

The Fairhaven Historic District, south of Bellingham, draws people from all over the country to the southern terminal for the Alaska Marine Highway, a cruise through the Inside Water Passages of Skagway in the Land of the Midnight Sun (dogs allowed! 360/676-8445; www.alaska.gov/ferry or www.akferryadventures.com). Alas, if you've heard of the famed Doggy Diner, it has gone out of business, but Fairhaven remains one of the dog-friendliest districts in an already dog-friendly city. The boardwalk at Taylor Avenue and 10th Street is a great place to take a scenic stroll along Bellingham Bay.

There's an abundance of pet-friendly businesses in this district. For example, in one building, you can walk indoors with pets from Village Books, through Paper Dreams cards and gifts, to clothing boutique LuLu2, and onto Pacific Chef, chock-a-block full of kitchen gadgets. Take a peek at the K-Nine Couture Collars at Four Starrs, and test out the sidecars at Chispa Scooters. Poke your heads into Jewelry Affairs and get a trim at The Barber Shop; you'll meet resident dogs in both these latter stores.

PARKS, BEACHES, AND RECREATION AREAS

🐾 Village Green

🐾🐾🐾 (See North Cascades map on page 326)

When all the talk of exercise has worn the Wieners out, they like to sun themselves on the lawn at this city square in Fairhaven central. They drink from the water fountain designed just for dogs, and sit on the bench next to the statue of Dirty Dan Harris, the area's first settler known for wearing his shirts well past their fresh-by date. Better smells waft from nearby outdoor tables for Colophon Café, and it is a written rule to greet dogs with a love pat as you pass. If you simply must exercise, you can join a section of the Interurban Trail, caddy corner across the street at 10th Street and Mill Avenue. Nap time!

Village Green is at the corner of 10th Street and Mill Avenue.

18 Post Point Lagoon Dog Park

🐾🐾🐾🐾🐕 (See North Cascades map on page 326)

A.k.a. Fairhaven Dog Park, or the dog park at Marine Park, or the dog park at the Port of Bellingham—call it what you want, this off-leash area is a brilliant use of land that might otherwise go to waste (pun intended), next to the sewer plant south of the city. It isn't fully fenced or gated; however, it is in a valley effectively hemmed in on all sides by steep hills covered with impassable blackberry bushes, by water, and by the tall fences of the treatment facility and a rail yard. From the gravel trail that leads down into the OLA, the park just keeps going and going, opening out onto a huge field. The path connects to a network of city trail systems, marked by brown mileage posts.

The lagoon was closed to dogs in 2006 to protect one of seven remaining pocket estuaries in the city. It is of great ecological importance as a habitat for salmon and bull trout, bald eagles, and a blue heron colony.

From I-5, take Exit 250 west on State Route 11, turn right on 12th Street, left on Harris, and watch closely to turn left on 4th Street. The OLA is on the right, 0.1 mile after you turn onto 4th Street. It's not marked, so watch for the parked cars, the bag dispenser and trash can, and the gravel path leading down into the patch of dog heaven. Bring drinking water.

19 Arroyo Park

🐾🐾🐾🐕 (See North Cascades map on page 326)

Arroyo Park is a piece of forested land managed by the city, connecting the Interurban Trail to Chuckanut Mountain Trails in Larrabee Park lands. Dogs are allowed off leash on the 0.75-mile connector trail that winds through Arroyo, and, even better yet, Chuckanut Creek courses through for crystal-clear water play along the streambed. The hike alone is great, hilly and narrow but manageable, across the creek on a footbridge. It will definitely be muddy in the rainy season. The city vanishes instantly when you step into the trees, and you're likely to meet locals who've been bringing dogs here for decades. Occasionally, horses and their riders take to the trail, and every few years salmon come up the creek to spawn. From Arroyo, you can leash up and hike for miles on the Hemlock and North Lost Lake trails. There are no facilities.

From I-5, take Exit 250 west on State Route 11, turn left on 12th Street, and left again on Chuckanut Drive. Continue for one mile and turn left on Lake

Samish Way. The first parking area is 0.1 mile after the turn on the right, a second lot is 0.3 mile after the turn.

20 Larrabee State Park

🐾🐾🐾 (See North Cascades map on page 326)

The 8,100 feet of saltwater shoreline along Washington's first state park are geared to a dog's sensibilities. While humans might prefer soft sand to tan on, canines are thrilled with this state park's smelly tidepools, gravel beaches, and piles of driftwood and seaweed to sort through. Humans tag along for the scenery, sunsets, and 2,683 acres of hiking trails through a forest so deep and enchanting, it had Cooper happily chasing shadows. Larrabee is a convenient access point for some choice treading ground on an additional 8,000 acres in the Chuckanut Mountain Trail System.

Fragrance Lake is the easiest to reach, with a trailhead right across the street from the main entrance to the state park. It's a 1.8-mile climb to the top, with a level lake loop to bring your heart rate down to normal before you descend. Take the quick detour to an overlook at the start of the trail for a breather and a great Puget Sound vista. Or, from the state park's main entrance, you can walk north on the Interurban Trail to Teddy Bear Cove Trail. At the bottom of this 0.9-mile switchback descent is a white sand beach from centuries of crushed clam shells. We can't recommend tent camping at Larrabee, because there's too much train and highway noise.

From I-5, take Exit 250 west on State Route 11. At 1.2 miles, take a left on 12th Street, and at the next block, take a soft left onto Chuckanut Drive.

There's limited trailhead parking at roadside pullouts. Open 6:30 A.M.–dusk.
360/676-2093.

21 Lake Padden Dog Park

👣👣👣👣🐕 (See North Cascades map on page 326)

In addition to more than five miles of off-leash trails, the 900-acre Lake Padden Recreation Area and Public Golf Course has the city's only fenced and gated off-leash exercise area, including a separate small-dog area. On the trails, it's another one of those places where it can be confusing to figure out where your dog is allowed off leash. That just means you'll have to visit more often, darn it, until it becomes second nature.

The off-leash area is a circular field with a cyclone fence and a clump of trees in the middle. It's big, several acres, and worth a visit for playtime, whether or not you take to the trails. There's a nearby restroom, garbage can and bags, and a water fountain if you've got a dish to fill.

The 2.5-mile trail around the lake, on leash, is a lovely walk on a level gravel path. On a narrow strip of marked beach adjacent to the ball field fence, dogs are allowed into the water. Essentially, the rest of the trails are off leash on the south end between the golf course power lines and the trailhead on Samish Way and in the woods west of Padden Creek Dam from the Ruby Creek entrance into the lake.

From I-5, take Exit 246; turn east onto Samish Way. At 1.3 miles, there is an unmarked, gravel trailhead parking lot for immediate access to the off-leash trails. The east entrance, the road to the golf course and to the fenced dog park, is at 2.5 miles. After you turn left into the park, follow the right fork in the road to the picnic area, 0.5 mile to the end, past the ball fields, to the OLA. The west entrance is at 2.7 miles, and the last entrance, at Ruby Creek, is at 3.0 miles. Open 6 A.M.–10 P.M. 4882 Samish Way.

22 Samish Park

👣👣👣🐕 (See North Cascades map on page 326)

Our enduring image of this terraced hillside trail is that it is steep. Really, very steep. The county's first park in 1968, Samish is 39 acres. Hard to tell, because most of it is on wild slopes, with switchbacks slithering back and forth like snakes on the map, through a dark and mysterious forest fortress, thick with ferns and moss.

The loop along the shoreline of Lake Samish is 0.7-miles, past the boat and fishing docks and an enclosed swimming area where dogs are not allowed. Dogs *are* allowed off leash on the 1.3-mile loop though the fir forest up and over the lake once used as a log-rafting pond for the timber industry.

From I-5 southbound, take Exit 246, and turn left at the stop sign. Drive 0.8 mile down North Lake Samish Drive, veer right at the Y in the road, and continue another 0.8 mile along the lakeside drive. The park is on your

right immediately before crossing the bridge. Open sunrise to sunset. www
.whatcomcounty.us/parks.

23 Squires Lake

🐾🐾 (See North Cascades map on page 326)

The toughest part of the hike is the first 0.3 mile, huffing up the connector trail
from the parking lot to the remote, miniature lake. At the top, you are treated
to a three-mile loop around a pretty lake, removed from all else. A short piece
of the trail follows the dirt road of an abandoned rail bed, and you can connect
to the slightly more challenging South Ridge loop and the easy Beaver Pond
circle. The water is a bit too scummy for swimming, even for dogs, and hard to
reach through the marsh. The hike is enough, in the kind of place where you
can have the peaceful forest and the wildlife to yourselves.

From I-5, take Exit 242 and turn east onto Nulle Road and continue 0.6 mile
to the gravel parking lot on the left. A portable potty and a garbage can are the
only amenities. Bring water and bags.

PLACES TO EAT

Colophon Café: The Dachshund Duo thoroughly enjoyed chowing down at a
restaurant whose legendary founder and mascot is Mama Colophon, the cow.
This deli, dairy, and ice cream counter is legendary for its dog-friendliness
and its unique and delicious daily soups. The soups are so varied that the restaurant has a monthly soup calendar. There are tables on the sidewalk at the
upper level, patio seating downstairs for the more elaborate restaurant, and
grass nearby in Fairhaven Village Green. 1208 11th St.; 360/647-0092; www
.colophoncafe.com.

Flats Tapas Bar: While dogs may be puzzled by the small plate phenomenon, people who like to share the finer things in life will love the variety of
flavors at Flats. Wine connoisseurs can enjoy many vintages by the glass from
a wine list which won a national award from *Wine Enthusiast* magazine. Dog
lovers can dine at a couple of elevated tables out front, sampling tasty dishes of
everything made from scratch, including sauces and desserts, something even
a dog can appreciate. 1307 11th St.; 360/738-6001;www.flatstapas.com.

Skylark's Hidden Café and Wine Parlour: Dogs are welcome on both
patios as you wine and dine on comfort food served anytime, breakfast, lunch,
and dinner until midnight. You might need doggie bags to take home leftovers
of your custom-made omelet or sandwich. 1308 11th St.; 360/715-3642.

PLACES TO STAY

Chrysalis Inn and Spa: Upscale and modern, this inn was fully remodeled in
2008, purpose-built for rejuvenation. Suites have spa tubs with pass-through
views into rooms with gas fireplaces, out onto patios with bay views. Breakfast
and use of the steam room are included in rates ranging $210–250. Pets under

20 pounds are generally allowed on the first floor only, for a $50 per visit pet fee. 804 10th St.; 888/808-0005 or 360/756-1005; www.thechrysalisinn.com.

Fairhaven Village Inn: At this refined Victorian-era hotel, two rooms are reserved for people with pets for a $20 fee. The designated dog rooms have washable cotton comforters on the beds, the only difference from standard rooms. If those two rooms are booked, the hotel will open up its other rooms for a $30 fee, to cover dry cleaning for the down bedspreads. This property is worthy on its own merits. It becomes irresistible when you discover that it's within walking distance of the city's best dog park and all of the Interurban and Chuckanut Mountain Trails. Rates are $160–220; save money with Park View rooms, as nice as Bay View rooms, only without fireplaces or balconies. 1200 10th St.; 360/733-1311 or 877/733-1100; www.fairhavenvillageinn.com.

Sedro Woolley

Historically an important trading post and lumbering town, Sedro Woolley is now the last large outpost before heading into the woods.

PARKS, BEACHES, AND RECREATION AREAS

2.4 Cascade Trail

🐾🐾 (See North Cascades map on page 326)

This 22-mile jaunt starts next to the highway, but doesn't stay next to it, which is nice. From Sedro Woolley on the west, it skirts behind farms and along the Skagit River, and winds gradually up a hill before ending east in Concrete. This banked railway is a fine-gravel multi-use path for pedestrian, equestrian, and cyclestrian users. It's kept in beautiful condition by Skagit County Parks and Recreation.

Park at the gravel lot at the intersection of Fruitdale Road and State Route 20, 0.1 mile west of milepost 67 on the south side of the highway. 360/336-9414; www.skagitparksfoundation.org.

PLACES TO STAY

Three Rivers Inn: The three rivers are the Sauk, the Cascade, and the Skagit. The three top reasons to stay here are convenience, cleanliness, and affordability. Medium or small pets preferred. Rates range $100–110. The pet fee is $20 per pet per stay. 210 Ball St.; 360/855-2626.

Concrete

Named for a cement plant now defunct, this small town is working hard to preserve its interesting heritage. East of Concrete, the population thins out drastically, replaced by alternating forest and scattered farmland.

PARKS, BEACHES, AND RECREATION AREAS

25 Rasar State Park

😼😼😼😼 (See North Cascades map on page 326)

Rasar, as in speed racer, is the newest all-season park in the state system. Open since 2000, it's been on the camping reservation system since 2004. Everything's still nice, especially the restrooms, covered shelter, and playground. Trails throughout the park include a paved, wheelchair-accessible path to the banks of the Skagit River. On the Skagit Trail Loop, after a quarter mile of woods, the path breaks out into a farming valley, surrounded by hills, becoming simply a mowed path through the field grass. It's about a half mile to the wide river and a big sandy beach with a smattering of river rocks. It's a compact park, only 128 acres, a quick and easy mountain playground that is rapidly growing in popularity. Eagle-watching is excellent in fall and early winter.

From State Route 20, 0.1 mile west of milepost 81, turn south on Lusk Road, go 0.5 mile, take a left on Cape Horn Road, and go an additional mile to the park entrance. Open 8 A.M.–dusk.

26 Mount Baker–Snoqualmie National Forest–Baker Lake Trail

😼😼😼 (See North Cascades map on page 326)

The nine-mile Baker Lake journey is for those who prefer a hands-on approach to nature, schlepping through shallow streams, crawling up, over, and under fallen logs, hopping a few boulders, that kind of thing. Trail conditions vary wildly from season to season, even from month to month; it's never the same

NATURE HIKES AND URBAN WALKS

On a walking tour of the **Fairhaven Historic District** in Bellingham, there are 24 historical markers and dozens of brick and sandstone buildings circa 1890–early 1900s. The Victorian architecture and character of the area's buildings are very appealing, filled with restaurants, galleries, and gift shops where trading posts, bordellos, and saloons once ruled a rowdy frontier town. Look for the Walking Tour Map of the Fairhaven Historic District.

The mountain village of **Concrete** is a fascinating aggregate of living, breathing community and eerie ghost town. Local deposits of limestone and clay became the basis of the cement industry, thriving by 1905, and closing finally in the 1960s. The name remains, as do abandoned poured-concrete buildings dating back to the 1920s and the massive concrete silos that welcome you into town, as unusual a "Welcome to" sign as you're likely to see. Self-guided walking tour brochures are available at 7460 S. Dillard St.; 360/853-7042.

trail twice. The tree cover is thick, and you usually can't see the lake until you're right up on it. There's a suspension bridge over the river at the north end that's thrilling if you don't suffer from vertigo. Also on the north end, you can hike up to a spot called Sulfite Camp, to a clearing where the sky is filled with the glaciers of Mount Baker and Mount Shuksan in all their glory.

If you are camping at Baker Lake, stay at one of the forest service campgrounds. The folks at Baker Lake Resort, run by Puget Sound Energy, are not dog enthusiasts. For the trail, check conditions at the ranger station before you go. Remember the backcountry hiking "Ten Essentials?" This is the time to bring them.

To reach the south trailhead from State Route 20, turn north on Baker Lake Road at 0.6 mile west of milepost 83, and travel 13.7 miles to Baker Lake Dam Road, Forest Road 1106. Turn right and continue 2.8 miles on the dirt road and over the dam to the trailhead. Parking is a $5 daily Forest Service Pass.

PLACES TO EAT

Birdsview Brewing Company: Yes, leashed dogs are allowed in the beer garden. No, children are not, but they are allowed inside, and they have a kids' menu. So, you are going to have to choose. Who do you love more? Just kidding. Hopefully, you won't be put in that position, but you will have to choose which of the seasonally made brews on tap to pour into your 64-ounce growler. Taco Tuesdays and biscuits and gravy are the big winners, but not necessarily together. On State Route 20, 0.1-mile east of Lusk Road, and just east of Rasar State Park; 360/826-3406; www.birdsviewbrewingco.com.

Cajun Bar and Grill: The jambalaya, blackened catfish po' boys, shrimp Creole and other Louisiana wonders at this restaurant are well worthy of your attention, even though no alcohol is served at the patio tables. 7296 Baker St.; 360/853-8518; www.cajunbarandgrill.biz.

PLACES TO STAY

Ovenell's Heritage Inn at Double O Ranch: Ovenell's is a working ranch first, with 200 head of cattle, wild turkeys, and two Clydesdales on 500 acres. The two log cabins that allow pets, Eagle and Wrangler, are about a mile from the main house in a country setting. They're equipped with gas fireplaces and kitchens, for great rates of $130–150. Eleanor, the leading lady of the house, will prepare travel itineraries in the area for you. Her grandpa was the first fishing guide on the Skagit River, so she knows her stuff. Meanwhile, her husband and five daughters run the ranch. Come up to the house and hang out with resident dogs Annie, Patches, and Molly, and feast on homemade jams and pumpkin, apple, and zucchini breads made for guests. The pet fee is $25 per night for one pet, $30 per night for two pets. 46276 Concrete–Sauk Valley Rd.; 866/464-3414; www.ovenells-inn.com.

Rasar State Park Campground: It's peaceful and quiet at this park, with

18 standard sites, 20 utility sites, and eight walk-in sites in the woods about a half mile from the Skagit River. Rates are $12–24; reserve at 888/226-7688 or www.camis.com/wa.

Rockport

Somewhere between 300 and 400 bald eagles come to the Upper Skagit area from mid-December to mid-January to snack on salmon that have come upriver to spawn. Starting in Rockport, there are four miles of wildlife viewing pullouts on State Route 20. Maps of the staffed viewing areas are available in Rockport at the Skagit River Bald Eagle Interpretive Center, one block south of State Route 20 on Alfred Street; www.skagiteagle.org.

PARKS, BEACHES, AND RECREATION AREAS

27 Rockport State Park
🐾🐾🐾 (See North Cascades map on page 326)

The old growth in this 670-acre park was never logged, leaving you with the rare experience of hiking and camping under a forest canopy so thick that sunlight might not reach the ground. Cooper says a blessing for the people at the Sound Timber Company who refused to log these giants, selling the land to the state instead for the princely sum of $1.

Use the small picnic area (which has dog hitching posts!) as a staging ground for a hike on the Evergreen Trail or on the ambitious Sauk Mountain Trail. Evergreen begins to the east of the restrooms in the picnic area and ends near site #28 in the campground. It's 0.7 mile to a rest stop called Broken Fir,

1.5 miles to a water break at Fern Creek, and 2.6 miles total to the campground. It's really an elaborate detour, because the campground is actually next to the picnic area.

The Sauk Mountain Trail starts at about 2,000 feet and climbs to 5,400 feet. You'll huff and you'll puff over 30 some-odd switchbacks in three miles and sit yourself down on plenty of resting benches before attaining the prized summit views you've earned.

The entrance to Sauk Mountain Road, Forest Road 1030, is at milepost 96, immediately west of the state park, and 0.4 mile from the campground and picnic area entrance to Rockport. The eight-mile gravel road to the trailhead can be pretty rough. Parking is $5 at the trailhead.

28 Howard Miller Steelhead Park

🐾🐾🐾 (See North Cascades map on page 326)

This county park's 1.4-mile trail is a manageable way to explore the back-country without getting too deep or steep into it. The path begins on the west side of the park, past campsite #36. You'll walk on a railway grade and across a footbridge to enter a big meadow with a view of snow-capped Sauk Moun-tain. For the first 0.5 mile, the trail follows the south side of the meadow to reach the water at the confluence of the Sauk and Skagit Rivers. The second half of the trail parallels the river through an old-growth forest, looping back to the footbridge. Underfoot, you can still see the railroad timbers embedded in the ground.

Camping is an open-meadow affair on the banks of the Skagit River. What it lacks in privacy, it makes up for in river and mountain views. Tent sites are $10, sites with electricity $15, and full hookup sites cost $18. 52809 Rockport Park Rd.; 360/853-8808.

From State Route 20, turn south on Alfred Street, 0.1 mile west of the inter-section of State Route 20 and State Route 530.

PLACES TO EAT

Cascadian Farms: Make a beeline for the seasonal berry shortcake, and worry about the soups, deli case sandwiches, and ice cream if you have room left over. This all-organic farm store specializes in jams and jellies and car-ries enough other foods to put together a splendid picnic lunch. Outside is a nice restroom, a shelter, umbrella-covered picnic tables, and lots of park-ing. Open May–October. Three miles east of Rockport on U.S. Hwy. 20; 360/853-8173.

PLACES TO STAY

Clark's Skagit River Resort: Robert De Niro stayed here, and Ellen Barkin, too. Your pet can join this prestigious list of guests, if, and only if, he can handle being around rabbits. We're not talking a couple of bunnies in a hutch, we're talking hundreds of them on the lawns all over the 125-acre property. Up to two pets are allowed in all of the 35 cabins, chalets, lodge rooms, and an Airstream trailer, each slightly different, decorated with themes that aren't too overdone (okay, just a little). They've got their own trails nearby and an eatery on the property. Cabins range $70–170, with a $10 pet fee. 58468 Clark Cabin Rd.; 360/873-2250 or 800/273-2606; www.northcascades.com.

Gracehaven: After a couple of days in one of these deluxe cabins, you may remember what it feels like to live without stress. Two of the five nearly identical cabins are pet-friendly (#4 and #5). The only difference is that they have vinyl floors instead of hardwood, and #4 has a tub in addition to a shower. The woodwork is beautiful in each log cabin, and the buildings are tucked away in a bend by the river. Please let them know you are bringing pets and keep your dogs on leash on the property. Rates are great, $85–105, and each pet is $5 per night. Bring as many as you want, within reason. This is a Christian retreat, open to the public. 9303 Dandy Pl.; 360/873-4106; http://wordofgraceministries.homestead.com/gracehaven.html.

Marblemount

This tiny burg has the last major services for 69 miles, and even they are more minor than major. You can get gas and coffee, fuel for your machine and your metabolism. Named for a nearby quarry, it began as a gold rush camp at the time of the Civil War.

PARKS, BEACHES, AND RECREATION AREAS

29 Pressentin Park

😺😺 (See North Cascades map on page 326)

Pressentin Park should be called Pressentin Meadows, and most of the one-mile trail is a mowed path through an open field. Chances are unlikely you'll meet anyone else traipsing through the wildflowers, and you'll certainly never have to fight for room. You'll pass through a bit of forest and get a peek at the river and connecting slough. If you have a member of a short species, your only risk is losing your pet if they leave the trail for the unmowed fields. Pressentin is a natural park with no amenities, unless you count the gas station's bathroom next door.

On State Route 20 in Marblemount, park at the Shell station and you'll see the signs for the park on the southwest side of the road.

PLACES TO EAT

Marblemount Drive-In Good Food: Yes, the Good Food is part of the name at this order window. The offerings include pizza, mountain burgers, fish and seafood baskets, Philly cheese steaks, and Cindy's soups. Eat at picnic tables on the grass while your pal plays with Junior, the blue heeler who will pace-set for him in the dog run on the premises. 59924 S.R. 20; 360/873-9309.

Newhalem

The mountain outpost of Newhalem is the last inhabited place you can reach on the Scenic North Cascades Byway before the road closes for the winter, usually between November and May. Listed on the National Register of Historic Places, it's a working company town for the Skagit Hydroelectric Project, which extends 40 miles north along the Skagit River from Newhalem to the Canadian Border. In addition to supplying the greater part of the electric power for Greater Seattle, the town has been a tourist destination since the 1930s, when people arrived by train from Rockport. It took two days to reach and tour the facility back then; you should be able to do it in a couple of hours with a self-guided tour brochure from the visitors center. Seattle City Light; 206/684-3030; www.cityofseattle.net/light, Skagit Tours link on the left navigation bar.

PARKS, BEACHES, AND RECREATION AREAS

30 Newhalem Trails
🐾🐾🐾 (See North Cascades map on page 326)

The core of town is one big park, a legacy of the power plant's first manager and his love for exotic greenery. There are a couple of short walks worthy of some tail-wagging time.

The Trail of the Cedars starts with a suspension bridge over the Skagit, which can be slippery when wet. The whole thing is a half mile at most; some of the trees are taller than the trail is long. This easy stroll has good interpretive markers telling stories of the power plant. From the company store in the center of town, walk straight back through the parking lot until you see the big arch that declares the trail.

Ladder Creek Falls also starts with a trek over a suspended bridge, and here the similarity with Trail of the Cedars ends. This quarter-mile trip through an elaborate garden involves navigating many stairs, wooden bridges, rock steps, a tunnel, and narrow trails, to view gardens clinging to cliffs behind the powerhouse. The falls is an exciting series of chutes and ledges, and you can get close enough to feel the spray. Showcasing the spark of electricity provided by the project, this unique garden is fully illuminated so you may walk at night. Even so, Isis warns you to watch your step.

To find Ladder Creek Falls, walk east to your left from the company store until you are in front of the powerhouse building. Cross the suspension bridge to the right of the powerhouse to begin the trail.

Mazama

The Methow Valley Sport Trails Association tells us that summer arrives up here a couple of months earlier than in Western Washington, meaning the sun comes out, even if temperatures are brisk. Pronounced MET-how, this high mountain valley has three small towns: Mazama, Winthrop, and Twisp. Harts Pass, above Mazama, is the highest point to which you can drive in the state, at 6,198-feet, but only if you can stomach the one lane, rocky road, without guard-rails, with death-defying drop offs and dizzying views into the valley below.

The valley is far enough from big population centers to keep it uncrowded for outdoor enthusiasts. Highway 20 is the preferred summer route; however, it closes annually from sometime in October to May, due to unmanageable snowfall and avalanche danger. During the winter, travelers must take High-way 2 or I-90 to Blewett Pass (Highway 97) and up, a drive of at least five hours. In addition to the Big Valley Trail below, Cougar Bait in the Rendezvous area and Lunachik Trail near Mazama are listed as dog-friendly hikes/ski trails.

PARKS, BEACHES, AND RECREATION AREAS

31 Big Valley Trail

🐾🐾🐾🐾 (See North Cascades map on page 326)

This mostly level trail comes highly recommended as a "good hike with dog," by the Methow Valley Sport Trails Association (www.mvsta.com). It's easy to get to, with a parking area right off State Route 20, between Mazama and Win-throp. This part of the Methow Community Trail ambles out to the Methow River and back, a little over five miles round-trip. It's a figure-eight loop, so you can cut the trail in half, doing only the first loop, for a quickie version.

If you start out to the right, you'll pass alongside farm fields planted with alfalfa and other grains you might find in your morning muesli. Soon you'll delve into the tree canopy on the 1,164 acres of Fish and Wildlife land, and then you break out into, well, a big valley. The sky is wide and bright, seemingly even when it's gray. It is a pretty well-traveled trail, so you'll probably have the company of other humans and dogs on your journey.

Big Valley Trail access is about five miles northwest of Winthrop off State Route 20. Turn left on Dripping Springs Road and follow it to the left to park. Help yourself to the vault toilet, poop bags, and garbage can at the trailhead.

PLACES TO EAT

Mazama Store: Well stocked with treats even gourmet foodies can appreciate, this gift shop, provisions store, and café pulls in locals as well as visitors for muffins and coffee cake, soup and sandwiches. We've seen a table out front once or twice; otherwise, pack your basket with goodies to go. 50 Lost River Rd.; 509/996-2855.

PLACES TO STAY

Freestone Inn: Pets are allowed in the 15 remote and romantic cabins, set near Early Winters Creek, with mountain and valley views. In classic northwest lodge style, they feature wood from floor to ceiling, river rock or iron grate fireplaces, period 1940s lodge furniture, and decks with Adirondack chairs. All have kitchenettes with microwaves and refrigerators; four larger cabins have stoves and dishwashers. A hot tub waits for you outside. Rates start at $175–300. The pet fee is $30 per stay, for a maximum of two pets. 31 Early Winters Dr.; 509/996-3906; www.freestoneinn.com.

Mazama Country Inn and Cabins: It's cabins again for pet-lovers, a whole bunch of them, and here's the list: A Cute Cabin, Fawn Creek, Firefly, Goat Wall Cabin, Goat Wall View, Happy Trails, Lost River, Ponderosa, and Triple J. Descriptions, rates, and pictures on their website provide all the details. Rates range $150–400, and the pet fee is $25 per pet per visit. Two-night minimums regularly, three-night minimums holidays and high seasons. This is where a dog belongs, out in the country. Often, you're out your door and onto the trails within a few steps. 15 Country Rd.; 509/996-2681; www.mazamacountryinn.com.

Winthrop and Twisp

Part wilderness and part cowboy country, there's just enough culture here to keep you active in the evenings, if your dog hasn't exhausted you for the day. Cross-country skiing and snowshoeing rules winter recreation. In the summer all those groomed schussing trails are converted for hiking and bicycling. Winthrop is a false-front Wild West town, Riverside Avenue is the main street. Twisp is more down-to-earth as the site of the lumber mill. Slowly, Twisp is evolving to become a center for arts and culture.

PARKS, BEACHES, AND RECREATION AREAS

32 Pearrygin Lake

🐾🐾 (See North Cascades map on page 326)

This state park puts up some pretty big numbers at more than 700 acres and 11,000 feet of freshwater shoreline. The sky is a big blue out here too, proving that Montana doesn't have a lock on the heavens. Old willow and ash trees offer shade over wide expanses of lawn. As for camping, there are 165 sites, and we suggest the East Campground loops for prettier tent spots. For all the room, it's a pretty laidback park, except for water sport action on the lake.

To reach Pearrygin from State Route 20 southbound, at the four-way stop in Winthrop go straight through the intersection and follow the main street up the hill. Travel north 1.2 miles as the road turns into East Chewuch Road. Turn right onto Bear Creek Road and drive 0.75 mile to the entrance of the

West Campground. For the picnic area, watercraft launch, park store, and East Campground, continue past the west entrance another 0.75 mile to the end of the pavement and turn right.

PLACES TO EAT

Boulder Creek Deli: They rotisserie-roast their own beef, turkey, and chicken for 15 specialty sandwiches at this deli in the Emporium Building. The Cowboy Calzones are big enough for Isis to move into, and the cookies and brownies are almost as big and thick. Lunch on deck, or take your sandwich to a blanket at nearby Pearrygin Lake or Mack Lloyd Memorial Park. 100 Bridge St., Winthrop; 509/996-3990.

Twisp River Pub: You can get pub grub such as nachos and buffalo wings at the favorite local watering hole, but they're better known for their soups and steak and seafood specials, so live it up a little. They're kid and dog friendly on the partially covered patio. 201 Hwy. 20, Twisp; 888/220-3360; www.methowbrewing.com.

PLACES TO STAY

Mount Gardner Inn: Pets are welcome in four inexpensive ground-floor rooms in the East Building, remodeled in 2005. It's centrally located in Winthrop and the rates are great at $60–90, plus a $10 pet fee. 611 Hwy. 20; 509/996-2000; www.mtgardnerinn.com.

WolfRidge Resort: Sitting pretty on 60 acres of Methow riverfront, staying at WolfRidge means you can step out your door onto an extensive valley trail system. You'll be about five miles from the center of Old West Winthrop. As a full-service resort, after you've had enough of lounging around on your hand-hewn log furniture, there's volleyball, a playground, a heated pool and hot tub, rec room, and plenty of picnic tables with barbecues. Rates are $90–200, $225–300 for the cabins. Pets are $10 per pet per night, plus a one-time $25 cleaning fee. 412-B Wolf Creek Rd.; 509/996-2828; www.wolfridgeresort.com.

Lake Chelan

For generations, station wagons and minivans crammed to the gills with families and gear have made the summer pilgrimage to this gigantic mountain lake for water play. Lake Chelan is 55 miles long, the third deepest in North America behind Tahoe and Crater Lake. Most of it is accessible only by boat or hiking in, and at one point it sits in a gorge deeper than the Grand Canyon. If you want to rent all manner of watercraft, check out www.cometothelake.com. Winter is a snowy wonderland, rated #1 in the state for snowmobiling, and superb for cross-country skiing and snowshoeing.

The surrounding Chelan Valley is also rapidly gaining a reputation for excellent wineries. The vine scene is amazing; bring an empty cooler, as you'll want to fill it with bottles for your cellar back home. In town, **Whaley's General Store** is your spot for pet supplies, including doggy life vests (hint, hint), and a choice treat selection (206 E. Woodin Ave.; 509/682-2216).

There are several informal pullouts along South Lakeshore Road where you can park and scramble over a few breakwater rocks into the water. Don Morse City Park and the adjacent city campground are off-limits to dogs from Memorial Day to Labor Day.

PARKS, BEACHES, AND RECREATION AREAS

33 The Riverwalk

🐾🐾🐾 (See North Cascades map on page 326)

This one-mile loop provides a great stroll along the Chelan River between the two main bridges, right in downtown sleepy Chelan. There are countless areas where it's feasible for all species to slip into the water for a swim.

At one end, 12-acre Riverwalk Park has everything else you need. There's parking, view benches, picnic lawns, shade trees, restrooms and changing rooms, and access to the loop. Coop's mom confesses to reading the entire last installment in the saga of Harry Potter's life on a bench in this park, several afternoons one summer. Cooper and Isis slept through all the excitement.

Riverwalk Park is at the corner of Emerson Street and Wapato Avenue.

34 Lakeside Park

🐾🐾 (See North Cascades map on page 326)

Not to be confused with Lakeshore Park, where dogs are not allowed in the summer, this smaller city spot is handy, next door to the Best Western, and right in town. Scoring a picnic table is a major coup, and blanket space is at a premium. The early dog gets the worm to roll in, and once put, you may as well stay for the day. Summers are hot and dry here, and sometimes it seems like this park's trees are the only ones providing shade in the valley. Dogs are not allowed into the water here, so sneak on over to the public swimming hole, marked by bright blue fence railings, next to the Forest Service Ranger Station at 428 W. Woodin Avenue.

Lakeside is on W. Terrace Avenue, off W. Woodin Avenue, past town toward the South Shore and Highway 97.

35 Echo Ridge Trail System

🐾🐾🐾 (See North Cascades map on page 326)

Groomed for Nordic Skiing and Snowshoeing, this trail grouping provides almost 30 miles of hiking and mountain biking pleasure in the summer, many with views of Lake Chelan and the Okanogan Highlands. Grab a map, get recommendations, and rent equipment (bikes, snowshoes, skis, etc.) at Uncle Tim's Toys onsite. Bring tons of water, keep an eye out for rattlesnakes,

DETOURS

The Dachsie Twins can recommend no fewer than seven dog-friendly wineries in the vintage-happy Chelan Valley. If they had to pick favorites, Isis would vote for Vin du Lac and Cooper would choose Nefarious.

At **Balsamroot,** you're invited to sit at the umbrella tables on the wooden deck or bring a blanket and picnic in the orchard. Don and Judy Phelps pride themselves on wines as a complete sensory experience. 300 Ivan Morse Rd.; 509/687-3000; www.balsamrootwinery.com.

Benson Vineyards Estate Winery has a trellised brick patio with a stunning view, perched on the hills of the North Shore. This family affair specializes in wines made exclusively from valley grapes. 754 Winesap Ave.; 509/687-0313; www.bensonvineyards.com.

Lake Chelan Winery has the largest winery gift shop in the state. Your four-legged friends are welcome on the tasting porch and for barbecue lunches and dinners at lawn tables. 3519 S.R. 150; 509/687-9463; www.lakechelanwinery.com.

The folks at **Nefarious Cellars** are "a chick, two guys, and a dog, striving to blow your mind." The dog, Lucy the Golden, was sprawled on the tasting room floor when we visited, with five people rubbing her tummy. Their Viognier is a must, enjoyed on the patio with another drop-jaw view. 495 S. Lakeshore Rd.; 509/682-9505; www.nefariouscellars.com.

At **Tildio Winery,** everybody is welcome in the airy tasting room, and the covered stone patio is a cool and elegant place to sip vino. 70 E. Wapato Lake Rd.; 509/687-8463.

Tunnel Hill Winery is a marvel of artisan stonework, with explosions of flower gardens sheltering café tables on a sunny plaza. All of the winemakers' dogs—Ginger, Cordie, Dancer, Dylan, and Boom Boom—are usually roaming the property. 37 Hwy. 97-A; 509/682-5695; www.tunnelhillwinery.com.

Last, and decidedly not least, **Vin du Lac** has a grape trellis covering an outdoor tasting bar, and a lawn with tables and peek-a-boo lake views. They serve the best bistro fare along with fat-flavored vintages. 105 Hwy. 150; 509/682-2882; www.vindulac.com.

and check yourself and your dog afterward for cheatgrass seeds and tick stowaways.

From downtown Chelan, take State Route 150 to the north side of the lake. Turn right on Boyd Road and follow the same signs to Echo Valley Ski Area. It's 9.75 miles to the parking area from downtown. Maps: www.lakechelannordic .org. Ski and snowshoe rentals: 509/687-8467; www.chelanrentals.com.

36 North Fork 25-Mile Creek

🐾🐾🐾🐾 (See North Cascades map on page 326)

Coop's totally cheating here, recommending three trails in one, grouped together in the Lake Chelan National Recreation Area. The big favorite is Trail #1265 along 25-Mile Creek, with plenty of shade and swimming holes along the path; but, due to a washout two miles in from the North Fork trailhead, you might want to start at the Lone Peak trailhead (#1264) to take a shortcut to the longer North Fork trail. Along the same forest road, the Pot Peak trail (#1266) is a four-mile climb through the forest, a workout worth the effort. Fires, floods, and general natural mayhem cause frequent trail closures and alterations. Check conditions before you go at the Chelan Ranger Station (428 W. Woodin Ave.; 509/682-2576).

To get to these forest service trails, drive 25 miles out along the South Lakeshore Road, and then follow the signs on Forest Road #5900, the Shady Pass Road, to the Snowberry Bowl Campground. The road is paved until 0.5 miles to the first trailhead. A $5 parking pass is required.

PLACES TO EAT

Blueberry Hills Farms: #1: This is an incredibly popular U-Pick berry farm. #2: It started with the waffles, rich Danish yeast waffles. It's really still all about the waffles. You can practically hear the call, echoing through the valley: "Attention! Waffles on deck!" #3: They have a penchant for using numbers and humor to illustrate points on their website and menus. #4: They love dogs. Dogs are welcome on the wraparound deck. 1315 Washington St., Manson; 509/687-2379; www.wildaboutberries.com.

Hungry Belly: As the name suggests, this is the perfect antidote to a grumbly tumbly. Forget that there's no outside seating, this deli is always so crowded that you'll want to call ahead and order to go anyway. The menu is overwhelming, printed around the room on blackboard walls. Don't worry, everything is good, especially anything from the grill and their noodle pad Thai-style dishes. Oh, and plan on splitting your huge to-go crate with at least one other person or dog. 246 W. Manson Way; 509/682-8630.

Sunshine Farm Market: Imagine a roadside fruit stand on steroids, and what you see might come close to rivaling Sunshine's choice selection of fruits, vegetables, and delectables, most of which are local and organic. To put together a picnic basket, Isis adores the homemade salsa and Cooper digs the yeasty, sourdough wheat Desem bread. 37 Highway 97A; 509/682-1350; www.sunshinefarmmarket.com.

The Vogue Lounge: Like a designer dog, this hip spot is the best of both breeds: coffee shop by day, wine bar and music lounge by night. Both can be enjoyed from tables out front, with the garage doors rolled up. A light menu of quiches, soups, and salads accent the espresso and wine. A variety of pastries and cakes call your name from behind the goody case. 117 E. Woodin Ave.; 509/888-5282; www.thevoguelounge.com.

PLACES TO STAY

Kelly's Resort: A family favorite for 60 years, this is the ultimate on-the-lake resort. They've got everything you want, including a beach and kayaks and canoes, and nothing you don't need, like cable TV or phones. Danish-style simplicity is featured in one-, two-, and three-bedroom cottages. Incessant barking and any other annoying behavior is strictly prohibited. Prices range $195–255 in the summer, $130–190 in the shoulder season; closed October–April. 12800 South Lakeshore Rd.; 509/687-3220; www.kellysresort.com.

Uncle Tim's Cabins: These hand-crafted and affordable beauties are nestled among the pine trees in Echo Valley. The Echo Ridge Trail System and Echo Valley Ski Area are literally steps from your front door, and so is your private patio hot tub and barbecue grill. All have some kitchen facilities and many have fireplaces and scenic views. They range from simple sleeper cabins for $70, one-bedrooms for $110–140 (sleeps four), to $190 for two-bedroom (sleeps 6); $20 pet fee. Rules: No dogs on beds and furniture, and no rottweilers or pit bulls (he's been bitten!). Tim's a character; watch out for his dry sense of humor, it'll bite you. He also rents skis, snowmobiles, bikes, and so on. 509/687-8467; www.chelanrentals.com.

Snowberry Bowl Campground: If you don't mind a lack of showers, or vault toilets instead of ones that flush, this national forest campground is gorgeous, with shiny new picnic tables and level tent-pitching pads. Nine sites are big, under trees far enough apart that you can't even see your neighbors. It's 3.7 miles southwest of 25-Mile State Park on Forest Road #5900. No reservations; $12 per night. 509/682-2576.

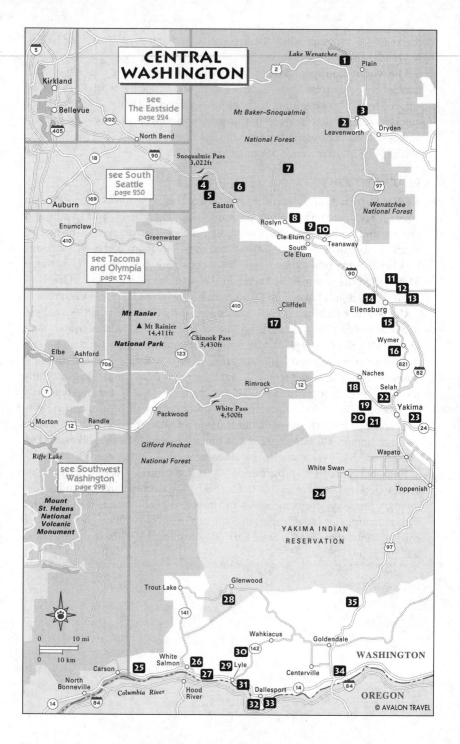

CHAPTER 13

Central Washington

This is volcano country. In the Cascade Mountain Range, extending from Northern California through Washington, there are 13 volcanoes with explosive potential. Of these, the three most famous are here: Mount Adams, Mount Rainier, and currently active Mount St. Helens, which regularly blows steam, smoke, and ash up to 33,000 feet high. While Mount Rainier National Park and Mount St. Helens National Monument are off-limits to dogs, the Mount Baker–Snoqualmie National Forest cuts a wide swath down the entire state, providing scenery and sport activities within easy driving distance of even latchkey city dogs. Trees easily outnumber people a hundred to one, and I-90 and U.S. Highway 2 are the only major roads that give you entry into this otherwise remote mountain playground.

On the east side of the Cascades, the Yakima Valley rests on lava fields up to 10,000 feet thick. It's hot out here, with an average 300 sunny days per year, and summer temperatures up to 100°F. The combination of rich volcanic soil, endless sun, and extensive man-made snowmelt irrigation combine to produce a fertile agricultural plain. More than five billion apples a year come

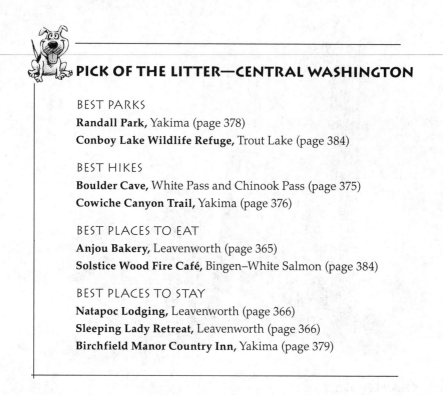

PICK OF THE LITTER—CENTRAL WASHINGTON

BEST PARKS
Randall Park, Yakima (page 378)
Conboy Lake Wildlife Refuge, Trout Lake (page 384)

BEST HIKES
Boulder Cave, White Pass and Chinook Pass (page 375)
Cowiche Canyon Trail, Yakima (page 376)

BEST PLACES TO EAT
Anjou Bakery, Leavenworth (page 365)
Solstice Wood Fire Café, Bingen–White Salmon (page 384)

BEST PLACES TO STAY
Natapoc Lodging, Leavenworth (page 366)
Sleeping Lady Retreat, Leavenworth (page 366)
Birchfield Manor Country Inn, Yakima (page 379)

from the area's 65,000 acres of orchards. Beer drinkers can appreciate knowing that 75 percent of the nation's hops are grown here. And, though wine country touring is technically beyond the scope of this book, it'd be a doggone shame not to mention that there are more than 300 wineries along I-82 headed east. You can savor the bounty of the valley while your dog enjoys its well-irrigated parks.

At the southern border, you'll both find something to appreciate in the striking Columbia River Gorge Scenic Area, whose walls span 80 miles and descend up to 4,000 feet, past cascading waterfalls, scenic overlooks, climbing trails, and explosions of wildflowers. The Columbia River, separating Washington and Oregon, is one of the world's top destinations for windsurfers and sailboarders, with regular wind gusts up to 85 mph and swells of 3–8 feet.

NATIONAL FORESTS AND RECREATION AREAS

Alpine Lakes Wilderness
😊😊😊😊

Nearly 700 lakes are tucked into the mountain peaks and valleys of this 394,000-acre wilderness jointly managed by the Mount Baker–Snoqualmie and Wenatchee National Forest Districts. There are 47 trailheads that access

615 miles of trails. You may need permits, maps, and advice on weather and trail conditions before you head into the backcountry. Start at the Snoqualmie Ranger District office in North Bend, 902 S.E. North Bend Way; 425/888-1421.

Wenatchee National Forest
😺😺😺

This forest covers 2.2 million acres, an overwhelming figure to contemplate. Fortunately, the Leavenworth and Lake Wenatchee Ranger Stations break it down for you with fun pamphlets including *Take a Hike!*, *Hikes on Highway 2*, and *Family Day Hikes*. In the districts in this chapter, dogs must be under control at all times, which includes voice control, although rangers strongly advise leashes, especially during hunting seasons, and leashes are required on groomed cross-country ski trails in winter. Always check for snow and avalanche conditions before heading out. Dogs are prohibited in the Enchantments Area and Ingalls Lake. Leavenworth Ranger District: 600 Sherbourne; 509/548-2550. Lake Wenatchee Ranger District: 22976 S.R. 207; 509/763-3103.

Pick up hiking and campground lists and directions for the White Pass and Chinook Pass Corridors at the Cle Elum and Naches Ranger Districts. Snow closure information is most important in the winter, and campfire restrictions and trail closures due to lightning-ignited fires are vital in the summer. Cle Elum: 803 W. 2nd St.; 509/852-1100. Naches: 10237 Hwy. 12; 509/653-1400; www.fs.fed.us/r6/wenatchee.

Yakima Box Canyon Recreation Area
😺😺

Between the cities of Ellensburg and Yakima, the Yakima River runs through valley walls of a deep box canyon. Along Canyon Road, State Route 821, the Umtanum Creek, Roza, Lmuma Creek, and Big Pines recreation sites are popular for fishing, camping, and floating the river. Daily parking fees range $2–5, and camping is free or $5 per day, depending on the site and season. Dogs are required to be on leashes not longer than six feet. For information, pick up campground and river access maps at the Naches Ranger Station, 10237 Hwy. 12; 509/653-1400.

Leavenworth

When all other sources of income dried up, new life for this ailing town began by reaching back to German roots to create a replica of a Bavarian Village as a way to draw visitors 90 miles into the mountains. It made sense in the heart of what some call the American Alps, where the only other major sign of civilization is the Stevens Pass Ski Area. Today, every building in the village, including the golden arches, must meet strict, legitimate Bavarian building codes. The local dogge shoppe is **A Paw Above,** although it's below, on the lower level in the corner building at 900 Front Street (509/548-3647; www. apawabove.us).

Leavenworth is at its finest during the winter holidays, when all of the intricate baroque woodwork is decked out to become the Village of Lights, chestnuts are roasted on open fires, Father Christmas and St. Nick wander through town smiling for photo ops, and, at dusk, everyone gathers to sing "Silent Night" in the town square. Cooper is absolutely smitten by Cinnamon Von Strudel, a tiny Dachsie who's made several bids to become the town mascot, gathering support from her own website at www.cinnamonvonstrudel .com (but does she have a MySpace page?).

Of note, dogs are prohibited in these nearby wilderness areas: Enchantment Lakes Area, Coney Lake, Ingalls Lake/Headlight Basin, and the Snow Lakes, Colchuck Lake, Stuart Lake, Eightmile Lake, and Ingalls Way trails.

PARKS, BEACHES, AND RECREATION AREAS

1 Lake Wenatchee State Park

🐾🐾🐾 (See Central Washington map on page 360)

Mountain crags, 489 acres of alpine meadows, and thousands of acres of national forest surround this glacier-fed lake high in Cascade Country. The state park has two distinct areas, one for swimming and boating, and another more rough and ready area for camping and hiking, lots and lots of hiking. The North River Trail and North Lake Loop are less than two miles each, plus there's the Riverview Loop Trail, interpretive trails, hiking-only trails, hiking and biking trails, forest service trails, and so on. There's a simplified map posted at the north entrance, and more precise maps are available from the campground host.

From U.S. Highway 2, turn north on State Route 207. The south entrance, to the swim beach and boat launch, is 3.5 miles up the road; the north entrance, for camping, picnicking, and hiking, is another mile beyond the first entrance. A Sno-Park permit is required during the winter recreation season, when sledding and snowshoeing replace hiking and swimming. 509/763-3101.

2 "The Dog Beach"

🐾🐾🐕 (See Central Washington map on page 360)

We put the name of this spot in quotes, because it isn't officially "dog" anything. On Wenatchee National Forest land, there's a lovely little beach on the Wenatchee River with a latrine and gravel parking lot. It has no name, and it is not marked except by a tiny brown Day Use Only, No Overnight Parking sign tacked to a tree. Local dog owners have adopted the beach, and they voluntarily maintain it in good condition in exchange for the privilege of having a swimming hole for all creatures great and small. In the Lake Wenatchee Ranger District, dogs are allowed off leash if they are under continuous voice control.

Watch carefully for the dirt road banking steeply down the hill, 0.3 mile east of milepost 97 on U.S. Highway 2, before you get into Leavenworth proper.

3 Waterfront Park and Blackbird Island

🐾🐾 (See Central Washington map on page 360)

Make no mistake, the Dachsie Twins love the oompah-band music piped through town. The peace and quiet of this tree-lined riverfront promenade is a nice contrast, that's all. On property once occupied by a sawmill operation, there are viewing benches and picnic tables, sandy beaches, a playground, and a river viewing platform. Short and sweet dog-walking trails are across a concrete bridge to the island, a pile of silt that accumulated in the river and sprung to life with trees and vegetation. Spend some quality time with your pup as she paws through the sand in search of the mythical treasure of Blackbird Island, not that your dog ever needed an excuse to paw through the sand.

As you enter Leavenworth on U.S. Highway 2 from Seattle, get in the right lane after Icicle Road to turn into the town loop on Front Street. From Front Street, turn right on 8th Street, and right on Commercial, two and a half blocks to the park. There's no visible sign, so look for the angled dirt parking on the left.

PLACES TO EAT

Anjou Bakery: As you wind your way to the parking area through a pear orchard, you'll notice lawns, pet waste bags, and a garbage can outside the old apple processing plant that houses the bakery. Inside are all manner of lovely baked goods, made from scratch daily. After enjoying quiche and tea on the front porch or at a picnic table, buy some of their famous fruit and nut crostini to take with you, then take a quick stroll before heading out again. The bakery is about 12 miles east of Leavenworth in Cashmere. 3898 Old Monitor Hwy.; 509/782-4360; www.anjoubakery.com.

The Gingerbread Factory: Cooper and Isis would have gladly changed their names to Hansel and Gretel to get their paws on this sweet shop's gingerbread cookies. Such drastic measures proved unnecessary. Owner Anita gives dogs free gingerbread biscuits because she doesn't like bad doggie breath. If dog breath is all it takes, Isis is golden. In addition to a lovely case of goodies, the Factory manufactures pasta salads and hot chicken and vegetable pockets in flaky crusts with cranberry sauce and sour cream. There's abundant outdoor yard and patio seating. 828 Commercial St.; 509/548-6592.

München Haus: Come to Munich House for all things traditionally German in a festive beer garden atmosphere. Apple sauerkraut, bratwurst, kielbasa, and bockwurst are brilliant paired with good beer or hot-spiced wine, enjoyed while lounging around the fire pits on heated patio tile floors. 709 Front St.; 509/548-1158; www.munchenhaus.com.

O'Grady's Pantry and Mercantile: On the grounds of Sleeping Lady Retreat, this deli and coffee shop is inclined toward the fresh and organic. The striped umbrellas tilt slightly over the patio picnic tables, and we bet your lab will be leaning toward your roasted turkey and field greens sandwich. 7375 Icicle Rd.; 509/548-6344.

Uncle Uli's Pub: Fondue, baby back ribs, hot broiler sandwiches, and salads are the specialties of the house at this restaurant with picnic tables tucked in an alley. 902 Front St.; 509/548-7262.

PLACES TO STAY

Destination Leavenworth: These higher-end rental properties allow pets in many of their cabins and homes. The management prefers only one pet but will make exceptions for two well-behaved dogs with advance notice. These vacation destinations are gorgeous, hidden all over the Leavenworth and Lake Wenatchee area. Rates range $155–295 (some priced for two people, some for four); the pet fee is $20 per visit. Office: 940 Hwy. 2; 866/904-7368; www.destinationleavenworth.com.

Evergreen Inn: This tiny motel is cute, if a bit dated; it's your best bet for staying in town with the most pet-friendly rooms. The dog-friendly lawn and entrance are off busy Highway 2. Don't bring a dozen; otherwise no restrictions. There's a $10 pet fee; rooms range $80–140. 1117 Front St.; 800/327-7212; www.evergreeninn.com.

Natapoc Lodging: Usually one pet is allowed, two with advanced permission, in each of the six lodges on 17 acres of riverfront property. These stunning log homes are all on the Wenatchee River in the woods 15 miles from Leavenworth. Special items are set out for pets, such as treats, pick-up bags, and a policy sheet, and crates are available to borrow. Dogs may be unleashed if under voice control, and the community beach on the river is awesome. The owners know and love dogs, and they have had many of their own. Skookum is the current dog overseer. You'll often see him riding the tractor with his dad, patrolling the grounds. Rates range $200–375 per night, with an additional $25 pet fee. 12348 Bretz Rd.; 509/763-3313 or 888/628-2762; www.natapoc.com.

Sleeping Lady Retreat: Dogs—one large or two small per room—get a royal welcome with doggie beds, bowls, and treats in six pet-friendly rooms in the Forest Cluster at this valley destination. Also environment-friendly, the Sleeping Lady features organic linens and hand-hewn, reclaimed log furniture, blending elegance with simplicity and rustic decor with cosmopolitan art and music. The large, wooded property is far enough from the city center to be a breath of fresh air, offering great spaces for dog walks. Summer rates include three gourmet meals; winter rates include two meals and easy access to winter sports. $300 May–October, $200 November–April. 7375 Icicle Rd.; 800/574-2123; www.sleepinglady.com.

More Accommodations: Please look under *Chain Hotels* in the *Resources* section for additional places to stay in this area.

Snoqualmie Pass

This mountain pass is only a 45-minute drive from Seattle, with popular Sno-Parks and ski slopes in the winter, hiking and mountain biking in the summer. Trails are muddy and variable, and you should be prepared for unexpected turns for the worse in weather at any moment.

PARKS, BEACHES, AND RECREATION AREAS

🐾 Asahel Curtis Nature Trail

🐾🐾 (See Central Washington map on page 360)

In 1897, nature photographer Asahel Curtis took 3,000 glass plates into the wilds of Washington and Alaska to document the Klondike Gold Rush. He was a strong advocate for the protection and responsible development of forest areas, especially Mount Rainier. The hike named in his honor is an easy 1.25-mile loop through a rare old-growth forest, crossing Humpback Creek on wooden bridges several times and heading into a grove that includes western red cedar, western hemlock, and Douglas fir. It gives you a feel for the moist nature of Northwest hiking, the kind that cultivates large ferns, mosses, and lichens and draws out the banana slugs that repel humans and attract dogs.

Take Exit 47 from I-90, go south and turn left on Forest Road 55, 0.5 mile to the trailhead parking lot. The trail starts at the east end of the lot.

🐾 Alpine Lakes Wilderness–Annette Lake

🐾🐾🐾 (See Central Washington map on page 360)

The Annette Lake trail is up the gravel road from the Asahel Curtis trail, and several notches up on the difficulty scale. This hike is a challenging 3.5 miles one-way, uphill, gaining 1,600 feet elevation along the way. The trail can be rocky and narrow, and you'll slop through mud and errant streams along the way. The toughest switchbacks are in the first two miles, then the slope mercifully levels out for the last mile. For fit folks, the ultimate reward is a crystal clear, icy lake at the top, surrounded by glacier-capped mountains. Cooper picked this trail out of the many available as one of the easiest to get to and one with fairly reliable conditions.

Take Exit 47 from I-90, go south and turn left on Forest Road 55, 0.5 mile to the Asahel Curtis parking lot. At the east end of the lot, go past the first trail, up and to the left.

PLACES TO STAY

Summit Lodge Hotel: The main lodge at Snoqualmie Pass allows dogs in first-floor rooms without restrictions, for $25 per pet per stay. After a refurbishment of carpets, drapes, and linens in time for the 2008 ski season, this former Best Western is still looking spiffy. Rates range $110–250. 603 Hwy. 90; 425/434-6300; www.snoqualmiesummitlodge.com.

Easton

Crumbling buildings and rusted railway cars are common sights in Easton, visible reminders of the town's history as an 1880s logging camp and the last station where trains could be serviced before climbing over the mountains. Although there's little commerce left, Easton is a great place to access the John Wayne Pioneer Trail. Like the legend it is named after, the trail is larger than life, capturing the biggest and best of the Northwest mountains (look for *Extended Trails* in the *Resources* chapter for more information).

PARKS, BEACHES, AND RECREATION AREAS

6 Lake Kachess

😸😸 (See Central Washington map on page 360)

This photogenic lake is popular with the canoeing and kayaking crowd, if you can call a couple of silent boats gliding along the water a crowd. Perhaps your dog is like Sweetheart, the shih tzu who loved nothing better in life than to sit in the canoe between her people, watching them do all the work. It brings new meaning to the phrase dog paddling.

Only four miles from the highway, picnic areas have perfect vistas of the lake surrounded by the mountain peaks, without development to spoil the scenery. Past the entry station to the right is the doggy beach, a tiny patch of sand to the east of the people's beach near the Gale Creek picnic area. If you head to the left, there's also easy water access near the Box Canyon picnic area. The Little Kachess Lake Trail, the only currently navigable one, also starts at Box Canyon and goes about 11 miles up into the hills. How far you go is up to you.

From I-90, take Exit 62 at Stampede Pass, follow the signs four miles to the lake campground. Day use parking is $6. Camping is $17 per night for primitive sites, without water or electric hookups. They've got flush toilets, but no showers. 877/444-6777; www.reserveusa.com.

PLACES TO EAT

Mountain High Hamburgers: There's outdoor seating and a drive-through at the home of the Mount Rainier burger with double meat, double cheese, and double bacon; 31 flavors of shakes; and blended ice cream and candy shakes called Avalanches. All the scrumptious burgers are named after local peaks, and they loom almost as large. Veggie burgers, fish and chips, a chicken club, and fried zucchini lighten up the menu, if only a little bit. 2941 W. Sparks Rd.; 509/656-3037.

PLACES TO STAY

Silver Ridge Ranch: There's one room with a shared bath at this bed-and-breakfast that accepts dogs, the Ghost Room, and it looks as no-nonsense as you'd expect it to on a working horse ranch. Instead of frills, they've spent money on the good stuff, including a big screen TV in the great room, a sunken tub in the bath, and picture windows with views of the two dozen or so horses roaming the pastures. Boarding horses are welcome, and snowmobile rentals are available in winter. Rates of $80 include a ranch-hand-sized breakfast; the pet fee is $10. 182 Silver Ridge Ranch Rd.; 509/656-0275; www.silver ridgeranch.com.

Roslyn

Before Roslyn played the part of Cicely, Alaska, in the quirky TV show *Northern Exposure*, it was a sleepy ghost town, the remnants of a coal mining community. The Coal Miners' Memorial on Pennsylvania Avenue is a powerful reminder of hard times, and the preserved "Cicely's Store" of better days. Now that the show has ended, the historic district benefits from its 15 minutes of fame, enjoying a modest celebrity status that brings in curious tourists looking for the moose on the wall of Roslyn Café at the corner of 2nd and Pennsylvania.

PARKS, BEACHES, AND RECREATION AREAS

❼ Wenatchee National Forest–Cooper River Trail

🐾🐾🐾 (See Central Washington map on page 360)

You're never very far from the sight or sound of the river along the four miles of this popular trail for day trekkers, starting with the series of running rapids within the first 0.25 mile. You'll roughly follow the river for 2.5 miles, descend deeper into the woods for a mile, then join up with a dirt road another 0.25 mile to Cooper Lake. Thick brush makes it challenging to get into the river, but once you reach the lake, head north of the Owhi Campground and boat ramp to find a few picnic tables and several convenient spots to take a dip. There's supposed to be a three-mile trail around the lake, but it is rough going, not maintained at all as far as we could tell.

Take Exit 80 off I-90, turn left on State Route 903, go east through Roslyn and 17 miles to Salmon La Sac. The trailhead is 0.5 mile on the dirt road past the campground. Parking is a $5 daily Forest Service Pass.

8 Roslyn City Park

😾😾😾 (See Central Washington map on page 360)

Cooper and Isis love city parks like this one, with a huge, empty field they can run in. Technically speaking, there is a leash law in town, but Lisa the dogcatcher only responds to complaints, so as long as you're not one of them, you should be okay. There's a pretty gazebo that provides the only shade other than two covered picnic tables. On the west side of the field is a wooden bridge that connects you to the middle of the Coal Mine Trail. Coop's only comment is to warn you that there are often unsupervised local dogs hanging around.

As you're coming east into town on State Route 903, it becomes First Street. Turn left on Idaho Avenue straight to the park. Idaho Ave. and 3rd St.; 509/649-3105.

PLACES TO EAT

Leftie's Eats: Thank goodness there's a place that offers healthy, organic, vegetarian choices. Even better that they taste good enough to fool the dogs, especially the no-chicken nuggets, black bean burritos, and vegan "tuna," not to mention the fresh-squeezed juices, smoothies, ice cream, and thick cookies. Adirondack chairs, benches, and a few tables out front make for comfy, if messy, eating. 107 Pennsylvania Ave.; 509/649-2909.

Roslyn Café: It's not often you get to eat at a place that's been around, more or less, in one form or another, since 1896. During a heyday in the 1970s it was a booming gathering place. It was made famous again in **Northern Exposure;** yes, it's the building with the camel painted on the side. After a complete remodel in 2004, it's living up to that reputation again, allowing you to enjoy a generous helping of history along with your comfort food at sidewalk tables. 201 W. Pennsylvania Ave.; 509/649-2763; www.roslyncafe.com.

Cle Elum

Nearby Cle Elum's population swelled when the TV crews moved in to Roslyn, but times are quieter now. Cle Elum has a ranger station for the Wenatchee National Forest: 803 W. 2nd St.; 509/852-1100; www.fs.fed.us/r6/wenatchee.

PARKS, BEACHES, AND RECREATION AREAS

9 Cle Elum City Park

😾 (See Central Washington map on page 360)

It'll do as a picnic spot, with lots of tall pine trees and unusual playground equipment, including a Model-T car and a climbing centipede designed and welded by hand. If you want an upper body workout, the do-it-yourself swing, where you pump with your arms to generate momentum, is big enough for grown ups. Tree stumps are made into tables with colorful tops. Keep dogs on leash to avoid problems with 2nd Street, the busy mainline between Roslyn and Cle Elum. Alpha Ave. and W. 2nd St..

🔟 Coal Mine Trail

😾 😾 😾 (See Central Washington map on page 360)

The former mining towns of Ronald, Cle Elum, and Roslyn are joined by another excellent trail, 4.7 miles one-way. It's tidy, easy gravel and dirt, with a slight incline as you head west. It alternates between open sun and deep shade, through forests and past town parks. It's a popular hangout. You'll meet lots of local dogs out for exercise with their owners along the way.

Trailheads and parking are located in all three towns, at the Ronald Fire Station, in Roslyn behind the City Park, and at Cle Elum's Flagpole Park. Call the city Chamber of Commerce for more information at 509/674-5958.

PLACES TO EAT

Gunnar's Coffee Cabin: Gunnar's is the spot for excellent espresso and design-your-own sandwiches and salads. How about ranch, Italian, blue cheese, with croutons? They pass out dog biscuits in the drive-through, and there are a couple of picnic tables out front. Cooper pants for their breakfast burritos, which are almost as big as he is. 115 W. 1st St.; 509/674-2524.

Thorp Fruit and Antiques: This big warehouse on the side of the road carries everything you need to put together an amazing picnic lunch. In addition to fruit, they specialize in locally made gourmet food products, including Anna's Honey. It's about 10 minutes past Cle Elum, on the highway to Ellensburg. 1503 Gladmar Rd., Thorp; 509/964-2474.

PLACES TO STAY

Aster Inn and Antiques: Pets are welcome without restrictions for a $10 charge at this tiny inn with lots of character that comes from individually decorated rooms furnished with brass beds, clawfoot tubs, and antiques (which are all for sale). Rooms surround a courtyard with barbecue grills and a lawn. Most rooms have kitchenettes at unbeatable prices of $75 a night, up to $125 for a hot tub room! There's a $10 pet fee. 521 E. 1st St.; 509/674-2551 or 888/616-9722; www.asterinn.com.

Cascade Mountain Inn: Dogs under 25 pounds can relax at this modern hotel with huge rooms and an equally massive fireplace in the lobby. Rates range from $75 for standard rooms to $130 for suites with spas, plus $20 per pet per night. 906 E. 1st St.; 509/674-2380.

Ellensburg

It is a four-legged animal of a different breed, the horse, that is most lauded in the famous annual Ellensburg Rodeo, held every Labor Day weekend since 1923. Cooper believes the annual Dachshunds on Parade, held in June, will soon become just as big a draw, pardner. To attend the former, call 509/962-7831 or visit www.ellensburgrodeo.com. You can find information on the latter at the visitors center (609 N. Main St.; 509/925-3138) as well as a self-guided Historic Ellensburg Walkabout Guide to the eclectic mix of 1889 brick buildings and preserved early 20th century architecture. An Ellensburg Outdoor Recreation Guide lists a dozen regional hikes, most a bit more ambitious than those the easily winded Wieners have listed here. For unique dog and cat collectables, visit **Wind River** (1714 Canyon Rd.; 509/933-4438; www.windrivergifts.com), one of the largest and best gift shops we've encountered on our travels.

PARKS, BEACHES, AND RECREATION AREAS

11 Reed Park

🐾🐾 (See Central Washington map on page 360)

This sunny sliver of a city park is at the top of the hill, on a crescent lawn carved out of the property next to the city's gigantic water tower. It's an ideal spot to catch some rays, along with fantastic views of the valley from a row of benches. A strategically placed doggie bag dispenser reminds you to do your part to maintain the public green space.

From Main Street, go east on 3rd Street 11 blocks to Alder Avenue. Turn left up the hill through a residential area to the center of the park, in front of the American Legion Post. 1200 E. Fifth Ave.

DOG-EAR YOUR CALENDAR

Ellensburg parties with the pups during dog events throughout the year. The **Doggie Easter Egg Hunt** is the Friday before Easter at the Kiwanis Park. If your Saint Bernard shudders at the thought of wearing bunny ears, perhaps he can pretend to be a wiener dog and march in **Dachshunds on Parade,** held in June, usually along W. 5th Avenue. That might be easier than drying him off after the **Dog Paddle** in the City of Ellensburg Pool, held in August before they close for annual maintenance. For information on all of Ellensburg's doggy doings, go to www.visitellensburg.com or call the Chamber at 509/925-3138.

12 Lions Mount View Community Park

🐾🐾 (See Central Washington map on page 360)

Any day is a good day for a dog at this two-block city park, even hot, hazy days with no mountain in sight. Your toughest decision will be whether you should take your lunch basket to the park's gliding bench swing or spread out on a blanket under one of several maple trees. Then it's up to your pup to decide where to wander in the bunches of sweet-smelling grass. Kids have the toughest choice of all: swing sets and playgrounds or the tennis courts converted to an inline skate park?

From Main Street, turn east on Manitoba Avenue and go 10 blocks to Maple Street. 1200 E. Seattle St.

13 Olmstead Place

🐾🐾 (See Central Washington map on page 360)

In 1875, Samuel and Sarah Olmstead crossed the Cascade mountains on horseback to homestead in the Kittitas Valley. For almost a hundred years, their dairy cows' butter was a prized commodity on the Seattle market, and their crops yielded hay, wheat, and oats. In 1968, their granddaughters Leta and Clareta deeded the 217-acre farm to Washington State Parks, to be maintained as a living historical farm for future generations to visit and study. On the property, their 1908 home is furnished as the family left it.

Even pampered city pets can experience what a working dog's life must have been like on the farm, walking with you through the hay and corn fields, past the cow and horse pasture, in the rose garden, and on the 0.75-mile path following Altapes Creek.

The farm is designed for kids to watch and participate in some of the farm chores, such as collecting chicken eggs, threshing wheat, churning butter, and picking vegetables. Free hay wagon rides run noon–4 P.M. Saturday and Sunday Memorial Day–Labor Day. No animals in the buildings, please.

Take Exit 115 from I-90, four miles east of Ellensburg in the town of Kittitas. Follow signs through Main Street, turn left on Patrick Avenue, go three miles, and turn left on Ferguson. 509/925-1943.

14 Irene Rinehart

🐾🐾🐾 (See Central Washington map on page 360)

The Yakima River runs thick and full past Ellensburg, and Rinehart is the city's woodsy riverfront park. From the southern entrance, there's a 0.5-mile gravel trail called Howard's Way that will keep your dog happily occupied. Birds rustle in the trees, yellow marmots scurry through the bushes, and there are plenty of convenient put-in spots on the river. Know your pet's limits; the currents are strong all summer.

Dogs are not allowed on the people beach or the groomed grass. This policy is strictly enforced by frequent police car patrols through the park.

From I-90, take Exit 109 to Canyon Road, take the first left turn on Ump-tanum Road, crossing under I-90 to the park entrance on the right. Turn left immediately into the south parking lot. 509/925-8638.

15 Thrall Gravel Pits Dog Area

🐾🐾🐕 (See Central Washington map on page 360)

The Kittitas County Off-Leash Association (KCOLA) has plans to develop a rough 17-acre site into a full dog park including "parking for 10–15 cars, an information kiosk, temporary restroom facilities, trails and paths, river access, open space, fenced area for small dogs and fencing around the perimeter of the park." However, the county's position is that the site may need to remain unde-veloped because it is prone to periodic flooding. Meanwhile, you can enjoy it as a diamond in the rough, marked by a fence with a ragtag sign and little else.

Within the boundary are 400 feet of Yakima River frontage, a few scummy ponds, an overgrown river rock, a dirt road, and scrub. Lots and lots of scrub. Because the area is a flood plain, it will essentially remain in this natural state, without turf, buildings, or potable water. It's an adventurous area to explore, as long as you're comfortable without infrastructure. Cooper begs you to be extremely careful around the river, as the currents are often high and swift.

Exit I-90 at Exit 109 and turn left onto Canyon Road. Follow Canyon Road for 3.3 miles and turn right at the second Ringer Loop sign. The park entrance is approximately 0.2 mile on your left side. Parking is roadside. At the far end of the OLA is a Fish and Wildlife recreation site with a vault toilet, boat ramps, and public fishing. Parking in this lot requires a Vehicle Use Permit, available at www.wdfw.wa.gov.

16 Yakima Box Canyon–Umtanum Creek

🐾🐾🐾 (See Central Washington map on page 360)

This BLM recreation site is a favorite high desert hiking trail. Sunglasses, sunscreen, bug spray, and drinking water are essential carry-ins. At the start of the hike, you'll cross a swaying wood and cable bridge over the river and some unmarked railroad tracks. After that, the hike is pretty straightforward. You'll follow and occasionally cross the creek, which attracts flowers, birds, and butterflies to the water from the parched surrounding hills. Be on the lookout for rattlesnakes.

The turnout to the trailhead is marked, 10 miles south of I-90 on State Route 821. Parking is $5 per day.

PLACES TO EAT

Dakota Café: Your dog will fondly recall any tidbits you sneak to her under the table from your sun-dried tomato and turkey sandwich, roasted chicken salad, or soup with incredible breadsticks. More power to you if you can keep your paws off the platter-sized cookies. 319 N. Pearl St.; 509/925-4783.

Ellensburg Pasta Co.: The Pasta Co.'s covered patio keeps you, your dog, and your salad greens from wilting in the heat as you dine on hearty portions of classic red- and white-sauce pasta dishes, soups, and spumoni ice cream. 600 N. Main St.; 509/933-3330.

PLACES TO STAY

Ellensburg Quality Inn: Nice lobby, cool colors, decent bedspreads; overall, a nice place with pet-friendly rooms located conveniently near Exit 109. Rates range $90–115, plus a $10 pet fee and your signature on a reasonable pet policy. 1700 Canyon Rd.; 509/925-9801.

More Accommodations: Please look under *Chain Hotels* in the *Resources* section for additional places to stay in this area.

White Pass and Chinook Pass

On the way up and over 4,500-foot White Pass, you'll pass through parts of the Wenatchee, Mount Baker–Snoqualmie, and Gifford–Pinchot National Forests. To the north, Chinook Pass is an even higher and more scenic destination, at 5,430 feet elevation. There are abundant hiking and mountain biking trails for you and your ambitious pups. The Naches Ranger Station (10061 Hwy. 12; 509/653-1416) has a long list of hikes and campgrounds along the White Pass and Chinook Pass Corridors. Furry breeds would enjoy the area's winter recreation as well, including groomed cross-country skiing trails and designated snowmobiling Sno-Parks.

PARKS, BEACHES, AND RECREATION AREAS

17 Boulder Cave

🐾🐾🐾 🦮 (See Central Washington map on page 360)

Boulder Cave is home to the only known population of Pacific Western big-eared bats. Bats?! Don't worry, they only use the cave as a place to hibernate in the winter. The trail and cave are closed October 31–April 1 to let them get their beauty sleep.

The remainder of the year, you and your dog can hike the easy, clear path 1.5 miles to the bat cave and back. Bring a flashlight for the 350-foot-long by 30-foot-wide cave. Don't be shy. We've seen babes in strollers manage it without fears or tears.

For those who prefer staying out in the open, a 0.75-mile fully accessible loop follows along the Naches River from the same trailhead. Resting benches and footbridges encourage lingering. The riverside picnic area is a pretty area for relaxing, pre- or post-spelunking.

The entrance to Boulder Cave is clearly marked, west of American River on State Route 410, 30 miles from Naches on Chinook Pass. Parking is $5.

PLACES TO STAY

Cozy Cat Bed and Breakfast: There's no pet-friendly place to stay, per se, going up and over either pass. However, well-behaved dogs on leashes are welcome at this comfy-casual home on the eastern end of White Pass, as long as they don't find it necessary to chase the resident cats or go fishing in the koi pond. The desert foothills beckon from the inviting front porch, and a trail out back leads through the pines to the Naches River. The Burgundy Cat room is $80 and the Mini-Suite is $90. 12604 S.R. 410; 509/658-2953.

Yakima

The valley's advanced farm irrigation techniques extend to Yakima's parks. Lawns are lush and trees are tall, a good trick in a desert valley where average summer temperatures easily reach 100°F. The name of the city, county, and valley are derived from the native tribe inhabiting the region, who use the spelling Yakama.

Yakima Greenway: This 10-mile, paved path follows the river and loops halfway around the city, through three parks, two lakes, and three boat landings. A map online or from the visitors center shows eight parking access points and distances from point to point. Open 6 A.M.–9 P.M. It is safer to walk in groups; not recommended after dark. Greenway Foundation: 509/453-8280; www.yakimagreenway.org.

Powerhouse Canal Pathway: Using old transit corridors and irrigation rights of way, this convenient multi-use trail bisects the city, 2.5 miles west to east. Parking is available at McGuinness Park at 1407 Swan Avenue (east) and Chesterley Park at the intersection of N. 40th Avenue and River Road (west). Open 6 A.M.–10 P.M. Yakima Parks and Recreation: 509/575-6020.

PARKS, BEACHES, AND RECREATION AREAS

18 Cowiche Canyon Trail

🐾🐾🐾🐾 (See Central Washington map on page 360)

No dog bones about it, this is a spectacular trail. It's Coop's kind of walk, wide and level, with no elevation gain unless you hike out of the canyon on the viewpoint spur. Along the three-mile one-way gravel road, you'll follow the course of Cowiche Creek, crossing over 11 sturdy wooden bridges built on former Burlington-Northern railroad trestles. You're close to the city, but you'd never know it, in a private universe of lush vegetation near the river, starkly contrasted by steep shale walls. There are places where your dog can sneak into the creek for a quick dip, and he'll get a kick out of testing the echo of his bark against the hillside. The Wieners walked the trail at sunset, with the moon rising on one side, and the sun burnishing the rocks to a bright gold on the other. For the first time in her little life, Isis was speechless. Bring drinking water, keep alert for rattlesnakes in hot weather, and stay away from poison ivy.

Take exit 33 off I-82 onto Yakima Avenue, jog north on 7th Avenue to Summitview. Travel seven miles past 40th Avenue in Yakima, turn right on Weikel Road, and go another 0.25 mile to the trailhead parking.

🐾19 Gilbert Park

🐾🐾🐾 (See Central Washington map on page 360)

At this city park, Cooper learned the difference between a maze and a labyrinth. In the classic sense, a labyrinth is a stone path, where you can see the whole pattern, meant to be walked with a certain meditation in mind. We suspect Coop walked it praying for a treat. Isis was distracted from her mantra by a bulldog in his own deliberations with a beach ball. The stone path is on the

DETOURS

While it's all well and good for your dog to drink out of the toilet, you might prefer more refined refreshment, say something served by the bottle or tasting glass? In that spirit, the Wonder Wieners' pack leaders suggest a trio of dog-friendly wineries to visit along "The Wine Highway," on Highway 82 east of Yakima. While there, the Best Western Inn at Horse Heaven in Prosser is a great place to overnight for about $100 (509/786-7977).

Bring your dogs for a stroll through the vineyard, picnic near the koi pond, and bring your thirst to enjoy the "little hobby that got out of hand" at **Bonair Winery** in Zillah. 509/829-6027; www.bonairwine.com.

Paradisos del Sol is one of the most relaxed dog- and kid-friendly wineries around. Let the dogs loose in the orchard while you try a rare, sweet Riesling wine. 509/829-9000; www.paradisosdelsol.com.

Meet Murray, the gentle giant yellow lab at **Hightower Cellars.** With high hopes and big talent, these husband and wife vintners uncorked their first estate vintages in 2007 in their beautiful tasting room perched high on Red Mountain. 509/588-2867; www.hightowercellars.com.

front lawn of an arts center, and the center's backyard is a gently sloping lawn, dotted with huge trees and tables. It's a simple park for a reflective afternoon.

From downtown Yakima, follow Lincoln Avenue past 40th Avenue to the park on the left at N. 50th Avenue and Lincoln Street. Open 6 A.M.–10 P.M.

20 Randall Park

😺😺😺😺 (See Central Washington map on page 360)

Cooper and Isis are impressed with the pedigree of Yakima's parks, especially at Randall, where the emerald lawns and ancient timbers are cultivated as carefully as the valley's grapes and hops. The dogs are glad park planners chose a sprinkler system over, say, Astroturf, for Randall's football-sized field on a plateau. The paved pathway around the park weaves through the tree canopy. Don't miss the section south of the parking lot down by the creek, the prettiest picnic area.

From I-82, take Exit 34 west on Nob Hill Boulevard to 48th Avenue, and go south on 48th to the park. Open 6 A.M.–10 P.M.

21 Emil Kissel Park

😺😺 (See Central Washington map on page 360)

Everything still has that new park smell in this city plot that became a park in 2004. There won't be any sun protection for a few years from the young trees and shrubs that have been landscaped. For the present, come to undiscovered Kissel to avoid the crowds or if you're lacking in vitamin D and are in need of southern exposure.

From I-82, take Exit 34 west on Nob Hill to 32nd Avenue, head south on 32nd to the park at S. 32nd Avenue and Mead Road. Open 6 A.M.–10 P.M.

22 Byrd Dog Park

😺🐕 (See Central Washington map on page 360)

These meager couple of acres have the barest essentials necessary for an off-leash park, that is, a five-foot chain-link fence with a gate, a picnic bench, and a garbage can. It was kind of Norman and Nellie Byrd to provide the funding for a dog park in 2000, and surely it looks better in a dog's eyes than a human's. Where we see parched dirt and bushes that leave seeds and burrs in fur, they see a place in the sun to run. While we struggle to find the @#$ place, they experience the sweet agony of anticipation. Finally, while we swelter in the shimmering heat, they pant and grin lopsidedly. Sometimes, it's good to see the water bowl as half full.

The dog park is at the Rotary Lake access point on the Yakima Greenway. Turn north on 1st Street from Yakima Avenue, and turn right on R Street. Turn left onto the frontage road immediately before R Street dead ends into the parking lot of Trail Wagons RV and Truck Sales. This dirt road curves around under the highway and then parallels it on the opposite side for about 0.25

mile before the park on your right. Parking is past the field on the left. Open sunrise–sunset.

23 Yakima Sportsman Park

🐾🐾🐾 (See Central Washington map on page 360)

Every dog can have his day at this 246-acre state park, created by the Yakima Sportsman Association for better game management, pollution reduction, and preservation of natural resources. These days, the only hunting you'll do is for the entrance to the river trail (between campsites 22 and 23). The park is expansive, richly green and forested with deciduous trees. Built on a floodplain of the Yakima River, it is a green zone in an otherwise desert environment. It's also a bird-watcher's delight; at least 140 different avian species have been identified on the grounds. No dog paddling in the wetlands! There are many species your dog could harm, and a few that could give her trouble.

From I-82, take Exit 34 east on Nob Hill Boulevard for a mile, turn left on Keys Road, and go another mile past the KOA campground to the park entrance. Open 8 A.M.–dusk. 904 Keys Rd.; 509/575-2774.

PLACES TO EAT

Essencia Artisan Bakery and Chocolaterie: The bakers will set out a sidewalk table or two, shaded by a tree or two, if time and weather permit. Meanwhile, inside, they're very busy laying out a spread of quiches, flatbread pizzas, daily soups and sandwiches, pastries, cookies, and homemade truffles. 4 N. 3rd St., 509/575-5570.

Marketplace Deli: If you can't find what you're craving on the list of 30 specialty sandwiches, you can always have it made to order. For a $10 minimum, they'll deliver. 304 E. Yakima Ave.; 509/457-7170.

Mercedes and Family: If you like it *caliente y picante* (hot and spicy), Mercedes' take-out window is the place for you. Grab authentic combination plates of tacos, tamales, chiles rellenos, or *sopitos* (a fat tostada), with rice and beans for $5 each on your way to Gilbert Park. At the corner of 56th and Tieton; 509/965-9193.

PLACES TO STAY

Apple Country Bed and Breakfast: The proprietors try to accommodate dogs whenever possible in their Picker's Cottage, a romantic hideaway steps away from the orchards. Call ahead and talk to Shirley to see what she can do for you. Unique perks include breakfast served outdoors in a hand-carved gazebo and the chance to pick and eat whatever is in season from the crops. The weekend rate is $95; weekdays are $80. 4561 Old Naches Hwy.; 509/965-0344 or 877/788-9963; www.applecountryinnbb.com.

Birchfield Manor Country Inn: Non-barkers are welcome in the Blue Willow, Sunrise, and Hunter's Glen guest cottages, in a separate building from the original manor. They're the nicest dog-friendly accommodations in the region by far, especially when you consider the lounging patios and room to roam on the groomed grounds. Rates of $140–180 include a gourmet breakfast. They don't charge pet fees. It's an altogether unexpected find. 2018 Birchfield Rd.; 509/452-1960; www.birchfieldmanor.com.

Sun Country Motel: Free snacks, such as popcorn, cherries, apples, and cookies, are always out for guests at this convenient motel with big, cool rooms and an outdoor pool. Let's hear it for cheap fun! Rates range $50–65, plus an $8 pet fee. 1700 N. 1st St.; 509/248-5650.

Quality Inn: This hotel lives up to its name, with a long list of desirable conveniences including free full breakfast, wireless Internet, HBO, and an outdoor pool. Rates range $80–120, plus a $10 pet fee. 12 E. Valley Mall Blvd.; 509/248-6924; www.qualityinnyakima.com.

More Accommodations: Please look under *Chain Hotels* in the *Resources* section for additional places to stay in this area.

Toppenish

Downtown Toppenish relishes its history in the Northern Pacific Railway Museum, the American Hops Museum, and the Yakama Nation Cultural Heritage Center (509/865-2800), which celebrates the people of the Yakama Indian Reservation, which covers 39 percent of the valley.

PARKS, BEACHES, AND RECREATION AREAS

🐾 Fort Simcoe Heritage Site

🐾🐾 (See Central Washington map on page 360)

This state park is a reminder of a positive chapter in the long struggle between Native Americans and settlers in the Pacific Northwest. Although the Army chose the camping ground of the Yakama people for the construction of a fort in 1856, it was peacefully abandoned in 1859 and turned over to the Bureau of Indian Affairs, serving instead as a Native American school and training facility. Ownership was returned to the Yakamas, and in 1956 they signed a 99-year lease with the state to allow the public entry to the site. Five of the original structures have been restored, several have been reconstructed, and the others are noted by markers around the 420-foot square parade ground.

If your dog doesn't get enough exercise walking the grounds with you, there is a trail around the fort, although it's hot and dry. Your pal can enjoy the shade, playground, and picnic area if you decide to tour the officer's quarters, 10:30 A.M.–3:30 P.M. April–September. The park is open 6:30 A.M.–dusk daily in the summer; weekends and holidays only October–March.

Fort Simcoe is 30 miles west of Toppenish in White Swan on the Yakima

NATURE HIKES AND URBAN WALKS

In the town of Toppenish, Washington, the city's most famous historical record is chronicled outdoors. Accompanied by piped country and western music, you can enjoy the **City of Murals,** so named for its 70 (and counting) larger than life pictorials of pioneer days on downtown buildings, on a walk with your pet. Artists come from all over the world to paint these full-color scenes. The Toppenish Mural Society occupies the same building as the visitors center, where you can get a free map to guide yourself through a colorful history lesson. Toppenish Ave.; 509/865-3262; www.toppenish.net.

Across the border, in The Dalles, Oregon, they one-up Toppenish with **Talking Murals,** although there are only two or three of them. You can purchase a key for $5 at the Chamber of Commerce office (404 W. 2nd St.; 541/296-2231 or 800/255-3385; thedalleschamber. com) to unlock the talk box for each picture. Though the mayor may not have given you the key to the city, you get to keep your souvenir.

Indian Reservation. The drive out is through fields of hops, grapes, and orchards. From U.S. Highway 97, turn west on Fort Road, left on Signal Peak Road, and right on Fort Simcoe Road. There is no fee for parking; donations are accepted to support historic preservation. 5150 Ft. Simcoe Rd.; 509/874-2372.

PLACES TO EAT

Pioneer Kitchen: No one is going to go away hungry from this tiny roadside joint that serves an immense menu of filling food, heavy on the meat and potatoes, for every meal of the day. Come on, we know you want that chicken fried steak and egg sandwich! At least we know your dog does. Although there are four picnic tables, bring an umbrella to make your own shade. 227 S. Toppenish Ave.; 509/865-3201.

PLACES TO STAY

In this area, chain hotels listed in the *Resources* section offer the best choices for dogs and their owners.

Carson

From here, it's a gorgeous, winding drive up Highway 30 north to Mount St. Helens, when not closed due to snow. Dogs can probably smell the sulfur for miles from the funky old hot springs facility in this equally funky old town.

PARKS, BEACHES, AND RECREATION AREAS

25 Dog Mountain Trail

🐾🐾🐾 (See Central Washington map on page 360)

Never mind that this trail is a real paw-bruiser, the Wonder Wieners would include this 3.1-mile climb on the merit of its name alone. We won't tell them it was named as such because starving pioneers ate their dogs to survive. An explosion of wildflowers in the spring and summer and views of Mount Hood, Mount Adams, and Mount St. Helens make all the panting worthwhile. The trail doesn't make you go all the way to the 2,948-foot summit, merely from the starting point at 60 feet above sea level to 2,800 feet.

The scenic route has better views and better meadows for the price of a steep, direct ascent. There's another trail that is a kinder, gentler route, adding 0.6 mile each way, leading you through more forests than fanfare, also more prone to rattlesnake crossings. To follow the pack leader and gut it out on the scenic route, stay to the right at the fork in the trail at 0.5 mile. Foot and paw traffic is very heavy mid-May through June and on summer weekends.

The trailhead is 13 miles east of Stevenson on State Route 14. The sign and the gravel parking area come up quickly between mileposts 53 and 54, so watch for them. For map reference, this is USFS Trail #147. Parking requires a $5 daily Northwest Forest Pass.

PLACES TO STAY

Sandhill Cottages: Individually decorated with homey touches, these small cabins aren't going to win any design awards, but that's not going to stop you from getting a good night's sleep. The #7 Coffee Company grinds grounds on the grounds of the property for one of the smoothest cups of coffee that'll ever wake you up in the morning, no wake-up calls necessary. Rates range $55–100; the pet fee is $15. 932 Hot Springs Ave.; 800/914-2178; www.sandhillcottages.com.

Bingen–White Salmon

Bingen is named for its sister city in Germany and White Salmon for the color the fish turn as they die after spawning, as described in the journals of Meriwether Lewis. Immediately west is the Hood River Toll Bridge, where $0.75 gets you over to said town on the Oregon side. West of that, exactly 0.1 mile west of Mile Marker 56, is Dog Creek Falls. From a marked gravel pullout, a quick walk down a few feet of rocky path leads you to the base of the falls and right into the streambed, for anyone in your expedition party feeling the call of the water.

DIVERSION

The **Happy Tails Boarding Kennel** in White Salmon, Washington, is so close to the Hood River Bridge that you can take advantage of its services whether you're on the Washington or Oregon side of the Columbia Gorge.

Each dog has an individual 5- by 10-foot inside run and a 5- by 5-foot outdoor romp. All are welcome to participate in exercise and playtime in the group play yards, and every pup is given individual love and affection, and a W-A-L-K every two hours, by resident staff in an American Boarding Kennel–certified facility.

Rates are $20 per night for one pet or $30 for two pets who share the same kennel. 70 Acme Rd.; 509/493-4255.

PARKS, BEACHES, AND RECREATION AREAS

26 Daubenspeck Park

(See Central Washington map on page 360)

As near as we can figure it, *Daubenspeck* roughly translates from the German as Bacon Stick, a name that thrilled the Dachsie Twins, who immediately set about looking for one. The playground doubles as a baseball field, and there are various picnic tables in the shade of wind-breaking poplars and under a covered shelter. A big log and the remains of a tree trough remind you of the town's sawmill history while you hang out and ham it up.

When State Route 14 becomes Steuben Street through town, look for Willow Street and turn north a half block to the park.

27 Sailboard Park

(See Central Washington map on page 360)

The Bingen Marina, in the Port of Klickitat, is a major dog hangout after their people get off from work in the late afternoon. As long as you have control of your dog, voice or otherwise, local leash enforcement is relaxed. The sniff-and-greet area is a long strip of lawn, which is also a landing pad for hang gliders. A rough dirt ramp leads down to a rocky shoreline. About the only thing not going on in Sailboard Park is sailboarding; enthusiasts prefer the windier conditions and easier put-in at Doug's Beach.

From State Route 14, turn south on Maple Street into the port industrial area, turn left on Lakeview Boulevard, right on N. Harbor Drive, and left on E. Bingen Point Way at the Sailboard Park sign.

PLACES TO EAT

Solstice Wood Fire Café: When it seems as though the rest of town is closing up shop and moving away, thank goodness this refreshing bistro is going strong. On a patio almost as large as the restaurant's interior, enjoy a brilliant salad of fresh organic greens with pears and sweet walnuts and an Italian sausage and dried cherry pizza with fresh goat cheese. Or, design your own thin-crust delight. Adults are welcomed with a local beer and wine list, children with a kid's play and art area. 415 W. Steuben St.; 509/493-4006; www.solsticewoodfirecafe.com.

Trout Lake

There's a Trout Creek in Trout Lake, but no Trout Lake. This is the last stop on State Route 141 before it dead-ends into the base of Mount Adams. Climbing permits, information, and human waste pack-out kits are available at the Mount Adams Ranger Station (2455 Hwy. 141; 509/395-3400), because there's no place to go on the rocks and snow above tree line. Maybe your dog will get a kick out of seeing you carry your own poop in a bag for a change. A climb to the summit requires technical equipment.

PARKS, BEACHES, AND RECREATION AREAS

28 Conboy Lake Wildlife Refuge

🐾🐾🐾🐾 (See Central Washington map on page 360)

An early homestead returning to the wild, Conboy delivered immediately on its promise as a hoot owl ushered us into the gravel parking area for the Willard Springs Foot Trail. Every red-blooded quadruped we know would love this three-mile walk through big-sky country, on leash in case the distractions prove too tempting. The soft pine needles are easy on the paws, there's wild scat to smell, marshes and field grasses to explore, and the sights and sounds of multiple bird and ground species. The scenery is equally easy on the eyes. The interpretive trail is a test of your photographic memory; there's a list of the markers posted at the entrance, but no brochures to take with you through it. There are restrooms and a makeshift picnic table. Bring drinking water.

The signs will guide you to the shortest route, also the most confusing. We vote instead for taking State Route 141 a little farther into Trout Lake, taking the right fork in the road, turning right on Sunnyside Road toward Glenwood, and following it 10.8 miles to Wildlife Refuge Road. It's another mile on the gravel to the parking area by the trailhead.

Lyle

Lewis and Clark are believed to be the first white men to visit this area along the Columbia, named for the town's 1876 postmaster, James O. Lyle. Lyle's economic mainstay over the years has been sheep and wool-shipping. Lyle's parks are wonderful for wheelchair users.

PARKS, BEACHES, AND RECREATION AREAS

29 Catharine Creek Universal Access Trails

🐾🐾🐾 (See Central Washington map on page 360)

Other than being too steep in a couple of sections for inline skates (yes, we tried), these two hillside loops are excellent for anything with wheels, feet, or footpads. The trail is a combination of asphalt and wooden bridges, and each loop is 0.75 mile. It's a nature stroll, with gorge views and wildflowers for humans, and nature and wildlife sightings crowded up against the trail for dogs. There are no facilities.

From State Route 14, turn north at the west entrance to Old Highway No. 8, immediately west of Rowland Lake, and travel 1.5 miles to the gravel parking area on your left and the trailhead on your right.

30 Klickitat Trail

🐾🐾🐾 (See Central Washington map on page 360)

This trail follows the route of the former BNSF railroad from Lyle to Klickitat, roughly paralleling State Route 142. It also follows the east shores Klickitat River for almost 11 miles. The first half of the 31-mile trail from Lyle to Klickitat is an improved, gravel surface that's wide and level. After that, a rougher grade heads up into the mountains on it's way to Goldendale, more remote and difficult to access. Abandoned structures dot the landscape among scrub brush, ponderosa pine, oak trees, and wildflowers.

It's hot and dry and there are no amenities. Poison oak and rattlesnakes are big concerns, so travel with others and stay on leash. We like to access the trail 0.9 mile up Highway 142 from the intersection of Highway 14 at Lyle. There's

a rough, unmarked dirt road off to the left that intersects the trail, leading to an unmarked public area next to the river where you can park. Maps and more information are available at www.klickitat-trail.org.

31 Balfour-Klickitat Park

🐾🐾🐾 (See Central Washington map on page 360)

This mile of riverfront and the surrounding hillsides were purchased in 1892 by English Lord Balfour, in need of a sunny break from his dreary homeland. He planted orchards and vineyards and built a castle on the hill. Only his name survives in this park, opened in June 2004. The nubby fruit of the Osage orange trees in the park are reported to be the first botanical sample the Lewis and Clark Expedition sent back to President Jefferson.

By its full name, the Balfour-Klickitat Columbia River Gorge National Scenic Area is on the west side of the muddy-brown Klickitat River. The parking lot, vault toilet, and smooth asphalt loop are easy for all users to navigate through the native ground cover to bluff picnic tables, watching river and train traffic along the gorge. The hills are alive at this community park, with prairie dogs piping, green dragonflies buzzing, and who knows what scurrying through the high grass, providing distractions for your dog.

From State Route 14 west of Lyle, turn north at the east entrance to Old Highway No. 8 and go up the hill 0.2 mile to the park entrance on your right.

PLACES TO STAY

Lyle Hotel: There are no TVs or phones, but they've got Wi-Fi at this tiny 1904 historic property, so you'll have to be self-entertaining. Your hosts can lead you to leash-free water play or a long walk on the Klickitat Trail. In the European fashion, hallway bathrooms are shared. The rate is $85 for two people, including breakfast. They also serve locally famous gourmet dinners. The pet fee is $10. 100 7th St.; 800/447-6310; www.lylehotel.com.

Dallesport

Once the Kittitas County seat (moved to Goldendale), this quiet community is perched on the bluffs at the east end of the Columbia River Gorge Scenic Area, with views of Mount Adams and Mount Hood. The toll-free Dalles Bridge crosses here, over to The Dalles, Oregon.

PARKS, BEACHES, AND RECREATION AREAS

32 Columbia Hills State Park

🐾🐾🐾 ◄► (See Central Washington map on page 360)

When the rising waters of the floodplain created by the Dallas Dam buried thousands of Native American petroglyphs on the canyon walls, a few examples were taken out and stored in the dam complex. They were eventually returned to the tribes, who graciously put them on display for everyone to see and appreciate at this state park. A cooperative effort between the Yakima Nation, Umatilla Reservation, Nez Percé, and tribes of the Warm Springs Reservation created the *Temani Pesh-wa* (Written on the Rock) Trail. You can see a few pictographs along an accessible pathway, but you would need to make advance reservations for the guided tour of the longer 0.5-mile trail, at 10 A.M. Friday and Saturday April–October.

You can enjoy the 338 acres of cool canyon cliffs, green picnic lawns protected by planted poplars, and 7,500 feet of Columbia riverfront all year. Open 6:30 A.M.–dusk. Call 509/767-1159 for tour reservations. At milepost 58 on State Route 14, near Maryhill.

33 Spearfish Park

🐾 🐕 (See Central Washington map on page 360)

The dogs wanted to include this hole-in-the-wall park because there are no leash rules to keep your dog from jumping in the lake to cool off in this dry hill country. There's not much infrastructure other than a boat ramp and a vault toilet. If you don't need anything more, you can catch a big trout for dinner and set up camp here free, with a four-day limit.

Turn east on Dock Road, from U.S. Highway 197, immediately north of the bridge to The Dalles. The paved road will become gravel as you travel through the Klickitat County Industrial Port. When you come to an unmarked fork in the road, take the left fork down a slight hill into the park.

Maryhill

No need to rub your eyes with your paws, for that is indeed a full-size replica of Stonehenge sitting on the bluff. It is America's first memorial to soldiers lost in World War I, built 1918–1929 by eccentric Quaker pioneer and engineer Sam

Hill. Your dog may walk around and through it with you while it is open to the public 7 A.M.–10 P.M. Sam Hill is also responsible for the classical building housing the Maryhill Museum of Art, built as a castle for his daughter Mary, on the hill. His visionary structures are the only part of Maryhill to survive; his hopes for a thriving Quaker community were never realized.

PARKS, BEACHES, AND RECREATION AREAS

34 Maryhill State Park

🐾🐾🐾 (See Central Washington map on page 360)

This is a wide, friendly park on the shores of the Columbia River at the easternmost point on the Gorge. Its lawns are a shockingly bright green in a sea of rolling brown hills, thanks to extensive watering. Check the sprinkler schedule on the board before you lay down a blanket if you don't want an unexpected shower. On the other hand, with temperatures often in the 90-degree range, you might not mind.

It's easy enough for you and your dog to dodge the sailboarders setting up and taking off from the beach into the wide, windy channel of the Columbia River. The sunny lawns are wide and the trees are tall, and dogs aren't allowed in the designated beach area anyhow. The restrooms have private changing facilities. Maryhill has camping, but we can't recommend it due to highway and train noise.

Follow the signs from State Route 14 going east or U.S. Highway 97 south from Goldendale. The park is 12 miles south of Goldendale. Open 6:30 A.M.–dusk.

PLACES TO EAT

Maryhill Winery: This vintner welcomes socially adept pets on the expansive patio under the grape arbor, if there aren't too many kids or other dogs around. The views of the Columbia River and gorge hillsides are superb from this vantage point. Biscuits are kept at the wine bar for beggar Potter, the resident dog, who may be willing to share. In addition to fine wines, there's a small selection of charcuterie, cheeses, crackers, chips and salsa, and chocolates available for sale and consumption. Regrettably, dogs are not allowed on the lawn for the summer concert series. Tasting room is open 10 A.M.–6 P.M. 9774 Hwy. 14; 509/773-1976; www.maryhillwinery.com.

Goldendale

The golden dales of this farming community are 35,000 acres of alfalfa and 25,000 acres of wheat. It's a good idea to fuel up your bodies and automobiles in Goldendale; the next services are 50 miles north and almost 100 miles east. Just south of town on I-97 is a viewpoint where you can see the tips of Mount Rainier and Mount St. Helens, all of Mount Adams, and most of Mount Hood.

There are no clouds to get in the way of the view from one of the country's largest public telescopes at Goldendale Observatory. Sky viewing hours change frequently, so it's best to call 509/773-3141 for information.

PARKS, BEACHES, AND RECREATION AREAS

35 Brooks Memorial Park

🐾🐾 (See Central Washington map on page 360)

This state park has nine miles of infrequently used hiking trails through high and dry alpine forests. Cooper seemed happy to let his webbed paws air out in a region that averages only 16 inches of rainfall per year, in contrast to Seattle's 36 inches on average. The picnic meadow is wide, with a couple of covered shelters. You'll catch glimpses of the Little Klickitat River and, if you make it to the top, views of Mount Hood. It's more popular for camping than as a day-use area. November through April, the park is a snowy playground for winter sports.

It's located 13 miles north of Goldendale on U.S. Highway 97.

PLACES TO EAT

St. John's: Proceeds from this bakery, coffeehouse, and gift shop benefit the sisterhood of the St. John's Greek Orthodox Monastery. You benefit from phenomenal handmade Greek food and desserts, including stuffed grape leaves, gyros, hummus and pita, coconut cake, and baklava. Eat at patio tables, then browse the gift shop for items made by the sisters and bring some pastries home for your lucky family and friends. 2378 Hwy. 97; 509/773-6650; www.stjohnmonastery.org.

PLACES TO STAY

Ponderosa Motel: Dogs are illogically charged by the pound at the Ponderosa; it's $7 for small, $10 for medium, and $15 for large; plus a $50 refundable deposit. If he sits and smiles sweetly at the manager, perhaps your dog will look lighter than he really is. The rooms are fair, with kitchens or kitchenettes, and fairly priced at $60–75. 775 E. Broadway; 509/773-5842.

Brooks Memorial Campground: This camping spot with 23 utility sites and 22 tent sites is unremarkable but for one notable exception—it is blissfully quiet, whereas almost every other campground along the Gorge has trains running by on one side and a highway on the other. It's only 12 miles inland and a good night's sleep away. 2465 Hwy. 97; 888/226-7688; www.camis.com/wa.

More Accommodations: Please look under *Chain Hotels* in the *Resources* section for additional places to stay in this area.

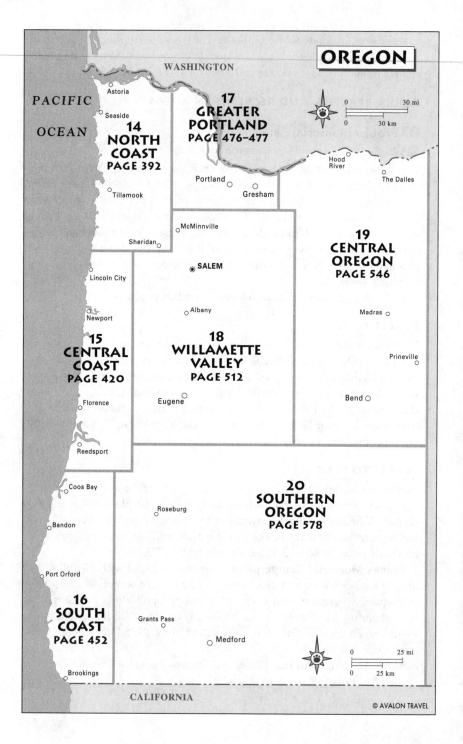

PACIFIC

OCEAN

WASHINGTON

OREGON

Astoria

Seaside

14 NORTH COAST PAGE 392

17 GREATER PORTLAND PAGE 476–477

0   30 mi

0   30 km

Hood River

The Dalles

Portland

Gresham

Tillamook

McMinnville

Sheridan

19 CENTRAL OREGON PAGE 546

◉ SALEM

Lincoln City

Albany

Madras

Newport

15 CENTRAL COAST PAGE 420

18 WILLAMETTE VALLEY PAGE 512

Prineville

Florence

Eugene

Bend

Reedsport

Coos Bay

20 SOUTHERN OREGON PAGE 578

Roseburg

Bandon

Port Orford

16 SOUTH COAST PAGE 452

Grants Pass

Medford

0   25 mi

0   25 km

Brookings

CALIFORNIA

© AVALON TRAVEL

Oregon

"Oregon is dogs' country," said a park host at a tiny county oasis in the Coquille River Valley. Well, if dog utopia is measured in trees, he's right—nearly 60 percent of Oregon, about 30 million acres, is forested. If dog heaven includes room to roam, Oregon wins again, with a population that's little more than half of Washington State's. There are extensive wilderness areas and rural farmlands. Extremely tough standards protect all of the state's natural resources. Much of Oregon remains wild, untamed at heart.

Water dogs seeking paradise will be beside themselves to learn that every inch of Oregon's 360 miles of beaches are public lands. The beaches fall under the jurisdiction of the State Park system, which requires pets to be on leashes of six feet or less. This rule is *absolute* in the campgrounds, but you'll see much more freedom of movement on the beach.

Also in state parks, a 2007 survey of 10,000 people showed an overwhelmingly positive response to allowing pets in yurts and cabins. A test program will allow pets for stays starting May 1, 2009, at South Beach on the Central Coast, Stub Stewart in the Willamette Valley, and LaPine in Southern Oregon. Reservations can be made by phone at 800/452-5687.

There are thousands of miles of riverfront waterways for swimming, boating, whitewater rafting, and the state's seemingly most popular pastime, salmon and steelhead trout fishing. Perhaps to avoid gender complications, the word fisherman has been universally replaced in Oregon with the word angler. If dogs had opposable thumbs, surely they would be anglers.

With the exception of the I-5 Highway Corridor, all roads are head-out-the-window scenic. Add in 14 national forests, almost 200 state parks, and dozens of dog events, and it sure starts to sound like somebody up above had canines in mind when designing Oregon.

Humans enjoy a few extra perks in the Beaver State, too. Most recreation areas have park hosts in the summer, valuable resources to answer your questions and help you with things like campfire wood and trail maps. In Oregon, all shopping is free of sales tax, and you don't have to pump your own gas. Actually, state law requires that attendants pump gas for you.

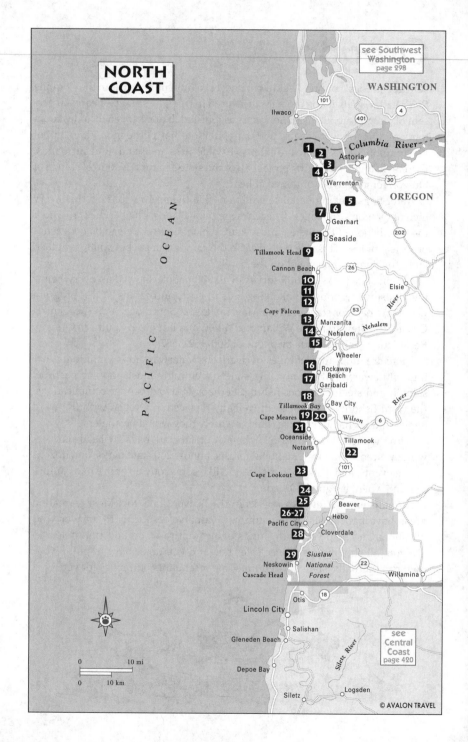

NORTH COAST

see Southwest Washington page 298

WASHINGTON

Ilwaco

101

401

4

Columbia River

1 2

Astoria

3

4

Warrenton

30

OREGON

5

6

7

Gearhart

202

8

Seaside

Tillamook Head 9

Cannon Beach

26

Elsie

River

10

11

12

Cape Falcon

13

Manzanita

Nehalem

53

14

Nehalem

15

Wheeler

16

Rockaway Beach

17

Garibaldi

River

18

Tillamook Bay

Bay City

Cape Meares 19 20

Wilson

6

21

Oceanside

Netarts

Tillamook

22

101

Cape Lookout 23

24

25

Beaver

26-27

Hebo

Pacific City

Cloverdale

28

29

Siuslaw

Neskowin

National

Cascade Head

Forest

22

Willamina

18

Otis

Lincoln City

Salishan

Gleneden Beach

Depoe Bay

Siletz River

Siletz

Logsden

see Central Coast page 420

PACIFIC

OCEAN

0   10 mi

0   10 km

© AVALON TRAVEL

CHAPTER 14

North Coast

Though they are die-hard Washingtonians, Isis and Cooper will be the first to admit that Oregon's coast is a beautiful place to play near big water. To keep the shores looking their best, more than 5,000 residents gather twice a year for massive beach cleanup work parties. Go to www.solv.org for more information if you'd like to participate in the Great Beach Cleanup.

There are so many fun parks and beach access points that the coast had to be split into three chapters. Even then, the dogs had an agonizing time choosing only the best. Basically, you can't lift a leg along the coast and miss a state park or public beach. Access to them may be limited in areas where uplands are private property, but once you are on the sand, there's nothing to stop you other than high tides, cliffs, and rocks. Well, that and the snowy plover. The tiny bird is on the endangered species list, and because it makes its nest in the soft, dry sand, your dog's freedom may be restricted in marked areas March–September.

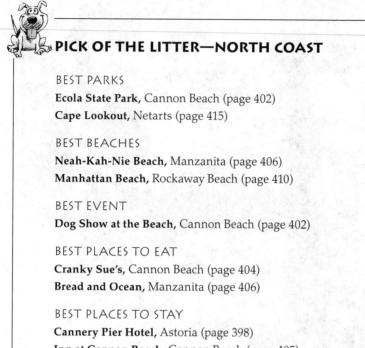

PICK OF THE LITTER—NORTH COAST

BEST PARKS
Ecola State Park, Cannon Beach (page 402)
Cape Lookout, Netarts (page 415)

BEST BEACHES
Neah-Kah-Nie Beach, Manzanita (page 406)
Manhattan Beach, Rockaway Beach (page 410)

BEST EVENT
Dog Show at the Beach, Cannon Beach (page 402)

BEST PLACES TO EAT
Cranky Sue's, Cannon Beach (page 404)
Bread and Ocean, Manzanita (page 406)

BEST PLACES TO STAY
Cannery Pier Hotel, Astoria (page 398)
Inn at Cannon Beach, Cannon Beach (page 405)
The Studio and The Lighthouse, Manzanita (page 409)
Inn at Cape Kiwanda, Pacific City (page 418)

You don't have to wait until summer to enjoy the quintessential coast experience. Lodging rates are much cheaper in the off-season. Winter storms produce shows of power and drama. Rare finds, such as Japanese glass floats and agates, are more likely to wash ashore during these turbulent times. If you get chilled, it is legal to have campfires on Oregon beaches unless a fire restriction is posted. You should be prepared for wet weather and ocean squalls at any time. Oregon's average coastal rainfall is higher than Seattle's, if you can believe that. Also, call ahead and keep in mind that business hours change dramatically with the seasons, and some shops and restaurants come and go with the ebb and flow of the economic tides.

Old-fashioned seaside resorts, working fishing ports, photographic natural landmarks, and the final destination of Lewis and Clark's great adventure—all of these await visitors to Oregon's coast. Of the 11 lighthouses on the coast, nine are on the National Register of Historic Places, seven of them open for public viewing and tours. Two are privately built and individually owned, open to the public only as sneak peaks from roadside viewpoints.

Astoria-Warrenton

Astoria is rich in history as the oldest settlement west of the Rocky Mountains. In 1792, explorer Robert Gray entered the mouth of the Columbia River, naming it after his ship, the *Columbia Rediviva*. It was here, in 1805, that the Lewis and Clark Expedition wintered at Fort Clatsop, waiting out the rain and preparing for their return journey. In 1811, American John Jacob Astor financed a trading post in what is now Astoria. As you walk through town, you can see the past in more buildings per square foot on the National Historic Register than any other Oregon location.

The Astoria Sunday Market along 12th Street, 10 A.M.–3 P.M. Mother's Day– October, has a long-standing reputation as a dog-friendly event (503/325-1010, www.astoriasundaymarket.com).

PARKS, BEACHES, AND RECREATION AREAS

1 Fort Stevens

🐾 🐾 🐾 (See North Coast map on page 392)

At the tip of the Oregon Coast, this state park starts things off with a bang. Constructed during the Civil War, it remained an active military post until after World War II. Eight concrete gun batteries are the focal point of a self-guided tour of the abandoned fort, the tip of the iceberg in this 3,700-acre park.

There are five major parking areas to reach miles of windswept beach. Parking Lot A is primarily for equestrian access, Lot C has an excellent long-range viewing platform for watching the kiteboarders and surfers, and Lot D reaches the most protected area around the bend where the Columbia River meets the ocean. It's the lot without a letter, however, that's the most popular. The southernmost access point takes you to the wreck of the *Peter Iredale*. The rusting hulk of this English sailing ship remains onshore, a hundred years after it ran aground.

For some, the beach is too windy and exposed. Take to the six miles of hiking trails in the park instead, especially the two-mile, hikers-only loop around Coffenbury Lake. Locals also recommend the Columbia River Beach, where there's typically fewer people and more dogs.

Take U.S. Highway 101 four miles south of Astoria. Turn west on Warrenton Road and follow the signs another five miles to the park. Parking is $3. 503/861-1671.

2 Carruthers Dog Park

🐾 🐾 🐕 (See North Coast map on page 392)

Contractor delays, a toppling giant spruce, and an errant car crashing into the fence did not stop Warrenton's determined dog owners from opening this off-leash area in 2008. Thanks to their perseverance, there's a new place for

NATURE HIKES AND URBAN WALKS

The **Fort Clatsop National Memorial** is a national park where dogs *are* allowed, except in the buildings. According to the park ranger, you may keep your traveling companion with you on the trails and grounds because Meriwether Lewis was never far from Seaman, his faithful Newfoundland, on his journey.

Together, you can walk the grounds and peek into the cramped spaces of this life-size replica shared by the 31 men, Sacagawea, and her papoose, from December 7, 1805 until March 23, 1806. The fort was re-created according to exact specifications described in Lewis's journals. At a site in nearby Seaside, the men made salt to preserve meats for the return journey, hunted, sewed moccasins, and traded frequently with Chinook and Clatsop Native Americans.

Open 9 A.M.–5 P.M. Entrance is $3 per person. Pets are free. 92343 Fort Clatsop Rd.; 503/861-2471; www.nps.gov/lewi.

dogs to run free on the coast. It's almost an acre of natural surroundings with shade trees. Separate, five-foot fenced areas for small and large rabble rousers allow free play. It remains to be seen how long the strong grass will last. Niceties include drinking water, an enclosed cement dog wash station, scattered benches, and pet waste disposal stations.

From downtown Astoria, head south on Highway 101 toward Seaside, across the Youngs Bay Bridge. Turn right on Harbor Street (State Route 104). You'll go straight at the stop sign as Harbor Drive becomes N. Main Avenue, and bear left at the fork in the road when it becomes N.W. Warrenton Drive on the way. It's three miles from the turnoff to the park, which comes up with little warning on the right. Open 6 A.M.–10 P.M. 503/861-2233; www.ci.warrenton.or.us.

⬛ Cathedral Tree Trail

🐾🐾🐾🐕 (See North Coast map on page 392)

From 28th Street and Irving in downtown Astoria, you and your pup can climb up past lofty Cathedral Tree to Coxcomb Hill and the Astoria Column. Or, you can start and the top and wander down into town. Where you start depends on whether you want to go uphill first or last, and if you have someone to pick you up at either end. It is a pleasant, manageable walk, 1.5 miles one-way. There are stairs and boardwalks for the steep parts, and plenty of benches for resting along the way. The tree is about halfway through; you can shorten the trip using it as a turnaround. Or, to lengthen your excursion, additional short trails spur off to the sides.

Street parking is very limited in town. You'll have better luck if you pay the buck to park at Astoria Column.

4 Astoria Column

🐾 ◄● (See North Coast map on page 392)

The park is called Astor Park, but it is known by its main feature, the 125-foot-tall Astoria Column, patterned after Rome's Trajan Column and Paris' Vendome. The bas-relief art of the column combines paint and plaster carvings to tell the story of Astoria's early white explorers and settlers.

Visitors crowd the column, leaving more room on the hillsides where your dog may better enjoy himself at view picnic tables and benches. The view from Coxcomb Hill, where the column sits, has always been stunning. It encompasses the wide mouth of the Columbia River, the grand Astoria-Megler Bridge, and the start of the Pacific Coast Scenic Highway, U.S. Highway 101. Naturally, it is the best place in town to watch sunsets.

From U.S. Highway 30, Marine Drive in town, turn north on 16th Street and follow the stencils of the column on the road. Parking is a $1 donation. Open daylight–10 P.M.

5 Youngs River Falls

🐾🐾 (See North Coast map on page 392)

Captain Patrick Gass of Lewis and Clark's Corps of Discovery recorded happening upon these 65-foot falls during a hunting expedition in March 1806. Today, this county park is an undeveloped picnic area with a gravel road and a few steps down to the bottom of the falls on the western fork of the Youngs River. Dogs can splash right into this local swimming hole and do some light hiking up and around the top of the cascade.

From U.S. Highway 30 in Astoria, take State Route 202 10 miles to Olney and turn south on Youngs River Falls Loop Road for another 3.8 miles.

PLACES TO EAT

Blue Scorcher: Kudos to Carlee and Jeff, the Dachsies' honorary Aunt and Uncle, for discovering this delectable bakery for breakfast, lunch, and beautiful breads. Being big on humane treatment for all beings, Coop 'n' Isis are happy to include this all-vegetarian and vegan hangout. The owners have turned a former auto body shop into a cool space where you simply want to hang out and eat your way to health and happiness. 1493 Duane St.; 503/338-7473; www.bluescorcher.com.

Bow Picker Fish and Chips: Order a half or full order of fish and chips right off the boat, only this 1956 wooden boat is moored in a field at the corner of 17th and Duane, across from the Maritime Museum. They serve seasonally, usually May–October, with a couple of picnic tables under a tree and beverages in a cooler. Cash only. 503/791-2942.

Wet Dog Café: Astoria Brewing Company's brewpub dishes up a massive menu of mondo burgers, including many involving seafood innards like catfish, swordfish, cod, and tuna. Okay, let's get real, you're here for the beer. Your dog's here because the patio is a party from Memorial Day until the rain blasts the siding off the walls. We couldn't pass up the Poop Deck Porter nor could we resist buying a Wet Dog hoodie. 144 11th St.; 503/325-6975.

PLACES TO STAY

Cannery Pier Hotel: Isis loves the three pet-friendly rooms at the glam CPH, opened in 2008, from its rooms with private, river view decks to the complimentary Finnish-inspired breakfast. She may have been swayed by the extensive pet goodie basket, which included treats and a squeaky toy. Isis' mom might also have been influenced by the claw foot tub, gas fireplace, complimentary wine happy hour and breakfast... oh, and the Finnish sauna. A single $40 charge applies to all pet stays. Rates range $170–300 for king and queen rooms; up to $350 for the suite. No. 10 Basin St.; 503/325-4996; www.cannerypierhotel.com.

Clementine's Bed and Breakfast: Judith welcomes dogs, has three of her own, and is happy to go with you on daily dog walks around town and lead you to the secret spots in the woods nearby. Her only request is that your dogs don't pee on her beautiful flowers; there's a park a few blocks away. Pets are allowed in the Riverview Loft ($135–165) and the two suites of the Moose Temple Lodge, next door to the main inn ($110–140 each, may be combined), plus a $25 cleaning fee per stay. 847 Exchange St.; 503/325-2005; www.clementines-bb.com.

Crest Motel: There are no pet fees at this Scandinavian-themed motel, and the only rules are that you keep your pets leashed on the property and don't leave them unattended in the rooms. Rates range from $60 for non-view queens to $115 for a view suite. 5366 Leif Erickson Dr.; 503/325-3141 or 800/421-3141; www.astoriacrestmotel.com.

Fort Stevens Campground: This campground is a city with 174 full-hookup, 302 electrical, and 19 tent sites in 14 loops. Rates are $13–22. Believe it or not, sites go fast in the summer. You'll need reservations. 100 Peter Iredale Rd.; 800/452-5687; www.reserveamerica.com.

More Accommodations: Please look under *Chain Hotels* in the *Resources* section for additional places to stay in this area.

Gearhart

Golf is the biggest attraction in this otherwise sleepy town, a tasteful and quiet oceanfront community that has been compared to old Cape Cod. There's a great lawn and beach access at the west end of Pacific Way, Gearhart's main street.

PARKS, BEACHES, AND RECREATION AREAS

6 Fort to Sea Trail

🐾🐾🐾 (See North Coast map on page 392)

At 6.5 miles one-way, this is a biggie, tracing the route that Lewis and Clark's men took from Fort Clatsop to the Pacific Ocean. It starts at Fort Clatsop visitors center and ends at Sunset Beach. In the summer, a shuttle will pick you up at either end and take you back. Otherwise, may we suggest breaking it into bite-sized pieces? For example, the one-mile round-trip down to Sunset Beach and back was definitely doable by the Dachsies. There's another one-mile loop that goes out and back from the fort side of things.

The fort and trail have seen some rough times, but they've prevailed. The replica of the fort burned to the ground in an accidental fire on October 3, 2005, and was completely rebuilt with safer materials and re-opened December 9, 2006. Then the trail was closed after extensive damage caused by a storm on December 3, 2007. It took eight months to clear away the debris and saw through the tree fall to recreate the trail, which reopened in August 2008. Come see what all the hard work has preserved.

From Highway 101, turn inland at the sign for Fort Clatsop, or turn west at the sign for Sunset Beach Lane, at milepost 13, south of Warrenton. Parking is $3 at the visitors center. www.forttosea.org.

7 Del Rey Beach

🐾🐾🐾 (See North Coast map on page 392)

At this State Recreation Site, you can experience the wonderful feeling of watching the rest of the world disappear. Once you climb over the sand dune that hides the parking lot, the only sight before you is the ocean and miles of flat, pristine beach. Light fog often obscures the town of Seaside and Tillamook Head, and even though cars are allowed on the wide, hard-packed sand, you'll watch the few that pass by shrink and fade in the distance. When the rest of the world seems too crowded and noisy, come to Del Rey to expand your horizons. Dogs appreciate the blissful simplicity of Del Rey's empty beach in the same way they can chase a single slobbery tennis ball until they drop.

From U.S. Highway 101, two miles north of Gearhart, turn west on Highlands Lane and continue straight onto the beach, or follow the left fork in the road until it dead-ends in the parking lot. There are no facilities at this beach.

PLACES TO STAY

Gearhart Ocean Inn: The cottage units at this 1941 restored inn are cool, crisp, and refreshing. The prices, ranging $100–165, are equally refreshing, only five blocks to the nearest beach. A maximum of two pets are allowed in units #3–5, 7, and 8, for $15 per pet per night. 67 N. Cottage Ave.; 503/738-7373; www.gearhartoceaninn.com.

Seaside

This beach city has attracted visitors for 150 years, and the antics of the seals at Seaside's famous aquarium have entertained people for more than 60 of those years. You get a glimpse of the old-time, carnival flavor of Oregon's first resort town along Broadway, a crowded arcade street with bumper cars, a restored carousel, and kitschy souvenir shops, ice cream parlors, and cotton candy and elephant ear vendors. Beach Books across from the Carousel Mall is a good find. Pop in for a lounge chair read and give Oz the cat a scratch behind the ears (37 N. Edgewood; 503/738-3500).

Sunset Boulevard, immediately south of downtown, is an aptly named place to park and watch the day descend into twilight, along a rocky, driftwood-scattered section of the beach. While in Seaside, your canine companion might enjoy a side trip to Oregon's largest tree, a 750-year-old Sitka spruce. The pullout is on U.S. Highway 26, 1.5 miles east of the junction with U.S. Highway 101.

PARKS, BEACHES, AND RECREATION AREAS

🐾 Seaside Promenade

🐾🐾 (See North Coast map on page 392)

The city's famous sidewalk promenade has been an institution since 1908. "The Prom" original was a boardwalk, replaced with a wide concrete structure in 1920. The aquarium marks the north end, and on the south you'll pass the site of Lewis and Clark's Salt Camp, with a historic re-creation of the seawater boiling operation. In the middle is an automobile turnaround commemorating the end of the Lewis and Clark Trail. There are excellent views of crashing waves all along the 1.5-mile one-way walk. Many resident and visiting canines cruise The Prom, along with walkers, joggers, bikers, and skaters. You can get down onto the beach at the turnaround.

Downtown public parking is easiest to find in the Trend West Tower at the intersection of 1st Avenue and Columbia Street. A one-block walk from there to the beach puts you right at the halfway point.

PLACES TO EAT

Big Foot Pub 'n' Grub: Patio dining at this bar and grill requires an extra level of vigilance. No matter how well-mannered, any canine culprit is going to be tempted to do a grab-and-dash, taking off with the juicy slab of prime rib that Big Foot is deservedly famous for serving. 2427 S. Roosevelt Dr.; 503/738-7009.

The Buzz: The Wonder Wieners bet you a box of chocolate-covered Twinkies that this is the most amazing candy store you'll ever see. Inside this magical emporium—home of the aforementioned confection—is floor to ceiling candy, from highbrow organic chocolates to giant lollipops in colors not found in nature. Don't count calories or dental fillings. Prefer to sip your sugar? Buzz carries 200 kinds of old-fashioned soda pop. Not enough for your sweet tooth? Next door is Chez Scoop, the ice cream shop. 406 Broadway; 503/717-8808.

Pirate's Cove General Store: Piracy is popular on the coast these days, and there's none more fun than this highway stop north of Seaside decked out as subtly as a theme park. The dessert and sundae list is longer than the main menu of burgers, salads, and sandwiches. Bring the whole family in for a Swiss Roast Beef Robinson and Pirate's Pig Out double banana split. There's outdoor seating under a covered patio at tables made from what just might be empty rum barrels washed ashore at nearby Fort Stevens. 90334 Hwy. 101; 503/861-7400.

PLACES TO STAY

Rivertide Suites: For those of you who prefer that new carpet smell to the odor of wet dog, this property, opened in 2008, is for you. You'll stay in designer condos, complete with kitchens fit for entertaining, gas fireplaces, big tubs, and flat-screen TVs mounted everywhere. Two dogs up to 75 pounds each are allowed, but it ain't cheap at $25 per pet per night. There's a pet goodie bag in the deal for you and a fenced relief area out back. Rates include four people, starting at $95–195 for studios, to $245–480 for 2-bedroom suites. 102 N. Holladay; 503/717-1100; www.rivertidesuites.com.

Sandy Cove Inn: An ambitious young couple has taken a derelict property in a brilliant location and turned it into a neat little beachside motel with charm and class. It's across from a pub, a block from a coffee shop, and two blocks to The Prom and Surfer's Cove. Eight ground-floor, pet-friendly rooms are furnished with antiques that you can buy out from under yourself. They openly welcome pets with a gift basket that includes treats and a gift certificate to a nearby pet boutique. Most of all, proprietors Mike and Betsy are down to earth, wonderfully friendly, and they've got their act together. Their affordable rates challenge the local Motel 6, ranging $45–130, plus a $10 pet fee. 241 Ave. U; 503/738-7473; www.sandycoveinn.biz.

More Accommodations: Please look under *Chain Hotels* in the *Resources* section for additional places to stay in this area.

Cannon Beach

Named for a cannon washed ashore in 1846 from the wreck of the schooner *Shark,* this booming community is the busiest destination on the North Coast. It has a reputation for its dramatic sea-stack rock formations, first-class lodging, and art from more than two dozen galleries and studio artists. The town bulges at the seams in the summer from the pressure of visitors and a growing number of permanent residents. For outdoor recreation with your dogs in and around Cannon Beach, the Dachshund Duo recommends the quiet season, October–April.

PARKS, BEACHES, AND RECREATION AREAS

🐾 Ecola State Park

🐾🐾🐾🐾 🐾 (See North Coast map on page 392)

Ecola smelled like a four-paw park from the moment Coop 'n' Isis drove through its 1,300 acres of forest, climbing up Tillamook Head to emerge at the first of many parking viewpoints at Ecola Point. The whole shebang is nine miles of ocean frontage, from Cannon Beach to Indian Head, following the coastal exploratory routes of Lewis and Clark.

The first hike you might want to try extends 1.5 miles from Ecola Point to Indian Head Beach, alternating between forests of mythical proportions and cliffside ocean views. You can also drive straight to Indian Head Beach to save your strength for more hiking.

The Clatsop Loop Interpretive Trail heads two miles north from Indian Head, with a brochure that traces the tale of a whale, where the Corps of Discovery, led by Lewis and Sacagawea, came upon Clatsop Indians carving and rendering whale blubber. At 1.5 miles, there is a hikers' camp, with primitive three-sided bunk cabins, a fire ring, water, and restrooms. Beyond the camp, the trail leads to the Tillamook Rock Lighthouse Viewpoint. All of the trails have areas of steep cliffs; leashes are a must.

Twelve miles out to sea, Tillamook Rock is the coast's most unusual lighthouse. The poor lightkeepers in this precarious spot were so battered by waves that the sentinel earned the nickname Terrible Tilly. It is the only registered historical lighthouse to be privately owned and it serves the unique purpose of being a Columbarium, a storage place for ashes of the deceased.

From U.S. Highway 101, turn off at the north Cannon Beach Loop exit onto

🐾 DOG-EAR YOUR CALENDAR

Your darling doesn't have to be a purebred to participate in the **Dog Show at the Beach** in Cannon Beach on the second Saturday in October. Pedigree isn't the point at this event, which features 1st-, 2nd-, and 3rd-place ribbons in more than 20 categories, everything from biggest ears to best tail wag. The event is sponsored by the Surfsand Resort, among others. There's no fee to enter, and any donations you wish to make will go to the Clatsop County Animal Shelter. Buy lots of raffle tickets! Find more information or make a donation at 800/547-6100 or www.cannonbeach.org.

Sunset Boulevard, bear right on 5th Street for a few blocks, and follow the signs to turn off on Fir Street into the park. Parking is $3. Open 6 A.M.–10 P.M. 503/436-2844.

🔟 Tolovana Beach Wayside

🐾🐾🐾 🦮 (See North Coast map on page 392)

This State Recreation Site is the largest beach access point in the city, giving beach walkers an entry point for a seven-mile stretch of active waterfront. Your dog can pal around with the *many* other dogs who'll be on the beach.

Haystack Rock, the universal symbol of Cannon Beach, sits onshore. The 235-foot monolith is a National Wildlife Refuge, home to a large colony of bright tufted puffins. You'll need to stay off the rocks, but you can investigate the tidepools around the other sea stacks, called the Needles.

There's a lot of action at Tolovana Beach. You can grab a cup of chowder at Mo's or catch a game of pickup volleyball. Strong winds make for good kite flying; in fact, you can tie a kite to your lawn chair and it'll fly itself. Although Cannon Beach city municipal code states that dogs are only required to be under good voice control, crowds may necessitate the dreaded leash.

From U.S. Highway 101, turn west on Hemlock Street, also called the Cannon Beach Loop. After 0.4 mile, turn left into the wayside parking lot. Open 5 A.M.–10 P.M.

11️⃣ Arcadia Beach

🐾🐾 (See North Coast map on page 392)

From the gravel lot, you can park and sit and look at the ocean through the trees, for starters. After a short walk and a few wooden steps, your dog will love feeling the soft sand in his paws and the water lapping at his forelegs in this pretty cove. You might as well leave your shoes in the car, too. The odd sandal or sock left on the sand is a frequent sight, evidence of the irresistible urge to let loose on the beach and leave your cares behind. The waves crashing against offshore rocks have a hypnotic effect, inducing deep states of relaxation.

There is a restroom and a picnic table on a patch of lawn at this day-use-only State Recreation Site, three miles south of Cannon Beach on U.S. Highway 101. Open 6 A.M.–10 P.M.

12️⃣ Hug Point

🐾🐾🐾 (See North Coast map on page 392)

You can trace the remnants of a treacherous stagecoach route carved into the cliffs that hugs the point on the north end of this glistening beach. You're free to walk along the historic roadbed, explore a couple of caves, and hike to a waterfall around the headland, but only at ebb tide. It's critical to know the tide table for the day, available free at the visitors center or most merchants in town, or you could find yourself stranded on the rocks as travelers of old often were.

The highway parking lot has drinking water and a vault toilet. This State Recreation Site is 4.3 miles south of Cannon Beach on U.S. Highway 101. Open 6 A.M.–10 P.M.

13 Oswald West

🐾🐾🐾🐾 🐾➤ (See North Coast map on page 392)

Oswald West, Oregon's governor from 1911 to 1915, is the man responsible for designating all of the state's beaches as public lands, preserving the coastal playground for all to enjoy. This 2,474-acre state park does him proud by honoring his memory and foresight.

As you drive into the park on U.S. Highway 101, there are a series of viewpoints as the road winds up and around Neah-Kah-Nie Mountain. From the southern parking lot, a 0.5-mile spur trail leads you down to Short Sands Beach, tucked into lush Smugglers Cove, a highly prized destination for surfers and boogie boarders chasing endless summer. The multiple waterways of Kerwin, Necarney, and Short Sands Creeks splash down the hillsides of Neah-Kah-Nie Mountain and Cape Falcon, the two headlands protecting the crescent beach. High-rise old-growth cedars, hemlocks, spruce, and firs hide a tent city of 30 hike-in sites; you can pass within feet of the campground and not see it.

From Manzanita to Arch Cape, a 13-mile stretch of the Oregon Coast Trail traverses the park. For you and your pup, two excellent trail sections break off from the beach spur. Cape Falcon is the easier trail, rising 300 feet in two miles to the tip of the headland to view the spectacle of the ocean below. The Neahkahnie Mountain Trail starts across a woozy suspension bridge, climbs switchbacks to a meadow, then crosses the highway on the way up to the summit at 1,631 feet. Up in this rarified air, every few footsteps lead you to another ocean vista.

Trail maps, wheelbarrows to transport camping gear, restrooms, and a drinking fountain are located in the larger parking lot on the east side of the highway. Oswald West is on U.S. Highway 101, 10 miles south of Cannon Beach. 503/368-3575.

PLACES TO EAT

Cranky Sue's: We don't know about Sue, but her famous "very crabby cakes," stuffed to the gills with succulent, sweet blue crab, put us in a fabulous mood. Seafood lovers, this corner café has to be on your "bucket list" of things to do before you die. Tables on the lawn out front are usually full, so take your cakes across the street to tables along Ecola Creek Park. Sue's dogs Cork and Rudy provide hilarious menu reviews. 308 Fir St.; 503/436-0301; www.crankysues.com.

Ye Olde Driftwood Inn: A kiss and a hug, apple pie á la mode, a dog and his human, seafood and steaks… there are some perfect pairs simply meant to go together. Enjoy them whenever you can. Especially when they include a full cocktail bar, and a railing on the porch to latch your pal to while imbibing. 179 N. Hemlock St.; 503/436-2439; www.driftwoodcannonbeach.com.

PLACES TO STAY

Arch Cape House: Dogs are usually permitted only in the Provence Room, an intimate suite on the garden level with its own entrance through elegant French doors. It's the only room at the inn with a terrace and a whirlpool tub. Darn. The rate is $200–220 per night; the pet fee is $35. 31970 E. Ocean Rd.; 503/436-2800; www.archcapehouse.com.

Inn at Arch Cape: This intimate retreat is perfectly placed between Hug Point and Oswald West. Rooms recall an earlier, gracious era when the well-to-do summered at the coast. Each has tongue-and-groove pine interiors and beach rock fireplaces, with wood provided. Two dogs are allowed in rooms #3–6, for $15 per pet per night. Rates vary $95–205 seasonally. 79340 Hwy. 101; 503/738-7373 or 800/352-8034; www.innatarchcape.com.

Inn at Cannon Beach: There's something to be said for staying at a private inn owned by savvy people with really good taste in things like HDTVs, gas fireplaces, big windows, and two-person jetted tubs. A welcome basket for pet guests includes linens, towels, bags, and biscuits. Of the 40 units, 16 allow a maximum of two pets. Guest pets will appreciate the doors opening onto a central courtyard with a pond and native plants. For the ultimate in luxury, inquire about oceanfront rooms at their sister property, the Ocean Lodge. Rates of $100–250 include a light buffet breakfast. The pet fee is $10 per pet per night. 3215 S. Hemlock St.; 800/321-6304; www.innatcannonbeach.com and www.theoceanlodge.com.

Lands End Motel: People book years in advance to return to "their" rooms at this property, owned by the same couple since the 1970s. The owners update the rooms frequently; when we checked in, it looked untouched and meticulously clean. The dogs love the friendly staff, the beach location can't be beat, and there's a wide choice of rooms. Rates range $140–295, plus a $15 one-time pet fee. Two-dog maximum. 263 2nd St.; 503/436-2264; www.landsendmotel.com

Shaw's Oceanfront Bed and Breakfast: From the back deck at Shaw's, you and your dog can step into the fenced backyard, through the gate, and onto the beach. This casual home includes a separate bedroom, living room, and kitchen for preparing meals and snacks, except for breakfast, which is made for you. The entire two-bedroom suite is yours for $200 a night, $185 per night for two or more nights. Pets are an additional $25 per stay. 79924 Cannon Rd.; 503/426-1422 or 888/269-4483; www.shawsoceanfrontbb.com.

Surfsand Resort: This large, cheerful family resort openly brags about their pet-friendliness by sponsoring Cannon Beach's annual Dog Show on the Beach. Dogs are welcome in all types of rooms except waterfront hot tub suites, for a $15 pet fee. Pet-friendly condos and vacation rental homes are available as well. Your dog will receive a basket of goodies at the front desk and there are "walking" papers everywhere for your convenience. Room rates range widely from $150–360; see the website for home selection and pricing. 147 W. Gower; 800/547-6100; www.surfsand.com.

Oswald West Campground: For a more pristine camping experience, try one of 30 walk-in tent sites. It's about a third of a mile down to the campground, and you can borrow a wheelbarrow for no charge. There are restrooms and drinking water, but no showers. Rates are $10–14. Open March–October on a first-come, first-served basis. 503/368-3575.

Manzanita

This smaller beach community at the foot of Neah-Kah-Nie Mountain is so popular with the canine crowd, it has earned the flattering nickname Muttzanita. One hotel owner quoted a 30 percent occupancy rate in the area, just for the dogs! There are a few choice shops, eateries, funky bookstores, and a lovely beach on a loop off the beaten highway. In Cooper's humble opinion, it's a resort town perfected.

PARKS, BEACHES, AND RECREATION AREAS

14 Neah-Kah-Nie Beach

🐾🐾🐾🐾 (See North Coast map on page 392)

With a beach this good, you only need one. Manzanita's city park goes on seemingly forever, seven miles actually, and has enough going on to keep you busy for a week. There are tales of buried treasure, of a Spanish galleon strayed off course and wrecked at the foot of the mountain. No one has unearthed gleaming gold bullion, but artifacts such as a wine cup and a beeswax candle prove the story. As for beach treasures, the early dog gets the best pick of seashells, agates, and driftwood, seaweed, flotsam, and jetsam. Beachcombers are allowed to take the treasures they find, unless in a protected refuge area or marked signs indicate otherwise. Let us know if you find galleons.

From U.S. Highway 101, turn west on Laneda Avenue through town, and turn onto Ocean Road. Park at any one of several roadside areas and walk straight onto the beach. Take advantage of the doggie bag dispensers and garbage cans at several beach entrance points. No parking 11 P.M.–5 A.M.

PLACES TO EAT

Bread and Ocean: A beautiful hand-carved picnic table on the lawn in front welcomes you to this bakery and deli, a harbinger of more good things to come. The display case is filled with artisan breads and bowls of couscous, wild rice, roasted beets, and caprese salads. Isis nearly died and went to heaven

DIVERSIONS

While in Astoria, pop into **LaDeDog!** (120 10th St.; 503/325-8337; www.ladedog.net), a dog boutique around the corner from the River-walk, where you can bring your bud to sample some delicious treats. Bring a photo of your pup for their album, and check their website for yappy hour events.

The pet boutique in Cannon Beach is called **Puppy Love by the Sea** (271 N. Hemlock; 503/436-9800). It's petite, but well stocked. While there, grab the local pet informer, the *Bow Wow* dog newspaper (bowwowdognews.com).

In 2008, perfect Manzanita got even better with the opening of the dog boutique **Four Paws on the Beach** (144 Laneda; 503/368-3436; www.fourpawsonthebeach.com). The large collection of practical, outdoor gear from RuffWear is most impressive.

when allowed a bite of grilled panini with Serrano ham, Manchego cheese, quince paste, and arugula. She loves saying the word arugula. 387 Laneda; 503/368-5823; www.breadandocean.com.

Left Coast Siesta: The Siesta puts together Southwest-Mex like the board game *Clue:* It was tequila lime chicken, smothered by burrito sauce, finished off with black olives and sunflower seeds, wrapped in a red chili tortilla, to be polished off on the deck. Get it to go, and take your game to the beach, as the patio is too crowded to allow pets. 288 Laneda; 503/368-7997.

Manzanita News and Espresso: Get informed while sipping your daily fix at this fixture in the center of town. This joint win's Cooper's vote for best coffee on the coast and the most interesting locals with whom to chat. Savories include quiches, Mediterranean gyros, and chicken sandwiches. No dogs on deck, and on leash only please, using the hitching post provided for the purpose. 500 Laneda Ave.; 503/368-7450.

Manzanita Seafood and Chowderhouse: To go, they have the largest fresh seafood market on the North Coast. To stay, we love their multi-level brick patio with its large, round, family-style tables. Steamed clams, whole crab, and fried oysters taste better in the sea air. For less adventurous kids, they'll make a fluffernutter sandwich (peanut butter and marshmallow cream) or grilled cheese. No credit cards. 519 Laneda; 503/368-2722.

PLACES TO STAY

Coast Cabins: Isis would like to hire the interior decorator and landscaper for these exceptional cabins, which would be right at home in the pages of *Metropolitan Home* magazine. A package of goodies await your pet, who is allowed in all five cabins. The property is a few blocks from the beach, luxury worth the walk. Rates range $125–375. A nightly $25 per pet fee buys you greenies and a squeaky toy, towels, bowls, and a pet bed. There is also a $30 one-time, deep cleaning fee. 635 Laneda Ave.; 503/368-7113; www.coastcabins.com.

OceanEdge Specialty Rentals: Dogs are accepted in half a dozen rental homes. They phone interview potential renters and ask them to sign a reasonable doggie contract, and, based on your needs, they find the perfect home for you. Because a cleaning fee is charged, these rentals are most economical for stays of at least a week. 503/368-3343; www.manzanitavacation.com.

Ocean Inn: It's out the door and onto the beach for you if you stay at these perky, airy oceanfront cottages, which allow a maximum of two pets in units 2, 3, and 4. Rates are really decent for oceanfront, ranging $135–165, plus $15 per pet per night. 32 Laneda Ave.; 503/368-7701 or 866/368-7701; www.oceaninnatmanzanita.com.

Manzanita Rental Company: This agency rents 38 pet-friendly vacation homes with a wide variety of capacities and rates. Each listing on its website clearly states whether or not pets are allowed. There's a $15 per pet nightly charge, and some have limits on the number of pets. It's easiest to call and discuss your desires and dog situation with an agent. Homes have a one-week minimum stay requirement in July and August. 686 Manzanita Ave.; 503/368-6797 or 800/579-9801; www.manzanitarentals.com.

San Dune Inn: Props to AlanBob™ (yes, he's trademarked his name) and his pup Popcorn for finding such a refreshing and inexpensive motel with honest character and warm hospitality, that's still well maintained and clean. A few blocks off the beach will save you and your dog some dough. All six standard rooms ($65–100) and eight suites ($75–140) welcome pets warmly. Perks for pets include treats, bags, and Frisbees; for humans, it's a complimentary VCR library, books, games, bicycles, and beach chairs. There is a one-time $10 pet fee. 428 Dorcas Ln.; 888/368-5163; www.sandune-inn-manzanita.com.

The Studio and The Lighthouse: Thanks to Stephanie and her pals Riley and Lola for turning us on to these rental properties, two little pieces of heaven across the street from the beach. Just for couples, these bright, sunny spaces have unbelievable ocean views. The Lighthouse is a loft with a romantic alcove bed. The two-story Studio was designed by an artist. One look at their pictures on the web and you'll fall in love. They run $130–150 each, plus a $10 per pet per night fee. In the lighthouse, you can add a downstairs room for an extra charge. Call for directions. Neither building is ADA accessible. 503/593-1736; www.the-studio-lighthouse.com.

Nehalem

There's little here other than any and all activities involving the beach or bay. You might want to visit the Nehalem Bay Winery, a couple of miles inland (34965 Highway 53, 503/368-9463, www.nehalembaywinery.com). For dining, there are many fabulous choices two miles north in Manzanita.

PARKS, BEACHES, AND RECREATION AREAS

15 Nehalem Bay

🐾🐾🐾 (See North Coast map on page 392)

It's easy to get to this ultra-popular State Park, and there's plenty to do once you've arrived. On the four-mile spit enclosing Nehalem Bay, there's a landing strip for fly-in campers, six miles of horse trails and a separate camp for equestrians, and two miles of paved, wheelchair-accessible trails for pedestrians and cyclists. If beachcombing isn't your thing, the waters are quieter on the east side of the spit. A boat ramp provides access to kayaking, crabbing, and fishing in the bay.

Any noise from the airstrip and the hectic campground fades away completely once you've climbed over a substantial dune to the ocean. Four miles of soft white sand and ocean views stretch along the Nehalem Spit to the south, and Neah-Kah-Nie Mountain towers overhead. Small dog warning: Winds here are strong. A kite tied to a collar will fly itself and Toto just might get whisked off to Kansas.

From U.S. Highway 101, the turnoff to the park is 0.8 mile northwest of the center of town in Nehalem (from the south, take a left at the blinking light), and another 1.2 miles to the entrance, marked with an unmistakable timber archway. Parking is $3. Open 6:30 A.M.–10 P.M. 503/368-5154.

PLACES TO EAT

The Bunkhouse Restaurant: The owners are relaxed about allowing dogs on the porches while you eat. At worst, if someone on the front porch would rather not eat with a dog nearby, they may ask you to move to the back porch.

After you're finished with your heaping plate of comfort food, you won't feel like moving anywhere. If you like caramels, you cannot live another moment without a box of Sarah Jo's, made next door. 36315 Hwy. 101; 503/368-5424.

PLACES TO STAY

Nehalem Bay Campground: This campground is a parking lot of 267 electrical sites, one big block party with a changing cast of characters. Pets of every breed abound. Sites are $16–20, and summer reservations are a necessity. 800/452-5687; www.reserveamerica.com.

Rockaway Beach

This resort community emerged as a getaway for Portlanders in the 1920s, focused entirely on the seven miles of sandy beach accessible from the center of town.

PARKS, BEACHES, AND RECREATION AREAS

16 Manhattan Beach

🐾🐾🐾🐾 (See North Coast map on page 392)

This State Recreation Site is thoroughly relaxing. The Wonder Wieners prefer this type of beach wayside, one without an attached campground and not in a city center. The beach is secluded, the parking lot is protected from the highway, and the picnic tables are tucked away from the wind in groves of shore pine. There are restrooms and one main path of about 50 feet to the beach. Once onshore, there's no development on the hill behind you, and nothing to interrupt the glorious view before you.

Turn west on Beach Street from U.S. Highway 101, two miles north of Rockaway Beach, and immediately turn left onto the park access road.

17 Rockaway Beach City Wayside

🐾🐾 (See North Coast map on page 392)

This city park provides beach access, pure and simple. There's a parking lot with room for about 50 cars, although it's not well protected from traffic. Amenities include a drinking fountain and restroom, outdoor shower, volleyball beach setup, and a few picnic tables and viewing benches in the parking lot area. The beach extends for seven miles along the homes, hotels, shops, and restaurants of town.

From U.S. Highway 101, turn west on S. First Street into the park.

PLACES TO EAT

Dragonfly Sisters Café: Dogs and kids love this place, with its fenced lawn, sandbox, and picnic tables crammed out back in the alley behind the store.

They only offer treats and baked goods, espresso and ice cream. For real food, they recommend takeout from Rick's Roadhouse across the street to bring back to the picnic tables. 127 Miller St.; 503/355-2300.

PLACES TO STAY

Tradewinds Motel: Gone is the trademark stucco siding of 15 years, replaced by hardy wood planking. Gone is the lawn, swallowed by the sand. What remains are big rooms with even bigger views. Two pets max are allowed per room, in six of the oceanfront suites. Rates range $95–160, plus $15 per night for your dog, up to a maximum of $40 per stay. There are picnic tables and barbecue grills by the beach in back. 523 N. Pacific St.; 503/355-2112 or 800/824-0938; www.tradewinds-motel.com.

Garibaldi

Captain Robert Gray was the first known U.S. explorer to spend time in this area on what is now Tillamook Bay. His crew of 12 men arrived on the sloop *Lady Washington* in 1778 and left hastily in a week after a skirmish with Native Americans onshore. A replica of his tall ship moors and sails from harbor in Aberdeen, Washington.

The pace of life is calm in this fishing and oystering village. The Boat Basin at the mouth of the Miami River is the primary hive of activity, for commercial and sport anglers. To see the boats in the harbor, and get some fresh fish or crab for dinner, turn west on 7th from U.S. Highway 101 to Mooring Basin Road.

PARKS, BEACHES, AND RECREATION AREAS

18 Barview Jetty County Park

🐾🐾 (See North Coast map on page 392)

The Barview Jetty protects the boats entering and exiting Tillamook Bay, a rich estuary nicknamed the Ghost Hole. One local said the nickname comes from the ghost shrimp harvested in the bay; another told us a tale of an elusive 1,000-pound sturgeon who lurks out of reach of anglers' lines; a brochure said it's haunted by the spirit of a disgruntled settler, crushed to death by a log he moved on the hillside. We think it's a tradition for each local to make up a different story to tell unsuspecting tourists. You decide.

It's fun to watch the waves crash against the jetty wall and the boats entering and exiting the harbor while your dog sniffs around the beach extending north. You'll have to time your beach walks for low tide, although you can meander through the sand dunes and campground anytime. 503/322-3477.

PLACES TO STAY

Barview Jetty Campground: The brave windblown trees on this beach jetty provide a decent amount of privacy in this 290-site county campground with hot showers and heated restrooms. Tent sites are $20, RV hookups are $25, and pull-through sites are $30. For reservations, call and leave a message at 503/322-3522 with your name, address, phone number, site request, and dates. P.S.: The manager gets grouchy when he sees dogs off leash. In this wild area, it really is for their safety.

Cape Meares

Separating from Highway 101 in Tillamook, the Three Capes Scenic Loop—to Cape Meares, Cape Lookout, and Cape Kiwanda—presents a quieter side of the Oregon Coast. Rush hour might be the morning launch of the dory fishing boats into the surf, and traffic congestion probably means there are cows blocking the road. This is life in the slow lane, where you can pull over to the side of the road to watch a blue heron nabbing fish in Netarts Bay or an oysterman hauling nets out of the sludge.

PARKS, BEACHES, AND RECREATION AREAS

19 Bay Ocean Spit

😺😺 (See North Coast map on page 392)

Hike the dike, with binoculars in hand, for a birding extravaganza. This sand spit is a migration stop that nature periodically builds and then takes away. Little trails shoot off in several directions through thick dune grass. For smaller dogs, it's like going on safari. In the early 1900s, eager developers tried to create "the next Atlantic City" on this spit. Over time, the ocean consumed all of the homes, a bowling alley, a natatorium, and, most likely, several saloons and brothels, although the historical sign doesn't confess to as much.

Turn west at 3rd Street in Tillamook and drive three miles to Bayocean Spit. Turn right onto the one-way dirt road and go 1.5 miles to the parking area.

20 Cape Meares State Scenic Viewpoint

😺😺😺 (See North Coast map on page 392)

Each of this cape's unique attractions are like small plates at a *tapas* bar, situated on a bluff 200 feet above the ocean. The paved path to the lighthouse is a quick 0.2-mile roundtrip. Next, a 0.4-mile out-and-back gravel loop leads to the Octopus Tree, a many-trunked Sitka spruce. Immediately to the north of the entrance is a 0.25-mile quickie that loops around another giant Sitka in a protected coastal old-growth forest. Then there's a picnic meadow to the south of the parking area, a neat surprise tucked between a rock alcove and the well-protected, fenced bluff. Many bird species nest in Cape Meares National Wildlife Refuge to the north and on the rock formations at sea, including peregrine falcons, a species slowly recovering from near extinction.

If all the sightseeing hasn't filled you up, there's a moderately difficult, two-mile trail down to a deserted beach that takes you through and under fallen old growth. For your dog's enjoyment, we can practically guarantee that this path will be muddy and plastered with giant banana slugs.

The Cape Meares Lighthouse is puny by most standards, only 38 feet tall. It was illuminated in 1890 and wasn't replaced with an automatic beacon until 1963. It has a gift shop and is open for tours April–October. Call 503/842-2244.

From the intersection of State Route 6 and U.S. Highway 101 in Tillamook, follow the signs for the Three Capes Scenic Loop, which begins on Netarts Highway. You'll bear right at Bayocean Road and travel four miles, then left on Cape Meares Loop for another two miles.

Oceanside

Look up! It's a bird... it's a plane... it's—actually, it's probably a hang glider, riding the wind currents down from this hillside to the beach below. In this quiet community, the most strenuous activities are usually hang gliding, paragliding, and kite flying.

PARKS, BEACHES, AND RECREATION AREAS

21 Oceanside Beach

🐾 🐾 (See North Coast map on page 392)

Located in town, this State Recreation Site offers some of the best agate-hunting on the coast in the winter storm season when outgoing currents strip away the sand. Agates are colorful gemstones, rounded by the sea and tossed onto the sand. They can be opaque in white, carnelian, red, blue-black, and

dark green. Many are translucent, and crystal formations can be seen inside when they are held up to the sun. Look for them in loose gravel at the tide line.

The beach has great views of the Three Arch Rocks National Wildlife Refuge. These offshore rock formations support Oregon's largest colony of tufted puffins and the largest colony of common murres outside of Alaska. The barking you'll hear isn't from dogs, but from the Oregon Coast's only breeding grounds for Stellar sea lions. The beach extends about a mile and a half in either direction. There are two parking levels, restrooms, and a hillside picnic table.

Oceanside is 11 miles west of Tillamook on the Three Capes Scenic Loop. You can approach from the south on Netarts Bay Road or from the north on Bayocean Road. Parking open 5 A.M.–11 P.M.

Tillamook

At Tillamook, the Pacific Coast Scenic Highway drifts inland for a short detour through rich dairy valleys, through countless cows to the Tillamook Cheese Factory, the Pacific Northwest's most famous purveyor of all things dairy.

PARKS, BEACHES, AND RECREATION AREAS

22 Munson Creek Falls

🐾🐾 ⬤ (See North Coast map on page 392)

It's an easy 0.5-mile out-and-back trot through ancient Sitka spruce and western red cedar to see the 319-foot falls, the highest in the Coastal Range. You'll follow rippling Munson Creek and pass by the world's second-largest recorded spruce, 260 feet tall and eight feet in diameter. It's a beautiful walk through this State Natural Site. Cooper only wishes it was longer.

From U.S. Highway 101, six miles south of Tillamook, turn west on Munson Creek Road. After 0.7 mile, the road becomes gravel, and you'll follow the signs to take first a left fork in the road, then a right, to reach the circular driveway at 1.5 miles.

PLACES TO EAT

Blue Heron French Cheese Company: The hens, roosters, turkeys, and pheasants are running amok in Tillamook, all over the grounds of this farmstead converted into a fantastic deli and gourmet food store. You can put together an amazing picnic basket full of food to go or eat in their picnic area, but keep your pet leashed to prevent him from chasing his own dinner. Kids like to buy oats in the store to feed the farm animals. 2001 Blue Heron Dr.; 503/842-8281; www.blueheronoregon.com.

Farmhouse Café at the Tillamook Cheese Factory: Although she would dearly love to join you, your dog will have to wait outside while you take the self-guided tour through the factory, but you'll be forgiven instantly if you sneak a couple of cheese curd samples into your pocket for her. There's a gourmet gift shop, ice cream counter, and deli in the factory, and you can share together after the tour on the lawn of the visitors center next door. 4175 Hwy. 101; 503/815-1300; www.tillamookcheese.com.

PLACES TO STAY

In this area, chain hotels listed in the *Resources* section offer the best choices for dogs and their owners.

Netarts

Bring cash and cocktail sauce. Look out for hand-painted "$5 for a Dozen Oysters" or "Live Crab" signs, and you've got yourself an instant beach party at Cape Lookout.

PARKS, BEACHES, AND RECREATION AREAS

23 Cape Lookout

🐾🐾🐾🐾 (See North Coast map on page 392)

Of the three trails available from the Cape Lookout Trailhead, the moderate, 2.5-mile Cape Trail is the most popular. For a nice change of pace, the trail starts at the highest point and gradually descends 400 feet to the tip of the cape, rambling through a coastal forest. When you reach the ocean, your grand view encompasses the ocean to the horizon, Cape Kiwanda to the south, and Cape Meares to the north. The South Trail is steeper, winding 1.8 miles down to a secluded beach south of the cape, and the 2.3-mile North Trail leads to the campground and the beach at Netarts Bay. There are steep drop-offs on all of the trails. Distances listed are one-way. Protect your dog by keeping her on a short leash at this stunning, 2000-acre state park.

If your dog would rather head right for the water, continue north of the trailhead entrance to the campground. There's a large day-use parking area, sheltered and viewpoint picnic tables, and a gorgeous beach.

From Sand Lake Road on the Three Capes Scenic Loop, turn onto Cape Lookout Road for 3.5 miles to the trailhead parking lot and another 2.5 miles to the campground. Parking is $3. Open 7 A.M.–9 P.M. 503/842-4981.

PLACES TO EAT

Schooner Oyster House and Lounge: Follow the locals if you know what's good for you, like chicken-fried steak trucker breakfasts, light and crunchy wood-fired mushroom pizza for lunch, or Cornish game hen for dinner. The place looks like a dive, the food tastes like a dream. Peek inside for a look at the beautiful bar carved out of maple. Hang with Radar, the owners' golden retriever, at the picnic tables on the paved lot, and enjoy his shenanigans. 2065 Netarts Bay Rd.; 503/815-9900.

PLACES TO STAY

Cape Lookout Campground: At this state park, sites closer to the sea are more open, in trees stripped bare of leaves by rough shore breezes. For privacy and peace, head to loops C and D. There are 38 RV and 173 tent sites, for $12–20. Reservations are wise in summer. 800/452-5687; www.reserveamerica.com.

Pacific City

Imagine a fishing village without docks, marinas, piers, or a wharf. On the south end of the Three Capes Loop, Pacific City is the home of the oceangoing dory fishing fleet, flat-bottomed boats that launch directly into the surf. When they've caught their load for the day, they return by running the boats full-throttle onto shore to a sand-slide stop. They have right-of-way, so you and your pooch better watch out!

Your dog will get a kick out of Pacific City's large population of domestic bunnies who have taken to the wild, hopping all over town. Kids can buy bunny food at the inn to feed them.

PARKS, BEACHES, AND RECREATION AREAS

24 Sand Lake
🐾🐾 (See North Coast map on page 392)

Sand Lake is a playground for all-terrain vehicles (ATVs), spinning and spitting their way through the sand dunes at the East Dunes and West Winds sites on the northwest side of the lake. For quiet dune hikes with your dog and playtime in the water, turn to the left as you enter the recreation area to the Fisherman Day-Use Area, where ATVs are not allowed. At high tide, there really is a lake, but when the tide is out, you can fool around on the mushy lake of sand and walk 0.75 mile out to the ocean. From Sand Lake Road on the Three Capes Scenic Loop, turn southwest on Galloway Road for 2.3 miles.

25 Clay Myers
🐾🐾🐾 (See North Coast map on page 392)

The 180 acres of Whalen Island became a state park in 2000, one of the most significant additions to State Natural Areas in 30 years. From a small, gravel parking loop, you can walk straight to a bayfront beach or estuary and wetland overlooks on short, wheelchair-accessible trails. Cooper recommends going the long way around on an easy, level, wood-chip trail that loops 1.4 miles through Sitka spruce, shore pine, and salal dripping with moss. At low tide, you can dig for sand shrimp or walk 0.75 mile along the tidelands to the ocean. In this pristine ecosystem, you can watch the salmon returning to spawn in the fall and the salmon smolts struggling back to the ocean in the spring. Whether or not you are a fan of state lotteries, you can thank the people of Oregon for voting to use lottery funds to purchase this public treasure.

The site is maintained simply, with a vault toilet and trail map. From Pacific City, follow the Three Capes Scenic Route north on Sand Lake Road for 5.5 miles and turn left at the sign for Whalen Island–Clay Myers.

26 Tierra del Mar Beach

😺😺 (See North Coast map on page 392)

Sometimes there's a bit too much going on at Cape Kiwanda, with the dory boats crashing on shore and cars driving on the beach, so families and picnickers come the tiniest bit north to this beach access point to escape the ruckus. The beach is wide and windy here.

Vehicles are prohibited on the beach to the north May–September, and on weekends and holidays all year. Tierra del Mar is on Kiwanda Drive about a mile north of Cape Kiwanda.

27 Cape Kiwanda

😺😺😺 (See North Coast map on page 392)

The golden, wave-carved sandstone cliff of Cape Kiwanda, jutting a half mile out to sea, is of one Oregon's most frequently photographed natural wonders. It is the smallest of the three capes, yet it's usually the most exciting. Heading north from the parking area, carefully climb to the top of the dune. From this perch, you can get a better view of the haystack rock and watch the surfers, boogie boarders, and dory boats launching into the ocean. At low tide, the beach extends four miles south to the tip of Nestucca Spit. Beachcombers on the cape can come away with a great selection of sand dollars.

At this State Natural Area, Tillamook County maintains the parking lot, a restroom, and a wheelchair-accessible ocean viewing deck. Cars are allowed on the beach during certain times of the year.

From U.S. Highway 101, take the Pacific City exit at Brooten Road. Follow it for 2.8 miles into town, and turn left on Pacific Avenue across the bridge. Turn right at the stop sign onto Cape Kiwanda Drive, and follow it another mile.

28 Bob Straub State Park

😺😺😺 (See North Coast map on page 392)

This undisturbed beach on the Nestucca River sand spit is a wonderful spot for a scenic beach walk. To the south, you can see Porter Point and Cannery Hill, behind you are the uninterrupted dunes you climbed over to reach the beach, and to the north is a haystack rock formation with good potential for watching wave action and nesting birds. On the bay side of the spit, the Nestucca River is the stuff of fishing legend, where it's not unheard of to hook a 50-pound Chinook salmon.

From Pacific City, turn west at the only four-way stop in town on Pacific Avenue, go straight through the next intersection, over the bridge, and immediately into the park. The park has restrooms and a drinking fountain.

PLACES TO EAT

Pelican Pub and Brewery: Burgers and pizza wash down nice and easy with cream ales, pales, stouts, or darks at this large, airy, and popular pub. If you want to get fancy, Isis recommends the crab cakes paired with the Scottish ale. Breakfast includes haystack burritos, stuffed French toast, and beer battered pancakes. It's gotta be noon somewhere. Just beyond the patio are posts for tying up, on the soft sand within view of the surf. You can't miss it—on the beach next to Cape Kiwanda. 503/965-7007; www.pelicanbrewery.com.

Village Coffee Shoppe: If Pacific Northwesterners weren't so obsessed with coffee, this restaurant might have a more descriptive name, such as the Village Home of the World's Largest Chicken-Fried Steak. At patio picnic tables, dogs are treated to free toast scraps while they wait for the leftovers from your large portions of steak and eggs or clam chowder. 34910 Brooten Rd.; 503/965-7635.

PLACES TO STAY

Inn at Cape Kiwanda: Every warm, light-filled room at the inn has an ocean-view balcony and a gas fireplace. In the hot tub rooms, the view is from the tub! The beach and the pub are right across the street, Stimulus espresso café is downstairs, and there's a bag dispenser, washing station, and dog walk on the north side of the building. Treats and extra blankets are provided at check-in. Room rates range $130–230, up to $280 for hot tub rooms. The pet fee is $20. A three-bedroom cottage is also available for rental. 33105 Cape Kiwanda Dr.; 503/965-7001 or 888/965-7001; www.innatcapekiwanda.com.

Sea View Vacation Rentals: This pet-friendly agency has an excellent, easy-to-navigate website that clearly lists which properties in Pacific City, Tierra Del Mar, and Neskowin allow pets. 6340 Pacific Ave.; 503/965-7888 or 888/701-1023; www.seaview4u.com.

Shorepine Village Rentals: Pets are welcomed with treats and towels at 18 very recent, individually-owned and decorated beach homes, each sleeping 4–10 people. They're fully outfitted and a few have fenced yards. There's a two-night minimum in the off-season, three-night minimum all summer, and you're going to want to stay longer, because the community's dune ramp to the beach is simply amazing. Go in with friends or extended family to cover the costs of $130–250 per night, plus a $65–85 cleaning fee and an additional $20 per pet per night surcharge (some leniency for longer stays). 5975 Shorepine Dr.; 503/965-5776; www.shorepinerentals.com

Whalen Island Campground: All 30 county park sites are beachfront, on the quiet estuary of this park adjacent to Clay Myers State Natural Area. This primitive campground with vault toilets is appropriate for small RVs or tents only on a first-come, first-served basis. Sits are $10–15 per night; closed in winter if no camp host is available.

Neskowin

After heading inland through Tillamook, the Pacific Coast Scenic Highway 101 meets up with the ocean again in this tiny town with posh cottages, two golf courses, a general store, and a restaurant. Slightly north, you can canoe and kayak in Nestucca Bay's estuary waters through strands of spruce and ocean views. It's a beautiful spot that escapes the tourist frenzy.

PARKS, BEACHES, AND RECREATION AREAS

29 Neskowin Beach
🐾🐾🐾 (See North Coast map on page 392)

The beach cove at Neskowin is dominated by the island known as Proposal Rock. The history of the island's name is vague, as it seems that no one remembers whether it was an Indian Chief's daughter, a sea captain's lover, or an early postmaster's daughter who received a proposal here. There's no forgetting the profile of the rock, half onshore and half in the water, topped with a hairdo of tall spruce trees.

After crossing the parking lot, which has a couple of picnic tables and a restroom, and carefully walking across Hawk Street, you'll walk to the beach on a sidewalk that starts out paved and rapidly becomes engulfed in the deep, silky sand. You'll share the tidepools and surf with local dogs who wander about and people from the nearby inn, but few others.

Turn west at the sign for Neskowin Beach Wayside on Hawk Street from U.S. Highway 101 in Neskowin.

PLACES TO EAT

Hawk Creek Café: Although the post in the front yard says No Pets, the owners will make exceptions for respectful, leashed dogs who can relax on the lawn and chat with local dogs who wander by. You can tuck into harvest potatoes and pancakes or lunch sandwich-and-salad plates at a nearby picnic table as well. The homespun food is great, so it's worth behaving to be allowed to hang out. 4505 Salem Ave.; 503/392-3838.

PLACES TO STAY

Proposal Rock Inn: Each room or suite is individually owned and decorated at this inn. Some have fireplaces, most have kitchens, and what they all have in common are balconies and patios with views of Hawk Creek or the ocean and the rock. A bridge crosses the creek to the beach. Room rates are fabulous, only $60–140; up to $175 for suites that sleep six. The best oceanfront prices on the coast get even better with two-for-one return-customer discounts. There's a one-time pet fee of $15, two pet limit. 48988 Hwy. 101 S.; 503/392-3115; www.proposalrockneskowin.com.

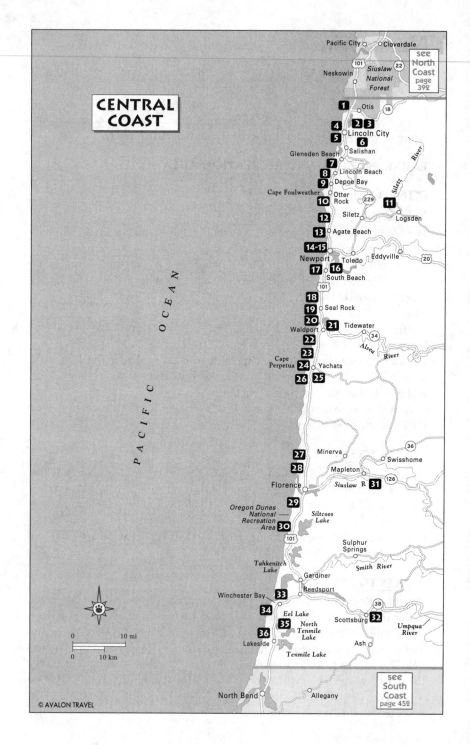

CHAPTER 15

Central Coast

Oregon's central coast is all about more—more lodging options, beachfront parks, tourists, and infinitely more sand in the Oregon Dunes, an ever-changing landscape at the whim of the winds and tides. This section of the coast begins with dramatic capes and cliffs to the north that give way to the graceful dunes.

Even the surf is higher, and more dangerous, causing nine wrecks of significant historical record from 1852 to 1912. Four of Oregon's nine historic lighthouses cling to the rocks along Central Oregon, the sentinels to protect other mariners from similar fates. Two of them are in Newport at Yaquina Head and Yaquina Bay, one at Reedsport's Umpqua River, and the most famous at Heceta Head north of Florence.

If you want more of the coast, you have to stay longer, and for that, the Dachsies recommend finding a private rental. For more than 30 pet-friendly properties for rent in Yachats, Waldport, Seal Rock, and other Central Coast locations, contact **Ocean Odyssey.** Pets are an additional $30 per pet per stay with a maximum of two pets. Cleaning up after your pets is especially vital,

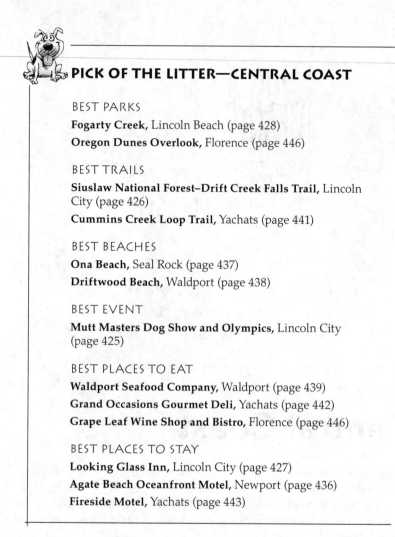

PICK OF THE LITTER—CENTRAL COAST

BEST PARKS
Fogarty Creek, Lincoln Beach (page 428)
Oregon Dunes Overlook, Florence (page 446)

BEST TRAILS
Siuslaw National Forest–Drift Creek Falls Trail, Lincoln City (page 426)
Cummins Creek Loop Trail, Yachats (page 441)

BEST BEACHES
Ona Beach, Seal Rock (page 437)
Driftwood Beach, Waldport (page 438)

BEST EVENT
Mutt Masters Dog Show and Olympics, Lincoln City (page 425)

BEST PLACES TO EAT
Waldport Seafood Company, Waldport (page 439)
Grand Occasions Gourmet Deli, Yachats (page 442)
Grape Leaf Wine Shop and Bistro, Florence (page 446)

BEST PLACES TO STAY
Looking Glass Inn, Lincoln City (page 427)
Agate Beach Oceanfront Motel, Newport (page 436)
Fireside Motel, Yachats (page 443)

as these are private homes. The office is in Clark's Market Plaza, 261 Hwy. 101, Yachats; 800/800-1915; www.ocean-odyssey.com (look for the pet icon on listings).

NATIONAL FORESTS AND RECREATION AREAS

Siuslaw National Forest
🐾🐾🐾🐾

The Siuslaw (Sigh-OOH-slaw) covers 630,000 acres from Tillamook to Coos Bay, bordered east–west by the Willamette Valley and the Pacific Ocean. Hardy Sitka spruce grow in the coastal zone, able to withstand ocean winds and dense fog. Inland, western hemlock grow under a thick canopy of Douglas fir. The "Trip Planning" section of the forest website, www.fs.fed.us/r6/siuslaw/ recreation, is an excellent way to find trails, campgrounds, swimming, and horseback riding opportunities. Hebo Ranger District: 503/392-5100.

Oregon Dunes National Recreation Area (ODNRA)

🐾🐾

The U.S. Forest Service manages a 47-mile sandbox between Florence and Coos Bay. While many use the dunes as a playground for off-highway vehicles (OHVs) or all-terrain vehicles (ATVs), approximately 27,200 of the park's 31,500 acres are reserved for people, dogs, and horses. The ODNRA Ranger Station is in Reedsport (Junction of Hwy. 101 and Hwy. 38; 541/271-3495 or 800/247-2155; www.reedsportcc.org).

Lincoln City

This coastal city is in the middle of everything. It's the halfway point between California and Washington, and it's on the 45th Parallel, the dividing line between the equator and the North Pole.

Lincoln City welcomes pets with open arms and good information about where to stay and local dog-oriented businesses. Call ahead for the Pet Friendly Vacation Guide, available at the visitors center (801 S.W. Hwy. 101; 541/996-1274; www.oregoncoast.org). You'll also want to grab a city map for 15 public beach access points along 14 miles of pristine beaches. The historic Taft District along S.W. 51st Street is a lively strip in town with the best outdoor food. Coop likes to practice his "arrgghh" at Captain Dan's Pirate Pastry Shop (5070 S.E. Hwy. 101 S.; 541/996-4600), while Isis prefers to "hang 20" for sunset barbecue at Tiki's (1005 S.W. 51st St.; 541/996-4200).

PARKS, BEACHES, AND RECREATION AREAS

🅱 Road's End

🐾🐾🐾 (See Central Coast map on page 420)

If you are on a mission to get to the beach, a couple of logs and some polished creek stones are all that separate you from the sand where the sidewalk ends. Then you're there, with the long-necked cormorants and sailboarders, on 14 miles of ocean stretching south through Lincoln City. There's only one catch: You have to fight for the right to park on busy summer weekends. A few picnic tables are placed in the parking lot, functional as opposed to scenic.

This State Recreation Site commemorates the end of the road for the Old Elk Trail, a route used by Native Americans for thousands of years to reach summer fishing grounds on the Pacific Ocean. From U.S. Highway 101, turn west on Logan Road and go to the end of the road. Open 6 A.M.–10 P.M.

DIVERSION

A little absence now and then can make the heart grow fonder. Renew your puppy love by giving you and her a break at the **Critter Cottage** in Lincoln City. Doggy day care is $15 per pup for 1–5 hours, and only $20 for up to 10 hours 8 A.M.–6 P.M., seven days a week and holidays. Overnight boarding is similarly well priced, and if she stays more than four days, they'll give your Bedlington a bath. You can also inquire about at-home pet sitting from Neskowin to Depoe Bay. Methods of payment are check with ID or cash only. 960 S.E. Hwy. 101; 541/996-7434; www.crittercomfortncare.com.

❷ Sand Point Park

(See Central Coast map on page 420)

Isis would be hard-pressed to choose a lakefront park when the ocean is so close, but this city park is a lovely place to enjoy the shores of Devil's Lake. There's a shady lawn—which you won't find on the beach—plus one picnic table in the sun and one in the shade. A wheelchair-accessible ramp leads down to a smidge of sand and a shallow swimming area. There's just enough room to launch a raft or do some dog paddling.

From U.S. Highway 101, turn at the north entrance to E. Devil's Lake Road and turn right onto Loop Road.

❸ Spring Lake Trail

(See Central Coast map on page 420)

About a mile's worth of hiking trails with spurs give your dog a hop, skip, and a jump through the woods around a pond in this open space. On your jaunt through a strand of birch trees with mossy limbs, you'll come to a sagging footbridge across the water and a few stairs. A portion of the trail goes up the ridgeline, too muddy and steep to tackle on the spring day we visited. All in all, just enough of a walk for the highway noise to die down.

Turn east on N.E. 14th Street from Highway 101. The trail marker is a quarter mile in on the north side, as 14th becomes West Devil's Lake Road, just west of Indian Shores and Regatta Grounds Park. There's pullout parking available for maybe three cars. Keep a tight leash for a few yards to get from the roadside to the trail.

❹ D River

(See Central Coast map on page 420)

At 120 feet, the shortest river in the Guinness Book of World Records doesn't need more than a single letter to name it. D River connects Devil's Lake to

DOG-EAR YOUR CALENDAR

Lincoln City's **Mutt Masters Dog Show and Olympics** celebrates our companions in ways that we can appreciate everyday, without having to worry about coiffure or conformation. Contests include best singing dog, tail wag champ, biggest ears, fastest eater, kid-dog look-alikes, and the sweetest smoocher. Come, sit, and stay in Lincoln City and strut your mutt at Mutt Masters. Usually held in late April or early May. It's a measly $2 per dog, $2 per parent, kids under 12 free. 541/996-1274 or 800/452-2151; www.oregoncoast.org.

the ocean at this tremendously popular city beach. The parking lot is akin to the mall at the holiday season, with cars jockeying for position. There's so little room off the sand that people hold impromptu tailgate picnics out of their car trunks.

If you are looking for some action, this state wayside is your beach. There are kites flying, beach volleyball games, families, kids squealing and running in the surf, boogie boarding, bubble blowing, you name it. D River is so reliably windy that the world's largest kite festivals are held here every spring and fall. It is a fun place, one you can escape a little bit by walking up to seven miles in either direction. People are very good about having their dogs on leash in this unpredictable environment.

The "D" is on U.S. Highway 101 in the middle of Lincoln City.

🐾 Siletz Bay

🐾🐾🐾 (See Central Coast map on page 420)

This city park is another people-packed destination. The gentle waters are protected by a sand spit, making them ideal for light canoeing, or for little tykes to toddle around in. Tough dogs can always walk around the bend to the north to reach the serious waves. It gets pretty muddy at low tide.

If you are lucky enough to find a spot, you can park along 51st Street, a popular restaurant and shopping strip paralleling the north side of the bay. That way, you can grab some chowder at Mo's or an ice cream cone at Eleanor's Undertow. There is a tiny patch of lawn and a covered picnic table in the city park at the entrance to 51st Street.

The Siletz Bay National Wildlife Refuge extends nearly the entire length of the bay along the east side of the highway. Trails, viewing platforms, and other opportunities for public use are in the planning stages. In the meantime, you can enjoy views of the salt grasses and brackish marsh from the road.

6 Siuslaw National Forest–Drift Creek Falls Trail

🐾🐾🐾🐾 (See Central Coast map on page 420)

Chipmunks, scurry for your life, 'cause Cooper's coming! Everyone we talked to in town recommended this 1.5-mile trail as a great dog walk. The hike packs a big punch for little effort. It's the pride and joy of the Hebo Ranger District, well maintained with gravel and hard-pack. A mild slope takes you down to a 240-foot suspension bridge looking out over a 75-foot, free-flowing waterfall. Your dogs will love the journey and you'll appreciate the reward at the trail's destination.

The drive to get there takes all the work, along 10 miles of twisty, one-lane road. At least it's paved. From U.S. Highway 101, 0.25 mile south of Lincoln City, turn west on Drift Creek Road. At the next intersection, bear right to stay on Drift Creek, then, for the next 11 miles, turn or bear left at every intersection and Y in the road to stay on Forest Road 17 until you see the large parking lot, vault toilet, and trailhead. Parking is $5. 503/392-3161.

PLACES TO EAT

Beach Dog Café: This joint serves dressed-up dogs to humans and human-shaped treats to dogs. Build your own bratwurst, kielbasa, kosher, and veggie dogs and chat with the owner who sidelines as the local paper's food and wine critic. Beach dog breakfasts feature specialty house potatoes, omelets, and pancakes. 1226 S.W. 50th St.; 541/996-3647.

Eleanor's Undertow: This café and ice cream parlor is hard to miss, with its bright pink building, 20-foot-tall candy canes, and mermaid fountain. The list of indulgences is long, including quarter-pound chocolate chip cookies, saltwater taffy, and anything you can make with ice cream. 869 S.W. 51st St.; 541/996-3800.

McMenamins Lighthouse Brewpub: The four tables on the lower deck only, which is basically the smoking section on the sidewalk out front, is one of your few dinner choices in town if you've got a dog in tow. Luckily, the Lighthouse serves up decent chow featuring hot sandwiches and pizza, famous brews, and Edgefield wines. Now that's the spirit. Colorable kid menu with crayons provided for the under-21 set. 4157 N. Hwy. 101; 541/994-7238; www.mcmenamins.com.

Sun Garden Café and Cyber Garden: Two restaurants in one, with soothing atmospheres to counteract the caffeine and the hum of the computers in the cyber section. The café side of the house serves fresh, vegetarian-only dishes. There is a tiny garden out back and abundant outdoor seating in front. 1816 and 1826 N.E. Hwy. 101; coffee house: 541/994-3067, café: 541/557-1800.

PLACES TO STAY

Coast Inn Bed and Breakfast: Pets, at least those who can remain off the furniture, are allowed in the Cordova Cottage Suite of this restored 1930s

Craftsman-style home. The room, with a private entrance from the front lawn, embraces the beach theme, with light periwinkle walls, a ceiling fan, and a tropical scene painted on the wall. It's $135 per night, with a refundable $25 cleaning deposit. 4507 S.W. Coast Ave.; 541/994-7932 or 888/994-7932; www.oregoncoastinn.com.

Ester Lee Motel: Each vintage 1940s unit is unique at this homespun property that proudly advertises its pet-friendliness as far away as Portland. Up to two pets are allowed, in the cottages only, for $9 per pet per night. Each unit has the comforts of a kitchen, gas fireplace, and fantastic views. Most have showers; ask for one with a tub if you want it. Prices range from a low season $55 studio rate up to a two-bedroom for $160 in the summer. 3803 S.W. Hwy. 101; 888/996-3606; www.esterlee.com.

Looking Glass Inn: The wood-shingled buildings, gazebo, and outdoor picnic area lend this little inn a warm, breezy feeling, matched by the exceedingly pet-friendly staff. Dogs are given a basket with extra towels, bones, and a monogrammed bowl that you can keep for $5. Spacious rooms are a block from Siletz Bay in the lively Historic Taft District. Room rates are $80–140 (plus a gorgeous suite for up to $240); the dog fee is $10. 861 S.W. 51st St.; 541/996-3996 or 800/843-4940; www.lookingglass-inn.com.

Sea Horse Lodging and Vacation Rentals: If the fabulous views and feel-good comfort of the Sea Horse Motel don't do it for you, rent one of the private vacation homes with ocean views and/or private backyards. Motel rates are $90–200, less mid-week during winter; pets stay free in select rooms. Homes that sleep four to six people are described on the website along with restrictions and rates. Pets are $10 extra. 1301 N.W. 21st St.; 541/994-2101 or 800/662-2101; www.seahorsemotel.com.

More Accommodations: Please look under *Chain Hotels* in the *Resources* section for additional places to stay in this area.

Gleneden Beach

Gleneden is pronounced as though it were two words, Glen Eden, the latter the same as the garden of Adam and Eve. It is a fitting name for an idyllic ocean village and its pretty beach. On the north end of the Gleneden Beach loop, turn west on Laurel Street to the end to find a public beach access point with a couple of parking spaces.

PARKS, BEACHES, AND RECREATION AREAS

7 Gleneden Beach
🐾🐾🐾 (See Central Coast map on page 420)

Wet-suited surfers come out in the morning to catch the best waves at this State Recreation Site with a quieter, more serious reputation, a 10-minute drive away from the craziness of Lincoln City. The surf is strong and the drop-off into the water is fairly steep. Joggers and their dogs take to the level, coarse sand above the high-tide line. Seals bob in and out of the surf, searching for supper. Cascade Head looms to the north and flanking you on either side of the beach are ochre sandstone cliffs, a fitting backdrop for a foggy morning beach walk or lovely evening sunset. There's a big parking lot with restrooms and picnic tables on a fenced hillside and landscaped lawns. Cooper prefers this reflective solitude, reached by a paved path through a grove of shore pines.

From U.S. Highway 101 seven miles south of Lincoln City, turn west on Wessler Street, the Gleneden Beach Loop, and follow the signs.

PLACES TO STAY

Salishan Lodge: A luxury golf resort and spa, Salishan captures that particular Northwest flair for cedar and stone and muted colors that complement the lush green of the links and surrounding forest. It's a lovely setting, if a bit large and impersonal. Traditional rooms range $200–250 and deluxe rooms with gas fireplaces and private balconies are $250–275. Pets, who are $25 each per stay, receive a letter with treats, beds, bowls, a generous roll of bags, and a guide to the running loops, beach access points, and nature trails on the 350-acre property. 7760 Hwy. 101 N.; 541/764-2371 or 800/452-2300; www.salishan.com.

Lincoln Beach

PARKS, BEACHES, AND RECREATION AREAS

8 Fogarty Creek

🐾🐾🐾🐾 (See Central Coast map on page 420)

A dog can learn to love this State Recreation Area, with acres of grass to sink his claws into and an abundance of bunny rabbits to chase. We like the large, protected areas of grouped picnic tables, places to get together with family, set up day camp, talk, and eat. The trouble with many other oceanfront parks is that there are no decent places to have a meal without getting sand in your food and other places we won't mention. You can reach these picnic areas from two parking lots, over the creek on wooden footbridges, through the Sitka spruce and Western hemlock.

To top it all off, there is a trail to an ocean cove, where the creek meets the sea. The beach is famous for bird-watching and observing tide pools, and it has the allure of steep headlands on either side and offshore rock formations. There can be lots of seaweed onshore, which you may not adore, but will keep your saluki's snoot occupied for hours.

Turn east off U.S. Highway 101 into either the north or south parking lots, two miles north of Depoe Bay. Parking is $3. Open 6 A.M.–10 P.M.

PLACES TO STAY

Pana Sea Ah Bed and Breakfast: The accessible downstairs Cozy Suite allows pets at this multilevel contemporary home across the street from Lincoln Beach. The interior is refined, and sunsets through banks of windows in the drawing room are divine. The fee is $120–150, plus a $25 fee per stay. There's hot and cold water outside the front door, use of beach towels, and easy access to a beautiful three-mile-long beach. 4028 Lincoln Ave.; 541/764-3368; www.panaseah.com.

Depoe Bay

The main beach access points are four miles north and south, so this seaside resort plays up the fact that you can watch migrating whales from vantage points along the city sidewalk on a rocky cliff above the ocean. Sure enough, Cooper and Isis saw their first gray whale nearby at Boiler Bay. In addition to gray whales that travel between summers in Alaska and winters in California, there are several hundred that hang out around the Oregon Coast year-round, not bothering to migrate.

Depoe Bay brags about having the smallest navigable port in the world, spouting water horns that shoot water geysers above the seawall promenade, and a street full of boutique shopping.

PARKS, BEACHES, AND RECREATION AREAS

9 Boiler Bay

🐾🐾🐾 (See Central Coast map on page 420)

The rusting hulk of a boiler that lends its name to this State Scenic Viewpoint can be seen at low tide, where it rests after the 1910 explosion of the steam schooner *J. Marhoffer.* Before U.S. Highway 101 cut through the cliffs, these steam ships transported people along the coastline.

Coop 'n' Isis saw their first gray whale from this bluff, trolling the bay for its shrimp dinner. Averaging 45 feet long and 35 tons in weight, a gray is a baleen whale, with fringed plates in its mouth to gather and filter its food from the mud, sand, and water. The whale slurps up an area of the seafloor about the size of a desk, filters out the junk, and scoops the amphipods off the roof of its mouth with its tongue, much in the same way your dog sucks peanut butter off the roof of his mouth. If you train your binoculars to the north for a moment, you'll see Lincoln City.

Boiler Bay has restrooms, a sunny picnic meadow, and a loop parking lot. Off U.S. Highway 101 a mile north of Depoe Bay.

PLACES TO EAT

Bay Station Café: Ready-to-serve breakfast is what the folks at Bay Station call their specialty; Coop 'n' Isis call it the best of the brunch buffet to go. Choose from eggs, biscuits and gravy, bacon and sausage, Belgian waffles, hash browns and country potatoes, cinnamon rolls and coffee cake, all until 10:30 A.M. For lunch, switch over to daily soups, chili, and salads. If it's any indication, and it usually is, the place is always packed with locals. Sorry, no outdoor seating. 433 N. Hwy. 101; 541/765-3430; www.baystationcafe.com.

Java Bean Espresso: The scones are unbelievably good, the coffee is hot, and the club is a major dog hangout. Help yourself to the water bowl and jar of dog biscuits by the door and get your dog's picture taken for the Mutt Mug bulletin board. 26 N.E. Hwy. 101; 541/765-3023.

PLACES TO STAY

Inn at Arch Rock: Rooms at the inn are crisp and suitably beachy with light woods and wicker. The setting is superb, perched above the ocean and rock formations. Rooms 6–8 allow pets; rates range $120–140 per night, plus a $10 pet fee. It's a good price that includes a continental breakfast, ocean views, and wooden deck chairs on the lawn overlooking the bay. 70 Sunset N.W.; 541/765-2560; www.innatarchrock.com.

Trollers Lodge: At this bright hotel, each suite has a different personality, looking more like mini–summer homes than rooms. They accept pets in three oceanfront cottages and in all suites except numbers 8, 9, and 11; and three oceanfront cottages. Pets are $10 extra in rooms, $15 in oceanfront homes. Call ahead to find out which suite is appropriate for your size and number of pets. Room rates are $65–100. 355 S.W. Hwy. 101; 541/765-2287; www.trollerslodge.com.

Otter Rock and Cape Foulweather

Mother Nature was having a bit of a spat on March 7, 1778, when English explorer Captain James Cook rounded the headland and named it Cape Foulweather. His published accounts aroused interest in the area, and the fur trade came soon after. Now, everyone refers to this area by its most prominent offshore formation.

PARKS, BEACHES, AND RECREATION AREAS

🔟 Devil's Punch Bowl

🐾 🐾 (See Central Coast map on page 420)

The various parts of this State Natural Area are spread out, offering more choices than are apparent at first glance. After turning onto Otter Crest Loop and then west on 1st Street, everyone heads to the overlook to see the geological formation that churns, swirls, and foams with sea water during high tide. From the windblown picnic tables above, you can also catch the action of the surfers to the south on Beverly Beach. Across the street are Mo's Chowder House, a local winery tasting room, and an ice cream truck.

Once you've filled your stomach and absorbed the views, take your dog to the beach and tide pools. Turn right onto C Avenue before the viewpoint, and park at the lot at 2nd Street and C Avenue to find a paved path and stairs to the Marine Garden. At low tide, you can climb over the rocks into the Punchbowl, where there are all kinds of sea creatures clinging to the rocks at dog nose level. A small lawn and restrooms are located on 1st Street between B and C Avenues.

From U.S. Highway 101, you can turn onto Otter Crest Loop from the north or south, approximately eight miles north of Newport.

PLACES TO EAT

Mo's West: People have been chowing down on Mo's clam chowder since the late 1960s. Today, the chain produces 500,000 gallons a year for various locations and grocery stores. Cups of the famous concoction come with every shrimp and oyster sandwich or dinner platter. Elbow your way through, get your food to go, and take your chowder hound across the street to Devil's Punchbowl picnic tables. 122 1st St.; 541/765-2442; www.moschowder.com.

Siletz

Pronounced with a soft "I," as in windowsill, this small community of about 1,500 people is the home of the Confederated Tribes of Siletz Indians.

PARKS, BEACHES, AND RECREATION AREAS

11 Moonshine Park

🐾🐾 (See Central Coast map on page 420)

For those times when the ocean is just too windy or noisy or cold or wet or whatever, come inland to escape. At this county park on the Upper Siletz River, tent sites with fireplaces and picnic tables are scattered on an 18-acre site, around a couple of decent open spaces for games of fetch. There's a boat launch and restroom facilities with drinkable water. Spend some quality time snooping around the area for the many swimming and fishing holes along this stretch of freshwater.

To reach this secluded spot, take Highway 229 to Siletz. Turn east onto Logsden Road and drive 7.5 miles to the Logsden Store. Cross the bridge and turn left onto Moonshine Park Road, and go another four miles to the park gateway.

Newport

Newport is the largest and reputedly friendliest city in the area, home of the Oregon Coast Aquarium and the Hatfield Marine Science Center. As Newport grew into a major commercial center, the character of its original neighborhoods was preserved in the Nye Beach promenade, with its art galleries, performing arts, and shops; and along the Historic Bayfront, which makes for a fun walk or drive, complete with unique shops and shamelessly cheesy Ripley's Believe It or Not, the Wax Works, and an Undersea Garden tucked in among legit seafood processing plants.

PARKS, BEACHES, AND RECREATION AREAS

🔟 Beverly Beach
🐾🐾🐾🐾 (See Central Coast map on page 420)

This state park is a zoo, no doubt because it is such a great beach. First of all, it is vast, extending from Yaquina Head to Otter Rock. The sand is soft and pliable for sandcastle building, the winds are strong and reliable for kite flying, and, on the north end of the beach, the waves are prime for surfers and kiteboarders. On a typical day, entire clans set up camp above the high-tide line.

DIVERSIONS

Stop by these fine establishments so you can answer in the affirmative when your dog cocks her head and gives you that look that says, "Did you bring me something?"

Paws on the Sand: Pets are welcome to shop with their people at Patty's boutique, which has been in Lincoln City for decades. She carries premium food lines as well as collars for every occasion, collar charms, bumper stickers, and signs that declare your canine tendencies to the world. 1640 N.E. Hwy. 101, Lincoln City; 541/996-6019.

Bella's Pet Boutique: Cashmere sweaters, beautiful necklaces, health and beauty aids, furniture, boating and camping equipment . . . yes, we're talking about a pet store, one that carries anything your little doggy's heart desires, and many wonderful things she never knew she desired. Bella's would be right at home on New York's 5th Avenue or L.A.'s Rodeo Drive. Lucky for you, it's on the beach. 1688 N. Hwy. 101, SeaTowne Courtyard, Newport; 541/574-8600.

Raindogs: Although mostly a people store, this great shop has a few toys and treats for your best friend, which is as good an excuse as any to come in for the unique jewelry, books, gifts, bath and body products, and so on for yourself. Raindogs has accumulated an eclectic selection that somehow just fits. 162 Beach St., Yachats; 541/547-3000; www.raindogsonline.com.

Reigning Cats and Dogs: This shop carries an unashamed extravagance of pillows, towels, stationery, and anything you can think of geared toward humans' celebration of their pets, and the largest selection of breed-specific gifts. 1384 Bay St., Old Town Florence; 541/997-8982.

If your dog can handle all this added stimulus, camp in one of Beverly Beach's 277 tree-sheltered spots and stay a while.

The day-use parking lot is to the left, just north of the campground entrance. A few picnic tables are practically in the parking lot, intended mainly for gulping down a bologna and cheese sandwich before running back to the beach. For a change of pace, there is a 0.75-mile creek trail that starts behind the gift shop.

Beverly Beach is seven miles north of Newport on U.S. Highway 101. Open 6 A.M.–10 P.M. 198 N.E. 123rd St.; 541/265-9278.

13 Yaquina Head

🐾🐾🐾 (See Central Coast map on page 420)

Yaquina Head (Yah-KWIN-nah) is an Outstanding Natural Area. That's not how the dogs rate it, that's its official name. It was formed by flowing lava around 14 million years ago, and the lighthouse perched on its outermost point is the tallest on the Oregon Coast, at 93 feet tall and 162 feet above sea level. The light, now automated, aids navigation along the coast and into Yaquina Bay. Call 541/574-3100 for visiting information (without your pooch).

There are five trails exploring the wildlife preserve, and your $5 pass is good for three days, so you should be able to do them all, except for the one around the lighthouse, which is off-limits to dogs. The walks are short, each less than a mile, and the steepest ones reward your efforts with great views.

Yaquina is full of noisy life, especially the thousands of squawking birds nesting on Colony Rock and the barking harbor seals on Seal Island. Another unique sound is the water tossing and tumbling beach cobbles, polished fragments of boiling hot lava that exploded upon impact with the cold water. About the time the Wieners hit Yaquina Head, they realized a common thread among Oregon beaches: They are windy, very and often. Birds taking off into a headwind fly backwards.

Yaquina Head is about 3.5 miles north of Newport on U.S. Highway 101. Open dawn–dusk.

14 Don Davis Park

🐾🐾🐾 (See Central Coast map on page 420)

This city beach park was rated by *Sunset Magazine* as the most romantic on the coast. Dogs don't know much about that; after all, their idea of romance is having you rub their tummies. For strolling couples, there are thought-provoking sculptures and built-in viewing benches along a stone paver pathway and rock wall that arches gracefully down to the beach. It's lighted at night by a host of lamps embedded along the walkway, which was built in honor of Vietnam veterans.

The icing on the cake is an indoor ocean-viewing conservatory, with wall-to-wall windows and cozy benches safe from the spray and freezing rain. It's the only public one on the coast, a choice place to watch sunsets and winter storms. Quiet, reflective dogs may join you in the rotunda.

From U.S. Highway 101, turn west on Olive Street to the end.

15 Yaquina Bay
😺😺 (See Central Coast map on page 420)

This State Recreation Site is the place to come for views. Of course, there is the ocean, which you can see even from the loop drive and parking areas. From the viewing platform, you can watch sailboats, speed craft, and commercial vessels navigating a constructed jetty system at the outlet of the bay into the sea. Towering above you is the historic Yaquina Bay Bridge, built in 1936, and behind you on the top of the bluff is the lighthouse.

The Yaquina Bay Lighthouse was lit for a mere three years, from 1871 to 1874, before it was outshone by its brighter neighbor to the north, at Yaquina Head. It experienced a second life of fame in a *Pacific Monthly* story from 1899, when Lischen Miller wrote about resident ghost Muriel in "The Haunted Lighthouse." In years since, it has been called to service as a Coast Guard lifeboat station and is now open for tours. Call 541/574-3129 or visit ww.yaquinalights.org for information.

Getting to the beach is a workout, first down a steep hill with several flights of stairs, and then through deep sand mounds before you reach the easygoing, hard-packed sand at the tide line. The park also has a playground, one of the few on the central coast; a fishermen's memorial sanctuary; and picnic tables in forested spruce and pine.

The entrance is immediately north of the Bay Bridge. Open 6 A.M.–10 P.M.

16 Mike Miller Park
😺😺😺 (See Central Coast map on page 420)

Between you, me, and the trees, Cooper gets tired of all these beautiful ocean beaches after a while. So, he'd like to thank the former parks commissioner Miller personally for such a great county park that packs a bunch of mini-ecosystems into a one-mile loop. The low-grade gravel path is an interpretive trail through a Sitka spruce forest, past old beaches, logging sites, and railway remains. While you read the brochure that corresponds to the numbered posts along the path, your dog will decipher the scent patterns left by local wildlife. In such a hustle-and-bustle beach town, this walk is a place of peace and quiet.

The educational trail is 1.2 miles south of the Yaquina Bay Bridge, at S.E. 50th Street on the east side of U.S. Highway 101. There's room for a couple of cars to park alongside the road.

17 South Beach
😺😺😺😺 (See Central Coast map on page 420)

This state park has a lot going on. At the north end of the park are horse trails, as well as surfing, scuba diving, and windsurfing for the very skilled. For $15 per person, kayak tours are booked at South Beach, launching five miles south at Ona Beach. The Oregon Coast Aquarium and Hatfield Marine Science Center are within walking distance of the park, and a hospitality store and information center are on the grounds, as well as a campground with 227 sites for RVers and seven primitive tent sites that are first come, first served for $9 per night.

In a dog's world, the best things in the park are free: miles of windswept beach and multiple park trails to explore. After a bit of a drive from the highway, turn left to reach the picnic area, restrooms, and beach. The Cooper Ridge Nature Trail is a 1.75-mile sandy loop around the perimeter of the campground, our Cooper's favorite because it's protected from high winds. The South Jetty Trail is an accessible, 10-foot-wide paved pathway that's two miles to the bay wall and back through the dunes. The Old Jetty trail is the least traveled, a wilder path that picks its way through shore pine and beach grasses. The trails are the best way to escape the park's summer crowds, especially the school buses that spit out dozens of summer camp kids primed to get rowdy.

South Beach is two miles south of Newport on U.S. Highway 101. 5580 S. Hwy. 101; 541/867-4715.

PLACES TO EAT

Café Stephanie: Three mini–picnic tables sit on the sidewalk outside a cute house on the quaint Historic Nye Beach loop. The lunch menu is consistently good with hot and cold sandwiches, fish tacos, and turkey wraps. Breakfast changes daily, featuring quiches, breakfast burritos, crepes, and homemade granola. 411 Coast St.; 541/265-8082.

Local Ocean Seafood: The LOS's sidewalk tables are perfect observation points for people and boat traffic going by. With all the things with fins, shells, and claws on ice in the case, you may be convinced that heaven is an underwater kingdom. Roasted garlic and lightly seared are adjectives to seek out on the daily fresh sheet. 213 S.E. Bay Blvd.; 541/574-7959; www.localocean.net.

Rogue Ales Public House: The vice president of this regionally famous brew pub is a black Lab named Brewer. Until the pub got called to the carpet by health inspectors, dogs were allowed everywhere. Now, your pal is limited to being hitched outside the beer garden fence. He'll still be treated as a special guest, with a personal water bowl and dog menu that includes pigs' ears, among other things. 748 S.W. Bay Blvd.; 541/265-3188; www.rogue.com.

South Beach Fish Market: Some of the best seafood you'll find anywhere is sold from this unassuming building attached to a convenience store, which is why it's hard to get a snout in edgewise at the white picnic tables on the parking lot patio. You'll sit next to the stew pots steaming with clams, oysters, mussels, and crabs. The market folks also smoke their own salmon, albacore, and oysters. If you want something waiting for you at home, they ship next-day to anywhere in the United States. 3640 S.W. Hwy. 101; 866/816-7716; www.southbeachfishmarket.com.

PLACES TO STAY

Agate Beach Oceanfront Motel: Owner Maynard calls his classic 1940s carport motel a little piece of paradise, with a $50,000 stairway to heaven down to the beach. It's a great discovery, with a protected lawn for room to run. Every unit welcomes one or two pets for an extra $10 per night. Says Maynard, "When people with pet allergies call, I simply apologize, because I can't turn down a friend with a pet in any of my rooms." Those rooms are lovingly restored and well kept, with ocean views, kitchens, and decks. Queen-size-bed rooms are $100–150, suites are $150–170. 175 N.W. Gilbert Way; 541/265-8746 or 800/755-5674; www.agatebeachmotel.com.

Driftwood Village Motel: Cooper and Isis fell in love with the owner of this motel, who obviously cares deeply about animals. He's added that friendly touch to this nine-room motel, where dogs are welcome everywhere. What it has are profoundly excellent oceanfront views at prices almost unheard of on the coast. What it doesn't have is glamour or pretense. Doesn't have? Stylish decor. Has? Private trail straight to the beach. Rates are $65 low end, topping out at $160; one-time $10 pet fee. 7947 N. Coast Hwy.; 541/265-5738; www.driftwoodvillagemotel.com.

Hallmark Resort: This super-sized, cheerful, oceanfront resort prefers to put dogs and their people in first-floor rooms with walk-out patios to the backyard and immediate access to the beach trail. Deluxe rooms (fireplace, spa, and kitchen) top out at $185; standard rooms at $140, plus a $15 dog fee. 744 S.W. Elizabeth; 888/448-4449; www.hallmarkinns.com.

Melva Company Vacation Rentals: Linda Lewis rents two absolutely stunning three-bedroom, two-bath vacation homes, one here in South Beach on a bluff, and another in Waldport directly on the beach. Both have fully fenced yards, and pets are welcome for a $200 fully refundable security deposit. Her business is too small to have a website, but if you call her, she'll mail you photographs, and we bet you'll be sold on them. Rates are $225 per night; ask about mid-week winter discounts. 503/678-1144.

Beverly Beach Campground: Sites are surprisingly private and quiet considering how huge the campground is, with an even split of 128 tent sites and 128 RV sites. Tent sites are in their own loops (C, D, and E) in the spruce to the east of the highway. Reservations well in advance are a must at this desirable park. Rates are $13–22; 800/452-5687; www.reserveamerica.com.

More Accommodations: Please look under *Chain Hotels* in the *Resources* section for additional places to stay in this area.

Seal Rock

The town of Seal Rock was platted in 1887, and a large hotel was built at the end of the Corvallis and Yaquina Bay Wagon Road, the first road to reach the coast from the Willamette Valley. None of the early development remains from land transferred over to the railroads in the 1890s and then by default to nature when the locomotives ceased their locomotion.

PARKS, BEACHES, AND RECREATION AREAS

18 Ona Beach

🐾🐾🐾🐾 (See Central Coast map on page 420)

Developed on a forested ocean flat around several tributaries of the Beaver Creek Estuary, this state park is a varied and interesting place to bring dogs. There's more room to relax than at most oceanfront spots. Pick your pleasure of the plentiful meadows under the protection of tall spruce trees, sheltered from the windy and wilder beach.

Ona has an accessible, paved trail to the ocean, ending in a wooden footbridge crossing above the creek. Where it empties into the river, the creek forms a shallow pool that's a good play place for younger children. Behind you and to the south are high sandstone cliffs.

Kayak tours of Beaver Creek are available. The boat launch is across the highway from the entrance to the park, on N. Beaver Creek Road. You can register and pay for the tours at South Beach State Park five miles north; call 541/867-4715.

Ona Beach is one mile north of Seal Rock on U.S. Highway 101.

19 Seal Rock

🐾🐾 (See Central Coast map on page 420)

There is no single rock formation that is Seal Rock; there is, however, one known as Elephant Rock, the largest of many interesting geological formations with exposed faults sitting offshore. There are plenty of live seals, sea lions, and sea birds; a great place to observe the active wildlife is the paved path along a high cliff of the shoreline and from two accessible viewing platforms.

Dogs get bored with watching, tending to tug you to the steep, switchback trail down to the beach. When the moon is full, pulling the tides farther out to sea, you can walk across the stones and driftwood to play among the rocks and get a closer look at the birds and the tide pool life. This is when the beach gets busier with people harvesting littleneck clams and seaweed, the good stuff that holds your sushi together. Otherwise, the slice of sand you can walk is somewhat cramped. The picnic area and restrooms are in a strand of shore pine, salal, and spruce.

Seal Rock is 10 miles south of Newport on U.S. Highway 101.

PLACES TO EAT

Kadi's Fudge: Get summer's four food groups here—caramel corn, ice cream, cookies, and homemade fudge—in a cute, tiny red building with seagull shutters and a couple of porch tables. Come on, you gotta have fudge. 10449 N.W. Pacific Hwy; 541/563-4918.

Waldport

South of busy Newport is this quieter, gentler town where it's easy to enjoy yourself for little or no money. Fishing and clamming are popular, and there is a free crabbing dock. Stop at the Alsea Bay Bridge Interpretive Center to learn about Conde B. McCullough, Oregon's most famous engineer. He designed and built many art-deco bridges along the coast in the 1930s. All are still in use, except the Alsea Bay Bridge in Waldport, which has been reconstructed true to his artistic vision.

PARKS, BEACHES, AND RECREATION AREAS

20 Driftwood Beach

🐾🐾🐾🐾 (See Central Coast map on page 420)

If Cooper and Isis had to choose their favorite place to reach the beach between Waldport and Yachats, this would be the one, with its perfect combination of nature and nurture. The nature comes in the form of five miles of wide, flat, unspoiled beach from Seal Rock to Alsea Bay. Despite the name, there's not too much driftwood, just enough to find the ultimate fetch stick. Nurture is in the details: a wheelchair-accessible path to the beach, flush toilets with changing areas, a large parking lot set back from the road, and two view picnic tables. Even from the parking lot, you have an uninterrupted view of the ocean.

Driftwood Beach is three miles north of Waldport on U.S. Highway 101. Open 6 A.M.–9 P.M.

21 Robinson Park on Alsea Bay

🐾 (See Central Coast map on page 420)

Pop in to this little park at Alsea Port at low tide and you might get to see the shrimp suckers in action. For 30 years, Alsea Bay's tidal flats have been a premier source of ghost shrimp, used not for human consumption but as bait for steelhead and salmon fishing. It's fun to watch the suction pumps mine the mud for these fish-tempting delicacies. You also have a great view of the Alsea Bridge, the harbor seals, and the brown pelicans that call the bay home. The park, funded in part by the National Oceanic and Atmospheric Administration, has protected picnic tables and easy bay access.

Turn east on Route 34 from U.S. Highway 101 and look for the Port Area sign, turning north on Broadway and west on Port Street. The park is on the far west side of the port, past the ramp and boat trailer parking.

22 Governor Patterson Beach

🐾🐾🐾 (See Central Coast map on page 420)

The state has gone to the trouble of doing some landscaping at this Memorial State Recreation Site, providing your pal with a good-sized lawn to sniff if he gets bored with the beach. Follow your nose to find the hidden picnic tables, each tucked into a private grove of thick dune vegetation, and most with great sea views. Several rough, short walkways take you to another fabulous swath of sand, running south from Alsea Bay for miles. Our only beef is that some of the lawns are too close to the highway for comfort.

The Guv'nor is one mile south of Waldport on U.S. Highway 101. Open 6 A.M.–9 P.M.

PLACES TO EAT

Sea Dog Bakery and Café: After she ate the "mess-a-puh-tatas" (herb roasted potatoes, onions, red peppers, cheese, and eggs) at the Sea Dog, Isis felt full, and fully justified in her bias toward any place that mentions her species. The folks at Sea Dog insist that real food tastes better, using natural and organic ingredients when available. Try the homemade granola with raisins and apricots. Sadly, there's no outdoor seating, so get it to go, and go the Guv', Governor Patterson Park that is. 180 Hwy. 101 at Willow, 541/563-3621.

Waldport Seafood Company: Same-day fresh shrimp, crab, oysters, and clams take center stage in soups, stews, sandwiches, and salads with homemade cocktail sauce and hot garlic toast. The tables out front are close to highway traffic; take your spoils of the sea and your ice cream out back to Kealy City Wayside on the bay. It's a Wi-Fi Hotspot; 310 S.W. Arrow St. (Hwy. 101); 541/563-4107; www.waldport-seafood-co.com.

PLACES TO STAY

Bayshore Rentals: This vacation service has an excellent selection of pet-friendly rentals in Waldport, Yachats, and more, typically for stays of three days to a week or more. Click the "Dog Friendly" link on the website or call 541/563-3162; www.bayshore-rentals.com.

Edgewater Cottages: Talk about location, location, location. If these nine cottages were any closer to the edge of the water, they'd be in it. All have sliding glass doors opening onto wind-protected sun decks, ocean views, beach access, kitchens, and fireplaces. They range from a tiny studio for two for $85 to a house that sleeps 14 for $315 per night, and any combination of "kids, dogs, and well-behaved adults" in between. They're popular enough to require a two-night minimum stay in the winter, up to a seven-night minimum July–September. Pets are $5–15 depending on the reservation. No credit cards. 3978 S.W. Hwy. 101; 541/563-2240; www.edgewatercottages.com.

Blackberry Campground: Oregon is famous for fat, juicy blackberries in late July through August. At this campground, 18 miles east of Waldport on Route 34, the only place that isn't plastered with prickly berry bushes is the area cleared for the sites and the boat ramp. Campsites are $15; the day-use fee is $5 per car. Sites #15–30 are along the river. Make reservations and get maps at the Waldport Ranger Station, 1094 S.W. Hwy. 101; 541/563-3211.

Yachats

Yachats (YAH-hots) is a laid-back village of 600 or so full-time residents, recently developing a reputation as a hotbed for artists and craftspeople. There remains less big-time tourist influence, more intimate lodging options and tiny shops with friendly owners. This charming community calls itself the Gem of the Coast, and the dogs agree, although they might express it as the Beef Marrow Bone with Peanut Butter Filling of the Coast, perhaps. Mountain scenery is unspoiled by development along miles of uninterrupted beaches. The section of U.S. Highway 101 between Yachats and Florence to the south is full of cliff-hugging, jaw-dropping oceanfront vistas and multiple highway pullouts for stopping and taking it all in. While here, take the one-mile Yachats Ocean Road scenic loop, and also stop by the Strawberry Hill and Bob Creek viewpoints.

PARKS, BEACHES, AND RECREATION AREAS

23 Smelt Sands

🐾🐾🐾 (See Central Coast map on page 420)

This turbulent section of coastline is designed not for playing in the surf, but for watching the surf play among the rocks and headlands. There are multiple blowholes, where waves crash up through holes carved in the rocks by thousands of years of water action.

Your dog will be content to join you on a sightseeing tour along the 804 Trail, a 0.75-mile, fine gravel path that is accessible for all users. Concerned citizens saved this piece of the former Road #804 for public enjoyment, and enjoy it they do, in large numbers. It's mere feet away from the crashing surf, and your pooch will meet lots of other dogs walking their owners along the way. Viewing benches along the trail give you front-row seats for divine ocean sunsets.

This State Recreation Site hosts the annual Smelt Fry in July, when you can watch thousands of the small, silvery relatives of salmon called smelt jump into catcher's nets.

Turn west on Lemwick Lane from U.S. Highway 101 into the parking lot, on the north side of Yachats.

24 Cape Perpetua Scenic Area

🐾🐾🐾🐾 🔷 (See Central Coast map on page 420)

There are 11 scenic hiking trails in and around Cape Perpetua, from 0.25 mile to 10 miles long, with a little something for everyone. The Wonder Wieners recommend the one-mile round-trip Captain Cook Trail and the 0.4-mile Restless Waters Loop for great views of an ocean spouting horn and chasm wave action, as well as for exploring tide pools. About the only thing you can't do at the cape is get to miles of sandy beach, but you only need to go 0.25 mile south to Neptune for that.

The guide at the interpretive center, open 9 A.M.–5 P.M., recommends the longer 6.5-mile Cook's Ridge/Gwynn Creek Loop Trail to explore old growth Sitka, Douglas fir, and cedar trees. About 1.5 miles in on the trail is an area called the Dog Hair Forest, where the trees grow so close and thick it looks like the hair on a komondor's back.

The Cape Perpetua Overlook is the highest viewpoint on the coast, and the U.S. Forest Service brags that it's also the best. A 1930s stone shelter, built for scouting enemy ships and planes during WWII, is used as a whale-watching lookout.

The entrance to the visitors center is three miles south of Yachats; it and the other areas of the park are well marked along U.S. Highway 101. Parking is $5.

25 Cummins Creek Loop Trail

🐾🐾🐾🐾🐕 (See Central Coast map on page 420)

The Cummins Creek Trail is a highlight of any journey down the coast. Dappled sunlight filters through mossy branches, presenting multiple opportunities for botanical photography. On a beautiful spring day on the level, gravel trail through a hushed forest, you might not meet up with anyone else, while the path you tread meets up with both the Oregon Coast Trail system and Cape Perpetua trails. It was only after making it to the visitors center that Cooper and Isis discovered that dogs are allowed off-leash on this one trail in the area. What a bonus!

It's 1.5 miles northbound to the Cape Perpetua visitors center from the trailhead. Along the way, you can break off to the east for a 6.25-mile loop. For even more exercise, walk as far as you want on the 10-mile loop that follows the ridgeline.

It's easy to reach the trailhead, 0.25 miles in on a dirt road with a clear sign off Highway 101 around mile 169, just north of the highway bridge between the two picnic areas of Neptune Beach. Even so close, there's no highway noise once you're on the trail.

26 Neptune Beach
🐾🐾🐾 (See Central Coast map on page 420)

Neptune North and Neptune South are one beach or two, depending on time and tide. At high tide, there are two slivers of sand to enjoy while you watch waves meet up with the reef. At low tide, which Isis prefers, you can walk from one beach to the other on firm, level sand, in and among the craggy formations. Just don't get caught in between as the tide is coming in.

The north parking lot of this State Scenic Viewpoint is not marked. It has one picnic table, a viewing bench, and a trail to the beach. The south parking lot is much larger, has restrooms, and stairs down to the sand. It is also set back farther from the highway and has a larger meadow for spreading out a blanket. Cummins Creek is a shallow stream that empties into the sea at the south beach.

Neptune is three miles south of Yachats on U.S. Highway 101.

PLACES TO EAT

Drift Inn: Order food to go from this restaurant and pub recommended by the folks at Fireside Motel. All the family dining staples are on hand for breakfast, lunch, and dinner. Live music, craft beers, and a full-service bar are available inside if you can score a dog-sitter. 124 Hwy. 101; 541/547-4477.

Grand Occasions Gourmet Deli: They must have perfected things on the catering side of the business and brought only the best into the café, and certainly the food tasted even better at outdoor wine barrel tables, overlooking the mouth of the Yachats River as it empties into the ocean. Coop can recommend the prosciutto on sourdough with mozzarella, greens, and vinaigrette. 84 Beach St.; 541/547-4409.

PLACES TO STAY

Ambrosia Gardens Bed and Breakfast: The Carriage House, up the stairs above the garage of this contemporary home, is a kid- and dog-friendly place with a full kitchen. Mary requests that there be no smoking, no pets in the bedding, and no peeing on the flowers. Her green thumb nurtures three acres of gardens around the house, and National Forest land is to the east and south for hiking. Take in the view of Sea Rose Beach across the highway from the outdoor hot tub. Rooms are $125 per night; no pet fee. 95435 Hwy. 101; 541/547-3013; www.ambrosia-gardens.com.

Fireside Motel: At this large motel, the rooms are predictable, yet it has many attributes which will impress the family pets. The buildings are set among a grove of trees with lawns and picnic tables. Steps from your patio door is the 804 walking trail with its tide pools and sandy ocean coves. The rocky coastline views are dramatic, with waves crashing into spray foam against giant boulders. The staff is ultra-friendly and the pet package includes towels and treats and pickup bags. Decent rates for view rooms range $90–140, non-view rooms start as low as $70, plus a $10 nightly fee per pet. 1881 Hwy. 101 N.; 800/336-3573; www.firesidemotel.com.

Shamrock Lodgettes: Pets are allowed in all of the seven vintage cozy cabins, in the modern Danish-influenced Sherwood House, all set in a four-acre park. Yachats Ocean Road Park is right outside your door along the bay. Prices start as low as $100 per night, up to $190, plus a $15 per pet per night fee; two-pet limit. 105 Hwy. 101 S.; 541/547-3312; www.shamrocklodgettes.com.

More Accommodations: Please look under *Chain Hotels* in the *Resources* section for additional places to stay in this area.

Florence

Florence is your spot for kitschy family fun. Break up the scenery with family bonding activities such as bumper boats, dune buggy rides, putt-putt golf, sea lion caves, and other goofy stuff. The Shell gas station in the center of town has buckets of dog biscuits next to the pumps. Head straight to Bay Street in Old Town Florence for the best local flavor, boutique shopping, and outdoor dining with dogs.

For more hikes and campgrounds than we have room to mention, stop by the Mapleton Ranger Station of the Siuslaw National Forest (4480 Hwy. 101; 541/902-8526). Avoid the Siltcoos Lake Recreation Area; when the dunes of this section aren't overrun by ATVs, they're off-limits for rare bird nesting. The best dune hikes are south of Florence. Keep in mind that distances are deceiving on the beach, longer than they look. Drink up! The wind wicks the moisture right out of you and your pets.

PARKS, BEACHES, AND RECREATION AREAS

27 Carl G. Washburn

🐾🐾🐾 (See Central Coast map on page 420)

What can we say? This memorial state park is yet another awesome beach along this stretch of coastline, with 1,100 acres, a big parking lot, large restrooms with changing areas, and surprise picnic tables hidden in the stunted trees of the fore dunes. U.S. Highway 101 bisects the park, with the campground

NATURE HIKES AND URBAN WALKS

Up and down the Oregon Coast there are so many geological formations named after the devil that Cooper and Isis wondered why the god of the underworld is so popular in Oregon. They may never know for sure, but they did hear a highly plausible explanation. The Native American inhabitants of the region believed that many spirits, evil and good, inhabited the natural world around them. The European settlers who arrived and translated these native place names into their language had only one. So Beelzebub became the default spirit given credit for the wilder aspects of the coast. Here's a sample of the wicked places where you can walk your dog.

Devil's Churn, Yachats

Devil's Elbow, Florence

Devil's Kitchen, Bandon

Devil's Lake, Lincoln City

Devil's Punch Bowl, Otter Rock

Seven Devils State Park, Bandon

to the east and the picnic area to the west. This beach is often foggy, with wisps of clouds clinging to the tops of the trees like cotton at Heceta Head to the south. You can take the China Creek Trail from the campground, which joins up with the Hobbit Trail and then the Heceta Head Trail, to travel the three miles down to the lighthouse.

This state park is located 14 miles north of Florence on U.S. Highway 101. 93111 Hwy. 101 N.; 541/547-3416.

28 Heceta Head Lighthouse

🐾🐾 🐾 (See Central Coast map on page 420)

The Heceta (Huh-SEE-duh) Lighthouse is the most photographed structure on the coast. Operational in 1894, it is perched on the brink of a 205-foot outcropping on 1,000-foot-high headland. The former keeper's quarters are in an equally picture-perfect building below. Common murres lay their eggs directly on the rocks offshore, and gray whales and their calves pass close by in May on migrations to Alaska.

A half-mile trail, with a gradual uphill incline, takes you to the lighthouse. Halfway up is a gift shop and the quarters, with a viewing bench that is perfect for a rest stop. Tucked into Devil's Elbow, the curve of land below the landmark, is a tiny crescent beach. Get up with the sun for an early session of wave chasing; otherwise, expect to share the trail and the beach with throngs of people.

The lighthouse is often open for tours, without your pet partner; call

541/547-3416 for information. Local tip: Pop into the bar for a beverage at Driftwood Shores Resort after playing on the beach at Heceta Head.

On U.S. Highway 101, 12 miles north of Florence. South of the park on the highway are several pullouts that offer the choicest areas to capture snapshots of the famous maritime building. Parking is $3.

29 Jessie M. Honeyman
🐾🐾🐾 (See Central Coast map on page 420)

Jessie was a spunky Scottish woman, a tireless advocate for the protection of Oregon's natural resources. At her memorial state park, it's tough to choose between the two major lakes, Woahink and Cleawox, so you might as well stay longer and enjoy both. The dogs might vote for the East Woahink picnic area, with its huge, rolling lawns and lengthy beachfront access, plenty of room for a dog to be a dog. It can be crowded with water sport enthusiasts.

You might prefer the more scenic and quiet Cleawox Lake, to the west of U.S. Highway 101 near the campground. Picnic tables are shaded in the woods and surrounded by high sand dunes, two miles of them between the lake and the ocean. Kids grab plastic saucer slides and sand boards to ride the dunes. There's a foot-rinse station that doubles as a dog wash.

Honeyman is two miles south of Florence on U.S. Highway 101. Parking is $3. Open 8 A.M.–8 P.M. 84505 Hwy. 101 S.; 541/997-3641.

30 Oregon Dunes Overlook

😽 😽 😽 🐾 (See Central Coast map on page 420)

The first marvel at this roadside stop are elevated platforms, with wheelchair-accessible ramps, that provide you with bird's eye views of the dunes and the ocean beyond. From there, a three-mile loop trail takes you first up and over the dunes, and then through coastal woods to the beach. The first half mile of this trail is also paved for accessibility. On the sand, the sky is so blue it hurts; think sunscreen, sunglasses, and extra water. Until you reach the forested fore dune, the only way to know you're on the right path is to follow the posts topped with blue bands.

As little as a hundred years ago the area was nothing but sand, until settlers planted the aggressive European beach grass in the 1920s to stabilize the shifting landscape. This led to quick development of the other vegetation you see today. If you're not accustomed to hiking through sand, you might need some sports cream for your calves later.

The overlook and trailhead are 10 miles south of Florence on U.S. Highway 101. Parking is $5.

PLACES TO EAT

Grape Leaf Wine Shop and Bistro: The "and Bistro" part of this wine bar in trendy Old Town may interest your pooch more than the floor to ceiling racks of bottles from all over the world. A single fresh sheet of dinner specials changes weekly, with a regular lunch menu and Sunday brunch. Enjoy the signature grape leaf salad and perhaps some penne pasta with asparagus and a pinot gris as you people-watch from sidewalk tables. 1269 Bay St.; 541/997-1646.

Side Street Bistro: As sophisticated a restaurant as you'll find in a big city, the Side Street has a brick patio with seating around a fire pit as well as tables. The menu is divided into small plates and large plates, with ingredients sourced whenever possible from local and organic artisans. Isis points out that, ironically, small plates give you larger variety. 165 Maple Street; 541/997-1195.

Siuslaw River Coffee: This company is primarily a bean roaster that serves coffee and baked good, and not much else, with a busy location in Old Town and two outdoor tables overlooking the river for which it's named. 1240 Bay St.; 541/997-3443.

PLACES TO STAY

Ocean Breeze: This inexpensive motel in the historic Old Town area is a cut above, with small rooms that sparkle in a crisp white building that's a breath

of fresh air. Decorator touches and a lawn with a picnic table out front are very inviting for weary dune hikers. There are five pet rooms, all nonsmoking, for $50–120, with a $10 pet fee. 85165 Hwy. 101 S.; 541/997-2642 or 800/753-2642; www.oceanbreezemotel.com.

Park Motel and Cabins: Several tiny and tidy rooms and two of the luxury cabins open their doors to pets at this throwback 1950s lodge with genuine pine paneling on the walls and pine trees out back. A disposal can and shovel are provided at a designated dog lawn. Standard rooms are $50–135; cabins are $165. The pet fee is $10. 85034 Hwy. 101; 541/997-2634; www.parkmotel florence.com.

Mapleton

Slather on the citronella lotion and head into the deep woods for a breath of fresh Oregon mountain air. This tiny outpost makes for a nice change of pace from the salty shores.

PARKS, BEACHES, AND RECREATION AREAS

31 Siuslaw National Forest–Sweet Creek Falls

🐾🐾🐾🐾 (See Central Coast map on page 420)

At a little over two miles out and back, this trail is an easy one to hike. The 20-foot falls at the end are mostly hidden behind the rocks, but you won't care because there are dozens of rapids and falls in the gorge along the way. The whole trail is dazzling, and the elevated steel platforms, with bridges that cling to the hillside and carry you over the creek, are most exciting. It can be muddy, it can be buggy, and you must stay on the trail to avoid poison oak.

From Florence, travel 15 miles east to Mapleton on Highway 126. Shortly after town, you'll turn south on Sweet Creek Road and go another 10.2 miles to the marked trailhead. Bring your own drinking water; a latrine is available.

PLACES TO EAT

Alpha-bit: Books, gifts, and a health food café share a sunny space in a little strip of shops that are the center of town in Mapleton. Turkey and tuna are the only meats on the predominantly vegetarian and vegan menu. It's all light and delicious. Even the ice cream is light enough to float in a tall, frosted glass of IBC root beer. A tiny county park out back has a picnic table waiting for you. 10780 Highway 126; 541/268-4311.

Scottsburg

Highway 38 is a great road, paralleling the Umpqua River from I-5 out to the coast at Reedsport. Somewhere along the way, you'll pass the town of Scottsburg before you even know it, but don't miss the park, it's a good 'un.

PARKS, BEACHES, AND RECREATION AREAS

32 Scottsburg Park

🐾🐾🐾 (See Central Coast map on page 420)

The rare Myrtlewood tree flourishes along the south shore of the Umpqua River at this county park, one of five tracts of land designated to protect the northern boundary of the Myrtlewood habitat. The park, with its playground, restrooms, and big grass plot, is a beautiful and quiet setting for a break in your travels or a picnic. It's a popular fishing spot for coho and Chinook salmon; the anglers get up early to put in from the boat ramp and floating docks.

The park is just west of mile marker 16 on State Route 38, about 15 miles inland from Reedsport.

Reedsport and Winchester Bay

Reedsport is at the heart of the Oregon Dunes. If you come into town from State Route 38, pull into one of the Dean Creek elk viewing platforms, three miles east of Reedsport, to see if you can catch any of the reserve's 100 or so Roosevelt elk in action.

From the center of Winchester Bay, Salmon Harbor Drive takes you to aptly named Windy Cove, a marina packed with thousands of recreational vessels, lodging, multiple beach access points, and some of the best food on the central coast. A mile south of Winchester Bay is a wayfinding point pullout, the only spot between Port Orford and Florence where you can get an unobstructed view of the Pacific Ocean. You'll spy the top of the Umpqua Lighthouse and the Triangle Jetty, where oysters and mussels are cultivated.

PARKS, BEACHES, AND RECREATION AREAS

33 Umpqua Lighthouse

🐾🐾🐾 (See Central Coast map on page 420)

Cooper can think of three reasons to visit this state park—the lake trail, the lighthouse grounds, and the whale-watching station—all of which are wheelchair-accessible. The first is a fun, easy, one-mile trail around Lake Marie beneath a tall forest with huckleberry bushes. The east half of the trail is paved; the west is gravel and dirt.

Dogs are allowed on the grounds of the lighthouse and Coast Guard station, and you can hear its distinctive two-tone foghorn anywhere in the park. The present lighthouse was operational in 1894 and still uses the original lenses crafted in Paris in 1890. Tour guides will take you to the top Wednesday–Sunday, where visibility is 19 miles out to sea. Call 541/271-4631 for lighthouse museum and tour information.

Next to the lighthouse is a whale-watching station, with spotting scopes ($0.50 for five minutes). Whales migrate anywhere between December and May, and you can watch the ATVs crawl over the sand from this lookout year-round.

Off U.S. Highway 101, six miles south of Reedsport. Open 7 A.M.–9 P.M. 460 Lighthouse Rd.; 541/271-4118.

34 ODNRA–Umpqua Dunes Recreation Area

🐾🐾🐾 (See Central Coast map on page 420)

The beach at Umpqua stretches far and wide, with sand the pleasing texture of superfine sugar. There are three large parking lots with beach access 20 feet from the pavement. Parking at the first lot is free, so you might as well stay there. There is a $5 fee to park in the second and third lots, used as staging grounds for off-highway vehicles. The only reason to go to the second lot is for a barrier-free beach trail with two excellent, accessible viewing platforms. The third lot has flush toilets and a covered picnic shelter, amenities not available at the others. ATVs are allowed on the dunes to the east of the access road; they are not allowed on the beach to the west.

From U.S. Highway 101, turn west on Salmon Harbor Road. Follow the Umpqua Dunes and Beach Road sign, past the marina and Windy Cove. Watch out for ATVs on the side of the road. Open 10 A.M.–6 P.M., until sunset in the summertime.

35 William H. Tugman

🐾🐾 (See Central Coast map on page 420)

If the beach is too windy and cold, this memorial state park provides good stomping grounds along the sheltered shores of 350-acre Eel Lake. It has big, big, green lawns for fetch, big trees for naps in the shade, and a big lake you can paddle around in, in a big canoe. On the north side of the picnic area is a trail that wanders about a mile, with several handy places for your dog to at least get his paws wet. Flush toilets and changing rooms make it nice if you or the kids decide to go for a swim. Your view of the lake from the handicap-accessible fishing dock isn't spoiled by any development, and there's no day-use fee at this state park. Eel Lake fishing nets crappie, largemouth bass, stocked rainbow trout, and steelhead and coho salmon.

Off U.S. Highway 101, eight miles south of Reedsport. 72549 Hwy. 101; 541/759-3604.

36 ODNRA–John Dellenback Trail

🐾🐾🐾🐾 (See Central Coast map on page 420)

This one-mile loop trail takes you to the highest dunes in the park, 500 feet tall or more, named in honor of someone instrumental in establishing the dunes as a recreation area. Our little dog goddess fancied herself Isis of Arabia as she climbed up to the top and viewed the immensity before her. The northern half of the trail is through coastal woods, making the discovery of the dunes all the more exciting as you emerge from the trees. You continue through deep sand on the south to return.

For the ambitious and incredibly fit orienteer, there is a six-mile loop—2.5 miles to the beach, 0.5 mile on the beach, and back. It is marked by posts topped with blue bands, the only way to tell if you're on the right track. This is a very difficult hike, slogging through deep sand and over high hills. We were also told that the last part of the trail may be under a foot or so of water during the rainy season. If you attempt the longer trail, we recommend dog goggles and booties, gallons of water and sunscreen, and protective clothing for the sting of the sand whipped against your skin by the wind.

Watch for the entrance to trailhead parking on U.S. Highway 101, immediately north of the turnoff for Lakeside. Parking is $5.

PLACES TO EAT

Anchor Grill and Oyster Bar: Everybody brags about having the best chowder on the coast; Anchor's is right up there. Their garlic lime prawns, fettuccini, and "Tsunami" appetizer platter aren't too shabby either. 208 Bayfront Loop, Winchester Bay; 541/271-2104.

Kitty's Kitchen Is Christmas Forever: Dogs are welcome on the fantastic back patio of Kitty's, an eclectic diner and kitschy holiday gift shop. The cooks make whatever suits them that day, might be meatloaf, could be egg salad, and there's always chili dogs and homemade pies and cakes. 110 Bayfront Loop, Winchester Bay; 541/271-1919.

Pah Tong's Thai Food: When you are craving the taste of Thai, no other flavors will do. Try Pah Tong's to go for a change of pace from the seafood all over the place. 460 Beach Blvd., Winchester Bay; 541/271-1750.

Sportsmen's Cannery and Smokehouse: Not to be missed are summer barbecues Friday, Saturday, and Sunday nights from Memorial Day to Labor Day, hosted by this seafood market, filling the parking lot with picnic tables. Red snapper, crab, cod, and oysters share the grill with land-based meats. For the rest of the year, order shrimp and crab cocktails, smoked fish, and oysters to go for your beach fire pit. 182 Bayfront Loop, Winchester Bay; 541/271-3293.

Sugar Shack Bakery: We love a place that tells it like it is. Beyond enough baked goods, doughnuts, cookies, and fudge to send you into sugar shock, there are good deli sandwiches, daily soups, ubiquitous espresso drinks, and seasonal blackberry pies. Order to go from the counter. 145 N. 3rd, Reedsport; 541/271-3514.

PLACES TO STAY

Loon Lake Lodge: Half the joy of staying here is in the getting here (the other half in doing nothing once here). After 13 miles of driving along Highway 38 paralleling the Umpqua River, you'll turn south and travel another eight miles on a narrow, curvy road hugging Lake Creek to reach this full-service resort. The cabins, yurts, and cottages are rustic, bunk bed affairs, separate from the restroom and shower building. Rates start at $75, plus a one-time $25 pet fee; 30-pound limit. Additional lake access is available at a couple of BLM Recreation sites nearby. This destination wins our out-of-the-way award for the Central Coast, with few signs of humanity. You'll pass some excellent elk viewing stations along the way. 9011 Loon Lake Rd., 20 miles outside of Reedsport; 866/360-3116; www.loonlakerv.com.

Winchester Bay Inn: Pets are welcome to "be our guests" in all except four rooms of this bright, modern, squeaky-clean motel. There are a wide range of prices and room types, including kitchenette rooms, suites, and spa rooms. Rates range $50–80, plus a $5 pet charge. 390 Broadway, Winchester Bay; 541/271-4871 or 800/246-1462; www.winbayinn.com.

Umpqua Lighthouse State Park Campground: It may be a sand dune underneath, but it is a forest on top, enough to give each of the 24 tent sites and 24 hookup sites decent seclusion. Rates are $16–20. U.S. 101, six miles south of Reedsport; 800/452-5687; www.reserveamerica.com.

More Accommodations: Please look under *Chain Hotels* in the *Resources* section for additional places to stay in this area.

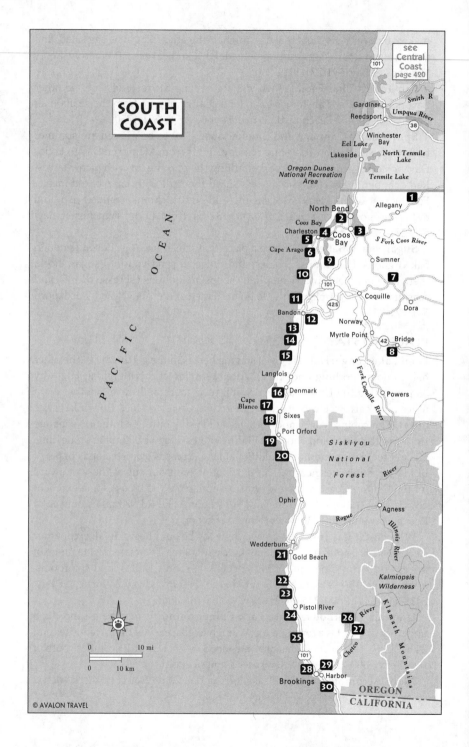

SOUTH COAST

see Central Coast page 420

101

Gardiner
Reedsport
Smith R
Umpqua River
38
Winchester Bay
Eel Lake
Lakeside
North Tenmile Lake

Oregon Dunes National Recreation Area

Tenmile Lake

PACIFIC OCEAN

1

Allegany

North Bend
2

Coos Bay
Charleston
4
5
3
Coos Bay
S Fork Coos River

Cape Arago
6
9
Sumner
7

10

101
425
Coquille
Dora

11

Bandon
12
Norway

13
14
Myrtle Point
42
Bridge
8

15

Langlois

16 Denmark
Cape Blanco
17
18 Sixes
Port Orford
19
20
Powers
S Fork Coquille River

Siskiyou
National
Forest
River

Ophir
Rogue
Agness
Illinois River

Wedderburn
21 Gold Beach

22
Kalmiopsis
Wilderness

23
24 Pistol River
26
River
27
Chetco River

25

101
28 29 Harbor
Brookings
30

Klamath Mountains

OREGON
CALIFORNIA

0   10 mi
0   10 km

© AVALON TRAVEL

CHAPTER 16

South Coast

The southern coast of Oregon is also called America's Wild Rivers Coast, where all of the major waterways that begin in the Cascades—Smith, Chetco, Pistol, Elk, Sixes, and mighty Rogue and Umpqua—empty into the sea, creating interesting lakes, estuaries, and Oregon's Bay Area, Coos Bay, along the way. The towns and recreation areas become less touristy the farther south you go. There's less saltwater taffy and more saltwater, exactly the kind of thing a dog pricks up her ears to hear.

In the forests south of the Umpqua River, your pet will have the pleasure of encountering the Oregon myrtlewood, a tree she's probably never smelled before. Famed for its multicolored burled wood and fragrant dark leaves that smell similar to bay, it grows only in this region of Oregon and the Holy Land in Israel.

If you travel in May and June, another exotic species your pup will meet is the *Vellela Vellela* (By the Wind Sailor), a member of the jellyfish family pushed ashore in massive numbers by west winds. Their fins are translucent, their

PICK OF THE LITTER—SOUTH COAST

BEST PARKS
Sunset Bay, Coos Bay (page 457)
Cape Blanco, Port Orford (page 465)

BEST BEACH
Seven Devils, Bandon (page 461)

BEST TRAIL
Oregon Redwood Nature Trail, Brookings-Harbor
(page 471)

BEST PLACE TO EAT
The Crazy Norwegian, Port Orford (page 466)

BEST PLACES TO STAY
Coos Bay Manor Bed and Breakfast, Coos Bay (page 458)
Tintagel by the Sea, Bandon (page 464)
Wild Rivers Motor Lodge, Brookings-Harbor (page 473)

bodies are cobalt blue, and, fortunately for curious wet noses, they don't have stingers or tentacles.

While the Dachsie Twins are not widely known for their hiking prowess, they recognize a great outdoor resource when they see one. They can therefore direct you to the Coos Regional Trails Partnership website at www.coostrails .com, and suggest you click the "Hiking Trails" link for a great clearinghouse of regional walks. Go ahead, knock yourself out.

Coos Bay

The Bay Area of Oregon refers to the city of Coos Bay and its suburbs North Bend and Charleston. Coos Bay is Oregon's largest bay, a significant commercial passage for coal at the turn of the 19th century, and later for lumber and seafood. The city is the coast's largest population center, and not a particularly memorable one, with a lumber mill and the Coquille Tribe's Mill Casino being the largest going concerns. A stroll along Coos Bay's boardwalk gives you the opportunity to gawk at the marina's working boats and pleasure craft.

Beyond that, the Dachshunds suggest you head straight through the city on Cape Arago Highway to Charleston, a fishing village that also serves as the gateway to three great beach parks, with their promontories and protected bays famous for blazing sunsets. Flower lovers come to the 743 acres of Shore Acres Botanical Gardens; however, this state park is off limits to dogs.

For a more scenic approach to Charleston from the south, leave Highway 101 and take W. Beaver Hill Road to Seven Devils Road through newly planted timberland.

PARKS, BEACHES, AND RECREATION AREAS

◻ Golden and Silver Falls
🐾 🐾 (See South Coast map on page 452)

Two trails, less than a half mile each, head off in opposite directions through an old-growth forest of maple, alder, Douglas fir, and myrtles to these cascades on Silver and Glenn Creeks. They are stunning, easy hikes. The 160-foot Silver Falls appears to rain straight out of the sky, and Golden Falls is only slightly less impressive. You've come all this way, so you might as well take to the 0.9-mile trail that climbs the edge of a steep cliff (leashes please) and gives you views of both falls. To reach the longer trail, head to the right from the parking lot, over a bridge, then left at the first trail junction.

The 24-mile drive inland from the coast to this State Natural Area is a roller coaster ride. From the Y intersection on the south end of Coos Bay, follow the sign to Allegany. Cross the bridge, turn north on 6th Avenue for 0.5 mile, and turn east on Coos River Road. The closer you get, the less of a road it is, and the last five miles are unpaved. Just when you're convinced that you can't possibly be on the right road, you'll see the sign to Glenn Creek Road indicating you have only three more miles to go. 541/888-3778.

◻ Empire Lakes/John Topits Park
🐾 🐾 🐾 (See South Coast map on page 452)

These woodsy lakes are surrounded by strip malls and superstores, but you'd never know it from walking or fishing along the forested paths of their shores. Tourists usually miss this 120-acre destination, so the friendly dogs you meet and greet are probably locals. The 1.25-mile path around the lower lake is paved and wheelchair-accessible, and there are additional unpaved and primitive trails around Upper and Middle Empire. These bayous are full of what dogs think of as everything nice: bugs, frogs, birds, and "Gone fishin'" bumper stickers on trucks.

From Newmark Street, the main east–west thoroughfare in North Bend, turn north on Hull Road to find a parking lot, trailhead, and restrooms. 541/269-8918; www.coostrails.com/traildescriptions/empirelakes/empirelakes.htm

DOG-EAR YOUR CALENDAR

Didn't have time to make a float? Don't have a pet? No problem! Kids with pets—of the live or stuffed-animal variety but preferably *not* of the taxidermy kind—are encouraged to participate in the **July Jubilee Parade** in North Bend. Awards are given in various categories, and entries are generously "judged" on creativity and the inclusion of at least one animal in the theme. Parade entry forms and rules and regulations are available at the Coos Bay or North Bend visitors centers (www.oregonsbayarea.org).

The Pacific Cove Humane Society in Coos Bay holds their largest annual fundraiser in October each year. The **Bite of the Bay** features about 10 chefs, local wines, and silent and live auctions, hosted at the Mill Casino. Go to www.pacificcovehumane.org for information or call 541/756-6522.

🐾 Mingus Park

🐾🐾 (See South Coast map on page 452)

Mingus is a truly lovely city park, with immaculate Japanese and rhododendron gardens surrounding a pond complete with water fountains (lighted from underneath at night), lily pads, and waterfowl. Even if you start out in a hurry, the peaceful grounds tempt you to stop to smell the flowers. The paved, accessible path around the pond is 0.4 mile, passing by viewing benches and crossing over a traditional arched bridge. There is a covered picnic gondola at the far end and a few minor wooded trails in an arboretum beyond.

From U.S. Highway 101, turn west onto Commercial Avenue and turn north on 10th Street. Pass the ball field and the skate park and cross the street to Chosi Gardens. 541/269-8918.

🐾 Bastendorff Beach

🐾🐾🐾 (See South Coast map on page 452)

No pets are allowed in the picnic area of this county park and campground, and camping is nicer at Sunset Bay anyway, so Coop 'n' Isis suggest driving right past the county property straight to the beach. The sun rises early on these shores, which curve two miles around to the north and east. You can park steps away from the beach in multiple places along a mile of road below the Coos Head U.S. Naval Facility. Walk your dog on the superfine sand for miles, from the jetty access to Coos Bay at the north end on down.

Take Cape Arago Highway west from U.S. Highway 101 and turn right at the sign for the county park onto Coos Head Road. 541/888-5353.

5 Sunset Bay

🐾🐾🐾🐾 (See South Coast map on page 452)

Partially enclosed by high sandstone bluffs and a narrow sea passage, this state park once played safe haven to vessels during storms, and as local lore has it, pirate ships waiting to spring on unsuspecting ships passing in the night. Waves are gentle behind the protected breakwall, and the water is shallow, making it a great place to play. The tide pools send dogs' noses and kids' imaginations into overdrive checking out the hermit crabs, sea anemones, starfish, limpets, urchins, and so on (eyes only, no touching please).

For hiking, complete with ocean vistas, primal forests, and wildflowers, you can pick up a two-mile section of the Oregon Coast Trail between Sunset Bay and Shore Acres. The trail marker is tucked behind the right side of the restroom in the picnic area. The park meadow is big enough for a hot-air balloon, as proved by Malcolm Forbes in 1973 when he took off on his successful transcontinental flight.

On Cape Arago Highway, 12 miles southwest of Coos Bay. 541/888-4902.

6 Cape Arago

🐾🐾🐾 (See South Coast map on page 452)

It's rewarding to simply drive or walk the loop at the road's end, gawking at incredible views, explosive surf, and sunsets beyond compare from a wheelchair-accessible lookout. Your dog will certainly appreciate it if you look for the multiple pullouts and markers indicating trails that wind through this state park. The Pack Trail, for example, is a 2.25-mile trip that gains 400 feet in elevation past WWII bunkers to the end of the cape. From another trail, you can catch a glimpse of the Cape Arago Lighthouse perched on the edge of the cliffs and hear its unusual foghorn. A third, paved switchback trail leads down to the South Cove, a sliver of beach with lots of smelly detritus washed onshore. (Oh boy! Oh boy!) If your dog thinks his bark is loud, he ought to get a load of the chorus of pinnipeds—that's seals and sea lions to us lay dogs— along Simpson Reef. Hundreds to thousands of them haul out on the rocks of Shell Island Refuge offshore to bask, bark, and breed in the sun.

Think "'ere I go" to correctly pronounce Arago, and to get there, take the Cape Arago Highway west from U.S. Highway 101, and watch for signs that say Charleston–State Parks. Cape Arago is the end of the road, 14 miles southwest of Coos Bay. Open 7 A.M.–6 P.M., until 9 P.M. in the summer. 541/888-3778, ext. 26.

PLACES TO EAT

Blue Heron Bistro: This restaurant specializes in two distinctly different types of cuisine: seafood and German food. If the shrimp, bacon-wrapped oysters, or blackened salmon sandwiches don't tempt you, perhaps the bratwurst, knockwurst, and sauerkraut will. You can squeeze into one of a couple of tiny sidewalk tables for lunch or dinner. 100 Commercial Ave.; 541/267-3933; www.blueheronbistro.com.

Charleston Station Donuts and Bagels: ... and ice cream, and espresso, and Laotian and Thai food. Odd combinations perhaps, but sometimes, out here in the boonies, you have to diversify to survive. Isis double-dog-dares you to order one of everything to go. 91120 Cape Arago Hwy., Charleston; 541/888-3306.

City Subs: A cut above any other sub shop we've encountered, City Subs in downtown Coos Bay par-bakes their own rolls daily, then finishes them when they make your sandwich, for pure fabulousness. Dustbuster (Dusty for short), the resident Bichon Frisee, says, "Order chef salads or low-carb wraps for the peeps if you must, but stick to the meatballs for the pups." For seating, a wide awning protects a row of café tables. 149 N. 4th St.; 541/269-9000.

Top Dog Espresso: With a name like that, of course this drive-through serves dog biscuits to canine backseat drivers. Try the espresso milkshake; it's good enough to growl for. 3636 Tremont (Hwy. 101 S.), North Bend; 541/756-6135.

PLACES TO STAY

Coos Bay Manor Bed and Breakfast: Innkeepers John and Felicia welcome mannerly dogs with open arms in all five rooms of their home, a stunning example of neo-Colonial architecture on the National Register of Historic Places. The original owner was a paper-pulp mill baron named Nerdrum, who settled in Coos Bay from Finland in 1912. Many famous families have since sheltered on the portico and front porch. Rooms are $135, combined suites are $220, and both include breakfast. 955 S. 5th St.; 800/269-1224; www.coosbaymanor.com.

Edgewater Inn: Coos Bay's only waterfront motel has big, ground-level rooms with sliding glass doors out to a nice strip of lawn by the bay. Rates range $90–135, plus a $10 pet fee. 275 E. Johnson Ave.; 800/233-0423; www .edgewater-inns.com.

Sunset Bay Campground: You'll need reservations for the 29 hookup, 36 electrical, and 66 tent sites in a sheltered cove, each with decent privacy thanks to tall trees and shrubbery. Spaces are $12–20, which includes free admission to nearby Shore Acres Botanical Gardens, where, alas, dogs are not allowed. 89526 Cape Arago Hwy.; 800/452-5687; www.reserveamerica.com.

More Accommodations: Please look under *Chain Hotels* in the *Resources* section for additional places to stay in this area.

Coquille and Myrtle Point

These two towns are off the radar, inland 20 miles from Bandon on the coast, and their combined population is probably less than 5,000. The countryside is serene, most notable for large groves of the exotic myrtle tree and the multiple winding forks of the Coquille River.

PARKS, BEACHES, AND RECREATION AREAS

7 LaVerne Park

😊😊😊 (See South Coast map on page 452)

When it's time to leave behind the tourist frenzy on the beaches and escape into the countryside, come to this beautiful county park. A broad playfield is bordered by tall Douglas firs and myrtlewood trees set on the banks of the North Fork of the Coquille River. The park has been around a while and has matured nicely into a pleasant rural getaway. No dogs are allowed on the designated swimming beach, which isn't much to brag about anyway. There are other spots along the river where your dog could sneak in for a quick swim.

From State Route 42 in Coquille, follow the signs to turn on West Central Boulevard, and east on Fairview Road 14 miles to the Upper North Fork Road. 541/396-2344; www.co.coos.or.us/ccpark.

8 Sandy Creek Covered Bridge Wayside

😊 (See South Coast map on page 452)

Just west of a town called Remote, 42 miles from Roseburg on State Route 42, is a covered bridge built in 1921 beside a circle of lawn, some good-sized pine trees, and a latrine. It may come in handy on the ride out to the coast if your backseat companion is giving you that special whine and you've got your legs crossed. You both can get out and stretch your legs while you look at the map of Coos County parks on display.

PLACES TO EAT

Figaro's Italian Kitchen and Sub Express: We bet your coonhound would happily serenade you with the famous refrain from the opera *Barber of Seville* for this Figaro's hot fajita or cool ranch chicken wrap. At the drive-through or on the wraparound porch, the restaurant's pizza, subs, calzones, ice cream, and frozen yogurt are tasty enough to entice your minstrel mutt to sing for his supper. 29 W. 1st St., Coquille; 541/396-5277.

PLACES TO STAY

LaVerne County Park Campground: The camping pads at LaVerne are gravel, and most sites have river views. It's first come, first served, and the park host recommends leaving the place to the locals on crowded Memorial Day and Labor Day weekends. Tent sites are $11, full hookups are $16; local checks only, so bring cash. 541/247-3719.

Bandon

The official name of this cute village is Bandon by the Sea. The first settlements were destroyed by fire in 1914 and again in 1936, and now, Old Town Bandon is generally what the place looked like after the latter, and hopefully last, fire. Bandon is also a sweet town, home of the best fudge on the coast (Big Wheel General Store; 130 Baltimore; 541/247-3719) and Cranberry Sweets, a company that makes a huge variety of jelly-fruit candies and gives out free samples.

Turn onto Beach Loop Drive, starting south of Bandon and ending in Old Town, for a scenic byway that winds you past most of the lodging and beach parks.

PARKS, BEACHES, AND RECREATION AREAS

🟦 South Slough National Estuarine Research Reserve

🐾🐾 (See South Coast map on page 452)

With a mouthful of a name that is easily shortened to South Slough, this 19,000-acre estuary is only a fraction of the larger 384,000 protected acres of the Coos Bay Estuary. An estuary is a rich wetlands environment where freshwater meets and mixes with saltwater, creating a biological stew perfect for infinite varieties of marine-, plant-, and birdlife. The 10-Minute Loop trail gives you a quick look at the local flora, labeled for easy identification. There are a variety of other trails and boardwalks, from 0.75 mile to three miles, for you and your curious pet to explore a variety of marshes full of frogs and snails and puppy dogs' tails (just kidding about that last one). They were all underwater when we visited; call ahead to the interpretive center for their status before you visit. 61907 Seven Devils Rd.; 541/888-5558; www .southsloughestuary.org.

🔟 Seven Devils

🐾🐾🐾🐾 (See South Coast map on page 452)

Seven is your gambling greyhound's lucky number. The Wonder Wieners give this beach wayside high marks for sticking to the KISS principle. You have instant access to the beach, the whole beach, and nothing but the beach, seven miles of it. A narrow strip of meadow is protected by cliffs that rise to either side, and a smattering of picnic tables have outstanding views. At seven miles off the highway, it doesn't get much action other than a few rockhounders looking for agates. Come up here and get away from the hubbub for a purist beach experience. Restrooms are available.

From U.S. Highway 101, 14 miles north of Bandon, turn west another seven miles onto Seven Devils Road. The approach to Seven Devils from the south is easier by far.

🔢 Bullards Beach

🐾🐾 (See South Coast map on page 452)

This state park has multiple picnic areas, parking lots, and campground loops along the wide mouth of the Coquille River as it dumps into the sea. The campground is a mile from the beach along a paved trail, and the three-mile Cut Creek Trail is a dirt track through flat grassland out to the Coquille River Lighthouse, built in 1896. The smallest lighthouse on the coast, it was officially decommissioned in 1939 and restored in 1979 with a solar-powered light in the tower to re-create the visual effect.

The best access to Cut Creek is between corrals #7 and #8 in the horse camp. If you're not interested in hoofing it alongside the horses, a road with parking leads directly to the beach and lighthouse. The campground at Bullards Beach is designed for RVs and horse trailers rather than tent campers. The turnoff is two miles north of Bandon on U.S. Highway 101. 541/347-3501.

12 Bandon City Park

😺 😺 🐾 (See South Coast map on page 452)

The rules listed on the secure gate at this off-leash area include a notation that your dogs owe their thanks to Edith Leslie for her donation that made possible the designated and fenced play area. There are a couple of picnic tables, a water faucet, trash can, and bag dispenser in an uneven acre of meadow with a stand of trees in the middle. In short, the OLA is a little piece of dog delight.

The larger city park is an oval, and traffic is routed one-way westbound on the north, eastbound on the south. The OLA is on the south, eastbound side of the loop. From U.S. Highway 101, turn west on 11th Street, go past Jackson Avenue, make the loop around the park, and look to your right. The Russ Sommers Memorial Playground and the skate park are worth detours from the dog park (dogs on leash) if you have kids.

13 Face Rock Wayside

😺 😺 (See South Coast map on page 452)

Don't be embarrassed if you can't see her face at first. It's like one of those Rorschach inkblots, where once someone points the picture out to you, you can't *not* see it. Nah-So-Mah Tribe legend says that the woman rising out of the water is Ewanua, a chief's daughter who swam into the sea and was turned to stone when she refused to look into the face of the spiteful god Seatka. When her faithful dog Komax swam out to rescue her, the monster petrified him as well (now that's evil), along with her cats and kittens, creating the string of rocks to the northwest.

The rock formations are viewed from a paved walkway above, and a long series of steps leads down to the beach proper. It's a favorite spot of joggers, beachcombers, and people who like to peer into the busy marine goings-on of tide pools.

From U.S. Highway 101, turn west on Beach Loop Road, one mile south of Bandon to this State Scenic Viewpoint.

14 Devil's Kitchen

😺 😺 😺 (See South Coast map on page 452)

Bandon State Natural Area is this park's official name; Devil's Kitchen is the colloquialism. At the southernmost Beach Access Road, you have to cross an ankle-deep river to reach the ocean. The trail down to the beach is on the north end of the parking lot, hiding behind some rocks. The second wayside has a shady picnic meadow, but the beach is over a very steep dune, covered with prickly bushes and spiky trees. The dachshunds never made it, having been distracted by turquoise dragonflies.

Of the three waysides, the northernmost gives you the easiest path to the sand, by way of a partially paved trail and series of wooden steps. It's also the largest and most developed, with rolling meadows, restrooms, picnic tables, and fire pits. The rock formations include a haystack rock, but it is not *the* Haystack Rock everyone talks about, which is farther north in Cannon Beach.

From U.S. Highway 101, five miles south of Bandon, turn on Beach Loop Road and follow the signs to reach the three park waysides.

15 New River ACEC

🐾🐾🐾 (See South Coast map on page 452)

An ACEC is an Area of Critical Environmental Concern, land granted federal status for the protection of unique ecosystems and wildlife. In this park, a reserve for globally important birding, three miles of trails take you through a variety of habitats, across a meadow, past ponds, into a forest, along the sand, and among marsh grasses. The trail surface varies, but is always easy and clear, and a small portion is paved for wheelchair accessibility. The New River separates you from the ocean, but as you approach you can hear the surf pounding and catch a glimpse of it from the top of the boat ramp. Car and boat access is restricted March 15–September 15 to protect the snowy plover. Trails are open all year, along with the Ellen Warring Learning Center, where kids can touch and explore exhibits about the creatures that live in the park (dogs not allowed inside the center). Isis and Cooper saw a brace or two of birds but were more impressed by the abundance of bunnies.

From U.S. Highway 101, 8.5 miles south of Bandon, turn west on Croft Lake Lane for 1.7 miles down a somewhat bumpy dirt road, and bear right at the fork in the road marked by a small brown sign with binoculars to reach the Storm Ranch entrance. Trail maps are available at the center. Open sunrise–sunset. 541/756-0100.

PLACES TO EAT

Bandon Baking Co. and Deli: This excellent deli specializes in made-to-order sandwiches for lunch, which you may not need after picking and choosing from the rows of cakes and baked goods and loaves of bread to take home. Cooper spied fat homemade dog biscuits. Cash only, unless you order online with a credit card. 160 2nd St.; 541/347-9440; www.bandonbakingco.com.

Bandon Fish Market: The rockfish fish-and-chips baskets, fish tacos, and chowder in sourdough bread bowls somehow taste better than usual when you're seated at outdoor tables with spiffy blue-and-white checkered tablecloths. There's a dog dish outside, a bucket o' biscuits at the counter, and you could buy your best friend a $2 dried salmon stick for a splurge. "They feed you too much," said one patron, who obviously didn't have a dog to take the excess off of his hands. 249 1st St. S.E.; 541/347-4282; www.bandonfishmarket.com.

Old Town Pizza and Pasta: The name is self-explanatory and the outdoor tables on the sidewalk patio are as red as tomato sauce, perhaps to get you in the mood. For fettuccini Alfredo, Cooper would be willing to come back as an Italian greyhound in his next life. 395 2nd St.; 541/347-3911.

Port O' Call: Owners of the largest breeds may want to keep an eye out for the dangerous combination of curious noses and paws around the claws of the live lobsters and crabs in the tanks at this authentic seafood market. Order your crustaceans steamed or served up in tomato broth for a spicy cioppino soup, while you sit at the outdoor oyster bar and sip bottled beer and wines by the glass. 155 1st St.; 541/347-2875.

PLACES TO STAY

Sunset Oceanfront: In the trade, ocean view means you can catch a glimpse of the ocean from your window and oceanfront means you can reach the beach from your door. This motel has both, and both recently renovated and a bit dated rooms, all facing Face Rock. Oceanfront rooms range $90–160; ocean views are noticeably cheaper at $65–90; non-view rooms $50–70; all require a $10 pet fee. 1865 Beach Loop Dr. S.W.; 541/347-2453; www.sunsetmotel.com.

Tintagel by the Sea: Tintagel is named after an headland in Cornwall, England; this one is a great-looking rental house, with private beach access, and "in your face" ocean viewing sunrooms on each level. The lower unit is perfect for a couple, with a couple of pets max, going for a song at $105–135 a night, plus a $10 per pet fee. The main house is even juicier, with a private master bedroom and bath with clawfoot tub ($200–250). One-week summer minimum stay. Neither unit is ADA-accessible; you must be able to handle 57 steps to get there. 1430 Beach Loop Dr.; 800/868-2304; www.tintagel bythesea.com.

More Accommodations: Please look under *Chain Hotels* in the *Resources* section for additional places to stay in this area.

Port Orford

After much strife with the land's earlier inhabitants, this port became the oldest European settled town on the coast in 1851. The coast's oldest continuously operating lighthouse is at nearby Cape Blanco, commissioned in 1870 to aid the ships transporting gold and lumber from the region.

PARKS, BEACHES, AND RECREATION AREAS

16 Boice-Cope at Floras Lake

🐾🐾 (See South Coast map on page 452)

In 1910, there were about 400 people living here on a developer's promise to build a canal connecting the lake to the ocean to create a thriving sea port. When they discovered that the lake is at a slightly higher elevation, and thus would drain out into the ocean if linked, the plan dried up and so did the people. The windsurfers don't mind a bit, making the lake a favorite place to practice because winds are steady at 15–25 knots, it's shallow, and water temperature averages 68°F.

You can walk around the lake on a sandy trail, and up over a single dune to the ocean on the far side from the parking lot/campground. Campsites at this county park are all together in a big meadow, for $16 per night. Windsurfing, kite boarding, and kayak rentals and lessons are available on the lake. 541/348-9912; www.floraslake.com.

Turn onto Floras Lake Loop from U.S. Highway 101, west onto Floras Lake Road, and west again on Boice-Cope Road. Parking is $2 per day.

17 Cape Blanco

🐾🐾🐾🐾 (See South Coast map on page 452)

Among some pretty stiff competition, Cape Blanco manages to stand out as a superb state park, the tip of which sticks out as the westernmost spot in the contiguous 48 states. It's got everything a dog dreams of: beach access along the south, picnicking in fields along the Sixes River, and eight miles of trails through a wide variety of ecosystems, from forest to tall grass dunes. For the people in your party, the views of the ocean surrounding three sides of the landmass are unbeatable. History buffs will appreciate the tours of the 245-foot Cape Blanco Lighthouse, the Victorian Hughes House on the National Register of Historic Places, and the remains of the church and cemetery. The lighthouse is the southernmost in Oregon, and the first to have a Fresnel lens installed in 1870. Call 541/332-6774 for information about hours and tours for the lighthouse and Hughes House, both of which have wheelchair-accessible areas.

The easiest beach access point is through the campground, next to site #A32. You can drive or walk down a winding lane that eventually crumbles right onto the beach, with a few parking places just before the sidewalk ends.

From U.S. Highway 101, nine miles north of Port Orford, go west on Cape Blanco Road to the end. 39745 S. Hwy. 101.

18 Paradise Point

🐾🐾 (See South Coast map on page 452)

Paradise, in this instance, is a parking lot with access to a coarse sand beach that extends several miles from the Port Orford Heads to Cape Blanco. Look closely, and you'll see that the beach is actually billions of tiny pebbles that have yet to be ground to the fine texture of sand. In most places, it is a steep slope of sand down to the water, making it tricky to walk long distances without feeling lopsided.

Look for the turnoff to Paradise Point Road about one mile north of town. Don't let the Dead End signs scare you; the road dead-ends into the State Recreation Site.

19 Port Orford Heads

😼😼😼 (See South Coast map on page 452)

From 1934 to 1970, this state park was one of the busiest Coast Guard stations on a stretch of treacherous water. The heads are prominent landmasses jutting over the ocean, providing the best viewpoint for sighting ships in trouble on the rocks, or to give you some fantastic views. Trails in the park are well groomed in soft wood-mulch that's easy to walk. The half-mile Headland Trail leads out onto the edge of the bluff, and from there, you can connect to the 0.75-mile Loop Trail that takes you past the site of the former lookout tower and the boat house where rescuers launched into the rough seas. While you read the placards telling the stories of the search-and-rescue station and check out the restored lifeboat, your watchdog can keep his eyes peeled for the black-tailed deer common to the area. You can't reach the beach at the heads, but you can look out over it for miles in every direction.

From U.S. Highway 101, follow the signs to turn west on 9th Street, and then south on Coast Guard Road. Open 6 A.M.–8 P.M.

20 Humbug Mountain

😼😼😼 (See South Coast map on page 452)

Rottweilers, get ready to rumble. Pull out those paw booties and take on the challenge of Humbug Mountain, a six-mile loop trail that climbs from the beach up to the summit at 1,748 feet. As you rest along the way, your pal can sniff out the subtle differences between myrtle, maple, and old-growth Douglas firs. Those who make the trek are treated to a northward viewpoint of Redfish Rocks and Port Orford and another south to Gold Beach. Trailhead parking is just north of the campground entrance. Isis has a tricky back that wasn't quite up to the rigors of the trail, but she did enjoy herself on the park's coarse gravel beach, north of the mountain, accessible along the banks of a creek starting near campsite #C7. The waves crash against the base of the mountain, and the surf has a wicked undertow.

To the south of the mountain is a picnic area, with its own parking and a meadow the length of a football field that's fun to run around on. Walk down the paved pathway along the stream to find it.

This state park is unmistakable, even before you get there on U.S. Highway 101, six miles south of Port Orford. Open 6 A.M.–10 P.M. 39745 Hwy. 101; 541/332-6774.

PLACES TO EAT

The Crazy Norwegian: As honorary Norwegians (grandmother on their maternal side), Isis and Cooper can say with tongue firmly in cheek that putting "crazy" and "Norwegian" together is a bit redundant. The cook will make you some insanely good fish-and-chips, salads, homemade cookies, burgers, sandwiches, and chowder to go. While you wait, you can experience the dry

Scandinavian sense of humor, reading the menu and learning the various meanings of the expression "Uff Da," including "Waking yourself up in church with your own snoring." 259 6th St. (Hwy. 101); 541/332-8601.

PLACES TO STAY

Castaway by the Sea: The major selling point at this little 13-room motel is the private, enclosed sun porch/storm watching veranda. Fantastic views, plain and simple. Rooms still look good after renovations in 2004; a "no pets on the furniture" policy helps keep them that way. A variety of room sizes are priced at $65–155. Pets are $10 each per night, no more than two, please. 545 W. 5th St.; 541/332-4502; www.castawaybythesea.com.

Cape Blanco Campground: A few of the 53 electric/water sites at this state park have water views, but most are neatly hidden from the water, and each other, widely spaced among the thick woods. It's miles to the main road through farm country; the only sounds you'll hear are the other campers, neighing from the neighboring horse camp, and the surf. Rates are $12–16 for first-come, first-served sites. 39745 S. Hwy. 101; 541/332-6774.

Gold Beach

This coastal community is where Oregon's most famous river, the Rogue, meets the Pacific Ocean. Ocean fishing charters for salmon and steelhead are at your beck and call and Jerry's Rogue Jets will speed you upriver. Coop 'n' Isis claim that the beaches between Brookings and Gold Beach are the best and most accessible on the Southern Coast. South Park and Kissing Rock provide two wheelchair-accessible ocean viewpoints, the former on the far south end of town, and the latter a mile south, on the south side of Hunter Creek. Even the visitors center has beach access, a playground, and picnic tables at South Beach Park (541/247-7526; www.goldbeach.org).

Although the dogs wouldn't technically list it as a park, Ophir rest stop is nine miles north of Gold Beach on U.S. Highway 101, giving you instant access to miles of unspoiled sand between Nesika Beach and a spot known as Sisters Rocks. All that, plus a potty and picnic tables.

PARKS, BEACHES, AND RECREATION AREAS

21 Buffington Park

🐾 (See South Coast map on page 452)

While everyone else is getting sand in their muzzles on the beach, you can escape to this cute community park in the center of town, with clean restrooms, covered and open picnic tables, and a Kid Castle playground.

From Ellensburg Avenue in town, turn on E. Caughell at the sign pointing to the library and community park. Open sunrise–sunset.

22 Cape Sebastian

🐾🐾 (See South Coast map on page 452)

The cape is a cliff you can climb for the widest ocean, shore, and mountain panoramas on the lower coast. Views start from the two parking lots, 200 feet above sea level, 40 miles to the north and Humbug Mountain and 50 miles as far south as California. From the southern lot, there is a 1.5-mile trail leading to even more panoramic vistas. The first half mile is paved, a real treat for wheelchair patrons (just about the best accessible views on the coast), and then it settles into a softer, paw-pleasing dirt trail through Sitka spruce with frequent clearings. It's essential to keep your pal on leash to avoid him going over the edge in his enthusiasm.

This State Scenic Corridor is seven miles south of Gold Beach on U.S. Highway 101.

23 Myers Creek Beach

🐾🐾 (See South Coast map on page 452)

Immediately south of a small bridge, exactly at mile marker 337, is a very large gravel roadside pullout. On the north end of the lot is an easy and quick trail directly to a gorgeous beach where the creek meets the sea, complete with rock formations, upland driftwood to sniff around, and extensive, smooth sand. Despite its proximity to the highway, small bluffs protect your scouting party from the silly people in cars who aren't stopping to smell the seaweed and get in touch with their inner beach bums. There are no amenities here.

24 Pistol River Sand Dunes

🐾🐾🐾 (See South Coast map on page 452)

In 1856, an infamous Native American–U.S. Army battle was fought here, and the park's name comes from a militia soldier rumored to have dropped his gun in the river in the heat of the fight. It'll be a slightly different park every time you visit. The sand dunes shift and grow in the summer, and the river has changed course several times in recent years. The big, bold surf is different every day, a boon for the many windsurfers. After a short climb over the sand dunes, you reach an open stretch of beach between Brookings and Gold Beach.

The pullout for parking is directly off U.S. Highway 101, 11 miles south of Gold Beach. There are no amenities at this State Scenic Viewpoint, only sand, sea, and sky.

PLACES TO EAT

The Cannery Building: This building is home to a bunch of options including the Coffee Dock (541/247-6158) for espresso, pastries, and fruit smoothies; Cone Amor (541/247-4270) for ice cream and sweets; Port Hole Café (541/247-7411) for family dining; and Fisherman's Direct Seafoods

DIVERSIONS

In the foyer at **Woof's Dog Bakery** in Gold Beach, treat samples are served at "Yappy Hour," 3–5 P.M. daily. At this divine doggy destination, two bakers work full time turning out treats that are far too beautiful for you-know-who to eat. More than a bakery, this is a full-service dog store featuring high-quality foods and an eye-popping selection of accessories and toys. 29525 Ellensburg Ave. (Hwy. 101); 541/247-6835; www.woofsdogbakery.com.

You ought to stop at **Dog Style Boutique's** "barkery," too, for treats and last-minute essentials when in Bandon. One of the owners of this pet boutique also makes and sells a raw food diet for animals at www.boneappetitrawfood.com. 95 S.W. 11th; 541/347-2504.

(541/247-9494), a cooperative of local boat operators offering live and cooked crab, shrimp cocktail, smoked salmon, and other fresh treasures from the sea. Outside, a few picnic tables are scattered around. 29975 S. Harbor Way.

Cutter and Co. BBQ Stand: Where's the beef? Call ahead to find out where the grill and picnic benches are parked this season, and order to share heaping plates of ribs, brisket, pork, and chicken from this authentic slow roaster of fine meats. Bring cash. 541/247-2271.

Rollin' 'n Dough Bakery and Bistro: The tiny white cottage with red trim looks humble, but locals say true gourmet food comes out of Patti's kitchen, but only 10:30 A.M.–3 P.M. daily, so time your visit accordingly. A Culinary Institute grad, Patti uses organic and local ingredients for artistic dishes such as pan-seared tuna or crab po'boys. Your pals can be secured to the back patio fence, or they can loll around on the lawn and make friends, human and canine. 94257 North Bank Road; 541/247-4438.

PLACES TO STAY

Ireland's Rustic Lodges: There's a surprising amount of room in the real log cabins, each one unique, with separate bedrooms and living rooms with fireplaces. Pets are allowed in cabins #1–8, but Cooper prefers the Hobbitish rooms out back (#24, #25, #26) because they have sliding glass doors that open onto a huge lawn and the beach trail. The price is more than right at $70–135 per night. Pets over 30 pounds are $10 per night; those under are $5. Their insurance prohibits Dobermans and pit bulls. In 2006, they added a sheltered hot tub deck (no dogs in tubs, please). 29330 Ellensburg Ave.; 541/247-7718; www.irelandsrusticlodges.com.

Turtle Rock Resort Cottages: Wipe your paws before entering these eight pet-friendly rentals. With carpets and furniture in tasteful neutral tones, the cottages look like shrunken town homes, nicely decked out with amenities in petite proportions. They're tightly grouped alongside the banks of Hunter Creek, or tucked up against a wooded hillside, which we prefer. They all have lofts, kitchens, and decks with barbecue grills; some have hot tubs and fireplaces. Rates range $140–180 per night, with a $15 fee per pet, two pet maximum. Check in the office for local restaurants that will deliver to the cottages. 28788 Hunter Creek Loop; 541/247-9203; www.turtlerockresorts.com.

Huntley Park Campground: This privately owned rustic campground is a super secret, seven miles up the Rogue River from Gold Beach. Spacious sites in a deep myrtle grove are only $10 a night. Bring quarters for the hot showers. Firewood and blocks of ice are also available for a small fee. Impromptu potlucks and sing-a-longs have been known to happen from time to time. No hookups. 96847 Jerry's Flat Rd.; 541/247-9377.

More Accommodations: Please look under *Chain Hotels* in the *Resources* section for additional places to stay in this area.

Brookings-Harbor

Only four miles north of the California border, Brookings benefits from weather patterns that give it the warmest average temperatures on the coast. The town is famous for its flowers, especially azaleas and Easter lilies, producing about 75 percent of all Easter lily bulbs grown in the United States. Vast fields of the tall white flowers are in full bloom in July, and the bulbs are shipped worldwide. You can reach this southernmost Oregon town only by coming down from U.S. Highway 101, or by dipping into California from Grants Pass and back up again on the famed Redwood Highway, U.S. Highway 199.

If the parks and trails listed here are too tame for your taste, there are literally hundreds of options in the **Kalmiopsis Wilderness,** with 197,000 acres of solitude and wildlife, 30 miles inland from Brookings. The Chetco Ranger Station in Brookings can give you all the details (539 Chetco Ave.; 541/412-6000; www.fs.fed.us/r6/rogue-siskiyou).

PARKS, BEACHES, AND RECREATION AREAS

25 Samuel H. Boardman

🐾🐾🐾🐾 (See South Coast map on page 452)

Sam Boardman was Oregon's first Superintendent of Parks, a visionary who led the effort to build a phenomenal system of preserved public lands. The acquisition of this State Scenic Corridor named in his honor was successfully negotiated as his last triumph before retiring. It's not so much a park as an adventure, a 12-mile long forest on rugged cliffs punctuated by small beaches. As you drive through the park on U.S. Highway 101, there are viewpoints, picnic areas, 300-year-old Sitka spruce trees, and beach access. If you'd rather explore the park on foot, 27 miles of the Oregon Coast Trail wind through its forests and along the coast.

The dynamic duo got a kick out of seeing how fast they could exhaust their humans, hopping in and out of the car at every viewpoint and wayside of the 1,471 acres. Of them all, the Whalehead Beach Trail is the paws-down winner. A narrow path winds through thick brush for about a half mile (in the spring, before feet have trampled down the brush, parts of the path are almost invisible). Undaunted trailblazing bulldogs are rewarded with the largest, most fabulous beach in the park.

You can't miss the park. U.S. Highway 101 drives straight through the middle, beginning four miles north of Brookings. You'll see signs for stops, including a good picnic area at Lone Ranch Beach and great viewpoints at Cape Ferrelo, House Rock, and Indian Sands. On your way, you'll cross over the tallest bridge in Oregon.

26 Oregon Redwood Nature Trail

🐾🐾🐾🐾 🐾 (See South Coast map on page 452)

This awe-inspiring one-mile trail takes you through the Pacific Coast's northernmost grove of redwood trees in the Siskiyou National Forest. You'll get a crick in your neck as you wonder at these giants, estimated to be between 600 and 800 years old. The path is generally easy, with a few steep, rocky, and narrow sections. Your pooch may not appreciate the height of the trees, but she'll certainly enjoy sniffing around their girth and in the equally large ferns on the forest floor. Pick up an interpretive map at the trailhead, which leads you counterclockwise around the trail.

From U.S. Highway 101, turn on the North Bank Chetco River Road and follow the signs. Parking at the trailhead is $5 per day, but if you're up to it, you can park free at Alfred A. Loeb State Park and take the 0.7-mile Riverview Trail connecting to and from this trail.

27 Alfred A. Loeb

🐾🐾🐾 (See South Coast map on page 452)

If you've worked your way along the coast, overdosing on ocean vistas, this state park in the deep woods is a welcome change of pace. Dozens of secluded picnic areas are tucked into a 200-year-old myrtlewood grove, the fragrant trees smelling like bay leaves. The meadows and trails and woods are next to the banks of the Chetco River, here a swift-moving, shallow stream in a wide bed of river rocks. Fish from the gravel bar for salmon and steelhead.

From the picnic area, the Riverview Trail travels 0.7 mile along the shore, connecting you to the Redwood Trail. Cooper highly recommends camping here in the peaceful forest by crystal-clear waters. Isis comes for the amazing variety of birds living in the grove. Note to dogs: Don't eat or play with the orange newts in the region, because their skin secretes a deadly toxin. Note to humans: Don't worry too much, as the newts are fast and can probably out-scamper your scamp.

From U.S. Highway 101, follow the signs to the state park, 10 miles in on the North Bank Chetco River Road. Open 7:30 A.M.–10 P.M. 541/469-2021.

28 Harris Beach
🐾🐾 (See South Coast map on page 452)

You begin to see the wonders of the ocean from the minute you drive into this state park. Unique rock formations loom from several pullout viewpoints, including Goat Island, the coast's largest offshore island. From this area, you can reach the first section of beach on the short Sunset Beach Trail.

Keep driving, and you'll pass the campground to reach the looped parking lot for the main picnic area and a second crescent of silky sand. Picnic tables are well placed for maximum views on a terraced hillside, wheelchair-accessible along a paved path. In between them is an outdoor shower where you and pup can rinse off after a frolic on the small beach. Cooper can't recommend camping here because the sawmill next door makes too much noise at night.

Harris Beach is directly off of U.S. Highway 101, just north of the main section of Brookings. Parking is $3 per day at the main lot. Open 8 A.M.–8 P.M. 541/469-2021.

29 Azalea Park
🐾🐾🐾 (See South Coast map on page 452)

This beautiful and unique city park is at its peak in mid-May, when the azaleas are in full bloom. Imagine the nuances a dog's nose must smell among 1,100 bushes of three species, some up to 300 years old. There are aspects of the park for you and your pets to appreciate all year: rolling hills, an accessible sidewalk and paths through the trees, sand-pit volleyball courts, viewing benches, and hidden picnic tables. Dogs are allowed to pull up a patch of lawn and enjoy summer concerts with you at the Stage Under the Stars and on the big playground called Kid Town. The fragrance from the riot of flowers is most heady in the center of the park, from the observation tower. There are no restrictions except to keep your pet on leash in the ball fields. Like Dorothy and her companions in the poppies, a drowsy afternoon here may lull you to sleep.

The park is easy to find by following the signs from U.S. Highway 101 just north of the Chetco River bridge.

30 McVay Rock
🐾 (See South Coast map on page 452)

This windy, brisk picnic spot is off the beaten path, a quieter place for your dog to explore the local flora and fauna while you take in the endless ocean views. From a gravel parking lot and a petite lawn, a very steep but short trail will take you down to the beach. It's mostly gravel, without water access because of the large rocks in the surf. The rock itself sits several stories tall behind you in someone's field of veggies.

There are no signs directing you to this state recreation site, so watch for Ocean View Drive on U.S. Highway 101, two miles south of Brookings. Turn left there, travel about a mile, and turn left again on Seagull Lane.

PLACES TO EAT

Boogie Board Bagels: Order one of 14 custom bagel sandwiches, or design your own, for breakfast and lunch. Jib Juice smoothies, green salads, and Sailin' Soups are made from scratch daily, just like the bagels. Call ahead to order and go through the drive-through, as there's no outdoor seating. 925 Chetco Ave.; 541/412-9050.

Slugs 'n' Stones 'n' Ice Cream Cones: Where there is moisture in the Northwest, there will be slugs, so why not celebrate them at an ice cream shop? Cooper says they can name themselves after giant Madagascar hissing cockroaches for all he cares, so long as they keep serving up free doggy cones, and big waffle cones of locally famous, more-than-31-flavors of hard scoop Umpqua ice cream. Open March–October. Lower Harbor Rd.; 541/469-7584.

Zola's Pizzeria at the Port: Please do not feed the birds from the patio or tables, asks the management. Feeding the dogs is up to you. Lots of folks in town recommended hanging out and feeding your face with buffalo wings, pizza pies, beer, and wine here at covered, heated, bright red picnic tables. 16362 Lower Harbor Rd.; 541/412-7100.

PLACES TO STAY

Wild Rivers Motor Lodge: The pet-friendliest place in town also happens to be a really excellent choice. Rooms in the newest wing, built in 2004, have granite countertops, big tubs, slate floors, and cherrywood furniture; but even the rooms in the 1970s wing and 1950s wing are great. The owners are a husband and wife team and their son takes care of maintenance. They believe in uncompromising cleanliness and superior customer service. It really shows. Second-floor rooms have distant ocean views. It's the best in town by a mile. At rates of $60–90, it's also a steal. A one-time $20 pet fee covers you for up to two pets and five days. 437 Chetco Ave.; 541/469-5361.

Alfred A. Loeb Campground: There are 48 electrical sites with water, flush toilets, and hot showers by the Chetco River in a grove of myrtlewood trees. Summer rates are $16 per site; in the off-season it's a measly $12. All sites are on a first-come, first-served basis. North Bank Chetco River Road, 10 miles northeast of Brookings. 541/469-2021.

More Accommodations: Please look under *Chain Hotels* in the *Resources* section for additional places to stay in this area.

CHAPTER 17

Greater Portland

It makes sense to be a dog lover in a metro area with 37,000 acres of parks and green spaces within city limits. Despite an annual rainfall that rivals Seattle's, Isis and Cooper can testify that Portlanders will tolerate wet dog smells and muddy paw prints to take advantage of the outdoors under *any* weather conditions. A total of 32 city parks have some off-leash opportunities. There are five full-time, fenced off-leash areas; the remaining 27 are unfenced open areas in specific city parks, and 19 of the 27 have seasonal or limited off-leash hours, some with annoyingly complicated schedules. These latter sites give dogs a place to exercise and play in open areas not designed for other uses. Look for the Exercising Your Pet Off-Leash sign. Good maps are also available at www.portlandonline.com/parks (under the "Recreation" tab, choose "Dogs") or call Portland Parks and Recreation's dog program hotline at 503/823-3647. The Wonder Wieners have included as many of these areas as reasonable, hoping you can find them and that there's at least some parking. They hope you'll go on a dog park tour of the city, exploring historic neighborhoods you might not see otherwise.

PICK OF THE LITTER—GREATER PORTLAND

BEST PARKS
Forest Park, Northwest Portland (page 485)
South Park Blocks, Downtown and Historic Waterfront (page 491)

BEST DOG PARKS
Chimney Park, North Portland (page 478)
Gabriel Park, Southwest Portland (page 500)
Hondo Dog Park, Hillsboro (page 502)
Hazeldale Dog Park, Beaverton (page 503)
Luscher Farm Dog Park, Lake Oswego (page 507)

BEST EVENT
Dogtoberfest, Southeast Portland (page 495)

BEST PLACES TO EAT
Tin Shed Garden Café, Northeast Portland (page 484)
St. Honoré Boulangerie, Northwest Portland (page 486)
The Lucky Lab Brew Pub, Southeast Portland (page 499)

BEST PLACES TO STAY
Ace Hotel, Downtown and Historic Waterfront (page 493)
Hotel deLuxe, Downtown and Historic Waterfront (page 493)
Hotel Lucia, Downtown and Historic Waterfront (page 493)
Jupiter Hotel, Southeast Portland (page 499)

When not braving the elements, the city's diverse populations cluster in ever-present neighborhood coffee houses and bookstores, the greatest of which is Powell's City of Books, the country's largest independent bookseller (1005 W. Burnside; 503/228-0540 or 866/201-7601; www.powells.com). When not drowning in mud, Portland natives also like to drown their sorrows in one of the city's several dozen craft breweries.

If you live in PDX, as locals call their town by its airport designation, you're either an Eastsider or a Westsider, depending on what side of the Willamette River you live on. As a visitor, you get to be a Topsider and take it all in. If you're only in town for a day or two, we suggest you stick around Northwest Portland and Downtown.

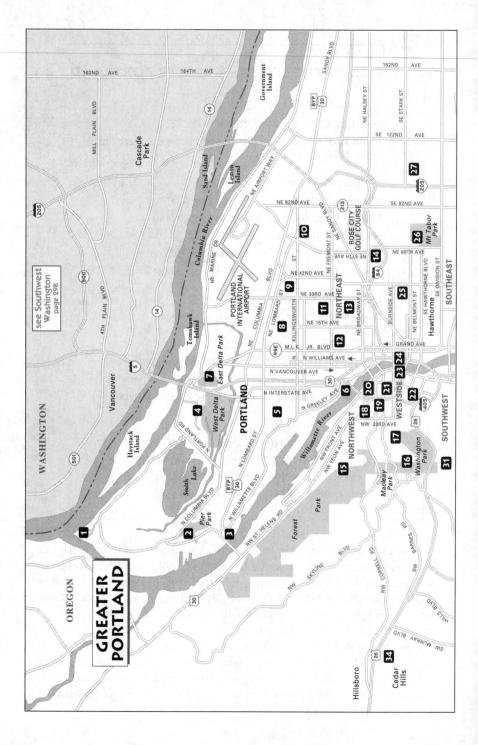

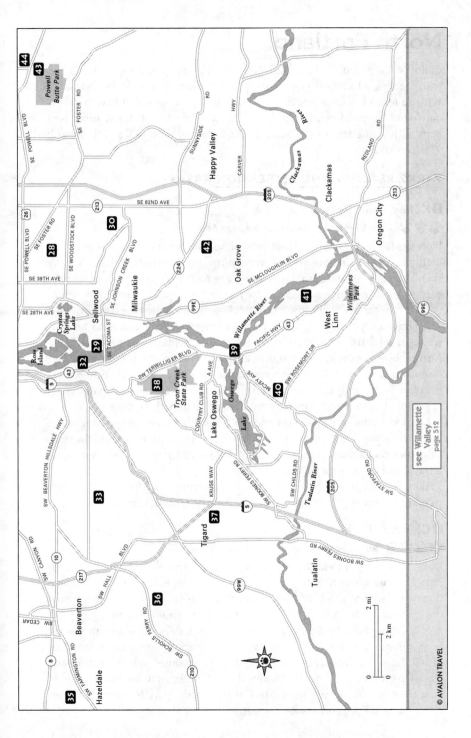

see Willamette Valley page 512

© AVALON TRAVEL

North Portland

Call it NoPo to sound like a local. North Portland is a heavy industrial area, with a couple of historic neighborhoods experiencing modest revitalization. With so few attractions to distract you, your dog hopes you'll have no alternative but to spend hours with her in the district's big off-leash areas, perhaps with a side trip to Tré Bone, a neat little dog shop (8326 N. Lombard; 971/255-0772).

PARKS, BEACHES, AND RECREATION AREAS

1 Kelley Point Park

🐾🐾🐾 (See Greater Portland map on page 476)

Pioneer Hall Jackson Kelley spent most of his later life trying to gain attention for his discoveries in the Oregon Territory. You, on the other hand, can happily spend hours going unnoticed in his 104-acre namesake park, built upon river dredgings. If anything, some spots are a little too private; we were tempted to whistle or wear bear bells to avoid stumbling upon clandestine trysts.

Among heavy tree cover, Kelley Point has paved walkways, woodchip pathways, gravel and dirt trails, and open fields dotted with tiny daisies and clover. Narrow beach coves are strewn with a natural obstacle course of rotting pier posts and driftwood. With the exception of a close-cropped picnic meadow, the place is generally unkempt and overgrown and there are multiple chances to get into Columbia Slough. In short, it's a brilliant park for dogs.

Located on the very tip of Portland, Kelly Point has two large parking areas. First is the south lot, the only place you'll see a worn map for the lay of the land. Dogs may prefer the second, or north lot, for its quick beach access, more open terrain, and massive picnic meadow.

Take Exit 307 from I-5 and go west on N. Marine Drive for 4.5 miles. Turn right into the park. Open 6 A.M.–9 P.M. N. Marine Dr. and Lombard St.

2 Chimney Park

🐾🐾🐾🐾 🐕 (See Greater Portland map on page 476)

Dogs are having a field day at the city's largest fenced and gated off-leash area. It's only a four-mile trip from downtown to get to this full-time 16-acre dog park. Two separately enclosed and gated plots are dedicated to dogs from the crack of dawn until it's too dark to see. The north side is a well-groomed, gently sloping hill with large, mature shade trees. It's also the side with a picnic table, poop bag supplies, and a garbage can. The south side is an uneven field of wildflowers infrequently mowed over. The groomed side is occasionally closed to give the grass time to breathe. Don't look for a tall landmark to guide you; the city's incinerator smokestack that gave the park its name has been removed. Bring your own water.

From I-5 northbound, take exit 306A. Go east on N. Columbia Boulevard for 4.5 miles. Turn left at the sign for the Stanley Parr Archives and Records Center. There's plenty of gravel parking behind the building. Open 5 A.M.–midnight. 9360 N. Columbia.

🔢 Cathedral Park

🐾 🐕 (See Greater Portland map on page 476)

Named after the graceful arches of the St. Johns Bridge overhead, this city park has an illustrious history as one of the camping sites for Lewis and Clark's men. Away from the boat launch and excessive boat trailer parking is a small, unsecured off-leash area, delineated by cable car tracks, the bridge, and Pittsburg Avenue. Cooper can't get excited about coming here for the OLA; he does, however, think the underside workings of the bridge are pretty keen, as are some interesting sculptures on park grounds. It's not too shabby as a picnic choice either, with its setting along the Willamette River and a dabbling of tables. Humans have a real restroom at the boat launch; poop bags and a can are stationed for dogs.

Exit 305B, go west on Lombard Avenue for four miles to the historic St. Johns neighborhood. Turn left on Baltimore and left on Crawford. Park along Crawford or turn right on Pittsburg and park on the street. Open 5 A.M.–midnight.

🔢 Portland International Raceway

🐾 🐕 (See Greater Portland map on page 476)

This off-leash area, formerly known as West Delta Park, has definitely got some quirks. The grounds may flood in the rainy season, the area is used for overflow parking for raceway events, and the winter wild geese population can overrun the field, leaving a whole mess of poop behind. Last, and most bizarre, the place smells like stinky cheese on hot days. It's an empty, three-acre field of scrubby bush, protected by a fence on the north and separated only by a guardrail on the south. There are no amenities.

Why do we bother to mention it? One, the only other OLA in the immediate vicinity closes November–April. Two, it's usually not crowded. And three, even a bad day at a mediocre dog park is better than a good day at the office.

From I-5, take exit 306B and follow the signs to Portland International Raceway. From N. Expo Road, turn left onto N. Broadacre Street. Gravel parking is available along Broadacre. Open 5 A.M.–midnight; check the event schedule at www.portlandraceway.com before you go. 1940 N. Victory Blvd; 503/823-7223.

🔢 Arbor Lodge

🐾 🐕 (See Greater Portland map on page 476)

As in many of the city's limited-hours off-leash sites, the dog area at Arbor Lodge is an unfenced, tree-filled section of a pretty city park. Although partially bounded by tennis courts, basketball courts, and paved pathways, you must have excellent voice control of your pet to protect him from residential traffic on all four sides. You'll need to provide bags and water for your dog. The people's potty is in the center.

From I-5, take Exit 304. Go west on N. Portland Boulevard 0.75 mile, turn right on N. Greeley Avenue and right on N. Bryant Street. The OLA is on the northwest corner of the park. Street parking is available on parts of Bryant. OLA hours are complicated and vary by the season; call 503/823-3647 or go to www.portlandonline .com/parks and select "Dogs" under the "Recreation" tab. N. Bryant St. and Delaware Ave.

6 Overlook Park

(See Greater Portland map on page 476)

The off-leash area at this city park overlooks the industrial workings of a busy city port and rail yards, the Fremont Bridge, and the downtown skyline. More suited to people than pets, it's a tiny triangle at the south end of the park. The view is the upside; the downsides are scarce parking, an unenclosed area without amenities, and a busy medical center next door. It's a panoramic potty stop and not much more.

From I-5, take Exit 303 and turn right on N. Alberta Street. Turn left at the next light and continue south on N. Interstate Avenue for 0.7 mile. You can pass Overlook Boulevard and turn right on N. Fremont Street to park in the cul-de-sac next to the OLA, if you're lucky enough to score a spot. Or, you can turn right on Overlook Boulevard to find easier street parking and walk south on leash until you see the OLA sign. June 15–August 31, OLA hours are 5–10 A.M. and 7 P.M.–midnight; open 5 A.M.–midnight the rest of the year. N. Fremont St. and Interstate Ave.

PLACES TO EAT

Equinox Restaurant: Much like the perfect balance between light and dark, this much-acclaimed restaurant manages to create food that seems light, yet is somehow completely filling. Their mission is to serve food that's fresh, organic, local, and in season, from a natural harvest in tune with the environment. We call it high-falutin' food brought down to earth. Leashed pets will be greeted with a water bowl on the stonework patio. 830 N. Shaver St.; 503/460-3333; www.equinoxrestaurantpdx.com.

PLACES TO STAY

In this area, chain hotels listed in the *Resources* section offer the best choices for dogs and their owners.

Northeast Portland–Airport

Northeast Portland provides room for the large facilities that can't be crammed into the downtown core on the Westside, such as the Portland International Airport and the Convention Center. Lloyd Center, Oregon's largest shopping mall, has 200 retail stores encircling an indoor ice rink. Only a few blocks farther out, the historic neighborhoods of Northeast Portland have distinct personalities, from the blowsy Hollywood area to highly starched Laurelhurst. The many wonderful city parks in Northeast Portland also share a signature look of rolling hills, thick carpets of grass, and a treasure trove of stately, mature deciduous trees that have guarded the city since its infancy.

PARKS, BEACHES, AND RECREATION AREAS

7 East Delta Park

🐾🐾🐕 (See Greater Portland map on page 476)

Across the street from a massive sports complex, this five-acre off-leash area is fully fenced and reserved for unfettered romping. Unfortunately, this OLA site isn't really year-round. It's open only May–October because it tends to be a swamp the rest of the year. Three gates lead into the rectangular space that features rough grass, a few trees, scattered water bowls, and a couple of picnic tables in the shade.

DIVERSION

There are times, no matter how close you are to your canine, that you will need or want to hop on a plane without her. For such times, the **AirPet Hotel** is a stroke of genius. This dog day-care and boarding service is located five minutes from Portland International Airport and offers shuttle services to park-and-fly lots and the flight terminal. Board your dog, park your car, and board your flight. It's that easy.

For a reasonable $30 per day (20 percent discount for multiple dogs), your pet sleeps in a comfy indoor kennel overnight, and during the day she gets to play in a supervised indoor playpen with dogs of similar temperament and size, and she is taken outside for at least five 10-minute potty breaks. She'll fall asleep each night exhausted, well fed, and happy.

Although normal business hours are 6 A.M.–10 P.M., the facility is staffed 24 hours a day. You can arrange early or late drop-off and pickup times by appointment for those red-eye flights. For once, your pet might not mind being left behind. 6212 N.E. 78th Court; 503/255-1388; www.airpethotel.com.

Other areas of the large city park make for good sunbathing and picnicking, but dogs must be leashed, and they are not allowed in the playgrounds, on paved trails, or on the sports fields.

From I-5, take Exit 307 and follow signs to Delta Park and Marine Drive East. Take a left on N. Union Court. The dog park is on the left. Open 5 A.M.–midnight May–October. N. Denver and MLK Jr. Blvd.

8 Alberta Park

🐾🐾🐾🦮 (See Greater Portland map on page 476)

The off-leash area at Alberta is comfortable and roomy. The lawn is soft, punctuated by big trees widely spaced apart. It's unsecured, with borders marked by park pathways along a fairly quiet side of the street. Restrooms, trash cans, water, and poop bag dispensers are available, although the latter are frequently empty. The sheltered basketball court and ball fields at Alberta get only moderate use, often leaving the park to the dogs.

From I-5, take Exit 303 and follow signs to N.E. Killingsworth Street. Go east a little more than a mile and turn left on N.E. 22nd Avenue. The OLA is on the east side of the park. Limited street parking is available alongside. Open 5 A.M.–midnight. N.E. 22nd Ave. and Killingsworth St.

9 Fernhill Park

🐾🐾🐾🦮 (See Greater Portland map on page 476)

The off-leash area at Fernhill Park is a vague, amorphous blob in the center of a 24-acre green space. Your dog will have her choice between open, gently rolling hills and gently rolling hills lightly covered with venerable trees. She's likely to meet new friends among the large group of local dogs who come here. There are no boundaries or fences of any kind to mark the OLA. However, it is big enough to stay a safe distance from the residential streets and the school sports fields. There are restrooms, water fountains, and playground areas. Bring your own bags. Heck, always bring your own bags.

From I-5, take Exit 303 and follow signs to N.E. Killingsworth Street. Go east almost two miles, turn left on N.E. 42nd Avenue and left on N.E. Ainsworth Street. Street parking is available between Ainsworth Street and Ainsworth Court. Open 5 A.M.–midnight. N.E. 37th Ave. and Ainsworth St.

10 Sacajawea Park

🐾🐾🦀 (See Greater Portland map on page 476)

Mornings and evenings, this lovely scratch pad of city greenery goes to the dogs, when kids are out of session at the neighboring head start center. Portland keeps its lawns in tip-top shape and this level plot adds a healthy set of mature trees to vary the funscape. The compact park is entered by a cul de sac and is further protected on two sides by fencing. A single can and a few straggly bags are there for your pick-up pleasure.

Take Exit 23B off I-205, going west on N.E. Killingsworth Street. Turn left on N.E. 82nd Avenue, right on Prescott Street, and right on 75th Avenue, which dead-ends at the park. OLA hours are complicated and vary by the season; call 503/823-3647 or go to www.portlandonline.com/parks and select "Dogs" under the "Recreation" tab. N.E. 75th and Roselawn St.

🐾 Wilshire Park

🐾🐾🐾🐕 (See Greater Portland map on page 476)

Portland's mature trees are alive and well in Wilshire Park in the off-leash area bordered by woodchip walkways, pleasing to the paws for leashed walks. Wilshire has the characteristic look of parks in this area: huge shade trees evenly spaced on lush lawns. The open area is a good size, on the northeast corner of the park bordered by Skidmore and 37th. It's near picnic tables and a children's play area. The nearby streets are not too busy, and the park doesn't seem to get heavy traffic from other users. You are on your own for water and bags, and the nearest garbage can is quite a walk away.

From I-5, take Exit 303. Go east on N.E. Killingsworth for 1.25 miles, turn right on N.E. 33rd Avenue, go 0.6 mile, turn left on N.E. Skidmore Street and right on N.E. 37th Avenue. Street parking is available. Open 5 A.M.–midnight. N.E. 33rd Ave. and Skidmore St.

🐾 Irving Park

🐾🐾🦮 (See Greater Portland map on page 476)

Irving Park is built on one of Portland's four defunct racetracks converted into city parks. Neighborhood dogs cut some racing tracks of their own on the park's hilly off-leash area, bordered by the horseshoe pits and the basketball courts on the west side of the park along 7th Street. Although not secured, the dog spot is a couple of blocks removed from the busiest side street. Irving is another park that is rich and green, sporting a healthy crop of tall trees. There are garbage cans and water fountains; as ever, bring poop bags.

From Highway 99E, go west on N.E. Fremont Street, right on N.E. 7th Avenue, and left on N.E. Siskiyou Street. The safest parking is available on N.E. 8th, 9th, and 10th Avenues, which dead-end into the south side of the park. June 15–September 1, off-leash hours are 5–10 A.M. and 6 P.M.–midnight, extended 4 P.M.–midnight the rest of the year. N.E. 7th Ave. and Fremont St.

🐾 Grant Park

🐾🦮 (See Greater Portland map on page 476)

This park is named in honor of the 18th president of the United States, Ulysses S., who began his career at nearby Fort Vancouver and continued to visit the city throughout his presidency. A celebrity in its own right, the park's setting has inspired many scenes in Beverly Cleary's children's books. There are so many varied activities going on at this community centerpiece that there's not much room left over for the off-leash area. It occupies a tiny, unsecured sliver on the north end at 35th Avenue and Knott Street beyond the soccer fields. Coop 'n' Isis enjoyed a leashed stroll on the park's paved walkways more than spending time in the OLA.

From Highway 99E/Martin Luther King Jr. Boulevard, go east on N.E. Knott Street. Turn right on N.E. 35th Place and park along this dead-end; you'll be directly in front of the dog area. OLA hours are complicated and vary by the season; call 503/823-3647 or go to www.portlandonline.com/parks and select "Dogs" under the "Recreation" tab. N.E. 33rd Ave. and U.S. Grant Pl.

14 Normandale Park

🐾🐾🐾🐕 (See Greater Portland map on page 476)

Double your pleasure and double your fun at this city park's identical twin off-leash sites. The two separately gated and fenced areas are both open in the summer, and one side or the other will close periodically in the rainy season for "turf restoration." The re-greening of these high-traffic dog sites is a lost cause. Lately the city has resorted to dumping piles of sand and wood chips in an attempt to mitigate the mud. Messy conditions do nothing to dampen Normandale's popularity; it's the closest full-time OLA to the city center. These dog parks are a 50–50 balance of open areas and tall conifers, and the sites share water and garbage facilities just outside the front gates. Bring your beloved to bond and smell butts in a lively canine social circle and join in on the turf wars.

From I-84, take Exit 2 into the right-most lane to go west on N.E. Halsey Street. Turn south on 57th to the parking lot at the intersection of N.E. 57th Avenue and N.E. Hassalo Street. Open 5 A.M.–midnight.

PLACES TO EAT

Cup and Saucer: This neighborhood haunt has healthy and filling food concentrating on vegan and vegetarian dishes, not to mention the biggest bowl of dog biscuits the Dachsie Twins have ever seen. It has its own picnic tables and is near Alberta and Fernhill parks. 3000 N.E. Killingsworth; 503/287-4427.

The New Deal Café: A very kid-friendly spot near Normandale Park, The New Deal Café has a small selection of natural foods on one side, tables with a play space on the other, and two picnic tables out front for Frenchie. A chalkboard touts the big breakfast menu, and soups, scrambles, hash, and sandwiches are featured on a daily short list. In the evenings, it's time for burgers and build-your-own pizzas. 5250 N.E. Halsey St.; 503/546-1833; www.thenewdealcafe.com.

Tin Shed Garden Café: Everything on the menu is called Goodness— Stacked Goodness, Scrambled Goodness, Sandwich Goodness, etc.—and oh my goodness, they aren't lying. Get this: There's even a Pet Goodness menu of Kibbles 'n' Bacon Bits (free-range beef), Ham "Barker" Helper (a garden burger), or Paw Lickin' Good (chicken), each with brown rice and garlic. It truly is a big tin shed, with an immense patio, heated by a live fireplace and covered by an authentic wavy garden roof. Humans, don't miss the Belly Pleaser, rice porridge made with coconut milk, spiced with cinnamon, ginger, and vanilla, and topped with mango. 1438 N.E. Alberta; 503/288-6966; www.tinshedgardencafe.com.

PLACES TO STAY

Portlander Inn: This motel is primarily for long-haul truck drivers, but they're good dog people, too. It's a city unto itself. You get a room for great rates starting at $85 per night, and you have access to a movie theater, shoe repair, laundry facilities, deli, country and western bar, gift shop, visitors center, gas station, chiropractor, convenience store, medical clinic, and hair salon. The pet fee is $5 per night for up to two pets, no more than $40 per stay. 10350 N. Vancouver Way; 800/523-1193; www.portlanderinn.com.

More Accommodations: Please look under *Chain Hotels* in the *Resources* section for additional places to stay in this area.

Northwest Portland

In this metro quadrant, there is a city park so large that a man and his daughter lived quite well in its woods for four years before anyone noticed. For hounds who love to hike, the words "Forest Park" may earn a place in the dog linguistic hall of fame alongside treat, ball, car, dinner, and walk.

PARKS, BEACHES, AND RECREATION AREAS

🐾 Forest Park

🐾🐾🐾🐾 (See Greater Portland map on page 476)

As if the 5,400 acres of Forest Park weren't enough, its most popular hiking trail doesn't even start within its borders! The 28-mile hikers-only Wildwood Trail begins near Washington Park's rose garden and wanders up through Hoyt Arboretum before it enters the deep woods of this city wilderness. From the moment you step onto any of Forest Park's trails, Oregon's largest city might as well not exist. Total hiking mileage on developed trails tops out near 70 miles, not including the cross-country trekking people also enjoy in the park. Leif Erickson Drive is the former road that winds 11 miles through the center, providing the widest and most visible path. It rises gently uphill and has handy markers every 0.25 mile to let you know how far you've come. You'll have to share Leif Erickson Drive with mountain bikers; leashes are required and helpful. There's a trail map and a water fountain at the start of Leif Erickson Drive.

From I-405, take Exit 3 and follow the N.W. Vaughn Street exit ramp. Get in the second to the right lane and turn left on N.W. 23rd at the bottom of the exit. Go one block and turn right on N.W. Thurman Street and follow it 1.4 miles to the end. Limited angled parking is available in front of the trailhead gate. Your best resource for park maps is at www.friendsofforestpark.org.

16 Hoyt Arboretum

🐾🐾🐾 (See Greater Portland map on page 476)

The $2 fee is a small price to pay for the map that provides peace of mind in this 185-acre tree museum's maze of vaguely marked trails. Twelve miles of hiking opportunities wind through about 1,100 species of trees, grouped by horticultural family. Starting at the visitors center, where a water bowl is thoughtfully provided for pets, the wheelchair-accessible Overlook Trail will take you and your dog to the dogwood collection. The rest of the park's trails are soft surface. Cooper recommends a seasonal approach to the Hoyt, visiting tree families at their showiest times of the year.

From U.S. Highway 26, 1.8 miles west of downtown, take Exit 72. Turn right on S.W. Knights Boulevard, pass the zoo and the forestry center, and turn right on S.W. Fairview to the parking lot. Grounds are open 6 A.M.–10 P.M.; visitors center hours are 9 A.M.–4 P.M. 4000 S.W. Fairview Blvd.; 503/865-8733; www.hoytarboretum.org.

17 Washington Park–International Rose Test Garden

🐾🐾 👣 (See Greater Portland map on page 476)

No proper visit to the City of Roses would be complete without a visit to the garden that started it all. Portland's International Rose Test Garden in Washington Park is one of the largest and oldest gardens in the country dedicated to the fragrant blooms of the romantic flower. At least 550 varieties are represented in 10,000 plantings on 4.5 acres, on a hilltop with city views. Picture-taking, stopping to smell the flowers, and walking on leash are encouraged, whereas pruning or digging is punishable by a $500 fine. There is a rose gift shop, and for the nose who thinks a rose by any other name wouldn't smell as sweet as a hot dog, there is a snack bar.

Beyond the rose garden, Washington Park includes many non-dog activities and sites, including the Oregon Zoo, the World Forestry Education Center, the Children's Museum (CM2), and a Japanese Botanical Garden.

Go west through downtown on W. Burnside Street. Although you'll see several signs to Washington Park, wait until S.W. Tichner Drive to make a sharp left-hand turn up the hill, then turn right on S.W. Kingston, following the more specific signs to the rose garden. 400 S.W. Kingston Ave.; 503/823-3636.

PLACES TO EAT

St. Honoré Boulangerie: The car turned, seemingly of its own will, toward this French café as we headed up to Forest Park. The soups, salads, and rows of éclairs and croissants are all stunning, and there's ample outdoor seating at umbrella-shaded tables. 2335 N.W. Thurman St.; 503/445-4342; www.sainthonorebakery.com.

Nob Hill

This high-profile neighborhood is also called the Northwest District or the Alphabet District, because the streets progress alphabetically north from Burnside. Its north–south avenues, especially 23rd and 21st, are full of trendy shops and a superb collection of outdoor eats. Your dog is sure to get extra pats and leftovers in this sophisticated and pet-perfect area to walk, window shop, and dine.

PARKS, BEACHES, AND RECREATION AREAS

18 Wallace Park

🐾🐾 🦮 (See Greater Portland map on page 476)

For years, Wallace Park has been known as the place to go for a pickup game of basketball. Since implementation of this park's off-leash area, a new breed of ball players are dribbling in the northeast corner, and the pickup action is equally hot. The whole park is only five acres, so the OLA is perhaps a tad larger than a regulation half-court. It has a chicken wire fence on three sides to protect it from busy side streets, and the fourth side is open to the interior of the park, with covered and open picnic tables for spectators. Bring your own bags; water and a trash can are provided.

Go west on W. Burnside Street, turn right on N.W. 23rd Avenue, left on N.W. Pettygrove Street, and right on N.W. 25th Avenue. The OLA is on the northeast corner at the intersection of 25th and Raleigh. Limited parking is available on side streets. OLA hours are 5–9 A.M. and 6 P.M.–midnight April–October, extended from 4 P.M. November–March. N.W. 25th Ave. and Raleigh St.

19 Couch Park

🐾🐾 🦮 (See Greater Portland map on page 476)

Rarely has so small a space received so much gleeful use by the four-legged patrons who call Couch Park home. And oh boy does it get muddy in the winter! The small, unsecured off-leash area is squished between a terraced play structure and a walkway on a slight slope on the north side on the park on Hoyt Street between the 19th and 20th Avenue blocks. It's hectic day and night in and around the park, across the street from a private school and only two blocks from one of the hottest street scenes in the city. Only the most civilized and completely voice-controlled dogs should be allowed off leash. Barking and street parking are at a premium in Couch Park.

Go west on W. Burnside Street, turn right on N.W. 21st Avenue and right

on N.W. Hoyt Street. OLA hours are complicated and vary by the season; call 503/823-3647 or go to www.portlandonline.com/parks and select "Dogs" under the "Recreation" tab. N.W. 19th Ave. and Glisan St.

PLACES TO EAT

Alotto Gelato: The only thing served at this storefront counter is gelato, up to 30 flavors of ice cream and sorbets, every day a little different. The line often goes around the block, and that's just the dogs. 931 N.W. 23rd Ave.; 503/228-1709.

McMenamins Blue Moon Tavern: People and their pets have been gathering at the sidewalk picnic tables of this hot spot since 1933 to drink pints of ale and down great burgers and fresh-cut fries. The Terminator Stout should impress even Guinness fans. 432 N.W. 21st Ave.; 503/223-3184; www.mcmenamins.com.

Papa Haydn: This sidewalk dessert bar is a Sunday brunch tradition. The small selection of lunch and dinner items is far outstripped by a menu of profanely rich cakes. Come for cake; the rest is an afterthought. 701 N.W. 23rd; 503/228-7317; www.papahaydn.com.

Yuki: This Japanese restaurant's menu is a struggle for the indecisive. The sushi menu alone takes up four pages, and that doesn't include the yakisoba noodles, teriyaki, tempura, and combinations of all of the above. Bento boxes are the perfect compromise, and they look like little works of art. 930 N.W. 23rd Ave.; 503/525-8807.

PLACES TO STAY

Park Lane Suites: This suites hotel is perfect for longer stays. Each unit is apartment-style, with full kitchens, living rooms with TV, onsite laundry, and business desks. One medium-sized dog per room is allowed for a $15 per night fee (negotiable for longer stays). It's in a desirable neighborhood surrounded by restored mansions, a block away from chic 23rd Street. Rates range $100–210. 809 S.W. King Ave.; 503/226-6288; www.parklanesuites.com.

More Accommodations: Please look under *Chain Hotels* in the *Resources* section for additional places to stay in this area.

Pearl District

Just north of downtown is the recently gentrified Pearl District, where industrial warehouses have been reborn into sleek loft apartments and galleries. To say that The Pearl is dog-friendly is to utter a profound understatement. Seemingly, life has been designed around the dog, including enough places to eat outdoors to fill four hollow legs. For in-city living and visiting, the Pearl is the cat's meow. Sorry dogs, it had to be said.

PARKS, BEACHES, AND RECREATION AREAS

20 "The Field" in the Pearl

🐾 🦴 (See Greater Portland map on page 476)

There's an unofficial off-leash area in The Pearl, and as this book went to press, it did exist, but there's no telling what'll happen in the future. The local condo construction company has been really cool about supporting The Pearl's extensive pet community, installing some benches, planting a few trees, and placing and maintaining several bag dispensers in the wide, open area. The ground cover consists of alternating patches of sand and grass, and there's

DIVERSIONS

Catering especially to petite canine clientele, **Lexidog** does it all. The boutique and social club hosts fashion shows, carries a high-end gift selection, has a bakery, and provides highly-supervised play groups. 416 N.W. 10th Ave.; 503/243-6200; lexidog.com. Feeling less than fresh? D'Tails in the Pearl next door will spiff you up with a pawdicure, body wrap, facial, or some soothing aromatherapy. 503/516-7387; dtailsdogsalon.com.

Dogstar is a big winner with long suffering, hard working pet parents, who can drop Darling off for daycare early and pick her up late when she's clean, tired, and happy to see you. Dogstar also charges only $10 for three hours of sitting from 6–9 P.M. on First Thursday, the Pearl District's popular art gallery walk. Check out explorethepearl. com. 1313 N.W. Kearney; 503/227-0292; dogstar.us.

some fencing, but don't count on it for security. All we ask is that you be extra conscientious of your dog's behavior here, to improve the chances of any part of it becoming an official dog park. There's no shade; bring your own water.

Go to the corner of 11th Avenue and N.W. Overton Street, and then look to the northeast to find the field, past the construction fencing. You'll see the bag dispensers and garbage cans, the only clue you're in the right place. There's paid parking along side streets, but do not park inside construction areas.

21 North Park Blocks

🐾 🐾 (See Greater Portland map on page 476)

These six park squares in The Pearl are close to the majority of downtown's vintage hotels, a handy place to walk your dog. If you see dogs veering automatically to the west at the corner of N.W. Everett Street, it's because they know treats await them at Urban Fauna. Also in the North Blocks, Portland dogs have their very own Benson Bubbler, a bottomless brass bowl of water on the west side north of N.W. Davis Street, created by the famous dog photographer William Wegman. Coop thinks he should've made it in the shape of a toilet bowl.

The North Park Blocks are on Park Avenue between W. Burnside Street and N.W. Hoyt Street. Metered street parking is $1.50 for up to 90 minutes. Open 5 A.M.–10 P.M.

PLACES TO EAT

Blue Hour: Seattleites Stacya, David, and Chester the Dog frequent this gourmet Mediterranean nightspot when in Portland. They enjoy being pleasantly surprised by the menu, printed daily to use the freshest seasonal ingredients and to please the chef's whim. Repeat after Isis: "Five star elegance—when eating your own dung simply will not do." 250 N.W. 13th Ave.; 503/226-3394; www.bluehouronline.com.

Paragon Restaurant and Bar: Coop 'n' Isis' mom has two words for you: signature cocktails. Here's two more: house-made desserts. At Paragon, truly fine Americana food is served outdoors on a covered, elevated platform. The restaurant gives a former warehouse building with rolling garage doors a second life, while their infused vodkas, tequila, and rums will give you a second wind for being the life of the party. 1309 N.W. Hoyt; 503/833-5060; www.paragonrestaurant.com.

Pearl Bakery: This patisserie and bistro excels in the French tradition of foods that make the difficult look easy and taste simply delectable. Try their meltingly rich brioche, chiffon cake, and eggplant, red pepper, and mozzarella sandwiches. We did. 102 N.W. 9th Ave.; 503/827-0910; www.pearlbakery.com.

Pop Culture: This shop makes frozen, fat free, lactose free, live culture yogurt treats that are as good for dogs' digestive systems as they are for yours. Imagine, guilt-free goodness! The "Home of the Pearl Swirl," a yogurt and fresh fruit extravaganza, has sandwiches and soups as well, plus a couple of outdoor tables. 900 N.W. Lovejoy St.; 503/477-9172; www.pcyogurt.com.

Rogue Ales Distillery and Public House: How about a burger, fries, and a carob-frosted cupcake? No, silly, that's the dog's menu, not yours! Rogue has a full specialty menu for your pooch. You can have a beer and, okay, your own menu on the patio, when joining your dog for a night out. 1339 Flanders; 503/222-5910; www.rogue.com.

Downtown and Historic Waterfront

Downtown Portland is ideal for dog-walkers. Built on a European model, using half-size city blocks, the city encourages exploration on foot. Smaller lots have left more room for pocket parks, water gardens, plazas, and plenty of foliage. Drinking water, too, is plentiful downtown in Benson Bubblers, 20 elegant freshwater drinking fountains commissioned at the turn of the 19th century by wealthy lumber baron and teetotaler Simon Benson. Pet-friendly lodging is equally abundant downtown. It's difficult to find a hotel that's *not* pet-friendly.

Portland's enhanced status as a pedestrian city may be due partially to the fact that getting around by car can be complicated. With the Willamette River cutting a wide swath north–south, and the Columbia River dividing Oregon and Washington, going across town requires crossing one of the area's 17 major bridges.

To take in the city in a nutshell, hang out with your dog in Pioneer Courthouse Square, Portland's outdoor living room. Walk along the waterfront park for the Portland Saturday Market under the Burnside Bridge, for more than 250 crafts booths, food, and music on Saturday (and Sunday) March–December 24th.

PARKS, BEACHES, AND RECREATION AREAS

22 South Park Blocks

🐾🐾🐾 (See Greater Portland map on page 476)

Leave plenty of time for walks along the city's South Park Blocks, an even dozen lawn-carpeted squares lined with aged elms from Salmon Street to

DETOURS

PDX Pedicabs allows dogs for no extra charge. While you relax on the comfy bench in back, a driver pedals the tricycle along the length of the Riverplace Marina area, pointing out the many stops for outdoor wining and dining. Our driver Leeman gave us great tips on where to eat while he worked off his calories, if not yours. 503/733-4222; www.pdxpedicab.com.

Jackson Street on Park Avenue. You'll pass through Portland State University and the heart of the cultural district, including the Portland Center for the Performing Arts, Arlene Schnitzer Concert Hall ("The Schnitz"), classical Portland Art Museum, historic First Congregational Church, and the Oregon Historical Society, with its multi-story, elaborate *trompe l'oeil* mural. You'll see all walks of life, and many manners of breeds, on your perambulations.

If you're slaving away at the computer, but your dog is waiting at your feet with his leash in his mouth, make a compromise. Check your email or surf the Internet from any park bench in the South Blocks. The whole area is a free Wi-Fi hotspot.

Parking is practically nonexistent along the South Park Blocks. Find a long-term lot downtown and walk. Open 5 A.M.–10 P.M.

23 Governor Tom McCall Waterfront Park

🐾🐾 (See Greater Portland map on page 476)

Waterfront Park is a mile-long sidewalk promenade built on top of Portland Harbor Wall, the single most expensive piece of infrastructure built by the city. It replaced rotting docks and dilapidated pier buildings in the 1920s. Buried within is the first sewer system on the west side of the river. From 2003 to 2006, another 1.2 billion dollars was spent on the Big Pipe project, to update the sewer system to handle modern population pressures. A master plan currently in place proposes $45 million in park improvements over the next 25 years.

The park is well used and it shows. What once were lawns have taken a repeated beating from Saturday Market booths and frequent city festivals. Goose poop takes over on the south end, and transients sleep here and there. It's still a languid stroll among statues and fountains, sculptures, and the occasional garden. We recommend crossing at the Hawthorne or Steel Bridges to join up with the Eastbank Esplanade. The south end of Waterfront Park expands to a grassy slope down to the beach. North of the Burnside Bridge, the Japanese Historical Plaza deserves a quick look-see. From the north end, the Pearl District is close, as is Powell's City of Books.

Tom McCall Waterfront Park is on Naito Parkway, essentially between the Broadway Bridge and the Marquam Bridge. We can recommend parking in a Smart Park Lot between N.W. Davis and N.W. Everett Streets.

PLACES TO EAT

Carafe: With an owner from Paris, this French bistro is as authentic as it gets. It serves escargot, smelly cheeses, and confit of duck, and *pomme frites* come with mayo, not ketchup. The outdoor seating is also traditional European, with all seats facing out toward the park plaza to observe the pulse of the city. 200 S.W. Market St.; 503/248-0004; www.carafebistro.com.

Kenny and Zukes: Borscht and blintzes and bialys, oh my! A delicatessen in the Jewish tradition, Kenny and Zuke's is the place to get your fix for old-fashioned flavors such as pastrami, liver, and corned beef on sandwiches bigger than Cooper's head. 1038 S.W. Stark St.; 503/222-3354; www.kennyandzukes.com.

South Park: Reservations are a must for dinner at this seafood grill and wine bar in the midst of the cultural center of town. You and your well-mannered dog will compete for patio tables with crowds from the symphony, theater, and college. South Park combines fresh local produce and catch of the day in creative ways, paired with a lengthy list of wines by the glass. 901 S.W. Salmon St.; 503/326-1300; www.southparkseafood.com.

PLACES TO STAY

Ace Hotel: Our dear friend Andrea and her golden Ellie turned us onto this unique and über-cool (as in, as cool as it gets) locale. Designer touches include Pendleton wool blankets, natural latex bedding, iPod docks, and art in every room. The Ace is awesome for connoisseurs of the spare and modern. From rooms with shared bathrooms as low as $95 to penthouse suites at $250, the choice to be among the cognoscenti is yours. The Ace doesn't charge a pet fee. 1022 S.W. Stark St.; 503/228-2277; www.acehotel.com.

Heathman Hotel: *Condé Nast Traveler* and *Travel + Leisure* have rated this luxurious hotel among their top favorites in the world, perhaps because its list of services and amenities is longer than a Great Dane's legs. The Heathman is perhaps most famous for doormen dressed like the guy on the Beefeater Gin bottle. Pets are welcome on the third floor for a $35 per night pet fee. A park is right behind the hotel for necessary business. Rates range $190–300. 1001 S.W. Broadway; 503/241-4100; www.heathmanhotel.com.

Hotel deLuxe: This 1912 boutique hotel near the PGE Stadium has gone Hollywood, in a historic renovation of what used to be the beloved but worse for wear Hotel Mallory. The deLuxe pays homage to Hollywood's heyday, decorating all floors and rooms with more than 400 black-and-white movie stills from the 1930s to the 1950s. You can be relaxing in throwback glitz, tempered by modern conveniences such as iPod docks, Wi-Fi, and flat-screen HDTVs watched from the comfort of your downy bed. Your pet is as pampered as a starlet with bottled water, a bag of treats, and the Furry Friend's Room Service Menu. Rooms run $170–250, and there's a non-refundable $45 pet fee per stay. 729 S.W. 15th Ave.; 503/219-2094 or 800/228-8657; www.hoteldeluxe.com.

Hotel Lucia: Cooper and Isis get into a tiff when we travel to Portland, because he wants to stay at this modern masterpiece of serenity, while she prefers the Studio-era Hollywood glam of Hotel deLuxe. Although opposites in character, the hotels are owned by the same group, one that welcomes pets without restrictions. Hotel Lucia's art collection alone is worthy of a visit, including 679 photographs of Pulitzer Prize–winner David Hume Kennerly. The dog bowls are on loan only, but you may keep the Aveda products and the jazz CD from your room. Rates range $125–195. 400 S.W. Broadway; 503/225-1717; www.hotellucia.com.

Hotel Monaco: A part of the always super dog-friendly Kimpton Hotel group, this hotel is part exotic and part whimsical, with a style featuring rich colors and Anglo-Chinois furnishings and decor. It's got every amenity you can imagine, including Art, the golden lab who is Director of Pet Relations. There are treats, waste bags, and bottled water for pets; there are no pet deposits, weight restrictions, or limitations. Three woofs for Kimpton! Humans, never fret, you are also taken care of exceptionally well here. Rates range $150–260. 506 S.W. Washington St.; 503/222-0001; www.monaco-portland.com.

Hotel Vintage Plaza: Lovely and luxurious, this upscale hotel is cared for as though it were a well-loved antique. The ambience is inspired by a French vineyard, bright enough to make you thirsty for a sip of the grape, and relaxing enough for you to nap peacefully afterward. This is a Kimpton Hotel, where dogs are always treated as first-class citizens; for example, there's a pet honor bar in each room stocked with treats and goodies rivaling yours. Rates range $130–270; there is no fee for pets. 422 S.W. Broadway; 800/263-2305; www.vintageplaza.com.

Mark Spencer Hotel: The Spence was famous as a traveling artists' hotel from 1907 to the 1960s. It was converted to apartments and then back to a hotel again, with a rooftop garden, tiny appliances, and walk-in closets left over from its apartment era. The hotel's frumpy Bohemian air is favored by the arts and theater crowd. While a bit worn around the edges, it's one of the few affordably elegant choices downtown, with rates ranging $100–190, and a name your price option when availability allows. 409 S.W. 11th Ave.; 503/224-3293; www.markspencer.com.

RiverPlace Hotel: Isis never knew that the royal treatment—bottled water, porcelain bowls, dog biscuits, and personalized notes delivered on a tray to the room—is standard for all canine guests. Humans are equally spoiled. Request a riverside or courtyard room for the best views. All rooms are open to dogs without size restrictions, except for a 30-pound limit in 10 condo units. A Doggie Diner menu is available from room service. Waterfront Park is the hotel's backyard. Rates range from $210 for a deluxe room to $525 for the grand suite; there is a $50 nonrefundable pet cleaning fee. 1510 Southwest Harbor Way; 800/227-1333; www.riverplacehotel.com.

More Accommodations: Please look under *Chain Hotels* in the *Resources* section for additional places to stay in this area.

Southeast Portland

Southeast Portland is perhaps best described as bohemian, honoring the hippie more than the hip. Hawthorne Boulevard and Belmont Street are the places to find an eclectic mix of retro storefronts, dining, and avant-garde theater. If

DOG-EAR YOUR CALENDAR

It's a dog-eat-dog world at the Berlin Inn's annual **Barktober-fest**, where the pooch sausage-eating contest is about technique, not quantity. On the second weekend in September, this restaurant hosts dog events and activities all weekend, complete with beer and bratwurst for canine chaperones. Funds raised benefit the humane society, dog rescue, and no-kill shelters. 3131 S.E. 12th; 503/236-6761; www.berlininn.com.

Dogtoberfest, otherwise known as the dog wash at the Lucky Lab, will celebrated its 15th year in 2009. The record is 600 dogs washed and $4,000 raised in one day to benefit local Dove Lewis Animal Hospital. Festivities include T-shirts, music, and a special brew, Dog Wash Pale Ale. Drink some suds while celebrity dog-washers suds up your pup. Usually held on a September weekend, it's just one of many annual events to support Dove Lewis, a pet hospital specializing in emergency and critical care, 365 days a year, 24 hours a day. Keep your eye on the events calendar for more fun, including DoveBowl, the Wet Nose Soiree, Pets in the Pearl, and Dine Out for Dove, at www.dovelewis.org or 503/535-3384.

you or your kids are science buffs, drop your pal at doggy daycare for a half day and visit the Oregon Museum of Science and Industry (OMSI). A stop into The Lucky Lab Brewing Co. is a must for dog lovers.

PARKS, BEACHES, AND RECREATION AREAS

24 Eastbank Esplanade

😺😺 (See Greater Portland map on page 476)

Located between the historic Hawthorne and Steel Bridges, this 1.5-mile waterfront promenade hugs the eastern banks of the Willamette River. It provides a superb unobstructed look at the city skyline and boasts a series of sculptures celebrating Portland's history. On the north end, a lower deck on the Steel Bridge provides bicycle and pedestrian access to Waterfront Park. The park's 1,200-foot floating dock is the longest in the United States, supported by 65 concrete pylons.

Your only hope for parking is on Carruthers Street, south of the Hawthorne Bridge. From I-5, take Exit 300 and get in the right lane to exit at OMSI/Central Eastside Industrial District. Turn right onto S.E. Water Street, go 0.7 mile, and turn right on S.E. Carruthers Street to the dead-end.

25 Laurelhurst Park

🐾🐾🐾🐾 (See Greater Portland map on page 476)

Laurelhurst is a city institution. Emanuel Mische of the famed Olmsted Brothers landscape firm created the park in 1912, the electric lights were lit for the first time in 1915, and, in 1919, it was named the most beautiful park on the West Coast. In 2001, it became the first city park to be listed on the National Register of Historic Places. The park is straight out of an impressionist painting, complete with parasol-shaded ladies and dapper gentlemen walking arm in arm under antique lighting fixtures. The pond has elegant swans and blue herons nesting under a weeping willow. The leaves fall gently as a yellow Lab runs screaming by after stealing a toy from his Doberman playmate. Yes, friends, as genteel as it may seem on the surface, Laurelhurst has had a regular base of boisterous canine clientele.

Dogs are fortunate to have an off-leash area in such a high-profile park. To help keep the privilege, it's critical that you and your dog respect the area's boundaries in the center on the south side, along Oak Street, defined by the walkways, and remain leashed while walking the rest of the park.

From Highway 99E, go east on E. Burnside Street to S.E. 39th Avenue, the eastern border of the park. Turn right on S.E. Oak Street. Parking is ad hoc, on the streets bordering the park perimeter. OLA hours vary by season and events; call 503/823-3647 or go to www.portlandonline.com/parks and select "Dogs" under the "Activities" tab. S.E. 39th Ave. and Stark St.

26 Mount Tabor Park

🐾🐾🐾 (See Greater Portland map on page 476)

Mount Tabor is an extinct volcano, which probably hasn't been active for about 3 million years. The dog scene, on the other hand, is very active at this city park. Only a tiny sliver of the 196-acre mountain is designated as an off-leash area, and it isn't even where the crowds tend to congregate. The city is trying to discourage the impromptu sniffing social on the west side of the mountain, above the largest reservoir, because the grass gets torn up, leading to runoff problems. You can help by sticking to the official, partially fenced area, on the south side near the Harrison Street entrance.

You can join the cruising canines hanging out of car windows on the loop drive to the 643-foot summit. On Wednesdays, the park is car-free, transforming the roads into bigger trails. For buns of steel, you and your Bernese can try climbing the stairs, essentially straight up. Multiple dirt paths cross and climb the point, and you can make up a different route every time you go, past the park's three reservoirs, the bronze statue by Gutzon Borglum (of Mount Rushmore fame), through the Douglas fir, around the crater amphitheater, and so on. Mount Tabor is a gathering place in the heart of Southeast Portland, and your dog can make multiple friends while you take in the great city views.

From I-84, take Exit 5 and turn right at the stop sign at the bottom of the exit ramp. Go one block and turn left on S.E. 82nd Avenue, go 1.1 miles, turn right on S.E. Yamhill Street, turn left on S.E. 76th Avenue, go 0.5 mile and turn right on S.E. Harrison Street, and follow the signs into the park. There is angled parking. Open 7 A.M.–9 P.M., www.taborfriends.com.

27 Cherry Park
🐾🐾🐾 (See Greater Portland map on page 476)

Cherry is long and skinny with a shaggy border—hey, like a Saluki! It's safely hemmed in on the two long sides by nice tall fences, and on the two short sides by residential dead-end streets. About two-thirds of the way through, you enter a dense forest, a veritable grove of trees. This city park has no facilities other than a few hand-hewn benches, providing a Spartan atmosphere for navel contemplation or tail chasing, your preference. The sand and gravel pit on the south side is a mild distraction; otherwise, there is nothing going on here. Cooper wants his buddies to know that Cherry Park has some serious squirrel action.

Take Exit 19 from I-205, going east on S.E. Division Street. Turn left on 112th Avenue, left on Market Street, and left on 106th Avenue to wind your way into the dead-end at the park.

28 Woodstock Park
🐾🐾🐾 (See Greater Portland map on page 477)

There are a bunch of neighborhood dogs who take advantage of the off-leash area at Woodstock Park on the west side of the park along 47th Avenue, south of Steele. It's slightly hilly and has neat green grass and big deciduous trees. In response to a problem complying with waste pickup laws, there are giant, blue plastic trash cans cabled to each of the trees bordering the OLA as a major hint. There is no fence around the area and you need to stay well clear of busy Steele Street. Playgrounds, a wading pool, and the restrooms are near the dog play area.

From Highway 99E, go east on U.S. Highway 26, S.E. Powell Boulevard. Turn right on S.E. 52nd Avenue, right on S.E. Steele Street, and left on S.E. 47th Avenue. Street parking is available along 47th. OLA hours are complicated and vary by the season; call 503/823-3647 or go to www.portlandonline.com/parks and select "Dogs" under the "Recreation" tab.

29 Sellwood Riverfront Park and Oaks Bottom Trail

🐾🐾🦆 (See Greater Portland map on page 477)

The off-leash area at Sellwood carves out a healthy center section of the nine-acre city park in the center of the intersection of S.E. Spokane and Oaks Parkway. You'll need excellent voice control of your dog, as there is no fencing nor natural features to separate the OLA from other park uses.

Many parts of Sellwood are worth exploring on leash. The riverfront part of the park is easy to reach by means of a ramp, and it extends around the bend all the way to Portland's historic Oaks Amusement Park, operating since 1904. The views of the city and Sellwood Bridge are great.

Sellwood also connects to the Oaks Bottom Trail, a 1.5-mile, soft-surface hike through a wildlife refuge packed with more than 140 species of birds, mammals, reptiles, and amphibians. You're most likely to see great blue herons, beavers, and muskrats in addition to the usual geese and ducks. It's a level and shady walk with late summer blackberries free for the picking.

From I-5, take exit 297 south on S.W. Terwilliger Boulevard for 0.9 mile, turn left onto S.W. Taylors Ferry Road for one mile, and right on S.W. Macadam Avenue 0.5 mile to the Sellwood Bridge. Cross the bridge and immediately turn left on S.E. 7th Avenue to S.E. Oaks Parkway. OLA hours vary by the season; call 503/823-3647 or go to www.portlandonline.com/parks and select "Dogs" under the "Recreation" tab.

30 Brentwood Dog Park

🐾🐕 (See Greater Portland map on page 477)

Although trees and grass have been planted, the fenced off-leash area at Brentwood City Park is a muddy patch of rectangular earth carved out of an existing park. It sits in a depression, gathering runoff from the sprinklers on the sports fields. After 15 minutes with her beloved soccer ball ("The ball, the ball, PUULEEEZ the ball!"), Isis came away with enough earth caked in her fur to bake four-and-twenty blackbirds into a mud pie. She suggests you give in to it and get covered head-to-toe. As any dog will tell you, that whole cleanliness-is-next-to-godliness thing is overrated. Bring your own bags, water, and a stack of towels.

From I-205, take Exit 17 west toward S.E. Woodstock, turn left at the next intersection on S.E. 92nd Avenue, then right on S.E. Duke Street, and left on S.E. 62nd. The OLA is on the southeast corner of 62nd Avenue and S.E. Rural Street. Street parking is on 62nd, south of S.E. Cooper Street. Open 5 A.M.–midnight. S.E. 60th Ave. and Duke St.

PLACES TO EAT

Berlin Inn: Dogs, that's *hunds* in German, have their very own Patio Pooch Menu for dining in the *biergarten* at this upscale Bavarian restaurant. Canine connoisseurs can select from items such as Lollipups, a peanut butter biscuit on a rawhide stick; a Bag-O-Bones sampler of treats; or Mutt Mix, two turkey hot dogs sliced and tossed with biscuits. Humans are treated to filling gourmet fare, fine wines, sponge cake tortes, and, of course, German beer. 3131 S.E. 12th; 503/236-6761; www.berlininn.com.

Cooper's Coffee: Our Cooper could barely maintain his composure when he discovered this fine establishment with lots of room for outdoor eating, named for another honorable furry four-legger whose portrait hangs on the wall. Fill out your sandwich order card with a grease pencil and hand it to the kind people behind the counter, or pick from a light menu of lasagna, quiches, and salads. Stop by after a visit to nearby Mount Tabor, and stay for evening acoustic music sets. 6049 S.E. Stark St.; 503/805-2835.

Dingo's Fresh Mexican Grill: Dingo's has dozens of picnic tables, a full bar, sit-down service, and inventive Mexican food, all on a hip street within a few blocks of Mount Tabor Park. The restaurant is popular for tequila samplers and breakfast, although perhaps not together. 4612 S.E. Hawthorne Blvd.; 503/233-3996; www.dingosonline.com.

The Lucky Lab Brew Pub: Some people would have a tough time choosing between beer or their dog as their truest best friend. Fortunately, they can have both, and decent grub, at this pub that's famous in canine social circles. Outside is a big, covered patio with dozens of picnic tables; inside, the walls are lined with photos of the many Labs and other breeds who have paid a visit. Add a little extra to your beer money to buy a Lucky Lab T-shirt or hat. 915 S.E. Hawthorne Blvd.; 503/236-3555; www.luckylab.com.

Two more locations celebrate life's good things: the Lucky Labrador Beer Hall at 1945 N.W. Quimby (503/517-4352) and Lucky Labrador Public House at 7675 S.W. Capitol Highway (503/244-2537).

PLACES TO STAY

Jupiter Hotel: Props go to the Jupiter for being the most mod, looking straight out of the 1960s after a 2004 update. In the Bohemian Hollywood District, the rooms fit right in, with unique murals, chalkboard art doors, and shag throw rugs. Don't let the kitsch fool you; modern amenities include Wi-Fi, HDTVs, iPod docks, and bamboo floors. This is not the place to stay for peace and quiet. It's a party town, especially weekends, with the largest independent music venue on the grounds (called Doug Fir) and wee-hour cocktails under the Dream Tent. The dog gift basket is unbelievable. Yours to keep are collapsible bowl and water bottle dispensers, a coupon book for pet-friendly businesses, bags, a box of designer treats, a map of local parks, and so on. Rates range $90–150. The pet fee is $30 a night, up to $90 per stay. 800 E. Burnside; 503/230-9200 or 877/800-0004; www.jupiterhotel.com.

Southwest Portland

Southwest Portland is green with money as well as trees. The real estate taxes in this area climb in direct proportion to the elevation, all the way to the city's highest point at Council Crest.

PARKS, BEACHES, AND RECREATION AREAS

31 Marquam Nature Trail and Council Crest Park

🐾🐾🐾 (See Greater Portland map on page 476)

On a very clear day at the 1,043-foot summit of Council Crest, you can see the city and the Mounts of Hood, Adams, Jefferson, St. Helens, and even Rainier. And, if you time it right, your dog can enjoy the off-leash area on the southeast hillside, although it's steep and has no fence or dog amenities.

The tip of Council Crest is panoramic in every direction, but the point of including this park in the book, according to Cooper, is to access the Marquam Nature Trail. It's a great city escape through a primal fern-filled canyon forest. On this steep, lung-capacity-challenging hike, there are so many things outdoor dogs love: trees, wildflowers, squirrels, and plump banana slugs, whose slime creates a favored hair gel for Isis. For stretches of the trail's 1.5-mile length, you'll feel lost in the woods, until you see the West Hill mansions tucked in the green space. On the trail, use the leash, pick up the poop, and don't pick the purple trilliums.

To corkscrew up the hill to Council Crest, take S.W. Broadway Drive south through downtown, stay in the far right to avoid the Barbur Boulevard/99W interchange, and follow Broadway another 1.3 miles. Turn left on S.W. Greenway Avenue, go another 0.7 mile, and take the right fork onto S.W. Council Crest Drive. Council Crest's OLA hours are 5–11 A.M. and 6–10 P.M. April–October, extended from 4 P.M. the rest of the year. The top of the hill within the boundaries of the circular drive is added to the OLA during these extended winter hours (bring the glow-in-the-dark toys). S.W. Council Crest Dr.

32 Willamette Park

🐾🐾🐕 (See Greater Portland map on page 477)

Willamette has a choice waterfront location, south of the city. The unfenced off-leash area is a good-sized landing strip, half open and half shaded. The grass is thick and green, a nice playground for those with paws. Soccer fields occupy the south end of the park, so the best time to enjoy this spot is midday weekdays, when there are no games. The only other users are boaters headed straight for the water; you can watch them unload and take off down the river while you play. If your loved one smells too much like a dirty dog after a day of play, the Wiggles and Wags Dog Wash is across the street (6141 S.W. Macadam; 503/977-1775).

From I-5, take Exit 299A and go south on S.W. Macadam Avenue and turn right on S.W. Nebraska Street. The OLA is on the north end of the park, to your left past the pay booth at the entrance. This park has a rare parking lot, which costs $3 per day Memorial Day–Labor Day and on weekends March–Memorial Day. Open 5 A.M.–10 P.M.

33 Gabriel Park

🐾🐾🐾🐾🐕 (See Greater Portland map on page 477)

The grass is soft and green on the rolling hills of Gabriel Park, no mean feat, even in the fully fenced off-leash area. We're talking some serious trees here, and the benches and chairs are comfy. It's definitely one of Portland's fanciest OLAs. The only drawback is that there are separate summer and winter areas to allow the turf to recover in the off-season. The summer area is bordered by the tennis courts, which had Isis doing the Wimbledon head wobble watching the balls go to and fro.

The two-acre winter site, dubbed "Little Gabriel," is unfenced, with fewer amenities, and it's a bit hard to find. Walk south of the summer area, down wooden steps and across a bridge to the paved path. When you come into a clearing, you are there, bordered by a baseball diamond and the community garden. The rest of the park's 90 acres provide amiable on-leash walks.

From I-5, take Exit 297 and continue straight onto S.W. Bertha Boulevard. Turn left on S.W. Vermont Street, pass the park, and turn left on S.W. 45th Avenue. There's a parking lot that's often full. To better your chances, continue south on 45th, turn left on S.W. Multnomah Boulevard, left on S.W. 40th

Avenue, and left on S.W. Canby Street to park by the winter area and sneak in the back way. Open 5 A.M.–midnight. S.W. 45th Ave. and Vermont St.

PLACES TO EAT

Fat City Café: The owners of this country café have four dogs, and they wish they could provide outdoor seating, but the sidewalk's too narrow and the codes are too strict in Historic Multnomah Village. They'll provide a water bowl and treats for your pet while he waits for you to order to go and take your homemade, good lovin' cookin' to Gabriel Dog Park around the corner. 7820 S.W. Capitol Hwy.; 503/245-5457.

PLACES TO STAY

Hospitality Inn: Both the motel rooms and the complimentary continental breakfast spread are cheery and large at the inn. Dogs up to 40 pounds are allowed. Rates range $80–100, plus a $10 pet fee. 10155 S.W. Capitol Hwy.; 503/244-6684; www.hospitalityinnportland.com.

Hillsboro

As an affluent suburb of Portland, Hillsboro brought considerable resources to bear in opening a beautiful dog park in 2007. During inclement weather, local dogs can be found at **Schroeder's Den,** an indoor dog park at a day-care and training facility (2110 N.W. Aloclek Dr., Suite 620; 503/614-9899; www.schroedersden.com).

PARKS, BEACHES, AND RECREATION AREAS

34 Hondo Dog Park

🐾🐾🐾🐾🐾 (See Greater Portland map on page 476)

Your water bowl runneth over, and not just from the water gushing out of the doggy drinking fountains in two of the three five-foot-high, black-vinyl-coated, chain-link-fenced, off-leash areas of this purpose-built dog park. It's the first ever OLA for this suburb, honorably named for the city's only, and we hope ever, K-9 dog officer to lose his life in the line of duty, commemorated by a plaque on-site.

Hondo is 3.75 acres in toto for Toto, separated into the main mixed-use dog area, a small/timid dog area, and a giant sandbox intended as a winter area to allow the grass to get some breathing time. Each space has fire-engine-red benches and garbage cans, bag dispensers, defunct and decorated fire hydrants, healthy grass, gravel walkways, and young trees that will grow up to provide decent shade. Everything is still shiny and new, so come and get it while it lasts. Humans get sloppy seconds in the form of a lowly portable potty. The water fountains are turned off in the winter.

Take Highway 26 west 11.5 miles from the intersection of Highway 405 to the Cornelius Pass Road South exit, Exit 62A. Take a left onto Cornelius Pass Road, a right on N.W. Evergreen parkway, and a right on N.W. 229th Avenue. The park will be on your left. Open dawn–dusk most days; opens at noon on Mondays and Thursdays to allow for maintenance. 4499 N.W. 229th Ave.; www.hillsborodogs.com.

PLACES TO EAT

Iron Mutt Coffee Company: Combining a love of coffee and canines, Iron Mutt provides a fenced-in side patio with gravel and wood-chip areas where lovable mutts can roam free while their owners IM using free Wi-Fi, eat panini and ice cream, and drink milkshakes and bubble tea and coffee. Inside, there are dog books on every surface and floor-to-ceiling shelves packed with treats, toys, and dog-themed gifts. A portion of proceeds goes back to non-profit animal organizations. 530 S.W. 205th; 503/645-9746; www.ironmuttcoffee.com.

PLACES TO STAY

In this area, chain hotels listed in the *Resources* section offer the best choices for dogs and their owners.

Beaverton

Beaverton is Oregon's fifth-largest city. Seven miles southeast of Portland, it is the heart of the state's "Silicon Forest," an economic artery pumping capital into a healthy business environment. Silicon or no, this forest is worthy of a side trip from Portland just for its dog park.

PARKS, BEACHES, AND RECREATION AREAS

35 Hazeldale Dog Park

🐾🐾🐾🐾 🐕 (See Greater Portland map on page 477)

This full-time off-leash complex devoted to the art of being a dog deserves all four paws, one for each of its four separate, fully fenced areas. There are two dog runs for the big boys and two for the little fellas. They're used in pairs, one set each for the summer and winter, allowing the opposites to repair themselves for half the year.

Each area is long and thin. There's some openness, but most of the space is covered with short, stocky pine trees for games of hide and seek. They are beautifully equipped. The fences are high and secure and there are double gates to create leash-transition zones. There are picnic tables, bags tucked in the fence, and water brought in bowls and buckets from elsewhere in the park. Perhaps best of all, the people and dogs are exceptionally friendly and take great pride in maintaining the OLA in tip-top shape.

From U.S Highway 26, exit to State Route 217, then exit on State Route 10

DOG-EAR YOUR CALENDAR

Beaverton has a beautiful dog park, and the city wants to keep it that way. Every August it holds a **Dog Day Afternoon** fundraiser at the Hazeldale Dog Park. There are vendor booths, a raffle, blessing of the animals, and contests and demos for lure coursing, agility, and flyball. Be a vendor, donate raffle items, or come and participate to raise rent and maintenance money for a great regional dog park. Email hazeldaledogpark@yahoo.com for more information.

westbound and follow it past Beaverton until you see signs for Aloha. Turn right on S.W. 192nd Avenue, then turn left on the third street, Prospect Street. There's plenty of parking. Everyone is vigilant about keeping their dogs on leash until inside the gates. Managed by Tualatin Hills Parks and Recreation, 503/645-6433.

PLACES TO EAT

Mingo's West: From the parking area, it's hard to see what everyone is getting so excited about. Pass through the archway, however, and everything becomes clear as you step onto a half-moon garden patio called The Round, with multiple canine-friendly culinary options. One look at the plump tomatoes and roasted garlic cloves at Mingo's had us salivating, an Italian grapefruit margarita drew us in, and gnocchi *alla Romana* sealed the deal. The bar menu, served 2–5 P.M., makes for the happiest of happy hours. 12600 S.W. Crescent; 503/646-6464; www.mingowest.com.

PLACES TO STAY

In this area, chain hotels listed in the *Resources* section offer the best choices for dogs and their owners.

Tigard

It's TI-gard, as in Tiger, and according to statistics on the city's Parks and Recreation website, approximately zero tigers and 9,200 canines call this Portland suburb home. Woof.

PARKS, BEACHES, AND RECREATION AREAS

36 Summerlake Dog Park

🐾🐾🐾🐕 (See Greater Portland map on page 477)

Suburban dogs idle away their days at Summerlake, a mid-sized field of a couple of acres, one of a few excellent off-leash areas created and maintained by the Tigard Dog Park Committee. Summerlake's off-leash area is crowded and friendly, with a large covered shelter that makes for a nice people hangout while the dogs go about their business. It's got all the goods, including garbage cans, pooper-scoopers and bags, running water, a secured fence with double-gated entry, and just enough tree cover for a bit of shade and a couple of suicidal squirrels.

From State Route 217 southbound, take Exit 4B (Exit 4 northbound), and go west on Scholls Ferry Road for a mile. Take a left onto 130th Avenue and go 0.4 mile, straight through a couple of stop signs, until the road becomes S.W. Winter Lake Drive. The OLA and the parking lot will be on your left, past the sports courts and the restrooms. Open dawn–dusk. 503/639-4171; www.tigard-or.gov/community/parks.

37 Potso Dog Park
🐾🐾🐾🐾 (See Greater Portland map on page 477)

Potso pups long for summer evenings and winter weekends, when this great part-time dog park is open to them for unleashed play. Potso is open 4:30 P.M.– dusk Monday–Friday May–Oct., and dawn–dusk on weekends and holidays all year. Cooper and Isis had a ball chasing balls in the open field's healthy green grass. They wanted to take a moment to thank the Bichon Frise who inspired this playground, as well as Coe Manufacturing for allowing a dog park to be built on their spare property.

Potso comes well equipped with poop bags, garbage cans, and sheltered picnic tables. It is completely fenced, with a double gate, and, as an extra bonus, has a separate off-leash area for smaller dogs (yip, yip, yippee!).

From State Route 217 southbound, take Exit 7, make a right onto 72nd Avenue, follow the cloverleaf and immediately turn left on S.W. Hunziker. Turn left on Wall Street in front of the Coe Manufacturing building. Park only in designated spots with giant paw prints painted on them. 7930 S.W. Hunziker; 503/639-4171.

PLACES TO EAT

Max's Fanno Creek Brew Pub: Nachos, fries, and mozzarella sticks are meant to be shared by human and dog alike, says Coop, and the proof is in the pub, or, rather, outside of it at multiple picnic tables packed with happy eaters from both species. Add a schooner of summer blonde or a pint of IPA and some caramel fudge pecan cake and discover what it means to be blissed out. 12562 S.W. Main St.; 503/624-9400; www.maxsfannocreek.com.

PLACES TO STAY

In this area, chain hotels listed in the *Resources* section offer the best choices for dogs and their owners.

Lake Oswego

As you approach this well-to-do bedroom community, you'll see forested landscapes and expansive views of the Willamette River, along with formal landscapes and expansive homes. The few blocks of downtown have a dense concentration of trendy shops, galleries, and a sculpture garden on A Avenue along the Millennium Plaza Park.

PARKS, BEACHES, AND RECREATION AREAS

38 Tryon Creek

😸 😸 😸 (See Greater Portland map on page 477)

There are eight miles of hiking tails in this 645-acre State Natural Area, plus three miles reserved for equestrians, and another three-mile paved path along the east edge. Pick any trail in the ravine and you'll enjoy plenty of shade among the cedar, fir, and big leaf maples, while your dog appreciates the mixed bouquet of the forest and occasional horse puck. If there's anyone in your group who thinks the last one in the creek is a rotten egg, the fastest route to the water is along the Middle Creek Trail from the nature center to High Bridge, returning on the Old Man Trail to make a quick one-mile loop. Many lunchtime and after-work joggers take to Tryon's hills; the park is strict about enforcing leash laws on the tight and narrow trails. The 0.4-mile Trillium Trail is fully accessible. There are drinking fountains and restrooms at the nature center, at the main entrance.

From I-5, take Exit 297 and stay in the right lane to cloverleaf around south onto S.W. Terwilliger Boulevard. The park entrance is 2.5 miles down on your right. Open 7 A.M.–dusk. 503/636-9886.

39 George Rogers Park

😸 😸 (See Greater Portland map on page 477)

Life is pretty relaxed on the swimming beach at this city park. Many of the park's 26 acres are taken up by baseball diamonds, tennis courts, a children's play area, and the formal, landscaped Memorial Garden. Pass all of that up and head down the hill to the sandy banks of the Willamette River to mingle with the geese at a natural open-space area.

George Rogers is the site of Oregon's first iron smelter in the 1890s. You can view the preserved historic chimney behind a fence on the grounds.

From I-5, take Exit 299A and travel south on State Route 43, S.W. Macadam Avenue, into Lake Oswego. The road becomes N. State Street through downtown; a few blocks later, watch closely for Ladd Street. Turn left, past the athletic fields, and then right at the Main Parking Lot sign. Open 6 A.M.–10 P.M. 611 State St.; 503/797-1850.

40 Luscher Farm Dog Park

🐾🐾🐾🐾🐕 (See Greater Portland map on page 477)

There's no getting up at the crack of dawn to milk the cows and feed the hens here. Well, there is, on the portion of land still maintained as a working farm, but the only chores you're likely to face are throwing a slimy ball a hundred times for your happy-go-lucky farm animal and picking up the fertilizer he leaves in the field.

Dogs will find any excuse to escape to the countryside if it means coming to this pair of popular off-leash parks in Hazelia Field. Gorgeous, and new in 2008, are two securely fenced and gated OLAs with generous field grass and woodchip trails around the inside perimeters. The timid-dog section is completely separate from the larger area, about a hundred yards away, so there's no barking at the fence.

There are clusters of trees in each OLA, with covered seating areas for humans to sit and shoot the breeze. It can be hectic, but you can get 40 dogs inside the fence and still have room to run. Each OLA has separate entrance and exit areas, to help with crowd control. A paved pathway winds around the farm if you want a leashed stroll to take the edge off. Biodegradable cleanup bags and water are provided. Decent restrooms and a playground are next to the larger field.

From I-205, take Exit 3 north on S.W. Stafford Road for two miles. Take a right on Overlook Drive into the park. A gravel parking lot is on the right. If you continue north on Stafford, it becomes McVay Avenue into downtown Lake Oswego. Open 6 A.M.–10 P.M.

PLACES TO EAT

Port City Pasta Co.: Get your turkey sandwich to go, take it one block south to George Rogers Park, and relish every bite of the focaccia bread that *Gourmet* magazine called "the Best in the West." Your dog would rather have bits of the turkey filling anyway. 333 S. State St.; 503/699-2927.

Zeppo: The salads are so gorgeous at this fine Italian eatery, you may never make it to the thin-crust pizzas, al dente pastas, or low-carb dinners. Your pup may join you on the piazza, a sunny brick plaza. 345 First Street; 503/675-2726; www.zepporestaurant.com.

PLACES TO STAY

Crowne Plaza: This swank property, favored by business executives, got full room renovations in 2008. They like to place pets in rooms on the second floor, saving other floors for those who may have allergies. Rates range $125–155; the pet fee is $20. 14811 Kruse Oaks Dr.; 503/624-8400; www.crowneplaza.com/lakeoswegoor.

More Accommodations: Please look under *Chain Hotels* in the *Resources* section for additional places to stay in this area.

West Linn

With a median household income approaching the six figure range, this afflu-ent suburban city survived fires and floods in the early years to emerge as a comfortable place to live and play. With a descriptive nickname, "The City of Hills, Trees, and Rivers," West Linn has no established commercial down-town, which doesn't hurt a dog's feelings at all. **The Dog Club** in West Linn is posh and well equipped for a day of play, a wash or groom, or to pick up quality chow, toys, and accessories (18675 Willamette Dr.; 503/635-3523; www.dogclub4u.com).

PARKS, BEACHES, AND RECREATION AREAS

41 Mary S. Young

🐾🐾🐾🐕 (See Greater Portland map on page 477)

If your dog is stir-crazy but you don't have time for a drive to the country, take her to the trails and the pet exercise area at this state recreation site. The off-leash area is a couple of acres, protected by a ring of trees on three sides. It's wide open and unfenced, yet remote enough to feel reasonably secure. There's some shade at picnic tables huddled in one corner, restrooms, and a water pump for dog drinking and bathing. Bring your own pickup bags.

The trail system is a bit vague in the forested section of the park. The city narrows it down to somewhere between five and eight miles of trails through the fir, maple, and alder. The paths you can easily find begin across the parking

DIVERSIONS

Fleece feels good on fur in these damper climes, and there's no better fleece dog sweater collection than the one at **Sellwood Dog Supply** (8334 S.E. 17th Ave.; 503/239-1517; www.sellwooddogsup-ply.com) in none other than the historic Sellwood neighborhood. The owners used to run Pacific City Beach Dog Supply on the Oregon Coast, but even that got too cold for their taste. Hence, perhaps, the sweaters.

A dog is not well and truly spoiled until she's paid a visit to **Bone-Jour GourMutt Bakery** (5656 Hood Street, Suite 107, Central Village; 503/557-2328; www.bonejourdogbakery.com) in West Linn for some of the most amazing treats ever created for those who are crated. The variety of savory and sweet biscuits laid out before her will look almost too pretty to eat. The store itself is decked out in soda fountain colors. Pearls before swine or divine for canine? She'll let you know, in between bites.

lot from the dog run, leading down to the southwest bank of the Willamette River.

From I-205, take Exit 8 north on Willamette Drive (State Route 43). Turn left toward Lake Oswego and go two miles. To find the OLA, drive past the athletic fields to the end of the circular parking loop. Open 7 A.M.–dusk. Mary S. Young is owned by Oregon State Parks and managed by West Linn Parks and Recreation, 503/557-4700.

PLACES TO STAY

Best Western Rivershore Hotel: Not only does this lovely hotel take dogs, but they've had a chimpanzee stay once. The only four-legged creatures they turn away are those with hooves. While your livestock may have to lodge elsewhere, your dog is welcome to join you for a $5 fee per night, soaking up Willamette River views from the balcony. Although technically in Oregon City, it is just across the river, and the highway, from West Linn. Rooms regularly go for $95–230 a night. 1900 Clackamette Dr.; 503/655-7141.

Milwaukie

Between Portland and historical Oregon City, this City of Dogwoods is a taste of small-town charm, close to the city.

PARKS, BEACHES, AND RECREATION AREAS

42 North Clackamas Park

🐾 🐕 (See Greater Portland map on page 477)

This fenced off-leash area is a prized privilege for Milwaukie dogs, even though it's smallish, a bit under two acres. Word of mouth says it can get really crowded on weekends, and Cooper thought the supervision was too minimal and play allowed here was too rough for his taste. There's even a local gang of Akitas who act tough in the after-work hours, so we're told. We're also told that a separate small-dog area is in the works for late 2008, but nothing has materialized yet.

It's a wood-chip area, a bit dusty in summer and certainly muddy the rest of the year. Through the double-gated entry, you'll find picnic tables and a muddy water pump. Bring pick up bags.

From Highway 99E, take State Route 224, the Milwaukie Expressway. Turn south on S.E. Rusk Road, and when this arterial road curves around to the left, continue straight to enter the park. To find the OLA, turn right at the Area A&B sign, pass the Milwaukie Center, and park behind the peaked-roof picnic shelter. Walk a few hundred feet west to the fenced area on your right. 5440 S.E. Kellogg Creek Dr.; 503/794-8002.

PLACES TO EAT

Bob's Red Mill Whole Grain Store: From the Milwaukie Expressway, you can't miss Bob's big red barn. This specialty mill grinds whole-grain, organic flours for sale at health food grocery stores around the country. There is a deli, whole-grain store, and visitors center on-site. Kids can watch the water wheel turn and sample Bob's breads and cookies. If the patio is iffy for pets, get your hearty sandwiches to go. 5000 S.E. International Way; 503/607-6455; www.bobsredmill.com.

Gresham

While these parks are still technically within Portland city limits, they are far enough east to use the heavy retail suburb of Gresham as a home base.

PARKS, BEACHES, AND RECREATION AREAS

43 Powell Butte Nature Park

🐾🐾🐾 (See Greater Portland map on page 477)

Pick a clear day when the mountains will be out and rain is not expected within 24 hours to head to the top of this 570-acre park, an extinct volcano with a nine-mile trail system for hikers, cyclists, and equestrians. In addition to the indigenous forest, trees include old apple, pear, and walnut orchards from the 1900s farm of Henry Anderegg. Powell Butte is exceedingly popular with mountain bikers, and you'll have to tolerate them buzzing by you at the beginning of the trail until you can break off onto a walkers-only path. There's a gravel parking lot with restrooms, a drinking fountain, and a trail map at the start. At the top is a rolling meadow where Anderegg's cattle used to graze within sight of Mount Hood and the tips of a few other peaks. Underneath it all is a 500-million-gallon reservoir, part of the Bull Run system, the primary water source for the Portland metro area.

From I-205, go east on S.E. Division Street for 3.5 miles. Take a right on S.E. 162nd Avenue and continue 0.7 mile to the park entrance. Open 7 A.M.–6 P.M. or later as the sun stays out. To protect the ecosystem from hillside erosion, the butte closes when measurable rain falls; call 503/823-1616 to get recorded status information before you go. www.friendsofpowellbutte.org.

44 Lynchwood Park

🐾🐾 🐾 (See Greater Portland map on page 477)

The Wonder Wieners will be the first to admit that this park is obscure. Its remote location and lack of other specific use are the very things that make it an ideal off-leash area. A grove of dense tree canopy forms a semicircle around the flat field, protecting it from the only adjacent road, which isn't very busy

anyway. The other three sides of the rectangle are enclosed by residential and school fences. You'll feel like the free fun zone on the east side of the park is your own secret discovery. Benches under the trees are the only amenities. You should go potty before you leave the house and bring anything you'll need, including bags, water, and your pooch's favorite UFO.

From I-205, go east on S.E. Division Street for four miles, take a right on S.E. 174th Avenue, and a right on S.E. Haig Street. Park along Haig where it dead-ends. OLA hours vary by the season; call 503/823-3647 or go to www .portlandonline.com/parks, and select "Dogs" under the "Recreation" tab.

PLACES TO EAT

Subs on Sandy: This tiny corner shop in the strip mall makes enough fat, messy sandwiches to order a different one every day of the month and teriyaki on weekends. An outdoor picnic table looked weary. 13912 N.E. Sandy Blvd.; 503/252-7827.

PLACES TO STAY

In this area, chain hotels listed in the *Resources* section offer the best choices for dogs and their owners.

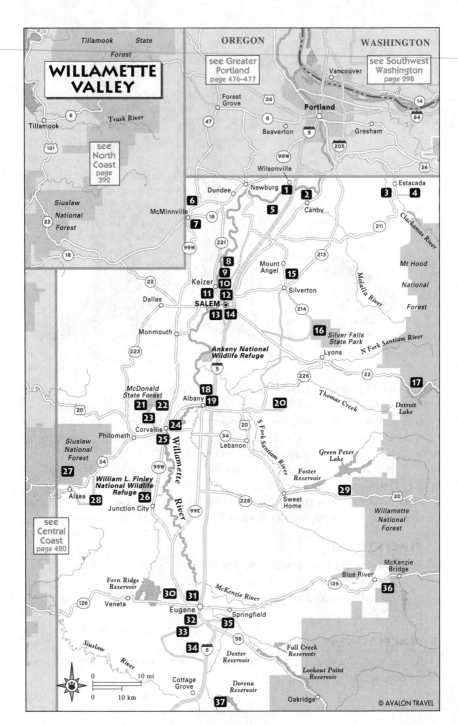

CHAPTER 18

Willamette Valley

From 1843 to 1869, a half million pioneers hitched up their wagons and traveled the 2,000-mile Oregon Trail from Missouri to reach the promised land of the Willamette Valley. As you travel through, you can see why they came, and reap the fruits of their labors. Tucked between the Cascade and Coastal mountains, the abundant valley sits on the same latitude as France's Burgundy wine region and is perfect for growing grapes. The climate is also ideal for hazelnuts, also called filberts, producing 99 percent of the nation's entire supply. Tree farms and nurseries line the rolling hillsides, with thousands of identical conifers in soldierly order. The valley's abundance includes a cornucopia of off-leash areas as well, within state parks and in the region's three major college towns of Eugene, Salem, and Corvallis.

PICK OF THE LITTER—WILLAMETTE VALLEY

BEST PARKS
Eagle Fern, Estacada (page 518)
Willamette Mission, Salem (page 524)

BEST DOG PARKS
Dog Runs at Keizer Rapids Park, Salem-Keizer (page 524)
Alton Baker Dog Park, Eugene (page 539)

BEST HIKE
Ridgeline Trail System, Eugene (page 541)

BEST EVENT
Silverton Pet Parade, Silverton (page 528)

BEST PLACES TO EAT
Bistro Maison, McMinnville (page 523)
Fleur de Lis, Cottage Grove (page 545)

BEST PLACES TO STAY
Wayfarer Resort, Blue River (page 544)
Village Green Resort, Cottage Grove (page 545)

Water is the source of life in the valley, and its rivers and reservoirs are the primary source of recreation. To cross the multiple tributaries of these major rivers, Oregon pioneers built bridges with buildings over them to protect the wooden trusses from accelerated decay in rainy weather. The state has preserved the largest number of historical covered bridges west of the Mississippi, most of them in the Willamette Valley, each county featuring a different design. Covered bridge tour maps from city visitors centers provide a perfect excuse to explore scenic roads.

The top two tourist attractions in Oregon are in the Willamette—the Champoeg and Milo McIver Pet Exercise Areas. No, actually they are Spirit Mountain Casino (www.spirit-mountain.com) and the upscale outlets at Woodburn Company Stores (www.woodburncompanystores.com), but dogs may beg to differ.

NATIONAL FORESTS AND RECREATION AREAS

Willamette National Forest
🐾🐾🐾🐾

This playground has more than 80 developed campgrounds and 1,700 miles of hiking trails. The forest service's interactive trip planning map, online at www.fs.fed.us/r6/Willamette, is a great way to find recreational opportunities far beyond what we have room to mention in this book. For the McKenzie River Recreation Area, along State Route 126, stop into the ranger station in McKenzie Bridge (57600 Hwy. 126.; 541/822-3381).

Wilsonville

This fast-growing city hosts corporate biggies like Xerox and Hollywood Entertainment. At the same time, it has a Tree City USA designation to keep it green.

PARKS, BEACHES, AND RECREATION AREAS

🚩 Memorial Bark Park
🐾🐾🐾🐕 (See Willamette Valley map on page 512)

This popular off-leash area is where local dogs come to blow off steam after a hard day's nap waiting for their humans to come home from work. The city says the 1.5-acre park has been left in its natural state except for the occasional mowing, but the Dachshund Duo found it to be in much better shape than many parks they've seen. Gopher holes are the main hazard, also providing something to stick a nose in for a snout full of rodent spoor. There's no long list of rules, merely the statement that only good dogs are allowed.

A chicken-wire fence surrounds the field with a perimeter path, tables in either corner, and gates on both ends. There are a few shade trees along one side and bag dispensers, which were all empty. Bring your own bags and water.

From I-5, take Exit 283 and go east on Wilsonville Road for 0.3 mile, turn right on Memorial Drive and almost immediately turn left. The OLA is around the corner to your left past the sports fields, down a short path from a gravel parking area. Open dawn–dusk.

PLACES TO EAT

Country Grains Bread Co.: It's only a couple of blocks from Memorial Bark Park, but you may want to eat at this deli's picnic tables to avoid mass

begging. In addition to sandwiches and low-carb choices, there's chili to go by the quart. Open Monday–Friday. 8553 S.W. Main St., in the Village at Main Street; 503/682-5857.

PLACES TO STAY

In this area, chain hotels listed in the *Resources* section offer the best choices for dogs and their owners.

Canby

Canby sits in the state's garden spot for tree nurseries, flax, and floral, the latter most visible in the summer at the Swan Island Dahlia Farm, the nation's largest dahlia grower. Other local landmarks include the Canby Depot Museum, one of the oldest remaining railroad stations in Oregon, and the Canby Ferry across the Willamette to Wilsonville.

PARKS, BEACHES, AND RECREATION AREAS

◘ Molalla River

🐾🐾 🐕 (See Willamette Valley map on page 512)

Since the last edition came out, the state park moved the pet exercise area to a four-acre sloped field. The park has land, lots of land, under starry skies above, with no fence to keep you in. If your dog is tempted to take off, he can go for miles on adjacent farmland before you can catch up with him. Also, it seems to the Dachsie Twins that the usability of the OLA depends on how ambitious the driver of the riding lawnmower is that week, carving a playground out of five-foot-high field grass. It's not very soft on the paws, and any animal with more hair than a Chinese crested is likely to come away with half the native groundcover stuck to his fur.

So, the Dachsie Twins give the off-leash area at this state park only one paw, with an extra paw thrown in for the riverfront trails. Starting west of the boat ramp, opt for a 0.75-mile hike along the Willamette River to where it joins with the Molalla then loops back around through the woods for a total of about 1.5 miles. There's a garbage can and bag dispensers, and running water nearby at a restroom drinking fountain.

A quarter mile downstream from the park is the Canby Ferry across the Willamette; pedestrians and bicycles cross for no charge, cars, with dogs allowed in them, are $1.25 each way. For information call 503/650-3030.

From Highway 99E northeast of Canby, turn right on N.E. Territorial Road, turn north on Holly Street, and travel 2.2 miles. The park entrance comes up suddenly on the left after a bend in the road. Open 7 A.M.–9 P.M.

Estacada

Estacada is the gateway city to the Clackamas River Recreation Area of the Mount Hood National Forest. Ask at the ranger station (595 N.W. Industrial Way; 503/630-6861) for a long list of scenic hikes and river boat ramps. Despite early years of logging and dam development to supply nearby Portland with hydroelectric power, the area remains beautiful for hiking, fishing, camping, and hounding around.

PARKS, BEACHES, AND RECREATION AREAS

🖪 Milo McIver State Park

😻😻😻😻 🐕 (See Willamette Valley map on page 512)

Sometime in the 1970s, according to a local historian, this state park hosted its first and only government-sponsored concert event, called Vortex. Supposedly, the goal was to keep all the hippie activists happy and busy, away from Portland while President Nixon was in town. Local farmers were reputedly paid to drop off bags of food and smokable plants for the 35,000 people.

While the flower power days of the 1970s may be over, at least your dog can enjoy a carefree existence at Milo McIver's off-leash pet exercise area. Even though the area is not fenced, the rest of the park's designated areas are miles away in this 951-acre sprawling park on the Clackamas River. There's a garbage can, a bag dispenser, and a huge, wide-open field of tender, green grass—real grass, not dirt or wood chips. You can enjoy the shade of one gigantic tree and an amazing view of Mount Hood while developing a case of tennis elbow from tossing.

It's easy to spend an entire vacation at this pet-friendly park and not get bored. There are miles of Milo along the riverbanks, hiking trails with long beaches and convenient splash points. Rafting down the river from Milo McIver to Barton Park is another popular pastime, plus there are equestrian trails, a campground, a fish hatchery, and several picnic areas.

From Estacada, travel southwest on State Route 211 for a mile, turn right on Hayden Road, and right on Springwater Road for another mile. The off-leash area is to the right along the main park road. Open 7 A.M.–sunset. Parking is $3. 503/630-7150.

◢ Eagle Fern

🐾🐾🐾🐾 (See Willamette Valley map on page 512)

The county's largest and most doggone divine park is tucked deep in the woods in one of the few remaining old-growth timber stands in the valley. There is an excellent kiosk of information presented by the forest service to give you an idea of the treescape around you. Each of many individual picnic areas along Eagle Creek has convenient water and garbage cans nearby. Across a bouncy suspension bridge are short and sweet hikes, from 0.5 mile to 1.25 miles each, through towering Western red cedars, Douglas firs, hemlocks, and maples. The water is inviting for fishing and dog paddling. It is a relaxed and relaxing atmosphere for people with pets.

From State Route 224, four miles north of Estacada, follow the sign to Eagle Fern Park/Dover District, turning on Wildcat Mountain Road and traveling two miles to bear right onto Eagle Fern Road and another 2.3 miles to the park. Open 6 A.M.–9 P.M. May–September, until 6 P.M. in the winter. A $3 parking fee is charged weekends and holidays Memorial Day–Labor Day. 503/794-8002; www.clackamas.us/parks.

PLACES TO EAT

Colton Café: It's the perfect little country café, a cheery yellow building with curtains in the windows and a picnic table on a side lawn shaded by a huge maple tree. The gravel parking lot is five times the size of the building, hinting at the restaurant's popularity for b'fast and lunch. 12 miles from Estacada; 21038 S. Hwy. 211; 503/824-5111.

PLACES TO STAY

Clackamas Inn: This friendly highway stop in Clackamas (Exit #12 off I-205) is the closest motel to Estacada. Management caters to seniors and pet owners, and non-smoking rooms are available. Rates range $70–100, plus a $10 pet fee. 16010 S.E. 82nd Dr.; 800/874-6560; www.clackamasinn.com.

Milo McIver Campground: The 44 electric sites at Milo are friendly for RVs or tents, for $13–17. There are also nine primitive tent sites available for a measly $6–9 per night. 800/452-5687; www.reserveamerica.com.

Newberg

This city was the boyhood home of Herbert Hoover, the 31st president of the United States. It's a popular stop along the "Wine Highway," State Route 99W, 25 miles southwest of Portland.

PARKS, BEACHES, AND RECREATION AREAS

5 Champoeg State Park

🐾🐾🐾🐾🐕 (See Willamette Valley map on page 512)

After her first visit to the pet exercise area at this state heritage area, your dog's tail will start wagging if you even think the word Champoeg (sham-POO-ee). The park's designated off-leash area is a five-acre field that seems much larger, in the middle of 615 acres of white oak forests, fields, and wetlands along the Willamette River. The pet area is not secured, but it is far enough removed from everything else to present no problems for well-managed dogs. The park sits on the site of the ghost town of Champoeg, where Oregon's first provisional government was established. The town was destroyed in an 1861 flood and abandoned after more floods in 1890.

There are other activities to enjoy with a leashed pooch. The Riverside Picnic Area is nearby, and if you walk on the trails west of the Pioneer Mother's Cabin, there are a few informal areas along the river to catch the drift. There is a four-mile paved trail from the park to the Butteville General Store, where you can rent bicycles for the day. A large campground, visitors center, historic buildings, hiking trails, and disc golf course occupy other areas of the large park.

We say phooey to the convoluted signs to Champoeg. Instead, take the Charbonneau exit (282B) from I-5, go west on winding Butteville Road for five miles, then bear right onto Champoeg Road for another three miles. To find the OLA, turn down the hill to the left toward the Riverside Area and Pioneer Mother's Cabin and go 0.7 mile to parking along a gravel lane at the far end of the field. Parking is $3. 503/678-1251.

PLACES TO EAT

Butteville General Store: First opened in 1863, Oregon's oldest continually operating store carries on the tradition of being the social center of a rural community. It's a deli, an art gallery, a historical museum of local photographs, a venue for local musicians, and a bicycle rental shop for treks to

DETOUR

Take your dog to a drive-in movie, before this endangered species becomes extinct. The **99W Drive In Theatre** in Newberg runs double features of first-run titles on summer weekends, with real-butter popcorn and original, restored 1950s trailers before the show and between features. Cash only; 503/538-2738; www.99w.com.

The drive-in's pet policy is priceless:

Question: Can I bring my dog/cat/ferret/elephant?

Answer: Yes, as long as the animal is harmless to the customers and our operation. Management reserves the right to refuse any animal (including human) admission. Elephants and other larger animals will be charged a single-occupant car admission due to the fact they would take up a car space by themselves. You will be solely responsible for damage caused by your animal to the drive-in, yourself, other drive-in patrons or property. You must keep your animal secured to your vehicle/parking space. NOTE TO ELEPHANTS AND GIRAFFES: Our ticket window height clearance is 8 feet.

nearby Champoeg. Plan your vacation to coincide with pizza or gourmet burger nights. Pets are warmly welcomed on the front porch or in garden seating. Open seasonally, May–September. 10767 Butte St.; 503/678-1605; www .champoeg.com.

PLACES TO STAY

Avellan Inn: This exquisite bed-and-breakfast is a haven of country peacefulness. Once you've lain down on the downy featherbeds and sat in a swinging chair on your private enclosed deck, you may never want to leave. Neither will your dog feel any desire to part from the hazelnut orchards and fields of the 12-acre property, where he's free to roam off-leash. Sally's Room is $125 per night, Emily's Room is $155 with a suite area and a private entrance for pet people. Children are also welcome. 16900 N.E. Hwy 240; 503/537-9161; www.avellaninn.com.

Champoeg Campground: There are 79 RV sites for $16–20, and six walk-in tent sites for $12–16 at this state park in a remote setting on the plains by the Willamette River. 800/452-5687; www.reserveamerica.com.

More Accommodations: Please look under *Chain Hotels* in the *Resources* section for additional places to stay in this area.

McMinnville

Historic downtown McMinnville, along 3rd Street, is an enjoyable place to stroll, shop, and eat. It's the hub for wine country tours of the valley, catering to travelers with its quaint bed-and-breakfast inns and a pretty city park.

PARKS, BEACHES, AND RECREATION AREAS

6 Joe Dancer Park

🐾🐾🐾 (See Willamette Valley map on page 512)

J.D. is a huge, sparkling city park, opened in 2008, with an excellent soft-surface perimeter trail, massive fields of tender manicured grass, and, someday, an official off-leash area at adjacent Kiwanis Marine Park. Isis was impressed by the landscaping, with giant stones lining all the newly paved roads and parking areas. While much of the park is reserved for ball fields, a skate park, and playgrounds where dogs are not allowed (officially, dogs must stay off the groomed lawn areas), at least check out the perimeter trail loosely following the South Yamhill River and lose a tennis ball or two in the back fields. There's plenty of space for every dog to have his day.

From 99W into downtown McMinnville, take 3rd Street east, which becomes Three Mile Lane. Turn left on Brooks Street into the park. The first pullout holds only a couple of cars; there are better spaces in the next lot and you can find join the trail a ways behind the skate park.

❼ McMinnville City Park

🐾🐾 (See Willamette Valley map on page 512)

Conveniently located at the end of the downtown historic district, this city park has two levels. Dogs are not allowed in the upper park, with a gigantic wooden play castle for the kids, sandwiched between the library and city pool. The lower level is more informal and dog-friendly, with a short walking path and picnic tables along woodsy Cozine Creek.

DETOURS

Oregon is deservedly gaining fame from wineries in the Willamette, several of which you can visit with your dog. The golden retriever, blue heeler and Pomeranian who live at **Elk Cove Winery** (503/985-7760, elkcove.com) will sit with you under a giant oak tree overlooking the La Bohème vineyard and brag to your dogs how they made it into the *Wine Dogs USA* picture book. Dog treats are available, but other begging is discouraged.

In what was once a decaying industrial area of McMinnville, Oregon, an old turkey processing plant, a grass seed company, and a steam-generated power plant have been converted to produce something that tends to get better with age. Owners of these upstarts call themselves either the "Pinot Quarter" or the "Wine Ghetto." At one of these wineries, Douglas Drawbond of **Anthony Dell** (503/910-8874; anthonydell.com) has produced 50 cases of 2005 Pinot Noir under the label Homeward Bound, and all sales benefit the local no-kill animal shelter of the same name. Enjoy a nice Oregon pinot noir, and help save the lives of shelter animals.

Dogs are also welcome in the picnic areas of **Duck Pond Cellars** (23145 Hwy. 99 W; 800/437-3213; duckpondcellars.com), and **Sokol Blosser** (5000 Sokol Blosser Ln.; 800/582-6668; sokolblosser .com), if they can get along with the winery dogs.

As you enter town from the north, State Route 99W becomes Adams Street southbound. The park is located at the intersection of 3rd and Adams Streets. If you are entering from the south, 99W merges onto Baker Street northbound. Turn left on Third Street and drive one block to Adams.

PLACES TO EAT

Bistro Maison: Deborah Chatelard, owner of this dog-friendly restaurant in McMinnville, called to invite us onto her beautiful patio to hang out with her boxer and indulge in a menu that won a Best of Fine Dining award from City-Search in 2006. It is a French menu, and as such, the *pomme frites* with saffron aioli are de rigueur. Reservations highly recommended. 729 N.E. Third St.; 503/474-1888; www.bistromaison.com.

Harvest Fresh Grocery and Deli: Hearty soups, fresh salads, and sandwiches of substance including tempeh, tarragon chicken, and turkey meatloaf are only the beginning at the deli side of this health food grocery store a couple of blocks from the city park. The fresh vegetable and fruit juice blends are refreshing, sipped at a sidewalk table. 251 E. 3rd St.; 503/472-5740.

PLACES TO STAY

Baker Street Inn: "Just be honest about your dogs," asks owner Cheryl Hockaday, and they will be welcome to stay in Le Petite Chateau, a two-bedroom, 700-square-foot cottage, fully renovated in 1994 and updated in 2004. They may choose to hang out with you on the back porch, and may stay in the chain-link-fenced dog run while you're away if they're comfortable in their own skin. Rates range $150–160; the pet fee is $20 total per stay. 129 SE Baker St.; 503/472-5575; www.bakerstreetinn.com.

More Accommodations: Please look under *Chain Hotels* in the *Resources* section for additional places to stay in this area.

Salem-Keizer

In 1864, the capital of Oregon was moved from Oregon City, near Portland, to its present location in Salem. Perhaps they realized how convenient this centrally located city is to all that the valley has to offer in Marion and Polk counties.

The gardens around the Salem suburb of Keizer are well known as the center of the world's iris industry. May and June are the months to see this tall flower in bloom.

PARKS, BEACHES, AND RECREATION AREAS

8 Willamette Mission

😼😼😼😼🐕 (See Willamette Valley map on page 512)

This 1,600-acre state park is a time capsule and a hands-on agricultural lesson, with an off-leash dog park thrown in for good measure. The history is visible against the sky in the form of ghost structures, metal sculptures that trace the outlines of the original Methodist mission, established in 1834 by Reverend Jason Lee. You can hike up to 12 miles through vineyards, fields of hops, mission roses, and habitat restoration projects, and, in the fall, you can gather hazelnuts in the picnic orchards. (Don't pick them off the trees; they're not ripe until they fall.)

As for the real reason you came here, to find the pet exercise area, turn left at the entrance booth and go a mile toward the picnic facilities, to the parking lot for the nation's largest black cottonwood tree. To your left is an unfenced off-leash area, another orchard with many trees to inspect. There's a garbage can and a bag dispenser. The OLA is close to group picnic areas, providing an opportunity to practice tough love to keep your German shepherd from snagging a bratwurst off someone's grill.

From I-5, take Exit 263 and drive two miles west on Brooklane Road. After a right turn on Wheatland Road, it's another 2.5 miles through hazelnut orchards and hops fields to the park entrance. Parking is $3. Open 7 A.M.–sunset. 503/393-1172.

9 Spong's Landing

😼😼 (See Willamette Valley map on page 512)

You'd never suspect that such a great countryside watering hole can be found five minutes from the commercialism of the main drag in Keizer. There is some serious running around going on, on the fields of Spong's Landing. It's also an excellent hidden river spot with bark dust trails down to a little beach on a wide bend in the Willamette River.

From River Road, turn west on Lockhaven Drive for 0.9 mile, right on Windsor Island Road for 0.7 mile, and left on Naples for 0.6 mile. Opens at sunrise; closes a half hour after sunset.

10 Dog Runs at Keizer Rapids Park

😼😼😼😼🐕 (See Willamette Valley map on page 512)

The city has grand plans for this park—building a boat ramp to connect it to regional river trail systems, creating a non-motorized transportation corridor, expanding it from 85 to 119 acres, you name it—but they did the most important thing first: They created an excellent dog park.

As canine celebrities, Cooper and Isis were granted access a couple of days early (they snuck in), as the field was being mowed before the grand opening on June 8, 2008. It's about time they leveled the playing field, literally, for Keizer canines, with kudos to Keizer Veterinary Clinic for financial support.

Bordered by rows of hazelnut orchards are two double-gated, fenced, wide-open areas blanketed with heavy-duty grass that might actually last a while under the punishment of happy paws. We guarantee that the field in the big-dog area is longer than the Salem-Keizer Volcanoes pitcher can chuck a ball. Cooper laughed to discover that the fence surrounding the small-dog area is shorter than the one for the big boys. There are cans and bags and we'll look for the city to add water and human perks such as shelter and real bathrooms in place of the portable potty as the park matures.

Take a moment to look in an information box for trail maps down to the river and peek at the park's grand master plan on the bulletin board. Enjoy the trails on leash, and watch out for poison oak.

Take Exit 260 from I-5 going west on Lockhaven Drive, and take the first left at the light after the railroad tracks onto Chemawa Road. Stay on Chemawa for 2.8 miles, until it ends at the park. You'll see the dog runs on your left; take the long drive past the fence to reach the gravel parking area. Open sunrise–sunset. 1900 Chemawa Rd. N.

11 Orchard Heights Park

🐾🐾🐕 (See Willamette Valley map on page 512)

Cooper and Isis pulled up, saw a small, unfenced, and roughly mowed field marked as a dog exercise area, and thought, "Ho hum, pretty ordinary." Then they crossed a bridge behind the tennis courts and their eyes went wide as a brief woodchip trail opened up to a hillside with the largest oak tree they'd ever seen, one of a hundred oak, alder, and cottonwood trees in this city park. The field is overgrown with waist-high grass, so all but very leggy and adventurous dogs typically stick to the gravel trail, leading back to a stream with several easy water entrance points. Parking, playgrounds, restrooms, mutt mitt dispensers, and garbage cans are all in close proximity.

From downtown Salem, go west over the bridge for State Route 22 West, staying in the right-most lane to peel off onto State Route 221 North. Go north toward West Salem and Dayton, and take a left on Orchard Heights Road. The park will be on your right at the corner of Parkway Drive and Orchard Heights Road. Open 5 A.M.–midnight. 1165 Orchard Heights Rd. N.W.

12 Salem Riverfront Park

🐾🐾🦴 (See Willamette Valley map on page 512)

We'll admit to the dogs up front that this park plaza is included primarily for your people. The main attraction is the Riverfront Carousel, with $1.25 rides on its colorfully restored horses. Wet-nosed ones won't mind the stroll along the Willamette River down to the *Willamette Queen* sternwheeler paddle-boat and the Eco Globe, a former acid tank for the Georgia Pacific paper mill transformed into a work of art using 86,000 mosaic tiles. The luxurious grass of the elevated amphitheater steps is tailor-made for picnic blankets.

From I-5, take Exit 256 and go west on Market Street through town and turn left on Front Street. Parking is immediately south, under the highway overpass.

13 Minto Brown Island Park

🐾🐾🐾🐕 (See Willamette Valley map on page 512)

Today, the former farmsteads of Isaac "Whiskey" Brown and John Minto have been combined into a 900-acre park with a 20-acre off-leash area. Through cooperative use agreements, some of the land continues to be farmed, while 12 miles of paved and soft-surface trails wind through the remaining wildlife areas. If there's a dog in your life who needs some space, this is an ideal place to bring him. The dog run at Minto Brown is just that, a long field, not fenced or secured, separated from the park road by a row of trees and large boulders. There's not much traffic to worry about in the middle of an island surrounded by low-usage orchards, gravel pits, timber, dense underbrush, and grassy meadows. Trash cans are provided; bring your own bags and water. A nearby trail, the A-Loop, is a good 1.5-miler.

Regular volunteer park patrols have significantly diminished the park's reputation as an unsafe place in the 1990s. It's still best to stick to the daylight hours in this remote area.

From I-5, take Exit 253 west on Mission Street. Turn left on Commercial Street and, shortly thereafter, turn right on Owens Road. Then you'll bear left onto River Road, and right onto Minto Island Road. The park entrance is a mile from the turn onto Owens Road. The dog run is between parking areas #2 and #3, 0.6 mile into the park. 503/588-6336.

14 Bush's Pasture Park

🐾🐾🐾 (See Willamette Valley map on page 512)

You can go for a long walk on the gentle bark-dust Outer Loop Trail of 95-acre Bush's Pasture. As the joggers pass you, you'll pass wide fields, mature oak trees and apple orchards, and a playground designed specifically for handicapped users. You'll skirt Willamette University's stadium and historic Deepwood Estate and Bush House Museums. You can detour through a 2,000-bloom rose garden and along Pringle Creek. Also at this city park is a track dedicated to Soap Box Derby racing; Salem is one of the few cities in the nation to have one. For a serious dose of lighthearted fun, check the schedule at www.salemsbd .org and catch a race. There's more here, but you get the idea. Salem dogs are lucky to have such a diverse urban park, and the Dachsie Twins thank them for sharing.

From I-5, take Exit 253 west on Mission Street, less than a half mile to the park on your left. Turn into the first parking lot for trail access. To find the

Municipal Rose Garden, continue on Mission and turn left on High Street. Open 5 A.M.–midnight.

PLACES TO EAT

Arbor Café: In the heart of the Capitol Mall area, this deli and bakery serves a half dozen daily specials in addition to a long list of delicious sandwiches and salads. Your eyes might glaze over as you gaze at the glazed tarts in the pastry case. There's plentiful courtyard seating. 380 High St.; 503/588-2353.

Gerry Frank's Konditorei: You can't miss the big sign that reads Extravagant Cakes Etc. on your way to Minto Brown park. The "etc." stands for traditional soups, salads, and sandwiches, but Isis couldn't take her eyes off the rotating pastry case of those aforementioned extravagant cakes. 310 Kearney S.E.; 503/585-7070.

La Margarita Express: This Mexican restaurant with colorful umbrella tables may very well be your elected government representative's favorite lunch haunt. It'll win your vote with vegetarian specialties and a light menu. 515 Chemeketa St.; 503/371-7960.

PLACES TO STAY

In this area, chain hotels listed in the *Resources* section offer the best choices for dogs and their owners.

Silverton

On your way to Silver Falls State Park, enjoy Silverton's excellent galleries, boutiques, and antique stores along its historic main thoroughfare, Water Street.

PARKS, BEACHES, AND RECREATION AREAS

🐾 The Oregon Garden

🐾🐾🐾 🖤 (See Willamette Valley map on page 512)

Isis was surprised to learn that the internationally renowned Oregon Garden opened only in 2001. It seems much more established and sophisticated than the years would indicate, located on 80 acres on the site of a former Arabian horse ranch in historic Silverton. Pets who won't pee on the flowers and people who pick up after their pets are welcome to walk together through 20 specialty gardens and around Oregon's only house designed by Frank Lloyd Wright.

Among the themed gardens is a pet-friendly educational garden designed to demonstrate how to keep pets from harm in the yard and from causing harm in the flower beds. There's information on edible plants and a take-home brochure listing toxic plants. Water bowls and a canine cooling station help those without sweat glands keep their cool.

DOG-EAR YOUR CALENDAR

The **Silverton Pet Parade,** on the third Saturday in May, is the longest running pet parade this side of the Mississippi. It was started by the American Legion as a way to get kids out for some fun after the Great Depression and has blossomed into a way to promote an animal-friendly community. The parade is free to enter and free to watch. The lineup starts at Coolidge McClaine Park and wanders through downtown Silverton. 503/873-5615; silvertonchamber.org.

For the famished, Wagger's Barkery dog treats are sold in the gift shop. Admission is $10 for adults, $8 for children. 879 W. Main St.; 503/874-8100 or 877/674-2733; www.oregongarden.org.

16 Silver Falls

(See Willamette Valley map on page 512)

There's no doubt that dogs will enjoy a hike on any stretch of the 18 miles of trails open to pets in the 8,700 acres of Oregon's largest state park. Yet, for their humans, it's a bit of a cruel tease, because pets are not allowed on the park's most famous trek, the seven-mile Canyon Trail loop, a.k.a. the Trail of Ten Falls. It is simply too crowded and too precipitous to allow dogs. As a condolence, there is an unfenced off-leash pet exercise area in the South Falls day-use area.

Despite the restrictions, you shouldn't pass up this park. You can see South Falls, the most popular, and two other falls from viewpoints accessible by car or along the 2.7-mile Rim Trail, where dogs are allowed. If possible, bring some

friends and tag-team it, a couple of you hanging with the dogs while the others take to the trail. The waterworks are truly spectacular, and you can walk behind four of the falls for the full sound-and-spray experience.

From downtown Silverton, the drive out State Route 214 to the park passes through beautiful farm country, rolling hills of tree farms and grass seed fields. After the park, the road loops down to intersect with State Route 22 in Salem. Park hours vary widely with the seasons; call 503/873-8681. Parking is $3.

PLACES TO EAT

Gingerbread House: Sure, it looks like a typical drive-through order window with burgers and fries, until you try the warm gingerbread with vanilla ice cream sprinkled with nutmeg. A blue X taped in the window is the secret code for the days when there's fresh banana bread. There are lounge chairs with side tables lined up out front. 21935 Gingerbread St.; 503/859-2247.

Silver Creek Coffee House: Just when you thought you couldn't stand to hear Coop go on about another coffee shop, in this case he feels justified, as Silver Creek serves full gourmet fare from a regularly changing seasonal menu. Additionally, this particular establishment does double duty for Howard Hinsdale Cellars wine tasting. So, please forgive the dog if he does go on. 111 Water St.; 503/874-9600.

PLACES TO STAY

Oregon Garden Resort: Moonstone properties built 17 cottages on a tiered hilltop meadow adjacent to the Oregon Garden, so that every room is a room with a view from private, landscaped patios. Six of the rooms in one building

DIVERSION

Lassie and Rin Tin Tin ain't got nothing on **Silverton Bobbie.** In one of the greatest true dog stories ever told, Bobbie was a Scotch collie who got separated from his family on a vacation to Indiana in 1923. Distraught, the family stayed in the area for a month trying to locate the dog, but left despondent and unable to do so. Six months later, Bobbie appeared on their doorstep, worse for wear but spirited, after covering nearly 3,000 miles on foot to find his way home. The story made national news, and over the next year, the family received letters with stories from people who remembered seeing and helping Bobbie on his journey. Stop in the visitors center to ask about his statue, doghouse and mural, located in town. There are more statues of him in the **Oregon Garden,** and several fiction and non-fiction books about this wonder dog in their gift shop. Visit silvertonbobbie.com for more.

will allow two pets per room. Opened in September 2008 with the latest in amenities, the rooms are luxuriously appointed and range $90–200, depending on the season; $15 pet fee. The garden theme is accented with occasional tables made from birdbaths and headboards that are modeled after garden gates. 895 W. Main St.; 800/966-6490; www.moonstonehotels.com.

Silver Falls Campground: There are 47 electrical sites open year-round for $16–20 and 46 tent sites open May–October for $12–16. 800/452-5687; www.reserveamerica.com.

Detroit Lake

It's torturous for the Dachsie Twins to limit what's in this guide, especially here in the North Santiam Canyon recreation area. There are dozens of picnic parks and campgrounds along the North Santiam and Little North Santiam Rivers. You could work your way into the Opal Creek Wilderness (www.opalcreek.org), or fish at the bend in the river in North Santiam State Park. Whatever you choose, as you travel State Route 22 southeast from Salem, it's along the river and through the woods you go to hound heaven.

PARKS, BEACHES, AND RECREATION AREAS

17 Mongold Picnic Area at Detroit Lake

😊😊 (See Willamette Valley map on page 512)

In and of itself, Detroit Lake is primarily designed for water recreation, with two beautiful boat ramps and a paved swim beach where dogs are not allowed. The Mongold day-use area has picnic tables all along the lake with great views, and a few tables tucked in the woods.

It's better to use this area to hike around and up above the lake. Pick up maps for the Tumble Creek Trail #3380, Dome Rock Trail #3381, and Stahlman Point Trail #3449 at the ranger station in Mill City on the way to the lake. Now you're talking.

The lake is four miles east of the town of Detroit on Highway 22. Detroit Lake has the only camping for miles. $3 day-use permit required. 503/854-3366.

PLACES TO EAT

KC's Espresso and Deli: The folks at Fodor's love KC's and the dogs do too, relaxing on the lawn by makeshift picnic tables. You can't miss the bright purple fence and you won't want to miss the old-fashioned milkshakes and made-to-order meatloaf sandwiches. You might meet the town mayor, coming in for his morning jolt. 210 Forest Ave.; 503/854-3145.

PLACES TO STAY

All Seasons Motel: Other than camping, this is it. The rooms are serviceable at prices of $50—70 per night. There's no charge for dogs yet, but they are toying with the idea of adding a flat $5 per visit cleaning fee. There are picnic tables and a propane grill out front for guests. 130 Breitenbush Rd.; 503/854-3421; www.allseasonsmotel.net.

Albany

Despite a difficult economy, residents of this historic town are working to restore the Victorian homes and the high concentration of covered bridges surrounding the city, reminders of a vital role this central town played in the trade and commerce of the early valley. Call 541/928-0911 for your copy of *Seems Like Old Times*, the self-guided tour brochure that will take you time traveling, walking or driving through the town's historic districts, including the Monteith House Museum, said to be the most authentic restoration project in Oregon.

PARKS, BEACHES, AND RECREATION AREAS

18 Simpson Park Trail

🐾🐾🐾 (See Willamette Valley map on page 512)

The Wonder Wieners were glad they went out of their way to visit this trail, reminiscent of a Sunday stroll down a quiet country lane. Neither the faint whiff from the wastewater treatment plant in the beginning nor the low hum of the highway in the distance or the occasional train whistle could deter them from their appointed rounds. The path is wide, level, easy, soft, and shaded, 1.3 miles each way, in between murky First Lake and the Willamette River. You'll end up in a field, with one very narrow, overgrown path heading to the river.

There are no amenities other than what nature intended, so humans go pee somewhere else first, bring bags and water, and pack everything in and out. From a parking circle, the trail curves around to the right, past the metal gate.

Take Exit 234 from I-5 and swoop into town on South State Route 99E, Pacific Boulevard. Exit onto Lyons Street, one-way into town. Turn north on 2nd Avenue, travel a mile, and turn left on Geary Street. Take a right on Front Avenue, which curves around to become Waverly Drive. Cross a one-lane bridge over Cox Creek to gravel parking on your left. Open 6 A.M.–10 P.M.

19 Takena Landing–Eagle Trail

🐾🐾 (See Willamette Valley map on page 512)

The picnic area and restrooms of this city park are under a highway overpass, but you lose the traffic noise after about a quarter mile on the Eagle Trail, named by default as the ongoing project of the local Eagle Scout troop. This 1.7-mile one-way walk parallels the Willamette River on the opposite shore from the city. The scouts are doing a good job maintaining the hard pack and

trimming back the blackberry bushes just enough to give you peek-a-boo water views. As for getting into the water, where there's a will, there are pathways. Your companionable river walk should be shady, serene, and private.

The park is a mile from State Route 99E. Turn west on Lyons, which crosses the bridge over the river and curves around to West U.S. Highway 20, and turn left onto North Albany Road. Open 6 A.M.–10 P.M. 541/917-7777; www.cityofalbany.net/parks.

20 Larwood Wayside

🐾🐾🐾 (See Willamette Valley map on page 512)

On a Linn County covered-bridge tour, pause at this countryside gathering place to soak up the timeless fun of a dog-day afternoon. The park looks much as it must have 70 years ago, when the Larwood Covered Bridge was wet with whitewash in 1939. Farm kids hang off the sides of the bridge, wave at passing cars, then jump into the water. Others float by on inner tubes past the ruins of the water wheel power plant on the riverbank. For sustenance, there's a U-Pick blueberry field two miles down the road and fishing. Once featured in *Ripley's Believe It or Not,* this is the only place in the United States where a river (Roaring River) flows into a creek (Crabtree Creek), instead of the other way around.

From State Route 226 east of Albany, Larwood is 6.7 miles down Fish Hatchery Road.

PLACES TO EAT

Loafers and Szabos: Primed to earn your vote for the hangout of the summer, this hybrid restaurant is a bread bakery and bistro by day, switching over to serve surf and turf (heavy on the turf) by night. They share the same historic building, the same boomerang-shaped patio with palm trees, and the same parking lot. The deli salads and dessert bars look especially good by day; see the specials board in the evening for chicken fried steak, a pound of shrimp, and halibut fish and chips with key lime pie and mile-high mud pie to top it all off. 222 S.W. Washington St.; 541/926-8183.

PLACES TO STAY

Peggy's Alaskan Cabbage Patch B&B: As retired Alaskans, Peggy and her husband, son, and two dogs are enjoying the not-so-cold weather and the company of lodgers in their two upstairs rooms: one lodge-themed, called Bear; and one frilly, called Wildflower. You can have either room for $75 with a shared hall bath, or for $125 to keep the bath to yourself. A six-foot fenced dog run is available in the unfenced yard, if you feel comfortable leaving your pet for a while. It's a no-frills, unfussy place to stay. No pet fees or restrictions. 194 S. Second St., in Lebanon, southwest of Albany; 541/258-1774; www.cabbage-patch-b-and-b.com.

More Accommodations: Please look under *Chain Hotels* in the *Resources* section for additional places to stay in this area.

Corvallis

Corvallis is the home of Oregon State University and their mascot the Beavers. It's fairly difficult to live in Oregon without being a rabid fan of the Beavers or of their riva from Eugene, the University of Oregon Ducks.

All city parks are open 6:30 A.M.–10 P.M. The Dachsie Twins applaud Corvallis for having six off-leash areas, although most of them can only be described as having rough ground cover, and they leave a bit to be desired in terms of creature comforts like shade, water, seating, and human facilities. On the other side of the coin, dogs are prohibited in Chintimini, Central, Franklin, Lilly, and Washington city parks. For heavier-duty hiking than the Wieners can manage, on primitive trails in the foothills, contact the OSU Research Forest Department regarding hiking trails in Dunn and McDonald State Forests. 541/737-4452.

One thing the dogs love about college towns is that there's a great variety of restaurants to serve a hungry student body. The highest concentration of prime outdoor eating is along 1st Street downtown, across from Riverfront Commemorative Park, and a block over on 2nd Street. For legit dog food and other goodies, visit **Animal Crackers** pet supply (949 N.W. Kings Blvd.; 541/753-4559; www.animalcrackerspetsupply.com).

PARKS, BEACHES, AND RECREATION AREAS

21 Martin Luther King Jr. Park

🐾 🐾 🐕 (See Willamette Valley map on page 512)

MLK Jr. Park was Walnut Park until a name change in 2005. At first, the designated off-leash area at MLK/Walnut is as clear as mud. From the parking lot, head due south about three-quarters of the way through a field. On the right, you'll see a painted brown wooden bridge and a Public Urban Stream Corridor sign. Cross the bridge and follow the gravel path, and you'll break out into a clearing with a post marking the dog area. It is effectively secured by the surrounding woods and a stream, with the added bonus of a landscaped private garden on the southern, fenced border. Once you've run the gauntlet to find it, you are rewarded with big meadows of wildflowers and field grass to play in, at least part of which has been mowed to dachshund height. There are no amenities other than a lonely shaded bench. A gravel path bisects the area, leading you back to the north end by the parking lot.

From 99W, turn west on Walnut Boulevard. The park is on the right as the road swings to the south, immediately as it becomes 53rd Street.

22 Chip Ross Park

🐾 🐾 🐾 🐕 (See Willamette Valley map on page 512)

This city park is composed of 125 acres of savannah, oak, and upland prairie in the foothills north of town. A 1.5-mile loop takes you through, and your sidekick will be thrilled to discover that he's allowed off leash on the trail. It's a bit of climbing to reach the summit, where you can connect to the Dan Trail in the McDonald Forest if, for example, your vizsla hasn't yet exhausted his supply of boundless energy. Cooper opted to rest and absorb the vistas of Coast and Cascade Mountains from summit benches before returning to a couple of picnic tables at the trailhead for a bite of bologna and cheese. You may pass horses and their riders along the hot, sunny trail. There are portable potties; bring your own drinking water.

From 3rd or 4th Streets, the main north–south thoroughfares through town, go west on Harrison Avenue to 10th Street. Follow 10th northeast through town until it turns north and becomes Highland Drive, and continue until the road starts to climb. Turn left on Lester Avenue, which dead-ends at the park. Closed November 1–April 15 for snow conditions.

23 Woodland Meadows

🐾 🐕 (See Willamette Valley map on page 512)

Rough and tumble pups only need apply at this city park. The off-leash area is essentially the back 40 of the farm, behind the historic Corl House. The field grass is like hay, and it's rarely, if ever, mowed. Any dog with hair longer than a Chinese crested is likely to come away with half the park's native groundcover stuck to his fur. The hilly area is not secured in any way, and is marked only by signposts. Things like shade, or a bench, or water have probably escaped the tight budgets of city planners. Avoid the side of the hill along Circle Avenue, a busy arterial street, and bring a wide-brimmed hat for self-made shade. The park on the west side of Circle Avenue only is off-leash, past the perimeter around the historic house.

From 99W, turn west on Circle Boulevard to the park. Turn north on Witham Hill Drive and right at the Corl House sign to the gravel parking lot.

24 Riverfront Commemorative Park

🐾 🐾 ◀● (See Willamette Valley map on page 512)

The banks of the Willamette River have served as the focus for commerce in Corvallis since the 1860s. Flour mills, grain warehouses, sawmills, rail lines, and even the city jail occupied the lots along the 11 city blocks of what is now the downtown core. In order to create a place for people to gather, the city had to remove 110,000 pounds of concrete rubble, asphalt, scrap metal, car bodies, and other debris as part of the riverfront restoration project.

The results speak for themselves. Even the garbage cans double as flower planters along this pretty city parkway. You and your mutt mate can stroll the promenade, day or night, to take in the gardens, artwork, and views of the river. Across the street are excellent restaurants, many with outdoor seating where your dog is allowed. Riverfront Park connects to Pioneer Park and Avery Park on the south. Dogs must be leashed, especially enthusiastic water dogs, to keep them from jumping into the spray fountain and scaring the toddlers.

The park is along 1st Street, from Washington to Van Buren. There's a large, free parking lot and restrooms south of the intersection of 2nd Street and B Avenue, and cheap metered parking along the walk.

25 Willamette Park

🐾 🐾 🐾 🐾 🐕 (See Willamette Valley map on page 512)

Coop 'n' Isis had encountered so many wonderful off-leash areas in the valley that they had become critical and jaded by the time they reached Corvallis—until they came here. At this big park close to downtown, the city has found a way for "civilized man" and "beast" to co-exist. It is complicated, so check the map at the north entrance information kiosk if you're unsure. Willamette is three parks in one. Dogs are always allowed off leash on Willamette Park trails, to the east along the river and in the Kendal Nature Park, the latter including informal trails to the west of the sports fields. Dogs are allowed off leash on the open Crystal Lake Sports Fields November–March. Dogs are not allowed off leash in the campground or south of Goodnight Avenue in the playground. Basically, stick to the trails until the whole park goes to the dogs in the winter. Behind the kiosk, only a short run from the parking lot, is a wide dirt ramp straight down into the wonderful Willamette River.

The off-leash areas and, more importantly, the map are easiest to reach from the north entrance to the park. From 99W, which is 4th Street downtown, turn left on Crystal Lake Drive, the opposite direction from Avery Avenue on the west. Curve around past the Evanite Glass Fiber factory and left into the park on Fisher Lane. 541/766-6918.

26 Bellfountain Park

🐾 (See Willamette Valley map on page 512)

A visit to Benton County's oldest park is worth a side trip from the highway for the unique and memorable experience of visiting the world's longest picnic table, a single slab of wood milled by the Hull Oaks Lumber Co. to 85 feet long and half a foot thick. With a peaked shelter covering the whole length, it even resembles an upside-down feed trough. The gleam in your dog's eye is him imagining the world's largest pot luck where all the humans have mysteriously disappeared, leaving him no choice but to save the food from spoiling.

From State Route 99W south of Corvallis, turn west on Dawson Road and travel 4.3 miles to the park entrance. To reserve the table for yourself, call 541/766-6871.

PLACES TO EAT

American Dream Pizza: Make your own pizza dreams come true with a huge list of meat and veggie combos served by the slice at a couple of picnic tables or to go. 214 S.W. 2nd St.; 541/753-7373. For delivery of whole pies to most of Corvallis, call the campus branch of the Dream at 541/757-1713.

Fox and Firkin: What we didn't know was that a firkin is a type of wooden keg. What we do know is that a menu of pub grub, including shepherd and vegetable pot pies, tastes best when washed down with one of the 46 beers on tap or 32 single malt scotches. The Fox has more seating outside than in, along the riverfront. 202 S.W. 1st St.; 541/753-8533.

New Morning Bakery: This shop is so much more than a bakery. It delivers the one-two punch, first with a glass case full of beautiful salads, then with even more beautiful desserts. 219 S.W. 2nd St.; 541/754-0181; www.newmorningbakery.com.

Sunnyside Up: Breakfast is the dogs' favorite meal of the day, especially when it is served all day at this café. The Sunnyside concentrates on organic, wholesome food served in very large portions, which shouldn't be a problem when you have a four-legged food-disposal device sitting at your feet. Outdoor seating and wireless Internet. 116 N.W. 3rd St.; 541/758-3353.

PLACES TO STAY

Hanson Country Inn: People flock to this former poultry farm for its rural setting, still within city limits. Charlie the dog and his feline friends, of the city's oldest and classiest bed-and-breakfast, are often out front to greet arrivals. Smaller or particularly well-mannered pets may be allowed in the posh, restored 1928 main house. The only slightly more rustic detached cottage is suitable for more rambunctious Rovers. There are extensive fields to roam if your dog is careful not to disturb the neighbors' sheep and chickens. Rates range $95–145. 795 S.W. Hanson St.; 541/752-2919; www.hcinn.com.

More Accommodations: Please look under *Chain Hotels* in the *Resources* section for additional places to stay in this area.

Alsea

Named for a native tribe that lived at the north of the river, Alsea is a gorgeous, second-growth wooded area that has recovered beautifully from early logging and settlement. Fishing, especially for steelhead, is the most popular pastime in local parks along the Alsea River.

PARKS, BEACHES, AND RECREATION AREAS

27 Siuslaw National Forest–Mary's Peak

😺😺😺 🐾 (See Willamette Valley map on page 512)

Even if you don't hike any of the 12 miles of trails on this peak, you owe it to yourself and your dog to visit Observation Point at the top of the 4,097-foot mountain, the highest in the coastal range. If you want to hoof it, come in at the north end, off U.S. Highway 20, to the Woods Creek Trailhead. From there, it is a heat-up-your-haunches 5.8-mile climb to the top on the North Ridge Trail. If you'd rather stick your heads out the window and drive 9.5 miles to the top, enter from the south, off State Route 34, to Mary's Peak Road. From the parking lot, it's a short, easy 0.5-mile walk to the tip top. Once there, you'll be so inspired by the 360-degree vistas you may want to circle the peak on the Meadowledge Trail, an easy 1.6-mile loop near the summit. Come for sunsets over the ocean; and, should you decide to stay overnight, there are two primitive, first-come, first-served campgrounds on the peak for $10 a night.

The signs are clear at the north entrance on Forest Road 2005, Woods Creek Road, and on the south from Forest Road 30, Mary's Peak Road. Mary's Peak Road is closed at milepost 5.5 December–April; foot traffic is welcome in the snow. Parking is $5. 541/563-3211.

28 Alsea Falls

😺😺😺 (See Willamette Valley map on page 512)

The coastal forest at the Alsea Falls Recreation Site is thick enough to grow in an arch over the road. As you hike along the South Fork of the Alsea River, 0.5 mile in one direction to the campground or a mile the opposite way to Green

Peak Falls, you can see the remains of old growth, last logged in 1945. Life persists, reclaiming the forest in thick carpets of springy moss, giant ferns, red vine maple, and sapling Douglas firs. The sun filters through the trees in dapple patterns, lending an air of enchantment.

The falls are a short series of segments tumbling over a wide ledge. How close you can get to the falls depends on mountain runoff. Picnic areas are hidden within their own private groves. On a hot day, Alsea offers cool relief in the river and a popular picnic spot. Camping at the falls is on a first-come, first-served basis, for $10 a night.

From the town of Alsea on State Route 34, turn south on State Route 201 for one mile and left on the Back Country Byway for nine miles, two of which are on a nicely graded gravel road.

Sweet Home

This small town of about 9,000 (not including dogs) is built on a vast, prehistoric petrified forest. While it may seem pointless to pee on petrified trees, it does make rock hounds happy to hunt for agates, jasper, and crystals.

Again, Cooper and Isis were forced to leave out many recreational opportunities, but you don't have to. The Sweet Home Ranger District (4431 Hwy. 20; 541/367-5168) publishes an excellent free guide to the hikes following the Santiam Wagon Trail along U.S. Highway 20 southeast from Albany, paralleling the South Fork of the Santiam River. A self-guided nature walk on Iron Mountain comes highly recommended, as does taking to the Tombstone Prairie nature trail, or just lounging around Foster Lake.

PARKS, BEACHES, AND RECREATION AREAS

29 Cascadia
🐾🐾🐾 (See Willamette Valley map on page 512)

This state park captures much of what makes the Pacific Northwest such a great outdoor destination. There's a quiet 25-tent campground in the woods behind the South Santiam River. The east picnic area has a wide, sunny field. The west picnic area is shaded under big trees. The paved Soda Springs Trail follows the springs, which divides the park east to west, and then down to the river. A 1.5-mile out-and-back trail runs along the creek to Soda Creek Falls. It's an easy magical mystery tour through a dense forest of ferns, moss, and old growth, a quintessential Northwest forest.

Cascadia is off U.S. Highway 20, 8.5 miles east of Green Peter Dam. The first-come, first-served campground, $14 per night, and east picnic area are open May–September. The west picnic area and the trails are open year-round. 541/367-6021.

Eugene-Springfield

Eugene is the birthplace of Nike (now headquartered in Beaverton), with a long-running tradition of long-distance runners that dates back to the 1970s, when Steve Prefontaine broke every record in the world for races of 2,000 meters and above. Needless to say, there's no shortage of places for your dog to get her exercise in the hometown of the University of Oregon Ducks. When it's time for a little time apart, pack Fido off to **Dogs at Play** for the day (590 Wilson St.; 541/344-3647). City parks are open 6 A.M.–11 P.M. unless posted otherwise.

In downtown Springfield, step into the alley on 5th Street between Main and A Streets to give your pet a moment to commune with the 11-foot by 16-foot mural titled *Bob the Dog Visits the Old Growth*.

PARKS, BEACHES, AND RECREATION AREAS

30 Candlelight Park OLA

🐾🐾🐾 (See Willamette Valley map on page 512)

Should you find yourself in the residential 'burbs of Bethel-Danebo west of downtown Eugene, there's a good-sized dog park out here, at the corner of Royal and Throne (we're not kidding!). An unofficial off-leash area since about 1991, now it's official with fence posts and mesh, gates, water pumps, and plastic pools for paw washing. There are two divided areas, the East and West Meadows, with a wood-chip trail around the inner perimeter. The West Meadow is reserved for small or timid dogs on Wednesdays and Sundays, and one of the areas may occasionally be closed in winter to allow turf to take a breather.

The leash-up area is nice and large, and an Eagle Scout built boxes around the dog parks to encourage people to recycle their home plastic bags. Not only does it save the city money, it's the environmentally responsible thing to do. Outside of the dog park are play fields, a playground, restroom, and picnic benches.

Take 6th Street west through town and stay on it until it becomes Highway 99 North. Turn left on Royal Avenue and go one block past Candlelight. Street parking is available along Throne. Royal Ave. and Throne Dr.

31 Alton Baker Dog Park

🐾🐾🐾🐾🐾 (See Willamette Valley map on page 512)

It is not easy to get to Alton Baker. Once there, you could try your dog's suggestion of never leaving, and, thus, never having to worry about trying to find your way back. This wonderful off-leash area has everything a dog park should. Its big, grassy fields are fenced with double gates for leash maneuvers.

DIVERSIONS

Eugene's historic 5th Street Public Market is famous for high-end designer shopping, and **Lexi Dog Boutique** is no exception. It's geared toward glamour and accessorizing (248 E. 5th Ave.; 541/343-5394; lexidog.com). Don't miss Yappy Hour on the patio, a mixer for both species featuring the valley's fine wines for the two-leggers. For a larger selection of everyday stuff in Eugene, The Healthy Pet is the place (2777 Friendly St.; 541/343-3411; www.thehealthypet.net).

It has covered picnic tables, shady benches, and hefty trees. There's water galore in the form of drinking fountains, water pumps, and wading pools to dunk in. Garbage receptacles and bags are plentiful. Outside the gates, you can connect to miles of Ruth Bascom's Riverbank Trail, paved multi-use pathways that follow the Willamette and Steve Prefontaine's four-mile soft jogging trails. As you can imagine, its popularity sometimes makes it a crazy place. The only time it's not good to visit is prior to and after a sporting event; get a list of game dates for the stadium at www.goducks.com to avoid rowdy sports fans.

If you're already in downtown Eugene, it's much easier to get to the park. Take 5th Street downtown heading east, follow the signs for I-105/206/Coburg Road, cross the bridge, and peel off to the right at the sign for Autzen Stadium/MLK Boulevard and right on Leo Harris Boulevard. Park at the Alton Baker Park Eastern Natural Area lot. Cross the wooden bridge to the dog area. Whew. 541/682-4800.

32 Amazon Dog Park

🐾🐾🐾 🐕 (See Willamette Valley map on page 512)

"Our dog has such a high ball drive, I don't know what we'd do without a dog park," said the owner of a 16-month-old black Lab Cooper met at Amazon's off-leash park. Although the smallest of the OLAs, this off-leash area is perfect for a game of toss. The wide field is level and open, fenced, and gated. In between rounds, there is a water station and plastic wading pools for cooling off. Our friend warned us that the park can get a little rough. People come to cluster around the single covered picnic table and chew the fat, and sometimes they don't pay enough attention to what their dogs are doing. If you're worried about the pack mentality getting out of hand, it wouldn't hurt to go up and introduce yourselves first and ask people to watch their charges around your timid or small dog.

From 6th and 7th Streets, the main east–west thoroughfares downtown, turn south on Pearl Street and stay in the right lane until the road merges onto Amazon Parkway. Continue in the right lane until 29th Street, then turn left into the parking lot behind the bus terminal. It's a total of two miles from the center of downtown.

33 Wayne Morse Ranch Dog Park

🐾🐾🐾🐕 (See Willamette Valley map on page 512)

This off-leash area is the place to perfect the precision of your throw to avoid tossing your dog's favorite ball or toy into the fenced-off, protected drainage areas in the middle of the park. There are three large, fenced meadows and lots of grass at Morse Ranch, with several gated entry points and natural bridges to cross in between. The ground in all three pastures is uneven and hilly; bigger trees to the west, and more open to the east, along Lincoln Street. Your Aussie can pretend he's patrolling the farm and then reward himself with a quick swim in the wading pools. There are historic buildings outside the OLA, several of which house Willamette Wildlife Rescue.

From 7th Street, eastbound downtown, turn south on Willamette Street and go 2.2 miles, then take a hard right up the hill on Crest Drive and go another 0.4 mile to the parking lot at the intersection of Crest and Arden, past the fenced-off areas. The east pasture is open shorter hours, 8 A.M.–8 P.M., to be kind to nearby neighbors. 595 Crest Dr.

34 Ridgeline Trail System

🐾🐾🐾🐾 (See Willamette Valley map on page 512)

We got the lowdown from a park maintenance supervisor in Eugene that this is where he takes his lab pal Zac for a jaunt out of town to a more relaxed environment. While our short-legged companions barely scratched the surface of these trails, they liked what they saw. Totaling about 14 miles from Spencer Butte to Mount Baldy, there are well-marked, regularly maintained treks from easy to challenging and everything in between. The hills are alive with the sound of barking.

To start at the Spencer Butte Park trailhead, turn south onto Willamette Street from downtown and go five miles, watching carefully to stay on

Willamette as it twists and turns. Plenty of parking and a couple of portable potties are available.

35 Howard Buford Recreation Area–Mount Pisgah

🐾🐾🐾🐕 (See Willamette Valley map on page 512)

You can see the mound of Mount Pisgah as you drive into HBRA, named for the Biblical summit from which Moses sighted the Promised Land. We say "Hallelujah!," for dogs are allowed to hike off leash on five of the 2,363-acre county park's seven trails. Only on Trails #1 and #2 are pups required to wear an eight-foot or shorter tether. Hikes are 0.7 to 3.9 miles in length, and some to the 1,531-foot summit are tougher than others that circle the base. Cooper can't promise your pet a religious experience, but he finds off-leash hiking to be nothing short of a revelation. One caution: Some trails are hiker only and some are designated for horses and hikers. Maps are available at visitors centers in town or at the bulletin board by the arboretum entrance. Hiking on the hill can be hot and dry. Bring plenty of water and poop bags.

From I-5, take Exit 189 to the east and go a block north on the frontage road. Turn right on Franklin Road for 0.4 miles, and left on Seavey Loop Road for 1.8 miles. Parking is $2 May–September; free in the off-season. www .bufordpark.org.

PLACES TO EAT

Hideaway Bakery: If local Jeannine and her miniature schnauzer hadn't shared their favorite spot with us, we never would have found it, living up to its name, hidden behind Mazzi's Italian Restaurant. The Mazzi's make amazing, rustic, baked goods in an earthen oven fired by recycled wood from a sawmill. Hideaway's trellis-covered patio is huge and warmed with heat lamps on cold days. People often have dogs with them, coming to and from Morse Ranch or Amazon Park to enjoy a pot of tea and piping hot panini. 3377 E. Amazon; 541/868-1982; www.mazzis.com/bakery.php.

Steelhead Brewing Co.: When the brewpub garage door is rolled up, it reveals a sidewalk sports bar, complete with TVs, homebrews on tap, and plenty of room for dogs to sit at their owners' elbows. The only thing missing is your lumpy couch. 199 E 5th Ave.; 541/686-2739; www.steelheadbrewery.com.

P.S.: The Lucky Noodle across the street is also a delicious choice.

Sweet Life Patisserie: It is indeed sweet to see row upon row of gleaming, gorgeous pastries in this bakery's case, with many good choices for people with food allergies, such as gluten-free, dairy-free, and vegan options. Sidewalk tables are open early and stay open late. They make cakes, tortes, and tarts, and yes, there really is a dessert called the Nipple of Venus. 755 Monroe; 541/683-5676; www.sweetlifedesserts.com.

PLACES TO STAY

Blue Rooster Inn: This is the place to stay if you want to visit the wineries in the valley. This 1865 historic farmhouse, 20 minutes from Eugene, is nestled on 68 acres where your dog is free to roam with Nancy's three dogs. It is absolutely postcard perfect. Turn-of-the-last-century antiques furnish a large lower room and parlor. The Garden Room upstairs may also be available. Call and discuss your dogs with her for details. Rates are $90 downstairs, $80 upstairs. 82782 Territorial Rd.; 541/684-3923; www.blueroosterbnb.com.

Campbell House: You have to really want to stay at this bed-and-breakfast, with its steep dog fee of $50 per pet per night, plus tariffs (that's British for rates) of $130 per night for the Frazer Room and $245–350 for the Celeste Cottage, the two rooms where pets are allowed. If you can swing it, you'll be a temporary resident at the most elegant address in town, a four-diamond property a few blocks from the desirable 5th Street Public Market. 252 Pearl St.; 541/343-1119 or 800/264-2519; www.campbellhouse.com.

Valley River Inn: This rambling, corporate motel is so pet-friendly, they like to say that The Pampered Pooch Pet Package is only $180, $200 for river view rooms, and owners stay free! Also just for pooch is a yappetizer menu of locally made gourmet treats in the gift shop. The motel's mall location seems a bit odd, but the back faces the banks of the river, with bike and jogging paths. Pets are allowed in ground-level rooms only. 1000 Valley River Way; 541/743-1000; www.valleyriverinn.com.

More Accommodations: Please look under *Chain Hotels* in the *Resources* section for additional places to stay in this area.

Blue River and McKenzie Bridge

From Eugene, State Route 126 leads you to the McKenzie River Recreation Area, 60 miles of swimming, boating, and fishing pleasure. The **McKenzie River National Recreation Trail** runs 27 miles along the whitewater tumbling down from the Cascades. From 11 well-marked parking areas, you can access 600-year-old stands of trees, waterfalls and turquoise pools, log bridge crossings, and hardened lava flows. The first trailhead is 1.5 miles east of McKenzie Bridge. Sahalie and Koosah Falls and Tamolich Pool are two highly recommended hikes. Directions and maps are available at the ranger station (57600 S.R. 126; 541/822-3381).

PARKS, BEACHES, AND RECREATION AREAS

36 Delta Old Growth Trail

😺 😺 (See Willamette Valley map on page 512)

This half-mile stroll through old-growth forest is a synopsis of the unique features of a Pacific Northwest temperate rainforest. Soft, pine-needle-carpeted trails and three wooden bridges take you past giant hemlock, fir, and cedar trees draped in moss. Your footsteps are hushed by the surrounding undergrowth of lichen and thick ferns. This trail is at the northern end of the Aufderheide Scenic Byway, a 19-mile drive through the Willamette Forest skirting the edge of the Three Sisters Wilderness.

From State Route 126 east of Blue River, turn on Forest Road 19 and, shortly thereafter, turn right into the Delta Campground. The trail is at the very end of the campground, 1.3 miles from the turnoff. Parking is $5.

PLACES TO EAT

Harbick's Country Store: If you forgot anything for your road trip along the river, Harbick's has it, including deli food and groceries for you and pet provisions for you-know-who. They also loan out narrated CDs or cassettes of the journey along the Aufderheide Scenic Byway; there's no charge if you return the borrowed disc or tape. 91808 Mill Creek Rd.; 541/822-3575.

PLACES TO STAY

McKenzie River Inn: Dogs may run free in the orchard and along 500 feet of riverfront at this bed-and-breakfast, as long as they are on leash in and around the buildings and other guests. The cabins are best for dog owners, with separate entrances and river-view decks, ranging $115–165 per night with steep winter discounts and no pet fees. 49164 McKenzie Hwy.; 541/822-6260; www.mckenzieriverinn.com.

Wayfarer Resort: Across a covered bridge and into the woods are 12 dog-friendly cabins, much too luxurious to be called cabins, on a 10-acre property surrounded by the McKenzie River and Martin Creek. Rates range $80–105 for studios for two, $290 for a house that sleeps six; there is a three-night minimum Memorial Day–Labor Day, and a $10 dog fee. Ironically, the only unit dogs are not allowed in is The Dogwood unit. There's a stocked pond where the kids can fish, tennis and basketball courts, and easy river access. Quiet dogs may be left unattended if crated. 46725 Goodpasture Rd; 541/896-3613; www.wayfarerresort.com.

Cottage Grove

This township is proud of its claim to fame as the location where Buster Keaton starred in the film *The General* in 1926. Today, it is known more as the starting point for a covered bridge scenic tour featuring five of Oregon's oldest covered bridges.

PARKS, BEACHES, AND RECREATION AREAS

37 Row River Trail

🐾🐾🐾 (See Willamette Valley map on page 512)

The river got its name from a row over cows, a dispute between two pioneer men over cattle-grazing rights in the 1850s. You can take it fast or slow on the paved 15.6-mile trail, originally the line of the Oregon Southern & Eastern railway nicknamed "The Old Slow and Easy." There are nine trailheads to reach trail segments from Cottage Grove to the mining and lumber towns of Dorena and Culp Creek. The most scenic part of the trail begins at Mosby Creek, three miles outside of town, passing the shores of Dorena Reservoir.

A trail map from the Cottage Grove visitors center shows restroom and water stops, trailheads, camping parks, and historic covered bridge sites along the trail. To reach the Mosby Creek Trailhead, take Exit 174 from I-5 and turn east at the bottom of the exit ramp onto Row River Road. Drive three miles and turn left onto Layng Road. Open dawn–dusk.

PLACES TO EAT

Fleur de Lis: An amazing painting of Notre Dame graces one wall, and outside, you'll be sitting alongside a trompe l'oeil park painted on boards covering up an empty lot between two buildings. The croissants and cakes in the pastry case are just as artistic at this bistro and bakery. Cooper couldn't decide between the chicken curry and pasta salads, so he ordered both. Meanwhile, Isis got up on her hind legs for the Princess Cake, a pink dome of marzipan covering raspberry jam, white sponge cake, and whipped cream. 616 Main St.; 541/767-0700; www.fleurdeliscafe.net.

PLACES TO STAY

Village Green Resort: "Pets stay free!" reads the ad at this older motel on 14 acres of theme gardens and walking paths. Moonstone Properties is slowly upgrading the rooms, so some look more dated than others. An entire building is reserved for dog and their people, and includes singles, doubles, smoking, and nonsmoking rooms. The staff are super dog friendly, handing out treats and love at check-in. Rates range $80–120; there's no pet fee, except a $50 penalty if you don't declare your dog at registration. 725 Row River Rd.; 541/942-2491; www.villagegreenresortandgardens.com.

More Accommodations: Please look under *Chain Hotels* in the *Resources* section for additional places to stay in this area.

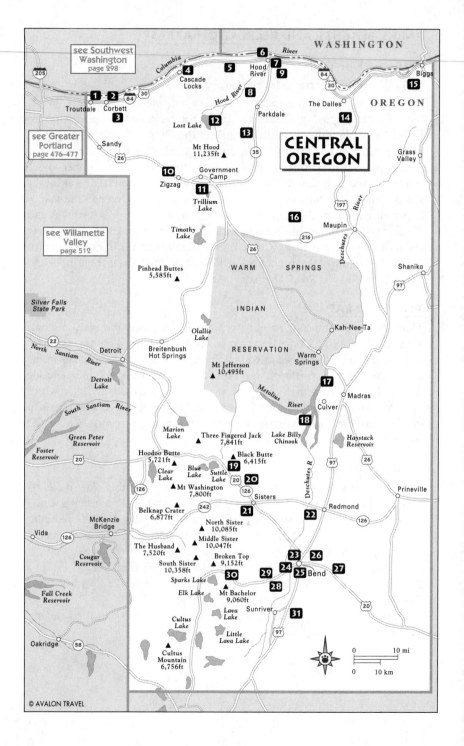

WASHINGTON

see Southwest
Washington
page 298

Columbia River

6

7
9

84
30

Biggs

15

OREGON

205

Cascade
Locks

4

5

Hood River

Hood River

8

The Dalles

14

1 **2**
84
30

Troutdale Corbett

3

Parkdale

Lost Lake

12

13

Grass
Valley

see Greater
Portland
page 476–477

Sandy

26

Mt Hood
11,235ft ▲

35

CENTRAL
OREGON

197

Deschutes River

Zigzag

10

Government
Camp

11

Trillium
Lake

16

Maupin

216

Shaniko

97

see Willamette
Valley
page 512

Timothy
Lake

WARM   SPRINGS

26

Pinhead Buttes
5,585ft ▲

INDIAN

Silver Falls
State Park

Olallie
Lake

RESERVATION

Kah-Nee-Ta

22

North Santiam River

Detroit

Breitenbush
Hot Springs

Warm
Springs

Detroit
Lake

Mt Jefferson
10,495ft
▲

Metolius River

17

Madras

South Santiam River

Culver

18

Lake Billy
Chinook

Green Peter
Reservoir

Marion
Lake

Three Fingered Jack
7,841ft
▲

Haystack
Reservoir

Foster
Reservoir

20

Hoodoo Butte
5,721ft ▲

Black Butte
6,415ft
▲

19

26

97

Clear
Lake

Blue
Lake

Suttle
Lake

20

126

Prineville

Vida

126

McKenzie
Bridge

▲ Mt Washington
7,800ft

126

Sisters

242

21

Redmond

22

126

Belknap Crater
6,877ft

North Sister
▲ 10,085ft

Cougar
Reservoir

The Husband
7,520ft ▲

▲ Middle Sister
10,047ft

Deschutes R

23 **26**

Fall Creek
Reservoir

South Sister
10,358ft ▲

Broken Top
▲ 9,152ft

24
25

Bend

27

Sparks Lake

30

29

28

Elk Lake

Mt Bachelor
9,060ft ▲

Sunriver

31

20

Oakridge

58

Cultus
Lake

Lava
Lake

97

Little
Lava Lake

Cultus
Mountain
6,756ft ▲

N

0   10 mi

0   10 km

© AVALON TRAVEL

CHAPTER 19

Central Oregon

From the high desert of the Oregon Outback in the south to Mount Hood and the Columbia River Gorge bordering Washington, Central Oregon is expansive and majestic, full of the kind of splendor that makes nature photographers drool like dogs. While traveling in this dry and sunny region, you'll often encounter more wildlife than people. Watch for deer on the road, elk in the mountains, and squirrels and chipmunks everywhere. Cooper has developed a deep, abiding love affair with the golden-mantled ground squirrel, small and striped like a chipmunk, numbering in the billions in Central Oregon's mountains and high plains.

The top boundary of the region is the Columbia River, the fourth largest river in the United States, with a water volume twice the Nile in Egypt. Before multiple dams and development, it is believed to have had the largest salmon runs in the world, between 6 and 10 million per year.

PICK OF THE LITTER—CENTRAL OREGON

BEST PARK
Mount Hood National Forest–Lost Lake Resort,
Mount Hood (page 558)

BEST DOG PARK
Big Sky Dog Park, Bend (page 571)

BEST EVENT
Fourth of July Pet Parade, Bend (page 572)

BEST PLACES TO EAT
Elliot Glacier Public House, Mount Hood (page 559)
Petite Provence, The Dalles (page 562)
Terrebonne Depot, Redmond (page 569)

BEST PLACES TO STAY
Columbia Gorge Hotel, Hood River (page 556)
The Dalles Inn, The Dalles (page 562)
Five Pine Lodge, Sisters (page 567)
Champagne Chalet at Cricketwood Country B&B,
Bend (page 575)

NATIONAL FORESTS AND RECREATION AREAS

Columbia River Gorge National Scenic Area
🐾🐾

Columbia River residents brag that their gorge is gorgeous, and they're not suffering from delusions of grandeur. In the 292,500-acre protected area, you can walk under waterfalls, wade through wildflowers, and retrace the route of Oregon Trail settlers in two states. You can windsurf until your lips turn blue and ski until you're blue in the face, on the same day. Nearly every hike is a bun-buster. You are, after all, hiking up out of a gorge that's 80 miles long and up to 4,000 feet deep. On the downside, access to much of the area's recreation requires four-wheel driving on rough dirt roads following vague directions. Weather conditions vary dramatically, often in the same day, and you and your pooch need to be safely equipped for the rigors of backcountry travel. Hood River Ranger Station; 541/352-6002; www.fs.fed.us/r6/columbia.

Deschutes National Forest
🐾🐾🐾🐾

The Deschutes invites 8 million people annually to come out and play in its 1.6 million acres (that's twice the size of the state of Rhode Island). Its diverse regions include the Crooked River National Grassland, Newberry National Volcanic Monument, eight wilderness areas, and the Pacific Northwest's largest ski area at Mount Bachelor. Its recreation opportunities could fill a library, much less a book. Where does a dog begin? In addition to our suggestions in this chapter, try the links under "Recreational Activities" at www.fs.fed.us/r6/centraloregon, or call the Bend–Fort Rock Ranger Station, 541/383-4000. On many trails, dogs are allowed off leash October–April.

Mount Hood National Forest
🐾🐾🐾

At the summit of 11,235-foot Mount Hood, the largest mountain in Oregon, is the grave of Ranger, a dog who was said to have climbed the volcano 500 times in his life from 1925 to 1938 with his owners and friends. Only 20 miles from Portland, this national forest is an easy recreation area for you to reach, following in Ranger's footsteps to create your own feats of athleticism on more than 1,200 miles of trails. Powder hounds can schuss and skijor on Mount Hood's five ski areas. www.fs.fed.us/r6/mthood. Mount Hood Chamber of Commerce: 503/622-3017; www.mthood.info.

Cascade Lakes Recreation Area
🐾🐾🐾🐾

From Bend, Century Drive leads to State Route 46, also called the Cascade Lakes National Scenic Byway. The nonprofit organization Scenic America has named it one of the Top 10 most important byways in the country, with extravagant views of mountain peaks, and access to alpine lakes, campgrounds, hiking, and skiing at **Mount Bachelor.** In the summer, dogs are allowed to ride the scenic chairlift and hike to the summit, led by a Forest Service Guide (541/382-7888; www.mtbachelor.com). For the drive, there's a cool downloadable Print-n-Go Map at www.byways.org (click "Explore Byways" and scroll down to "Oregon").

Troutdale

This period town welcomed travelers in their new-fangled Model Ts when the Columbia River Highway opened in 1915. Travelers rested up in auto courts, predecessors to today's motels, before their adventures on the King of Roads. Merchants in Troutdale sold tyres (tires), fuel, and parts, now replaced by antiques, gifts, and clothing boutiques. Isis barked at the dog on the *Hitchin' a Ride* bronze sculpture at the corner of Dora Avenue on Main Street.

NATURE HIKES AND URBAN WALKS

On the Historic Columbia River Highway, between Exit 22 and Exit 35 from I-84, you can drive or walk to 10 **Columbia Gorge waterfalls.** Half of them require fancy footwork to see; the rest are visible from highway stops.

Upper and Lower Latourell: It's a short walk from the parking lot viewpoint to the base of 249-foot Lower Latourell Falls. A 2.3-mile circuit takes you to 100-foot Upper Latourell, where you can walk behind the falling water and through the peaceful picnic area of Guy W. Talbot Park. On Highway 30, 3.4 miles west of Exit 28 from I-84.

Shepperds Dell: Two tiers of falls can be viewed from the bridge crossing. The upper tier is a straight plunge of 35 feet, the lower is a horsetail formation, falling 60 feet. From I-84, take Exit 28 and drive 2 miles west on Highway 30.

Bridal Veil: There's a mile hike down steep switchbacks and stairs to the base of Bridal Veil, which plunges twice—first 100 feet, then another 60 feet. The basalt formation Pillar of Hercules can be seen from a separate wheelchair-accessible path around the cliff above Bridal Veil. The falls is in a state park that includes a picnic area and restrooms. Near milepost 28 on Highway 30, accessed from I-84 at Exit 28.

Wahkeena: These 242-foot fantail falls are described by the Yakima tribe's word meaning "most beautiful." They can be seen from a picnic area, or you can walk 0.2 mile to a bridge viewpoint, close enough to feel the spray. Wahkeena is 0.5 mile west of Multnomah Falls on Highway 30.

Multnomah: The highest and most famous of the falls, Multnomah cascades 620 feet in two sections from the top of Larch Mountain to the Columbia River. Two million people crowd the 0.2-mile trail to the bridge viewpoint each year. Fewer hardy souls climb the 1.2 miles from the visitors center to the top of the falls, and those of you with haunches of steel may want to tackle the six-mile trail to the top of Larch Mountain or trek the equally long loop to Wahkeena Falls and back. Multnomah has a lodge, restaurant, gift shop, and snack bar. Exit 31 from I-84; 503/695-2372.

Horsetail and Ponytail: This 176-foot swisher can be seen from a turnout on Highway 30, 2.5 miles east of Multnomah Falls. Viewing the smaller Ponytail Falls requires a short, steep hike.

Oneonta and Triple Falls: Starting at Horsetail Falls Trailhead (#438), it's a mile uphill to Oneonta Falls, with the added treat of a footbridge over Oneonta Gorge on the way. From there, it's a 1.7-mile climb on Trail #424 through wild canyon scenery to the log bridge viewpoint of Triple Falls, with parallel chutes ranging from 100 to 135 feet. Round-trip is 5.4 miles.

Dogs are prohibited at nearby Glenn Otto, Oxbow Regional, Blue Lake Regional, and Dabney State parks.

PARKS, BEACHES, AND RECREATION AREAS

1 Lewis and Clark State Recreation Site

🐾🐾🐾🐕 (See Central Oregon map on page 546)

About a third of the grounds at this state recreation site is designated as a pet exercise area. While there are no fences to separate the space, signs clearly mark where your dog may be off leash. It's hemmed in on three sides by bushes, an inviting place to spend a leisurely afternoon on the grass under the shade trees by Sandy River. There are restrooms, picnic tables, and interpretive signs for the Lewis and Clark Trail.

Across the street from the park is the easiest access to the Sandy River. You'll see cars parked in the dirt and in the roadside pullout before the Troutdale bridge. Portlanders bring their dogs here to walk along the river and go for a swim.

From I-84, take Exit 18 and turn left at the bottom of the cloverleaf exit ramp. You'll see the recreation area to your left around the bend under the railroad trestle. Closes at 9 P.M.

PLACES TO EAT

Jack's Snack 'n' Tackle: Drive or step up to the window at this tackle shed that's been semi-converted to a sandwich place. Fresh-squeezed lemonade, power smoothies, and zero-carb drinks taste so good when slurped at a picnic table around the corner from Lewis and Clark's off-leash area. 1208 E. Historic Columbia River Hwy.; 503/665-2257; www.jackssnackandtackle.com.

Troutdale General Store: This double-duty shop has good taste, both in the food they serve on a covered sidewalk patio and in the gifts and goodies they carry inside. The apple and bacon breakfast casserole is a great choice, and the smoked salmon chowder comes highly recommended for lunch. 289 E. Historic Columbia River Hwy.; 503/492-7912.

PLACES TO STAY

In this area, chain hotels listed in the *Resources* section offer the best choices for dogs and their owners.

Corbett

For the best gorge views, the curviest section of the Historic Columbia Gorge Highway, and the highest concentration of waterfalls in the United States, take Exit 22 from I-84 and follow the signs to Corbett. Your first stop should be the Portland Women's Forum, and then you'll rise to Crown Point and the Vista House.

PARKS, BEACHES, AND RECREATION AREAS

🐾 Rooster Rock Pet Exercise Area

🐾🐾🐾🐕 (See Central Oregon map on page 546)

Dogs are allowed off leash in this state park, as are unclothed people; Rooster Rock is one of Oregon's two public clothing-optional beaches. There are some restrictions: Dogs are not allowed on the nude beaches to the far east of the park, and nude sunbathers are not allowed in the dog area to the far west of the park. The dogs definitely got the better end of the deal.

The off-leash area is a lengthy, hefty field, partially shaded by old-growth trees, yet open enough to break into a run after a ball. The only oddity is that the state is waiting for funds to replace the decayed wooden tops and benches of the picnic tables, leaving the concrete bases as mini-monoliths for your dog to sniff and lift a leg on.

From I-84, Exit 25 is an exclusive road into the park. Parking is $3. Park closes at 10 P.M.

🐾 Larch Mountain

🐾🐾🐾 (See Central Oregon map on page 546)

On a clear day at the Sherrard Viewpoint picnic area, at an elevation of 4,055 feet, you can see Mount Rainier, Mount St. Helens, Mount Adams, Mount Hood, Mount Jefferson, and the Columbia River Gorge. It's as if you're in an airplane with a much bigger window. From the parking area, it's only a 0.25-mile climb to the picnic spot.

For a true test of endurance, you can hike 6.6 miles straight up Larch Mountain from Multnomah Falls to this glorious spot. Bring plenty of water and protein bars. This is summer and fall recreation only; the road is snowed in half the year.

From I-84, Take Exit 22 and follow the signs to Highway 30. Go east from Corbett to Larch Mountain Road, turn right and follow the main road 14 miles to the viewpoint sign.

Cascade Locks

If you get as excited by technical marvels as you do by wonders of nature, let the dogs take a backseat and drive through the grounds of the Bonneville Locks and Dam and watch the fish play chutes and ladders.

Native American oral history tells of a natural bridge across the Columbia created by a landslide, but evidence of the crossing was lost by the time Lewis and Clark arrived, and the explorers had to portage over a difficult section of rapids. The more recent Bridge of the Gods is a steel toll bridge, costing $1 to drive over to Stevenson, Washington.

PARKS, BEACHES, AND RECREATION AREAS

4 Marine Park

😽 😽 (See Central Oregon map on page 546)

This scenic city park is the site of frequent weddings and also the port for Sternwheeler paddleboat cruises along the gorge. There's a rose garden, pristine lawns, and a seawall walk along a fishing canal. The coolest part of this park is the trek over to Thunder Island, a man-made berm once part of an elaborate and expensive boat locks system that was never fully successful. A historical museum and interpretive signs tell the saga of humans' attempts to control the forces of nature, from the Lewis and Clark expedition to the crossing of Oregon Trail pioneers and the debacle of building and tearing down the locks.

From WaNaPa Street in Cascade Locks, turn north on N.W. Portage Road, down the hill and under a tunnel with a 12-foot clearance to enter the park. Open a half hour before sunrise to 10 P.M.

PLACES TO EAT

Johnny's Ice Cream and Deli: All hail the spud, one of the most popular lunch items on the menu, next to burritos, soup, and other simple, homemade, tummy-filling food. Johnny's is not fancy, so don't worry about your dog putting his paws up on the secondhand dining room sidewalk furniture. 424 WaNaPa St.; 541/374-0080.

PLACES TO STAY

Bridge of the Gods Motel: A surprising number of amenities are packed into the rooms at this laid-back mom-and-pop motel in the locks. Cheerful hanging flower baskets provide a signature welcome. Inside, you'll find jetted tubs, HDTV, Wi-Fi, and kitchenettes in tidy rooms. Smaller rooms upstairs are $70 and larger rooms with kitchenettes downstairs are $90 a night; $10 pet fee. 630 WaNaPa St.; 541/374-8628.

More Accommodations: Please look under *Chain Hotels* in the *Resources* section for additional places to stay in this area.

Hood River

Vibrant and outdoorsy, this city is a magnet for young and energetic sailboarders and kiteboarders pumped to ride the crests of the Columbia River. To hang out and watch the boarders, ask for directions to The Hook or The Spit. Between town and the mountains is an agricultural valley you can tour with a

DIVERSIONS

When you go away, the very least you can do is take your four-legged kids to **Cascade Pet Camp** to stay. They can bed down in the bunkhouse or in private cabins, some with patios and, um, even TVs tuned to Animal Planet. Daytime includes a heavy schedule of play, cuddles, treats and snacks, and naps, and can include special services such as training, grooming, and therapeutic massage. The facility must be seen to be believed. It is gorgeous and state–of–the art. Your little darling will want for nothing, other than you, of course. Day camp is $24 weekdays, $32 weekends. Overnights are $30–50, depending on accommodations. Check online for the whole list of optional services and goodies. 3085 Lower Mill Dr., Hood River; 541/354-2267; www.cascadepetcamp.com.

Fruit Loop brochure from the visitors center (405 Portway Ave.; 541/386-2000; www.hoodriver.org). While most places prefer that you leave pets in the car, your dogs can relax in the picnic area at Hood River Vineyards while you enjoy wine-tasting (4693 Westwood Dr.; 541/386-3772; www.hoodriver vineyards.us).

The **Gorge Dog** (412 Oak Ave.; 541/387-3996; www.gorgedog.com) is in town for accessories for your best friend. They can recommend great hiking in the area, and you can check their website for local pet-friendly services. **Hannah's Great Dog Store** (2940 West Cascade Ave.; 541/386-8844, www .hannahs4dogs.com) is another great stop, just west of downtown.

PARKS, BEACHES, AND RECREATION AREAS

5 Starvation Creek

🐾🐾 (See Central Oregon map on page 546)

It's easy to miss this tiny spot as you whiz by on I-84, especially since it can be accessed only via the eastbound lanes. If you seek it out, what you'll find is an enchanting forest glade, with three lovely picnic areas beside a stream underneath a cascading waterfall. This magical pixie-sized park gets its dramatic name from a band of holiday train passengers who were trapped here for three weeks in a snowstorm. Nearby residents rallied to their aid, snowshoeing in supplies. Everyone emerged safely, if a bit thinner.

You can work on trimming your figure on the park's spur trails that head straight up the gorge walls a mile on the Starvation Ridge Trail to Warren Falls and six miles to Mount Defiance. For an easier, accessible stroll, follow the restored mile of the Historic Columbia River Highway State Trail eastbound to Viento State Park. At least walk to the gently cascading waterfall.

Exit 54 from I-84 is available eastbound only, 10 miles west of Hood River.; westbound, take Exit 51 and return three miles on the eastbound side.

6 Port Marina Park–Port of Hood River

🐾🐾 (See Central Oregon map on page 546)

The port's a busy place, with boat builders, surfboard rentals, docks, and the Hood River County Historical Museum. All the activity makes for good people-watching: novice sailboarders trying to take off from a nearby sand spit, toddlers with water wings splashing in the shallow cove, a Chihuahua swimming on leash as her owner wades alongside. The picnic tables are in front of the surfboard shop, and a huge lawn by the museum is popular with the Frisbee crowd.

From I-84, take Exit 64 and turn north toward the river. Before you cross the Hood River Bridge, turn left into the marina and follow the signs to the left. Closes at 10 P.M.

7 Wilson Park

🐾🐾 (See Central Oregon map on page 546)

"There are always dogs at Wilson," said Jessie at the visitors center. There's a little bit of shade and a little bit of sun on an Irish-green lawn, with primary-colored playground equipment and just enough room to throw a ball around. The park is out of the way on a quiet residential street with a fence along one side.

From Oak Street, turn south on 13th Street and left on May Street to 2nd Street.

8 Tucker Park

🐾🐾🐾 (See Central Oregon map on page 546)

Tucker is tucked into a bend in Hood River, offering camping with showers and flush toilets, which is pretty swank for a county park. When views of the river simply won't suffice, there's a quickie river trail across the picnic meadow from the parking lot. Water dogs will find several swimming holes while picking their way along the sandy and rocky trail. Tent sites are $13 a night.

From Oak Street, turn south on 13th Street, which will merge into Tucker Road. The park is 5.5 miles from the Oak Street turnoff.

9 Mark O. Hatfield–Mosier Twin Tunnels Trail

🐾🐾🐾 (See Central Oregon map on page 546)

Before this old section of the Historic Columbia River Highway was restored and paved, trail users were 80 percent off-leash dogs and 20 percent mountain bikes. Now, it's 80 percent bicycles and 20 percent dogs *on* leash. Either way, you get 100 percent of the best views in the gorge. Dog activists in town are trying to secure a couple of off-leash hours per day; so far, no luck. We say, if you can't beat 'em, join 'em. Rent a bike at Mount View Cycles in Hood River (205 Oak St.; 541/386-2453) and pedal the 10-mile round-trip with your dog jogging along-side. You'll pass through two radically different climate zones, from lush forest to arid desert, two rock tunnels with windows on the gorge, and an engineer-ing marvel designed to keep rocks from falling and crushing trail users.

The two trailheads are named for Senator Mark O. Hatfield, who was active in promoting highway restoration and park projects. From I-84, take Exit 69 and turn left on Rock Creek Road to the East Trailhead. In Hood River, take Exit 64 and turn right at the Historic Columbia River Highway State Trail sign for the West Trailhead. Plentiful parking is $3 per day, and there are restrooms and water at both ends. This trail is excellent for wheelchair users.

PLACES TO EAT

Double Mountain Brewery and Taproom: You can never have too many brewpubs, insists Cooper, although it seems Hood River is pushing the limit. The dogs' choice appears to be the sidewalk outside the brew room here, where garage doors are rolled up to reveal seating, a stereo blaring, and content humans drinking and eating from a short menu of pizza, brats, and the like. Dinner only; lunch on weekends. 8 Fourth St.; 541/387-0042; www.double mountainbrewery.com.

Mike's Ice Cream: Mike's Adirondack chairs, picnic tables, and glass-topped café tables rest on a corner lawn that is probably the busiest patch of turf in town. You and your malamute have it made in the shade, slurping down ice cream, shakes, malts, and floats. 504 Oak St.; 541/386-6260.

South Bank Kitchen: Passionate foodies will be in gourmet deli heaven at South Bank. Salads have dreamy combinations such as spinach and pears, pralines and chicken, and Asian noodle and cabbage. Sandwiches are dressed in spreads; for example, curried chicken with golden raisins or cranberry tur-key and hazelnut cream cheese. Wraps, cookies, and pastries, plus daily soup specials and shelves of delicacies, help you pack the picnic basket. Pass the Grey Poupon. 404 Oak St.; 541/386-9876; www.southbankkitchen.com.

PLACES TO STAY

Columbia Gorge Hotel: This 1921 grande dame is the Hope Diamond of hotels, voted the most romantic in Oregon year after year, and the site of more than 100 weddings annually. For $35 per stay, dogs receive treats stored in a Waterford crystal jar, blankets, and a dog dish to keep. An original Otis Elevator, with an operator, whisks you to your timeless, antique-filled room with a Mount Hood or Columbia River view. The price of your room, rang-ing $200–250, includes a five-course farm-style breakfast and afternoon

champagne and caviar. The grounds are a park in themselves, with 208-foot Wah Gwin Gwin Falls and lavish formal gardens. Go on, your dog deserves it! 4000 Westcliff Dr.; 541/386-5566; www.columbiagorgehotel.com.

Hood River Hotel: The best rooms in this historic hotel are reserved for dogs, three ground-floor suites that have been graciously restored into vintage masterpieces with antique reproductions, wood floors, and four-poster beds. Suite rates are $90–170; the pet fee is $15. 102 Oak St.; 541/386-1900; www.hoodriverhotel.com.

Hood River Vacation Rentals: The great thing about renting a house is that you can find one with a fenced yard if you'd like to sneak away for a movie or to shop without your terrier in tow. This property listing service has eight dog-friendly homes from two to four bedrooms, in a variety of price ranges, available nightly or weekly. Dog fees are $8 per night or $50 per week. 541/387-3113; www.hrvacations.com.

Pheasant Valley Bed and Breakfast: Dogs who can be sociable with resident dogs, cats, and namesake pheasants can stay with you in The Cottage, a stylish two-bedroom apartment in the pear orchard of this winery, farm, and inn. The private deck can be securely fenced to give your dog a comfy place to hang out. Nightly rate is $135, and there's no pet fee as long as they don't have to clean up after your dog; the five-day minimum in the summer rents for $500. 3890 Acree Dr.; 541/387-3040; www.pheasantvalleywinery.com.

More Accommodations: Please look under *Chain Hotels* in the *Resources* section for additional places to stay in this area.

Mount Hood

In the Mount Hood Territory, you can start a hike to Mexico on the Pacific Northwest Trail or watch the birds migrate there on the Pacific Flyway. You can water ski in the morning on the Columbia River and snowboard in the afternoon on the largest night ski area in the nation. Dogs are not allowed to stay at the historic Timberline Lodge, but if you *had* to leave your loved ones at home and needed a fix, stop by and pet the lodge's Saint Bernards Bruno and Heidi. Each village has its own name—ZigZag, Rhododendron, Welches, Government Camp, Brightwood, Parkdale—but ask even Portland natives where Welches is, and they'll scratch their heads. It's all Mount Hood to them.

PARKS, BEACHES, AND RECREATION AREAS

10 Wildwood Recreation Site

🐾🐾🐾 (See Central Oregon map on page 546)

There is something for every ability and interest at this family-oriented interpretive nature site. The biggest draw for the kids is the underwater fish-viewing window on the 0.75-mile Cascade Streamwatch Trail. Adults may enjoy the Wetland Boardwalk Trail more, suspended over the ponds and marshes. Both trails are wheelchair accessible, and picnicking spots are nearby. If you and your dog are looking for a better workout, the Boulder Ridge trail climbs 4.5 miles one-way up steep and narrow switchbacks into the Mount Hood wilderness. Open 8 A.M.–sunset May–September. Parking is $3. 503/622-3696.

11 Trillium Lake

🐾🐾🐾 (See Central Oregon map on page 546)

Mount Hood towers in all its glory above the crystal-clear lake, easily one of the best views of the mountain in the region. Only two miles off State Route 35, this mountain gem has an easy mile loop around the lake, alternating between hard pack, pavement, and boardwalks. There are dog-paddling opportunities galore. Drive past the Day Use/Boat Ramp sign to another parking lot by the dam to reach the lake loop trailhead.

The lake entrance is 0.25 mile west of the junction of State Route 35 and U.S. Highway 26. Parking is $3. Winter use of the Trillium Sno-Park for snowmobiling and cross-country skiing requires a separate permit November 15–April 30.

12 Mount Hood National Forest–Lost Lake Resort

🐾🐾🐾🐾 (See Central Oregon map on page 546)

This destination deep in the woods of Mount Hood National Forest is full of perks for all, from spectacular views of the lake and Mount Hood to pockets of old-growth cedars and firs and plenty of places to take a swim. The hike around the alpine lake is an easy 3.2 miles on soft dirt track and alternating boardwalks, starting from the viewpoint parking lot. There's a general store, paddleboat rentals, cabins, and camping at the lake as well. It's peaceful; motorboats are strictly prohibited and cell phones stop working about a quarter mile before the park. The picnic area closes at 9 P.M. Maps are available at the general store for a half dozen additional hikes in the area. September is a stunning time to visit after the crowds have thinned.

From Oak Street in Hood River, turn south on 13th Street, which merges onto Tucker Road. Follow Tucker as it becomes State Route 281 into Dee. From there, the only way to avoid getting lost on the 28-mile journey to Lost Lake is to carefully follow the signs as the road twists and turns to your destination. Parking is $6 per day; the Northwest Forest Pass does not apply. Closed October–May.

13 Mount Hood National Forest–Tamanawas Falls Loop

🐾🐾🐾🐾 (See Central Oregon map on page 546)

Dog owners at both the Gorge Dog boutique and the visitors center recommended this moderate trail through a cool forest glade along Cold Spring Creek to the falls viewpoint. It's four miles round-trip, with only a few huff-and-puff sections. First, you cross a springy suspension bridge over the East Fork of the Hood River, then turn right after the bridge. Stay to the left at the remainder of the trail junctions to stay on the Tamanawas Trail #650A. The hike is typically doable April–November. It's a beautiful hike, one that's easy to get to, and it provides several places where your dog can go for a quick swim in the creek.

From I-84, take Exit 64 and go south on State Route 35 for 25.3 miles to a gravel parking area on the right side of the road. The trailhead entrance is 0.2 mile north of the Sherwood Campground.

PLACES TO EAT

Elliot Glacier Public House: It's dog central on the lawn out back by the patio seating of this brewpub, where your pal can hang with the local ruff-raff. The food tastes great and it's cheap; Monday night is $1 taco night! Don't miss the porter brownies. 4945 Baseline Rd., Parkdale; 541/352-1022.

Soup Spoon: Gourmet soups and daily specials are served in a pretty garden setting behind the Heart of the Mountain gift shop. Shop, slurp, and go home happy. Well-behaved dogs are welcome. 67898 E. Hwy. 26, Welches; 503/622-0303.

PLACES TO STAY

Lost Lake Resort: Lost Lake has private tent sites available for $15 per night, $20 if you want a lake view on F loop. All campsites are on a first-come, first-served basis. Showers are coin operated. If you'd rather stay warm and dry, dogs are allowed in the seven cabins, $60–120 per night; $10 pet fee. They are various sizes, sleeping 2–10 people, and guests must provide their own cooking utensils and bedding. There's a two-night minimum on weekends and holidays. Lost Lake; 541/386-6366; www.lostlakeresort.org.

Old Parkdale Inn: Mary puts out a whole spread for dogs, including bowls, bags, blankies, treats, and a letter of behavioral expectations. The gorgeous Monet Suite has a kitchen, and breakfast can be served in your room, so you don't have to worry about leaving your pal unattended. Dogs are allowed free on the acre property, but please stay out of the pond and away from the resident cats. The room is $135–145 per night; the pet fee is $25 per stay. 4932 Baseline Rd., Parkdale; 541/352-5551; www.hoodriverlodging.com.

Resort at the Mountain: The Scottish were the first to play golf, so it's appropriate that this resort on the grounds of the first golf resort in Oregon (a nine-hole hayfield in 1928) has a Scottish theme. Thankfully, the tartan isn't overdone, nor is the snob factor. The older Croft Rooms allow two pets for a $25 fee per stay; rates are $90–100. In 2004, the resort opened a few fancier rooms to pets, ranging $100–185. 68010 E. Fairway Ave., Welches; 503/622-3101; www.theresort.com.

More Accommodations: Please look under *Chain Hotels* in the *Resources* section for additional places to stay in this area.

The Dalles

We're pretty sure this is the only city in the United States that officially has the word "the" as part of its name. The French translation of the town's unusual moniker means "river rapids flowing swiftly through a narrow channel over flat, basaltic rocks." The rapids have disappeared, drowned in the rising waters of The Dalles Dam, locks, and irrigations systems. The dam visitors center is open 10 A.M.–5 P.M. Wednesday–Sunday April–October. 541/296-1181.

Cars can pick up another segment of the Historic Columbia River Highway from The Dalles to the east in Mosier. It's another stunner, with a terrific viewpoint at the Rowena Crest Overlook. From this apex, you'll descend again in loops that Agent 007 would love to take on in his Aston Martin.

PARKS, BEACHES, AND RECREATION AREAS

14 Sorosis Park

🐾🐾🐾 (See Central Oregon map on page 546)

Never mind that it sounds like that disease of the liver, drinking in the intoxicating sights and smells in this city park can only be good for you. The buzz starts right in front of the park at the Kelly Viewpoint, with a panoramic vista that includes the Columbia River and Gorge and the city of The Dalles below. It continues at the park entrance with a fragrant and beautiful rose garden, in the center of which is a towering water fountain, given to the city in 1911 by Maximillian Vogt. Kids will get giddy just looking at the Treetop Play Park, one of those gigantic playground castles that'll keep them occupied for days.

Finally, it's the soft grass and the trees—immensely tall and fat pines thickly grouped together—that make dogs dizzy with delight. We're not sure how they managed it, but it looks like the city cleared 15 acres of forest floor and laid a carpet of sod, without touching a single tree.

From the city center on 3rd Street westbound or 2nd Street eastbound, turn south on Union Street, right on 9th Street, and left on Trevitt. Continue on Trevitt past 17th Street, where it becomes W. Scenic Drive, winding up several spirals into the foothills before you'll see the park on your right and the viewpoint on your left. Open 6 A.M.–dusk.

15 Atiyeh Deschutes River Trail

🐾🐾 (See Central Oregon map on page 546)

Oregon's thirty-second Governor, Victor Atiyeh, was a smart man who led an effort to combine public and private funds to protect the lower 18 miles along the Deschutes River as public land in 1987. Now everyone can responsibly enjoy their piece of the 8,320 acres along both sides of the river without bugging anyone else.

Horses have their 22-mile round trip, bicycles have a 32-mile loop on the abandoned railroad grade, and hikers have several 2–4 mile loops of their own. The two-mile Lower Atiyeh Trail wins the dogs over for having the most shade and places to jump in the water in a valley where 100–110 degree summer heat is common. The trails begin at the back of a field, past the picnic grounds and campground, where the Deschutes meets the Columbia River. Watch for rattlesnakes and check for ticks after hiking.

The trimmed and watered greens of the day-use area are a delicious place to relax before, after, or instead of a hike, scoping the river from under the

NATURE HIKES AND URBAN WALKS

At the start of the **Lewis and Clark Riverfront Trail** in The Dalles, there are authentic covered wagons to fuel your imagination as you travel what was a treacherous final section of the Oregon Trail for thousands of pioneers. Your journey along the Columbia River should be a much easier one, up to five miles one-way on a smooth asphalt path, and you won't have to lug provisions other than plenty of drinking water. The starting point is the Columbia Gorge Discovery Center, and the trail ends at the boat basin downtown, near Riverfront Park. It's also a great way to observe the present, watching the commercial freighters and tugs navigate the river.

From I-84, take Exit 82 and go west on U.S. Highway 30 to Discovery Drive. 541/296-8600.

protection of the white alder tree canopy. The dogs envied the anglers floating in armchair inner tubes, launching at Heritage Landing across the river. Serious hikers can pick up a spur of the original Oregon Trail; couch canines can read the excellent interpretive markers about the Trail's history.

Deschutes State Park is 17 miles east of The Dalles on State Route 206. Heading eastbound on I-84, take Exit 97; westbound, take Exit 104 at Biggs Junction; and follow the signs. 89600 Biggs-Rufus Hwy.; 541/739-2322.

PLACES TO EAT

Big Jim's Drive In: Big Jim's has held its own against the golden arches for 40-plus years, promising hamburgers, chili, and chowder made with love, and ice cream made 50 ways to sundae. As tastes have leaned toward the leaner side, they've added chicken, fish, shrimp, and salads to the menu. Dogs can take their rightful place at the drive-through or on patio seating. 2938 E. 2nd St.; 541/298-5051.

Holstein's Coffee Co.: Who knew this many specialty drinks could come from a bean and an udder? If the Holy Cow, with three shots of espresso with ground chocolate and steamed milk, doesn't take you to a higher plane, nothing will. While chewing your cud, check your email on wireless Internet. Moo if you like outdoor seating! 811 E. 3rd St.; 541/298-2326.

Petite Provence: Soak up the sunny flavors of Southern France while basking in the glow reflected off the distinctive bumblebee-inspired facade of this full restaurant. The victuals are certainly inspired, as are the intricate pastries and breads. 408 E. 2nd St.; 541/506-0037.

PLACES TO STAY

Cousins Country Inn: On the outside, this motel invokes the relaxed comfort of a country home with a big red barn replica housing the lobby and restaurant. Inside, it's fairly standard. They have no official restrictions, but said, "Please don't bring herds." Rates are $65–110; pet fee is $10. 2114 W. 6th St.; 541/298-5161; www.cousinscountryinn.com.

The Dalles Inn: Isis was psyched to find out that the #1-rated property in town welcomes dogs in the back building. After staying here, this is what she knows: The rooms are lovely and the staff will take good care of you. Other items worthy of mention are that your room or suite will be close to historic downtown for great strolls, breakfast includes D.I.Y. Belgian waffles, and the outdoor pool opens Memorial Day. The pet package includes bowls, towels, treats, and scoop bags for use at a small pet exercise area. Rates start at $90; $10 pet fee. There are no pet restrictions. 112 W. 2nd St.; 541/296-9107; www.thedallesinn.com.

More Accommodations: Please look under *Chain Hotels* in the *Resources* section for additional places to stay in this area.

Maupin

The main draw in Maupin is the Deschutes River Recreation Area for life-vest-wearing, rubber-raft-carrying crowds intent on fording the river's low-level rapids and fishing its swells. None of the local companies allow Rover to raft with you. For that, try Ferron's Fun Trips on the Rogue in the *Southern Oregon* chapter. For rafting, fishing, horseback riding, camping, and hiking along the banks of the Deschutes, check out the Bureau of Land Management's information center at 7 N. Hwy. 97; 541/395-2778.

PARKS, BEACHES, AND RECREATION AREAS

16 White River Falls

🐾🐾 (See Central Oregon map on page 546)

The river lives up to its name in the hottest months as melting glacial water deposits silt and sand into the water. This turbulent waterfall is the site of a former hydroelectric plant, built in 1901 to power the gristmill of the Wasco Warehouse Milling Company, grinding the grain from local farmers into flour. In the picnic area above the falls, each tree guards its own picnic table, providing precious shade. Your dog's reward for waiting patiently while you look at the falls lies across a wooden bridge and down a rough, short trail to a swimming hole below, near the stone remains of the mill. For a quick peak at the one-mile round-trip down into the canyon, see the hiking guide at www.nwhiker.com. As they obviously note, rattlesnakes in the area don't make good playmates for your dog, so leashes are vital.

From U.S. Highway 197 in Maupin, travel 10 miles north and turn east on White River Road for 3.8 miles to the State Park.

PLACES TO EAT

Imperial River Company: This business is a triple treat of white-water rafting rental company, excellent restaurant, and great lodge. Dogs are not allowed in the picnic area of Maupin City Park, so walk on over to the picnic tables on the lawn or the backyard patio tables, where you and your dog will be warmly welcomed and well fed with steaks, burritos, chicken, pastas, and other big-appetite pleasers. 304 Bakeoven Rd.; 541/395-2404; www.deschutesriver.com.

PLACES TO STAY

Imperial River Company: Dogs are allowed in rooms #3, #4, #11, and #12 on the ground floor of this nonsmoking lodge. Also pet friendly, the Bunkhouse for $110 per night and the Imperial Suite with kitchen, TV, fireplace, and private deck for $150 are modern with a Western flair, as big as the open prairie. The pet fee is $10. 304 Bakeoven Rd.; 541/395-2404; www.deschutesriver.com.

Madras-Culver

A drive along U.S. Highway 197 through the golden wheat fields of this arid desert region is a cure for feeling overcrowded. It looks like the plains extend to the Cascades without interruption, and until you're right on the brink of it, you can't see the immense Crooked River Canyon extending from Madras to Culver. For better canyon views, less traffic, and quicker park access, drive the **Cove Palisades Tour Route.** Maps are available in Madras (366 5th St.; 541/475-2350).

PARKS, BEACHES, AND RECREATION AREAS

🐾🐾 Round Butte Overlook

🐾🐾 (See Central Oregon map on page 546)

Thanks to the Portland General Electric Company, park visitors can look into the workings of the dam and the hydroelectric power it produces to learn much about the history of the Warm Springs Indians, including Billy Chinook and Chief Simtustus. Next to the free educational center, there's probably more exquisite shade on the spruced-up grass than in the rest of the valley combined.

From Madras, turn west on Belmont Lane and south on Mount View Drive, following the signs to the park. Open 10 A.M.–8 P.M. Thursday–Monday.

🐾🐾🐾 Cove Palisades

🐾🐾🐾🐕 (See Central Oregon map on page 546)

It took a darn big dam to create this watery playground in the Crooked River Canyon. The majority of people come to this state park for the water sports on Lake Billy Chinook, named for the tribesman and scout to Captain John C. Fremont on his explorations of the Oregon Country in 1843. Water sport rentals of all kinds are available at the marina.

This rambling 5,200-acre park has two campgrounds and its own pet exercise area. The off-leash area is a fenced and gated acre of rarely mowed field, simple and desirable for a leisurely stroll and sniff. There's no immediate parking; park at the Upper or Lower Deschutes day-use areas and walk a short ways on a trail to the dog area.

After you drive your way down into the canyon, you can hike your way back out on the Tam-a-Lau Trail. It's a difficult, steep, hot hike topped off with seven stunning mountain peaks, one for each mile of the seven-mile loop. There are thousands of harmless whiptail lizards living in the area, an added bonus and distraction for dogs.

From U.S. Highway 97, turn west onto State Route 361, the Culver Highway, and follow signs six miles to the park. Parking is $3. 7300 Jordan Rd.; 541/546-3412.

PLACES TO EAT

Beetle Bailey Burgers: The restaurant selection isn't huge in Culver. This burger shed on the way to Cove Palisades is about it, which is probably why the half dozen picnic tables out front are always packed. 403 W. 1st, Culver; 541/546-8749.

PLACES TO STAY

Hoffy's Motel: Hoffy's rooms are neat, comfortable, and inexpensive at $50–60, plus $12 per pet per stay. 600 N. Hwy. 26; 541/475-4633.

    Cove Palisades Campground: Cooper highly recommends sites #B18–#B22 in the Deschutes River Campground, five miles into the park. They are pleasantly shady, and, most importantly, they line up against the fence of the off-leash area. There are a total of 92 tent sites and 82 hookups in Crooked River and the Deschutes Campgrounds, both in the park. $13–21; 800/452-5687; www.reserveamerica.com.

Sisters

The Three Sisters—Faith, Hope, and Charity—are mountains, tremendous and snow-capped year-round. In the valley below, the town has cultivated the Western frontier look, where you might expect the sheriff to stroll around with his six-shooters and shiny star. It is the gateway to the Metolius River Recreation Area and the Three Sisters Wilderness.

In the winter, downhillers come to **HooDoo Ski Area** (541/822-3799; www.hoodoo.com) and cross-country skiers and snowmobiles share the trails at Corbit and Ray Bensen SnoParks. You'll see evidence of a massive 2007 fire as you drive and hike through this area.

Dogs are required to be on leash July 1–September 30 in the following areas of the surrounding Deschutes National Forest: Moraine Lake, Green Lakes, Todd Lake, and Broken Top with its associated trails. Otherwise, voice control is acceptable. For trail details, call the Sisters Ranger District at 541/549-7700.

PARKS, BEACHES, AND RECREATION AREAS

19 Deschutes National Forest–Black Butte Trail

🐾🐾🐾 (See Central Oregon map on page 546)

Occasionally, Cooper and Isis like to include more challenging trails for their longer-legged friends, and this calf-burning climb takes you 1,585 feet up to the top of a 6,436-foot cinder cone. The reward for climbing to this high point is the 360-degree vista of the Metolius Valley, the Three Sisters, and all of the nearby Cascade Peaks from the historic fire lookout.

Take U.S. Highway 20 four miles west of Sisters and turn right on Green Ridge Road (Road 11). The sign says Indian Ford Road/Green Ridge Road/Indian Ford Campground. Follow the signs 3.8 miles to Forest Road 1110, turn left and travel 4.2 miles to Forest Road 700, turn right and continue 1.1 miles to the trailhead. All this driving means there's less climbing, but not much. Bring lots of refreshing water.

20 Metolius River Recreation Area

🐾🐾🐾 (See Central Oregon map on page 546)

Eons ago, the green ridge volcanic fault cracked open, releasing the Metolius River to the surface from its glacially fed source high in the Cascade Mountains. The temperature and flow rate are cold and constant, producing a crystal clear waterway to play in and around. From the Head of the Metolius Observation Point, you and your trail hound can walk for miles through ponderosa pine and Douglas fir in the 4,600-acre corridor, jumping in and out of the river at will. Brrrrr. The level trail is easy for all ability levels.

From U.S. Highway 20, take the Camp Sherman Road (Road 14) and follow the Campground signs. To pick up the trail, park in the observation point lot, go back out across the road and a few yards down, across from the Riverside Campground. Additional trailheads start at the Wizard Falls Fish Hatchery and the Canyon Creek Campground off Forest Service Road 1420. Metolius Recreation Area maps are available at visitors centers in the area. Metolius Recreation Association: 541/595-6711; www.metoliusriver.com.

21 Village Green
😺 (See Central Oregon map on page 546)

In the village of Sisters, population 2,000, this block of picnicking green is a welcome respite from the heat. It has restrooms, picnic tables, and… a good sprinkler system, as Coop 'n' Isis unexpectedly found out early one morning.

The park is on Elm Street, two blocks south of State Route 20/126, which is Cascade Avenue through town.

PLACES TO EAT

Martolli's: Order hot subs, calzones, and authentic, hand-tossed pizza by the slice, or create your own pie to wolf down at the restaurant's outdoor tables, for takeout, or to take and bake yourself. 220 W. Cascade St.; 541/549-8356.

Ski Inn: Rumor has it that breakfasts at this classic greasy spoon are bountiful and wonderful. As for lunch, the tiny inside of this hut was crammed when we stopped for fat burgers and fries, which made us especially thankful for the much larger lawn, outdoor order window, and bright blue metal picnic tables covered with Pepsi umbrellas. 310 E. Cascade; 541/549-3491.

PLACES TO STAY

Cold Springs Resort: All of the privately owned rental cabins allow pets for $8 per pet per night. Each modern, fancy cabin sleeps six people. You can fight over who gets the loft, the separate bedroom, or the queen-size sofa bed in the living room. The river is right outside your doorstep, burbling by your private deck, and you can pick up the Metolius River Trail to follow it. Winter rates are $120 for two people, up to $155 for six. Summer rates range $165–195. 25615 Cold Springs Resort Ln., Camp Sherman; 541/595-6271; www.cold springs-resort.com.

Five Pine Lodge: The Harrington and The Hitchcock, a.k.a. classic cottages #20 and #21, are as grandiose as they sound, with pillow-top king-size beds, two-person Japanese soaking tubs (the water comes from the ceiling!), wet bars, 52-inch flat-panel TVs, gas fireplaces, and authentic Amish Craftsman furniture. It doesn't get any better than this, folks. For Fido, hiking trails are out your patio door, past your Adirondack chairs. For you, there's a pool, an athletic club, and Shibui Spa. As an added bonus, you and your pal are also welcome on the patio at the brew pub. The rates are amazing for what you're enjoying, at $150–210, plus a $20 pet fee, limit two pups. 1021 Desperado Trail; 541/549-5900; www.fivepinelodge.com.

Lodge at Suttle Lake: Of the resort's pet-friendly options, Isis votes for the Falls Cabin ($200–300), originated in 1929 and renovated in 2008. It's closest to the water along Lake Creek and has the best front deck. Cooper's choice is the authentic 1959 Ranger Guard Station ($215–250), with its summer camp character and backyard seclusion. The other six are rustic camping cabins ($100–130), what our folks used to call Mattress Camps, without kitchens or bathrooms, fun to reserve in groups if everyone is down with trudging to the bathhouse.

You'll have easy access to trails all the way around the lake from Cinder Beach, and the day-use area is open 7 A.M.–9 P.M.; you can use it even if you're not staying at the resort. The pet fee for up to two dogs is a hefty $40 a night; it includes a package with mats, bowls, and treats. 13300 Highway 20; 541/595-2628; www.thelodgeatsuttlelake.com.

More Accommodations: Please look under *Chain Hotels* in the *Resources* section for additional places to stay in this area.

Redmond

While it may not be as glamorous Bend or as scenic as Sisters, Redmond is a central location to use as home base for exploring the region. It's also the site of Central Oregon's only commercial airport. On your way through, stock up on chow at **The Feed Barn** (2215 Hwy. 97; 541/923-3333; www.feedbarn.net).

Although energetic people are crawling all over the walls at nearby Smith Rock State Park, an internationally famous, technical rock-climbing Mecca, we chose not to include it because it's not a dog-friendly destination. Shade is hard to come by; the rim of the main developed hike is called Misery Ridge for a reason. The local ranger's biggest pet peeve is an off-leash dog and he'll slap you with a $104 fine if your terrier is caught off his tether.

PARKS, BEACHES, AND RECREATION AREAS

22 Dry Canyon
😊😊😊 (See Central Oregon map on page 546)

The Dry Canyon cuts through the middle of the city, providing a three-mile paved path that you'll share with cyclists and inline skaters out for exercise or their morning commute. Dogs may prefer the narrow dirt track that parallels the main trail to the west. This single track will give your dog a more interactive experience with the gully's natural environs. It's not marked, but you'll easily see it leading from the south end of the trailhead parking lot. There are no restrooms or water in the gulch. However, right about mid-point in the trail is a road that leads up to West Canyon Rim Park. Relax, water, and refresh yourselves at this green space before descending again from the rim.

From U.S. Highway 97 north of Redmond, turn west on Pershall Way and travel a mile to the trailhead entrance sign on your left by the City of Redmond Water Pollution Control.

PLACES TO EAT

Terrebonne Depot: One sip of the basil-infused orange martini sent us over the moon. One bite of the seared ahi tacos with mango cabbage left us clamoring for more. Suffice it to say that even if they didn't put water bowls on the wide and sunny deck for the pooches, we'd be back for this bistro's new American menu and long cocktail list. The curb appeal of the beautifully restored, 100-year-old railroad station adds to the ambiance. 400 N.W. Smith Rock Way; 541/548-5030; www.terrebonnedepot.com.

Bend

Bend is gorgeous, a high-desert playground stacked against the Cascade Mountains. Locals who moved here years ago to get away to a quiet mountain town are bemoaning the fact that Bend has become "the Aspen of Oregon." Nothing this good stays undiscovered for long, and Bend draws as many mountain bikers, hikers, and anglers in the summer as nearby Mount Bachelor calls boarders and skiers to the slopes in winter. Bendites are a highly fit, outdoorsy bunch who have dogs in tow where e'r they go. Official city stats say 49 percent of households have 1.2 dogs. Downtown, along four blocks of Wall and Bond streets, is packed with hip shopping and delicious outdoor dining.

Dogs are allowed in all city parks as long as they are on a leash and you pick up after them. To assist you in this task, Bend Parks and Recreation has installed Dog E Rest Stops, bag dispenser stations with a witticism borrowed from Smokey the Bear: "Only *you* can prevent dog piles." Pick up an Urban Trails Map at the visitors center (917 N.W. Harriman, 541/382-8048, www .visitbend.com).

PARKS, BEACHES, AND RECREATION AREAS

23 Sawyer Park

🐾🐾 (See Central Oregon map on page 546)

Robert W. Sawyer River Park, which was a state park and is now part of the City of Bend, is a sampler platter of regional recreation. It has interesting rock formations, picnic benches under ponderosa pines, a bridge over the Deschutes

DIVERSIONS

There are a couple of great options for dog shopping in Bend. For high-end glamour and fanciful dog treats, toys, and accessories, **Downtown Doggie** is the place, near the Old Mill district. 55 N.W. Wall St.; 541/389-5138; www.downtown-doggie.com.

For a huge selection of all things pet, there are two locations of **Bend Pet Express.** The Eastside store has self-serve dog wash stations and the Down Dog Bakery for homemade-with-love treats. Eastside: 420 N.E. Windy Knolls; 541/385-5298. Westside: 133 S.W. Century Dr.; 541/389-4620; www.bendpetexpress.com.

Bend is the headquarters for RuffWear, a national retailer of serious outdoor gear for active pets on-the-go. Your best bet is to shop online at www.ruffwear.com. Also manufactured here are safety dog collars and leashes at Tazlab (www.tazlab.com) and ultra-impressive dog-powered scooters and trikes and skateboards (www.dogpoweredscooter.com). Get your dog to pull you; he needs more exercise than you do!

river, and an outstretched circle of turf over the hill with a Dog E Rest Stop bag dispenser. A piece of the Deschutes River Trail follows the water, past squirrels and wildlife popping in and out of ground holes. You can get your fill and be wanting more a few hours later.

From U.S. Highway 97/20 North, turn left on O. B. Riley Road and left into the park.

24 Shevlin Park

🐾🐾🐾 (See Central Oregon map on page 546)

This hillside of shady pines became a city park in 1920, the same year as Drake Park below. Its six miles of looped paths are a popular spot for trail runners and joggers. Mountain bikers take their cycles for a spin on parallel, separate tracks. Tumalo Creek rambles through the park, with bridges to cross here and there. Shevlin is on the outskirts of town, but not for long. As high-profile housing developments pop up around it, its sampling of the Oregon Outback topography will be appreciated even more by canines who prefer parks to pavement.

Turn west on Business 20 from U.S. Highway 97. Stay in the right lane to remain on Newport, which leads to Shevlin Park Road. The park is 4.8 miles from the turnoff onto Business 20. 18920 Shevlin Park Rd.

25 Drake Park

😸😸😸 (See Central Oregon map on page 546)

Isis thinks this gorgeous park, named for Bend founder Alexander M. Drake, should be renamed Mrs. May Arnold Park, for it was she and early women of Bend who were responsible for its establishment in 1920. They gathered 1,500 signatures in a fledgling town of 5,400 to convince the city council to purchase the land.

No mere asphalt will do for strolling the greens centered around Mirror Pond—the walking paths are of intricate flagstone. Over an arched wooden footbridge in the middle of the 13-acre park is Harmon Park, with a playground for kids and placards telling the early history of the pond's famous Swan Pageant. The pageant is no more, but the swans and geese remain, as does their prodigious poop.

Dog E Rest Stops are found on the Harmon end of the footbridge and the west end of the park, which is where the dogs tend to hang out, a bit farther away from downtown.

Follow the signs from U.S. Highway 97 to downtown and turn west on Franklin Avenue from Wall Street. If you can't find street parking, there is a public lot on the east side of the park. It's free for the first two hours, $1 per hour thereafter.

26 Pilot Butte

😸😸😸 (See Central Oregon map on page 546)

About 19,000 years ago, a cinder cone erupted, leaving this peak in the middle of the flats. Civilization has overtaken the butte, and now it's an oddly located State Scenic Viewpoint in the middle of a busy suburban area on auto row. There are two ways to hike to the top of Bend's natural answer to the Stairmaster: alongside the road on a one-mile trail, or up the shorter but steeper 0.8-mile nature trail. You'll see all of the city and the mountains beyond. It's a fine place to catch the high country's colorful sunsets.

For dogs who would rather stick their heads out the window on a drive to the top, the summit access road is 0.75 mile east of the trailhead entrance.

From U.S. Highway 97, turn east on Greenwood Avenue and follow it to Summit Drive and the Trailhead Parking signs.

27 Big Sky Dog Park

😸😸😸😸 🐕 (See Central Oregon map on page 546)

Bend's first and largest off-leash park is a four-acre, fenced playground on the east side of town. It's a rough-and-tumble, natural park among the juniper trees and sagebrush behind the youth sports complex. Short trails from a

🐾 DOG-EAR YOUR CALENDAR

If your pup is feeling patriotic, she can prance in the annual **Fourth of July Pet Parade** in Bend. The organized chaos starts at Drake Park at 9 A.M. and winds through downtown on Bond and Wall Streets. It's huge. Estimated attendance in recent years counts more than 6,000 walkers and another 6,000 onlookers participating in a tradition that dates back to the 1930s.

Although dogs are the primary species, there have been lizards, rats, goldfish, cows, donkeys, llamas, and more on parade with kids walking, pulling wagons, and riding bicycles and tricycles. Everyone is welcome to come in costume, and kids can join in with a stuffed animal if there are no live, tame animals in the family. All participants get a collector's button and Popsicle at the finish line. There's no registration, no fees, and no solicitation. It's a free-for-all in every sense. 541/389-7275.

Dogs are also welcome to hold down their corners of the picnic blanket at **Free Summer Sunday Concerts** in the Old Mill District (www.theoldmill.com). Gates open at 1 P.M., concerts start at 2:30 P.M.; B.Y.O. lunch or get your delicacies at food court vendors. See www.bendconcerts.com for the full list of sweet, soothing music.

couple of double-gated entry points lead down to a centralized open space with a picnic table and a water spigot.

The area can be dry and dusty, prickly and brambly, and overrun by chipmunks. In short, the Dachsie Twins loved it. You're likely to come away coated in fine red dust in the summer and rich mud after a rain.

Turn east on Olney from 3rd Street/Business 97. Continue onto Penn, which becomes Neff Road. Follow Neff until you see the park, 3.5 miles from the turnoff at 3rd. Pass the BMX track and the fields to the end of the parking lot marked with large rocks and a Dog E Rest Stop bag dispenser. 21690 Neff Rd.; 541/389-7275; www.bendparksandrec.org.

28 Farewell Bend Park
🐾🐾🐾 (See Central Oregon map on page 546)

Bend used to be called Farewell Bend until a lazy postmaster decided plain ole Bend was enough. Easily four out of five cars are unloading dogs at the city's namesake park, but you may be puzzled at the lack of people on the wide, groomed lawns. It's because most of them are saying farewell to the city and heading around the bend. They're taking to the Deschutes River Trails, crossing the bridges and hiking upriver starting at this easy-access point in the Old Mill District. Some are even launching self-propelled watercraft and floating the water from put-ins along the shores. Either way, we suspect this is how the lazy postmaster chose to spend his summer afternoons.

From downtown, take Wall Street southbound. Go straight through the light at Arizona, then take the roundabout to the left onto Industrial Way. Stay on Industrial Way as it curves to the right to become Bond Street. Follow Bond all the way around the Mill District, and take the roundabout to the right onto Reed Market Road.

You can only access the four-hour parking lanes along the park from Reed Market Road westbound.

29 Upper Deschutes River Trails
🐾🐾🐾🐾🐸 (See Central Oregon map on page 546)

You can walk a little or a lot on this easy, family-friendly trail system closely following the banks of the tumbling Deschutes. There are seven trailheads, two picnic areas, and three waterfalls (Dillon, Lava Island, and Benham), along a 10-mile stretch from Bend south to Sunriver. Hiker, biker, and horse trails are separated to give you room to spread out. Dogs have to be on leash May–September, darn it, because the trails are so popular; otherwise, voice control is acceptable. The drier and hotter the weather, the more you'll come away with a fine sheen of red dust on your skin or fur from the dusty paths.

Patrick, CEO of RuffWear, takes his dogs Otis and Gordo to the Meadow

Camp Picnic Area, six miles west of U.S. Highway 97 on Century Drive (follow the signs toward Mount Bachelor). Immediately before the Widgi Creek Golf Course, turn left on the gravel road with the little brown park sign. Local Justin and his dog Shadow recommend going another mile, past the Seventh Mountain Resort, and turning up Forest Road 41 for the other trailheads. Parking is $5 at all marked trailheads: Lava Island, Aspen Falls, Big Eddy, Dillon Falls, and the Slough.

🐾 Tumalo Falls

🐾🐾 (See Central Oregon map on page 546)

The amount of work it takes to see these beautiful falls depends on the time of year and the snow pack. When melted, the gates to the 2.5-mile dirt road are opened, and you may drive along Tumalo Creek all the way to the impressive waterfall. In winter, the road becomes part of the fun for the very fit, either on snowshoes or cross-country skis.

Out this way, in the Deschutes National Forest, there's a whole mess of trails for hikers and cyclists, some of them many miles, leading from both the trailhead and the falls. Your journey will be somewhat shaded by pines, junipers, and alder trees and there are opportunities to slip into the water for a quick swim or to fish for rainbow trout, but watch those currents.

For the falls and the trails, take Exit 137 from U.S. Highway 97, and go straight south on Wall Street. Take a right on Franklin Avenue, which becomes Riverside Boulevard almost right away. At the stop sign, take a right on Tumalo Avenue and go straight through the roundabout onto Galveston Avenue. On your 10-mile journey out to the trailhead, it will become Skyliners Road, then Tumalo Falls Road. Parking is $5.

PLACES TO EAT

Bendistillery Martini Bar and Sampling Room: Sidewalk seating at the martini bar in the alley overlooking Drake Park is the nightspot in Bend, with a dizzying list of specialty martinis and everything from chichi appetizers of brie and fruit to comfort food interpretations. Patrons 21 and over only, please; that's about three in dog years. 850 N.W. Brooks St.; 541/388-6868; www.bendistillery.com.

Cascade Lakes Brewing Company Lodge: The dudes who came up with the clothing line featuring stick people enjoying the good life had to have been inspired by a heated brewpub patio such as this one, on the way to and fro all the recreational wonder of the Cascade Lakes. Drink some beer, grab a burger. Guzzle some brew, devour a taco. Sip a cold one, shred a brat. You get the idea. 1441 S.W. Chandler Ave.; 541/388-4998; www.cascadelakes.com.

Kebaba: A small restaurant that serves modern Middle Eastern food, Kebaba is all about choice. Choose your meat and veggies on a skewer or in a pita; select beer or wine from a daily list; pick between flagstone patio seating or a handy drive-up and drive-off option. Whatever you decide, don't miss the great "fries" made out of sliced and spiced flatbread. 1004 Newport Ave.; 541/318-6224; www.kebaba.com.

Merenda Wine Bar: Please your palate with more than 60 wines by the glass, and hors d'oeuvres and small plates with interesting combinations like fennel, grapefruit, and avocado salad or asparagus and prosciutto pizza. It's sidewalk dining at its finest. 900 N.W. Wall St.; 541/330-2304.

Mother's Juice Café: Mother wants to make sure you eat your apple a day, provided with every sandwich. But the health-conscious flock to Mother's mainly for the list of more than 30 fruit juice and smoothie blends, made from whole, fresh fruit. An impressive list of metabolic accessory nutrients, stuff like spirulina, psyllium, echinacea, and ginseng, can be added for that extra performance punch. 1255 N.W. Galveston St.; 541/318-0989.

Soba Asian Bistro: Everything is made to order and served in a bowl, be it a rice dish, a noodle dish, or a salad. Recipes are from all regions of Asia; there's sure to be something your shar-pei will love. You'll love the shaded sidewalk tables and cold Asian beer or ginger-peach iced tea on a hot day. 945 N.W. Bond St.; 541/318-1535; www.eatsoba.com.

Strictly Organic Coffee Co.: The cement patio is huge at this fair-trade coffee cooperative, but even it pales in comparison to the size of the breakfast burritos and lunch wraps. It feels good to sit in the sun and eat good food and drink strong brew with a clear conscience. 6 S.W. Bond; 541/330-6061; www.strictlyorganic.com.

Victorian Café: There's usually a dog or two hanging out on the lawn beside glass-topped patio tables where people enjoy a comfy-casual menu of breakfast scramblers with thick hobo potatoes and hot sandwiches and fresh salads for lunch. So popular, it can be hard to eke out a spot. 1404 N.W. Galveston St.; 541/382-6411.

The Village Baker: You'll be thrilled you took the time to hunt down this little storefront, even if you have to wait in line for superb sandwiches and baked goods. 1470 S.W. Knoll Ave.; 541/318-1054.

PLACES TO STAY

Absolutely Bend Vacation Homes: For a variety of pet-friendly rental properties, for longer stays on long summer days, the Cascade, Honeysuckle Lane, Bear's Den, and Kingston are pet friendly. There's no pet fee as long as there's no damage and no hair all over the place. 541/280-1813; www.abvhs.com.

Champagne Chalet at Cricketwood Country B&B: Heated Italian tile floors, two-person hydrotherapy tub, see-through gas fireplace, these the humans in your party can appreciate while the pups experience what a guest once called "Disneyland for dogs." Your pal can cavort in the five-acres of native grasses and wildflowers on a fenced, rural property down a dirt road with very little traffic. A rate of $150 per night covers you and your dogs;

breakfast is not included, but you have your own kitchen to DIY. It's a straight shot down Hamby Road to the Big Sky Dog Park. It's bliss, is what it is. 63520 Cricketwood Rd.; 541/330-0747; www.cricketwood.com.

Entrada Lodge: You can feel your stress level decrease a notch or two as soon as you enter the warm, fuzzy lobby of this quiet lodge on the west side of town, mere steps away from the Cascade Lakes Scenic Byway and the Deschutes National Forest. Rates range $80–100. There's a short list of reasonable pet rules and a $10 pet charge. Continental breakfast is included. 19221 Century Dr.; 888/505-6343; www.entradalodge.com.

Hillside Inn: The Studio Suite is your sweet spot on the west side of town, a desirable, modern destination with a separate entrance and private patio. It's got the you-thought-of-everything factor, with kitchenette, Internet, Satellite TV, DVD, and hot tub for $170 a night, plus a $20 pet fee. It's a half mile from Drake Park, and closer still to great outdoor seating and eating. 1744 N.W. 12th St.; 541/389-9660; www.bendhillsideinn.com.

Riverhouse Resort: This extensive, popular hotel is always busy thanks to superior service and Danish-influenced rooms with sliding glass doors onto patios overlooking the Deschutes River. If you sign a simple pet policy, there is no charge for your pets. Rates range $100–135, higher for suites. 3075 N. Business Hwy. 97; 866/453-4480; www.riverhouse.com.

More Accommodations: Please look under *Chain Hotels* in the *Resources* section for additional places to stay in this area.

Sunriver

There are those who make an annual pilgrimage to the 3,300-acre resort town of Sunriver, due south of Bend, as a required homage to sun worship. What's there? Golf courses, tennis courts, 35 miles of paved bike paths, swimming pools, athletic clubs, stables, a marina, a nature center, and a shopping/dining village.

PARKS, BEACHES, AND RECREATION AREAS

31 Newberry National Volcanic Monument–Lava Cast Forest

🐾🐾 ◀🐾 (See Central Oregon map on page 546)

It's not every day that you get to walk on a lava field, especially if you're not in Hawaii. A mile-long interpretive trail takes you through a forest where the trees are gone, but their impressions, molded in lava, remain. The trees acted as casts around which the molten lava surged when the Newberry Volcano erupted about 6,000 years ago. The path is paved, but the nine-mile road to the site is not. For the price of a bumpy ride on a washboard dirt road and a $5 parking fee, you're treated to one of the most unusual geological sites you're likely to see. The peaks of the Cascades accentuate the stark beauty, and in the spring, fiery Indian paintbrush and purple prairie lupine flowers contrast with the hardened black lava. Your dog will be too busy enjoying her leashed stroll to question the point of going to a treeless forest.

Travel south on U.S. Highway 97 and turn east on Forest Service Road 9720, directly across from the Sunriver exit. The trail is wheelchair accessible. Closed due to snow cover in winter. 541/593-2421.

PLACES TO STAY

Sunray Vacation Rentals: As the pet-friendliest agency in the Sunriver resort, Sunray believes you should be able to bring your loved ones with you for these rites of passage. There's a list of about 50 rentals that allow pets under "Pet Homes" on the left navigation bar. Find a handful that look good online, and then call and chat with a representative for availability and their recommendations. 56890 Venture Lane; 800/531-1130; www.sunrayinc.com.

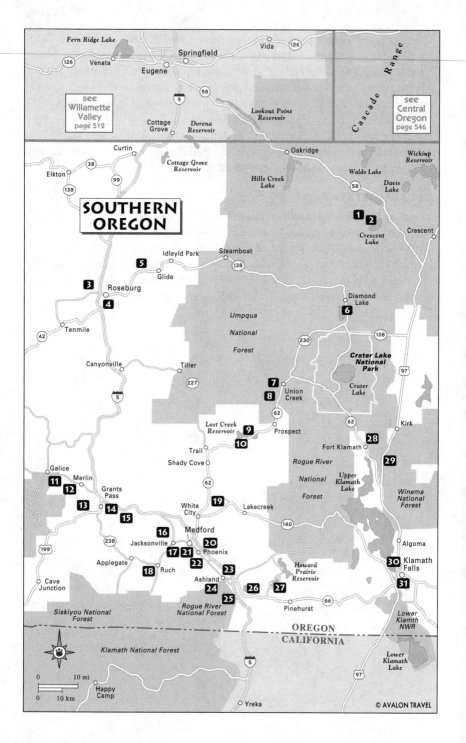

CHAPTER 20

Southern Oregon

The mighty Rogue and Umpqua Rivers, named for regional Native American tribes, are the source from which fun flows in Southern Oregon. The rivers begin high in the Cascade Mountains, winding and tumbling down to the ocean, providing hikes, campgrounds, and water sports of infinite variety along the way. Salmon, trout, and steelhead fishing and white-water rafting on the Rogue draw people from all over the world. Even so, except for a few hotspots, Southern Oregon is not as crowded as, say, the Oregon Coast. Rules are more relaxed, areas more open, and the lifestyle resonates in a lower key. While visitors crowd Crater Lake and the Oregon Caves National Monument—both places where dogs are *not* allowed—you can recreate unhampered in the backwoods.

The rivers connect to lakes, hundreds of them, and dozens of those have lake resorts. In addition to providing lodging or camping or both, they are complete destinations, offering boat and bicycle rentals, general stores, restaurants, and more places to picnic, play, and hike. The topography shifts from fertile valleys in the west to the Cascade Mountains as you head east. Be prepared with

PICK OF THE LITTER—SOUTHERN OREGON

BEST PARK
Whistler's Bend, Roseburg (page 584)

BEST DOG PARKS
Bear Creek Dog Park, Medford (page 596)
Ashland Boyd County Dog Park, Ashland (page 598)

BEST OFF-LEASH BEACHES
Crescent Lake Recreation Area, Crescent (page 582)

BEST TRAIL
Rogue Gorge Trail, Union Creek (page 587)

BEST EVENT
Puss 'n' Boots Costume Ball, Ashland (page 598)

BEST PLACES TO EAT
Blue Stone Bakery and Coffee Café, Grants Pass (page 592)
Allyson's Kitchen, Ashland (page 600)

BEST PLACES TO STAY
Sutherlin Inn, Roseburg (page 585)
Jacksonville Inn, Jacksonville (page 595)
Anne Hathaway's Garden Suites, Ashland (page 601)
CrystalWood Lodge, Fort Klamath and Crater Lake (page 603)

traction tires and/or snow chains for any elevation above 1,000 in the winter months, and ask for local road conditions before traveling.

NATIONAL FORESTS AND RECREATION AREAS

Rogue River–Siskiyou National Forests
🐾🐾🐾

The two million acres of the Siskiyou and the Rogue are managed together, and cover parts of Southern Oregon and Northern California. Biologists will tell you that it's the most floristically diverse forest in the nation and includes the carnivorous *Darlingtonia californica,* the fly-eating Cobra Lily. The "Recreation" section of the National Forest Website (www.fs.fed.us/r6/rougue-siskiyou) provides information on everything from guides and outfitters to detailed trail information. Or, stop into the Prospect Ranger Station (47201 Hwy. 62; 541/560-3400) and the Ashland Ranger Station (645 Washington St.; 541/552-2900).

Umpqua National Forest
🐾🐾🐾🐾

The Umpqua covers almost a million acres on the western slope of the Cascade Mountains. This forest's most popular recreation opportunities are Diamond Lake, included in this chapter, and a 79-mile hiking and mountain-biking trail following the North Umpqua wild and scenic river. Playing with the interactive North Umpqua Trail Map online is almost as much fun as hiking the trail itself. The map is also available in print at the Roseburg Visitors Center and at the North Umpqua Ranger Station in the tiny town of Glide: 18782 N. Umpqua Highway; 541/496-3532; www.fs.fed.us/r6/umpqua.

Fremont-Winema National Forest
🐾🐾

On the eastern slope of the Cascades, the 1.1 million acres of the Winema are wild and rugged, with fewer developed recreation opportunities. The two main trails, sections of the Pacific Crest Trail and the Mount McLoughlin Trail, are in Winema's wilderness. Mount McLoughlin isn't so much of a trail as it is a rock scramble guided by unreliable spray paint markers on loose boulders. You and your experienced trail dog really need to know what you are doing to wander in the Winema. The ranger station in Klamath Falls has more information: 1936 California Ave.; 541/883-6714; ww.fs.fed.us/r6/frewin.

Crescent

If dogs awarded sainthood to humans, Ronda Bishop would be on the short list. As the recreation program manager for the Crescent Ranger District of the

Deschutes National Forest, she has designated eight off-leash play areas around the beach at Crescent Lake.

Winter activities in the area include alpine and nordic skiing at the Willamette Pass Ski Area and miles of roads and trails for snowmobiling, snow shoeing, and skijoring. Crisp air and warm summer days are ideal for fishing, hiking, swimming, and taking to all those trails on a mountain bike.

PARKS, BEACHES, AND RECREATION AREAS

1 Crescent Lake Recreation Area

😺😺😺😺 🐕 (See Southern Oregon map on page 578)

Do doubt about it, this is dogtopia. Cooper and Isis had to pinch each other to make sure they hadn't died and gone to doggy heaven. Crescent Lake is a 4,000-acre, crystal-clear, glacially fed water playground surrounded by silky sand beaches and mountain peaks that make you want to sing, "The hills are alive!" Keep your pets on leash when they are in the campgrounds and wear your mosquito dope in June and July. Day-use areas are open 6 A.M.–10 P.M. Crescent Ranger District: 541/433-3200.

Take the Crescent Cut-Off Road from the center of town in Crescent on U.S. Highway 97, turn right toward Oakridge on State Route 58, and go 3.5 miles to Road 60, to Crescent Lake Campgrounds-Resort-Marina. It's another 2.2 miles to the Y junction that is the start of all recreation around the lake. From Eugene, the lake is 70 miles southeast on State Route 58. The off-leash areas (OLAs) are:

North Simax: This is the only OLA on the south shore. There is paved parking, a latrine, picnic tables, and the most beautiful wide and long beach you can imagine with a gentle slope into the water. Go straight to the left when the road forks right to the campground.

Crescent Lake Campground: This area is only practical if you are staying in the campground. It is small and steep, to the right of the old boat launch. It's .3 mile to the right of the Y junction. There is a $5 parking fee at this area.

Day-Use Areas: There is limited dirt parking in two pullouts. If you're the first ones there, you'll probably get to keep the area to yourselves. No facilities. Go right at the Y intersection, 3.3 miles.

Tranquil Cove: The cove has picnic tables, garbage, gravel parking, a potty, and a designated swimming beach marked by posts driven into the ground. The OLAs are to the outsides of the pylons, left and right. Head right at the Y, four miles.

Tandy Bay: Walk a few yards through the woods at this bay to the beach, to a single picnic table with a phenomenal lake view and a peek at Diamond Peak behind you. The whole area is off leash. Right at the Y, 4.5 miles.

Spring Campground: This is the last access area off of the paved road. The OLA is to the right of the boat launch. In addition to a lovely crescent of beach, there are high grass fields for olfactory exploration. Right at the Y, 5.5 miles. There is a $5 parking fee at this area.

Contorta Point: The lake saves its best for last. This beach is an interesting mix of sand and crumbly volcanic pumice. Views of Diamond Peak take up the entire skyline. As of press time, there was no charge to stay at the undeveloped campground. Right at the Y,

7.5 miles, left at Cortorta Point turnoff, and 0.5 mile to the first campground road and OLA. The last two miles are on a dirt road.

② Diamond Peaks Wilderness–Fawn Lake Trail
🐾🐾🐾 (See Southern Oregon map on page 578)

The official distance to Fawn Lake from the trailhead was three miles on the sign, but someone had crossed that out and written in four. It sure seems longer, perhaps because of the continuous elevation gain and hot, dusty trail. The higher you go, the better the views get, so the moderately steep trail isn't the only thing that will take your breath away. Signs will direct you if you want to branch off in the direction of Pretty Lake, Stag Lake, and Diamond Peak Lake for even more mileage and vistas. Water and some form of bug deterrent are essential traveling companions.

Park at the Crescent Lake Campground and watch for the busy road you must cross at the beginning of the hike. Parking is $5.

PLACES TO EAT
KJ's Café: Sure, dogs are allowed on the covered porch, where they can plead earnestly for a bite of your omelet, pancakes, burger, sandwich, or salad. KJ's also has a lengthy kids' menu, great chili, ice cream, and milk shakes. Milepost 69, Hwy. 58; 541/433-2005.

PLACES TO STAY
Crescent Lake Campground: Of the 44 tent/RV sites, #37 is the choicest spot, with direct access to the off-leash beach. Fees are $13 for premium lakefront sites and $11 for the rest, on a first-come, first-served basis. Follow the signs to the campground from Road 60. 541/433-3200.

Roseburg

Roseburg is the center point of The Land of Umpqua, a major river system that provides public parks, hiking trails, and campgrounds that are a source of dog delights in every form. The Roseburg visitors center (410 S.E. Spruce St.; 800/444-9584; www.visitroseburg.com) publishes a self-guided tour map that takes you in four directions, literally and figuratively—Historic South, Wine West, Cultural North, and Scenic East. Isis pointed her paw due east for the best outdoor adventures.

PARKS, BEACHES, AND RECREATION AREAS

③ Singleton Park
🐾🐾 (See Southern Oregon map on page 578)

The story goes that would-be farmer George Singleton had his eye on a plot of land owned by farmer Charles Curry. Charles finally relented and sold it to

George, when George did him a favor by fixing a cantankerous Curry farm tractor. Not a bad way to become landed gentry, especially of such a choice plot at the confluence of the North and South Umpqua rivers. This postage-stamp-sized park was the first land purchased by Douglas County in 1951. A jug of wine, a loaf of bread, and dog need be your only companions as you rest in the shade of the dark green leaves of the myrtlewood trees.

Part of the park's appeal is that it's out a ways, past vineyards, orchards, and farms. Take Garden Valley Parkway west, turn left on Curry Road and right on North Curry Road to the end.

4 Riverside Park

😸 (See Southern Oregon map on page 578)

When everyone is hot, sweaty, and tired from driving the super slab of I-5, you can all dog-pile out of the car onto the shady green lawns of this park in the backyard of the Roseburg visitors center. The grass slopes to the water, but your entrance is blocked by thick brush and trees, so you'll have to enjoy the river simply for its cooling breezes and refreshing sound. The gardens surrounding the park and center are full of rhododendron bushes, especially pretty in bloom in May.

From I-5, take Exit 124 onto State Route 138 and turn right on S.E. Oak Street, following the signs to the visitors center. Open dawn–dusk.

5 Whistler's Bend

😸😸😸😸 (See Southern Oregon map on page 578)

Like Cooper, your dog may gleefully and vocally greet the many sheep, wild deer, and turkeys you'll encounter on the rolling foothills surrounding this county park. The Wonder Wieners highly recommend this remote, beautiful spot along the North Umpqua River. The picnic area is on the north side of the bend, with front row seats on the wide, strong water. Watch the current carefully if you or your dog decide to take a dip. The swings and slides are shaded by myrtlewood and pine trees, which are also used as obstacles for a very challenging disc golf course. The only flush toilets are in the campground, around the bend on the south side, far enough away that you'll want to hop in the car to reach them.

The road to the park is 12 miles east of Roseburg on State Route 138. Follow the sign to turn on Whistler Park Road and travel patiently until it dead-ends into the park.

PLACES TO EAT

Anthony's Italian Café: Dine out or takeout, lunch and dinner at this pasta place feature at least 20 specialty dishes, plus pizzas, subs, soups, antipasto, and salads. Sip Chianti or bottled and tap beer with your meal on the large concrete patio. You won't regret accepting the challenge to save room for Mama Carole's cheesecake. 500 S.E. Cass Ave.; 541/229-2233.

Gay '90s Ice Cream and Deli: We don't know if the name of this café is referring to the 1890s or the 1990s. Your dog certainly won't care as long as you feed him bits of your sandwich and legendary Umpqua ice cream at one of three outdoor tables. 925 W. Harvard Ave.; 541/672-5679.

PLACES TO STAY

Big K Guest Ranch: City dogs looking for a taste of the country will find that this is as authentic as it gets, about an hour's drive northwest from Roseburg. The "driveway" winds along a dirt road for four miles through a 2,500 acre working ranch with 200 head of cattle, 400 ewes and lambs, and free-range turkeys. As you round the final bend, spread before you are a lodge and 20 cabins on a plateau among the hills overlooking the Umpqua River. The 10,000-square-foot lodge is grand in every way, with a dining hall, river rock fireplace, and a game room all flanked by stunning views through banks of massive windows. The wheelchair-accessible cabins are simple, with various bed arrangements. Plan to eat in the lodge, because there's nothing else for miles, and meals feature steak, salmon, quail, catfish, chicken, and homemade desserts. If your dogs are prone to wandering or chasing wildlife, you might want to keep them leashed, it's up to you. Rates range $325–340 per night, including meals. Hwy 138 W., Elkton; 800/390-2445; www.big-k.com.

Sutherlin Inn: Although it's 15 minutes north of Roseburg, we had to include this spotless motel, which offers the best quality for the price in this entire book, including Wi-Fi, cookies and bagels, cable TV, tubs, and a guest laundry, at rates starting at $40 (40 bucks!), plus a $10 pet fee. Rooms are spare and modern, and the beds are "chiropractor-approved." A lawn out back is handy for pit stops. 1400 Hospitality Pl., Sutherlin; 541/459-6800.

More Accommodations: Please look under *Chain Hotels* in the *Resources* section for additional places to stay in this area.

Diamond Lake

Diamond Lake has the most developed national forest facilities in Oregon. For more information before you go, call the visitors center at 541/793-3333.

PARKS, BEACHES, AND RECREATION AREAS

6 Umpqua National Forest–Diamond Lake

🐾🐾🐾 (See Southern Oregon map on page 578)

The crystal waters of the lake sparkle at 5,182 feet, a mile above sea level. For sea dogs, there are boat rentals of all breeds—pedal boats, patio boats, dinghies with dinky motors, kayaks, canoes, and bumper boats. For landlubbers, an 11-mile paved, multi-use trail circles the entire lake. Humans can rent bicycles at the lake's resort to do the double-digit mileage. Resort management is low-key about allowing dogs off leash to run around the ball field and go swimming, but the trail passes through several government-managed campgrounds where you should leash up. Winter recreation includes innertubing, ice skating, and snowmobiling.

Diamond Lake is five miles north of Crater Lake on State Route 138.

PLACES TO STAY

Diamond Lake Resort: Dogs are welcome in both the durable cabins and rooms in the lodge for $5 each per night. Thick-furred animals will do fine in the cabins, heated only by woodstoves. Italian greyhounds and Chihuahuas might prefer the warmer lodge. The resort includes restaurants, a general store, and boat and bicycle rentals (snowmobile and Sno-Cat tours in winter). Motel rooms are $85–100, cabins are $150–190 for up to six people. 350 Resort Dr.; 800/733-7593; www.diamondlake.net.

Steamboat Inn: For a small dog, Isis has a fairly large vocabulary, yet even she ran out of adjectives to describe the beauty of this area along the North Umpqua River and this historic fly-fishing camp, revamped as an upscale haven for recreational activities near Crater and Diamond lakes. It's 38 miles east of Roseburg on Highway 138, and about 45 miles west of Diamond Lake. Pets are allowed in the glamorous Hideaway Cottages, 0.5 miles of solitude down the road from the main inn; and in the practical Camp Water Houses, leased from Oregon State Parks and the U.S. Forest Service. There are no pet fees or restrictions. Rates for two people are $210 a night. Dinners at the inn are legendary and cost $50–85 per person extra. Hiking and fishing excursions are often arranged for guests. 42705 N. Umpqua Hwy. 138, Steamboat; 800/840-8825 or 541/498-2230; www.thesteamboatinn.com.

Union Creek

Pick a trail, any trail, and you can't go wrong. All of them follow the splashy spectacle of the Rogue River and Union Creek, through rapids and waterfalls, lava tubes, beaver dams, and log jams. Some lead you to volcanic rock formations and pumice flats, or deep into canopies of Douglas fir. The trails can be accessed reliably June–October; during winter months, the region is a popular snowmobile and cross-country skiing playground. While hiking, you'll probably need to exercise restraint, otherwise known as a leash, to keep your dog out of the water. The adjectives used to describe the river—such as wild, raging, and swift—do not exaggerate, and no one wants to see their dog get swept away by strong currents.

PARKS, BEACHES, AND RECREATION AREAS

7 Natural Bridge Trail

😼😼😼😼 🐾 (See Southern Oregon map on page 578)

The Natural Bridge is a lava tube, carved through rock by the molten flow. The Rogue River now follows the same path, disappearing underground for several hundred yards before emerging in a roiling rage downstream. Viewpoints around the formation are accessible on a paved walkway. Near the viewpoint bridge is a trailhead that leads to a 3.5-mile trail following the Westside of the Upper Rogue River south to Woodruff picnic area. Much of the time you'll be treading on mossy lava rock, alternating between sheltering old-growth forest and open brush.

Travel nine miles north on State Route 62 from Prospect and look for signs to the Natural Bridge Viewpoint. If you crave more, continue south another 4.6 miles to the River Bridge campground, along a section known as the Takelma Gorge Trail.

8 Rogue Gorge Trail

😼😼😼😼 🐾 (See Southern Oregon map on page 578)

On a 0.25-mile paved loop, there are four scenic viewpoints that demonstrate the power of water over time to slice through solid rock. It is simply spectacular, even more so during spring runoff in June. A 3.5-mile trail starts at the southern end of the loop, traveling along the east side of the river down to the Natural Bridge area. The sometimes rocky, mostly level trail is easy, featuring rock formations called potholes, carved by churning river currents. Your dog will get a kick out of watching you drool for a change, your mouth agape, awed by the scenery.

Travel north on State Route 62 approximately 12 miles from Prospect to the parking lot. A latrine is the only amenity.

PLACES TO EAT

Beckie's Restaurant: Although they are tasty, no one would blame you if you skipped past the burgers, sandwiches, and chicken-fried steak and went straight to the homemade pies. Dogs feel no guilt when eating dessert first, nor for chowing down on steak and eggs for breakfast, and they've been doing it here for more than 80 years. Order to go and eat at the tables in front of the ice cream shop next door. 56484 Hwy. 62; 541/560-3563.

Prospect and Shady Cove

These tiny burgs are mere spots of community along the Rogue-Umpqua Scenic Byway (State Route 138), also known as the Highway of Waterfalls, leading to the wilderness, forests, and high mountain lakes of the Oregon Cascades. The area has drawn famous anglers, including Western novelist Zane Grey, to its fishing holes and nature trails. Pick up USFS maps for the hikes along the Rogue River at the Prospect ranger station (47201 Hwy. 62; 541/560-3400).

PARKS, BEACHES, AND RECREATION AREAS

🔟 Lost Lake Trail

🐾🐾🐾 (See Southern Oregon map on page 578)

The Dachsie Twins prefer skipping the crowds at Joseph Stewart State Park and traveling the far side of the lake on this trail instead. It's 2.4 miles from this trailhead to a viewpoint called The Grotto. Pick up a U.S. Army Corps of Engineers map of all the trails around Lost Creek Lake at the state park on your way. On the back of the map is a species list of hundreds of birds, mammals, flora, and fauna you may see. While you should leash your dog to keep her paws out of the poison ivy, there are places where she can slip into the water for a quick dip.

Start at the Lewis Road Trailhead, reached by traveling north of the state park on State Route 62, and turning left onto Lewis Road for a mile.

🔟 Joseph H. Stewart State Park

🐾🐾 (See Southern Oregon map on page 578)

This State Recreation Area is the place to go for family reunions and big gatherings. The whole place is like one big, happy family in the summer anyway, parked on wide, open plains aside Lost Creek Lake. It's a big park, mostly taken up by endless campsites. Dogs will undoubtedly prefer the separate day-use area, southwest of the campground, with room to roam along the lake, and a store, café, marina, and boat launch. There are 5.5 miles of trails in the park along the south shore, from the dam to the picnic area and up to the campground.

Take State Route 62 from Shady Cove northeast to Lost Creek Lake. Parking is $3. Open 6 A.M.–7 P.M.

PLACES TO EAT

Phil's Frosty: Bunches of umbrella-shaded picnic tables are outside the order window. Inside the hot pink shed is the standard fare you're supposed to eat on summer vacation. There are hot dogs, burgers, burritos, fries, and onion rings for the main course; doughnuts and hard and soft ice cream are for dessert. 22161 Hwy. 62, Shady Cove; 541/878-2509.

PLACES TO STAY

Edgewater Inn: The Rogue River runs right past your room at this spiffy motel, and your pooch can do the same at the dog run in the back. The rooms are fresh and simple with white pine furniture and Danish accents. Continental breakfast is included. Summer rates range from $115 for parking lot views up to $170 for a room with a king-size bed, spa, and patio on the river; winter rates are lower. The pet fee is $7. 7800 Rogue River Rd., Shady Cove; 541/878-3171; www.edgewaterinns.com.

Prospect Historical Hotel, Motel, and Dinnerhouse: Behind the original 1892 stagecoach inn is a simpler motel that is more suitable for families with dogs and children. Nice, clean canines (even gorillas, according to the policy) are allowed in the motel rooms at no charge. Dog treats are provided at check-in with a map of where to play and potty. There's a huge groomed field with a little creek to wade in. Rooms are $80–110, $10 pet fee per visit. 391 Mill Creek Dr., Prospect; 800/944-6490; www.prospecthotel.com.

Merlin and Galice

These two villages mark a section of the Rogue River that is most famous for rafting and salmon and steelhead fishing. Drive the historic Rogue River Loop, between Exits 61 and 71 off of I-5, to trace the struggles between early pioneers and native inhabitants during the Rogue Indian Wars of 1852–1856. The battles erupted largely due to the Oregon Donation Land Act, passed by congress to allow settlers to stake claims to Native American lands without consent or treaties. Today the river remains as turbulent as the area's history. Dozens of scenic pullouts line the waterfront, with fishing access near river riffles, which Isis learned is water lingo for miniature rapids. However, as a miniature dachshund, she does not feel it is appropriate to call her a *diffle*.

PARKS, BEACHES, AND RECREATION AREAS

11 Indian Mary Historic Reservation

🐾🐾🐾 (See Southern Oregon map on page 578)

What was once the smallest Native American reservation in the United States is now a 61-acre, well-kept county park. Indian Mary filed a homestead application in 1884 and was granted the land in honor of her father, known as

Umpqua Joe, who had warned settlers of a planned massacre, saving the lives of settlers and Native Rogues. The county purchased Mary's property from her descendants in 1958.

It is a showpiece park with lawns of golf-course-green perfection. Wet noses go into overdrive sniffing the many varieties of trees, including Japanese fern, maple, flowering cherry, Port Orford cedars, pines, fir, oak, walnut, and Pippin apple trees from an old orchard. Isis spent most of her time inspecting the tall grape arbor that divides the RV sites from the tent camping area. The park is on the banks of the Rogue River, with the picnic area closest to the water, and the campground loops above. The hosts who care for this park obviously take great pride in keeping it well maintained. Its level spaces are excellent for handicapped users. There are accessible camping plots and an ADA-rated fishing platform.

From I-5, take Exit 61 and follow Merlin-Galice Road five miles north of Galice. www.co.josephine.or.us (click "Parks" under "Departments").

12 Griffin Park

😺😺 (See Southern Oregon map on page 578)

Despite the Swim at Your Own Risk signs, the river is long and calm beside this quiet, cozy park. And, leash laws aside, we saw dogs chasing Frisbees at their own risk, as well. Griffin pales in comparison to Indian Mary, but then again, it's not as crowded. Plastic climbing equipment and a wooden bridge over a tributary creek provide the kind of simple pleasures kids and dogs appreciate.

From U.S. Highway 199, go north on Riverbanks Road for six miles and turn right on Griffin Road.

PLACES TO EAT

Backroad Grill: The quality and variety of the gourmet food available at this restaurant "on the road to the Rogue" comes as a bit of a surprise is such a tiny, unassuming town. Even better yet, if you are staying at a place with an oven, many dishes are available in individually sized take-and-bake options. Try Chinese pork with peppers, pineapple, and water chestnuts; chicken Divan with Mornay sauce and Parmesan; or eggplant moussaka with feta, tomato, and béchamel sauce. After roughing it on the river, it doesn't get any better than this. Open 4–8 P.M. Wednesday–Sunday May–December 15. 330 Galice Rd.; 541/476-4019.

Galice Resort: Lunches are simple and filling at this roadside stop. Try a famous river burger, for example, the Widowmaker, with Swiss cheese and jalapeño peppers. The dinner menu adds great choices like vegetarian lasagna, breaded fantail shrimp, and homemade strawberry shortcake. In the summer, there's a big barbecue spread Friday and Saturday nights and a famous Sunday brunch buffet. Open seasonally, May–November. 11744 Galice Rd.; 541/476-3818; www.galice.com.

PLACES TO STAY

Indian Mary Campground: This county park has been named one of the 10 best camping spots in Oregon. There are 91 spaces, 35 of which are for tents on amazingly level, tidy plots. Tent sites are $13 in the off-season and $15 April–October. If you call ahead for reservations—and you'll need to in the summer—there is an additional $5 fee. 800/452-5687; www.reserveamerica.com.

Grants Pass

An 18-foot-tall caveman on the lawn of the visitors center (1995 N.W. Vine St.; 541/476-5510; www.visitgrantspass.org) welcomes you to this city, commemorating the oldest inhabitants of the area. Grants Pass brags about its ideal climate that gets warmer earlier than the rest of the valley but stays cooler as the summer heat beats down farther south. Parks in and around the city showcase the Rogue River, the whitewater rafting capital of Oregon. For a change of pace and more local color, travel the Rogue River Highway (State Route 99), which roughly parallels I-5 through the area.

PARKS, BEACHES, AND RECREATION AREAS

13 Schroeder Park

🐾🐾🐾 (See Southern Oregon map on page 578)

Schroeder County Park is a great destination that manages to give off a country vibe, even though it's within whistling distance of downtown. Separate areas of the park are neatly divided by rows of towering trees, hills, fences, and sculpted shrubs, adding to the secluded feel. The sports fields and playground are first, fenced off and with a separate parking lot. Next is the campground, a

DIVERSION

Ferron and Junior the mostly black Lab are co-owners of the only rafting guide service along the Rogue River that allows you to bring your dog along for the ride. **Ferron's Fun Trips** are aptly named, as long as your idea of fun includes getting wet. You can rent your own floating craft or take a tour guided by Junior and Ferron, which Cooper highly recommends. Ferron is a character who knows much about local wildlife, ecosystems, and history. Junior is an experienced guide dog who has been featured on an *Animal Planet* TV special. Take a fishing expedition for game fish, steelhead, and Chinook salmon or a mild Class 2 whitewater trip on the infamous Rogue. Guided raft trips are $50 per person for a half day, $80 for a full day, and include lunch. 541/474-2201; www.roguefuntrips.com.

loop with a large lawn in the center designed for croquet or badminton. Most dogs make a beeline for the picnic area, with about the dimensions of a football field, down the hill and alongside the river. There's a barrier-free fishing platform for anglers with special access needs.

From U.S. Highway 199 west of the city, turn right on Willow Lane for a mile to Schroeder Lane. 541/474-5285.

14 Riverside and Baker Parks
🐾🐾🐾 (See Southern Oregon map on page 578)

Several recreation areas along the Rogue River share the Riverside name, but this one is the coolest among them, especially for a picnic. The grass goes on for 26 acres, mature trees provide soothing shade, and the river burbles alongside.

The grounds include the Josephine County Peace Memorial, a rose garden, decent restroom facilities, and plenty of picnic shelters to go around. The big playground has a real tractor, scoop truck, and steamroller to climb on. Wheelchair-accessible pathways wind through the trees, and there are ample parking places. Across the parking lot, Baker Park adds a public boat ramp and more restrooms into the appealing mix.

From I-5, take Exit 58 to State Route 99, which becomes N.W. 6th Street through town. Cross the river and turn onto E. Park Street. Open 7 A.M.–10 P.M.

15 Tom R. and Watta B. Pearce Park
🐾🐾🐾 (See Southern Oregon map on page 578)

This 108-acre county park is elongated, providing multiple meadows, woods, fields, and trails along the Rogue River. There were dogs everywhere the day Coop 'n' Isis visited, including an agility course for corgis set up at the far end. The river access trail is short and sweet. You have to stay away from the little Wildlife Sanctuary, which leaves you about 107 other acres to enjoy. Caution: The river is faster and deeper than it looks. There's plenty to do without getting in the water.

Take Exit 55 from I-5. Turn left on Agness Avenue. At the stop sign, turn left on Foothill Boulevard. Take the right fork in the road onto Pearce Park Road when Foothill turns to go under the highway. It's an additional 1.1 miles to the park entrance. Open 8 A.M.–8 P.M. Parking is $2. 3700 Pearce Park Road.

PLACES TO EAT

Blue Stone Bakery and Coffee Café: The Blue Stone's menu is more extensive and healthier than a typical coffeehouse, with fabulous soups and choices like stuffed potatoes, chicken burritos, and the "Yougonnalikeit," a deluxe sandwich that approximates a Thanksgiving dinner between two slices of bread. Okay, so the pastries, cakes, and puddings aren't exactly healthy, but they are so fine! Outdoor seating and free wireless Internet are available. 412 N.W. 6th St.; 541/471-1922.

La Burritta: This restaurant serves large portions of all your Tex-Mex favorites, plus a wide selection of Mexican beers and margaritas, at your covered patio table. The management requests that you sit with your dog along the edge of the deck. The menu features an entire page of fajita and seafood specialties with plenty of zing. 941 S.E. 7th St.; 541/471-1444.

PLACES TO STAY

Redwood Motel: Three ground-floor rooms in the older section of this tidy motel are reserved for pets. Rooms are big, the TVs are huge, and the grass out back is wide and soft. Rates range $80–125 per night; the pet fee is $10, which buys a couple of biscuits at check-in. 815 N.E. 6th St.; 541/476-0878; www .redwoodmotel.com.

Riverside Inn: This resort is a grand affair, covering three city blocks. It's the only lodging on the river in town, and the five pet-friendly rooms have river views. Standard rates are $125–150, but there are often specials. The dog fee is $10. 971 S.E. 6th St.; 541/476-6873 or 800/334-4567; www.riverside-inn.com.

Schroeder County Park Campground: This is a serene and outdoorsy campground close to the city with 54 sites, 22 of them designated for tents in a separate loop. $15 for tents or $20 for hookup sites; 800/452-5687; www.reserveamerica.com.

More Accommodations: Please look under *Chain Hotels* in the *Resources* section for additional places to stay in this area.

Jacksonville

This well-preserved historic district was founded in 1852 by gold prospectors. When the railroad bypassed the town in the 1890s, so did commercial development, leaving the town captured in time. Citizens with excellent foresight began preserving and restoring this history in the 1960s, and now more than 100 of its buildings are listed on the National Historic Register. People have thoughtfully placed water bowls outside the homes and businesses everywhere to refresh your thirsty pup. You might want to avoid the town on Britt Music Festival Nights (www.brittfest.org), when throngs of concertgoers, without dogs in attendance, take up all the parking spots in town.

PARKS, BEACHES, AND RECREATION AREAS

16 Sarah Zigler Interpretive Trail

🐾🐾🐾 (See Southern Oregon map on page 578)

This mile-long trail follows the Jackson Creek, where gold was first discovered in 1851. An excellent and extensive brochure and map is available. It's a good idea to follow the city's request to keep your dogs on leash, because poison oak grows heartily in the area (remember, "Leaves of three, let it be"). Coop saw lots of poop on the trail, so please do your part not to add to the problem.

From Oregon Street southbound into Jacksonville, turn right on C Street. The trail begins across the street from the visitors center parking lot, at the entrance to Britt Park.

🔟 Albert "Doc" Griffin Park

🐾 (See Southern Oregon map on page 578)

Dogs don't mind tagging along on trips to this tidy and pretty park, designed mainly with kids in mind. Those kids will tell you that the "bestest" part of Doc's is the Spray Park, custom designed for water play on hot summer days. Dogs will have to settle for stray spray while sitting on the nearby lawn. There's also a big playground, a picnic pavilion, and clean restrooms.

Doc's is on Pine Street between 4th and 5th Streets.

🔢 Cantrall-Buckley

🐾🐾🐾 (See Southern Oregon map on page 578)

Don't rely on first impressions to judge this county park in the country. The initial pull-out is an uninspiring dirt lot, with a single picnic table hidden in tall grass and a sandy riverbank down to a swimming hole. That's just a tease. Keep going, across a single-lane bridge, and you'll come to a campground on the left and an 88-acre picnic area on the right.

You'll want to go all the way down past the group picnic shelters to the south lawn on the banks of the Applegate River, where there's fun play equipment,

NATURE HIKES AND URBAN WALKS

When gold was discovered in Rich Gulch in 1851, the town of Jacksonville sprang up around the prospectors and the gold diggers hoping to profit from them. Development and modernization passed by when the railroads bypassed the town in favor of Medford, and the early character of Jacksonville remained largely unchanged as surrounding communities grew. In 1966, the charm of the city was permanently preserved when the entire town was designated as a National Historic Landmark.

Walk through the past on the **Jacksonville Historic Landmark Walking Tour,** with a brochure from the visitors center (N. Oregon and C Streets) or try a Jacksonville Woodlands Map ($2), listing 15 walking paths and woodland trails around the city, from 0.3 mile to one mile each. 541/899-8118; www.jacksonvilleoregon.org.

bathrooms and showers, a trail, and shade trees. It wouldn't be surprising to find a rope swing somewhere out over the 1.75 miles of river frontage.

Take State Route 238 west from Jacksonville, turn left on Hamilton Road, for about a mile. Parking is $3. Open 10 A.M.–dusk. 541/899-7155.

PLACES TO EAT

Lutrell's Mustard Seed Café: A rose garden marks the entrance to Lutrell's outdoor patio. The food is named after family and friends; Pop's Covered and Smothered is hash browns and biscuits with sausage gravy, Renee has her own chicken burger, Joel's BLAT is a BLT with avocado, and Millie has a killer Philly. 130 N. 5th St.; 541/899-2977.

MacLevin's Whole Foods Deli, Bakery, and Ice Cream Parlor: This authentic Jewish deli is the place to nosh on pastrami, knishes, and potato latkes, oy vey! All-day breakfast and lunch are served at a couple of outdoor tables. Or, you could take your matzo ball soup, herring in sour cream, borscht, and lox to go. 150 W. California St.; 541/899-1251.

PLACES TO STAY

Jacksonville Inn: Cooper and Isis are on their very best behavior at this glamorous inn. It is rare that an establishment of this caliber accepts pets, and they'd like to keep it that way. Two guest rooms and one cottage combine tasteful Victorian opulence with modern conveniences in the heart of town. The owner requests that she be allowed to meet every dog, that they sleep in their own beds, not hers, and that they not be left alone in the room, which goes without saying. The inn has an elegant restaurant, casual bistro, and wine shop. Rooms are $160–200; decadent cottages are $270–465. You get what you pay for. 175 E. California St.; 541/899-1900; www.jacksonvilleinn.com.

Stage Lodge: Well-behaved pets are welcome at this "anti-motel" with real colonial furniture and designer bath fixtures. Rooms are all nonsmoking. Rates are $100–115; honeymoon suites with fireplaces and jetted tubs are $175. 830 N. 5th St.; 800/253-8254; www.stagelodge.com.

Cantrall-Buckley County Park Campground: It costs $10 to overnight at this quiet county campground, not including quarters for the coin-operated showers. The 42 first-come, first-served sites are well shaded, but too close together to be private. www.jacksoncountyparks.com.

Medford

The working-class cousin of Ashland, Medford is the largest and most commercial city in Southern Oregon. It is surrounded by a rich agricultural valley dominated by pear orchards and vineyards. Many of the region's delectable goodies can be found at famous **Harry and David** (1314 Center Dr.; www.harryanddavid.com). Medford is a good central location from which to explore the Applegate Valley, named for pioneers Jesse and Lindsay Applegate, trailblazers of Southern Oregon in 1846. Not as quaint as Ashland or Jacksonville, Medford has its merits in less expensive lodging and nearby winery tours.

North of Medford in Eagle Point is the oldest and largest training facility for hearing-assistance dogs in the nation. Tours of **Dogs for the Deaf** are free, but you are welcome to make a donation to the privately funded facility. See how rescued pups are trained for a higher calling as service dogs for the deaf and hearing-impaired. There are areas where your pup can wait for you; visiting dogs would be too disruptive to those in training (10175 Wheeler Rd.; 541/826-9220; www.dogsforthedeaf.org).

PARKS, BEACHES, AND RECREATION AREAS

19 TouVelle State Park

🐾🐾🐾 (See Southern Oregon map on page 578)

So much of this region calls for activity—trails to hike, mountains to climb, rivers to navigate—that it is refreshing to come across a park tailor-made for doing little other than lying in the shade of a tree alongside a quiet river. This State Recreation Site is one of the few places where the Rogue calms down, gliding past the foot of the Table Mountains. Large trees shade the rolling grassy slopes dotted with picnic tables. Even when busy, there's plenty of room for everybody. Relaxation runs rampant.

From State Route 62, turn west on Antelope Road and right on Table Rock Road. Parking is $3 per day.

20 Bear Creek Dog Park

🐾🐾🐾🐕 (See Southern Oregon map on page 578)

Bear Creek Park is a 100-acre expanse of rolling hills with a litany of fancy amenities, including a skate park, amphitheater, playground, tennis courts, barbecue areas, a BMX bicycle track, and restrooms. Best of all, it is the location of Medford's only off-leash area, a good-sized two acres, secured all around by a sturdy, tall fence with a double-entry gate. A blend of open field and tree-covered shade, bushes to sniff, and a dirt path around the perimeter suit every dog's needs. There's a garbage can, a picnic bench, and water to sip, but we didn't see a bag dispenser, so come prepared. We visited at the peak of the dry season, yet the grass was still lush, watered, and maintained.

The main parking lot is on Siskiyou Boulevard, but there's a back way to sneak in directly to the off-leash area. From I-5, take Exit 27 east onto Barnett Road. Turn left immediately on Alba Drive in front of the Dairy Queen and park at the Little League field. Follow the signs across a wooden footbridge to reach the dog park entrance. Hours are 6 A.M.–10:30 P.M. 541/774-2400; www.playmedford.com.

21 Alba Park

🐾🐾 (See Southern Oregon map on page 578)

It's easy to imagine this lovely little park as the social center of downtown Medford. Dedicated to the city by Charles and Callie Palm in 1934, it has the formal quadrangle design of that era, with a gazebo and a fountain in the center of diagonal sidewalks. Next to the fountain is a statue of a young man, surely it's Charles, kneeling to pet two Irish setters. The thick maple trees lining the square lawn must have been around since the beginning. As the historic heart of downtown Medford is rapidly being restored, Alba revels in its former glory. This rarified atmosphere is appropriate for a walk, but probably not for mutts who want to mess around.

Alba Park is at the corner of Holly and Main Streets.

22 Hawthorne Park

🐾🐾🐾 (See Southern Oregon map on page 578)

There's room to roam at Hawthorne, enough for Friends of the Animal Shelter to hold a benefit parade annually on the expansive lawn. Picnic tables are smartly placed under the few shade trees. Isis adores the elaborate rose garden, where No Pruning signs admonish humans tempted to take flowers home. Dogs, that means no digging, either.

The park is across the street from Medford Center Mall, which has a Cold Stone Creamery ice cream shop. At the corner of Jackson and Hawthorne Streets. Open 6 A.M.–10:30 P.M.

PLACES TO EAT

Corks Wine Bar and Bottle Shoppe: Drink outdoors and enjoy antipasti, cheese and fruit plates, hummus and crackers, and chocolate truffles with your dog at a patio table or even up on the roof deck, near the restored Craterian Ginger Rogers Theatre. Corks carries only the best Washington and Oregon wines, of which there are many to please your palate. 235 Theater Alley; 541/245-1616; www.corks-wineshoppe.com.

PLACES TO STAY

In this area, chain hotels listed in the *Resources* section offer the best choices for dogs and their owners.

Ashland

This cultured, artistic town is world famous thanks to a guy named Bill who wrote great plays. Founded in 1935, the Oregon Shakespeare Festival has grown and evolved to present music, dance, and theater far beyond the Bard. The Plaza, a triangle in the center of town, is the hotspot for theater, shopping, and an entire row of restaurants with "creekside dining," a block-long outdoor patio. It's public space, where dogs can join you while you dine.

It's a shame that dogs are not allowed in Ashland city parks, excluded even from famous Lithia Park. However, the dirt roads and trails in the mountains above the town are fair game, and you'll meet many canine locals up in them thar hills. Gardening is a high art in evidence everywhere, especially at the many lovely B&Bs.

PARKS, BEACHES, AND RECREATION AREAS

23 Ashland Boyd County Dog Park

🐾🐾🐾🐾 🐕 (See Southern Oregon map on page 578)

The ABCD park, for short, is completely fenced, grassy, and graced by shade trees and scattered bushes. There's a covered shed (with a couch inside) for waiting out the rain, and a plastic swimming pool and water fountains for both species. A dozen or so lawn chairs are scattered around for impromptu seating in addition to a couple of picnic tables. Smack dab in the middle is a built-in trash bin with a bunch of garden shovels leaning against it. Why bother with bags or mitts when you can simply shovel the you-know-what?

The OLA is two parks in one: a two-acre, sloping lawn for the big boys, and a separately fenced, little spot with its own entrance for small or timid dogs. Cooper figures that now is as good a time as any to reveal his darkest secret: He is afraid of dog parks. Gasp! How can it be? For starters, practically everybody is bigger than he is and, sadly, his scars bear witness to prior dog attacks before he was rescued. What a treat to have his own space, complete with a miniature copse of trees for him to anoint.

From the center of town, turn east onto Oak Street for about a mile, turn left on Nevada, and right onto Helman, which looks like a driveway, past the

DOG-EAR YOUR CALENDAR

Every year in late October, the Friends of the Animal Shelter (FOTAS) in Ashland host an annual **Puss 'n' Boots Costume Ball** and silent auction to benefit the Jackson County Animal Shelter in nearby Phoenix, Oregon. The cost is a worthwhile $35 per person, with all funds raised going to pay the salary of a full-time coordinator who wrangles more than 100 volunteers to keep the shelter running smoothly.

In nearby Jacksonville, the annual **Mutt Strut** parade is held in May, sponsored by the Jacksonville Animal Hospital, with all funds raised also going to FOTAS. 541/774-6646; www.fotas.org.

Ashland Greenhouses. You can also connect to the Bear Creek Greenway Trail from this location. Open dawn–dusk. 541/488-5340; www.abcdogpark.com.

24 Ashland Watershed Area

😊 😊 😊 (See Southern Oregon map on page 578)

It took some digging in the dirt, but Cooper and Isis finally got the local sheriff to spill the beans on the best kept secret in these parts. We're not sure what to call these wooded areas above town, but eat your heart out long-distance dogs, there's probably 20 miles of dirt roads and trails up here, free for all. Sheriff said to be aware of the homeless people that sometimes camp up here, and you're even more likely to encounter and be bothered by prolific poison oak, so stay on the dirt pack.

Don't mind the green gate, past it is an old rock quarry you can roam around; don't mind the yellow gate, past it are old police training grounds you can use as an impromptu agility course. Another trail, just before both gates, leads beside, over, under and in Asford Creek.

From State Route 99 southbound into town, as soon as it becomes E. Main Street turn right on Granite Street, one street north of the plaza. Drive out Granite about 1.5 miles or until you can't go any farther, past the water tank, past where the pavement ends, and just to the right at the intersection with Glenview Drive. There are several head-in parking areas. Even if you don't make it to the trails, the Ashland Creek Loop dirt road above town provides a bird-dog's-eye view of the city, frequented by local joggers and their sidekicks.

25 Siskiyou Mountain Park and Todd Oredson Woods

😊 😊 😊 (See Southern Oregon map on page 578)

If you enjoy the nightlife, shopping, and culture of staying in Ashland *and* you want to do some more serious trekking, you're in luck. Above the city on the west side are 270 acres of single-track trails connecting the Pacific Crest Trail and the Creek to Crest Byway (no animals on the byway, by the way). You can't really tell where the "woods" leave off and the "park" starts; it's all one big, happy, hiking ground. Just stay on the trail and off private property when signs request, and you're good to go. You might want to leave a trail of breadcrumbs to eat on your way back, as most of this area is unmarked.

South of town, Highway 99 becomes Siskiyou Boulevard. Take the right fork in the road to stay on Siskiyou when you pass the turnoff for State Route 66 to stay. Park on Park Street before Dragonfly Lane, being careful to curb your wheels on this very steep hill. Tamarack Place is another parking possibility; be courteous of the residents and their driveways and mailboxes. Walk uphill on the left fork of the gravel trail, then on the left fork of the dirt trail, to access the woods.

26 Emigrant Lake

🐾🐾🐾🐕 (See Southern Oregon map on page 578)

Word on the street is that Emigrant Lake is packed with local dogs on weekends. The catch is that they're not allowed in the County Recreation Area, a.k.a. the RV park. Go past the park entry and you'll see at least a half dozen dirt roads with Day Use Area signs. The roads are rough, you're lucky if there's a latrine, and parking is in a dirt patch. Yet, persevere! Rediscover what it means to bound around. Indulge your dock-dog fantasies. There are no leash restrictions; there *are* meadows filled with wildflowers and lots of comfortable entry points along the lake for dog paddling; and you don't have to pay the $3 that dogless people are paying to park in the RV park. Songer Wayside has the best parking.

From I-5, take Exit 14 west on State Route 66 about six miles to the lake. Park closes at sunset.

27 Hyatt Lake

🐾🐾🐾🐾 (See Southern Oregon map on page 578)

The Hyatt Lake Recreation Complex is located a dizzying mile above sea level, so unless you're from Colorado, don't be alarmed if you're a little out of breath. Here's another tip: The higher you go in altitude, the less alcohol it takes to get buzzed. The lake is crystal clear, remote, and surrounded by wilderness and snow-capped peaks. The playground and picnic areas are rudimentary except for a large fire ring, ideal for a bonfire and weenie roast. Cooper suggests you spend time hiking the section of the Pacific Crest Trail that parallels the west side of the lake, accessible from behind the park office. It's especially awe inspiring to play in the winter snow up here in this rarefied air.

From Ashland, take State Route 66 east for 17 miles, past the top of Green Springs Pass. Turn onto Hyatt-Prairie Road and follow the signs. Parking is $3.

PLACES TO EAT

Allyson's Kitchen: It's predictable in this town for things to be named after Shakespearean characters, and Allyson has followed suit in dubbing her sandwiches MacBeth, Shylock, King Lear, etc. Clichéd names aside, they are otherwise exciting and really good. Daily specials are even better, such as chicken and pumpkin tortellini. Order downstairs and they'll bring your food to your sidewalk table. 115 E. Main St.; 541/482-2884.

Greenleaf Restaurant: Of all the restaurants on the plaza, Isis favors this one. The menu is five pages long, with something for even the pickiest palates. Food dishes lean toward the healthy side, and it's all fresh and delicious. 49 N. Main St.; 541/482-2808.

Pangea Grills and Wraps: Meals wrapped in tortillas make for handy, on-the-go lunches and dinners. Get your taste buds tingling with Greek and Mediterranean flavors, then cool down with a mango or peach smoothie.

Order at the counter and relax at a sidewalk table. Your food is brought to you, along with a water dish and some dog biscuits for your dining companion. 272 E. Main St.; 541/552-1630.

Water Street Café: It's a great concept, well suited to a resort town: open-air dining with healthy food ordered from an outdoor bar. Salads, wraps, smoothies, and espresso soothe the savage stomach. Open April–November. Downtown at the corner of Water and Main Streets; 541/482-0206.

PLACES TO STAY

Anne Hathaway's Garden Suites: Guests with pets who opt for the Garden Suites across the street from the main house will find spacious rooms, private entrances, decks overlooking an English garden, kitchenettes, whirlpool tubs, and continental breakfast in a clubhouse. We like Viola, with an enclosed sun porch, and Calla, with its front porch. Everyone will experience the unforgettable, warm hospitality of the innkeepers, which extends to the pets in the form of treats, pick-up bags, and a welcome letter from resident chocolate Lab Cappy. All this brilliance comes at amazing rates as low as $115 in the off-season to $160 in the summer, plus a $10 nightly pet fee. No pets on the antique beds or furniture please. 586 E. Main St.; 800/643-4434 or 541/488-1050, www.ashlandbandb.com.

Ashland Creek: Isis feels she is expensive, but worth it; thus, she finds the Taos Suite ($200/$250/$325 depending on season) at this top-of-the-line establishment to be in suitably good taste. A cool Mexican tile floor graces all 1,200 square feet of the California-king bedroom, two full baths, kitchen, and living and dining rooms. The deck overhangs the creek where the waterwheel used to enter the old mill. Pets may be welcome in other suites on a case-by-case basis, but never on the furniture or beds. The pet fee is $10. 70 Water Street; 541/482-3315; www.ashlandcreekinn.com.

Green Springs Inn: The road to get here, about 17 miles east of Ashland, is worth the price alone. State Route 66 inspires adjectives such as precipitous and convoluted as it winds through deep forests above green valleys to arrive at the top of Green Springs Mountain. Two lodge rooms, #2 downstairs with an outdoor jetted tub and #5 upstairs with an indoor one, are icing on the cake. The rooms are recovering from neglect under new owners in 2008, but they are fine for people who don't want to rough it for recreation at Hyatt Lake. Dogs enjoy almost infinite walking opportunities. Rooms are $120, and there's no pooch tariff. Steaks at the inn's restaurant and summer bonfires add to the enjoyment. 11470 Hwy. 66; 541/482-0614; www.greenspringsinn.net.

Lithia Springs Resort and Gardens: About five minutes north of town, the Lithia Springs' unique garden setting with a backdrop of forested hills is an ideal location for pets who need room to stretch their legs. The owner began allowing dogs in 2008, choosing Irish Suite #4 and ADA-accessible English Cottage #12 for them. Both are roomy and have easy access to the backyard for birding, hiking, and general lolling about. Rates range $140–250; $20 one-time pet fee. 2165 W. Jackson Rd.; 800/482-7128; www.ashlandinn.com.

Plaza Inn and Suites: The Plaza is a sophisticated, modern choice in downtown. Dogs under 60 pounds are allowed in a second building, smaller but equally fancy. Cascade Rooms rates range $90–220 and include a European breakfast. The pet fee is $25. 98 Central Ave.; 541/488-8900; www.plaza innashland.com.

Hyatt Lake Campground: Tent sites are on an opposite shore from the RV sites, with walk-in or drive-in availability. Sites are deeply wooded and widely spaced apart for privacy. Most have views; #T15 is the best. Available June–October. Fees are $12 Monday–Thursday and $15 Friday–Sunday. Hyatt–Howard Prairie Rd. off Hwy. 66; 541/482-2031; www.blm.gov/or (see "Outdoor Recreation" under "Visit Us" on left navigation bar).

More Accommodations: Please look under *Chain Hotels* in the *Resources* section for additional places to stay in this area.

Fort Klamath and Crater Lake

Crater Lake is Oregon's only national park, and as such, your dog is not allowed on trails or in buildings. She can still experience the best part of this natural wonder with you, a 33-mile Rim Road drive encircling the 4,000-foot-deep basin, the remnants of the Mount Mazama volcano that erupted an estimated 7,700 years ago. You have to travel the route slowly as the curves hug the mountains and the water, leaving lots of time for her to hang her head out the window and take in the territory. The full drive is open only during the warmest summer months; the southern entrance and a short drive up to a lake viewpoint and historic lodge are open year-round. The entrance fee is $10 per vehicle (www.nps.gov/crla).

PARKS, BEACHES, AND RECREATION AREAS

28 Jackson F. Kimball

🐾🐾 (See Southern Oregon map on page 578)

Locals will tell you that the best time to visit this State Recreation Site is in September, after the first hard frost kills off the mosquitoes that will drink you dry during spring and summer. A 50-foot path leads to the Wood River Headwaters; on one side is a creek not much wider than a road, and on the other is a panorama of snow-capped mountains and towering pines that our host at CrystalWood Lodge said was "straight out of a John Wayne Western." Despite including a river and a marsh, it is called a dry camp, because none of the water is drinkable. Bring some with you on this short, sweet stop.

From State Route 62, north of Fort Klamath, turn west on Dixon Road and left at the T intersection onto Sun Mountain Road.

29 Collier Memorial

🐾🐾🐾 (See Southern Oregon map on page 578)

The main attraction at Collier is the logging museum, with the largest collection of equipment in the country on 147 acres of state park land. The museum is outdoors, allowing your dogs to enjoy it with you. Self-guided tour brochures are available. The rusting hulks of machinery are left in situ, rain or shine, although it doesn't rain much in this high, dry country. Across the highway, the poor trees in the campground look thirsty and scrawny. The picnic area is greener, with watered lawns leading to the banks of the Williamson River and Spring Creek. Cooper was driven to an ecstatic frenzy by the excess of chipmunks and tiny prairie dogs in the park. If he hadn't been on leash, Isis doubts she would have ever seen him again.

Collier is 30 miles north of Klamath Falls on U.S. Highway 97. Open dawn–dusk. 541/783-2471.

PLACES TO STAY

CrystalWood Lodge: Every detail of this B&B is designed to welcome dogs. After all, owners Liz and Peggy have 21 dogs of their own. You are welcome to meet the troops, 14 of whom who finished the 2008 Iditarod dogsled races in 14 hours. Copies of *Fido Friendly* and *Bark* magazine are in every room, as are kennels, lint/hair remover brushes, and designer doggie-bag holders. You are not required to use the kennels. Extra sheets are provided if your dogs sleep in bed with you. The property encompasses 130 acres, with five miles of trails your hosts have cleared and access to the 10-mile Klamath Lake Canoe Trail. The lodge, an original homestead, is also a phenomenal place for bird-watchers, anglers, and hunters. It's easy to reach, yet secluded between the Winema National Forest and the Upper Klamath National Wildlife Refuge.

You won't mind being sent to the doghouse here, full of games for kids and a self-service dog-wash station. The room rates, ranging $85–215, include unparalleled hospitality and breakfast. In short, Coop 'n' Isis think it's one of the best place for dogs to stay in the region. 38625 Westside Road; 866/381-2322; www.crystalwoodlodge.com.

Klamath Falls

In the Oregon High Country, the only way you and your dog will get cabin fever is by staying in too many of them. Between the Rogue Valley and Klamath Falls are the Cascade Mountains, famous for more than 100 alpine lakes, at least a dozen of which have cabin resorts on their shores.

Klamath County is a high-desert region. You'll leave behind the dreary, drippy Pacific Northwest to an average of 300 days of sunshine yearly. The heat rises up through the ground as well, as most of the city is warmed by underground geothermal energy, a pleasant reminder of an explosive volcanic legacy. In winter, when it's not sunny, it's snowing. Keep traction tires or chains on hand.

PARKS, BEACHES, AND RECREATION AREAS

30 Link River Nature Trail

😽 😽 😽 (See Southern Oregon map on page 578)

In the summer, a morning stroll along this 1.7-mile gravel trail is best, before it gets too hot to enjoy the meandering river and the many birds. For longer walks, the Link Trail connects to the Lake Ewauna Wingwatchers Nature Trail for another mile. You might see blue herons, white pelicans, mallards, and red-winged blackbirds.

To reach the trailhead parking lot, turn west on Nevada Avenue from U.S. Highway 97. The small, gravel parking area is on the left, shortly after the road becomes Lakeshore Drive and before you round the bend and cross the bridge. Dog walking has recently been allowed in Moore Park as well, further down the same road.

31 Veterans Memorial Park

😽 😽 (See Southern Oregon map on page 578)

In this hot, dry town near the California border, this city park may be the only place where you can picnic in the shade of large trees. The football-field-sized lawn also has steps for sitting in the sun, restrooms, and big steam engine trains on display.

It's on the south end of downtown at the bottom of Main Street, which has a couple of great places to grab a picnic lunch before heading to the park.

PLACES TO EAT

Café Paradise: Mexican food and American fare sit side-by-side on the extensive menu, and it's all good. Cooper is biased toward the Mexican side of the border, with to-drool-for quesadillas and deep-fried ice cream. There's easy ordering through a to-go window. 1401 Esplanade; 541/850-2225.

The Daily Bagel: The custom bagel sandwiches, named after big-city U.S. newspapers, are so fat they're almost impossible to fit your mouth around. You're highly likely to drop sandwich filling from your sidewalk table, and nothing would please your pooch more. This news-worthy stop also offers daily soups and Ben and Jerry's ice cream bars. 636 Main St.; 541/850-1809.

PLACES TO STAY

Maverick Motel: This downtown establishment prefers to accept dogs for a couple of days only, not weeks or months. Each pet is $6 per stay, and rates

DIVERSION

You don't have to roam the wilds of Alaska to experience the thrill of dogsled racing. At **Briar's Patch Sled Dogs,** veteran musher Liz Parrish and her team of long-distance racing dogs will take you on an extreme sport wilderness trip, where you'll get to enjoy all of the excitement without doing any of the work.

You won't forget the thrills, from the tension-building moment the dogs are harnessed, bootied, and put into position to the bedlam that erupts as the command is given to "GO!" After whooshing through the forest, you'll return with rosy cheeks and a serious case of perma-grin without the perma-frost. Even in the summer, these eager work-ing dogs are happy to pull you in a rugged, all-terrain cart.

One-hour rides ($60 adult/$35 child) include warm refreshments; half-day ($170 adult/$80 child) and all-day ($300 adult/$145 child) excursions also include lunch. Talk to Liz about dog-sitting for your pups while you're out. 38625 Westside Rd. (based at CrystalWood Lodge); 541/892-3639; www.briarspatchsleddogs.com.

range $60–100. Rooms are crisp and clean, with a full list of amenities includ-ing continental breakfast and afternoon cookies and milk. Afternoon naps are also encouraged. 1220 Main St.; 541/882-6688 or 800/404-6690; www.maverickmotel.com.

Running Y Ranch Resort Lodge: If you enjoy running with a high-brow crowd, as Isis certainly does, you'll love this upscale Western ranch on the grounds of Oregon's only Arnold Palmer–designed golf course. Everything is as nice as you'd expect, from the leather furniture, timbered ceilings,

and flagstone floors to the views of the greens and surrounding mountains. Rates are $180–210 per night, plus a $25 pet fee. Pet-friendly vacation rental homes are also available. 5500 Running Y Rd.; 541/850-5500 or 888/850-0275; www.runningy.com.

More Accommodations: Please look under *Chain Hotels* in the *Resources* section for additional places to stay in this area.

Canada

To a dachshund, which is pronounced DASH-hound up north, Canada seems like an awfully big place. So much of the Great White North requires sled dogs to visit, and taking your mush team on vacation is a subject for a different book entirely. Knowing you'd have your paws full with Washington and Oregon, the Wonder Wieners decided to include only three key destinations in the province of British Columbia: Whistler, Vancouver, and Victoria. Even then, in these incredibly dog-friendly cities, their stubby little legs only got them so far, hardly scratching the surface of the region's dog parks and other recreation possibilities. They spent their short quality time focusing on the urban off-leash areas and a few must-see provincial treasures.

In general, Canada is very dog-friendly and more relaxed than the States. In many parks, having your dogs under voice control is comparable to having them on leash. Restaurants were the only places where the Dachsie Twins found Canada to be as strict as the United States; B.C. health code does not allow dogs on restaurant patios.

Hotel rates vary drastically between seasons and dramatically based on how full they are in these popular international destinations. Exchange rates vary less so, but we've listed all rates for hotels and other expenses in Canadian dollars. The whole region has geared up to host the 2010 Winter Olympics, which would not be a good time to visit, as rates will be exorbitant, if there's any availability left at this point at all. On the other paw, there may be bargains before and after the games, in order to fill vacancies created by the added capacity.

If your canine wants to blend in like a true Canuck, she can start by adding the expression "eh?" at the end of every bark. For example: "Sure is good Canadian maple syrup, eh?" or "I'm renting my house out for the 2010 Olympics for ten grand. Good idea, eh?"

Prior to 9/11, crossing the border from the United States to Canada was a more casual affair, usually requiring only a driver's license or picture ID. Today the rules are strict and uniformly enforced. United States travelers must have a photo ID, like a driver's license, *and* proof of citizenship: either a passport, a NEXUS card, a birth certificate, a naturalization certificate, *or* a citizenship certificate. For canines crossing the border from the United States to Canada, proof of rabies vaccination is required. Bring proof of other shots and a health certificate from your dog's veterinarian, just in case.

CHAPTER 21

British Columbia

In Canada, there are provinces instead of states, and thus, provincial parks instead of state parks. In the province of British Columbia, with the exception of parks listed here, check in advance before visiting regional or provincial parks. Some parks prohibit dogs in the high season, generally May–August, and most prohibit dogs on public beaches June 1–September 15.

The best times for a dog to visit British Columbia are April–May and September 16–October. Lodging establishments call this the shoulder season, and room rates are significantly cheaper than in the high season. This is when provincial parks open up beaches to dogs, but the weather isn't uniformly gray. Vancouverites and Victorians insist they don't get as much drizzle as Seattle; Isis might raise an eyebrow at that, if she had one.

Vancouver and Victoria are within easy reach of the United States, the former a three-hour drive from Seattle, and the latter by a ferry ride from Seattle;

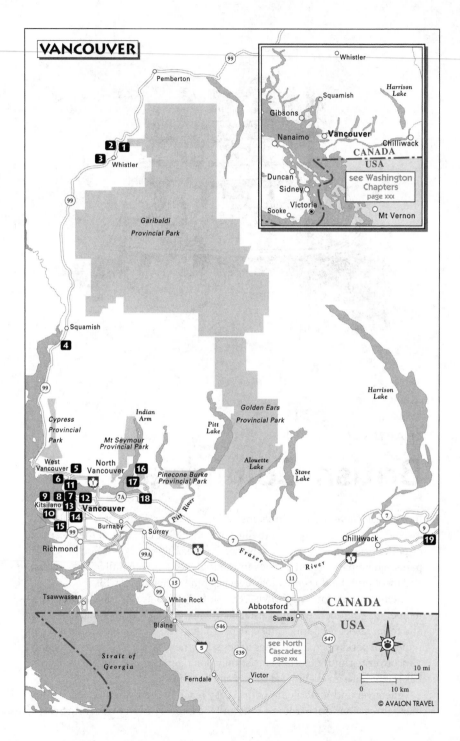

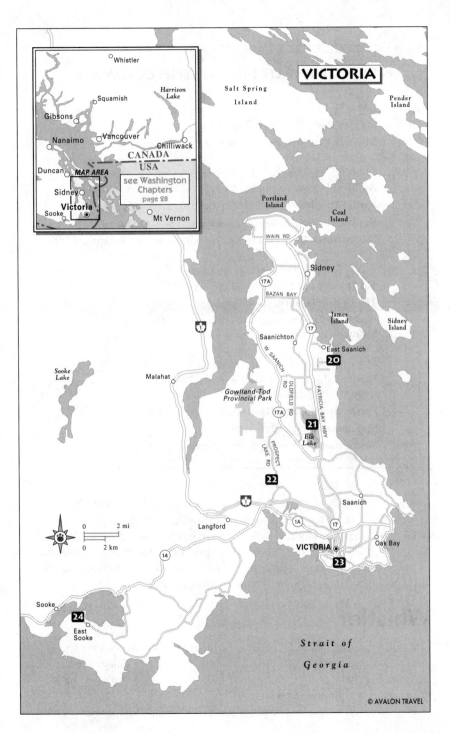

VICTORIA

PICK OF THE LITTER—BRITISH COLUMBIA

BEST PARKS
Stanley Park, West End (page 619)
Belcarra Regional Park, Tri-Cities Area (page 628)

BEST DOG PARKS AND BEACHES
Ambleside Beach and Dog Park, West Vancouver (page 618)
Vanier Dog Beach, Kitsilano (page 620)
Buntzen Lake Dog Beach, Tri-Cities Area (page 627)
Dallas Beach Dog Area in Beacon Hill Park, Victoria (page 635)

BEST PLACES TO EAT
Val D'Isere Brasserie, Whistler (page 614)
The Urban Barkery, Tri-Cities Area (page 629)
Waddling Dog Bar and Grill, Sidney and the
Saanich Peninsula (page 633)

BEST PLACES TO STAY
Pacific Palisades Hotel, Downtown Vancouver and
Gastown (page 625)
Pacific Spirit Guest House, Cambie (page 626)
Magnolia Hotel, Victoria (page 636)
Sooke Harbour House, Sooke (page 640)

Port Angeles, Washington; or Vancouver. Whistler, farther into the imposing mountains, is about a six-hour drive from Seattle, the latter part on the Sea to Sky Highway, a twisty two-lane road sandwiched between the cliffs and the water. This road's dangerous beauty requires attentive driving, preferably in the daytime, although improvements are being made to accommodate the 2010 Olympics. Tires and snow chains are required in winter.

Whistler

The resort municipality of Whistler is an internationally famous ski and golf destination, and everything is priced accordingly. Whistler Village is compact, designed to explore on foot, with a pedestrian-only Village Stroll leading to all the shops, restaurants, and resorts.

Schussing and slicing are two activities not particularly high on a dog's wish list, due to the technical difficulties. To allow you to engage in skiing fun with minimal guilt, hire a pet-sitter from Nannies on Call, who come take care of your "kids" in your hotel room. They charge the same rate for pets, kids, or a combination of both (604/938-2823; www.nanniesoncall.com).

Whistler resorts spoil pets, as does the abundance of open space and fresh mountain air, not to mention a few treats and pats from shops in town. Dogs are required to be on leash in the municipality. They are not allowed on beaches, except ones reserved for them, and they are not allowed on trails on Whistler Mountain or in nearby Garibaldi Provincial Park.

Valley Trail: This paved multi-use path connects all things throughout the valley, including the parks a dog might wish to visit. You can rent bikes and strollers in Whistler Village if walking the 30 kilometers (19 miles) gets too long. There are excellent trail markers at all points along the trail, and most maps of Whistler include the path.

PARKS, BEACHES, AND RECREATION AREAS

◻ Canine Cove at Lost Lake Park

🐾 🐾 🐾 ➤ (See Vancouver map on page 608)

Within walking distance from Whistler Village on the valley trail, Lost Lake Park offers barbecues, picnic areas, sandy beaches, a concession stand, plenty of grassy spots, floating docks, and walk-on docks from several locations around the lake.

The Lost Lake Loop, a wide gravel road, is a great walk. If you start on the

DOG-EAR YOUR CALENDAR

If you are a dachshund fan and your travel plans are taking you anywhere near British Columbia in mid-August, you can experience more than 200 wieners first-hand at the **Annual Picnic and Wiener Walk** organized by the Western Dachshund Club at Winskill Park in Tsawwassen, British Columbia. Since 1998, these hot dogs have been coming—many in costume—to show off in a parade and play games. Stampede! Find out more on the unofficial Canadian dachshund lovers' websitw at www.wienerdogs.org.

In the resort town of Whistler, **DogFest** is held every April, the last weekend of the TELUS World Ski and Snowboard Festival. There's a dog parade, booths, contests, raffles, and general merrymaking and mayhem to support Whistler Animals Galore (WAG) and the Canadian Avalanche Rescue Dog Association (CARDA, www.carda .bc.ca). For this and more WAG events, call 609/935-8364 or go to www.thewagway.com.

trail, to the right around the lake from the main parking lot, you'll reach a private dog beach at about 0.25 mile. Canine Cove has a sandy beach, sitting logs, a bag dispenser, and its own floating dock with a ramp dogs can climb. This exclusive area is a real treat.

Cooper recommends Lost Lake as the most scenic of the three lakes near town, with the best unpaved, easy trails as well. You can get a map online or at visitors centers, but the soft-surface trails winding around south of the lake aren't very long, and eventually you'll hit the Lake Loop or the Valley Trail or Fitzsimmons Creek to get your bearings again. It's a relatively safe area in which to lose yourselves in the woods for a time. In winter, the whole shebang gets converted into a cross-country skiing trail network. Check www.tourism whistler.com and click "Things to Do" for a map.

2 Barking Bay at Rainbow Park

🐾 🐾 🐕 (See Vancouver map on page 608)

Rainbow Park is on the west side of Alta Lake, a large lake south of Whistler Village with several parks. Along Alta, there are long, sandy beaches with walk-on docks, picnic areas with barbecue grills, volleyball courts, and a heritage site with three log cabins. Lucky dogs will find their reward at the end of the Rainbow, at Barking Bay, a private, miniature dog beach and picnic area. The bay has a couple of petite lawns with tables and a sliver of sandy beach. Dock dogs will love their private floating pier. Beyond Barking Bay, dogs must

leash up. If it gets too busy during the summer, dog beach hours may be limited; watch for signs.

One of the most scenic sections of the paved Valley Trail travels between Rainbow Park and Meadow Park, following the river of golden dreams. To protect Whistler's water supply, dogs are not allowed on the Rainbow/Madely Trails above the park.

From Highway 99, 2.7 miles south of the center of Whistler Village, turn west on Alta Lake Road and travel three miles to the paved parking lot. To reach the off-leash beach, go right from the parking lot, through the Railway Crossing bars, across the wide wooden footbridge, and to the right around the lake a few hundred feet.

3 Alpha Lake Park

🐾 🐾 (See Vancouver map on page 608)

A leashed stroll around this small lake is an attractive option for a walk, across a suspended bridge and through light wooded areas. Children get a charge out of the tree-house playground, a focal point of the park. Dogs are allowed in the picnic area, but not on the main beach.

For dogs, water access at Alpha Lake is a fluid concept: Sometimes there is a designated dog area, and sometimes there's not. Occasionally, there's a dog beach with limited hours. It depends on the season, the crowds, and the number of complaints the municipality gets from residents. Watch for any signs, and behave accordingly. Facilities include restrooms and a doggy bag dispenser.

Alpha Lake Park is located in Creekside, 2.5 miles south of Whistler Village. From Highway 99, turn west on Lake Placid Drive, around the bend only about 0.1 mile to the gravel parking area on your right. You can reach the park from the Valley Trail.

PLACES TO EAT

Citta Bistro: Ask a local for a not-too-stuffy place to eat in the Village, and you'll hear Citta nine times out of 10. Best people-watching, best hangout, best patio—Citta wins again. The menu changes regularly, leaning toward lighter fare. The patio is covered and heated for year-round outdoor eating, and dogs have their own hangout area nearby. 4217 Village Stroll; 604/932-4177; www.cittabistro.com.

Dubh Linn Gate Pub: This great Irish bar is one of the most crowded après-ski spots, right at the base of the mountain. The bar stocks 30 draft beers, 28 single-malt scotches, and, without question, Guinness on tap. Although famed for its crab-and-Guinness soup, the pub will serve you food without alcohol in it, if you insist. There's a large outdoor patio, and dogs can tie up nearby, within sight. Whistler Village, Pan Pacific Lodge; 604/905-4047; www.dubhlinngate.com.

Val D'Isere Brasserie: This full-service French restaurant is one of your most elegant dog-friendly choices in town, with patio tables in the summer season only. Ask to be seated around the border of the patio, where there is a low rock wall your dog can relax up against and a couple of lampposts where you could secure his leash if needed. 4314 Main Street; 604/932-4666; www.valdisere-restaurant.com.

Zogs Dogs: At summertime kiosk locations in Whistler Village and at the Sundial Lodge, Zogs serves a signature dog smothered in spaghetti sauce and mozzarella cheese (don't knock it until you've tried it), fries smothered in gravy, and "beaver tails" (fried dough in various cheesy and spicy flavors). There's lots of smothering going on at Zogs. This is an order-at-the-window, sit-outside kind of affair. Village Stroll, 4340 Sundial Cres; 604/938-6644.

PLACES TO STAY

Adara Whistler: Let's face it, sometimes Whistler can come across as a little stuffy, a wee uptight, which is what makes Adara so refreshingly different by comparison. It is for the young and relaxed, the hip and contemporary. It felt, finally, as though they weren't taking everything quite so seriously. They're smart to set themselves apart from the pack, even choosing a name at the beginning of the alphabet, starting things off on the right foot. Pets are free, and they're going to love the atmosphere, the cheeky furniture, the dog biscuits, bed, and bowl. Now, mind you, all this modernity still comes with high-class amenities at no lower rates than the other four-star wonders, ranging $120–600 per night. 4122 Village Green; 604/905-4009; www.adarawhistler.com.

Crystal Lodge: This mid-range hotel is at the base of both Whistler and Blackcomb Mountains. Dogs are greeted with a welcome letter and pet beds, in rooms on two of the three floors. All rooms are nonsmoking. Rates range $150–400 for traditional rooms, higher for suites; the pet fee is $20, max two dogs. 4154 Village Green; 800/667-3363; www.crystal-lodge.com.

Delta Whistler Village Suites: The policy states pets should be under 50 pounds, yet the reservationists we spoke to had never turned away a four-legged friend (the front desk is full of dog lovers). The cookie basket for humans is always full at the registration desk, and bellhops are notorious for carrying pet treats in their pockets. The Delta has a center courtyard with grass, and the trails of Lost Lake are about 10 minutes away. As suites, the units are typically booked for longer stays, and as such, the pet fee is calculated at $35 every five nights; rates are $150–240 for the smallest studios, up to $400–630 for king suites. 4308 Main St.; 604/905-3987; www.deltahotels.com.

Fairmont Chateau Whistler: This five-star Fairmont property is high on the luxury scale. The pet fee is $25 total per night, and they'll allow a couple of pets per room, as they said, as long as there's no fighting among them. The hotel will send up biscuits, water bowls, and beds for pet guests. You'll lack nothing. Rates range $235–1500 for standard rooms, depending on the season. 800/606-8244; www.chateauwhistler.com.

Four Seasons Whistler: You will want for nothing at this, the only five-diamond resort in Canada. Nestled in the Upper Village at the base of Blackcomb Mountain, you can be sure this is where visiting dignitaries will be housed, come the 2010 Olympics. Treat bags and dog beds are lovingly provided. Dog-sitters, walking services, and perhaps any other service you care to pay for are arranged for visitors by expert concierges without the bat of an eye. There are no pet fees or restrictions for those able to lavish $295–1500 per night, with five-night minimums during holidays. 4591 Blackcomb Way; 604/935-3400; www.fourseasons.com/whistler.

Summit Lodge: The contemporary furnishings at this four-star Kimpton boutique hotel are designed to help you and Rover relax and restore. A secluded walkway behind the hotel meanders along Fitzsimmons Creek. Dog lovers get treats and bags at check-in, and there are no pet fees or limits, but you must ask specifically for a nonsmoking room if you want one. Rates range $110–475. 4359 Main Street; 604/932-2778 or 800-KIMPTON; www.summitlodge.com.

Tantalus Lodge: The Tantalus Lodge has large, fully equipped, two-bedroom, two-bath suites, which are good for families, and 6.5 acres of property, good for pets. The Delta hotels in Whistler, including the Tantalus, go the extra mile to let people know they are pet friendly, with a full set of pet goodies and convenience items listed on the website. Rates are based on four-person occupancy and range widely, based on season and demand, $100–700. There is a $35 one-time cleaning fee for a maximum of two medium-sized pets. 4200 Whistler Way; 604/932-4146 or 888/633-4046; www.tantaluslodge.com.

Squamish

In a country legendary for outdoor recreation, this town's claim as Canada's capital of outdoor recreation seems excessive. Then again, after climbing Stawamus Chief Mountain, you may feel like you've done all of Canada. When heading to Whistler, some people choose to stay in Squamish, about 45 minutes south, for cheaper accommodations and all kinds of hiking, biking, rafting, golfing, bird-watching, horseback riding, and other things you can do with dogs.

PARKS, BEACHES, AND RECREATION AREAS

🐾 Shannon Falls Provincial Park
🐾🐾 🐾 (See Vancouver map on page 608)

People are falling all over themselves to get to Shannon Falls. At 335 meters (1,105 feet), it is British Columbia's third-highest falls, one of the most popular picnic spots along the Sea to Sky corridor. It's worth a look to see the spray foam and tumble over the smooth granite walls, even though your pup might feel the pinch of the crowds during all but the earliest days of spring or the last gasps of fall. There are 500,000 annual visitors in the park but only 50,000 on the hike up Stawamus Chief Mountain, a great place to take a fit canine if you want to cut the crowds.

This monolith is internationally famous among climbers, and its smooth granite face has appeared on more than its share of outdoor-type magazine covers. There are three summit points you can hike to, depending on how far—or rather how high—you choose to go. The hikes range from four to seven miles round-trip. The trails can be reached from the parking lot and viewpoint at Shannon Falls, where there is a basic and a topographic map of the trails. The hikes are all challenging, steady climbs that will really get your and your pooch's blood pumping.

Shannon Falls Provincial Park is located two miles (three km) south of Squamish and 16 miles (25 km) north of Horseshoe Bay on Vancouver's North Shore. Parking is $1 per hour or $3 per day by automated ticket machine. Open 7 A.M.–10 P.M.

PLACES TO EAT

Cheekye Bar and Grill: This restaurant is out there, out near the Cheekye River, close to great fishing and rafting at the Sunwolf Outdoor Centre. The owners always play blues music, frequently smoke their own salmon and chicken and make their own bread and burgers, and often seem to have dogs around the picnic tables in the garden below the outdoor deck. 70002 Squamish Valley Rd.; 604/898-4011.

PLACES TO STAY

Sunwolf Outdoor Centre: Come to the Sunwolf's cabins when you want to escape. This is where nightlife is a hoot owl and rush hour is the rushing waters of the Cheekye, Cheakamus, and Squamish Rivers. This mountain resort and river rafting tour company is situated on 5.5 acres of park and wooded land, where dogs get a new lease on life by being unleashed and by jumping into the water if the spirit moves them. The Sunwolf is an equal-opportunity pet facility, accepting snakes, cats, llamas, etc., in addition to good old Snoopys. Five cabins have kitchenettes, and all 10 renovated cabins have showers, cathedral ceilings, gas fireplaces, fir floors, and handcrafted pine furniture, nothing more or less than you need. The main lodge is a perfect place to meet, gather information, and plan an outing. Basic cabins are $90 per night; cabins with kitchenettes are $100. There is a flat $10 fee per visit for pets. 70002 Squamish Valley Rd.; 604/898-1537 or 877/806-8046; www.sunwolf.net.

North Vancouver

Although it was once called "Moodyville," after lumber baron Sewell Prescott Moody, North Vancouver has been an incorporated city, separate from Vancouver, since 1907. The main draw here is the Capilano Bridge tourist attraction, one that visitors can enjoy with their pets.

PARKS, BEACHES, AND RECREATION AREAS

5 Capilano Suspension Bridge and Park

🐾 🐾 ◀● (See Vancouver map on page 608)

The Capilano Suspension Bridge is Vancouver's biggest attraction, surrounded by the serenity of a 300-year-old West Coast rainforest. Even dogs with strong stomachs will appreciate that today's bridge is held up by steel cables, capable of supporting two fully loaded 747s, as opposed to the twisted hemp ropes used in the first bridge, built in 1889. Capilano Bridge is a dizzying 230 feet above the canyon floor and a dazzling 450 feet across. Each step creates a wave of action on the bridge surface.

Capilano Park continues to preserve and show the art and culture of First Nations artists, ever since Native people were invited to place totem poles and life-size red cedar statues in the park in the 1930s. The collection of totems and the ongoing work at the Big House Carving Centre are areas you shouldn't miss on a visit. If you have kids of the two-legged variety, every area has extensive

THINK GLOBALLY, BARK LOCALLY

The British Columbia Society for the Prevention of Cruelty to Animals (BCSPCA) has six thrift stores in and around the Vancouver area that contribute valuable funds each year for the operation of animal shelters. The **SPCA Thrift Stores** receive donations, similar to Goodwill, and volunteers run the stores. The couple of locations in Vancouver are below. More stores and information is available at www.spca.bc.ca.

- **Vancouver (West)**
  Furniture: 3626 West Broadway; Clothing: 3606 West Broadway
  604/736-4136, 10 A.M.–6:30 P.M. Monday–Sunday

- **Vancouver (East)**
  5239 Victoria Drive (at 37th)
  604/321-8144, 10 A.M.–6:30 P.M. Monday–Sunday

displays to teach and entertain them. The West Coast Rainforest trails, short walks through old-growth evergreens, will round out the adventure for Rover.

From downtown Vancouver, cross through Stanley Park over the Lions Gate Bridge and travel north one mile on Capilano Road. Dogs are allowed everywhere except on the Treetop Adventure, in the gift shop, or in the Bridge House Restaurant. The park is open every day except December 25. Summer hours are 8:30 A.M.–dusk; winter hours are 9 A.M.–5 P.M. Cost is $23.50 per day for adults; dogs aren't charged. 3735 Capilano Rd.; 604/985-7474; www.capbridge.com.

PLACES TO EAT

Canyon Café and Logger's Grill: From May through September, this food stand in Capilano Park cooks up beef, chicken, and salmon burgers and feeds hungry park-goers with homemade pizza, muffins, and cookies. It's an over-the-counter affair, with plenty of open seating. 3735 Capilano Rd.; 604/985-7474; www.capbridge.com.

West Vancouver

The city of Vancouver and surrounding cities and suburbs have an extensive network of full-time and part-time off-leash areas. In all, there are 31 off-leash parks in Vancouver for responsible owners and well-behaved dogs. These dog beaches and parks are rarely secured by fences or gates, reinforcing the expectation that you have complete voice control of your dog. You are required to pick up after your dog, carry a leash at all times, and observe the designated boundaries and time limits. There are excellent aerial photographs of the off-leash boundaries on the Vancouver Park Board website. Go to www.city .vancouver.bc.ca/parks, select "ParkFinder," and choose "Dog Off-Leash Areas" in the search engine. Of a few outstanding dog destinations, West Vancouver starts it all off with one of the best.

PARKS, BEACHES, AND RECREATION AREAS

6 Ambleside Beach and Dog Park

🐾🐾🐾🐾🦮 (See Vancouver map on page 608)

Parts of this district park are off-limits to dogs, whether leashed or not, but almost nine acres of it is all for the dogs, whether leashed or not. The eastern half of Ambleside is a beautiful sandy off-leash beach, with extensive fields, bunches of trees, and a paved path for dogs' human companions, with views of Vancouver, Stanley Park, Lions Gate Bridge, and Burrard Inlet. Your dog will agree it's a great place to watch sunsets over Vancouver Island, especially if you got there in time for sunrise the same day.

The off-leash area is bordered by the end of the parking lot, the pitch and putt course with a high fence, the railroad with a high fence, the Capilano River, and the inlet. Bags, water bowls, and seawall bench seating are scattered around.

Cross the Lions Gate Bridge north through Stanley Park, turn left on Marine Drive, and left on 13th Street, down the hill and curving to the left into the park. To reach the off-leash area, stay on the road until you can't go any farther, and at the end of that parking lot will be the west end of the OLA. There will be parking problems on sunny weekends and holidays.

West End

Beaches, big parks, and sidewalk cafés abound in the West End, all good news for those whose pleasures come cheap in the form of trees, dirt, and water. On the opposite end of the spectrum, the West End is particularly famous among visitors for Robson Street, a fashionable boutique dining and shopping thoroughfare, good news for those whose designer passions are a bit more dear.

PARKS, BEACHES, AND RECREATION AREAS

7 Stanley Park

(See Vancouver map on page 608)

Stanley Park is Vancouver's first park, established in 1888. At about ("a-boot" as the Canadians say) 1000 acres, it is North America's third-largest urban park. There are so many things to do and see in this city park, it shouldn't concern you that many of them don't involve dogs. The internal hiking trails, the gardens, and the lagoons can take days to explore, if you have the luxuries of time and stamina. Drawing an estimated eight million annual visitors, Stanley Park is never quiet; nothing this good ever is.

Cooper and Isis chose to get to the heart of what's best about the park by staying around its perimeter, on the 5.5-mile Seawall Promenade. To them, everything else is the white chocolate coating on the biscuit. It took nearly six decades to complete the seawall, from the 1920s to the 1980s. For most of the way, the paved trail is divided to separate pedestrians and leashed dogs from cyclists and inline skaters. Every section of the trail adds another vista or attraction to the list, some of which can be enjoyed simply from a drive through the park.

From downtown, take Georgia Street W., Highway 99/1A, west to Stanley Park Drive, find the nearest parking lot, and start walking. Parking is $4 per day. Parking lots are open 6 A.M.–9 P.M. April–September, 7 A.M.–6 P.M. October–March. 604/257-8400.

Kitsilano

"Kits" is one of the younger, hipper neighborhoods in Vancouver, with rows of California bungalows, Craftsman-style homes, lining its fashionable streets. Our coverage of dog parks in Vancouver proper starts in this area, with a whopper of an off-leash beach.

PARKS, BEACHES, AND RECREATION AREAS

8 Vanier Dog Beach

🐾🐾🐾🐾 🦀 (See Vancouver map on page 608)

Dogs are loving life at Vanier. As designated dog areas go, it doesn't get much better than this. The off-leash area of the park includes a large lawn on the bluff, a portion of the waterfront trail, and prime beachfront real estate, which is where you'll find all the barkers clustered. The leash-free zone is the area behind and to the west of the Vancouver Maritime Museum. The beach itself is down a short set of stairs; just follow the splashing sounds. Large driftwood logs give you a place to relax, close enough to the water to keep you from injuring your stick-throwing arm. From Vanier, you can leash up and walk along the water all the way through Hadden Park to Kitsilano Beach Park. Vanier Park hosts Bard on the Beach, Shakespearean outdoor theater, in the summer; however, dogs are not allowed in theater areas, not even those who can bark in verse.

From downtown, cross the Burrard Bridge and bear to the right onto Cornwall Avenue. Turn right almost immediately on Chestnut Drive to the end. It costs $1.25 per hour, maximum of four hours, to park in the museum lot in front of the OLA. If it's not too crowded, you may be able to find street parking by turning left on Ogden in front of the museum and left on Maple a block down.

Off-leash hours are 6–10 A.M. and 5–10 P.M. May–September and 6 A.M.–10 P.M. October–April. 1000 Chestnut Street; 604/257-8689.

9 Kitsilano Beach

🐾🐾 (See Vancouver map on page 608)

The city's fashionable people have been coming to Kits Beach for more than a hundred years to soak up the sun and, honestly, to check each other out. While dogs aren't allowed on the sand, canines are a trendy accessory for picnickers up on the wide lawns, judging by the number of fur-wearers basking alongside the bikinis and board shorts. Walking along the waterfront around Kits, leash in hand, is a good way to meet Vancouver's young and restless. When your dog stops to sniff that cute stranger's dog, it's a natural segue to strike up a conversation about the great views of the North Shore mountains and downtown, your need for a knowledgeable tour guide while visiting the city… that sort of thing.

From downtown, cross the Burrard Bridge and veer to the right on Cornwall Avenue. Turn right on Arbutus Street. Parking is $1 for two hours, $3 all day, by automated machine. 1499 Arbutus Street.

PLACES TO EAT

Bean Brothers: Sidewalk seating is a natural at this casual café and coffee shop, serving light lunches and dinners and pizza by the slice. 2179 West 41st Ave.; 604/266-2185.

Incendio West: The sidewalk café tables with colorful umbrellas lend such a European air to this brick-oven pizzeria and fresh pasta shop that it has frequently been used for on-location TV and film shooting as "an unspecified city somewhere in Italy or France." It's easy for your dog to sit with you at the Kitsilano location: 2118 Burrard St.; 604/736-2220. A second Gastown location has an enclosed patio, where dogs would have to sit on the other side of the railing: 103 Columbia St.; 604/688-8694; www.incendio.ca.

The Smoking Dog Bistro: This classy restaurant wins accolades and awards for its authentic French cuisine. The outdoor dining scene is hot at *Le Chien Qui Fume,* and neither you nor your dog have to light up to enjoy it. 1889 West 1st Ave.; 604/732-8811; www.thesmokingdog.com.

Three Dog Bakery: Cooper and Isis have no qualms about advertising this franchise, the original, and still one of the best, dog-exclusive bakeries in North America. 2186 W. 4th Ave.; 604/737-3647.

Point Grey

PARKS, BEACHES, AND RECREATION AREAS

🔟 Spanish Banks West Dog Beach

🐾🐾🐾 🐸 (See Vancouver map on page 608)

As you pass miles of beach parks along West Point Grey—Jericho, Locarno, Spanish Bank East—your dog will be sorely tempted to jump out of the car and run to the water. At the very least, he'll beg to walk along the seaside trail, which he's welcome to do on leash. But if he can wait just a bit longer, he can taste freedom and be left to his own dog devices on the off-leash zones of Spanish Banks West.

In the off-leash area, across the wide lawns and picnic tables, past the willow trees, and beyond the paved waterfront walk is a long and narrow beach, with choice sand and gentle lapping waves. The park has great views of the water and mountains and is far enough from downtown to avoid the worst of the crowds, canine and otherwise.

From downtown, take the Granville Bridge and go west on 4th Avenue W., past Jerico Beach Park. At the sign for Spanish Banks, bear right onto N.W. Marine Drive and patiently follow the road all the way to the end of the last parking lot you see before Acadia Beach and Pacific Spirit Regional Park. From there, the entire area in front of you is the OLA. Off-leash hours are 6 A.M.–10 P.M. 4801 N.W. Marine Dr.; 604/257-8689.

1️⃣1️⃣ Pacific Spirit Regional Park

🐾🐾🐾 🐕 (See Vancouver map on page 608)

The Greater Vancouver Regional District takes the intelligent approach that dogs are great companions for exercise, safety, and socializing in parks. To welcome an average of 360,000 (!) dog visits per year at Pacific Spirit Regional Park, the GVRD has created a map to designate three levels of hiking options—no dogs, dogs on leash, and leash-optional hiking—to educate and enforce good canine etiquette and to protect the park's sensitive areas and wildlife.

Sure, lots of dogs visit Pacific Spirit, but it's a big park, 1,800 acres with 34 miles of trails. It takes some studying of the park map, available online, before you can figure it out. Cooper likes to start on the north end of the park, from the small parking area immediately to the west of Spanish Banks Park. All the trails up into the woods are leash optional from this starting point. Along the waterfront, dogs are prohibited March–August.

Follow the directions to Spanish Banks West, going past the city's parking lot to a gravel lot for the GVRD park. Open 8 A.M.–7 P.M., as late as 11 P.M. in the summer. 604/224-5739; www.gvrd.bc.ca/parks/PacificSprit.htm.

Granville Island

This hidden spot is a great place to spend a few hours. Dozens of outdoor shops and market stands sell seafood, jewelry, crafts, fresh fruit and vegetables, and cut flowers. There are food vendor kiosks where you can grab a bite to eat and sit on a bench to watch the other people and dogs go by. Several stores are dog friendly, especially Blackberry Books (1666 Johnston St.; 604/685-4113; bbooks.ca), which offers dog treats.

Parking is tough on Granville Island, so your best bet is to take the inexpensive and fun False Creek Ferry. It's a short ride from downtown on the north to Granville, and as an added bonus, there's a tiny off-leash dog beach next to the north ferry terminal at Sunset Beach. Ferries run continuously 7 A.M.–10:30 P.M. in summer, until 8:30 P.M. in winter. 604/684-7781; www.granvilleislandferries.bc.ca.

PARKS, BEACHES, AND RECREATION AREAS

12 Sutcliffe Park and the Island Park Walk

🐾 (See Vancouver map on page 608)

There's no chance Isis would allow your dog to be stuck on an island with no place to pee. For a dog who weighs 12 pounds soaking wet, she manages to wet more than her fair share of blades of grass in pursuit of the perfect piddle. She declares these petite gardens, ponds, and stone-paver promenades will do nicely, thank you, discreetly hidden between the shops of Granville Island and the condos surrounding it.

As you drive onto Granville Island on Anderson Street, Sutcliffe Park and the Island Park Walk are to the right. The closest parking is near the Woofles and Meowz pet specialty diner, what a coincidence, or in front of The Cat's Meow.

PLACES TO EAT

The Cat's Meow: Vancouverites do indeed consider this diner with American flair to be the cat's meow. Your bow-wow can sit along the fringes of the patio, lassoed to a wooden railing, consoled with a water bowl. 1540 Old Bridge St.; 604/647-2287; www.thecatsmeow.ca.

Dockside Restaurant: Dining al fresco is possible for more of the year at Granville Island Hotel's patio, with sun umbrellas, overhead gas heaters, garden flowers, and colorful tablecloths, plus views of False Creek, Vancouver City's skyline, and the Coastal Mountains. The transition from the patio to Granville Island's brick streets is pretty seamless, allowing dogs to sit nearby and graciously accept the water bowls and treats put out for them. 1253 Johnston St.; 604/685-7070; www.docksidebrewing.com.

Granville Island Brewery: The taproom and gift shop at the GIB are dog friendly, and you can taste limited release beers from Canada's first microbrewery. 1441 Cartwright St.; 604/687-2739; www.gib.ca.

Woofles and Meowz: This specialty store on Granville Island is where dogs and cats go to grab a bite to eat. Located in a caboose, still parked on a section of unconnected track, this pet deli prides itself on 100 percent natural treats and an unusual assortment of accessories and customized toys. 1496 Cartwright St.; 604/689-3647; www.wooflesandmeowz.com.

PLACES TO STAY

Granville Island Hotel: The pet-friendly rooms at this boutique hotel with a modern bent have marble floors, and most have views of Vancouver and the surrounding waters of False Creek. Rates range $150–230. The pet fee is $25. 1253 Johnston St.; 604/683-7373 or 800/663-1840; www.granvilleislandhotel.com.

Downtown Vancouver and Gastown

Of all the things to do in downtown Vancouver, shopping and dining on Robson Street hits the top of the list, followed in short order by a visit to Gastown, the birthplace of Vancouver and the location of Vancouver's most-photographed icon, the Gastown Steam Clock (www.seegastown.com).

PARKS, BEACHES, AND RECREATION AREAS

13 CRAB–Portside Dog Park

🐾🐾🐾🦀 (See Vancouver map on page 608)

From your perch on a big rock, a driftwood log, or a bench, you can sit and reflect on life, watching the tugboats tug and the container ships being loaded and the few dogs running circles around each other. This medium-sized park has the closest off-leash area to the downtown core, but locals say it's not heavily used. It's nice enough, with gently sloping green lawns, a crushed-rock walkway, and restroom, water fountain, and garbage facilities. It could be underutilized because it's in an industrial area or because the water doesn't meet safety standards for people to swim in it. It serves a dog's purposes perfectly, as long as you're comfortable with your canine cavorting in an unfenced area.

From downtown, go north on Main Street, Highway 99A/1A, through Chinatown, over the bridge and around to the left onto Waterfront Road. The park will be to your right. The only parking for miles is a pay lot a block to your left. It's $2 per hour, $4 per day. That little devil sitting on your shoulder, suggesting you might as well stay longer, looks surprisingly like your dog. No dogs are allowed within 15 meters (50 feet) of the playground. Off-leash hours are 6–10 A.M. and 5–10 P.M. 101 E. Waterfront Rd.; 604/257-8400.

PLACES TO EAT

Brioche Urban Baking and Catering: This Italian-meets-West-Coast casual eatery apologizes for its big selection and inventive daily specials, knowing that doesn't make it easier for you to choose between dashing in for a pastry and a cuppa to go or a full meal made from scratch, relaxing with furry friends at summertime sidewalk tables. 401 Cordova St. W.; 604/682-4037; www.brioche.ca.

PLACES TO STAY

Georgian Court Hotel: All of this hotel's roomy quarters combine gracious, old-world style with newfangled amenities such as pillow-top mattresses and high-speed Internet. Two small pets are welcome for a flat $30 cleaning fee per visit. Nightly rates in high season (May 1–Ocober 15) range $260–340; low season (October 16–April 30) rates range $200–270. 773 Beatty St.; 800/663-1155; www.georgiancourt.com.

    Pacific Palisades Hotel: Located on trendy Robson Street in downtown Vancouver, the Pacific Palisades has South Beach Florida–inspired decor to brighten up those rainy, gray Vancouver days. Citrus-colored interiors look out to great views of the mountains, city, or harbor. This boutique embraces the legendary pet-friendliness of all Kimpton hotels, featuring a Four Paws Program. Dogs receive a Doggie Bag including freshly baked dog biscuits, plastic bags, a souvenir orange flying disc, and discount coupons for local pet stores. Pet owners will receive a complimentary glass of wine and, through the concierge, can arrange for day care or an appointment at a local grooming salon (for their dogs or for themselves). Rates range $160–250. 1277 Robson St.; 800/663-1815; www.pacificpalisadeshotel.com.

    More Accommodations: Please look under *Chain Hotels* in the *Resources* section for additional places to stay in this area.

Cambie

PARKS, BEACHES, AND RECREATION AREAS

🔟 Queen Elizabeth Park Dog Area
🐾🐾🐾 (See Vancouver map on page 608)
The top of this posh and straight-laced 130-acre city park is the highest point in the city, 505 feet above sea level. From the lookouts, about 6 million visitors a year admire the 360-degree view of the Vancouver skyline. These throngs then head to the North Quarry Garden to find nearly all trees native to Canada, exotic plants from other countries, and the Bloedel Conservatory's floral displays.

Meanwhile, on the south end of the park and worlds away from the social awareness of the multitudes, local dogs and a few tail wags "in the know" happily romp in peace and quiet in QE's off-leash area. The designated dog area is a plain affair, an open plateau of grass bordered by a few small trees and protected by the ritzy homes of this desirable residential neighborhood. The OLA is kept hush-hush, not listed on the brochures or maps given to the general public. It'll be our little secret.

The off-leash area is bordered by 37th Avenue, the tennis courts, a pitch and putt course, and the driveway into the parking lot. There are minimal facilities in this section of the park.

From downtown Vancouver, take Cambie Bridge south and stay on Cambie Street until you see signs to the park. Turn left on W. 33rd Avenue, bear right on Kerrsland, turn left on W. 37th Avenue, and left into the parking lot east of Columbia Street. Off-leash hours are 6 A.M.–10 P.M. 4600 Cambie St.; 604/257-8689.

PLACES TO EAT

Meinhardt Fine Foods: This gourmet market gives the Dachsie Twins' mom fits of pleasure. Put together a picnic or meal of your dreams from the store shelves. If you aren't in a do-it-yourself mood, get prepared delicacies from the deli counter or the affiliated mini-café, **The Picnic Table.** 3002 Granville St.; 604/732-4405; www.meinhardt.com.

PLACES TO STAY

Pacific Spirit Guest House: When Coop 'n' Isis were putting the book together, this bed-and-breakfast held the honor of being Vancouver's only certified pet-friendly facility, a new program in Canada that recognizes establishments where your pets are as welcome as you are. The Garden Room and the Cedar Room are West Coast casual and instantly comforting, sharing a living room with a wood-burning fireplace and a bath with a full tub. Pets will cost you a total of $20 per night, which covers a list of Very Important Pet services too long to include here and a $5 gift certificate to Three Dog Bakery. Plus, the Guest House is a block away from the regional park of the same name, the largest off-leash park in the city. Rooms start at $100 per night. 4080 West 35th Ave.; 604/261-6837 or 866/768-6837; www.vanbb.com.

Kerrisdale

It's worth a stroll along West 41st Street in this district to find many cute cafés with outdoor seating, where you can stake out a prime people-watching spot. Vancouverite dogs socialize at the **Fetch** dog boutique during yappi hour, while their owners paw over the latest in all things dog related (5617 W. Boulevard; 604/879-3647; www.fetchstore.ca).

PARKS, BEACHES, AND RECREATION AREAS

15 Fraser River Dog Park

🐾🐾🐾 🐕 (See Vancouver map on page 608)

This neighborhood park allows dogs free reign over the whole park territory for select hours. The gigantic fields on the east end are well suited to any activity involving dogs who believe people were put on the earth for the sole purpose of throwing something for them to fetch. Marsh boardwalks and docks and a waterfront trail are great for scenic walks, looking out on the north arm of the Fraser River, fashionable homes on the north side, and the Vancouver International Airport and container barges to the south. It's a good bird-watching spot, with blue herons that don't seem the least bit intimidated by the dogs.

The only drawback is a lack of convenient water access. Against the banks of the river are large granite boulders, called rip-rap, to act as channel and bank erosion control. The sharp rocks are too big and too plentiful to scramble over safely. There are convenient restrooms, water fountains, and garbage bins.

From downtown, take Granville Street south, turn right on 70th Avenue W., left on Barnard Street, and right on W. 75th Avenue to Angus Drive. Off-leash hours are 6–10 A.M. and 5–10 P.M. 8705 Angus Dr.; 604/257-8689.

Tri-Cities Area

You might as well roll over and play dead if you come all the way up to Vancouver and don't go the extra kilometer to day-trip destinations in the Coquitlam, Port Coquitlam, and Port Moody area, some of the biggest and brightest dog and people parks in the region, about 18 miles outside the city.

PARKS, BEACHES, AND RECREATION AREAS

16 Buntzen Lake Dog Beach

🐾🐾🐾🐾 🐕 (See Vancouver map on page 608)

When dogs dream, they dream of Buntzen Lake, their legs churning in time to the count of the steps it takes to run from the gate to the water. The lake sure looks like a piece of heaven, with crystal-clear waters and clean sandy beaches with a mountain backdrop. You'd never suspect that it's an artificial reservoir; it has even fooled the cameras for misty morning and late-night shots in *X Files* episodes.

Try not to be put off by all the Dogs Prohibited signs in the rest of the recreation area. It's hard enough to manage the masses of petless people who want to lap up the sun and water of Buntzen. The designated dog beach is a special place, one of three off-leash options in the park. When you pass the park gates, go into the first parking lot to your right, to the end, to the trail leading to the off-leash beach. After a trot of maybe 0.1 mile, you'll see the gate. It's fenced on three sides, with the fences extending into the water to neatly divide dogdom from the main south beach area. The sand is soft, there are trees and picnic benches, and Buntzen Creek burbles through. Past the last main parking area is another off-leash section for dogs who would rather sink their claws into the turf, but it doesn't have quite the same curb appeal as the beach. There's a 0.6-kilometer out-and-back off-leash trail from the parking lot to the equestrian area. Skip it. Any part of the extensive hiking and biking system around the lake is better, and leashed dogs are welcome on all trails.

Exit the Trans-Canada Highway on Ioco Road and follow the signs to wind up and over on Heritage Mountain Boulevard, Parkside Drive, East Road, and Sunnyside Road. Turn right at the T intersection on Sunnyside Road to get to Buntzen. Hours change with the seasons. Avoid Buntzen and Belcarra on sunny summer days. The parks get so crowded that there are quotas, so you may be turned away at the gates. 604/469-9679; www.bchyrdo.com/recreation.

🔟🖤 Belcarra Regional Park

🐾🐾🐾🐾 (See Vancouver map on page 608)

Covering more than 2,600 acres, this provincial park is in every sense a huge destination for Vancouverites. Like nearby Buntzen, Sasamat Lake turns away all but the earliest arrivals from its crowded shores. Unlike Buntzen, there are no dog areas designated on the beach. Dogs are limited to leashed hikes on the many park trails, limits any dog we know would be willing to accept. Detailed maps are available from the park's concession stand. Cooper recommends the easy 1.5-mile Sasamat Lake Loop, the moderate four-mile Cod Rock Trail, and the moderately difficult three-mile Jug Island spur, the last only if you're up for the ups and down of hills and stairs. There are views everywhere you look.

Exit the Trans-Canada Highway to Ioco Road and follow the signs to wind up and over on Heritage Mountain Boulevard, Parkside Drive, East Road, and Sunnyside Road. Turn left at the T intersection on Sunnyside Road to Bedwell Bay Road. Signs will guide you the whole way. 604/432-6359; www.gvrd.bc.ca/parks/Belcarra.htm.

🔟🖤 Rocky Point Park

🐾🐾🐕 (See Vancouver map on page 608)

For those dogs among us who need a little extra reinforcement to keep them nearby when allowed off leash—and you know who you are—Cooper and Isis decided to toss in this little off-leash area, the only one included that is fenced and gated. The dog run has the full complement of necessary items, including a bag dispenser and garbage, benches, a double-gate with a leash-up area, and a water pump. The surface is dirt and sand, with grassy patches holding on for dear life in the corners. A few trees surround a natural gully where all the tennis balls end up, ensuring the balls are muddy *and* slobbery when you get them returned to you by eager retrievers.

For the scenic route from Vancouver, take Hastings Street E. from downtown all the way out. It will become Highway 7A. After you see the Port Moody signs, take the left exit onto Clark Street, turn left on Moody Street, cross the bridge and cloverleaf around, turn left on Murray Street, and travel 0.2 mile past the main park entrance and the skate park to the fenced OLA. There's room for three or four cars to park on the gravel.

PLACES TO EAT

Anducci's: It's a lovely day and you're looking for a patio, a place to enjoy the good life with your best friend. This authentic Italian restaurant hits the spot, with fresh salads and pastas, and different food and drink specials every day for lunch and dinner. 2729 Barnet Hwy.; 604/468-9002; www.anduccis.com.

The Urban Barkery: Sorry, kids, you've had your share; these bakery treats are for dogs only. The pastry case is full of lovingly handmade, all-natural treats, and the store carries raw and natural pet foods, stylish gear, and funky toys for your fuzzy buddy. 1410 Parkway Blvd.; 604/945-3647; www.urban barkery.com.

Chilliwack and Harrison Hot Springs

About an hour and a half east of Vancouver, Chilliwack is a popular vacation getaway for Vancouverites. In the hot springs resort town of Harrison, dogs are welcome anywhere on the lake except the small lagoon. The world's most talented sand sculptors come to Harrison Hot Springs every September to create new inventions for the annual World Championship Sand Sculpture Competition. With your dog, you can enjoy the sculptures from outside the fence; you'll have good views and you won't have to pay the entry fee.

PARKS, BEACHES, AND RECREATION AREAS

19 Bridal Veil Falls Provincial Park

😾 (See Vancouver map on page 608)

To dogs, it's a little jaunt in the woods, capped by a 300-meter-high, cascading drinking fountain at the end. A half-mile looped dirt trail, uphill to the falls, downhill back, takes visitors to the park's signature feature, worth seeing if you're a waterfall buff and for a photo op. Coop 'n' Isis's Grandmom, who visited it with us, said it was her favorite part of the trip; if you're an active dog looking for a serious romp, maybe not. There were eight picnic tables near the foot of the trail, but with busloads of people pulling up to see the lacy falls, it's not a very secluded stop. Bridal Veil Falls is prone to freezing during colder winters, which results in the formation of an unstable ice wall. During this time, the base of the falls is a hazardous area.

The park is located on the south side of the Fraser River, 16 kilometers east of Chilliwack. Take Exit 135 off the Trans-Canada Highway and follow the signs.

PLACES TO EAT

Harrison Pizza: The outdoor tables are naturally warmed by the heat coming from the pizza ovens. If you're not a pizza fan, go for the salads, ice cream, tasty fried chicken, and jo-jos (those thick fried potato wedges). 160 Lillooet, Harrison Hot Springs; 604/796-2023.

Miss Margarets: This to-go deli in the lobby of Harrison Hot Springs Resort shares outside tables with the hotel bar. Get your sandwich, salad, pastries, and drinks to go and sit at a table around the patio perimeter. 100 Esplanade Ave., Harrison Hot Springs; 800/663-2266.

PLACES TO STAY

Harrison Hot Springs Resort and Spa: This hotspot sits at the end of the road in a valley surrounded by mountains on the shores of Harrison Lake. It is gorgeous and unspoiled, and the views are stunning. The rooms are decent, but did we mention the views? The grounds of the resort include a fully fenced private garden with a fitness course trail and a trellis walkway that provide a good place for your Irish setter to stretch his legs. The three outdoor and two indoor pools fed by the springs are for humans only, but your dog doesn't need to feel left out. He can run right outside the entrance to the lobby and across the street for a quick dip in the chilly lake. Dogs under 50 pounds are allowed in designated rooms of the lodge for an additional $100 nonrefundable cleaning fee, but here's a secret: There are 10 tiny cabins out back, nestled against the hillside, that allow any size dog for no additional fee, and you have full use of all the facilities; one of them has a kitchenette. Rates range $120–190 in the main lodge; $180–280 for the cabins. 100 Esplanade Ave., Harrison Hot Springs; 800/663-2266; www.harrisonresort.com.

More Accommodations: Please look under *Chain Hotels* in the *Resources* section for additional places to stay in this area.

Sidney and the Saanich Peninsula

The charming town of Sidney-by-the-Sea is the largest community on the Saanich Peninsula, a thumb of land north of Victoria. Sidney is two kilometers south of Swartz Bay, where the Tsawassen Ferry from Vancouver arrives, and the Washington State Ferries to Anacortes and the San Juan Islands. The town got its start in 1894 when the Victoria–Sidney Railway began service.

DIVERSIONS

In 1904, Jennie Butchart began a lifelong project to transform a barren limestone quarry into a garden. More than 100 years later, her vision has blossomed into 55 acres of world-renowned gardens on a 130-acre estate. If you are going to Vancouver Island, you really must go to **Butchart Gardens.** There's a different stunning floral explosion to see each month, although a late afternoon stroll, around 3 P.M., from mid-June to mid-September can be best to enjoy pleasant weather. Pets on a six-foot leash are welcome, except during fireworks displays on Saturday evenings, which they'd hate anyway. Summer night strolls are magical, when underground wiring installations set the gardens aglow. Adult entrance fees are $26.50 and hours change seasonally; there's no charge for your pet. Inside the gardens are cafés with courtyard seating. Butchart Gardens are 12.5 miles north of Victoria. 800 Benvenuto Ave, Brentwood Bay; 866/652-4422; www.butchartgardens.com.

On the mainland, leashed dogs may join you at **Minter Gardens,** 32 acres of show gardens featuring 11 different themes, a labyrinth, and some surprising floral topiary sculptures. Spring highlights daffodils and 100,000 tulips imported from Holland. More than 1,000 rhododendron bushes explode around May, and the rose garden blooms fragrantly through August. Autumn features chrysanthemums, blooming cabbages, and pansies. Outdoor covered seating is available with an á la carte menu at The Garden Café. The gardens are open April–October. Hours vary seasonally. Admission is $15 for adults, $9 for youth 12–18, $6 for children. Exit #135 off Highway #1. 52892 Bunker Road, Rosedale; 888/646-8377; www.mintergardens.com.

Downtown has shops, marinas, and diving facilities protected by its break-water wall.

The peninsula's regional parks allow unleashed dogs under voice control, except at Francis/King Park and the Lochside Regional Trail, where they must remain leashed due to these parks' popularity. The regional park's definition of under control means that your dog returns to you immediately when called. There are no fences to contain misbehavers who ignore commands to "Come!" For complete regulations at each of the regional parks, go to www.crd.bc.ca/parks and look for the "Pets in Parks" link under "Find a Park." On the same website, looking for parks under "By Activity" allows you to find some great spots for hiking.

Lochside Regional Trail: The rails stopped carrying cars in 1924, and now the re-graded line carries people, bicycles, and, in some places, horses a total of 29 kilometers (18 miles) from Swartz Bay to Victoria. This civilized paved and gravel path traverses mostly urban areas and pastoral farmland. It connects to the Galloping Goose Trail, a wilder neighbor to the south in Victoria. For a good access point, with a couple of parking spaces, take Royal Oak Road west from Highway 17, and turn right down the dead-end of Lochside Road. Please respect the No Parking signs near private property.

PARKS, BEACHES, AND RECREATION AREAS

20 Island View Regional Park

🐾🐾 (See Victoria map on page 609)

For four months out of the year, a walk along the dirt road trails of this regional park is good clean fun. It's a chance to hike above the beach, off leash if you prefer, on a straight and level trail on Cordova Bay, looking out at James and Sidney Islands. You have far-reaching sight on the path, so you can see what's coming and leash up if necessary to pass other walkers and dogs.

September 15–May 31, Island View gets bonus points, because that's when dogs are allowed to get on the beach and get mucky in the water. The beach is sandy enough; it's just that saltwater somehow adds extra pungency to that wet dog smell.

From Victoria or Sidney, take Provincial Highway 17 to Island Drive Road and go east for 1.7 miles to the parking lot. Open 6 A.M.–11 P.M.

21 Elk and Beaver Lake Parks

🐾🐾🐾 (See Victoria map on page 609)

A thousand acres or so (442 hectares) is pretty big for a regional park, and this is one of the prettiest, with two lakes available for water sports. Any or all of the perimeter 6.25-mile trail is given high paws ratings by area dogs. It alternates between forest, fields, and wetlands, with bountiful lake views. Dogs may hike this trail off leash under voice control, as well as on the maze of short trails southeast of Beaver Lake. Near the Beaver Lake entrance, off to the right, is an unmarked field that's perfect for a game of fetch.

In the off-season, September 15–May 31, dogs have the added bonus of free time on the lake's beaches and on the grassy slopes of the picnic areas. During the summer, pupsters may pass through on leash but are not allowed to remain in the picnic or beach areas.

From Highway 17, turn west on Haliburton Road, and for less crowded parking and better trail access, follow the frontage road south to the Beaver Lake parking area. 250/478-3344.

22 Francis/King Park

😸😸😸 (See Victoria map on page 609)

Freeman "Skipper" King, a local naturalist and scout leader, and homesteader Tommy Francis worked together to donate this farm to the community. Freeman designed and dedicated a 750-meter accessible nature trail for his wife Elsi, who spent her last years in a wheelchair.

The Elsi King Trail makes up a tiny fraction of the walking trails available in this nature park. The map on the diamond kiosk at the park entrance tallies up the trails to 11 kilometers (not quite seven miles). The longest, the Centennial Trail, is a moderate loop around the park that'll take about an hour for well-conditioned legs of either species.

From the Trans-Canada Highway, take Exit 8 and go west on Helmcken Road. Turn left on Burnside and travel almost a mile, turn right on Prospect Lake Road, and take the left fork in the road to Munn Road, a total of another mile to the park entrance. Open 8 A.M.–9 P.M. 250/478-3344.

PLACES TO EAT

Third Street Café: This comfy diner is a long-standing favorite, with a huge list of breaky (endearing Brit slang for breakfast) specialties and hot lunch sandwiches. The staff are professed dog lovers, giving scraps and pats to dogs. A bunch of sidewalk tables are up for grabs out front. 2466 Beacon Ave.; 250/656-3035.

Waddling Dog Bar and Grill: At the Quality Inn Victoria, the Waddling Dog Bar and Grill is the casual pub option, with sidewalk seating where your dog can fall in love with new foods, perhaps steak and kidney pie or salmon Wellington in a puff pastry. 2476 Mt. Newton Cross Road; 800/567-8466.

PLACES TO STAY

The Cedarwood: The simple rooms of this motel, both standard units and suites with kitchens, are on landscaped grounds with a great beach walk right across the street. A small off-leash area at Tulista Park is right up the street. There are 10 nonsmoking pet rooms available within five blocks of the specialty shops of Sidney's downtown. The website states that only small dogs are allowed; in practice, the Cedarwood stretches the definition of small infinitely; up to three dogs per room are allowed. Rates range from $90–120 in winter to $125–205 in summer. The dog fee is $15. 9522 Lochside Dr.; 877/656-5551; www.thecedarwood.ca.

Waddling Dog: "The Dog" is now a Quality Inn, but it retains a unique character, embracing a basset hound theme and going all out with Tudor style and imported British antiques. It's close to Sidney and the ferries. Dogs have the added convenience of a fenced yard behind the property in which to run about, and there's usually a resident basset to play with. Guest dogs are not required to be bassets; all breeds are welcome for a $10 fee per pet per night. Four dogs maximum, please. Rates range $95–130. 2476 Mt. Newton Cross Road, Saanichton; 800/567-8466; www.qualityinnvictoria.com.

More Accommodations: Please look under *Chain Hotels* in the *Resources* section for additional places to stay in this area.

Victoria

The architecture and style of Victoria, with its afternoon high teas and dou-ble-decker buses, emphasizes the British in British Columbia. Hurrah for the local dog advocacy group Citizen Canine (www.citizencanine.org), which conducted a pilot program 2005–2007 allowing off-leash dog hours in nine city parks, a big step up from the city's only existing designated dog areas in Bea-con Hill Park. See more of this beautiful city park and the historic buildings of downtown Victoria than you could on foot with a horse-drawn **Victoria Carriage Tour** (877/663-2207; www.victoriacarriage.com). Calm, leashed, lap

dogs are welcome to join you on 30-minute or 90-minute guided tours starting at $70 for the carriage, which holds 4–6 people. Tours operate daily 9 A.M.–midnight, weather permitting.

Galloping Goose Regional Trail: This 55-kilometer (35-mile) trail passes through urban, rural, and wilderness scenery from Victoria to Sooke. Named for the ungainly, gas-powered passenger car that carried people and mail during the 1920s, the Goose is part of the Trans-Canada Trail System, linking large sections of the country, coast to coast. From downtown Victoria, you can start at the corner of Warf Street and Pandora Avenue, cross the Johnson Street Bridge in the pedestrian lane, and turn right on the paved path that intersects Harbour Road. The trail doesn't require dogs to be on leash, but it is heavily used by cyclists. For many more trailheads, download maps from www .gallopinggoosetrail.com.

PARKS, BEACHES, AND RECREATION AREAS

23 Dallas Beach Dog Area in Beacon Hill Park

🐾🐾🐾🐾🐕 (See Victoria map on page 609)

Beacon Hill Park is as old as the hills, its 200 acres set aside in 1858 by governor James Douglas and officially established as a park in 1882. On a leashed stroll of this gorgeous city park, you and your pup may come across a strutting peacock, bald eagles, or a great blue heron among the lilies of Goodacre and Fountain Ponds. You might pass a horse-drawn carriage, children playing at the petting zoo, or a civilized game of cricket.

But, wait, what is that sound interrupting your reverie? It could be the thundering paws of the scores of dogs beating a path to Dallas Beach, Beacon Hill's off-leash area. Dogs can play where it all begins, at the Kilometer Zero marker for the Trans-Canada Highway, leading 7,349 kilometers to St. John's, Newfoundland. Victoria's main dog park comes complete with a great view, on headlands where settlers erected twin beacons to guide seafarers around dangerous waters. It extends around the bend to a headland called Clover Point, and, September–April, further still to Gonzales Beach.

Although it's called a beach, the largest land masses in the OLA are green fields of grass, divided by clumps of short trees and natural shrubs. There's a bunch of room for games involving your dog's flying object of choice. Be aware, as there are no fences separating your dog from a busy road. From the bluff, careful footing is required to get down to two beach coves, both rough and rocky. Once on the cobble beaches, your dog's not going anywhere; the steep headlands are behind you and cliff rocks on either side keep you tucked in.

There are restrooms nearby, a water fountain, garbage cans, and benches. Your only responsibility is to bring bags. Before you wear him out completely, you might want to walk on leash with your dog around the full bluff trail for maximum views.

The Trans-Canada Highway and Provincial Highway 17 merge into Douglas Street a block before Beacon Hill Park. Follow Douglas until it dead-ends into Dallas and turn left onto Dallas. The off-leash area is located south of Dallas Road between Douglas and Cook Streets. Angled parking is available along the majority of Dallas Road.

PLACES TO EAT

Murchie's: This venerable institution has been serving high tea in Victoria since 1894. The counter cases are filled with legendary cakes and tarts on one side and pasties, sandwiches, and savories on the other. Murchie's vegetable strata, in Italian veggie lasagna or Mexican styles, takes your taste buds to a new stratosphere. Murchie's sidewalk seating is along a popular people-watching boulevard. 1100 Government Street; 250/383-3112; www.murchies.com.

PLACES TO STAY

Abbeymoore Manor: This mansion was built in 1912 and sits among the castles and gardens of Old Victoria, where governors, merchant barons, bankers, and architects built elaborate homes to show off their wealth. Pets are welcome in the Garden Suites only, and please let them know you have pets when making reservations, which you should always do to ensure that your pets will get along with the resident pets. There is a $15 pet fee per day for short-term stays, which includes a freshly washed pet blanket, food bowls, and gourmet doggie treats. Rates range $120–230. 1470 Rockland Ave.; 888/801-1811; www.abbeymoore.com.

Abigail's Hotel: This hotel is a five-star bed-and-breakfast accommodation, frequently rated Victoria's best small hotel by Frommer's Travel Guides. It's a warm and comfortable Tudor-style house with country furnishings and English gardens. Dogs are welcome in the Coach House Suites, three rooms on one floor that require navigating narrow stairs. Abigail's is four blocks from the Dallas off-leash dog beach. Rates range $190–340. The pet fee is $25 per dog per stay. 906 McClure Street; 866/347-5054; www.abigailshotel.com.

Magnolia Hotel: Selected as one of the top three in all Canada by *Condé Nast Traveler*, this 64-room luxury boutique hotel in the heart of downtown Victoria highlights colonial style with fat duvets and soaker tubs. Some rooms have fireplaces, harbor views, and decks, but it's the Pooch Package your pup will be most interested in hearing about. Your room comes with a doggie dish and mat, poop and scoop bags, gourmet treats, a toy, monogrammed towel, and perhaps the most precious prize of all, a map of Victoria's dozen off-leash areas. Dallas Road, a 24-hour dog Mecca, is about a klick away—a kilometer in local lingo. Rates range $200–300 a night, with a $60 per night discount for multiple nights. The pet fee is also $60 total per stay, so stay more than one night, and the pet fee pays for itself. 623 Courtney St.; 877/624-6654; www.magnoliahotel.com.

DIVERSIONS

Should your travels take you farther afield in Victoria than the Inner Harbor, you'll want to know about **Paws in Parks,** a program established in June 2005 to allow designated off-leash areas and times in neighborhood parks. It started with six parks and now there are nine freedom zones in addition to the Dallas Beach/Clover Point/ Gonzales Beach strip originating in Beacon Hill. For full details and maps of the OLAs listed below, go to www.victoria.ca/dogs.

Alexander Park, 6–10 A.M. and 4–10 P.M.

Arbutus Park, 6 A.M.–10 P.M.

Banfield Park, 6–9 A.M. and 5–10 P.M. April–September; 6 A.M.–10 P.M. October–March

Oswald Park, 6 A.M.–10 P.M.

Pemberton Park, 6 A.M.–10 P.M.

Redfern Park, 6–10 A.M. and 4–10 P.M.

Songhees Hilltop Park, 6 A.M.–10 P.M.

Topaz Park, 6–10 A.M. and 4–10 P.M. Monday–Friday; 6–8 A.M. and 5–10 P.M. weekends

Victoria West Park, 6 A.M.–10 P.M.

Paul's Motor Inn: This motel has a bright copper roof and rooms that are retro-hip, even more hip because the retro is original. It's right downtown, within walking distance of everything. Paul's has won awards for genuine hospitality at an unbeatable price. Pets under 30 pounds are allowed in 14 rooms for a $15 fee per stay. Children under 12 stay for free, and two adults can stay for $80–125. 1900 Douglas Street; 866/333-7285; www.pauls motorinn.com.

Prior House Bed and Breakfast: The Prior House accepts pets with well-behaved owners, up to two pets per room, providing them with treats, walk bags, and, most importantly, a welcome environment in a lavish home with ocean views. The Hobbit Garden Studios are pet friendly, each unique, with private entrances and furnished patios on a secluded lawn surrounded by award-winning gardens. There is a $20 pet fee per stay during the summer, no fee the remainder of the year, and the basic courtesies apply. Pet-sitting can be arranged with advance notice. Rates range $160–260. 620 St. Charles; 877/924-3300; www.priorhouse.com.

More Accommodations: Please look under *Chain Hotels* in the *Resources* section for additional places to stay in this area.

Sooke

The drama of the Pacific Ocean and the wildness of a towering rainforest come together here on the southern tip of Vancouver island. Sooke seems much more remote than it is, easily accessible via a 45-minute drive from downtown Victoria. It was a thriving settlement of Coast Salish Indians until an 1864 gold rush brought European settlers. Today's residents experience an annual invasion of summer vacationers who want to experience the great outdoors.

PARKS, BEACHES, AND RECREATION AREAS

24 East Sooke Regional Park

🐾🐾🐾🐕 (See Victoria map on page 609)

This park's coastline trail, pocket beaches, timeless woods, and tide pool coves come with a lot of caveats. This is a wilderness park, a rugged experience you can enjoy if you are confident of your hiking skills and the capabilities of your canine. Let's just say that East Sooke's 1,463 hectares—that's 3,511 acres—are more than a walk in the park. To handle any of this regional park's 30 miles of trails, come prepared with maps and backcountry essentials, and allow more

time than usual to return to your vehicle before dark. Imagine your dog's embarrassment if the rangers have to send a rescue dog to find him!

Anderson Cove is the starting point for hiking trails to the uplands, Babbington Hill, and Mount Maguire. You and your dog might share views of the Strait of San Juan de Fuca and the Olympic Mountains with bald eagles, turkey vultures, and red-tailed hawks. Pike Road, the westernmost access point, is the best place to pick up the Coast Trail, a vigorous, seven-hour hike to private beaches, rocky bays, and tide pools for hours of exploring.

In a park where only voice control is required, leashes are still highly desirable, due to a greater likelihood of running into deer, black bears, and cougars. We'll let you off with one more warning: Do not allow your dog to swim in an area where seals or sea lions are present. It can disrupt the pinnipeds' breeding patterns, and, more importantly, the sea mammals will attack and can kill. Cooper and Isis don't want to scare you away from Sooke; they merely want you to come fully prepared to safely enjoy this spectacular experience.

From the Trans-Canada Highway starting in Victoria, take Exit 10 to Colwood. Go to your left to follow the Old Island Highway, which becomes Sooke Road. From Sooke Road, turn left on Gillespie Road. When you reach the T intersection on East Sooke Road, turn right to reach the park entrances at Anderson Cove and Pike Road, or turn left to Aylard Farm, off Becher Bay Road. Dogs are never permitted *in* Aylard Farm pond and they are not allowed on the Aylard Farm beach and picnic area June 1–September 15. Open 7 A.M.–sunset. 250/478-3344; www.eastsookepark.com.

PLACES TO EAT

17 Mile House Pub: The lanterns of 17 Mile House welcome you as you round the bend from East Sooke Regional Park, not much changed from 1894, when weary gold panhandlers and settlers rode up on horseback. The hitching post is still there, and the pub sticks to its traditional purpose to quench the thirst of weary travelers with cold beer, wine, ciders, coolers, spirits, and liqueurs. It also fills empty bellies with salads, a couple of sandwich selections, pastas, and burgers. At the owner's discretion, dogs are allowed to sit at outdoor tables nearest to the lawn. Come into the restaurant and ask a server how to get around back to the patio. Takeout is also available all day, seven days a week. 5126 Sooke Road; 250/642-5942; www.17milehouse.com.

Tugwell Creek Farm–Mead Tasting Room: This honey farm and meadery keeps things laid back and friendly, allowing leashed dogs who can keep a respectful distance from the hives and goats, mainly so they don't get stung or kicked. The latest and greatest product of the honey farm is mead, a heady brew made from honey and local berries. Sample the brew and buy honey products noon–4 P.M. Wednesday–Sunday. 8750 West Coast Rd.; 250/642-1956; www.tugwellcreekfarm.com.

PLACES TO STAY

Amazing Vacation Homes and Cottages: This rental agency has a wide selection of oceanfront vacation homes and cottages, the only rental properties in the area that allow pets. These houses and cottages all have acres of land surrounding them and feature such goodies as private hot tubs, fireplaces, large sun decks with panoramic views, private beaches, lovely gardens, fully equipped gourmet kitchens, and washers and dryers. Rates range $85–800 per night; weekly, monthly, and low-season rates are also available. Children are welcome, as well as pets. All homes have a fee of $10 per pet per night, up to a maximum of $50; ask about pet fees for longer-term rentals. 250/642-7034 or 877/374-8944; www.amazingvacationhomes.com.

Sooke Harbour House: Art, natural beauty, and artful food will surround you and your spoiled pets at this phenomenal property. Pets are allowed in all 28 rooms. Take your pick from ocean views or garden rooms with antiques, original paintings and sculpture, and extravagant amenities. The remote location, scenery, and walks on Whiffen Spit will restore your spirit. It's a feast for all the senses. After you've stayed a day or two, leaving may be the hardest thing you ever do. Dogs are allowed on leash everywhere on the property, except around the world-famous cafés. Caution: Rates are not for the faint of heart, at $330–570; the pet fee is $40 per night, but there are no restrictions. 1528 Whiffen Spit Rd.; 250/642-3421 or 800/889-9688; www.sookeharbour house.com.

RESOURCES

Emergency Veterinary Clinics

For better geographic coverage, this list includes clinics that have an emergency veterinarian on call in addition to 24-hour animal clinics.

WASHINGTON

SAN JUAN ISLANDS

Ark Veterinary Clinic: Doctor on call. 262 Weeks Rd.; Lopez Island; 360/468-2477.

Islands Veterinary Clinic: Doctor on call. 850A Mullis St., Friday Harbor, San Juan Island; 360/378-2333.

Orcas Animal Clinic: Doctor on call. 429 Madrona St., Eastsound, Orcas Island; 360/376-7838.

Pet Emergency Center: 5 P.M.–8 A.M. weekdays, 5 P.M. Friday–8 A.M. Monday, and holidays. The islands refer to this clinic on the mainland. Avon Allen Rd. and Memorial Highway, Mt. Vernon; 360/848-5911.

OLYMPIC PENINSULA

Angeles Clinic for Animals: Doctor on call. 160 Del Guzzi Dr.,
Port Angeles; 360/452-7686.

Olympic Veterinary Clinic: Doctor on call. 1417 E. Front St.,
Port Angeles; 360/452-8978.

Sequim Animal Hospital: Doctor on call. 202 N. 7th Ave.,
Sequim; 360/683-7286.

KITSAP PENINSULA

All Creatures Animal Hospital: 24-hour service.
4091 S.R. 3 West, Bremerton; 360/377-3801.

Animal Emergency and Trauma Center: 24-hour clinic.
320 Lindvig Way, Poulsbo; 360/697-7771. In Bremerton, call 360/475-3077.

Central Kitsap Animal Hospital (VCA): 24-hour clinic.
10310 Central Valley Rd. N.E., Poulsbo; 360/692-6162.

PUGET SOUND ISLANDS

North Whidbey Veterinary Hospital: Doctor on call. 1020 NE 7th Ave.;
Oak Harbor; 360/679-3772; After-hours number is 360/320-1182.

Pet Emergency Center: 5 P.M.–8 A.M. weekdays, 5 P.M. Friday–8 A.M. Monday,
and holidays. The islands refer to this clinic on the mainland. Avon Allen Rd.
and Memorial Highway, Mt. Vernon; 360/848-5911.

EVERETT AND VICINITY

Animal Emergency Clinic of Everett: 24-hour clinic. 3625 Rucker Ave.,
Everett; 425/258-4466.

NORTH SEATTLE

Alderwood Companion Animal Hospital: Open 7 days a week, plus
doctor on call. 19511 24th Ave. W., Lynnwood; 425/775-7655.

Veterinary Specialty Center: 24-hour emergency and critical care, plus a
referral service. 20115 44th Ave. W., Lynnwood; 425/697-6106 or 866/872-5800.

CENTRAL SEATTLE

Animal Critical Care and Emergency Services: 24-hour clinic.
11536 Lake City Way N.E., Seattle; 206/364-1660.

Emerald City Emergency Clinic: After-hours 6 P.M.–8 A.M. and weekend
clinic. 4102 Stone Way N., Seattle; 206/634-9000.

EASTSIDE

Aerowood Animal Hospital: 24-hour clinic. 2975 156th Ave. S.E., Bellevue; 425/641-8414.

Alpine Animal Hospital: 24-hour pet hospital. 888 NW Sammamish Rd., Issaquah; 425/392-8888.

Animal Emergency Services East: After-hours clinic open 6 P.M.–8 A.M. Mon.–Fri., and noon Sat.–8 A.M. Mon. 636 7th Ave., Kirkland; 425/827-8727; www.animalemergencykirkland.com.

SOUTH SEATTLE

After Hours Animal Emergency Clinic: Open after-hours weekdays, 6 P.M.–8 A.M., and weekend clinic from noon Sat.–8 A.M. Mon. 718 Auburn Way N., Auburn; 253/833-4510.

Five Corners Animal Hospital (VCA): 24-hour clinic. 15707 1st Ave. S., Burien; 206/243-2982.

TACOMA AND OLYMPIA

Animal Emergency Clinic: 24-hour clinic. 5608 S. Durango St., Tacoma; 253/474-0791.

Olympia Pet Emergency: Open after hours 6 P.M.–7:30 A.M. weekdays; 6 P.M. Fri.–7:30 A.M. Mon. 4242 Pacific Avenue S.E.; 360/455-5155.

SOUTHWEST WASHINGTON

Emergency Veterinary Service: 24-hour clinic and critical care specialists. 6818 E. 4th Plain Blvd., Suite C, Vancouver; 360/694-3007.

St. Francis 24-Hour Animal Hospital: 12010 N.E. 65th St., Vancouver; 360/253-5446.

Willapa Veterinary Services: Doctor on call. 231 Ocean Ave., Raymond; 360/942-2321.

NORTH CASCADES

Animal Emergency Care: Open nights, weekends, and holidays. 317 Telegraph Rd., Bellingham; 360/758-2200.

Pet Emergency Center: 5 P.M.–8 A.M. weekdays, 5 P.M. Fri.–8 A.M. Mon., and holidays. Avon Allen Rd. and Memorial Highway, Mt. Vernon; 360/848-5911.

CENTRAL WASHINGTON

Airport West Animal Clinic: Doctor on call. 5804 W. Washington Ave., Yakima; 509/966-8460.

Mt. Stuart Animal Hospital: Doctor on call. 807 E. 8th Ave., Ellensburg; 509/925-2332.

Pet Emergency Service: 24-hour emergency phone service with rotating doctors on call. 5 P.M.–8 A.M. Mon.–Fri., weekends and holidays. 509/452-4138.

OREGON

NORTH COAST

Cloverdale Veterinary Clinic: Doctor on call. 34610 Hwy. 101, Cloverdale; 503/392-3322.

Emergency After-Hours Hotline: Shared answering and referral service for Cloverdale/Tillamook area. 888/437-5278.

Pioneer Veterinary Hospital: Doctor on call. 801 Main Ave., Tillamook; 503/842-8411.

The Tillamook Veterinary Hospital: Doctor on call. 1095 N. Main St., Tillamook; 503/842-7552.

CENTRAL COAST

Animal Medical Care of Newport: Doctor on call. 162 N.E. 10th, Newport; 541/265-6671.

Oceanlake Veterinary Clinic: Doctor on call. 3545 N.W. Hwy. 101; Lincoln City; 541/994-2929.

Osburn Veterinary Clinic: Doctor on call. 130 E. Railroad Ave., Reedsport; 541/271-5824.

Osburn Veterinary Clinic: Doctor on call. 1730 Kingwood, Florence; 541/902-2013.

Emergency Veterinary Hospital: These coastal communities also refer people to the 24-hour clinic in Eugene-Springfield. 103 W. Q St., Springfield; 541/746-0112.

SOUTH COAST

Gold Beach Veterinary Clinic: Doctor on call. 94211 3rd St., Gold Beach; 541/247-2513.

Hanson and Meekins Animal Hospital: Walk-in only, no appointments. Doctor on call after hours. 45 E Lockhart Ave., Coos Bay; 541/269-2415.

Morgan Veterinary Clinic: Doctor on call. 230 Market Ave., Coos Bay; 541/269-5846.

Ocean Boulevard Veterinary Hospital: Doctor on call. 1710 Ocean Blvd. N.W., Coos Bay; 541/888-6713.

Town and Country Animal Clinic: Doctor on call. 15740 Hwy. 101 S., Brookings; 541/469-4661.

GREATER PORTLAND

Dove Lewis Emergency Animal Hospital: 24-hour clinic. 1945 N.W. Pettygrove, Portland; 503/228-7281. Southeast location: after hours 6 P.M.–8 A.M., Mon.–Fri. and weekends. 10564 S.E. Washington St. in Plaza 205; 503/262-7194; www.dovelewis.org.

Southeast Portland Animal Hospital (VCA): 24-hour clinic. 13830 S.E. Stark, Portland; 503/255-8139.

WILLAMETTE VALLEY

Dallas Animal Clinic: Doctor on call. 135 Fir Villa Rd., Dallas; 503/623-3943.

Emergency Veterinary Hospital: 24-hour clinic. 103 W. Q St., Springfield; 541/746-0112.

Newberg Veterinary Hospital: Open seven days a week, plus doctor on call after hours. 3716 Hwy. 99W. Newberg; 503/538-8303.

River's Edge Pet Medical Center: 24-hour animal emergency service. 202 N.W. Hickory St., North Albany; 541/924-1700.

Salem Veterinary Emergency Clinic: After hours 5 P.M.–8 A.M. and weekends only. 3215 Market St. N.E., Salem; 503/588-8082.

Willamette Veterinary Clinic/Animal Emergency and Critical Care Center: 24-hour clinic. 1562 S.W. 3rd St., Corvallis; daytime: 541/753-2223; after-hours emergency: 541/753-5750.

CENTRAL OREGON

Animal Emergency Center of Central Oregon: After hours 5 P.M.–8 A.M. and weekends only. 1245 S. Hwy. 97, Suite C3, Bend; 541/385-9110.

Sisters Veterinary Clinic: Doctor on call. 371 E. Cascade Ave., Sisters; 541/549-6961.

SOUTHERN OREGON

Animal Emergency Service: Doctor on call. 2726 S. 6th St., Klamath Falls; 541/882-9005.

Basin Animal Clinic: Doctor on call. 1776 Washburn Way, Klamath Falls; 541/884-4558.

Southern Oregon Veterinary Specialty Center: 24-hour clinic. 3265 Biddle Rd., Medford; 541/282-7711; www.sovsc.com.

CANADA

BRITISH COLUMBIA

Animal Emergency Clinic: After hours and weekends only. 6325 204th St., #306, Langley; 604/514-1711.

Animal Emergency Clinic: 24-hour emergency clinic. 1590 W. 4th Ave., Vancouver; 604/734-5104.

Central Victoria Veterinary Hospital: 24-hour clinic. 760 Roderick St., Victoria; 250/475-2495.

Coast Mountain Veterinary Services: Doctor on call. 2011 Innsbruck Dr., Gateways Plaza, Whistler Creek; 24-hour emergency number: 604/932-5391.

Elk Lake Veterinary Hospital: Doctor on call. 4975 Pat Bay Hwy., Sidney-Saanich; 250/658-5922.

Pet-Friendly Chain Hotels

The following chains are generally pet friendly; but not every location of every chain allows dogs. If a specific location is listed below, you can expect a warm welcome for your weimaraner; for any unlisted location, call ahead and check with management before arriving with your dog in tow. The listings are organized as follows: restrictions on size, number, or location of pets; pet fees (pet fee is per pet per night unless stated otherwise); and nightly room rates.

BEST WESTERN

The largest hotel chain in the world has a good track record of accepting pets, but not all Best Westerns take pets, and their fees and regulations vary. 800/528-1234; www.bestwestern.com.

WASHINGTON

Bainbridge Island Suites: Dogs 25 pounds or less; $50 per stay fee; from $130; 350 N.E. High School Rd.; 866/396-9666.

Bellingham–Heritage Inn: Two dogs; $20 pet fee; $90–150; 151 E. McLeod Rd.; 360/647-1912.

Bellingham–Lakeway Inn: A renovation in 2008 has this hotel looking very modern. Five pet-friendly rooms; two dogs, 25 pounds or less; $10 pet fee; $90–200; 714 Lakeway Dr.; 360/671-1011; www.bellingham-hotel.com.

Chehalis–Park Place Inn and Suites: Dogs are not allowed in suites; two dogs, 20 pounds or less; maximum three-day stay; $10 pet fee; $85–140; 201 S.W. Interstate Ave.; 360/748-4040; www.parkplaceinn-suites.com.

Ellensburg–Lincoln Inn and Suites: First floor only; two dogs, 25 pounds or less; $25 pet fee; $90–200; 211 W. Umptanum Rd.; 509/925-4244.

Friday Harbor: Dogs 25 pounds or less; $20 pet fee; $110–360; 680 Spring St.; 360/378-3031.

Gig Harbor–Wesley Inn: Very pet friendly, with a pet package including treats; two dogs; $10 pet fee; $155–275; 6575 Kimball Dr.; 253/858-9690; www.wesleyinn.com.

Kelso–Aladdin Motor Inn: Dogs 10 pounds or less; $80–130; 310 Long Ave.; 360/425-9660.

Lake Chelan–Lakeside Lodge: An all-suite hotel in a park setting on the lake; 22 pet-friendly rooms, two of them suites; small pets at manager discretion; $10 flat fee; $90–330; 2312 W. Woodin Ave.; 509/682-4396; www.lakesidelodgeandsuites.com.

Leavenworth–Icicle Inn: Dogs 25 pounds or less; $25 pet fee; $90–250; 505 Hwy. 2; 509/548-7000.

Prosser–Inn at Horse Heaven: One dog under 50 pounds (sometimes more if smaller), in Building B only; $10 pet fee; $80–220; 259 Merlot Dr.; 509/786-7977.

Mount Vernon–College Way Inn: Dogs not allowed in pool area and must be kept on leash at all times in public areas. Two dogs; $20 pet fee; $85–105; 300 W. College Way; 360/424-4287.

Mount Vernon–Cottontree Inn: First floor pet-friendly rooms; two dogs; $25 per stay flat fee; $100–140; 2300 Market St.; 360/428-5678.

Toppenish–Lincoln Inn: Two dogs, 15 pounds or less; $10 pet fee; $70–180; 515 S. Elm St.; 509/865-7444.

Best Western–Tumwater Inn: Two dogs, no more than 40 pounds; $15 pet fee; $90–105; 5188 Capitol Blvd. S.E.; 360/956-1235.

Union Gap–Ahtanun: One dog under 50 pounds; $10 pet fee; $80–220; 2408 Rudkin Rd.; 509/248-9700.

Yakima–Lincoln Inn: Two dogs, 30 pounds or less; $15 pet fee; $80–200; 1614 N. 1st St.; 509/453-8898.

OREGON

Albany–Albany Inn: No restrictions; $10 pet fee; $60–130; 315 Airport Rd.; 541/928-6322.

Ashland–Bard's Inn: Two dogs; $15 pet fee; $90–225; 132 N. Main St.; 541/482-0049.

Ashland–Windsor Inn: No restrictions; $15 pet fee; $80–180; 2520 Ashland St.; 541/488-2330.

Astoria–Lincoln Inn: Three dogs, at managers discretion for size and temperament; $10 pet fee; $80–325; 555 Hamburg Ave.; 503/325-2205.

Bandon–Inn at Face Rock: Dog rooms do not have ocean view, but the beach is dog friendly. No restrictions; $15 for the first dog, $5 each additional dog, per stay; $110–300; 3225 Beach Loop Rd.; 541/347-9441; www.innatfacerock.com.

Bend: No restrictions; pet fee $10, $50 if not declared; $80–150; 721 N.E. 3rd St.; 541/382-1515.

Brookings–Beachfront Inn: No restrictions; $5 pet fee; $120–295; 16008 Boat Basin Rd.; 541/469-7779.

Cascade Locks–Columbia River Inn: No restrictions; $10 pet fee; $80–150; 735 Wanapa St.; 541/374-8777.

Coos Bay–Holiday Motel: Two dogs under 35 pounds; $10 pet fee; $95–180; 411 N. Bayshore Dr.; 541/269-5111.

Corvallis–Grand Manor Inn: Dog-specific rooms, closer to side rooms; $10 pet fee; $85–225; 925 N.W. Garfield; 541/758-8571.

Eugene–Greentree Inn: Two dogs, small pets only, special treat bag given at check-in; $30 deposit per dog, refundable depending on room condition; $90–105; 1759 Franklin Blvd.; 541/485-2727.

Eugene–New Oregon Motel: Two dogs, do not leave dog unattended, special treat bag given at check-in; refundable $30 deposit per dog, depending on room condition; $90–105; 1655 Franklin Blvd.; 541/683-3669.

Eugene South–Creswell Inn: No restrictions; small off-leash area on property; $10 flat fee for all dogs; $75–130; 345 E. Oregon Ave.; 541/895-3341.

Eugene (Springfield)–Grand Manor Inn: No restrictions, do not leave pets unattended; $10 pet fee; $95–175; 971 Kruse Way; 541/726-4769.

Florence–Pier Point Inn: Two dogs; $10 pet fee; $90–400; 85625 Hwy 101 S.; 541/997-7191; www.bestwestern.com/pierpointinn.

Grants Pass–Grants Pass Inn: Content, well-behaved dogs may be left unattended for short periods, such as dinner. Biscuits given at check-in. No restrictions; $10 flat fee per stay; $80–140; 111 N.E. Agness Ave.; 541/476-1117.

Grants Pass–Inn at the Rogue: Grassy hill for on-leash walks; no restrictions; under 20 pounds is $10 per dog per night and $30 refundable deposit; over 20 pounds is $20 per dog per night, and $50 refundable deposit; $65–100; 8959 Rogue River Hwy.; 541/582-2200.

Gresham–Pony Soldier Motor Inn: Small and medium dogs only; no pet fee; $80–130; 1060 N.E. Cleveland Ave.; 503/665-1591.

Hillsboro (Forest Grove)–University Inn and Suites: No restrictions; $10 pet fee; $90–200; 3933 Pacific Ave.; 503/992-8888.

Hood River–Hood River Inn: Treats given at check-in; no restrictions; $12 pet fee; $80–180; 1108 E. Marina Way; 541/386-2200.

Klamath Falls–Klamath Inn: No restrictions; no pet fee; $80–120; 4061 S. 6th St.; 541/882-1200.

Madras–Rama Inn: Treat bag given at check-in. Pets under 30 pounds, four dogs, no pit bulls; $20 per dog per stay; $70–100; 12 S.W. 4th St.; 541/475-6141.

McMinnville–The Vineyard Inn Motel: Limited pet rooms, must call ahead; $10 pet fee; $99–141; 2035 S. Hwy 99W; 503/472-4900.

Medford–Horizon Inn: Across the street from Medford's off-leash dog park; $20 pet fee; $85–130; 1154 Barnett Rd.; 541/779-5085.

Newport–Agate Beach Inn: Treats, dog sheets/bedding given at check-in; two dogs; $15 per dog per stay; $100–225; 3019 N. Coast Hwy.; 541/265-9411.

Portland–Inn at the Meadows: Biscuits available at front desk. Two dogs, 50 pounds or less; $25 flat fee per stay; $70–160; 1215 N. Hayden Meadows; 503/286-9600.

Roseburg–Garden Villa: Bags are available at the front desk and there is a walking trail behind hotel; $15 per dog per stay, plus credit card or $125 cash refundable deposit; $75–120; 760 N.W. Garden Valley Blvd.; 541/672-1601.

Roseburg–Rice Hill: Two pets maximum; $10 pet fee; $70–95; 621 John Long Rd.; 541/849-3335.

Salem–Black Bear Inn: No restrictions; $12 pet fee; $70–110; 1600 Motor Ct. N.E.; 503/581-1559.

Salem–Pacific Highway Inn: Two dogs; $20 pet fee up to $40 maximum per stay; $90–95; 4646 Portland Rd. N.E.; 503/390-3200.

Sandy–Sandy Inn: Two dogs; $10 pet fee; $85–125; 37465 Hwy. 26; 503/668-7100.

Seaside–Oceanview Resort: Treat bags given at check-in. Dogs not permitted in whirlpool suites; $20 pet fee; $90–300; 414 N. Prom; 503/738-3334; www.oceanviewresort.com.

Sisters–Ponderosa Lodge: Very pet-friendly. Doggie basket given at check-in with sheets, towels, bags, and treats. Lodge is near Deschutes National Forest and has walking trails next to pet wing. Two dogs; $15 per dog per visit; $90–240; 500 Hwy. 20 W.; 541/549-1234.

St. Helens–Oak Meadows Inn: Four dogs depending on size; $10 per dog per visit; $75–145; 585 S. Columbia River Hwy.; 503/397-3000.

The Dalles–River City Inn: Small dogs only, two dogs; $10 pet fee; $65–110; 112 W. 2nd St.; 541/296-9107.

Tigard–Northwind Inn and Suites: Four dogs, each less than 30 pounds, at discretion of front desk staff; $10 pet fee; $80–170; 16105 S.W. Pacific Hwy.; 503/431-2100.

Tillamook: Ground-floor rooms only, two per room; $10 pet fee; $90–170; 1722 N. Makinster Rd.; 503/842-7599.

Wilsonville–Willamette Inn: Two dogs under 25 pounds; no pet fee; $90–100; 30800 S.W. Parkway Ave.; 503/682-2288.

Woodburn: One dog per person; $10 pet fee; $70–130; 2887 Newberg Hwy.; 503/982-6515.

BRITISH COLUMBIA

Abbotsford–Bakerview Inn: No pet fees or restrictions; $110–150; 1821 Sumas Way; 604/859-1341.

Burnaby–Kings Inn and Conference Center: Small pets less than 20 pounds; $15 pet fee; $115–200; 5411 Kingsway; 604/438-1383.

Chilliwack–Rainbow Country Inn: Limit three pets per room, 20 pounds or less; $10 per pet per stay; $100–230; 43971 Industrial Way; 604/795-3828.

Langley–Langley Inn: Newly renovated; pets of knee height (said the clerk at the front desk); $15 pet fee; $100–130; 5978 Glover Rd.; 604/530-9311.

Mission–Mission City Lodge: No restrictions; $15 pet fee; $90–140; 32281 Lougheed Hwy.; 604/820-5500.

Sidney/Victoria–Emerald Isle Motor Inn: Main floor only, two per room; $15 pet fee; $110–170; 2306 Beacon Ave.; 250/656-4441.

Port Coquitlam–Poco Inn and Suites: $10–20 pet fee depends on size; $110–180; 1545 Lougheed Hwy.; 604/941-6216.

Richmond–Abercorn Inn: Pets up to 35 pounds; $110–250; 9260 Bridgeport Rd.; 604/270-7575.

Squamish–Mountain Retreat Hotel: No restrictions; $25 pet fee; $100–170; 38922 Progress Way; 604/815-0883.

Vancouver–Downtown: One dog 20 pounds or less; $20 pet fee; $100–225; 718 Drake St. at Granville; 604/669-9888.

Vancouver–Sands: Limit four small or two large dogs; $10 pet fee; $120–260; 1755 Davie St.; 604/682-1831.

Victoria–Carlton Plaza Hotel: Dogs cannot be left unattended in room; $10 pet fee; $80–250; 642 Johnson St.; 800/663-7241.

Whistler–Listel Hotel: Small pets only in first-floor rooms; $25 pet fee; $170–450; 4121 Village Green; 604/932-1133.

COAST HOTELS

BRITISH COLUMBIA

Vancouver–Coast Plaza Hotel and Suites: Pamper Your Pooch package includes accommodations for two adults and dog, overnight parking, a great little welcome gift for your dog, and a $25 gift certificate for the Doggy Style Deli on Denman. Four dogs; $160–250; 1763 Comox St.; 604/688-7711; www.coasthotels.com.

Vancouver–Airport: Dog dishes available onsite, park close by; $20 pet fee; $120–150; 1041 S.W. Marine Dr.; 604/263-1555; www.coasthotels.com.

COMFORT INN AND SUITES

Not all Comfort Inns allow pets, and each location's rules and fees vary. The fees assume payment with credit cards in case of damages. Cash transactions may require additional refundable deposits. 800/228-5150; comfortinn.com or petfriendlyhotels.choicehotels.com.

WASHINGTON

Ellensburg: Two dogs; $10 dog fee; $85–160; 1722 Canyon Rd.; 509/925-7037.

Port Orchard: Dogs up to 25 pounds; $25 per visit; $100–110; 1121 Bay St.; 360/895-2666.

Wenatchee: Two dogs under 50 pounds; $10 per dog per stay; $75–130; 815 N. Wenatchee Ave.; 509/662-1700.

Yakima: Limit four small dogs, 25 pounds or under; $15 per dog per stay; $90–230; 3702 Fruitvale Blvd.; 509/249-1900.

OREGON

Albany–Suites: No restrictions; $15 pet fee, or $30 per stay; $65–160; 100 Opal Ct. N.E.; 541/928-2053.

Coos Bay: Two dogs under 25 pounds; $15 per night; $70–170; 1503 Virginia Ave.; 541/756-3191.

Cottage Grove: No restrictions; $10 pet fee; $65–120; 845 Gateway Blvd.; 541/942-9747.

Eugene/Springfield: No restrictions; $25 pet fee; $100–160; 3550 Gateway St.; 541/746-5359.

Garibaldi: Under 50 pounds, maximum two pets; $20 pet fee; $60–160; 502 Garibaldi Ave.; 503/322-3338.

Grants Pass: No restrictions; $10 pet fee and $100 refundable deposit; $60–130; 1889 N.E. 6th St.; 541/479-8301.

Gresham: No restrictions; $15 pet fee; $75–100; 2323 N.E. 181st Ave; 503/492-4000.

Klamath Falls: No restrictions; $10 pet fee; $60–150; 100 Main St.; 541/882-4666.

Lincoln City: Pets under 20 pounds; $20 pet fee; $80–350; 136 N.E. Hwy. 101; 541/994-8155.

McMinnville: Three dogs under 50 pounds; $10 pet fee; $100–160; 2520 S.E. Stratus Ave.; 503/472-1700.

Seaside: Under 50 pounds; $25 per stay; $80–350; 545 Broadway; 503/738-3011.

The Dalles: Two dogs under 20 pounds; $10 pet fee; $65–145; 351 Lone Pine Dr.; 541/298-2800.

Wilsonville: Three dogs; $15 pet fee; $80–140; 8855 S.W. Citizen Dr.; 503/682-9000.

BRITISH COLUMBIA

Chilliwack: Comfort Inn by Journey's End, main floor only; caters to nearby dog shows, so allows many pets in one room; pet fee is $5 flat fee per night; $100–140; 45405 Luckakuck Wy.; 604/858-0636.

DAYS INN

Rules and regulations vary. 800/DAYS INN (800/329-7466); www.daysinn.com.

WASHINGTON

Days Inn Auburn: One dog under 35 pounds; $110–140; $15 pet fee; 1521 D St. N.E.; 253/939-5950.

Bellingham: No restrictions; $20 pet fee; $65–140; 215 N. Samish Way; 360/734-8830.

Bellevue: Under 50 pounds, two maximum; $25 pet fee; $85–115; 3241 156th Ave S.E.; 425/643-6644.

Federal Way: Pets under 30 pounds; $20 first night, $5 each night thereafter; $80–100; 34827 Pacific Way S.; 253/838-3164.

Kent: Under 20 pounds; $15 pet fee; $100–130; 1711 Meeker St.; 253/854-1950.

Mount Vernon, Casino Area: No restrictions; $10 pet fee; $90–110; 2009 Riverside Dr.; 360/424-4141.

Port Orchard: Under 55 pounds; $20 pet fee; $70–160; 220 Bravo Terrace; 360/895-7818.

Yakima: No restrictions; $15 pet fee; standard rate is $75; 1504 N. 1st St.; 509/248-3393.

OREGON

Bend: Two small to medium pets only; $6 pet fee; $70–100; 849 N.E. Third St.; 541/383-3776.

Corvallis: First floor only; $5 pet fee; $60–82; 1113 N.W. 9th St.; 541/754-7474.

Eugene: No restrictions; $10 pet fee; $55–113; 1859 Franklin Blvd.; 541/342-6383.

Gresham–Days Inn and Suites: Limit four dogs, $10 pet fee; $60–75; 24134 Stark St.; 503/465-1515.

Portland–North: Limit three dogs; $15 flat fee per stay; $65–85; 9930 N. Whitaker Rd.; 503/289-1800.

BRITISH COLUMBIA

Days Inn on the Harbour: No restrictions; $10 flat pet fee; $70–215; 427 Belleville St.; 250/386-3451; www.days-innvictoria.com.

ECONO LODGE AND RODEWAY INN

Rules and regulations vary. 800/55 ECONO (800/553-2666); www.econolodge.com or www.petfriendlyhotels.choicehotels.com.

WASHINGTON

Bellingham–Rodeway Inn: No restrictions; $10 pet fee; $65–120; 3710 Meridian St.; 360/738-6000.

Centralia: No restrictions; $10 pet fee; $60–80; 702 Harrison Ave.; 360/736-2875.

Kelso: No restrictions; $20 pet fee; $50–100; 505 N. Pacific Ave.; 360/636-4610.

Long Beach: Two dogs; $7 pet fee; $70–130; 115 3rd St.; 360/642-3714.

Sequim: One dog; $10 pet fee; $70–160; 801 E. Washington St.; 360/683-7113.

Woodland: Two dogs; $44–74; $10 per dog per stay; 1500 Atlantic Ave.; 360/225-6548.

OREGON

Albany: Two dogs; $10 pet fee; $55–90; 1212 S.E. Price Rd.; 541/926-0170.

Bend–Roadway Inn: No restrictions; $10 pet fee; $60–100; 437 N.E. 3rd St.; 541/382-7711.

Corvallis: Quantity allowed depends on size, call ahead; $5 pet fee; $45–50; 345 N.W. 2nd St.; 541/752-9601.

Klamath Falls: No restrictions; no pet fees, but deposit required if paying with cash; $35–110; 75 Main St.; 541/884-7735.

Lincoln City: Dogs under 25 pounds, but no rottweilers, Doberman pinschers, or pit bulls; $15 pet fee low season, $25 pet fee high season; $40–150; 1713 N.W. 21st St.; 541/994-5281.

Medford/Ashland: Two under 20 pounds; $10 pet fee; $55–90; 50 Lowe Rd.; 541/482-4700.

Newport: No restrictions, don't leave unattended; no pet fee; $39–99; 606 S.W. Coast Hwy.; 541/265-7723.

Portland/Hillsboro: One dog under 50 pounds; $10 pet fee; $50–70; 622 S.E. 10th Ave.; 503/640-4791.

Salem–Rodeway Inn: Three dogs; $5 pet fee; $45–100; 3340 Astoria Way N.E.; 503/393-6000.

HOLIDAY INN, HOLIDAY INN EXPRESS

Pet room availability and rates may vary for special occasions. 800/HOLIDAY (800/465-4329); www.holiday-inn.com or www.ichotelsgroup.com.

WASHINGTON

Bellingham–Express: No restrictions; $15 one-time charge; $120–150; 4160 Meridian St.; 360/671-4800.

Ellensburg–Express: Opened 2008. Limited pet rooms available, no size or quantity restrictions; $10 pet fee; $110–130; 1620 Canyon Rd.; 509/962-9400.

Poulsbo: Limit three dogs under 25 pounds; $10 pet fee under 10 pounds, $20 for 10–20 pounds, $30 over 20 pounds; $90–170; 19801 7th Ave. N.E.; 360/697-2119.

Renton: One pet of 40 pounds or less per room; $50 refundable pet deposit; $100–135; One South Grady Way; 425/246-7700.

SeaTac: One pet of 20 pounds or less per room; $20 pet fee per stay; $75–120; 17338 International Blvd.; 206/248-1000.

SeaTac–Express: Lake across the street for walks; two small dogs; $50 per stay; $100–135; 19621 International Blvd.; 206/824-3200.

Seattle Downtown–Crowne Plaza: No restrictions; $50 pet fee per stay; $130–180; 1113 6th Ave.; 206/824-3200.

Yakima–Express: First floor rooms only, two dogs under 25 pounds; $10 pet fee; $55–85; 1001 East A St.; 509/249-1000.

OREGON

Albany–Express: Three dogs; $15 pet fee per night, or $30 per visit for longer stays; $85–160; 105 Opal Ct.; 541/928-8820.

Astoria: Two dogs; $15 pet fee; $80–180; 204 W. Marine Dr.; 503/325-6222.

Bend: No restrictions; $10 pet fee; $85–130; 20615 Grandview Dr.; 541/317-8500.

Corvallis: First-floor rooms only; $25 pet fee; $90–110; 781 N.W. 2nd St; 541/752-0800.

Cottage Grove: No restrictions; $15 pet fee; $75–95; 1601 Gateway Blvd.; 541/942-1000.

Eugene/Springfield–Express: Designated rooms only; $10 pet fee; $80–120; 3480 Hutton St.; 541/746-8471.

Grants Pass: No restrictions; $10 pet fee; $80–130; 105 N.E. Agness Ave.; 541/471-6144.

Portland–Airport (I-205): Two dogs, lower floors only; $25 non-refundable deposit per stay; $105–275; 8439 N.E. Columbia Blvd.; 503/256-5000.

Roseburg: First-floor rooms; $10 pet fee; $70–95; 375 W. Harvard Ave.; 541/673-7517.

Troutdale: Quality Excellence Award Winner; pets up to 50 pounds; $10 first night, $15 additional nights; $90–110; 1000 N.W. Graham Rd.; 503/492-2900.

Wilsonville: No restrictions; $15 pet fee; $80–125; 25425 S.W. 95th Ave.; 503/682-2211.

BRITISH COLUMBIA

North Vancouver–Holiday Inn Hotel and Suites: Torchbearer Award Winner; two dogs; $120–170; $25 pet fee; 700 Old Lillooet Rd.; 604/985-3111; www.hinorthvancouver.com.

Vancouver–Airport: Torchbearer Award Winner; two dogs under 50 pounds; $20 pet fee; $110–170; 10720 Cambie Rd.; 604/821-1818.

Vancouver–Centre: Two, if well-behaved; $15 pet fee; $95–230; 711 W. Broadway at Heather; 604/879-0511; www.holidayinnvancouver.com.

Vancouver–Express: No restrictions; $15 pet fee; $160–190; 2889 East Hastings St.; 604/254-1000.

KOA CAMPGROUNDS

Aggressive dogs of any breed are not welcome at any KOA. If your dog shows behavior that is protective and unfriendly to strangers, please leave it at home. If you bring your dog and it exhibits this type of behavior, the owner or management of the KOA will ask you to find other camping accommodations. KOA Kampgrounds have policies against accepting breeds that have been identified by its insurance provider as having a history of unfriendly and aggressive behavior to other dogs and humans, specifically pit bulls and pit bull mixes, rottweilers, and Doberman pinschers.

KOA does not charge pet fees. Dogs are not allowed in Kamping Kottages or Kabins. 406/248-7444; www.koa.com.

WASHINGTON

Anacortes/Burlington: Tents $25–35; 6397 N. Green Rd.; 360/724-5511.

Bay Center/Willapa Bay: Tents $20–25; 16 miles S. of Raymond on Hwy. 101; 360/875-6344.

Bellingham/Lynden: Tents $25–35; 8717 Line Rd.; 360/354-4772.

Concrete/Grady Creek: Tents $25–30; 7370 Russell Rd.; 360/826-3554.

Ellensburg: Tents $20–30; 32 Thorp Hwy. S.; 509/925-9319.

Leavenworth/Wenatchee: Tents $25–60; 11401 Riverbend Dr.; 509/548-7709.

Long Beach/Ilwaco: Tents $20; 1509 S.R. 101; 360/642-3292.

Port Angeles/Sequim: Tents $25–35; 80 O'Brien Rd.; 360/457-5916.

Seattle/Tacoma: Tents $35–50; 5801 S. 212th, Kent; 253/872-8652.

Winthrop/North Cascades National Park: Tents $25–35; 1114 Hwy. 20; 509/996-2258.

Yakima: Tents $25–30; 1500 Keys Rd.; 509/248-5882.

OREGON

Albany/Corvallis: Very dog-friendly. Tents $25–35; 33775 Oakville Rd. South; 541/967-8521.

Astoria/Seaside: Tents $25–55; 1100 N.W. Ridge Rd.; 503/861-2606.

Bandon/Port Orford: Tents $25–30; 46612 Hwy. 101; 541/348-2358.

Bend/Sisters: Tents $30–45; 67667 Hwy. 20 W.; 541/549-3021.

Cascade Locks/Portland East: Tents $25–30; 841 N.W. Forest Ln.; 541/374-8668.

Klamath Falls: Tents $25–30; 3435 Shasta Way; 541/884-4644.

Lincoln City: Tents $25–35; 5298 N.E. Park Ln.; 541/994-2961.

Madras/Culver: Tents $20–30; 2435 S.W. Jericho Ln.; 541/546-3046.

Medford/Gold Hill: Tents $25–30; 12297 Blackwell Rd. (Gold Hill Exit 40); 541/855-7710.

Oregon Dunes: Tents $20–35; 68632 Hwy. 101; 541/756-4851.

Salem: Tents $25–30; 8372 Enchanted Way; 503/363-7616.

Waldport/Newport: Tents $20–35; Alsea Bay Bridge, Waldport; 541/563-2250.

LA QUINTA

There are no restrictions or pet fees at the following locations, unless otherwise noted. 800/NU ROOMS (800/687-6667); www.laquinta.com or www.lq.com.

WASHINGTON

Bellingham: Limit three medium dogs; no pet fee; $70–150; 125 E. Kellogg Rd.; 360/671-6200.

Federal Way: Two dogs under 50 pounds; $180 refundable pet deposit; $110–120; 32124 25th Ave. S.; 253/529-4000.

Kent: One dog under 25 pounds; $60–90; $10 flat fee per stay; 25100 74th Ave. S.; 253/520-6670.

SeaTac: Three dogs; $85–110; 2824 S. 188th St.; 206/241-5211.

Wenatchee: No restrictions; no pet fee; $75–100; 1905 N. Wenatchee Ave.; 509/664-6565.

OREGON

Albany: Limit four dogs; no pet fee; $70–140; 251 Airport Rd. S.E.; 541/928-0921.

Ashland: No restrictions; no pet fee; $70–140; 434 S. Valley View Rd.; 541/482-6932.

Bend: Four beings per room (pets and people); no pet fee; $60–150; 61200 S. Hwy. 97; 541/388-2227.

Eugene: No restrictions; no pet fee; $80–135; 155 Day Island Rd.; 541/344-8335.

Grants Pass: Two dogs per person; no pet fee; $60–130; 243 N.E. Morgan Ln.; 541/472-1808.

Newport: Two dogs; no pet fee; $65–150; 45 S.E. 32nd St.; 541/867-7727.

Portland–Lloyd Center: Two dogs; no pet fee; pets may be left unattended if crated; $75–130; 431 N.E. Multnomah St.; 503/233-7933.

Portland–Northwest: No restrictions; no pet fee; $70–130; 4319 N.W. Yeon Ave.; 503/497-9044.

Wilsonville: No restrictions; no pet fee; $80–90; 8815 S.W. Sun Pl.; 503/682-3184.

Woodburn: Two dogs; no pet fee; $65–85; 120 N. Arney Rd.; 503/982-1727.

MARRIOTT

Rules and regulations vary. The Marriott chain includes Courtyard by Marriott, Residence Inns, SpringHill Suites, and TownePlace Suites. 800/228-9290; www.marriott.com.

WASHINGTON

Bellevue–Residence Inn: No restrictions; $75 per stay; $180–200; 14455 N.E. 29th Pl.; 425/882-1222.

Kent–TownePlace Suites: Less than 30 pounds; $10 pet fee; $175–200; 18123 72nd Ave. S.; 253/796-6000.

Redmond–Residence Inn: Two dogs; $100 per stay; $160–180; 7575 164th Ave. N.E.; 425/497-9226.

Renton–Springhill Suites: No restrictions; $100 per stay; $150–160; 300 S.W. 19th St.; 425/917-2000.

San Juan Island–Courtyard Suites Friday Harbor: No restrictions; $20 per day and above depending on type and size; 275 A Street; 360/378-3033; www.courtyardsuites-fridayharbor.com.

Vancouver–Residence Inn: No restrictions; $75 nonrefundable fee; $100–160; 8005 N.E. Parkway Dr.; 360/253-4800.

OREGON

Eugene-Springfield–Residence Inn: No restrictions; $75 nonrefundable fee; $150–180; 25 Club Rd.; 541/342-7171.

Hillsboro–Residence Inn: No restrictions; $10 pet fee; $180–200; 18855 N.W. Tanasbourne Dr.; 503/531-3200.

Hillsboro–TownePlace Suites: Two dogs; $10 pet fee (changes for longer stays); $90–160; 6550 N.E. Brighton St.; 503/268-6000.

Lake Oswego–Residence Inn: No restrictions; $80–160; $75 nonrefundable pet fee; 15200 S.W. Bangy Rd.; 503/684-2603.

Portland–Downtown RiverPlace Residence Inn: Two dogs; $10 pet fee; $150–220; 2115 S.W. River Pkwy.; 503/552-9500.

Portland–Lloyd Center: No restrictions; $75 per stay; $105–175; 1710 N.E. Multnomah St.; 503/288-1400.

CANADA

Whistler–Residence Inn: One dog; $25 per night, maximum of $75; $400–700; 4899 Painted Cliff Rd.; 604/905-3400; www.whistler-marriott.com.

MOTEL 6

Official policy for Motel 6 is that all properties accept one pet per room, exceptions are noted below. There are no pet fees, unless listed otherwise below. There is a 10 percent discount for booking online. 800/4MOTEL6 (800/466-8356); www.motel6.com.

WASHINGTON

Bellingham: Three dogs; $50–70; 3701 Byron St.; 360/671-4494.

Centralia: $40–55; 1310 Belmont Ave.; 360/330-2057.

Everett–North: $50–70; 10006 Evergreen Way; 425/347-2060.

Everett–South: $50–70; 224 128th St. S.W.; 425/353-8120.

Fife: $50–65; 5201 20th St. E.; 253/922-1270.

Issaquah: Two dogs; $65–75; 1885 15th Pl. N.W.; 425/392-8405.

Kelso: $45–65; 106 N. Minor Rd.; 360/425-3229.

Kent: $50–70; 20651 Military Rd. S.; 206/824-9902.

Kirkland: $65–75; 12010 120th Pl. N.E.; 425/821-5618.

SeaTac–North: One dog under 20 pounds; $50–70; 16500 International Blvd.; 206/246-4101.

SeaTac–South: $50–70; 18900 47th Ave. S.; 206/241-1648.

Tacoma–South: Two dogs; $45–70; 1811 S. 76th St.; 253/473-7100.

Tumwater: One medium, two if small; $40–55; 400 W. Lee St.; 360/754-7320.

Vancouver: One dog free, second dog is $10 per night; $40–70; 221 N.E. Chkalov Dr.; 360/253-8900.

Yakima: $35–50; 1104 N. 1st St.; 509/454-0080.

OREGON

Albany: $45–70; 2735 Pacific Blvd. S.E.; 541/926-4233.

Bend: Two dogs; $45–80; 201 N.E. 3rd St.; 541/382-8282.

Coos Bay: No restrictions; $45–85; 1445 Bayshore Dr.; 541/267-7171.

Corvallis: $45–65; 935 N.W. Garfield Ave.; 541/758-9125.

Eugene–South: No restrictions; $45–70; 3690 Glenwood Dr.; 541/687-2395.

Gold Beach: Really nice, looks like a lodge. No restrictions; $50–75; 94433 Jerry's Flat Rd.; 541/247-4533.

Grants Pass: Two dogs; $40–65; 1800 N.E. 7th St.; 541/474-1331.

Klamath Falls: Two dogs; $40–65; 5136 S. 6th St.; 541/884-2110.

Lincoln City: $45–85; 3517 N.W. Hwy. 101; 541/996-9900.

Medford–North: Two small dogs; $50–75; 2400 Biddle Rd.; 541/779-0550.

Medford–South: $40–70; 950 Alba Dr.; 541/773-4290.

Portland–Airport: One dog free, second dog $10 per night; $45–65; 9225 S.E. Stark St.; 503/255-0808.

Portland–Central: Two small dogs; $45–70; 3104 S.E. Powell Blvd.; 503/238-0600.

Portland–North: One under 30 pounds, extra dogs $10 each; $45–65; 1125 N. Schmeer Rd.; 503/247-3700.

Redmond: Two small dogs; $60–85; 2247 S. Hwy. 97; 541/923-2100.

Roseburg: Pets and Wi-Fi are free. National award winner. $45–70; 3100 N.W. Aviation Dr.; 541/464-8000.

Salem: Three dogs; $40–60; 1401 Hawthorne Ave. N.E.; 503/371-8024.

Seaside: $45–90; 2369 S. Roosevelt Dr. (Hwy 101); 503/738-6269.

Springfield: Two small; $45–70; 3752 International Ct.; 541/741-1105.

The Dalles: One dog free, second dog is $10 per night; $40–80; 2500 W. 6th St.; 541/296-1191.

Tigard: One dog free, second dog is $10 per night; $45–60; 17950 S.W. McEwan Ave.; 503/620-2066.

Troutdale: $40–60; 1610 N.W. Frontage Rd.; 503/665-2254.

QUALITY INN

Rules and regulations vary. 800/228-5151; www.qualityinn.com.

WASHINGTON

Bellingham–Baron Suites: Up to two dogs; $25 flat rate; $85–200; 100 E. Kellogg Rd.; 360/647-8000.

Goldendale: A few pet rooms available; $10 pet fee; $80–145; 808 E. Simcoe Dr.; 509/773-5881.

Kelso-Longview: Two small or one large to medium pet; $25 first night, $15 additional nights; $80–110; 723 7th Ave.; 360/414-1000.

Leavenworth: Up to two dogs, 50 pounds each; $15 pet fee; $80–200; 185 U.S. Hwy. 2; 509/548-7992.

Mount Vernon: Only on first and third floors. $10 pet fee; $80–170; 1910 Freeway Dr.; 360/428-7020.

Port Angeles: Two dogs per room, up to 30 pounds; $10 pet fee; $80–220; 101 E. 2nd St.; 360/457-9434.

Sequim: They have nine designated pet rooms; maximum two pets; $10 pet fee; $80–190; 134 River Rd.; 360/683-2800.

Vancouver: No restrictions; $10 pet fee; $60–90; 7001 N.E. Hwy. 99; 360/696-0516.

OREGON

Albany: Dogs up to 14-inch shoulder height (that's what they said); $10 pet fee; $80–105; 1100 Price Rd. S.E.; 541/928-5050.

Bend: No restrictions; $10 pet fee; $110–140; 20600 Grandview Dr.; 541/318-0848.

Eugene/Springfield: Three dogs; $5 pet fee; $80–180; 3550 Gateway St.; 541/726-9266.

Klamath Falls: No restrictions; $10 pet fee; $85–135; 100 Main St.; 541/882-4666.

Roseburg: Three dogs; $10 pet fee, plus a $50 refundable deposit; $70–100; 427 N.W. Garden Valley Blvd.; 541/673-5561.

RAMADA INN

Rules and regulations vary. 800/2RAMADA (800/272-6232); www.ramada.com.

WASHINGTON

Tukwila: Smoking rooms only; $20–40 pet fee depending on size; $90–180; 13900 International Blvd.; 206/244-8800.

Yakima: No restrictions; $15 pet fee; $80–115; 818 N. First St.; 509/453-0391.

OREGON
Medford: No restrictions; $20 pet fee per stay; $75–95; 2250 Biddle Rd.; 541/779-3141.

RED LION

There are no restrictions or fees for pets at these locations, unless stated otherwise below. Booking online guarantees the lowest available rates. 800/RED LION (800/733-5466); www.redlion.com.

WASHINGTON
Bellevue: Under 25 pounds; $25 pet fee; $140–180; 11211 Main St.; 425/455-5240.

Kelso: $20 pet fee; $130–175; 510 Kelso Dr.; 360/636-4400.

Olympia: Under 30 pounds; $20 pet fee; $105–125; 2300 Evergreen Park Dr. S.W.; 360/943-4000.

Port Angeles: $15 pet fee; $80–145; 221 N. Lincoln St.; 360/452-9215.

Seattle–Airport: Two dogs; $35 deposit, $20 of which is refundable; $65–155; 11244 Pacific Hwy. S.; 206/762-0300.

Seatte–5th Avenue: They have a full doggie program, including goodies, toys, waste bags, food and water tray, pillow, reference guide, and a "Doggie Napping" door hanger to avoid surprising housekeeping. One dog, under 30 pounds; $50 one-time fee; $140–300; 1415 5th Ave.; 206/971-8000; www.redlion5thavenue.com.

Tacoma: Dogs under 25 pounds only; $20 pet fee; $65–85; 8402 S. Hosmer St.; 253/548-1212.

Vancouver–Red Lion at the Quay: Two dogs; $25 per day pet fee; $100–160; 100 Columbia St.; 360/694-8341.

Wenatchee: Two dogs; $20 total per night; $90–155; 1225 N. Wenatchee Ave.; 509/663-0711.

Yakima: Three dogs; $10 pet fee; $85–150; 818 N. 1st St.; 509/453-0391.

OREGON
Astoria: Limited to two small dogs or one medium to large dog; $20 total per night; $99–179; 400 Industry St.; 503/325-7373.

Bend: No restrictions; $10 per night; $85–125; 1415 N.E. 3rd St.; 541/382-7011.

Coos Bay: Under a 100 pounds, max two; $10 per night; $135–190; 1313 N. Bayshore Dr.; 541/267-4141.

Eugene: Under 30 pounds; $20 per night; $90–250; 205 Coburg Rd.; 541/342-5201.

Hillsboro: "No elephants or snakes"; $20 per night; $90–170; 3500 N.E. Cornell Rd.; 503/648-3500.

Klamath Falls: No restrictions; no pet fee; $60–90; 3612 S. 6th St.; 541/882-8864.

McMinnville: Five pet-friendly rooms; $10 pet fee; $100–135; 2535 N.E. Cumulus Ave.; 503/472-1500.

Medford: No restrictions; $10 pet fee; $110–130; 200 N. Riverside Ave.; 541/779-5811.

Portland–Airport: $15 per dog per stay; $100–130; 5019 N.E. 102nd Ave.; 503/252-6397.

Portland–Jantzen Beach: $35 one-time flat fee; $110–130; 909 N. Hayden Island Dr.; 503/283-4466.

Salem: Maximum two pets, under 30 pounds each; $20 total per visit; $80–135; 3301 Market St. N.E.; 503/370-7888.

SHILO INNS

There is a standard limit of two pets per room at these locations, unless stated otherwise below. Shilo's standard pet fee is $25 total per stay. All Shilo Inns have 3- by 4-foot dog beds available; just ask at the front desk. 800/222-2244; www.shiloinn.com.

WASHINGTON

Ocean Shores: First floor only; $140–230; 707 Ocean Shores; 360/289-4600.

Tacoma: $105–150; 7414 S. Hosmer St.; 253/475-4020.

OREGON

Astoria-Warrenton: $100–260; 1609 E. Harbor; 503/861-2181.

Beaverton: $100–155; 9900 S.W. Canyon Rd.; 503/297-2551.

Bend: $100–240; 3105 O.B. Riley Rd.; 541/389-9600.

Eugene/Springfield: $80–150; 3350 Gateway; 541/747-0332.

Grants Pass: $70–120; 1880 N.W. 6th St.; 541/479-8391.

Klamath Falls: $110–200; 2500 Almond St.; 541/885-7980.

Medford: $90–115; 2111 Biddle Rd.; 541/770-5151.

Newberg: $90–125; 501 Sitka Ave.; 503/537-0303.

Newport: $115–200; 536 S.W. Elizabeth; 541/265-7701.

Portland–Rose Garden: Three dogs; $90–180; 1506 N.E. 2nd Ave.; 503/736-6300.

Salem: $115–130; 3304 Market St. N.E.; 503/581-4001.

Seaside: Under 50 pounds; $90–190; 900 S. Holladay Dr.; 503/738-0549.

The Dalles: $130–170; 3223 Bret Clodfelter Way; 541/298-5502.

Tigard: $100–1365; Washington Square, 10830 S.W. Greenburg Rd.; 503/620-4320.

Tillamook: $115–150; 2515 N. Main St.; 503/842-7971.

STARWOOD HOTELS

In 2003, all Starwood Properties, including Sheraton, Westin, and W Hotels, made it corporate policy to accept and pamper pets after an independent study proved how loyal pet owners are to accommodations that accept their four-legged loved ones. There are no fees and no restrictions unless stated otherwise below. www.starwoodhotels.com.

WASHINGTON

Bellevue–Sheraton: Two dogs; $170–410; 100 112th Avenue N.E.; 425/455-3330.

Bellevue–Westin: Two dogs, 40 pounds and under; $50 refundable pet deposit; $180–260; 600 Bellevue Way N.E.; 425/638-1000.

Seattle–Westin: Very dog-friendly. Lots of treats and goodies, dog beds, and tips for owners. $210–300; no pet fee; Downtown District, 1900 5th Ave.; 206/728-1000.

Seattle–Sheraton: Two dogs; $200–240; 1400 6th Ave.; 206/621-9000.

OREGON

Portland–Sheraton Airport: $25 nonrefundable pet fee; $120–180; 8235 N.E. Airport Way; 503/281-2500.

Portland–Sheraton Four Points Waterfront: Two dogs under 60 pounds; $50 fee per stay; $150–210; 50 S.W. Morrison St.; 503/221-0711; www.fourpointsportland.com.

Portland–Westin: Two dogs; $160–240; 750 S.W. Alder St.; 503/294-9000.

SUPER 8

Rules and regulations vary. 800/800-8000; www.super8.com.

WASHINGTON

Bremerton: No restrictions; $25 deposit per dog, $10 of which is refundable; $70–100; 5068 Kitsap Way; 360/377-8881.

Ellensburg: No restrictions; $10 flat fee for pets; $75–110; 1500 Canyon Rd.;
509/962-6888.

Federal Way: No restrictions; $10 per dog per day, $30 maximum; $80–110;
1688 S. 348th St.; 253/838-8808.

Ferndale: No restrictions; $20 flat fee; $65–85; 5788 Barrett Ave.;
360/384-8881.

Kelso: No restrictions; $10 flat fee; $65–95; 250 Kelso Dr.; 360/423-8880.

Lacey: No restrictions; $25 refundable deposit; $70–85; 112 College St S.E.;
360/459-8888.

Long Beach: Dog biscuits at front desk. No restrictions; $10 pet fee; $80–110;
500 Ocean Beach Blvd. S.; 360/642-8988.

Port Angeles: Two dogs; $25 refundable deposit; $65–85; 2104 E. 1st St.;
360/452-8401.

SeaTac: Two dogs; $25 refundable deposit; $75–100; 3100 S. 192nd St.;
206/433-8188.

Union Gap: No restrictions; $15 pet fee; $75–90; 2605 Rudkin Rd.;
509/248-8880.

OREGON

Bend: Two dogs; $10 per pet per stay; $75–85; 1275 S. Hwy 97;
541/388-6888.

Corvallis: Three dogs; $10 pet fee; $70–90; 407 N.W. 2nd St.; 541/758-8088.

Grants Pass: No restrictions; $25 refundable deposit; $50–75;
1949 N.E. 7th St.; 541/474-0888.

Gresham: Two dogs; $10 dog fee; $60–80; 121 N.E. 181St Ave.;
503/661-5100.

Klamath Falls: No restrictions; $25 refundable deposit; $60–75;
3805 Hwy. 97 N.; 541/884-8880.

Portland–Airport: No restrictions; $10 pet fee; $65–90;
11011 N.E. Holman St.; 503/257-8988.

Redmond: No restrictions; $5 flat fee; $65–80; 3629 S.W. 21st Pl.;
541/548-8881.

Roseburg: Pride of Super 8 award; no restrictions; $10 pet fee; $55–70;
3200 N.W. Aviation Dr.; 541/672-8880.

Salem: No restrictions; $10 pet fee; $60–80; 1288 Hawthorne Ave. N.E.;
503/370-8888.

The Dalles: Three dogs; $10 pet fee; $60–85; 609 Cherry Heights Rd.;
541/296-6888.

Wilsonville: Limit four, 30 pounds or less; $10 pet fee; $65–75; 25438 S.W. Parkway Ave.; 503/682-2088.

Woodburn: No restrictions; $10 pet fee; $60–70; 821 Evergreen Rd.; 503/981-8881.

TRAVELODGE

Rules and regulations vary. 800/578-7878; www.travelodge.com.

WASHINGTON

Auburn: $10 per pet per night, but no more than $30 per pet per week; $80–120; 9 16th St. N.W.; 253/833-7171.

Edmonds: Limit three small or two medium dogs; $25 per dog per stay; $80–150; 23825 Hwy. 99; 425/771-8008.

Everett–City Center: Two dogs under 75 pounds; $5 pet fee; $65–85; 3030 Broadway; 425/259-6141.

Fife: No restrictions; $50 refundable deposit, plus $10 per pet, per day; $55–65; 3518 Pacific Hwy. E.; 253/922-0550.

Longview: No restrictions; $15 pet fee; $50–60; 838 15th Ave.; 360/423-6460.

OREGON

Grants Pass: One dog under 35 pounds; $5 pet fee; $75–130; 1950 N.W. Vine St.; 541/479-6611.

Newberg: Allowed in specific rooms only; $7 pet fee; $65–90; 2816 Portland Rd. (99W); 503/537-5000.

Portland–Airport: One dog; $10 pet fee; $65–100; 3828 N.E. 82nd Ave.; 503/256-2550.

Roseburg: Two dogs under 30 pounds; $10 pet fee; $75–90; 315 W. Harvard Ave.; 541/672-4836.

Salem: Two dogs, in selected rooms only; $65–80; $10 pet fee; 1555 State St.; 503/581-2466.

BRITISH COLUMBIA

Sidney-Victoria Airport: Two dogs; no alligators, boa constrictors, or tarantulas; $10 pet fee; $105–165; 2280 Beacon Ave.; 250/656-1176; www.airporttravelodge.com.

Vancouver–Lions Gate: Pets stay free in designated rooms; $140–160; 2060 Marine Dr.; 604/985-5311.

Transportation

WASHINGTON

Guemes Island Ferry: A tiny ferry that takes about 10 minutes to go from Anacortes to Guemes Island, this county boat allows dogs in the car, or leashed on the open-air deck. Cost is $5.75 for vehicle and driver round-trip. 360/293-6356; www.skagitcounty.net, click on "Guemes Island Ferry" link.

Kenmore Air: This floatplane service flies to six airports in the San Juan Islands, leaving from floating airports on Lake Union and Lake Washington in Seattle. Dogs are welcome in the cabin with you and, if they are 23 pounds or under, can sit in your lap for no extra charge. Dogs 24 pounds and over are required to buy their own seats at child's fare rates. Kenmore will also transport animals in travel carriers without humans to accompany them; call for more information. Round-trip prices range $156–199 for adults, $149 for kids and dogs. 6321 N.E. 175th St., Kenmore, WA, 98028; 800/543-9595 or 425/486-1257; www.kenmoreair.com.

Victoria Clipper: The Clipper is a high-speed boat, passenger only, that goes between Seattle, Washington, and Victoria, British Columbia. The ride takes 2.5 hours each way. Dogs are allowed in airline-approved kennels, and they are strapped to an outside deck. It could get a little chilly for them; bring their favorite blanket and put short-coated dogs in their coats. Cost for dogs is $10 each way; adult round-trip tickets range $106–133. 800/888-2535; www.victoriaclipper.com.

Washington State Ferry Association: This is the largest ferry system in the United States. There are 10 routes, served by 29 boats; all but one are car ferries, but you can walk on as a passenger or bicyclist on any of them:

- Seattle to Bainbridge Island
- Seattle to Bremerton, Kitsap Peninsula
- Seattle to Vashon Island (passenger only)
- West Seattle to Vashon Island
- West Seattle to Kitsap Peninsula
- Edmonds to Kingston, Kitsap Peninsula
- Anacortes to the San Juan Islands and Sidney, B.C.
- Mukilteo to Whidbey Island
- Whidbey Island to Port Townsend, Olympic Peninsula
- Tacoma to Vashon Island

Dogs can stay in the car or be on leash outside on the outer lower car deck. They can't go upstairs onto upper decks, even outside. Ferry schedules and pricing changes quarterly. 888/808-7977; www.wsdot.wa.gov/ferries.

OREGON

Broadway Cab: This taxi company in Portland will allow dogs if you call and let the driver know in advance. 503/227-1234.

BRITISH COLUMBIA

BC Ferries: Pets are allowed on most of the BC ferries, including the route from Vancouver to Victoria. These ferries depart from Tsawassen, south of Vancouver, and arrive at Swartz Bay, north of Victoria near Sidney. Dogs are allowed on the open-air car deck and must stay in your car or tied in a designated pet area. Owners must stay with their pets. The travel time for this route is approximately an hour and 35 minutes. Guide dogs and certified assistance dogs are not required to stay on the car decks. From outside British Columbia: 250/386-3431; from anywhere in British Columbia: 888/BCFERRY (888/223-3779); www.bcferries.com.

Extended Trails

REGIONAL

Pacific Crest Trail: Crisscrossing California, Oregon, and Washington on its way from Mexico to Canada, this American National Scenic Trail extends 2,650 miles. It transverses six ecozones, from high desert to old growth and arctic alpine. The Oregon section is typically wooded, generally the shortest and easiest terrain of the trail. Through the North Cascades, the Washington section boasts dramatic mountainous scenery and notoriously fickle weather patterns. The Pacific Crest Trail Association is in California: 5325 Elkhorn Blvd., 5325 Elkhorn Blvd.; PMB #256, Sacramento, CA 95842-2526; 916/349-2109; www.pcta.org.

WASHINGTON

Iron Horse State Park/John Wayne Pioneer Trail: Iron Horse is essentially 1,613 acres of easement through which the 100-mile-long John Wayne Trail passes from Vantage to North Bend. The trail is a wide dirt and gravel road that served as the right-of-way for the old Chicago–Milwaukee–St. Paul–Pacific Railroad. The mild grade is family-friendly, and it's easy to get to, never too far from the highway. Yet you can disappear from civilization quickly into varied scenery and encounter cool things like high trestles and spooky tunnels (bring a flashlight). Along the way, you pass from mountains and valleys thick with forests to sagebrush desert and scrubland, as well as charming farm country.

It intersects a handful of other state parks in the region where you can rest and camp and has campgrounds and trailheads of its own. In the summertime, you'll share the trail with horses and cyclists. In winter, bring paw booties, dog sleds, cross-country skis, and/or horseshoes to join snowmobiles on the trail. Dogs are welcome on an eight-foot or shorter leash.

You'll see signs that say Iron Horse State Park, John Wayne Pioneer Trail, or both. There is a $5 daily fee at all trailheads. While the trail is clearly marked and easy to follow, you can pick up maps for $2 at Lake Easton State Park, Exit 70 from I-90. Kiosks with trail information are located at Rattlesnake Lake in North Bend, and in Hyak, Easton, South Cle Elum, Thorp, and Kittatas. For trailhead directions, click the "Iron Horse" link at www.parks.wa.gov.

OREGON

Willamette Valley Scenic Bikeway: The entire route is 130 miles, separated into five sections on the website. It runs generally north–south, from Champoeg State Park near Newburg to Armitage County Park, just above Eugene. It largely highlights the agricultural history of the lush valley, passing vineyards, hazelnut orchards, fruit orchards one after another. Any segment can be walked on leash with dogs. Call the Oregon DOT Bike and Pedestrian program at 503/986-3555 or go to www.oregon.gov/oprd/parks/bike.

Oregon Coast Trail: This is a 360-mile route from the tip of the state at the mouth of the Columbia River to the bottom at the California border. The majority of the trail is on the beach, sometimes so close you need a tide table to cross headlands when the tide is out. Some of it wanders inland through state forests and parks, and in between, landowners along the coast have generously provided easements and permits through property to make connections. Some of it is dirt and gravel, some paved, and some so narrow through brush you need a scent hound to pick up the trail. If you want to take on the whole thing, or major portions of it, buy a detailed point-to-point guide available at bookstores and magazine outlets. Select the "Maps and Publications" link on the Oregon State Parks and Recreation website at www.oregonstateparks.org and look for the 2005 Coast Trail Brochure.

OC&E Woods Line State Trail: At 100 miles long, this state trail is Oregon's longest linear park, stretching from Klamath Falls east to Bly and north to Sycan Marsh. The wide, level path is built on the rail bed of the Oregon, California, and Eastern Railroad (hence the OC&E). It's open to all nonmotorized travelers, so be prepared to yield right-of-way to horses and bicyclists, inline skaters, and joggers. The farther you go, the more you'll run into the farm and ranch lands of the Klamath Basin, with great views of Mount Shasta to the south. The first 15 miles of the trail are paved, but softer paws will prefer the wood-chip trail that parallels the asphalt. 800/551-6949; www.oregon stateparks.org.

Useful Organizations

NATIONAL PARKS AND FORESTS

Recreation.gov: The feds have established a new, easy-to-remember website to consolidate information and reservations for public lands such as National Parks and National Forests. Find a recreation spot on a massive, interactive map, get wilderness permits, and make campground reservations at the National Recreation Reservation Service (NRRS). www.recreation.gov.

WASHINGTON

Department of Fish and Wildlife: Contact this organization for fishing, shellfish gathering, and hunting licenses. Main Office: 360/902-2200; License Division: 360/902-2464; www.wdfw.wa.gov. Make license purchases online at www.fishhunt.dfw.wa.gov.

Washington State Parks: Dogs are required to be on an eight-foot or shorter leash. State park camping costs $23–32 for RVs and $17–23 for tents, $1 less in the winter. For parks that require camping reservations, call 888/CAMPOUT (888/226-7688) or go to www.camis.com/wa.

Kitsap Peninsula

Kitsap Dog Parks, Inc.: A nonprofit organization working with Kitsap County to develop and maintain peninsula dog parks at Bandix and Howe Farm; www.kitsapdogparks.org.

Puget Sound Islands

FETCH!: Free Exercise Time for Canines and their Humans is dedicated to providing Island County dog owners areas where they are free to exercise their pets without disturbing others. They promote and maintain five dog parks on Whidbey Island. 360/321-4049; www.whidbey.com/fetchparks.

Central Seattle and North Seattle

COLA: Citizens for Off-Leash Areas promotes and maintains city dog parks. www.coladog.org.

The Eastside and South Seattle

SODA: Serve Our Dog Areas is the off-leash group that manages and volunteers at Marymoor Off-Leash Area in Redmond and Grandview Dog Park in Kent. 425/881-0148; www.soda.org.

Southwest Washington

DOGPAW: Dog Owners' Group for Park Access in Washington works to increase the availability of safe off-leash areas for dogs in Clark County and to promote awareness and acceptance in the community at large. www.clarkdogpaw.org.

North Cascades

Grateful Dogs: What a great name for the organization that promotes responsible dog ownership and off-leash opportunities for canines in Bellingham. 360/671-4193; www.gratefuldogs.org.

OREGON

Department of Fish and Wildlife: Contact this organization for angling, shellfish gathering, and hunting licenses. Print an application online and fax to 503/947-6117. Main phone: 503/947-6000 or 800/720-6339; Licensing: 503/947-6100; www.dfw.state.or.us.

Oregon State Parks: Oregon calls its state parks by many names, and only a few charge a $3 daily parking fee. Camping fees vary by location. Dogs are required to be on a six-foot or shorter leash. Reservations are made by calling 800/452-5687 or through www.reserveamerica.com.

North Coast

Bow Wow Dog News: This free newspaper is distributed in Oregon Coast and Southwest Washington beach locations. Also available online at www.bowwowdognews.com.

Greater Portland

PDX DOG: For pets and their peeps, www.pdxdog.com is a social networking site for dog lovers who want to share—photos, tales, tips, hints—you name it. PDX is the airport designation for Portland, used locally as a nickname for the city. You can find local dog businesses that advertise on the site.

Portland Pooch: This online guide to the Portland dog scene has great information and the best descriptions and directions to all of the area's dog parks. www.portlandpooch.com.

Southern Oregon

FOTAS: Friends of the Animal Shelter holds benefits and dog events in and around Ashland, Medford, and Jacksonville to raise funds for the county animal shelter. www.fotas.org.

BRITISH COLUMBIA

Citizen Canine: An off-leash advocacy group in Victoria; www.citizencanine.org.

RainCity Dogs: An online guide for Vancouver dogs; www.raincitydogs.com.

WAG: If you have a lost pet, or find one, in Whistler, B.C., contact Whistler Animals Galore at 604/935-8364; www.thewagway.com.

INDEX

A

T

UV

WY

Acknowledgments

First and foremost, I want to express my abiding love and gratitude to Dread Pirate Steve for saying "As you wish" to every demand made of him.

I'd like to extend thanks to my PCC Natural Markets peeps Mike, Jill, and Nancy for tolerating my bizarre and constant schedule requests. Apologies go to all my family and friends, who regularly watch me disappear into the wilds of the Pacific Northwest, and into the depths of my home office, never knowing when I might emerge from either.

To Pam, Tana, Loni, Robin, Christine, and anyone else whose name I've lost in computer email crashes, thank you for housing, feeding, and touring our traveling dog and pony show.

Kudos to everyone, everywhere, who works or volunteers in animal rescue, spay and neuter education, and land conservation. Finally, this book would be greatly diminished if it weren't for the efforts of every dog advocate who campaigns for, creates, and cleans up off-leash areas.

Keeping Current

Note to All Dog Lovers:
While our information is as current as possible, changes to fees, regulations, parks, roads, and trails sometimes are made after we go to press. Businesses can close, change their ownership, or change their rules. Earthquakes, fires, rainstorms, and other natural phenomena can radically change the condition of parks, hiking trails, and wilderness areas. Before you and your dog begin your travels, please be certain to call the phone numbers for each listing for updated information.

Attention Dogs of the Pacific Northwest
Our readers mean everything to us. We explore the Pacific Northwest so that you and your people can spend true quality time together. Your input to this book is very important. In the last few years, we've heard from many wonderful dogs and their humans about new dog-friendly places, or old dog-friendly places we didn't know about. If we've missed your favorite park, beach, outdoor restaurant, hotel, or dog-friendly activity, please let us know. We'll check out the tip and if it turns out to be a good one, include it in the next edition, giving a thank-you to the dog and/or person who sent in the suggestion. Please write us—we always welcome comments and suggestions.

The Dog Lover's Companion to the Pacific Northwest
Avalon Travel
1700 Fourth Street
Berkeley, CA 94710
www.dogloverscompanion.com